THE
CROWN'S
SILENCE

THE
CROWN'S
SILENCE

THE HIDDEN HISTORY OF SLAVERY
AND THE BRITISH MONARCHY

BROOKE N. NEWMAN

MUDLARK

Mudlark
HarperCollins*Publishers*
1 London Bridge Street
London SE1 9GF

www.harpercollins.co.uk

HarperCollins*Publishers*
Macken House, 39/40 Mayor Street Upper
Dublin 1, D01 C9W8, Ireland

First published by HarperCollins*Publishers* 2026

1 3 5 7 9 10 8 6 4 2

© Brooke Newman 2026

Brooke Newman asserts the moral right to be
identified as the author of this work

Designed by Chloe Foster

A catalogue record of this book is
available from the British Library

HB ISBN 978-0-00-867095-5
PB ISBN 978-0-00-867098-6

Printed and bound in the UK using 100% renewable
electricity at CPI Group (UK) Ltd

For Greg, and in memory of all those impacted
by the transatlantic slave trade

My present was the future that had been created by men and women in chains, by human commodities, by chattel persons. I tried hard to envision a future in which this past had ended, and most often I failed.

—SAIDIYA HARTMAN, *LOSE YOUR MOTHER*

For a long time, truly, a great doubt has held me: Should I be silent or should I speak?

—QUEEN ELIZABETH I, SEPTEMBER 5, 1566

CONTENTS

ILLUSTRATIONS

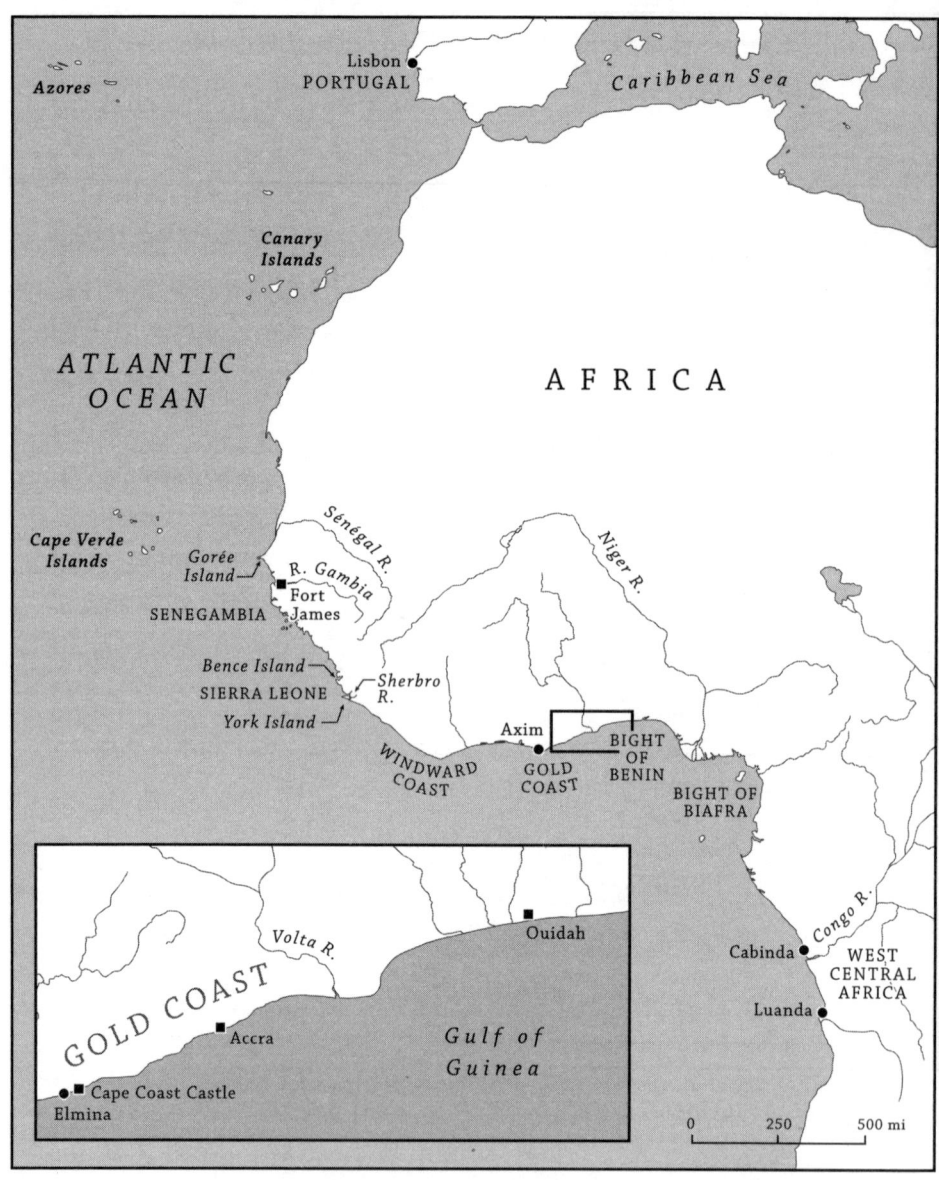

Key Atlantic Regions and Ports in West Africa. MAP BY ERIN GREB CARTOGRAPHY.

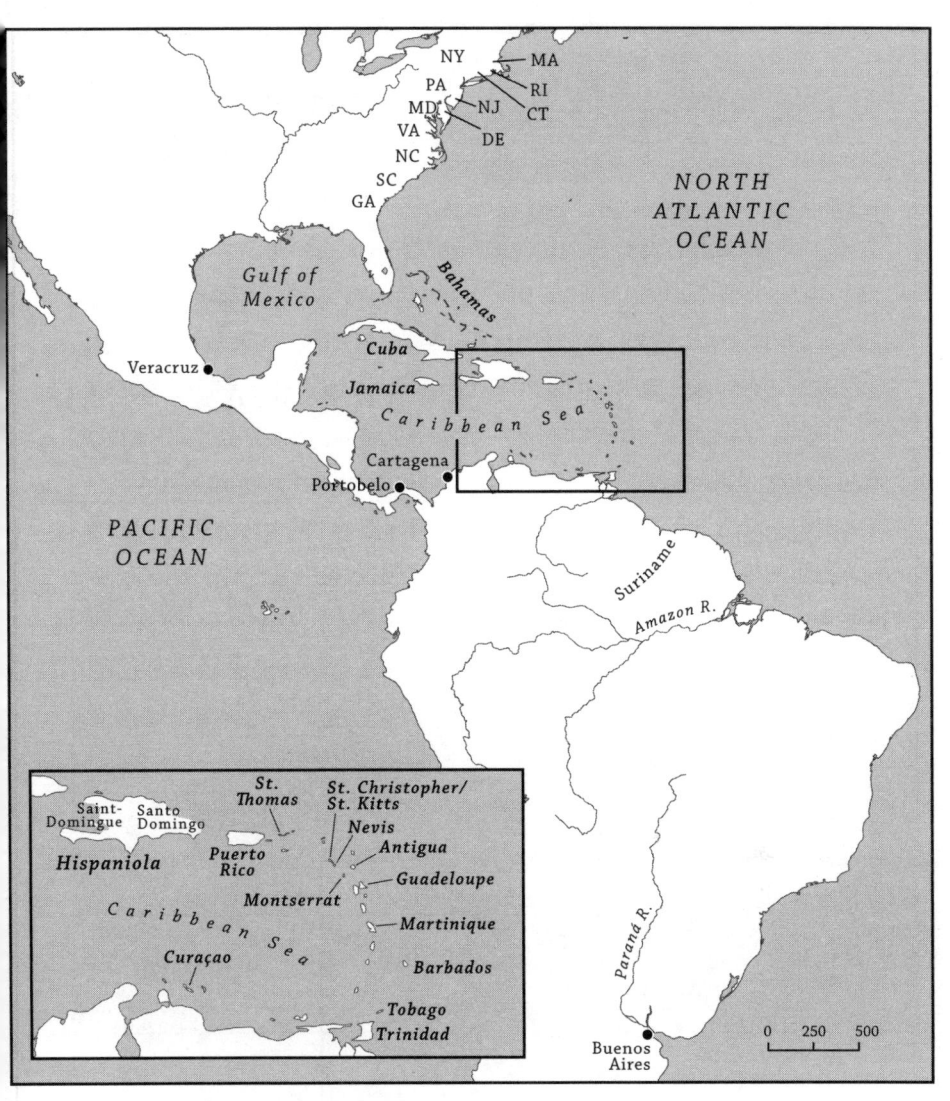

The Americas, 1732. MAP BY ERIN GREB CARTOGRAPHY.

The British Atlantic World, 1763. MAP BY ERIN GREB CARTOGRAPHY.

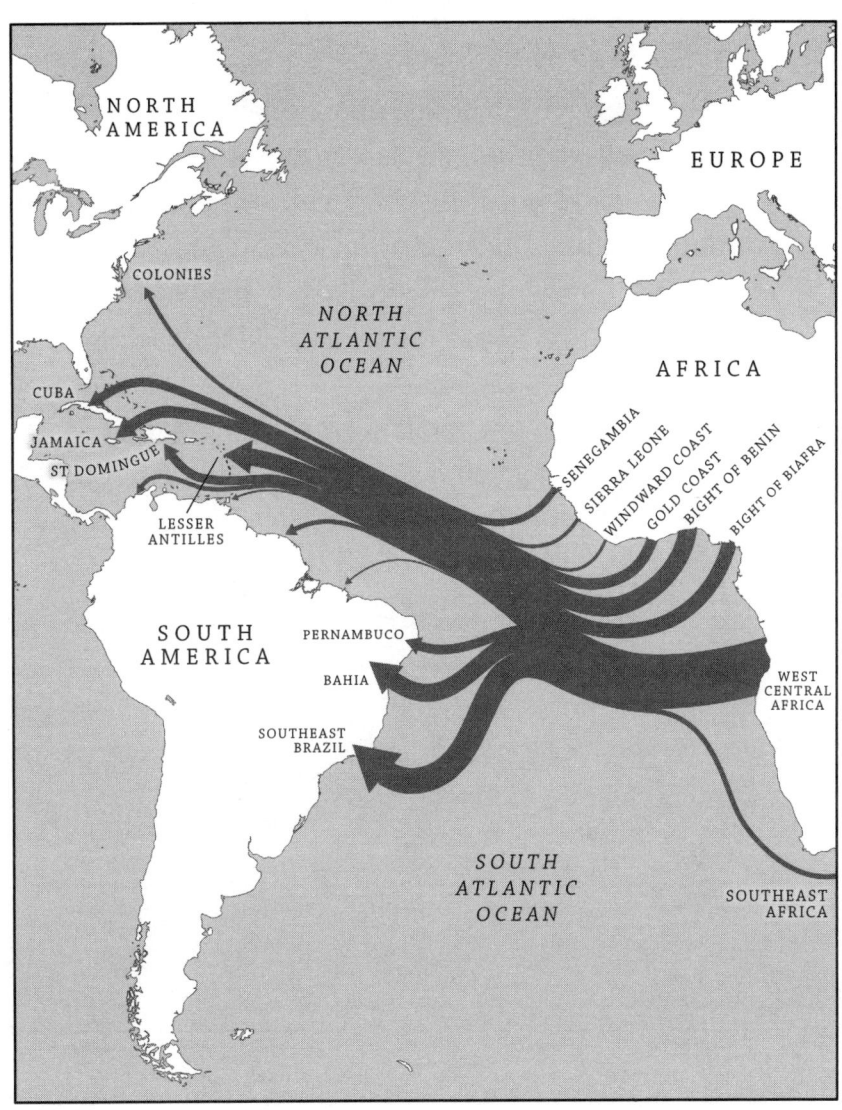

Volume and Flow of the Transatlantic Slave Trade. MAP BY ERIN GREB CARTOGRAPHY.

AUTHOR'S NOTE

Among scholars, the terminology surrounding slavery has shifted in recent years. As historian Vanessa Holden explains, "the word *slave* emerges as an artifact, an accounting of historical record-keeping"; but for "scholars who are interested in uncovering the silences, it is not a word for the people who endured enslavement." I have generally substituted the terms *enslaved person* or *bondsperson* for *slave,* as well as *enslaver* for *slaveowner.* However, in some instances I have used historical terms such as *slave trader/holder* to more accurately capture power relationships in the past.

The story that unfolds in the following pages is based on a wide-ranging documentary record that stretches across four centuries. While the paper trail of Crown involvement in the transatlantic slave trade and colonial slavery is fragmentary and incomplete, it is nonetheless extensive. Direct empirical links are scattered across multiple archives, embedded in the voluminous records of slave-trading companies and in state and parliamentary papers; in royal grants, charters, treaties, portraiture, and private papers and financial receipts; in the extant correspondence of government ministers and the proceedings and publications of the pro-slavery lobby; and in manuscript and printed accounts produced by abolitionists, anti-slavery activists, former enslaved people, and free Blacks, among others.

I have lightly edited and modernized spelling in quoted material and expanded abbreviations for clarity's sake. With the exception of the years, the dates remain exactly as they appear in the original sources. Before 1752, the British used the Julian calendar and considered March 25 the start of the new year. The years referred to in this book have been modernized to align with the post-1752 Gregorian calendar, recognizing January 1 as the start of a new year. Throughout the book I have capitalized *Black* and *Native/Indigenous* but not *white*. Derogatory premodern racial terminology is cited and retained in quotations solely for illustrative purposes. We must grapple with what historical actors did as well as what they said.

And we must never forget.

THE
CROWN'S
SILENCE

I SEE AND KEEP SILENT

T reading cobblestones warmed by the midsummer sun, Diego Guzmán de Silva, the canon of Toledo and King Philip II of Spain's newly appointed English ambassador, arrived at Westminster on July 24, 1564. Royal stewards led him into the presence chamber, a great hall hung with exquisite tapestries where the sovereign held court, dined in state, and received foreign envoys. Queen Elizabeth I awaited Silva on a throne positioned beneath a rich cloth-of-gold canopy of estate. Adorned in an elegant black velvet gown embroidered with gold thread and pearls, her face painted white to cover the scars from a near-fatal brush with smallpox two years earlier, she greeted Silva warmly. Elizabeth had twice met with the tall Spanish cleric since his arrival in London the previous month and had hosted him at a masque performed in her honor.

This visit carried a different sense of urgency. Silva had received intelligence that Captain John Hawkins, a Plymouth-based merchant adventurer, intended to embark on an illicit transatlantic slaving venture to West Africa and the Spanish Caribbean. Hawkins had conducted a previous voyage following the same route in 1562–63, kidnapping Africans from Portuguese slaving vessels and then crossing the Atlantic to sell his captives to Spanish colonists. His actions constituted a flagrant violation of Philip II's royal decree prohibiting foreigners from trading in Spanish America without Crown license. As a result of his brazenness, Hawkins and his investors had netted approximately £3,000—a significant sum at the time—and secured a place at the top of Philip II's watch list.

Alerted to Hawkins's covert preparations by his network of spies, Silva knew that men high in status and official station at the English court had backed the Plymouth merchant's upcoming slaving venture. The syndicate sponsoring Hawkins included wealthy London businessmen and members of the queen's privy council, including Sir William Cecil, Elizabeth's principal adviser, and her confidant and favorite Lord Robert Dudley, the first Earl of Leicester. That powerful men in the queen's inner circle would openly sponsor Hawkins's illicit expedition troubled the Spanish ambassador. On behalf of his royal master, Silva pressed Elizabeth for details regarding the impending voyage. Would she guarantee that whatever business Hawkins sought to undertake on the coast of West Africa, plundering the king of Spain's empire in the Americas was not on his agenda? Elizabeth assured Silva that she had granted Hawkins her royal approval for an innocent mercantile venture. His voyage posed no threat to the Crown of Spain. "I will try to have her promises carried into effect," a skeptical Silva reported to Philip.

The Spanish ambassador was right to view the English queen's pledge with suspicion. An often underestimated female monarch with a savvy geopolitical and religious agenda, Elizabeth knew the precise scheme Hawkins had envisioned. Building on the success of his previous transatlantic slaving expedition, Hawkins intended to profit from the capture, forcible transport, and sale of enslaved Africans to labor-hungry colonists in Spanish America. Elizabeth not only comprehended his design but had also encouraged it and offered material assistance. When Hawkins returned from the Spanish Caribbean in September 1563, the holds of his ships bursting with gold coins, jewels, sugar, and animal hides, news of his triumph reached the queen's ears. Elizabeth offered to loan him one of the largest warships in her modest royal navy of thirty-four vessels. In exchange, she expected to receive a share of the profits in his next transatlantic slaving venture. The queen's treasury was empty. Hence her willingness to invest in a high-risk overseas commercial enterprise bound to provoke the wrath of the Iberian Catholic powers. When questioned, both before and after the expedition, Elizabeth denied prior knowledge of Hawkins's true intentions.

The queen's gamble paid off. Hawkins's second slaving voyage more than met his investors' objectives. After raiding the West African coast and crossing the Atlantic with hundreds of Africans chained in the dark hold of the queen's ship, Hawkins sold the terrified survivors into slavery in the Spanish Caribbean. When he returned to England, his ships bore "over 50,000 ducats [around £16,000] in gold and some pearls, hides, and sugar, as the payment for his slaves," Silva wrote to Philip II. Contemporary estimates suggest that Hawkins and his patrons—including Queen Elizabeth—each received a staggering 60 percent return on their investment. His daring slave-trading venture enriched the royal coffers, securing Elizabeth I's historical legacy as the first English monarch to profit directly from the transatlantic slave trade.

Emboldened by the scale of the profits, the queen loaned Hawkins two royal warships for a larger, grander transatlantic slaving scheme in 1567. Hawkins's third voyage would prove the most ambitious and heavily funded English transatlantic slaving venture of the sixteenth century. But calamity struck the third expedition. Ambushed by the Spanish fleet off the coast of Mexico on the return voyage, Hawkins lost four out of his six ships. He limped home across the North Atlantic with only a fraction of the men who had embarked with him on the voyage and nothing but enormous losses to show for his troubles. By crushing Hawkins's fleet, the Spanish had dealt England's fledgling slaving industry a devastating blow, setting it back by many decades. Yet Hawkins and Elizabeth I had established a precedent for English merchants and monarchs seeking to profit from the trafficking and enslavement of African men, women, and children for centuries to come.

On March 27, 2007, nearly 450 years after Elizabeth I feigned ignorance of John Hawkins's slaving designs in her presence chamber, thousands gathered in Westminster Abbey for a national service commemorating the two hundredth anniversary of Britain's Act for the Abolition of the Slave Trade. In attendance were Queen Elizabeth II, Prince Philip, Prime Minister Tony Blair, and other notable political figures and clerics. Following the singing of hymns and scripture readings, Rowan Williams, the archbishop of Canterbury, delivered a sermon on the evils and ubiquity of slavery. Acknowledging the "hideously persistent" global legacies of slavery, he lamented the continued existence of human trafficking and enslavement in the twenty-first century. The archbishop's sermon did not shy away from addressing the historical roots of worldwide present-day racial inequities. "We, who are the heirs of the slave-owning and slave-trading nations of the past, have to face the fact that our historic prosperity was built in large part on this atrocity," he observed. "Those who are the heirs of the communities ravaged by the slave trade know very well that much of their present suffering and struggling is the result of centuries of abuse."

The archbishop of Canterbury then pivoted from the universal to the particular—to Britain's past sins. "But today it is for us to face our history," he admonished the congregation; "the Atlantic trade was our contribution to this universal sinfulness." Although modern Britons had, admittedly, not engaged in the cruel traffic themselves or held anyone in bondage, the stain of racial injustice that the forced migration and enslavement of Africans left behind saturated everyday life. Its legacies were unavoidable, and they disproportionately impacted communities of African descent. "Human beings are born into an inheritance of one kind or another," the archbishop continued. Attaining either individual or collective spiritual freedom in this life "means facing the legacy we inherit without fear, excuse, or untruthfulness. Often, so often, that means asking others to tell us the truth we can't see for ourselves." He then invited worshippers—including the queen, the prime minister, and members of multiple African-descended communities in attendance—to kneel for the prayer of confession.

Just then, a Black protester wearing a colorful African dashiki interrupted the solemn national service. He dashed in front of the altar, shouting, "You should be ashamed! This is an insult to us!" Gesturing to the congregation, he stared directly at Queen Elizabeth, Blair, the bishop of London, the Anglican archbishop of the West Indies, and the archbishops of Canterbury and York. The queen, her face impassive, watched as security guards and ushers rushed to surround the protester, Toyin Agbetu, founder of the Afro-British human rights organization Ligali. Collaborating with other Black British activists based in Bristol, Agbetu had developed Operation Truth 2007, a counter African-centered interpretation of the 1807 Abolition Act that rejected official events attached to what activists dubbed "Wilberforce 2007." The British government had determined what the nation would remember about the transatlantic slave trade and slavery, proponents of Operation Truth 2007 contended: "'They freed us, we should be grateful, commemorate and move on.' Box ticked."

As the guards hauled him toward the exit, Agbetu's shouts echoed through the still abbey. He pointed to Elizabeth II and again yelled, "You, the queen, should be ashamed! You should say sorry!" In keeping with her own protocol and that of her namesake, Elizabeth I, whose motto was "*Video et taceo*" ("I see and keep silent"), the queen said nothing. She maintained her silence long after the event, leaving those who saw Britain's abolition bicentennial as a missed opportunity to issue a formal state apology for slavery further disappointed.

But commemorative events intended for mass consumption rarely grapple with the messiness of the past or the contested nature of collective memory. Exercises of state power, official commemorations contribute to a process of national mythmaking that in turn shapes public opinions of the nation's character. "They impose a silence upon the events that they ignore," argues the Haitian scholar Michel-Rolph Trouillot, "and they fill that silence with narratives of power about the event they celebrate." In 2007, Britain deemed abolition worthy of recognition and the country's centuries-long investment in the trafficking and enslavement of millions of Africans and people of African descent fit for erasure.

During his arrest outside of Westminster Abbey, Agbetu held an impromptu press conference. Asked why he disrupted the national service, Agbetu said the British monarchy owed a long overdue apology and redress for the forced migration and enslavement of Africans. Motivated by profit, the queen's distant royal ancestors had initiated England's involvement in the transatlantic slave trade—what reparations activists refer to as the *maangamizi* or *maafa*, Swahili words that mean "destruction" or "disaster." Without official acknowledgment of the monarchy's complicity in slavery, there could be no national healing or forgiveness. "The queen has to say sorry. It was Elizabeth I. She commanded John Hawkins to take his ship," Agbetu explained. "The monarch and the government and the church are all in there patting themselves on the back."

Dismissed as a crazed "madman" by many British commentators at the time, Agbetu later wrote that he could not watch "the British monarchy, government and church—all leading institutions of African enslavement" commemorate abolition when they had "collectively refused to atone for their sins." "I was moved to make a collective voice heard at the commemorative ritual of appeasement and self-approval," he noted. Through his unsolicited contribution to the national conversation, Agbetu attempted to offer Queen Elizabeth II and Britain's foremost political and spiritual leaders, in the words of the archbishop of Canterbury, "the truth we can't see for ourselves."

Although a lone voice in Westminster Abbey that day, Toyin Agbetu called out for what African-descended individuals and communities have requested for centuries: a formal apology from the British monarchy and government for the atrocities associated with slavery and colonialism coupled with financial and material restitution and restorative justice. In 1961 members of Jamaica's Rastafarian community petitioned Elizabeth II for slavery reparations to fund their repatriation to Africa, after a telegram sent to Buckingham Palace in 1958 to the same effect went unanswered. From then on, Rastafarians have appealed regularly to the queen and the United Nations for international repatriation under the Universal Declaration of Human Rights Charter—to no avail.

In February 2002, Queen Elizabeth visited Jamaica on the first leg of her international Golden Jubilee celebrations. During her state visit, which coincided with the island's fortieth anniversary of independence, Rastafarians renewed their request for the queen's assistance receiving compensation for slavery from the British government and repatriation to Africa. The High Commission, the office that represents the Crown in former British colonies, issued a response rejecting their appeal. "We regret and condemn the inequities of the historic slave trade, but these shameful activities belong to the past," the High Commission replied. "Governments today cannot take responsibility for what happened over 150 years ago." Over the course of her seventy-year reign, Elizabeth II never addressed the foundational role of the monarchy, as both an institution and a family, in Britain's transatlantic slave trade and mass enslavement of Africans. Her reticence to discuss the matter was strategic.

The queen's silence did not go unnoticed, however. On November 30, 2021, Barbados, a Caribbean nation known as both "Little England" and the birthplace of British slave society, celebrated the fifty-fifth anniversary of its political independence by removing Elizabeth II as head of state. Attending the ceremony in his capacity as heir apparent, then–Prince Charles watched as his mother's royal standard was lowered at the stroke of midnight, never to fly again over a state building in Barbados. The fourth and most recent Caribbean nation to shed the final vestiges of

British imperial rule, Barbados has lit the way for other Commonwealth realms to renounce the monarchy. Jamaica, once the most valuable colony in Britain's former eighteenth-century Atlantic slave empire, is poised to follow.

Queen Elizabeth II's death on September 8, 2022, only exacerbated the collective soul-searching of the Commonwealth realms that continue to recognize the British sovereign as their head of state. Her passing frayed the emotional bonds forged anew among Britain's remaining overseas dependencies and the monarchy after the violent collapse of the British Empire. Yet the cocoon of silence the queen erected around the issue of slavery had already begun to sever the most fragile of these links during her final years. The release of a ten-point reparation plan by the Caribbean community (CARICOM) in 2014; the Black Lives Matter protests that swept the United States, the United Kingdom, and the world in 2020; slavery apologies issued by British institutions (ranging from major corporations and High Street banks to city authorities and universities); and mounting calls in Commonwealth realms to cut ties to the Crown had all heightened pressure on the British monarchy.

To protect the revered centuries-old institution she embodied from controversy, Elizabeth II said nothing and took negative action. She chose *not* to acknowledge her royal predecessors' instrumental role in launching and expanding past coercive systems of forced migration and labor that enriched the Crown, facilitated Britain's rise as a global power, and perpetrated violence on millions of enslaved Africans, Indigenous people, and their descendants. Preserving her policy of silence until the bitter end, the queen went to her grave with her lips permanently sealed on the subject of the monarchy's historic links to slavery.

But silence, however seemingly effective in the moment, cannot erase the past or expunge its enduring impacts. The imposed silence that surrounds the British monarchy and continues to haunt the royal family carries its own weighty significance. It is time to place the British Crown at the center of our analysis of the transatlantic slave trade, its legacies, and the pursuit of reparatory justice for slavery—where it belongs.

PART I

ORIGINS

CHAPTER 1

THE FIRST ROYAL SLAVE TRADER

In April 1561, Emanuel Aranjo, a Portuguese envoy, arrived at Whitehall and pressed for an audience with Queen Elizabeth I, then a young woman of twenty-seven. During their private interview he laid before her the Portuguese Crown's complaints related to English incursions in Africa. By right of first discovery, Aranjo explained, the king of Portugal held political jurisdiction and sole authority over trade with Africa's Atlantic coast and adjacent islands. He entreated Elizabeth to prohibit her subjects from venturing to North and West Africa and piratically seizing Portuguese vessels and crews. In her formal response to Sebastião I, the boy king of Portugal, and his grandmother, Catherine of Austria, the queen regent, Elizabeth adopted a polite but firm tone. She agreed to submit to Aranjo's requests on his master's behalf, she noted, "although unprecedented." Forwarding her royal order granting the Portuguese safe conduct, the queen directed English merchants not to sail into any African ports in which the king of Portugal "hath dominion, obedience, and tribute."

On April 30, the queen commanded her Lord Admiral to issue orders that preparations for voyages intended for Africa cease and desist until they obtained his prior approval. Elizabeth, on the surface at least, made a show of regulating English involvement in the African trade in accordance with her promises to the Portuguese Crown. Yet rather than forbid her subjects from undertaking such voyages, she instructed them only to avoid ports controlled by the king of Portugal. By this she meant sites already under effective Portuguese sovereignty and occupation, which left vast swathes of Africa's Atlantic coast apparently up for grabs.

Based on eyewitness reports from English mariners, Elizabeth and her advisers surmised that the Portuguese presence in West Africa was unevenly distributed on the ground and concentrated at a few strategic outposts in the Gold Coast region of what is now Ghana. To protect their interests and dominate West Africa's gold trade, the Portuguese had erected a considerable fortress at Elmina (literally, "the mine") in 1482, supplemented by smaller forts clustered nearby at Axim, Shamma, and Accra. Local rulers tolerated the erection of Portuguese forts in exchange for payments and to facilitate trade, not as evidence of more extensive Portuguese claims along the coast. If African rulers agreed to conduct business with her subjects, the queen reasoned, Portugal's pretensions to sovereign rights over the entirety of West Africa amounted to nothing more than empty words.

That summer Elizabeth herself promoted a commercial venture to West Africa, loaning four vessels from her modest Royal Navy—the warships *Minion* and *Primrose* and two small pinnaces, *Brigantine* and *Fleur de Lys*—to a syndicate of merchant adventurers planning an expedition. Backed by leading London merchants Sir William Chester, Sir William Garrard, Sir Thomas Lodge, Edward Castlyn, and Anthony Hickman, and two naval officials, Benjamin Gonson and William Winter, the voyage was formally described on paper as bound for parts of Africa outside the king of Portugal's dominion. Captain John Lok, a merchant who had participated in previous African voyages during the reign of Mary Tudor, commanded the venture. The adventurers departed on September 11, 1561, intent on conducting trade and scouting for a suitable location on the Gold Coast to build an English fort.

Iberian emissaries in England rapidly learned not only of the prospective English venture to West Africa but also, and more concerning, of the involvement of the queen's ships. Alvarez de Quadra, the Spanish ambassador in England, informed Phillip II of Spain that when he questioned Elizabeth, she professed ignorance of the voyage and its intended aim. The queen and her chief adviser, William Cecil, ever mindful of the need to avert international conflict that England could ill afford, declared she had sold the four royal vessels to certain merchants. Queen Elizabeth's hands were thus tied. She could not forbid the ships' new owners from "going to buy and sell their wares where they think fit," Cecil claimed. In his dispatches to Philip II, Quadra explained the English Crown's reasoning but did not mask his cynicism. It was not long before the Spanish ambassador's doubts were borne out. His spy network reported that 15 percent of the profits of the expedition were to be paid into the hands of Gonson, the treasurer of the queen's navy, who also held a personal stake in the venture.

To Queen Elizabeth and the English merchant adventurers who backed these precarious voyages, the risk of alienating the Iberian powers was well justified if their vessels returned home laden with valuable African commodities. The English craved access to African gold, ivory, and malagueta pepper, a cardamom-like spice also known as Guinea pepper or Guinea grain. Lok's Guinea expedition in the fall of 1561 proved unlucky, however. Shortly after departing the English coast, the queen's ships hit a fierce gale in the Straits of Dover; *Minion* and *Primrose* collided in the thick fog, forcing a return home for repairs. With the ships now damaged and the season already well advanced, Lok postponed the venture until after the new year.

Within months a modified consortium, headed by Thomas Lodge, the Lord Mayor of London, signed a new contract with Queen Elizabeth. In exchange for providing *Minion* and *Primrose*, newly repaired and seaworthy, the queen would receive one-sixth of the profits of the voyage. Captained by William Rutter, the expedition departed Dartmouth on February 25, 1562, headed for the Canary Islands and the Gold Coast. After receiving intelligence of the voyage, the king of Portugal responded with both force and diplomacy, dispatching two heavily armed galleons and four caravels in pursuit of "not only the merchant ships, but the Queen's also." At the same time, he ordered João Pereira Dantas, the Portuguese envoy in France, to hasten to the English court to defend Portugal's exclusive claim to the African trade in no uncertain terms. Captain Rutter's expedition, chased and fired on by Portuguese armed squadrons on the Gold Coast, ultimately brought back an underwhelming 166 tusks, twenty-two butts, or casks, of malagueta pepper, and a clutch of desperately ill seamen.

From the Iberian perspective, however, more galling incursions were yet to come. During the same period, John Hawkins, an enterprising Plymouth merchant and sailor, conducted a far more brazen and lucrative venture of his own accord, one that encroached upon the respective spheres of influence of the Crowns of both Portugal and Spain. Rather than pursue the customary trading opportunities on the Gold Coast, like his fellow English adventurers, Hawkins hunted for Africans to capture and sell into bondage in the Spanish Caribbean. When he returned to Plymouth from his first profitable transatlantic slaving venture in August 1563, England's mercantile community and bureaucrats took notice. So did Queen Elizabeth. Slave trading, it turned out, was a profitable business. By the following winter, Hawkins had secured the queen's support for his next trafficking scheme to West Africa and the Spanish Indies. In 1564, Elizabeth I became the first English monarch to invest directly in the transatlantic slave trade, fully aware of the aim of Hawkins's venture and its human costs.

Why did Queen Elizabeth agree to sponsor John Hawkins's slaving voyages during the first decade of her reign? In the late eighteenth century, abolitionists perpetuated the claim that the queen loaned ships from her Royal Navy to Hawkins despite her religious proclivities and strong personal misgivings about selling Africans into slavery. In a private meeting with Hawkins, she reportedly said that if he carried away Africans without their consent, such an act "would be detestable and call down the vengeance of heaven upon the undertakers." Hawkins, an unscrupulous merchant adventurer intent on fame and fortune, ignored the queen's concerns. He captured and enslaved Africans by force, thus commencing England's—and, ultimately, Britain's—investment in the trafficking of Africans. Hawkins alone was to blame, not the queen, her government, or the institution of the monarchy. Yet the quote famously attributed to Elizabeth I, popularized by the abolitionists Anthony Benezet and Thomas Clarkson and repeated countless times since, stems from a naval history of Britain published in 1756 by John Hill, who failed to attribute his source. In other words, to understand the queen's motivations, her supposed qualm about enslaving innocent Africans is a dead end, not a starting point.

Considering the sixteenth-century geopolitical and religious context in the British Isles, continental Europe, and the broader Atlantic world offers more accurate insight into Elizabeth's ambitions. Age twenty-five at her accession, Elizabeth I had barely survived the reign of her elder Catholic half-sister, Mary Tudor. She inherited an island kingdom mired in debt, religious strife, and political factionalism. Her royal predecessors, particularly her father, Henry VIII, had harbored grand imperial ambitions. But Tudor England was a second-rate power compared to Spain, Portugal, and France. Divided over religion, England remained resource poor and vulnerable to invasion by the wealthier, more populous Catholic nations in Europe.

Between 1553 and 1558, Mary Tudor forcibly wrenched the country away from Protestantism. She collaborated with the papacy to reverse the Protestant religious transformations initiated in the wake of Henry VIII's break with Rome two decades earlier. A devout Catholic, Mary reestablished the Catholic Mass and papal authority, married the equally fervent Philip of Spain, returned lands taken by the Crown to the Catholic Church, and persecuted Protestant dissenters. Mary and Philip, in a nod to papal authority and Philip's own imperial interests, prohibited English merchants from encroaching upon overseas trade and territories claimed by other European monarchs. In the final year of Mary's reign, England's medieval ambitions in Europe, reinvigorated by Henry VIII's expensive yet disappointing military campaigns, were dashed after the seaport of Calais, just across the Channel from Dover, fell to the French. Losing Calais, England's only territorial foothold on the Continent and a crucial link to European markets, dealt a crushing blow to national honor and weighed heavily on Elizabeth I at the start of her reign.

England's Protestant queen faced numerous obstacles upon her accession, the Crown's weak fiscal position chief among them. Her treasury was virtually empty and burdened with an inherited debt equal to a year's income. The revenue sources that made up two-thirds of her regular, ordinary income—the royal lands and customs duties—proved inadequate to meet the Crown's mushrooming annual expenditures. Finding extra-European markets for English goods and increasing the funds at her government's disposal was a top priority. That the country possessed only a minute fraction of global trade frustrated England's mercantile community. The queen shared this concern. She was cognizant of both the immense value of overseas trade and her own vulnerability as the Protestant female head of an impoverished island kingdom. "For whosoever commands the sea, commands the trade," acknowledged Sir Walter Raleigh, one of Queen Elizabeth's most infamous favorites; "whosoever commands the trade of the world commands the riches of the world, and consequently the world itself." Unlike its Iberian Catholic neighbors, Elizabethan England commanded neither the sea nor trade. And certainly not the world and its riches.

In stark contrast, Spain claimed sovereignty over lands, commerce, and mined resources in the Americas, and the Spanish Crown received one-fifth of the profits from the distribution of Spanish American gold, silver, pearls, and precious stones throughout the world. Portugal asserted its dominance over the flourishing gold trade with West Africa, the spice trade with the East Indies, and Brazil's sugar and wood trade. As early as 1486, King João II of Portugal had assumed the title "Lord of Guinea" to trumpet his subjects' premier access to West African gold markets. The Portuguese Crown enriched itself by declaring the African trade a royal preserve, which required merchants to obtain a royal license and pay one-fifth of their profits to the state. In addition to exporting substantial quantities of African gold, the Portuguese purchased enslaved Africans to work in the sugarcane fields of the Atlantic islands, including Madeira, Azores, Cape Verde, Canaries, and São Tomé. Portuguese traders sold Africans into slavery in Lisbon and Castile and pioneered the transatlantic slave trade to Spain's possessions in the Caribbean and Central and South America.

After 1492, the European invasion of the Americas had offered unprecedented opportunities to acquire vast territories, exploit natural and human resources, and expand Christendom overseas. The Iberian imperial project was a military, legal, and religious enterprise, sanctioned by both temporal and spiritual leaders. Approved by Pope Alexander VI in 1494, the Treaty of Tordesillas divided the world into Spanish and Portuguese spheres of influence. Lands east of the imaginary north-south meridian dividing the Atlantic Ocean fell under Portugal's purview, while territories to the west became the exclusive preserve of Spain. What the Indigenous inhabitants of these regions thought of such a demarcation was considered irrelevant. To assert and defend their title to newly discovered territories, Spain and Portugal drew on papal bulls, reports of the submission of Indigenous peoples, and the Roman legal notion of possession, which posited that a possessor of a thing, or territory, only needed to show that they had a better claim than a competing power. These events and presumptions set the stage for Spain's and other European countries' subsequent colonization of the Americas and the enslavement and decimation of Indigenous populations.

In the decades after Christopher Columbus first made landfall in the Bahamas, Spanish explorers, raiders, and settlers captured and consigned hundreds of thousands of Indigenous people to slavery. The dispossession and enslavement of Native peoples went hand in hand with European colonization in the Americas. Some Indigenous captives were transported back to Europe, to be auctioned off in the markets of the Mediterranean; others were dispersed throughout the Spanish colonies and compelled to serve as miners, plantation laborers, guides, translators, pearl divers, servants, and unwilling sexual partners. In the circum-Caribbean, cultural and linguistic differences between the Arawak or Taíno peoples of the Greater Antilles and the supposedly warlike "Caribs" of the Lesser Antilles were exaggerated to create categories of enslaveable Indians. The Spanish launched slaving raids, both royally sanctioned and legally ambiguous, against resistant Native peoples and Caribs living in so-called "useless" islands lacking in gold deposits.

Although the Spanish monarchy banned Native slavery in most instances in 1542, Spanish colonists flouted the new royal laws and justified their continued enslavement of Indigenous peoples by invoking "just-war doctrines." According to this line of thought, resistance to Spanish Christian rule by Native peoples merited their subjugation through war and bondage.

An illicit Indigenous slave trade flourished alongside legal trades, encompassing the circum-Caribbean, South America, and North America as far north as the Chesapeake. While a lack of surviving records makes it difficult to track the full extent of the Native slave trade, Indigenous slavery played a central role in the development of Spain's empire in the Americas, and the practice persisted in illicit form for centuries. Vocal criticism of Spanish mistreatment of Native peoples by clerics such as Bartolomé de Las Casas gave rise to the Black Legend, a myth perpetuated by other European powers, particularly the English, to undermine

Spanish colonial rule. Even as the transatlantic slave trade altered the demographic makeup of the sixteenth-century Spanish empire, enslaved Africans frequently lived and worked alongside enslaved people of Native descent.

What were the English doing during this early period of unparalleled Iberian overseas expansion and resource exploitation? In the 1480s, while the Portuguese were constructing their stronghold at Elmina on the Gold Coast, the English sought to establish their own trading relations with West Africa. In February 1481, Edward IV sought permission from Pope Sixtus IV for two merchants, John Tintam and William Fabian, to undertake a venture to West Africa on behalf of the duke of Medina Sedonia. The English king informed the pope that he "willingly permits his subjects to pass over to any parts of Africa for traffic and the exchange of baser merchandise for nobler," intimating that this trade had occurred in an unofficial capacity prior to his request for papal permission. When news of the intended venture reached the ears of King João II of Portugal, he dispatched an ambassador to England to proclaim Africa as his master's exclusive sphere of influence. Edward acquiesced to João's claims of sovereignty over the West African trade and prohibited the expedition. This 1481 incident suggests why the English, a minor player on the world stage, preferred to operate in regions where the Iberian powers held little to no influence.

The lure of overseas trade with non-Christians and uncharted lands rich with untapped natural resources fascinated the Tudor monarchs. In 1496 and again in 1498, Henry VII granted letters patent, or open letters under the royal seal, to the Italian navigator John Cabot and his sons to sail westward in search of "regions or provinces of the heathen and infidels whatsoever they be, and in what part of the world soever they be, which before this time have been unknown to all Christians." Like his Iberian counterparts, Henry VII would receive one-fifth of the net profits of the enterprise, though the king invested no money of his own. Cabot made landfall on the northeastern coast of present-day Newfoundland, claiming the previously unknown land for the English Crown. Henry rewarded Cabot with £10 and a pension of £20 per year and began plotting more ambitious exploratory ventures to the tropical southern oceans.

Pedro de Ayala, the Spanish ambassador in England, watched these developments with unease. He warned King Ferdinand and Queen Isabella that Henry hoped to profit at their expense. While the English might claim sovereignty over territory in the western hemisphere by right of Cabot's find, "what they have discovered or are in search of is possessed by Your Highnesses," Ayala wrote. The Spanish Crown refused to let English claims of first discovery in North America go uncontested. In 1498, Christopher Columbus stumbled upon South America, a mysterious landmass later described by Amerigo Vespucci as "an enormous land, to be found in the south, of which at present time nothing has been known." As recognition of the existence of vast continents between Europe and Asia dawned, English promoters pointed to Cabot's landfall on the far northern mainland as evidence of their Crown's title to North America. Henry VII granted new letters patent for an Atlantic crossing to an Anglo-Portuguese syndicate based in Bristol in 1501. But nothing came of the voyage. Spain, meanwhile, worked to consolidate and defend its burgeoning empire in the Americas.

Henry VIII concentrated his attention on mounting expensive military campaigns in France rather than encouraging overseas trade or westward expeditions across the Atlantic. The mercantile community, however, assumed that the nation's economic future depended on the global expansion of English commerce. Merchants from Bristol and London tapped into preexisting Anglo-Iberian commercial networks, particularly with the principal ports of southern Spain. Granted special privileges by the duke of Medina Sidonia, the hereditary lord of Sanlúcar de Barrameda, hundreds of traders relocated to Seville, Sanlúcar, and Cádiz, where they were well positioned to take advantage of trading opportunities. English merchants made fortunes through participation in Iberian Atlantic commerce, including the West African slave trade. Resident in the Mediterranean, Englishmen purchased and sold enslaved captives from North and sub-Saharan Africa and exploited the labor of enslaved individuals in their homes and businesses. Despite Henry VIII's rejection of papal authority in the 1530s, English merchants continued to profit from engagement with Anglo-Iberian commercial networks.

Yet the English mercantile community aspired to attain direct access to overseas markets over which the Spanish and Portuguese claimed exclusive dominion. Merchants based in Plymouth and Southampton penetrated the coasts of both Brazil and West Africa, where they traded for pepper, ivory, and brazilwood (used to make red dye). In the early 1530s, William Hawkins, father of John Hawkins, made three expeditions to Pernambuco, Brazil, calling first at Guinea for elephant tusks and other commodities. During his second voyage, Hawkins left behind a crew member, Martin Cockeram, in Brazil as surety for an Indigenous man identified as "one of the savage kings of the country." The Brazilian *cacique*, or chief, sailed with Hawkins to England and was presented to Henry VIII at Whitehall, "at the sight of whom the king and all the nobility did not a little marvel." Although the Indigenous man died en route to Brazil the following year, the Native Brazilians honored their arrangement with Hawkins and released Cockeram. In 1536, Hawkins wrote to Thomas Cromwell, Henry's chief minister at the time, requesting the king's sponsorship for a transatlantic trading venture. "I doubt not to do such feats of merchandise as shall be of great advantage to the king's custom," he assured Cromwell.

By midcentury, English merchants were pursuing opportunities to import coveted foreign goods straight from their source rather than through commercial intermediaries. The Barbary trade in North Africa offered Englishmen the opportunity to obtain luxury grocery wares, mainly sugar, without passing through Iberian spheres of influence. Weakening Portuguese control along the Atlantic coast in Morocco, where French interlopers had challenged Portugal's monopoly over trade, influenced the first wave of documented English ventures to the region. In 1551 and 1552, Thomas Wyndham, the master of naval ordinance, commanded expeditions to Agadir and Safi in Morocco, trading English merchandise for sugar, molasses, dates, and almonds—foreign products that commanded high prices at home.

African gold, however, was the ultimate prize. Locating it demanded more ambitious ventures to West African coastal areas where the Portuguese held sway and resisted any commercial challengers with violent reprisals. On August 12, 1553, during the first weeks of Mary Tudor's reign, a voyage sponsored by a consortium of London merchants departed Portsmouth for Guinea and the kingdom of Benin. Wyndham again captained the venture, seconded by Anthonie Anes Pinteado, a Portuguese naval commander. The expedition consisted of two royal vessels, the 240-ton *Primrose* and *Moon*, a pinnace, chartered from the government of Edward VI prior to his death. Pinteado, having lost the favor of the Portuguese Crown and defected to England, claimed that an abundance of gold and other profitable commodities awaited them on the West African coast, and his pilot, Francisco Rodrigues, knew the way. Months later the expedition returned home with 150 pounds of gold and eighty tons of pepper. But the loss of life was staggering. Only forty of the original 140 crew members survived the voyage, and both captains succumbed to fever and died in the Bight of Benin.

Undeterred, leading London merchants prepared to launch another West African trading venture. The expedition set out in October 1554 captained by John Lok, a relatively inexperienced seaman from one of the leading merchant families in London. Investors' faith in Lok was not entirely misplaced. He avoided stopping in Madeira or other Portuguese possessions and went ashore to trade solely on the Gold Coast, rather than risk loss of life by sailing farther south. Lok's expedition fared well, returning home with a valuable cargo of pepper, ivory, and roughly four hundred pounds of gold, with only twenty-four men lost. Lok recounted how one crew member, Martin Frobisher, had fallen into Portuguese custody after volunteering to serve as a trading hostage—the cost of doing business—in the town of Shamma. Frobisher remained in his captors' hands until 1556, when he returned to England with vital first-hand knowledge of Portuguese-controlled West Africa and stories of the famed Northwest Passage to Asia. Lok's 1554 venture generated profit and skewed misperceptions of African coastal kingdoms and peoples. A description of the voyage, later published by Richard Hakluyt, characterized West and West Central Africa as an alien, sun-scorched land populated by "Moors and Negroes, a people of beastly living, without a God, law, religion, or commonwealth."

These remarks belied the true state of West and West Central African kingdoms in the sixteenth century. Europeans were heavily dependent on the African coastal brokers who negotiated cross-cultural trade and on local rulers for security. While English seafarers and merchants may have expressed disdain for the unfamiliar communities and peoples they encountered in West Africa, the English coveted the commodities produced by those societies. And none more so than gold. Since the eleventh century, West African gold producers had provided the gold that financed the expansion of Mediterranean economies and allowed for the growth of Iberian empires. Tudor monarchs and England's mercantile community, cut off from African gold supplies except for occasional haphazard trade, lacked access to capital accumulation in the form of gold bullion. England's sluggish start in the development of extra-European trading networks compelled private merchants to borrow royal naval vessels and sponsor repeated incursions into West African coastal areas, regardless of the perils.

The Portuguese fiercely resisted English efforts to grab a share of the West and West Central African trade. For more than a century, Portugal had monopolized European access to the African gold trade, through which it had attained wealth and international esteem. Now, with the arrival of other European powers in the region, that dominance was under threat. After repeated English voyages to the Gold Coast in the early 1550s, the Portuguese ambassador presented a formal complaint regarding "the unlawful traffic of English merchants in Guinea" to Queen Mary and her husband, Philip of Spain. Philip took the lead in these discussions and determined that his English subjects, whatever their objections, must honor the terms of previous agreements granting Portugal dominion over the African trade. On July 18, 1555, in response to a royal directive, the Privy Council ordered the Lord Mayor of London to command all merchants to refrain from further traffic to West Africa, "for that the King of Portugal makes a claim to that navigation." Preparations for trading ventures to the region continued quietly, nonetheless. At the end of the year, the Privy Council directed a London syndicate to abandon a planned expedition to Mina (in present-day coastal Ghana) and hand over its cargo to the Crown in exchange for compensation.

As the English state under Mary and Philip prohibited voyages to West Africa, London's mercantile community petitioned the queen to resist Portuguese pressure to bar English subjects from the African trade. They insisted that free access to overseas markets and friendly extra-European trading partners formed part of their natural rights under "the common usage of the world." Honoring Portugal's exclusive rights to trade in West

African waters diminished England's ability to remain competitive in a rapidly globalizing world, they argued. Still, the Crown did not reverse course. In 1556, Philip II succeeded to the Spanish throne and inherited a vast empire spanning Europe and the Americas. By upholding the Portuguese Crown's monopoly of West African trade, Philip implicitly supported his own transoceanic claim to exclusive dominion.

That English merchants paid little heed to the monarchy's directives is evidenced by repeated Privy Council attempts to prevent expeditions to West Africa from launching throughout 1556. In July, the Privy Council redistributed a second order to all the major city and port authorities prohibiting English merchants from trading on the Gold Coast or other Portuguese-controlled regions of Africa. Royal efforts to prevent trading ventures to West African coastal areas, and assurances of compensation for voided expeditions, continued for the remainder of Mary Tudor's reign.

English attempts to penetrate the West African trade accelerated after November 17, 1558, when a new Protestant monarch ascended the throne following the death of her childless half-sister, Mary. A young, unmarried queen, Elizabeth I stood on uncertain ground. She had inherited a government deep in debt and a stagnant economy. Her island kingdom was riven with political instability compounded by religious strife. Elizabeth began her reign as she had lived the initial decades of her life: on a knife's edge. Catholics refused to recognize the divorce of Henry VIII and Catherine of Aragon or the legitimacy of Henry's marriage to Elizabeth's mother, Anne Boleyn. In their eyes Elizabeth was a bastard and a heretic, unfit to rule. Protestants, meanwhile, desired revenge following the religious persecutions of Mary's reign and public burnings of some three hundred Protestants condemned for heresy. English Protestants rejoiced in Elizabeth's accession but questioned whether she had the stomach for the task ahead. She was, after all, a woman. But Elizabeth, an astute and cautious ruler, stayed violent hands, preventing her most zealous Protestant subjects from turning upon their prior tormentors. She worked with Parliament and her Privy Council to implement policies designed to promote religious unity and replenish her government's coffers.

Her Tudor predecessors had bequeathed to Elizabeth a nearly bankrupt treasury and depreciated currency. Since her father's reign, the precious metal content in the kingdom's coinage supply had plummeted. Henry VIII and Edward VI had repeatedly debased the English coinage, ordering the Royal Mint to adulterate silver and gold coins with cheaper inferior metals, such as copper, to increase the amount of money in circulation to fund foreign wars. Raising revenue for the Crown and redeeming the debased coinage by bringing bullion into the country topped Elizabeth's list of priorities. To tackle these pressing issues, the queen readily encouraged and invested in overseas trade and shared the aims of England's mercantile community.

From the outset, Elizabeth's government promoted a series of expeditions to West Africa, embracing opportunities to acquire precious metals overseas at the expense of rival European nations. When the Portuguese envoy João Pereira Dantas crossed the English Channel in May 1562 to defend his master's exclusive claim to the African trade, Elizabeth and her advisers sought fresh intelligence. To assist the queen in determining the true extent of Portuguese influence on the West African coast, the Privy Council sent for Martin Frobisher. Frobisher's nine months of captivity at the Elmina fortress on the Gold Coast in the mid-1550s held the potential to benefit his queen.

Though his information was dated, Frobisher possessed useful firsthand knowledge of conditions on the ground. He declared that the king of Portugal had only a few trading outposts dotted along the African coastline stretching south from Cape Verde to Benin. The Portuguese dared not stray far from their forts, he claimed, because "none of the people other than such as inhabit under the said fort, or within gunshot of the same, owe any obedience, neither be they at the commandment of the Portuguese." Regarding the Portuguese Crown's efforts to convert the native Africans to Christianity, Frobisher observed that at the central castle of Elmina "not the fourth person of them [are] christened;" and, other than the occasional Mass, "there is neither priest nor preacher to convert anyone." His opinions confirmed the assumptions of Elizabeth and her councilors. While the Portuguese ambassador might bluster and threaten, his master held only a light grip on Africa. Unchartered regions and trading partners beckoned, and the Portuguese were incapable of mounting a campaign of resistance along the entire West African coast.

Elizabeth responded to the Portuguese Crown's growing concerns about English interlopers in Africa with incredulity. If all the kingdoms in Guinea and on the Gold Coast owed obedience and tribute to the Crown of Portugal, she pressed, why did Africans engage in trade with other European nations, including the French and the English? Additionally, if the Portuguese king wished to spread Christianity overseas, as Dantas maintained, why would he forbid her Christian subjects from trading in his dominions on the coast of Africa? Surely "the more Christian people that shall resort to the Gentiles and Saracens, the more shall the faith increase," Elizabeth wrote in her reply. She could not countenance "that more regard should be had to the enriching of any particular person by monopolies and private navigations than to the public utility of the whole body of Christendom." Dissatisfied with the outcome of his diplomatic mission, Dantas submitted a thorough rejoinder to England's Protestant queen. He defended his master's sovereignty and conversion efforts and accused English merchants of seeking to traffic in Africa solely "upon the ambition of profit, and whose least thought is to increase the knowledge of God."

Still, Elizabeth's mind remained unchanged. The queen and the Portuguese ambassador went back and forth over the matter of the African trade for several weeks. Taking exception at the king of Portugal's pretensions to sovereignty over vast stretches of the West African coast, Elizabeth deemed it incomprehensible that Christian sovereigns on friendly terms should prevent their subjects from trading freely throughout their dominions. She also protested attempts by Dantas to link the rights of Portugal in Africa to those of Spain in the Americas. "He joins the name of the King Catholic to that of his master's," Dantas responded, "because in this matter the rights of one cannot be violated without prejudice to the other." Dantas's argument proved prescient. Just as the queen concluded their discussions and sent the discontented Portuguese envoy back to his master, one of her seafaring subjects was preparing to undertake an audacious transatlantic voyage: a voyage calculated to trespass on the exclusive spheres of both Iberian powers—to his own and England's benefit.

Born around 1532, John Hawkins grew up in one of the wealthiest merchant households in Plymouth, a strategic seaport perched at England's southwestern-most tip, where the English Channel flows into the Atlantic

Ocean. He spent his youth surrounded by influential men and hardened seafarers, raised on a diet of incredible tales of distant, unknown lands and exotic commodities, as much at home on the ocean as on the docks. His father, William, a successful businessman and ship owner, held several important positions in Plymouth, including town treasurer, mayor, and member of Parliament. He had made a fortune importing foreign products from Iberia, France, the Canaries, and Newfoundland. The elder Hawkins's maverick ambitions had compelled him to look for profit much farther afield, on the coast of West Africa and in Brazil, which brought him to the attention of the English Crown.

Encouraged to cut his teeth in the family business at a young age, John Hawkins made regular voyages from Plymouth to the Canary Islands to exchange English goods for wine and sugar. After his father's death in 1554, he inherited a fleet of ships and an extensive overseas commercial network. In Tenerife, the largest of Spain's Canary Islands, Hawkins forged a close trading partnership with Pedro de Ponte, a merchant with connections in Hispaniola and knowledge of the slave trade to the Spanish Indies. Hawkins, informed "that Negroes were very good merchandise in Hispaniola, and that store of Negroes might easily be had upon the coast of Guinea," determined to undertake a transatlantic slaving venture of his own. Such was his drive to turn a profit and make a name for himself at Elizabeth's court that Hawkins readily shifted his focus from importing foreign products to the coerced trafficking of human "merchandise."

With assurances in hand from Pedro de Ponte, who agreed to provide him with supplies and an experienced pilot to help guide him along the coast of Guinea and to the ports of Hispaniola, Hawkins looked for investors. He first approached Benjamin Gonson, treasurer of the Royal Navy since 1549 and his future father-in-law. Well-connected and moneyed, Gonson organized a consortium of London businessmen willing to back Hawkins's proposed transatlantic slaving venture. Investors included Sir Lionel Ducket, a sheriff and member of the Mercers' Company, one of London's oldest and wealthiest livery companies; Sir Thomas Lodge, a grocer and then–Lord Mayor of London; and William Winter, master of naval ordnance, among others.

In October 1562, as Queen Elizabeth fought a life-threatening case of smallpox at Hampton Court Palace, Hawkins set out from Plymouth. He captained three small ships totaling 260 tons—*Saloman, Jonas,* and *Swallow*—and a crew of less than a hundred men. Joining the voyage was his young cousin Francis Drake, sailing as a common sailor. Drake would later circumnavigate the globe and achieve wealth, fame, and a knighthood.

Hawkins's first stop was the island of Tenerife, where his business partner, Pedro de Ponte, awaited the fleet with food and water and a Spanish pilot, Juan Martinez of Cádiz. Ponte also facilitated Hawkins's trade by informing contacts in Hispaniola that the English merchant would soon arrive with enslaved Africans for sale. From Tenerife the squadron sailed to Cape Verde and south along the Guinea coast. Once in Sierra Leone, as Hawkins noted in characteristically vague language twenty years later, "he got into his possession, partly by the sword, and partly by other means, to the number of 300 Negroes at least, besides other merchandise, which that Country yieldeth." According to Portuguese witnesses, Hawkins and his men took multiple Portuguese ships containing valuable goods, such as ivory and wax, and stole away with around three hundred African captives awaiting forced transport to the Spanish Indies.

After dispatching one ship home laden with African commodities to sell in England, Hawkins and the remainder of his fleet crossed the Atlantic to vend their human cargo to Spanish colonists. During the eight-week voyage, Hawkins crammed the enslaved captives into the holds of his ships, subjecting them to unsanitary conditions and a near-starvation diet of beans and minuscule amounts of water. Many doubtless perished during the horrific crossing. Hawkins's slaving fleet arrived in Hispaniola in early April. He conducted a brisk trade at northern ports before leaving behind roughly one hundred unsold Africans, too sick or frail for purchase, to reclaim at an unspecified future date. To transport hides and sugar acquired in Hispaniola that would not fit on his ships, Hawkins sent his excess wares in two borrowed caravels to Spain, hoping to sneak the freight past royal customs officials. But authorities in Seville seized his cargo and sent word to officials in Hispaniola to confiscate the African women, men, and children Hawkins had left behind. Unaware of these developments for the time being, Hawkins and his small fleet returned to Plymouth in late August 1563, bearing gold and silver, pearls, hides, and sugar for his investors.

News of Hawkins's profitable slaving voyage, and the subsequent confiscation of his two additional cargoes in Spain, soon reached the queen's court. Elizabeth offered Hawkins her royal support. She penned letters to Philip II and the English ambassador in Madrid on Hawkins's behalf, pressing for the return of his stolen slaving proceeds in Seville. The queen had previously informed the Spanish ambassador of her resolution to treat cases of stolen ships or merchandise from the king of Spain's subjects "as if the matter was between her own subjects." She entreated Philip to likewise answer "as justice may require." The Spanish king dismissed Elizabeth's appeals for redress on behalf of an Englishman he regarded as a heretic pirate. Yet Hawkins's star rose rapidly at court. Capitalizing on his newfound fame, he initiated preparations for a second transatlantic slaving expedition, this time with additional heavy-hitting sponsors. Investors included two former lord mayors, influential merchants, members of Elizabeth's inner circle such as William Cecil and Robert Dudley, and even the queen herself.

CHAPTER 2

UNDER THE QUEEN'S COMMAND

I n tracing the monarchy's historic links to slavery, 1564–65 is a watershed year. It was then that Elizabeth I moved beyond either tacit or diplomatic support for Hawkins. The Tudor queen invested directly in the capture, coerced transatlantic transport, and sale of Africans into bondage in Spanish America. In exchange for a sixth-part share in the anticipated profits of the slaving venture, she loaned Hawkins an armed, fully equipped vessel from her Royal Navy: the 700-ton *Jesus of Lübeck*. The tonnage of the *Jesus*, a venerable warship originally purchased in 1545 by Henry VIII, was more than two and a half times that of Hawkins's entire first fleet. Although the *Jesus* had seen better days, naval assessors valued the lumbering warship at £2,012.15s.2d, and the Admiralty required payment of a £500 bond for use of the queen's ship. Commanding the *Jesus* and flying the queen's royal standard gave authority and prestige to Hawkins's second fleet, impressing potential enemies and trading partners alike. Hawkins could legitimately claim—and did—that his privately organized transatlantic slaving venture had Crown sanction; that he acted under the command of the queen of England and as her official representative.

Queen Elizabeth's sponsorship proved useful to Hawkins in multiple ways—financial, pragmatic, and symbolic. As he saw it, royal favor held the potential to assist his quest to break into the tightly controlled transatlantic slave trade to Spanish America. Bypassing the members of the Consulado and the Casa de Contratación, the merchants and officials in Seville who regulated the official slave trade on behalf of the Spanish Crown, Hawkins intended to sail directly to the Caribbean with his unlicensed cargo of African captives. Once his fleet reached Spanish waters, he

Figure 2.1. *Jesus of Lübeck.*

would obtain trading licenses from local authorities, pay the required royal taxes, and conduct business with Philip II's colonial subjects. Hawkins sought to prove to the Spanish Crown that he held honorable intentions: lawful, mutually beneficial trade. Not piracy. It mattered little to Hawkins that his scheme flouted Philip II's declarations forbidding foreigners from trading with his western possessions without prior permission. Hawkins aspired to impress the Spanish king with his seafaring skills, business acumen, and bravado, thereby securing a special royal grant permitting him to participate in the transatlantic slave trade to Spanish America.

In July 1564, Guzmán de Silva, the newly arrived Spanish ambassador in England, heard news of an impending Guinea voyage captained by John Hawkins with Crown support. Writing to Philip II, Silva explained that Queen Elizabeth had offered him assurances that Hawkins would not plunder Spain's American possessions. Elizabeth's words provided cold comfort to the Spanish king. Philip commanded Silva to activate his spy network in England and hinder the voyage if possible. Yet Hawkins had the queen's backing and the support of powerful, wealthy men at court.

The Spanish ambassador lacked the means of fulfilling his master's wishes. When Aires Cordoso, a Portuguese envoy, arrived in London in November equally intent on halting the slaving venture, he discovered to his dismay that Hawkins and his fleet had recently sailed. He was too late. Cordoso's urgent request that Elizabeth "command the said ships to be stayed and unarmed, and that those who have already sailed may be punished," came to nothing. The queen rebuffed the ambassador's concerns as unreasonable. Her subjects, she emphasized to the Portuguese king, ventured to trade in regions of Africa outside his dominion.

By this point, Hawkins's fleet of four ships—the queen's flagship, *Jesus*, Hawkins's 140-ton ship *Salomon*, and two nimble vessels for ferrying to and from shore, the 50-ton *Tiger* and the 30-ton *Swallow*—had refreshed supplies at Tenerife and were nearing the West African coast. Once the fleet reached Cape Verde, Hawkins divided his crew into raiding parties and sent them ashore. But the passage of another English fleet on its way to trade for gold in Guinea had alarmed the local people, who avoided Hawkins's men. For the next two months, as recounted by the merchant John Sparks in his narrative of the second voyage, Hawkins's fleet sailed along the coast of Sierra Leone, hunting for potential Africans to capture and enslave.

In December they stopped at an island Sparks called Sambula, most likely the Isle de Los off the site of present-day Conakry, to conduct slaving raids. "In this island we stayed certain days, going every day on shore to take the inhabitants, with burning and spoiling their towns," he noted bluntly. Sparks understood that Hawkins and his crew had arrived at an island whose inhabitants had undergone a recent violent upheaval. Although muddling their names, he described how the Mendes, or "Manes," a Mande-speaking people, had invaded the island three years earlier, conquering and enslaving the Sape peoples. Hawkins's slaving fleet likewise arrived with aggressive intentions. While the Mendes fled, his men captured the Sape, "of whom we took many in that place," said Sparks.

After departing the Isle de Los, Hawkins and his crew sailed north and anchored *Jesus* and *Salomon* at the mouth of the Calousa River. While cruising upriver in *Tiger* and *Swallow* in search of potential targets to kidnap, the Englishmen encountered two Portuguese slave ships at anchor.

Hawkins, as Sparks put it, "dispatched his business, and so returned with two caravels, laden with Negroes." Portuguese traders advised him of a nearby town in which gold and women and children were loosely guarded, "so that if he would give the adventure upon the same, he might get a hundred slaves." Guided by Portuguese informants, Hawkins took forty men and set upon the village. Scattering to ransack huts in pursuit of gold, of which they found none, his men were set upon by the retaliating villagers. They killed seven Englishmen and wounded many more, driving Hawkins and his surviving men, who had taken only ten captives, back to their ships. Soon afterward members of his crew began to fall ill, prompting Hawkins to cut his losses and depart Sierra Leone on January 29, 1565. His fleet headed west across the Atlantic, bound for the Spanish Caribbean with more than four hundred Africans chained together and crowded into the dismal holds of *Jesus* and *Salomon*.

By March 9, the fleet had reached the eastern Caribbean and went ashore for fresh water in Dominica. The Englishmen kept their stop brief, fearful of encountering the island's Native population due to their reputation, perpetuated by previous Spanish explorers, as man-eating cannibals. Hawkins called first to trade at the island of Margarita, where the governor not only refused to grant him a license to traffic but also promptly notified the viceroy in Santo Domingo of Hawkins's arrival. The viceroy, fearing Philip II's wrath, issued instructions throughout New Spain "that no man should traffic with us, but should resist us with all the force they could," Sparks recounted. This prohibition, though unsurprising, angered Hawkins. He sailed on toward the Spanish Main, prepared to force a trade if necessary.

Arriving at Borburata, a struggling port town on the Venezuelan coast, Hawkins informed local officials that fate, not design, had driven his fleet to their shores. He commanded "an armada of the queen's majesty of England," bound for Guinea and other parts, but was "forced by contrary winds to come into those parts, where he hoped to find such friendship as he should do in Spain." Due to the precarious state of his crew and the enslaved Africans he had forced to cross the Atlantic, he could not leave their port without first trading for essential supplies and money. After two months confined in the ships' holds with scant food and water, many of the enslaved Africans had grown emaciated and sickly; he needed to sell his human cargo posthaste. Through a combination of haggling and threats, Hawkins convinced the governor to grant him a license to trade. But they disagreed over the price of his captives, and Hawkins balked at paying both the king's custom duty of thirty ducats and a 7.5 percent tax per each African he sold.

After Hawkins threatened to descend on the town with one hundred armed men, trade finally commenced. He sold the remainder of his cargo, including approximately three hundred African individuals, in Río de la Hacha on Colombia's Caribbean coast before calling at Newfoundland for fish and crossing the North Atlantic and returning home. As Sparks concluded, the fleet arrived in Cornwall on September 20, "God be thanked, in safety, with the loss of twenty persons in all the voyage, and with great profit to venturers of the said voyage, and also to the whole realm, in bringing home both gold, silver, pearls, and other jewels in great store." The queen's slave trader had accomplished a daring feat of mercantile prowess, encroaching upon overseas territories claimed by the Iberian powers.

John Hawkins returned to England with most of his crew intact and substantial profits for his investors, including Queen Elizabeth. The immense proceeds of his second slaving expedition, which had cost about £4,990 to mount (not including the cargo or value of the ships), aroused the fury and resentment of the Iberian ambassadors and the admiration of his fellow countrymen. Guzmán de Silva reported that the syndicate more than doubled its investment, though no detailed financial account of the voyage survives. The reactions of Hawkins's English contemporaries are suggestive of his success. Characterizing Hawkins as a man of "courageous worth and famous enterprises," William Garvey, Clarenceux king of arms, granted Hawkins a coat of arms featuring a nude and bound African on the recommendation of William Cecil.

The Spanish ambassador invited John Hawkins to dinner. He was keen to take the measure of the Englishman who had repeatedly defied his master. After their meeting, Silva wrote to Philip II of the need for immediate action. The profitability of Hawkins's brash venture, he learned, "has encouraged some of the merchants here to undertake other like voyages and even that Hawkins will return in May." Hawkins had chattered like

Figure 2.2. Arms of Sir John Hawkins, c. 1568.

a magpie about his illicit transatlantic slaving expedition. His success had induced other English traders to emulate him through similar high-risk exploits and made him determined to set out again himself. Deterring the English mercantile and seafaring community from exploiting the Spanish Crown's empire in the Americas was fast becoming an issue of paramount importance.

Guzmán de Silva kept a close eye on the ambitious Plymouth merchant. The men dined together again three months later, in February 1566. Hawkins, anticipating a special license from Philip II, offered his services to the Spanish Crown. He said that though he faced pressure from eager investors in England to captain another transatlantic slaving venture, he would not undertake a third voyage without Philip's permission due to the dangers of the business. But Silva remained skeptical. "The trade of capturing Negroes in Guinea and taking them to the Indies is considered very profitable," he wrote to the king of Spain. "It seems advisable to get this man out of the country, so that he may not teach others." The following month Hawkins visited the Spanish ambassador again, offering the use of four ships for a slaving venture, besides "another vessel belonging to the queen, who he thought would willingly give it to him for that purpose." Silva feigned interest to keep Hawkins talking. "I am keeping him in hand," the Spanish envoy wrote to Philip, "because I understand that there are many people urging him to make another voyage like the last." The overconfident English slave trader was a growing liability to Spain.

John Hawkins, having recently wed Katherine Gonson, daughter of the treasurer of the navy, had in mind a different plan, a scheme that would prove no less displeasing to the Spanish king. Remaining in England, he dispatched a fleet of four vessels to Guinea and the Spanish Indies under the command of a cousin, John Lovell. Shortly before the fleet departed, Hawkins and three other key investors each posted a £500 bond agreeing to prevent their ships from venturing into Caribbean waters privileged by the king of Spain. In official terms, the bonds let the queen and her government off the hook for any damage her subjects might inflict upon Philip. But from the Spanish Crown's perspective, damage was certain. Hawkins had dispatched his kinsman to West Africa and the Spanish Caribbean intent on repeating the successes of previous unlicensed slaving voyages. Lovell, based in Tenerife for a time as the Hawkins family resident agent and knowledgeable about the route, lacked Hawkins's verve and business acumen. His venture included another relative, Francis Drake, who sailed again as a common seaman.

Lovell spent several months on the Guinea coast trading, capturing Africans, and seizing Portuguese ships, though scant evidence survives regarding the details of the journey. He returned to Borburata on the Venezuelan coast to sell his enslaved captives to Spanish colonists, assuming the license granted to Hawkins the previous year would smooth his way. However, the governor refused. Local officials in Río de la Hacha and Hispaniola likewise rebuffed Lovell. The Spanish Crown had forbidden trade with foreigners on pain of death; only threats and acts of violence could impel local authorities to defy the king. Unofficial business dealings with various Spanish colonists nonetheless still took place, clumsily forced by Lovell who, Hawkins later admitted, "knew not how to handle these matters." In the end, Lovell's voyage brought home minimal profit at great expense. His actions worsened relations with Spain and, as Hawkins later discovered, laid the groundwork for hostile opposition to future English incursions in Spanish America.

Optimism for slaving ventures nevertheless remained high in England. Two years later Hawkins announced his readiness to command a third transatlantic commercial expedition to West Africa and the Spanish Indies. He promised Queen Elizabeth substantial profits in gold and other precious metals if she reinvested. Writing to the queen, Hawkins spelled out his intention "to load Negroes in Guinea and sell them in the West Indies, in truck of gold, pearls and emeralds, whereof I doubt not but to bring home great abundance to the contentment of your highness." Elizabeth approved of his design to profit once again at the expense of the Iberian Crowns, loaning him two warships from her Royal Navy: *Jesus* and *Minion*.

On October 2, 1567, Hawkins set out on his third slaving expedition with six ships and 408 men, certain of his success. His cousin Francis Drake sailed with him again, this time commanding one of the smaller vessels. After a storm scattered the fleet several days into the voyage, Hawkins reconnected with the missing ships at Tenerife before continuing toward the West African coast. By the third week of November, Hawkins and his men had arrived at Cape Verde. Meeting with limited success, Hawkins pushed southward. His fleet clashed with Portuguese slaving vessels in the Cacheu River in modern Guinea-Bissau before departing to explore the coast of what is now Guinea and Sierra Leone.

By Christmas, although Hawkins had relied on his usual aggressive tactics to round up as many African captives as possible over the previous month, his crew failed to net sufficient enslaved individuals to justify an Atlantic crossing. The situation grew more urgent as sickness swept through his fleet, killing nearly a quarter of his men. Hawkins weighed his options. An opportunity to acquire additional captives emerged when two local leaders who served as slaving intermediaries requested his assistance in an assault on a rival chief on the island of Conga in the Tagarin River of Sierra Leone. It is challenging to identify the warring African forces that Hawkins took advantage of for his own purposes. They most likely included the Mendes and the Temnes, the latter of whom lived along the Tagarin River and were conquered by the Mendes around this time. During the siege, which occurred in early January 1568, Hawkins and his allies captured roughly 850 prisoners, all of whom were supposedly promised to Hawkins in exchange for his aid of men and firepower. But immediately after the attack, his Native allies disappeared in the night along with 650 prisoners. Hawkins felt duped. But with nearly five hundred enslaved Africans in hand, "we thought it somewhat reasonable to seek the coast of the West Indies," he later clarified in *The Third Troublesome Voyage*.

Back in London, Guzmán de Silva met with Queen Elizabeth to complain of Hawkins's unfolding slaving venture. His spies had learned that Hawkins's fleet, after stopping in the Canaries, had embarked for Guinea in November. The expedition was bound to culminate in Hawkins crossing the Atlantic with his human merchandise and trespassing in the king of Spain's western dominions, Silva pointed out. Elizabeth, who knew full well the intent of Hawkins's third voyage, tried to soothe the Spanish ambassador's mind. "She made me great promises about it," he informed Philip II, "and said she would cut off Hawkins's head if he exceeded by one tittle the orders that had been given to him." The queen convinced Silva that she had given Hawkins strict instructions not to enter areas prohibited by the Spanish Crown, under threat of severe punishment for disobedience. Pleased by this intelligence, Philip directed his envoy in England to "thank her for forbidding Hawkins and his companions from going to my Indian territories." Elizabeth excelled at offering underhanded assistance to her subjects while simultaneously denying responsibility.

Naturally, Hawkins and his fleet were headed straight for the king of Spain's dominions in the Caribbean. After reaching Dominica on March 27, 1568, he spent four months cruising around the Caribbean and Spanish Main conducting business. As Hawkins later recounted, the Spanish Crown's crackdown on unlicensed foreigners did not prevent him from finding "reasonable trade, and courteous entertainment, from the isle of Margarita unto Cartagena." His luck took a turn for the worse in late July, when his fleet, laden with gold, silver, jewels, and hides, departed

Cartagena and set course for Florida—at the start of hurricane season. A violent storm descended upon them and "beat the *Jesus*," disabling the rudder and weakening the timber until the warship sprung many leaks. With his flagship severely damaged and taking on water, Hawkins sought refuge in San Juan de Ulúa, then the principal port of New Spain, located in modern Veracruz, Mexico.

Hawkins's arrival in San Juan de Ulúa on September 16 was ill-timed. Port officials had long anticipated the arrival of the Spanish fleet bearing the fourth viceroy of New Spain, Don Martín Enríquez. On September 17, the Spanish fleet, consisting of thirteen ships, appeared on the horizon. Enríquez, outraged to discover that the ships anchored in the port belonged to English pirates, feigned civility. He informed Hawkins they would enter the port in peace. But it soon became clear the Spanish intended to attack. In the ensuing battle, the queen's damaged warship *Jesus* and several other vessels were abandoned; only *Minion* and *Judith* escaped. Hawkins, aboard *Minion*, found himself in a tight predicament. The ship, which now carried its own men and others who had fled the lost ships, was running severely low on food and water. He put the question to his crew and half opted to take their chances on shore in Florida. After leaving around a hundred men behind, Hawkins staggered back to England, arriving on January 25, 1569, a few days after Drake, who captained *Judith*. And just in time: Elizabeth's advisers and Hawkins's older brother, William, feared the worst and had nearly given him up for dead.

Once home, Hawkins attempted to clamp down on rumors regarding the failure of his third slaving voyage. In a letter to William Cecil, Hawkins blamed his heavy losses on "the treason of the Spaniards," who had feigned civility to the English fleet but with ill intent in mind. The venture "hath had infelicity, misfortune, and an unhappy end," he admitted. Hawkins penned an account of the voyage and requested that Cecil reserve judgment until he had examined his version of the events that had transpired in Spanish waters. In March 1569, Hawkins and six others who had invested in the transatlantic slaving expedition appeared before the High Court of Admiralty. In an attempt to secure redress from the Spanish Crown, they drew up a schedule of losses. The lengthy list of goods and human merchandise for which Hawkins and his fellow investors sought compensation included twenty-seven items, totaling nearly

£28,000. The two most substantial claims were the queen's ship, *Jesus*, and its equipment, guns, and cannons (worth £7,000) and fifty-seven enslaved Africans "of the best kind of stature," valued at a minimum of £9,120.

Queen Elizabeth, though undoubtedly disappointed by the poor outcome of the slaving venture, did not reprimand John Hawkins. She supported his formal complaint against the Spanish, including the claim for financial recompense for goods and equipment lost at San Juan de Ulúa. While Hawkins may not have received advance permission from Philip II to conduct business in his empire in the Americas, local Spanish authorities had granted him permits to trade. As the English saw it, Hawkins had acted in good faith. Moreover, the queen and her advisers denied the pope's right to apportion the world into exclusive spheres of influence controlled by the Iberian Catholic powers. Elizabeth's contentious response to Hawkins's depredations in both Portuguese-controlled West Africa and Spanish America heightened Anglo-Iberian political tensions.

The Portuguese Crown countered with its own demand for legal redress and reimbursement for losses. Hawkins, the king's representatives contended, had stolen "a great spoil of ivory, wax, and Negroes" from Portuguese slaving vessels in West Africa. It was of no consequence that his venture netted losses of 50 percent, besides a majority of the sailors. "In the two years 1567, 1568," the Portuguese envoy wrote to the queen, Hawkins "has taken more than 200,000 ducats"—worth roughly £66,000 at the time. Elizabeth demurred to all the allegations. She refused to reimburse the Portuguese for damages, to forbid her subjects from voyaging to the West African coast, or to castigate Hawkins according to the Crown of Portugal's wishes. "The king is pricked to the heart that she refuses immediate recompense to his subjects for piracies committed by the English, and again demands that she will do so," his ambassador retorted.

John Hawkins's Crown-sponsored third voyage had ended in catastrophe and considerable loss of life. However, it neither dampened enthusiasm for the African trade in England nor tarnished his reputation among his countrymen. The English celebrated Hawkins as an intrepid slave-trading hero who dared to challenge the commercial monopolies of two of the most powerful Catholic nations in Europe. Throughout the 1560s, Hawkins had assumed he could demonstrate his worth to Philip II and consequently receive special treatment in Spain's empire in the Americas.

No more. His harrowing experience in San Juan de Ulúa in 1568 crushed that fantasy, engendering in its place a profound and lasting hatred of the Spanish. Hawkins spent the rest of his political career, serving as a member of Parliament for Plymouth and treasurer of the navy, seeking revenge against Spain for the undignified end to his transatlantic slaving voyages.

In the 1570s, tensions between Protestant England and its Catholic neighbors intensified. On February 25, 1570, Pope Pius V issued the bull *Regnans in Excelsis*, excommunicating Queen Elizabeth I from the Catholic Church as a "heretic and an abettor of heretics." The bull released all those who subscribed to the "true faith" from their allegiance to the English queen, ordering them not to obey Elizabeth or her commandments on pain of incurring the sentence of excommunication themselves. In the eyes of the queen and her council, the bull transformed every Catholic in her kingdom into a potential traitor. It also further emboldened her government to ignore acts of predation directed against Catholic foreign powers. Consequently, the 1570s saw a marked increase of English piracy against Iberian shipping and Spanish possessions in the Caribbean, and the deterioration of Anglo-Iberian relations. Portuguese diplomatic interventions and military opposition to English commercial activities in West Africa ranging from Sierra Leone to the Benin coast led to the temporary abandonment of the Guinea trade.

In August 1578, however, the death of King Sebastião of Portugal in a crusading battle in Alcazar in Morocco provoked a dynastic crisis that nullified earlier Anglo-Portuguese trade agreements. Two years earlier, Muhammad al-Mutawakkil, the sultan of Morocco, had crossed into Iberia and requested Portuguese aid after his uncle, Abd al-Malik, deposed him from the throne. Sebastião, an idealistic, fervently devout Catholic, had long aspired to reclaim parts of Atlantic Morocco from which the Portuguese had been driven out in the 1540s. He seized the opportunity to embark on a new crusading campaign to North Africa. But Abd al-Malik's army, aided by Ottoman forces, crushed the childless, twenty-four-year-old king and his army of crusaders. Sebastião was succeeded by his elderly granduncle, Cardinal Henrique, who died without issue in 1580. With the male line of the Portuguese royal family extinct, Philip II took the opportunity to conquer Portugal and annex it to Spain. In April

1581, Philip II became Philip I of Portugal, uniting the Iberian Peninsula and its extensive global dominions under one ruler until 1640. The Iberian union strengthened England's greatest rival, posing a serious threat to Queen Elizabeth. It also made previous trade agreements with Portugal moot. In June 1581, Dom António, an exiled claimant to the Portuguese throne, arrived in London to seek English military aid. Dom António needed assistance to prevent Philip from taking the Azores, the only Portuguese territory still claiming loyalty to him. Lacking coin, he offered Elizabeth the fortress of Elmina as security until he repaid her. This concession was purely academic, as the Gold Coast and its trade remained well protected by Portuguese forces. Although nothing came of Dom António's request for English military support, his arrival catalyzed calls by English merchants to resume the West African trade. To finance his campaign to recover the Portuguese throne and pay off debts accumulated in England, Dom António struck a deal with West Country and London merchants. In exchange for a £500 license to conduct business on the Senegambian coast, a merchant syndicate known as the Senegal Adventurers agreed to recognize Dom António as the lawful king of Portugal and pay him a duty of 5 percent on the profits of all goods acquired there.

In May 1588, the same month the Spanish Armada set sail from Lisbon to invade England, Queen Elizabeth issued a royal charter to the Senegal Adventurers. She granted them a ten-year monopoly of English trade with Senegambia. Per the terms of a separate contract signed between the Adventurers and Dom António, it was understood that they would sail in the company of his agents and a Portuguese pilot. Limited by her meager financial resources, the queen was willing to turn Dom António's cause to her own and her subjects' advantage so long as open war with Philip II did not result from supporting the Portuguese pretender. But a Spanish seaborne force would soon be on her doorstep nonetheless. From late July to August, Queen Elizabeth faced the most dangerous threat to her reign. The Spanish Armada attempted to assail the English coastline and depose the Protestant queen, but the Spanish ships were intercepted and beaten back by the English fleet.

Meanwhile, Dom António's imperfect knowledge of Senegambia became apparent. The Portuguese had minimal influence in the region as commercial go-betweens, having erected only limited outposts on the coast. Senegambian rulers preferred to trade directly with the French and the English, dismissing Portugal's pretensions to commercial dominion. The English lacked sufficient motivation to uphold the terms of the 1588 agreement privileging Dom António. In 1589, his fortunes worsened when an ill-fated English expedition to Iberia intended to install him on the Portuguese throne failed. Dom António, his political prospects now permanently dashed, was unable to hold his Anglo trading partners to account. English merchants familiarized themselves with Senegambia and ignored their prior agreement with the Portuguese pretender, refusing to pay him a cent.

Intermittent, privately sponsored English commercial ventures to coastal Benin and other regions of West Africa outside the area specified in the charter also continued after 1588. In 1592, the queen granted Thomas Gregory of Taunton and his associates a ten-year monopoly on traffic to Sierra Leone. English merchants, both licensed and unlicensed, set out for Senegambia and Sierra Leone with a range of wares, including linen, woolen goods, copper bracelets, and glass beads. They returned with ivory, pepper, palm oil, and cotton, and in some cases they were accompanied by Africans who had agreed to sail to England voluntarily or were seized from slaving vessels. In 1598, the queen renewed the ten-year monopoly charter for the Senegambian trade for two courtiers, declaring "we think it advisable that the trade should still be so continued." It appears, however, that the royal grant was not acted upon. For the moment, the Gold Coast—the site of the most profitable trade in gold and enslaved captives—remained out of reach of English hands. But Elizabethan merchant adventurers had made inroads in West Africa upon which future generations would build.

By the final decade of Elizabeth's reign, a small but highly visible community of African descent resided in England. The household of the queen herself included two African children, probably gifted to her by well-connected aristocrats or merchants with ties to the Iberian or West African trades. Concentrated in the capital and southwestern port communities, the Black population, though minuscule in comparison to other foreign groups, appeared significant to contemporaries. By the 1590s, harvest failure, famine, and rising unemployment across England heightened anti-alien hostility in the capital. Londoners exhibited recurrent, sometimes violent opposition toward aliens, even if they posed no real economic threat. Africans and people of African ancestry made easy targets. Noticeable on city streets as well as in the households of ruling elites, African-descended aliens may have appeared to pose a more overt risk to the state and social order. Yet the treatment of Africans as human commodities in the Iberian empires also enhanced the strategic international value of their presence in Elizabethan England.

In the context of pervasive anti-alien hostility, Queen Elizabeth sent open warrants to the Lord Mayor of London and other public authorities ordering the expulsion of so-called "blackamoors" from her kingdom on three separate occasions, twice in 1596 and again in 1601. By calling for the deportation of "blackamoors," and using the additional descriptor of "negars" to clarify her target, the queen singled out sub-Saharan Africans, whose association with Iberian slaving and bondage was well established. As Walter Raleigh later clarified in his *History of the World*, the English called African "negroes" by the name "black-moors." Yet the queen's edicts are not indicative of the presence of large numbers of persons of African ancestry in London. Rather, they suggest the extent to which the queen and her advisers viewed Black individuals as noticeably foreign and fit for enslavement in the Iberian empires. The alien status, physical distinctness, and known enslavement of Africans qualified them for compulsory removal from England and use as diplomatic bargaining chips.

On July 11, 1596, the queen and her Privy Council ordered the deportation of ten "blackamoors" recently brought into the country as political prisoners by Colonel General Sir Thomas Baskerville. The previous fall, Baskerville had set out with Francis Drake and John Hawkins under secret orders to raid a Spanish treasure ship grounded in San Juan, Puerto Rico. Consisting of twenty-seven ships and twenty-five hundred men, the expedition to San Juan failed, and Hawkins died of fever during the campaign. Drake and Baskerville, loathe to return home empty-handed, laid siege to Rio de la Hacha, burning the town to the ground. Although most of the inhabitants fled, the English raiders took an unspecified number of Spanish soldiers and "Negroes" prisoner before Drake succumbed to dysentery and was buried at sea.

After Baskerville's return to England, Elizabeth's regime targeted his

African-descended prisoners of war, whom they suspected of being in league with the Spanish, for forcible removal to Iberia. Grappling with mounting economic and social discontent in her kingdom, the queen attempted to placate her subjects. Her pronouncement that "there are of late diverse blackamoors brought into this realm, of which kind of people there are already here too many," offered a potentially straightforward means of incurring public favor. "Her Majesty's pleasure therefore is that those kind of people should be sent forth of the land."

Later that year, Elizabeth expanded on her initial edict ordering Baskerville to transport out of the country ten African prisoners from the war with Spain. She issued an open warrant to the Lord Mayor of London and other public authorities calling for the expulsion of "blackamoors" from the realm, this time as remuneration for services rendered to her government. Casper van Senden, a Lubeck merchant, had secured the release of eighty-nine English subjects imprisoned in Spain and Portugal and brought them home at his own expense. Appealing to the queen for recompense, Van Senden asked for permission to "take up so much blackamoors here in this realm and to transport them into Spain and Portugal." Elizabeth would have known that Van Senden intended to profit from their sale into slavery. Pronouncing his offer a "very good exchange," the queen remarked that there were already too many of "those kind of people" in England while her own Christian subjects "perish for want of service." As her support for slaving ventures early in her reign indicates, Elizabeth held no qualms about facilitating the seizure and sale of Africans into bondage in the Spanish empire.

Still, her royal edict calling for the expulsion of "blackamoors" lacked force. It permitted Casper van Senden to capture and deport any Africans or people of African descent he discovered in England, so long as he received the consent of their enslavers. In other words, the queen's instructions left too much room for interpretation and individual will. "The masters of the blackamoors, however, seeing by his warrant that he could not take them without the master's good will, would not suffer him to have any one of them," Van Senden complained in a letter to Elizabeth. Nonetheless, after securing the release of an additional two hundred English prisoners in Lisbon, he proposed another exchange with the English queen. "In consideration of these services and seeing that all the blackamoors in England are regarded but only for the strangeness of their nation, and not for service to the queen, and may be very well spared out of the country," Van Senden wrote that he "prays again for license to take up and carry away into Spain and Portugal all the blackamoors he shall find, without interruption of their masters or others." Elizabeth once again accepted his offer as an expeditious form of debt repayment but left the onus of the task to Van Senden.

In 1601, two years before her death, a draft proclamation circulated among Elizabeth's government ministers ordering the deportation of "negars and blackamoors" from England. These individuals, it claimed, had "crept into" the queen's kingdom "since the troubles between her highness and the king of Spain." But it is likely that Elizabeth never signed off on the 1601 expulsion proclamation. By the end of the Elizabethan era, the Crown could not simply expunge Afro-diasporic peoples from England. Repeated forays into West Africa and the Americas in search of new markets and bullion had led to a steady stream of Africans entering the realm and becoming embedded in parishes and households across the country. People of African ancestry held a range of occupations, serving as court musicians, royal pages, servants, maids, goldsmiths, and skilled laborers. They also worked in the households of Spanish and Portuguese merchants and envoys living in London.

People of African origin and descent were in England to stay, but their legal status remained ill defined. As the reign of the Tudors came to an end, English imperial aspirations became increasingly intertwined with the territories, bodies, and labor of Native and African peoples. In time, the Stuart monarchs would build on and greatly expand Queen Elizabeth's incursions into the Iberian-controlled transatlantic slave trade. The dispossession of Indigenous peoples and forced migration and enslavement of Africans would ultimately give rise to a seventeenth-century English Atlantic empire.

CHAPTER 3

THE WORLD OF 1619

Around three in the morning on March 24, 1603, Queen Elizabeth I died at Richmond Palace after a brief illness. She had reigned nearly forty-five years, longer than any other Tudor monarch. Eyewitness accounts of her final moments varied. But English narratives agreed on the matter of greatest dynastic significance. On her deathbed, the queen named, either verbally or by gestures, James VI of Scotland as her successor. News of the queen's demise must have shocked her subjects. Although Elizabeth passed away at the advanced age of sixty-nine, she had long since mastered the art of disguising signs of her mortality and projecting timelessness to the public.

Immediately after Elizabeth's death, Sir Robert Carey, the queen's godson, rode north to Scotland. He hoped to incur favor by being the first to bear the news of the queen's passing to her successor. At midnight two days later a bruised and bloodied Carey, who had fallen off his horse in his haste to reach Edinburgh before any other messenger, knelt before King James at the Palace of Holyrood. As Carey later claimed, he presented James with a sapphire ring, the prearranged sign that Elizabeth I had breathed her last. The ring summoned the Scottish king southward to claim the throne of England.

Many had feared that the passing of a childless queen might provoke bloodshed and anarchy. Elizabeth's Privy Council, led by Sir Robert Cecil, smoothed the way, proclaiming the accession of James VI by hereditary right in Whitehall and throughout the capital within hours of her death. James set out for his new kingdom the following week. The king—now James I to his English subjects—proceeded slowly and deliberately to London, creating over three hundred knights and building public enthu-

siasm along the way. Across the country, the English lit celebratory bon-
fires, announcing the passing of a queen and the inauguration of a new
sovereign's reign. James and his retinue entered the capital on May 7 amid
great excitement and pageantry, despite his foreign status and largely unknown character.

As king of Scotland, James VI had used the authority of the royal
word to disseminate his ideas in print, and London stationers raced to
reprint the new monarch's publications. His works included volumes of
poems, treatises on witchcraft, political theory, and divine right monarchy,
and a manual on kingship written in the form of a private letter to his
eldest son and heir, Prince Henry. James had authored these texts while
king of Scotland but with a greater aspiration in mind: succeeding Queen
Elizabeth I and uniting the English and Scottish thrones under his rule.
To grasp their new sovereign's views on church and state, his English
subjects needed only to acquaint themselves with his published works.
"Monarchy is the true pattern of divinity," James wrote in *True Law of
Free Monarchies*; consequently, "betwixt the king and his people, God is
doubtless the only judge." For James, kingship entailed God-given powers. His accession ushered in an era of Stuart royal attempts to expand the
power of the monarchy in England and, ultimately, its budding overseas
territories.

King James envisioned his reign as the harbinger of not only a perpetual Anglo-Scottish union but also an era of abundance and broader European concord. A "righteous and just king," James proclaimed in his speech
on the opening of his first Parliament in March 1604, will "acknowledge
himself to be ordained for the procuring of the wealth and prosperity of
his people." Building a prosperous Christian commonwealth necessitated
amity with foreign powers, "for by peace abroad with their neighbors the
towns flourish, the merchants become rich, [and] the trade doth increase,"
he pronounced. In another royal proclamation, James informed the public
that his official title would be "King of Great Britain." By his lineal descent from the ancient royal bloodlines of both realms, James had reunited
"these two mighty, famous, and ancient kingdoms of England and Scotland, under one Imperial Crown."

Hostility with Spain, which had dominated Elizabethan foreign policy
since 1585, came to an end in 1604. James annulled letters of marque

and ordered ship captains not to molest the subjects of the king of Spain
or any other foreign prince on pain of prosecution for piracy. After diplomatic discussions that nearly broke down over the two powers' claims
to commercial rights in the Caribbean, James signed a treaty with the
Spanish king, now Philip III, establishing free commerce between England and Spain as it had existed before the war. Yet the major sticking
point of the negotiations from the perspective of England's mercantile
community—free trade with the Spanish Indies—went unsatisfied. Intent on peace, James capitulated to the Spanish Crown's insistence that
its overseas territories remain out of bounds for the English. In exchange,
Philip III agreed to refrain from attempting to reestablish Catholicism in
England.

The king's pacific stance ran counter to the global commercial interests of his ambitious seafaring subjects. Elizabethan sailors and merchant
adventurers had adopted privateering as a way of life and profited from
two decades of Anglo-Spanish conflict. Dissatisfied with the terms of
the Anglo-Spanish treaty, English merchants resented the prohibition
on their commerce in Caribbean waters. Because the Dutch Netherlands
continued its quest for independence from Catholic Spain and fell outside
the Anglo-Spanish agreement, English corsairs offered their services to
the Dutch in exchange for letters of marque granting them permission to
seize the property of the Spanish. Even the royally sanctioned activities
of English merchant syndicates and chartered companies held the potential to threaten the fragile peace arrangement with Spain if mariners
overstepped the prescribed limits. The result was that mainland North
America and the rumored gold mines of Guiana, on the eastern edge of
the Spanish empire, received greater mercantile and royal attention.

While James prohibited his subjects from committing maritime of-
fenses against the property and subjects of Philip III, he defended England's right to claim areas of North America outside the bounds of
Spanish control. Persuaded that the English could encroach upon the
outer limits of the Spanish empire, the king loaned his support to privately funded colonizing enterprises along the northeastern seaboard of
North America. James recognized Spanish hegemony over occupied territories in the Americas but saw the so-called vacant lands uninhabited
by European powers as fair game for English conquest and settlement.

Neither James nor his subjects took the presence or sovereignty of Native peoples in North America into account. When the English acknowledged that the lands they sought to colonize were already inhabited, they cast themselves as Christian civilizing agents. English colonizers would bring beneficial trade and the true religion to the heathen Natives of the Americas and in so doing prevent further abuse of Indigenous populations by Catholic Spaniards.

The Stuart monarchy and mercantile community recognized the perceived benefits of planting overseas colonies in the western hemisphere. Establishing English Atlantic settlements would, proponents maintained, generate profits and steady revenue for the Crown; expand overseas commerce and navigation; establish a base from which to trade with Asia and Spanish America; employ the idle and ease poverty at home; spread Protestantism among Indigenous peoples; and enhance English prestige on the world stage. The historian and geographer Richard Hakluyt had made similar arguments a generation earlier in "A Discourse Concerning Western Planting," a pro-colonization treatise presented to Queen Elizabeth in 1584. Hakluyt articulated a strong case for English colonial settlement in the Americas as a means of preventing the Catholic Iberian powers from monopolizing global trade. But the English Crown lacked the financial resources to spearhead overseas colonizing ventures. A century of inflation had eroded the Crown's real revenue, and Elizabeth died some £300,000 in debt. James inherited this debt, and though he avoided foreign wars, the king proved a poor steward of limited resources. To launch English colonization ventures, a joint-stock arrangement, in which a pool of private investors shared the financial risks and potential rewards, offered the only recourse.

As private individuals and companies descended on the Stuart king's court proposing overseas colonizing experiments designed to tap novel sources of wealth, royal support proved essential. Obtaining a royal charter granted patent holders a legal title to any lands claimed in the king's name, with freedom to travel to and from the colony and govern and defend it on behalf of the Crown. Charters included practical benefits such as tax breaks and other settlement incentives, which were handy if a colonial venture proved viable. Colonists were also guaranteed the same rights as the king's natural-born subjects in England. Yet royal charters meant absolutely nothing if the enterprise failed on the ground, leaving patentees with exclusive rights merely on paper. As the historian Philip Stern points out, "overseas charters projected their authority into places where the Crown, legally and pragmatically, had none." To secure the king's support constituted the first step of many in an overseas colonizing enterprise.

Revisiting the first successful English settlement in North America lays bare the possible paths available to colonists and the Stuart monarchy at the time. The spread of slavery regimes from the tobacco plantations of the Chesapeake many decades later was far from inevitable. Yet over the course of the seventeenth century, English colonists accelerated their reliance upon and commitment to African slavery. How this economic transformation came about and to whose benefit is a critical part of the story.

On April 10, 1606, King James granted a royal charter to two separate groups of patentees vying to colonize the eastern seaboard of North America. The Virginia charter authorized merchants from the West Country ports of Plymouth, Bristol, and Exeter, known as the Plymouth Company, to take possession of the coastal region between modern Philadelphia and Bangor, Maine. London investors calling themselves the Virginia Company made up the other group, which received permission to plant a colony to the south, from modern Cape Fear to Philadelphia. The monarchy, as in previous letters patent, reserved the right to one-fifth of all precious metals discovered. James required both companies to set up governing councils with authorization to levy taxes on goods bought and sold in the prospective colonies, the proceeds of which were to remain in the colonies for twenty years before reverting to the Crown. He also granted a seven-year exemption from customs and duties on the export of goods shipped to the colonies from England. Of the two groups of competing patentees, the Virginia Company alone established a colony, dispatching three ships that landed at the Jamestown site, within the bounds of the chiefdom that Native people called Tsenacommacah, on April 26, 1607.

The Virginia Company's aim was to plant a successful colony in North America, locate and exploit profitable mineral deposits and raw materials, and conduct trade with Native people. But for the bulk of the initial adventurers, hopes of finding gold served as the principal motivation. Not counting the crew, between a third and a half of the 144 Englishmen who embarked for the region they called Virginia were described as gentle-men; the rest were ex-soldiers, privateers, craftsmen, and artisans. What-ever their backgrounds, the first Jamestown colonists arrived unwittingly in the paramount chiefdom of Wahunsonacock. English observers called Wahunsonacock "king," "emperor," or "the Powhatan" and the people sub-ject to his rule "Powhatans," regardless of the distinct group to which they belonged within the alliance. The English also characterized the various Algonquian dialects spoken in the region as the "Powhatan" language. Five of the more than thirty tribes in the Tsenacommacah chiefdom survive today and are recognized by the state of Virginia: the Pamunkeys, Mattaponi, Rappahannocks, Nansemonds, and Chickahominy. For ease of understanding, the Native peoples within Wahunsonacock's chiefdom will be referred to as Powhatans.

The English adventurers who arrived in 1607 brought with them vir-tually no knowledge of the region or its Native inhabitants and equally limited supplies. Fortune frowned on the initial wave of ill-informed, underprepared colonists, only a third of whom survived the first year in Tsenacommacah. The majority succumbed, in the words of the settler George Percy, to "cruel diseases, as swellings, fluxes, burning fevers, and by wars, and some departed suddenly, but for the most part they died of mere famine." Describing the general state of misery, John Smith, an early leader of the colony, wrote that after Captain Newport sailed for England for fresh supplies within two months of their arrival, "God (being angry with us) plagued us with such famine and sickness, that the living were scarce able to bury the dead." While the surviving colonists managed to build a triangular fort and ramshackle chapel at the Jamestown site, the famished English grew increasingly reliant on their Powhatan neighbors for corn. To secure larger investments and exert more direct authority over the struggling settlement, the Virginia Company petitioned the king for a revised charter, which he granted in May 1609.

The winter of 1609–10 proved especially brutal at Jamestown. Survi-vors later described this period as the "starving time." Half the colony's residents perished from starvation, sickness, and attacks by their Native neighbors. New arrivals, disembarking with little more than the clothes on their backs and fantastical visions of gold mines, were appalled by what they found. Persuaded by the Virginia Company's promotional literature—which promised prospective settlers "houses to dwell in, with gardens and orchards, and also food and clothing at the common charge of the joint stock"—colonists arrived expecting a land of abundance and opportunity. What they found was anything but. None had hazarded a perilous voyage across the Atlantic to an unknown continent to face the toil, famine, disease, and daily calamities colonists encountered in the fledgling settlement.

According to Jamestown's leaders, colonists' idleness and lack of religious devotion had placed the settlement in dire straits, not the Virginia Company. John Smith, elected president in 1608, put it bluntly to his fellow colonists: "the greater part must be more industrious or starve." Desperation led to the dispersal of the emaciated English away from the Jamestown fort to forage for food. Moving to areas with greater supplies of wild game and berries seemed like their only chance of survival. This policy, in turn, fueled conflict with the Powhatans, upon whom the colonists depended for food and other necessities. Although technically at peace with the local Indigenous people, the frantic colonists encroached upon Native homelands and hunting grounds, leading to increased Anglo-Indian contact and hostilities. Both sides committed violent acts against the other and took captives to gain the upper hand.

In July 1609, *Sea Venture*, the sinking flagship of a nine-vessel English supply fleet carrying much-needed food, livestock, and 150 new settlers to Jamestown, ran ashore on the uninhabited island of Bermuda after a hurricane. Surviving on the island's abundant natural resources, including feral hogs, fish, and turtles, the shipwrecked passengers built two vessels to carry them to Virginia. They departed ten months after landing in Bermuda, arriving in Jamestown only to discover a shocking scene: sixty emaciated colonists, a dilapidated fort and crumbling houses, and an incalculable number of fresh graves. Everyone else had perished. The fortunate arrival of a new supply fleet saved the Virginia colony from utter ruin. But Bermuda was now on England's radar as an island worth colonizing, especially given its lack of an Indigenous population. In 1612, a subgroup of Virginia Company investors received a royal charter to subsume Bermuda under the company's purview. Bermuda's first colonists arrived ready to clear and farm the land. Its semitropical climate boded well for the growth of staples that would enrich both the Virginia Company and the Crown and serve as a supply lifeline for the struggling Virginia colony. Within three years, the company had peopled Bermuda with six hundred settlers. Although they had not yet hit on a lucrative staple crop, the position of the colonists in Bermuda was night and day compared to those barely eking out a subsistence existence in Virginia.

Conditions were so bleak in Virginia that in 1613 colonists kidnapped Wahunsonacock's married teenage daughter, Metoaka, referred to in English sources by her childhood nickname, Pocahontas. They demanded corn and the release of English prisoners in exchange for her freedom. Wahunsonacock attempted to negotiate with the English but did not redeem his daughter from captivity. She remained a hostage at Jamestown, receiving instruction in the English language, religion, and customs until her eventual conversion to Christianity and baptism as Rebecca. In 1614, Wahunsonacock granted permission for his daughter to marry John Rolfe, dissolving her previous marriage per Powhatan custom. The diplomatic marriage established a kinship bond between the Powhatans and the English, halting Anglo-Indian hostilities for a time.

On both sides of the Atlantic, English observers praised John Rolfe for marrying a Native woman. He had, they alleged, sacrificed his own self-interest for the good of the colony. The social commentator John Chamberlain characterized the Jamestown colonists' kidnapping of Pocahontas, "the daughter of a King who was their greatest enemy," as a master stroke of pragmatic diplomacy. Colonists such as Ralph Hamor commended Rolfe for marrying a "savage" to save Jamestown. No man, Hamor concluded, had sacrificed as much for the English colony as Rolfe: "witness his marriage with Powhatan's daughter, one of rude education, manners barbarous and cursed generation, merely for the good and honor of the plantation." Rolfe himself, in a letter to Virginia colony governor Dale, claimed that he wed a Native woman not for "the unbridled desire of carnal affection: but for the good of this plantation, for the honor of our country, for the glory of God, for my own salvation, and for the converting to the true knowledge of God and Jesus Christ, an unbelieving creature, namely Pocahontas."

At the behest of the Virginia Company, Rolfe and Pocahontas visited London in 1616. Dressed as an Englishwoman, with her English Protestant husband at her side, Pocahontas embodied everything colonial promoters had long touted. Her appearance on the streets of the capital and at court offered material proof that the English could tame the Americas and spread Christian civility to Native peoples rather than be transformed by them. John Smith declared that Pocahontas, "rejecting her barbarous condition," had wed Rolfe after recognizing the superiority of English customs and religion. Reflecting on her visit to London, he wrote that those who met the "Lady Pocahontas" saw her conversion and marriage to Rolfe as a sign of divine will, and "it pleased both the king and queen's majesty honorably to esteem her."

For King James, a monarch concerned about the infiltration of what he deemed "savage" practices into his kingdom, Pocahontas's visit to England must have offered reassurance. He saw her with his own eyes when she attended a court masque by Ben Jonson, clothed in English attire. "The Virginian woman, Pocahontas, with her father's councilors, has been with the king and graciously used," observed Chamberlain, "and both she and her assistant well placed at the masque." Pocahontas's father, Wahunsonacock, viewing the journey to London as a scouting mission, had sent a Powhatan priest with her to take the measure of the English and their monarch. To the English, Pocahontas's visit to London confirmed the supposed superiority of their own cultural practices, religious beliefs, and civilization. Still, the kinship link Pocahontas established between the Powhatans and the English was short lived. She died in March 1617, aged only twenty, at the start of her return journey to Virginia and was buried in Gravesend.

The diplomatic marriage between John Rolfe and Pocahontas had brought peace but not abundance to Jamestown. The Virginia colony teetered on the edge of financial ruin until it was saved by the cultivation of a single cash crop: tobacco. In 1612, Rolfe discovered that tobacco native to Central and South America grew readily in Virginia. Tobacco had risen in popularity in England since its first introduction in the mid-sixteenth century. Proponents, including physicians, promoted tobacco as a miraculous panacea capable of treating all manner of ailments, from colds and toothaches to hunger and thirst. In 1586, the English colonists who returned home after the failure of the Roanoke settlement brought along samples and tales of tobacco. Among them was the naturalist and mathematician Thomas Hariot, who had witnessed the use of tobacco by Native Americans firsthand.

In *A Briefe and True Report of the New Found Land of Virginia* (1588), the first book in English published about North America, Hariot praised tobacco's extraordinary medicinal properties. After detailing how the local Algonquian-speaking peoples prepared and smoked tobacco—a leaf of "so precious estimation amongst them, that they think their gods are marvelously delighted therewith"—Hariot explained that he and his fellow adventurers followed their example. "We ourselves during the time we were there used to suck it after their manner, as also since our return, and have found many rare and wonderful experiments of the virtue thereof," he noted. Hariot joined a chorus of writers promoting tobacco, a foreign plant associated with the Indigenous peoples of the Americas, as a "sovereign remedy" worthy of emulation by Englishmen.

Critics of tobacco feared its growing fame as a heathen cure-all in England. Tobacco consumption by members of all social classes threatened to erode the physical and mental well-being of individual smokers and English civilized society. In 1602, *Work for Chimny-Sweepers*, a tract staunchly opposed to tobacco usage, was published under the pseudonym Philaretes. Philaretes railed against "Indian tobacco"—a "venomous and poisoned substance" first introduced by the devil and his priests in the Americas "and therefore not to be used of [by] us Christians." A pamphlet war over tobacco ensued in London for the remainder of the year, with multiple tracts defending "the great indignities offered to that innocent tobacco," as one author put it. The controversy failed to dampen tobacco's popularity among the English public, however.

In May 1603, when King James first arrived in London, he may have noticed plumes of tobacco smoke emerging from the mouths of his new subjects and wafting through the streets of the capital. English merchants imported about twenty-five thousand pounds of tobacco that year from Spanish America—produced by the labor of enslaved Africans and Indigenous people. This total did not include the vast quantities of tobacco smuggled into the country to meet the rising demand. James expressed disdain for the latest fashion. In *A Counterblast to Tobacco* (1604), the first tract written specifically for his English subjects, James mocked those who championed tobacco—a heathen weed—as a universal antidote. "And now good Countrymen," he exclaimed, "what honor or policy can move us to imitate the barbarous and beastly manners of the wild, godless, and slavish Indians, especially in so vile and stinking a custom?" If the English scorned to emulate the manners of their European neighbors, "shall we, I say, without blushing, abase ourselves so far, as to imitate these beastly Indians, slaves to the Spaniards, refuse to the world, and as yet aliens from the holy Covenant of God?" In the king's view, copying Native customs and smoking a diabolical plant imperiled the souls of his subjects. To allow idolators to influence the habits of Englishmen undermined Christian colonizing efforts in the Americas.

Early Stuart material and literary culture linked tobacco with Indigenous Americans and enslaved Africans years before the English employed enslaved laborers in the Chesapeake and Caribbean colonies. A painted wooden sign featuring a Black boy smoking a pipe became a common fixture outside the shops of London tobacconists. To advertise their wares, tobacconists and other shopkeepers also adopted the imagery of a stereotypical Native American man holding a pipe or tobacco leaf. After the Portuguese introduced tobacco to their African trading partners in the sixteenth century, its cultivation had spread throughout West Africa, transforming spiritual ceremonies and social activities. Using tobacco as a trade good to acquire enslaved Africans for their own use and for the Spanish empire, Portuguese merchants purchased and transported African bondspeople to Brazil and elsewhere in the Americas to begin the cycle anew.

Published in 1617, Richard Brathwait's pamphlet *The Smoaking Age* captures tobacco's intertwined association with African and Native peoples in early Stuart England. The title page features a Black man standing in a tobacconist's shop sucking on a pipe; in a tavern next door, three Englishmen smoke pipes beneath a painting of figures inhabiting a foreign landscape. At the end of the text, the medieval poet William Chaucer returns to England only to find his homeland unrecognizable, shrouded in a haze of tobacco smoke. Appalled by the proliferation of *"Indian* weed," Chaucer berates his fellow countrymen as "English Moors," too willing to adopt "a late Negro's introduced fashion, / Who brought his drugs here to corrupt our nation."

King James despaired that tobacco, a foreign plant enjoyed by Native peoples and Africans, had infiltrated his kingdom, corrupting its habits and morals. Although the king doubted tobacco's medical value, physicians routinely prescribed it to patients. Londoners could purchase tobacco on virtually every street. Barnaby Rich, a fierce tobacco critic and former soldier turned author, estimated in 1614 that the capital boasted seven thousand shops selling tobacco—from apothecaries and grocers to taverns and licensed tobacconists. Rich conceded that tobacco might hold medicinal value, though he added cheekily, "if all be diseased that do use to take tobacco, God help *England*, it is wonderfully infected, and his Majesty hath but a few subjects that be healthful in his whole dominions." Another writer lumped together taverns, tobacco shops, and brothels as sites of "devilish and drunken merriments." A cloud of smoke had descended over the nation, he wrote, "yea, as our life is but a breath and a vapor, so the very smoke and vapor is sufficient to choke us." The English rage for tobacco was precisely what colonists in Virginia aimed to exploit, as James understood all too well.

Strong personal misgivings aside, the king needed money, and tobacco's profitability was undeniable. Crown finances remained a sore spot in early Stuart England. In a few short decades, violent conflict would erupt between the monarchy and Parliament, exacerbated by the king's desire for money free of parliamentary oversight. In 1604, Lord Treasurer Robert Cecil initiated the Farm of the Great Customs, a fiscal scheme intended to boost royal revenue. The monarchy lacked a functional bureaucracy to collect the customs proceeds that formed a key component of royal income. Underreporting was pervasive, and Cecil's plan entailed King James farming, or contracting, the right to collect the customs duties on imports and exports to a syndicate of merchants. They would bid for the privilege and pay the king an annual rent in exchange for pocketing the customs revenue they collected. Cecil, however, heavily indebted from renovating Hatfield House, a Jacobean money pit, awarded the contracts to some of his largest creditors. Many customs farmers held a stranglehold on royal officials such as Cecil, whose debts placed them at the mercy of their creditors. The actual royal revenue derived from customs duties depended on the level of trade and the honesty and diligence of the collectors.

As the cultivation of tobacco offered an economic boon to England's struggling Virginia colony, the stewards of the royal treasury plotted how to use the fashionable weed to benefit the king's near-empty coffers. Royal control over tobacco importation and licensing, whether from Virginia, Bermuda, or the Spanish colonies, held the potential to boost Crown income. Schemes to place tobacco profits into the king's hands were quickly put into effect. According to the Venetian ambassador, the English spent exorbitant amounts on tobacco—so much so that "the duty on it alone yields the king 40,000 golden crowns yearly." The king needed this additional customs revenue to flow into his depleted coffers. Tobacco was a money maker, heathen weed or no.

But King James needed more coin than even tobacco could provide. In March 1618, Sir Thomas Edmondes, treasurer of the royal household, reported that James was saddled with debts of £800,000 and an average annual expenditure that exceeded his ordinary income by £120,000. King James, never one for frugality, struggled to rein in his personal and domestic spending. The modest curtailment of royal household expenses, as his financial advisers recommended, did nothing to lessen the king's ballooning debts. English territorial expansion and lucrative staple crop farming in the Americas fed into and supported the king's immediate goal of augmenting his revenues.

In the Virginia colony, composed of fragile English outposts in Powhatan territory, the laborious process of tobacco cultivation demanded numerous field-workers. Drawn by the pull of potential land ownership and economic prosperity, Englishmen, and some -women, arrived in the region as free settlers and indentured servants. Bond labor, mostly contractual and temporary, underpinned the growth of tobacco cultivation from the outset. In a colony fraught with disease and malnourishment, many planters worked their servants into early graves. Reports of abuse and high mortality rates among indentured servants made their way back to England, discouraging prospective workers and dampening the Virginia Company's recruitment efforts. Planters seeking field laborers exercised other options, such as the employment of enslaved Africans, whenever they became available.

In the early years, the colony obtained bonded African laborers primarily in the aftermath of opportunistic assaults on Iberian shipping by privateers and pirates. The most well-known incident occurred in August 1619. John Rolfe described how Dutch privateers, after attacking the Portuguese slave ship *São João Baptista*, arrived in Virginia looking to fence stolen African captives intended for sale in New Spain. English colonial authorities traded food supplies for the ship's cargo of "20. and odd Negroes" who came from Luanda, the Portuguese capital in Angola. While the Angolan men and women subsequently worked alongside English indentured servants cultivating tobacco for their owners, they did so in the absence of labor contracts. Unlike indentured servants, the first enslaved Africans in colonial Virginia were purchased under the assumption that they, like bondspeople in the Iberian empires, would labor for life. A Virginia census conducted in March 1620 suggests that the "20. and odd" enslaved arrivals from Angola joined a handful of other Africans: a total of thirty-two individuals out of a population of 982.

By the seventeenth century, the English had long associated Africans not only with coerced labor and commodity production for European markets but also with dark skin that signified difference and, increasingly, inferiority. Similar cultural trends and assumptions about blackness had evolved in Scotland. Prior to taking the English throne, James VI featured several Black entertainers at his court. Upon the entry of his new wife, Anne of Denmark, into Edinburgh in 1590 she was met by a group of men with blackened faces dressed as "blackamoors," supposedly led by an actual person of African descent carrying a ceremonial sword, who cleared a path for her carriage. Known for her pale skin and blond hair, Anne adopted motifs of blackness and femininity as a means of accentuating her own whiteness and regal status, and she took these associations with her to England.

On January 6, 1605, Queen Anne herself wore blackface in a controversial masque performed before the king and court at the Banqueting House at Whitehall. Author Ben Jonson and choreographer Inigo Jones created *The Masque of Blackness* in response to Anne's request that she and her ladies appear onstage disguised as "blackamoors." Costumed as the stunning daughters of Niger, the queen and eleven of her ladies-in-waiting perched in a giant seashell with their faces and arms blackened with paint up to their elbows. In the masque, Niger's beautiful dark-skinned daughters, scorched by the sun's harsh rays, travel to Britain in search of fair skin. Once exposed to the temperate and refined rays of Albion's sun, allegorically identified with King James, their skin is blanched white and their beauty perfected. Yet Anne and her ladies remained in blackface after the performance ended. Traditionally, English performers representing African characters wore a removable vizard, or mask, of black velvet and gloves and leggings. The inability of the queen and her ladies to remove their thick black makeup by the masque's finale scandalized the court. To Sir Dudley Carleton, a courtier and diplomat, the women's "black faces and hands, which were painted and bare up to the elbows, was a very loathsome sight" and an embarrassment to the English court.

Anne spent a fortune staging her elaborate court masque and likely would have dismissed such criticism out of hand. The queen prided herself on her exquisite taste and ancestral pedigree, surrounding herself with artwork, flags, pendants, and banners advertising her Danish royal bloodline. A full-length hunting portrait commissioned by Anne and painted by the Flemish artist Paul van Somer in 1617 depicts her standing in the grounds of her palace at Oatlands, a residence she frequented during the summer months. Highlighting recent updates to the palace grounds, including a classical stone gate and newly planted vineyard, Anne is dressed in riding clothes and accompanied by five greyhounds and an unidentified, partially obscured Black groom. Richly clothed in the scarlet and gold livery of the Danish House of Oldenburg, like the queen's caparisoned horse whose reins he holds, the unnamed Black groom gazes fixedly at Anne, awaiting her command. Directly above her head floats a scroll inscribed with the queen's favorite motto, "*La mia grandezza dal eccelso*" ("My greatness is from on high"). Anne hung the portrait at Oatlands, inviting visitors to contemplate her regal status and hereditary preeminence as the daughter, wife, and mother of kings.

Queen Anne's appropriation of Black bodies extended well beyond her theatrical performances and portraiture. Her personal income, supported mainly by revenue generated from the rents and fines associated with her jointure lands and estates, was supplemented by her annual lease of the import duties on slave-produced sugar, worth £5,000 per year. During her lifetime, England imported most of its sugar from Brazil, the dominant sugar producer in the western world by 1600. While Indigenous people comprised the majority of enslaved laborers in the sugar fields in the sixteenth century, Brazilian sugar producers increasingly relied on the agricultural toil of enslaved Africans in the seventeenth century.

Known for her extravagance, Queen Anne enjoyed the fruits of en-

Figure 3.1. *Anne of Denmark and a Groom.* Paul van Somer, 1617.

slaved labor, purchasing jewels, plate, cloth of gold and silver, fine silks and linen, and interior furnishings with her annual allowance. The queen's profligacy left her in a constant state of debt, contributing to King James's overall financial difficulties. Following Anne's death from dropsy in March 1619, her jeweler, George Heriot, received the annual rent on sugar impositions for three years as payment for a debt of £14,529 owed to him by the late queen. Heriot later collected the rent on an additional half-year of sugar duties in payment of a remaining debt from Anne of £2,295. In death as in life, the queen encouraged the perception among her subjects that enslaved people in the Americas labored on behalf of their European superiors and that it was the monarchy's right to exploit Africans and to own them.

CHAPTER 4
TOBACCO AND GOLD

As King James and English investors contemplated the future of the Virginia colony, they cared little for who labored in the tobacco fields so long as profits rolled into their coffers. The Stuart monarchy regulated the tobacco trade entirely by royal proclamation during the first decades of the seventeenth century. After 1619, as demand for tobacco surged at home, sales of Virginia-grown tobacco equaled and then surpassed sales of Spanish tobacco in London. Parliament aided the public shift to Anglo-American tobacco by levying duties on foreign tobacco.

Under the pretense that a monopoly would limit tobacco consumption among his subjects, particularly of the unhealthiest sort grown in the British Isles, King James prohibited its cultivation at home. A report released by the College of Physicians backed the king's assertion, concluding that the most wholesome tobacco derived from warm countries to which it was indigenous. Yet the motivating factor for royal tobacco regulation was above all financial, not medical. The king increased his revenues through the sale of tobacco monopolies and the collection of customs duties. Smuggling also cut into the king's share of tobacco revenue, leading to proclamations forbidding the sale of tobacco "before the customs and import thereof due were paid."

Colonists in Bermuda also jumped on the tobacco bandwagon. However, on a small island with limited acreage and unpredictable winds, inexperienced planters struggled to cultivate and cure tobacco that could compete with higher-grade Spanish tobacco. Tobacco's popularity in England, where consumers purchased more than £200,000 worth of tobacco annually, offered a strong incentive to keep trying. Leaders of the Somers

Islands Company, which managed the Bermuda colony, resolved to bring enslaved Africans and Native peoples versed in tobacco cultivation from Spanish America to Bermuda to teach the island's struggling planters their methods. They also sought to exploit Bermuda's natural resources by purchasing enslaved pearl divers from the Spanish Caribbean.

To acquire skilled enslaved laborers required Bermudians to either engage in an illicit trade with Spanish colonists or to conduct unsanctioned peacetime raids in the Spanish Crown's territories. In the spring of 1616, the Somers Islands Company dispatched the ship *Edwin* to the Spanish Caribbean to trade for livestock, tropical plants, and enslaved divers to hunt for pearls. *Edwin* returned with "one Indian and a Negro (the first these islands ever had)." Over the next five years, English ships landed periodically in Bermuda to sell colonists dozens more enslaved Africans versed in tobacco cultivation, "a most necessary commodity for these Islands." By the time the first African captives reached Virginia in 1619, Bermuda had between fifty and one hundred African-descended residents, accounting for between 5 and 10 percent of the colony's population. Somers Islands directors also required Bermudians to raise livestock and plant crops for food in addition to cultivating tobacco, minimizing the colony's reliance on imported food supplies.

In contrast, colonists in Virginia invested heavily in growing and exporting tobacco to the detriment of the soil and local food supplies. Virginia farmers overplanted tobacco, stripping the ground of nutrients. To maintain tobacco yields, they pushed westward and cleared new fields, further souring relations between colonists and the Powhatans. English settlers encroached upon Powhatan lands while simultaneously demonstrating an inability to feed themselves. They banked on neighboring Native peoples to supplement their meager food supplies. To exacerbate matters, the Virginia Company sent hundreds of apprentices to the colony with minimal provisions and no survival skills. As the English population in Virginia swelled as more colonists landed, food supplies became scarcer. Recurrent epidemics of typhoid, dysentery, and salt poisoning ravaged the colony, killing both new arrivals and seasoned colonists. The Powhatans, aware of the English dependence upon them, refused to provide food to the desperate colonists. These untenable conditions triggered a violent Powhatan assault against the colony that not only destroyed Anglo-Indian relations but also radically altered official policy toward the Powhatan chiefdom and Native peoples generally.

On March 22, 1622, Powhatans from several different neighboring villages converged on Jamestown and other English settlements along the James River, seemingly to trade. According to eyewitness accounts, they brought turkeys, deer, fruit, and fish and sat down with the English at their breakfast tables. Sometime during midmorning, the "Native infidels" suddenly turned on the English, grabbing whatever tools or weapons they could find and killing every colonist they encountered, sparing none. The unanticipated assault resulted in the deaths of nearly four hundred colonists. Characterizing the attack as a "barbarous massacre," English reports of the event blamed the "treachery of the savages" and called for swift retaliation. The Natives were at fault, not the English. The English Crown, Edward Waterhouse argued, had exercised control over Virginia as its "lawful and rightful kingdom" since John Cabot claimed North America for Henry VII in 1498. The "savages" merely resided there on sufferance, permitted to remain only so long as they proved useful to the colony and receptive to English conversion efforts. But the situation had entirely changed and "hands which before were tied with gentleness and fair usage, are now set at liberty by the treacherous violence of the Savages." The events of March 1622 irrevocably altered English perceptions of and relations with the Powhatans and Native peoples.

In the wake of the 1622 surprise attack, the English government together with the Virginia Company adopted an offensive position. English commentators, no longer persuaded of the inevitability of Native redemption, called for the extermination of the Powhatans. In his published poem inspired by the massacre, the poet Christopher Brooke argued that only "extirpation of that Indian crew" and a "war unto the dead" would secure the safety of the colony. "For, but consider what those creatures are, / (I cannot call them men)," he wrote; "Errors of nature, of inhumane birth, / The very dregs, garbage, and spawn of Earth." No longer would the English consider the Native peoples of Virginia worthy of friendship—a shift that made their eradication from the region more palatable.

Reflecting on the events of March 1622, John Smith condemned the Powhatans as a "perfidious and inhumane people." Some saw a silver lining in the assault, he remarked, "because now we have just cause to destroy them by all means possible." According to Smith, the Virginia colonists should have "beat the savages out of the country" years before the attack, assuring their own long-term safety and prosperity. From the vantage point of recent events, Spain's cruel treatment of Native peoples appeared prudent rather than heartless. "And you have twenty examples of the *Spaniards* how they got the *West-Indies* and forced the treacherous and rebellious infidels to do all manner of drudgery work and slavery for them," he noted. "This will make us more circumspect and be an example to posterity." If Native Americans could not be trusted as allies, Smith suggested, the English would benefit more from their dispossession and enslavement.

The Virginia Company's plan of attack involved securing arms from England and bolstering the colony's defenses against the "treacherous savages." Company leaders requested old cast arms stored in the London Tower, "which though they were altogether unfit and of no use for modern service, might nevertheless be serviceable against that naked people," clarified the Privy Council. King James consented to this request while harboring concerns about European weapons falling into Native hands and being turned against his subjects in Virginia and other English-occupied regions of North America. In November 1622, James issued a proclamation forbidding interlopers to trade in New England as a means of preventing Englishmen from selling weapons to "the savages." Relations had soured, and English colonists armed themselves in preparation for future hostilities.

The Virginia Company sent hundreds of new colonists to replace the English men, women, and children killed in the attack, but these replacements did not last long. Diseases and pestilence spread among the recent arrivals and throughout the settlement, killing at least a thousand settlers between 1622 and 1623. Grievances against the Virginia Company poured into London from planters and others on the ground in Virginia. In response to accusations of mismanagement, King James appointed a royal commission to investigate the state of the colony and the affairs of the Virginia Company. According to a census dated February 1624, despite an influx of about six thousand migrants in total since the colony's founding, only 1,275 persons resided in Virginia, including twenty-two individuals of African descent. But the council in Virginia reported that conditions in the colony had steadily improved and that the king was misinformed. As of the spring of 1624, the colony boasted good health, sufficient provisions, and laborers at work producing staple commodities—particularly tobacco. Nonetheless, King James revoked the Company's charter. On May 24, 1624, Virginia became the first royal colony, brought under the king's direct control and dependent upon his good favor.

Thousands of miles east from England's developing plantation colonies in the Atlantic, naval men and courtiers in London looked to West Africa and the expertise of a handful of merchants to satisfy their thirst for gold. Gold, in the form of bars, currency, dust, or nuggets, was a crucial global commodity, and Europeans who could trade in gold rather than less desirable goods had an edge in international markets. Prior schemes to locate gold mines and untold riches in the Americas had failed, resulting instead in piratical raids on Spanish shipping and territories that outraged King James. After Sir Walter Raleigh returned to London in March 1618 following his final failed attempt to locate the mythical golden city of El Dorado in Guiana, the king accused him of deliberately provoking war between England and Spain. Raleigh, a victim of his own ambitions, subsequently lost his head. While the whereabouts of untapped overseas deposits of precious metals remained elusive, English investors did not lose their appetite for gold-hunting schemes. They simply shifted focus to a different gold-bearing region of the globe: Africa.

In 1618, King James granted the Company of Adventurers of London Trading to Gynney and Bynney (known as the Guinea Company) exclusive control over English trade with West Africa, though the practical emphasis remained on Senegambia and Sierra Leone. Preceded by decades of intermittent English ventures to the region sponsored by individual investors or small collectives, the Guinea Company was the first English joint-stock company to enter the African trade. The patent listed thirty-six founding members with various lofty connections, to the Jacobean court, the navy, Parliament, and other overseas trading ventures, including the East India Company and the Virginia Company. The royal patent conferred trading privileges on the company with the aim of encouraging commerce in Africa that "will not only be beneficial to our said Realms and dominions but also profitable to us in advancement of our customs."

As the king understood, the company aspired to sail up the Gambia River, reach the goldfields of the West African interior, and establish profitable new trading links with local African partners.

Beginning in 1611, a consortium of London merchants led by Humphrey Hanford and Christopher Lanman operated from a trading station established near the mouth of the Senegal River. Their factors probed inland and sailed upriver in pursuit of trade but remained confined to Senegambia. After its launch, the Guinea Company shifted focus to the Gambia River, sponsoring a total of four ventures between 1618 and 1621, none of which proved profitable or managed to reach the gold markets of the interior. Setting a disastrous tone, the first expedition resulted in loss of life and property when the company's 120-ton vessel *Katherine* was attacked on the Gambia River and "taken, and most of the men slain." In 1623 Richard Jobson, a company factor, published *The Golden Trade* based on his experiences voyaging up the Gambia River in 1620–21 on the third venture. Jobson's narrative described how, with the assistance of four local guides, he led a small expedition of canoes on a reconnaissance mission to explore the higher reaches of the river. His team traveled a significant distance upstream before halting due to low water levels and diminishing provisions.

Jobson and his men never located the goldfields, though he claimed that Buckar Sano, the principal trader in the region, assured him that they lay within reach. Sano boasted of "a great town" with houses overlaid with gold, less than four days' journey from Tinda. In the interim, he offered Jobson "certain young black women" for consideration, "which he told me were slaves, brought for me to buy." Jobson declined, explaining that "we were a people who did not deal in any such commodities, neither did we buy or sell one another, or any that had our own shapes." Jobson's response, far from the whole truth, must be considered in its contemporary context. He aimed to advertise the company's immediate and principal objective—gold. Jobson needed Sano and other leading local traders to understand the primary commodities the Guinea Company desired, and at that moment human beings were not on the list. White men seeking to purchase enslaved captives for resale in Europe or the Americas "were another kind of people different from us," Jobson clarified.

By the time of the publication of *The Golden Trade*, the Guinea

Company's failure to turn a profit or locate goldfields in the West African interior had imperiled its future. Internal competition over the African trade also heightened conflict within the company. Humphrey Slaney, a London merchant and company member, lodged a formal complaint with the Privy Council against fellow member John Davies for attempting to exercise sole authority over the African camwood, or redwood, trade. Since the 1610s, Davies had engaged in the redwood trade in Sierra Leone, after first dabbling in the transatlantic slave trade. West African redwood attracted English merchants seeking to circumvent the Iberian monopoly over brazilwood and cochineal, Europe's principal sources of high-quality red dye. In 1614, Davies requested an individual monopoly over the African redwood trade, claiming he had spent the previous seven years experimenting with different types of coastal dyewood. The Privy Council denied his request. King James granted no monopolies over trade in West Africa until the Guinea Company received its patent in 1618.

The Guinea Company struggled to rein in members' private commercial pursuits as well as the activities of interlopers. Humphrey Slaney and John Davies, equally intent on dominating England's redwood trade, proved particularly problematic. Both men backed West African ventures sponsored by the company but concentrated on their own more profitable private trading interests. While Slaney centered his redwood trade in the Sherbro River south of Davies's commercial base in Sierra Leone, Davies resented sharing a trade that he alleged to have initiated with his chief rival. Meanwhile, the bankrupt company borrowed money on the strength of individual members' reputations but could not afford to repay its loans. John Davies, spying an opportunity to tighten his grip on West African commerce, offered to assume the repayment of the debt in exchange for complete control of England's redwood trade. Davies fined the master of one of Slaney's ships £500 for trafficking within his jurisdiction, defending his right to keep the redwood trade in his "sole hand." An outraged Slaney petitioned the Privy Council, which ruled in his favor. It noted that King James "utterly dislikes that his gracious favor intended for a general good should be charged into the nature of a monopoly for the private turn of one man."

By the mid-1620s, the deeply indebted Guinea Company was teetering on the brink of dissolution, its monopoly condemned by the House of

Commons. In a few short years it had acquired a reputation for overhyped and unmet promises, scandal, and financial disaster. Critics called into question the legitimacy of its exclusive rights to the Guinea trade. The king had extended the patent based on fraudulent claims that founding members such as John Davies had pioneered a new African trade, although "there were English traders there eighty years before the patentees who pretended to discover it." The Guinea Company's issues snowballed in 1624 after a ship purchased for a Gambia venture proved rotten and incapable of sailing, leaving the company in a perilous financial position and further disgraced in the public eye. The House of Commons, opposed to monopoly companies as a matter of principle, denounced the company's patent as a "grievance in creation and execution." The royal monopoly "restrains trade to merchants of this kingdom, where foreign people trade there at pleasure," undermining the public good.

A Monopolies Act passed that same year terminated the power of the monarchy to grant monopolies to individuals, though not to corporate bodies. This exemption left the Crown free to continue selling commercial monopolies to chartered companies—a loophole King Charles I would repeatedly turn to his advantage to increase royal revenues in the years ahead. The financial problems that James faced on his accession had worsened by the end of his reign. His successor inherited a substantial Crown debt that grew rapidly as a result of wars with France and Spain. Coin was in short supply in England. Overseas trade and colonization, and the customs revenue it generated for the Crown, offered a potential financial lifeline to the Stuart monarchy. Although the Guinea Company managed to survive the parliamentary attacks and staggering financial losses of the 1620s, it was in no position to enforce its monopoly. Spotting weakness, English interlopers increasingly ventured to West Africa to pursue trading opportunities. At the same time, the establishment of English plantation colonies in the Caribbean encouraged a marked shift toward coerced labor and investment in the transatlantic slave trade.

CHAPTER 5

OPPORTUNISTIC ENSLAVERS

Upon the death of James I, following a stroke and severe attack of dysentery on March 27, 1625, his surviving second son ascended to the throne as King Charles I at age twenty-four. Charles's older brother, Henry Frederick, the dashing and popular Prince of Wales, had died at age eighteen of typhoid fever. The Crown's financial situation remained dire; but the new king spared no expense on his father's funeral, which cost upward of £50,000. Charles began his reign embroiled in a costly war with Spain after failing to procure a Spanish bride. Parliament, initially supportive of the war, retracted its support after Charles's first military offensive on Cádiz ended disastrously.

The national mood worsened when Charles married the French Catholic princess Henrietta Maria, the younger sister of King Louis XIII of France. Charles secretly pledged to relax enforcement of anti-Catholic laws in exchange for French help in restoring the German Palatinate to Protestant rule under Charles's sister Elizabeth and his brother-in-law, Frederick. Frederick had naively accepted the Bohemian throne, disrupting the balance of power in Europe, then fled to Holland in exile after a Spanish army invaded the Palatinate. France reneged on its promise of assistance, however, dooming Charles's military campaign on the Continent and paving the way to open hostilities between the two nations. Parliament outright rejected Charles's pleas for additional tax revenue. The new king was left to finance the war effort and maintain commitments abroad without parliamentary support.

Charles I and his Privy Council pushed the royal prerogative to the limit, raising money for his continental wars and campaigns without recourse to Parliament. The king turned to forced loans, pawned many of the crown jewels, and revived ship money—a demand that towns and counties provide the king with warships for naval and coastal defense or their cash equivalent. Charles also sought to extract revenue from expanding overseas trade and higher duties on imported goods. The king knew that increasing the yield of the customs would boost permanent royal revenues and satisfy his pressing need for nonparliamentary funding sources.

Charles maintained prohibitions on the cultivation of tobacco in the British Isles and the importation of foreign tobacco. He proposed making the purchase and distribution of Virginia tobacco a royal monopoly, but tobacco growers and retailers were able to secure free trade in exchange for paying import duties and licensing fees to the king. Although Charles retained his father's animosity toward tobacco and worried that Virginia was "wholly built upon smoke," he brought in a minimum of £10,000 a year in much-needed royal revenue from tobacco retail licenses.

Beginning in the late 1620s, King Charles added customs revenues on staple crops produced in newly established English colonies in the Caribbean, including St. Christopher, Nevis, Antigua, Montserrat, and, most important, Barbados, to his royal income. English privateers and pirates had been patrolling Caribbean waters hoping to intercept Spanish treasure ships since the Elizabethan era. "The chief spring from whence the main current of treasure flowing into all Christendom hath his original is in the Indies," observed one contemporary. Spain's inability to defend its interests in the Caribbean also inspired entrepreneurial individuals to establish commercial bases in the region and engage in colonizing enterprises. Charles supported these schemes and boosted his royal income by freely handing out letters patent to favorite courtiers in exchange for lump sums. In the case of the island of Barbados, the king granted separate patents to the earl of Carlisle and Sir William Courteen, leading to confusion and violence throughout the 1620s until the earl of Carlisle's claim stuck.

Early Caribbean planters concentrated on clearing the land and cultivating tobacco, aided by an influx of English migrants, predominantly young male indentured servants. Barbados attracted thousands of indentured servants in the 1630s. Working conditions on the island were notoriously bleak, however—even by seventeenth-century standards. Scant food, a punishing work regime, physical abuse and corporal punishment, and the adverse disease environment ensured that many indentured servants failed to outlive their terms of service. Bound by an indenture signed in England or drawn up on arrival, servants' contracts could be bought, sold, traded, or willed to others in the colonial labor market. Masters exercised near total control over indentured servants' lives and treated them as declining assets for the duration of their contracts. Servants had limited recourse against mistreatment by their employers; in a colonial society dominated by planters at every level, the customs of the country prevailed. Once word of the conditions of servitude in Barbados spread to England, increasing numbers of emigrants sought out other destinations. Desperate for agricultural workers, planters turned to enslaved Africans whenever opportunity struck.

As the demand for servile labor in Virginia and the English Caribbean rose, Nicholas Crispe and other leading London merchants with overseas commercial interests took the reins of the Guinea Company in hand. In September 1626, King Charles loaned the company his ship *St. Anne* for a trading venture to West Africa in exchange for a share in the proceeds. The king also requested specific African commodities, including "an elephant's head with the teeth [tusks] very large; a river horse's [hippo's] head; strange sorts of fowls; birds and fishes' skins; great flying and sucking fishes; all sorts of serpents, dried fruits, shining stones, etc." Charles wanted to fill his royal coffers with precious metals acquired through the West African trade, but he was also drawn to exotic commodities that would garner public attention and prestige at court.

Interloping English merchants remained a thorn in the Guinea Company's side. In the summer of 1627, private traders complained that the volume of the company's trade with West Africa was insufficient to warrant a royal monopoly. Charles disagreed. The Privy Council issued instructions reiterating the king's pleasure that all persons trading in Guinea and Benin "who are not allowed by the patentees for the sole trade thither shall be restrained and not suffered to go out." Unfazed, interlopers continued to operate illicit voyages. English merchants and sailors seeking to circumvent the Guinea Company's monopoly also engaged in the transatlantic slave trade. As Crispe and others complained in 1627, for instance, several interlopers had fitted out a ship intending "to trade upon the coasts of Guinea and to take nigers and to carry them to other foreign parts." In response, the Admiralty ordered the stay of the vessel until the merchants involved submitted proof that their slaving venture would not breach the company's patent.

In May 1631, the king issued the Guinea Company a new monopoly charter over trade with West Africa for a thirty-one-year period. The terms of the patent prohibited members of the six-person consortium led by Nicholas Crispe from engaging in private trade. According to the Guinea Company, the king received £10,000 in gold in exchange for granting the monopoly, which he subsequently announced to the public by royal proclamation. In 1632 the company conducted an expedition to the Gold Coast, resuming English commercial engagement with this region for the first time in sixty-seven years. Between 1632 and 1634 Crispe financed the building of the first permanent English settlement in present-day Ghana, Fort Cormantin. In the fall of 1636, one of the company's ships returned with gold and other sought-after commodities, including redwood, ivory, animal hides, and grains valued at £30,000. Evidence such as iron shackles inventoried at Fort Cormantin indicates that the Guinea Company readily diversified its portfolio. In addition to engaging in the transatlantic slave trade, it purchased land in Barbados. Planters based in Virginia and Barbados paid their debts to the company in the form of tobacco and cotton, presumably for the purchase of enslaved Africans to serve as coerced laborers.

At the same time that English merchants and planters were recognizing the profit potential of slave trading and enslaved labor, the Caroline court adopted the iconography of the exotic African "other" embraced by Charles I's deceased mother, Anne of Denmark, in both portraiture and performance. Created around 1630, Daniel Mytens's painting *Charles I and Henrietta Maria Departing for the Chase* depicts the royal couple in the foreground standing together before the hunt dressed in riding clothes. Eight eager hounds, two of which are restrained by Henrietta Maria's court dwarf, Jeffrey Hudson, yap at their feet. Above their heads a cherub parts the clouds, showering the royal couple with flowers, while the hunting party awaits the king and queen in the background. Like the earlier hunting portrait of Queen Anne, the painting of Charles and Henrietta Maria includes a young groom of African descent holding the reins of a

Figure 5.1. *Charles I and Henrietta Maria Departing for the Chase.*
Daniel Mytens, c. 1630–32.

caparisoned horse. The Black groom featured here appears markedly different, however. Much smaller in stature than the royal couple, the groom is partially clothed in a simple white and gold tunic trimmed with leopard skin and leather sandals with lace-up ties, recalling classical attire.

Portraiture and theatrical performances enabled foreign-born queen consorts to exert their influence over the English court and evolving notions of racial and sexual difference. In 1632, Henrietta Maria commissioned the courtier Walter Montagu to compose a pastoral drama for the queen and her ladies to perform for the king's birthday. The resulting masque, *The Shepherds' Paradise*, was performed before Charles I in January 1633. Departing from convention, it featured Henrietta and her troupe playing both male and female parts; it also contained a secondary blackface plot reminiscent of Anne of Denmark's controversial *Masque of Blackness*.

In the third act, the noblewoman Fidamira disguises herself as Gemella, a Moor, to gain entry to the Shepherds' Paradise, a pastoral refuge to which women apply for admission by recounting the sufferings they have endured. When the women of Shepherds' Paradise later elect the virtuous Gemella queen in the fourth act, the decision is challenged due to her dark skin. According to tradition, the queen is "to be chosen principally for her beauty"—a requisite custom "now violated in the choice of the Moor Gemella." But the current queen, Bellessa, played by Henrietta Maria, is aware of Gemella's blackface disguise. She pulls off Gemella's veil, revealing her true identity as Fidamira, a white woman worthy of succeeding her as the queen of Shepherds' Paradise.

As representations of blackness and bondage influenced court culture in Stuart England, the transition to African slavery in the English plantation colonies arose not from the attitudes or demands of planters but from more ready access to enslaved Africans. In 1630, English Puritans founded Providence Island, a small volcanic island off the coast of Nicaragua, during the same period they settled the Massachusetts Bay colony. In less than a decade Providence Island would fall to the Spanish—but not before it had become the first English colony to engage in the large-scale use of coerced African labor. The Puritan-managed Providence Island Company intended the colony to serve as a godly plantation focused on tobacco cultivation. Private land ownership was forbidden. But when the first batch of indentured servants' contracts began to end in 1633, recruitment efforts failed to attract new English servants.

Providence Island's colonists supplemented the dwindling labor supply with enslaved Africans purchased from Bermuda and passing privateers. The company supported the turn toward coerced labor with caution, insisting that enslaved individuals be well treated and their presence limited. But colonists ignored this advice, acquiring hundreds of enslaved men and women, some of whom ran away to the island's hilly interior. After bondspeople launched a rebellion, the first in any English colony, on May 1, 1638, authorities attempted to thin the population of enslaved people on the island. Nonetheless, when the Spanish conquered Providence Island in 1641, they found more enslaved Africans than English colonists.

By the 1630s, as European markets for tobacco became heavily saturated, sugar offered English planters the potential for much greater profits. But its successful cultivation required extraordinary capital, land, labor, and processing equipment. In 1637, the Dutch captured the Portuguese stronghold of Elmina on the Gold Coast, transforming the fortress into their own base for supplying the labor necessary to operate sugar plantations in Brazil. Portugal's involvement in the transatlantic slave trade steadily declined thereafter, opening opportunities for English traders to supply England's Atlantic plantation colonies with enslaved laborers.

The Scottish also sought to profit from the West African trade. In 1634, King Charles granted four Scottish courtiers a thirty-one-year monopoly of traffic between Scotland and Africa. Although the parallel monopoly patent threatened the English Guinea Company's commercial position, the king adopted the position that Scotland was excluded from English trading regulations. With the assistance of three foreign-based merchants, the Guinea Company of Scotland launched *Golden Lion* and *St. Andrew* for West Africa in late 1636. But the voyage proved disastrous. The Portuguese seized *St. Andrew* on its return voyage, killing the crew and stealing £10,000 worth of gold. While Scottish merchants and sailors continued to work for other trading companies, Scotland abandoned its attempt to break into the African trade for the time being.

Meanwhile, in the Caribbean, sugar production led to the concentration of land and capital in the hands of a small number of ambitious Englishmen who could afford to invest and innovate. They understood that obtaining an adequate supply of workers to plant and harvest cane, a laborious process that took many months and entailed backbreaking labor, was mandatory. Planters employed whatever laborers turned up: indentured servants and convicts from the British Isles, Indigenous captives from the circum-Caribbean and mainland North America, and enslaved West Africans. While the duration of servants' contracts varied, nearly all African and Indigenous laborers arrived without preexisting arrangements. Colonial planters used this legal ambiguity to their advantage to create restrictive local customs. In 1636, Governor Henry Hawley of Barbados and his council declared "Negroes and Indians, that came here to be sold, should serve for life, unless a contract was before made to the contrary." As non-Christian foreigners, people of African and Native descent lacked the rights and legal protections of English subjects; planter needs alone determined the (permanent) nature of their servitude.

The 1640s proved a critical pivot point for the expansion of the English transatlantic slave trade and slavery in the Caribbean colonies. Merchants with experience in the Americas bought plantations in the Caribbean islands and remained active in subsidiary trades, often illicit, to supply themselves and the other sugar producers with coerced labor. When the Englishman John Scott visited Barbados in 1645, the island already contained an estimated 5,680 enslaved Africans. "I believe they have bought this year no less than a thousand Negroes," he observed, "and the more they buy, the better able they are to buy, for in a year and half they will earn (with God's blessing) as much as they cost." Purchasing thousands of enslaved Africans and subjecting them to permanent bondage left many questions unresolved, including the fate of their future offspring. There was no English slave law to guide colonists' hands. As relations between King Charles and Parliament deteriorated at home, Caribbean planters devised self-serving local customs and statutes to profit indefinitely from enslaved people's productive and reproductive labor.

The tumultuous decade of the 1640s saw civil war in Britain and Ireland, Parliament's execution of Charles I for treason in 1649, and the birth of a short-lived English republic. Political upheavals in the metropole coincided with the emergence of a regular traffic in African captives to England's plantation colonies, a trade in which the Guinea Company took part. When Nicholas Crispe, a supporter of King Charles, lost his position in Parliament and his controlling stake in the Guinea Company, other partners took the lead. They reoriented the Guinea Company toward the transatlantic slave trade and the establishment of English forts on the West African coast. The overthrow of monarchal authority prompted the Council of State to revoke its royal patent nonetheless. Interlopers attempting to exploit the Guinea Company's shifting fortunes contested the resumption of its monopoly but were outmaneuvered. In April 1651, the Council of State renewed the patent, persuaded by claims that the Guinea Company offered the best means of securing English commercial interests in West Africa. By then, English traders operating both legally and illicitly had carried approximately thirty-four thousand enslaved Africans to the Americas since 1626.

The leaders of the English Commonwealth governed an Atlantic empire with enormous economic promise but limited naval strength with which to defend it. Consequently, the new government prioritized trade and the expansion of the navy. Between 1649 and 1653, England's merchant and naval fleets more than doubled. Still, the Dutch stood in the way, leaching commerce and profits away from the English republic. Enacted by Parliament in October 1651, the first Navigation Act launched a new era of aspirational metropolitan control over the colonies. The act stipulated that goods from the Americas or East Indies could be imported into England only in vessels owned and manned by the English or English colonists. Additionally, continental European goods could be imported only in vessels owned by the English, English colonists, or the country of origin—thus cutting out Dutch middlemen. War between England and the Netherlands, Europe's two major Protestant commercial powers, broke out in May 1652 and lasted until 1654. The war concluded with a nominal English victory and a lenient treaty for the Dutch, whose goods were still freely purchased by English colonists in violation of the Navigation Act.

Despite increased competition from private traders and rival European powers, the Guinea Company continued to operate and expand its slaving operations throughout the 1650s. The Council of State permitted the company's monopoly to run for another fourteen years but restricted its ventures to an area running twenty leagues to the north of its headquarters at Cormantin and twenty leagues south of the fort at Sierra Leone; private English traders were permitted to conduct business along the remainder of the West African coast. In September 1651, the Guinea Company instructed its chief factor, James Pope, to trade for wax, hides, ivory, and gold. Dispatching the vessel *Friendship* to the Gambia, the directors also requested that "15 or 20 young lusty Negers of about 15 years of age" accompany the vessel on its return voyage; "bring them home with you for London." The presence of African bondspeople in the capital, the Guinea Company hoped, would inspire prospective patrons to invest in future slaving ventures already in the works. Pope was instructed to buy two hundred enslaved Africans the following year for an Atlantic crossing to Barbados.

The Guinea Company sought to capitalize on the recent sugar boom in Barbados, which had led to a skyrocketing demand for coerced African labor. Three months later the directors ordered ship captain Bartholomew Haward to purchase "so many negers as your ship can carry" and then hasten to Barbados "for the sale of your negers." Once he docked at the island, Haward would be met by Francis Soane, a Guinea Company factor specially appointed to receive and manage the sale of disembarking enslaved people. Aware of the potential for uprisings during the hazardous Middle Passage, the Guinea Company provided Haward with "30 pairs of shackles and bolts for such of your negers as are rebellious." It instructed him "to keep them under" in the dark hold of the slaving vessel "and let them have their food in due season that they rise not against you, as they have done in other ships." The coercive nature of this transatlantic enterprise was undeniable to all involved.

The potential threat of seaboard insurrections was one of many impediments to the Guinea Company's midcentury slaving operations. In March 1652, Prince Rupert raided the company's vessels in the Gambia on behalf of King Charles II—then exiled on the Continent in the wake of his father's execution. Rupert's revenge entailed siphoning coin away from the English republic by disrupting lucrative international trade. Company agents aboard *Friendship* reported that while the vessel was anchored in the Gambia River, Rupert's fleet of six ships suddenly "assaulted and took it, with the goods, negroes, &c. on board." The Guinea Company calculated £3,200 as a conservative estimate of the damages for *Friendship* alone, not including lost interest, goods, mariners' wages, and the pinnaces also taken in Rupert's assault. It petitioned the Council of State for redress but struggled to recover financially. Waves of attacks by privateers, interlopers, and foreign adversaries torpedoed business; by 1657 the Guinea Company was sunk and essentially inoperative.

Watching these developments with interest, the East India Company attempted to gain its own share of the Guinea trade. Ships calling on the West African coast en route to India could exchange a cargo of European manufactured goods for gold and ivory. Supplying bullion in the form of African gold to East India factories in Surat, Madras, and Bengal helped to maintain company operations in India. In December 1657, two months after being awarded a new charter and collecting subscriptions, the East India Company secured the monopoly of the West African trade by purchasing the remainder of the Guinea Company's lease for £1,300.

Directors prohibited company agents from participating in the transatlantic slave trade to the English plantation colonies. Avoiding conflict with the Dutch and preserving cordial relations with local African leaders was vital to trade. Yet East India directors permitted the transport of thirty-five enslaved Africans to labor in their factories in India, St. Helena, and Bantam, so long as the individuals agreed to serve the company. English traders maintained their transatlantic slaving operations in an illicit capacity, responding to changing geopolitical circumstances and the rising demand for coerced labor in the Caribbean.

In 1654, after reconquering Ireland and subduing Scotland, Oliver Cromwell was named Lord Protector of the three kingdoms. His government, equipped with a dramatically expanded navy and greater finances than the early Stuart monarchs, set out to challenge the Spanish Crown's empire in the Americas. Cromwell's "Western Design," as his plan became known, involved sending a fleet of thirty-eight warships bearing seven thousand men to the Spanish Caribbean. His aim: to seize and colonize either Cuba or Hispaniola, after which the rest of Spanish America and its treasures would fall to the conquering English. Cromwell's plan was bold and unparalleled in the history of English colonization in the Atlantic world. The design, Cromwell assured his skeptical advisers, "would cost little more than laying by the ships, and that with hope of great profit." Neither of his Stuart predecessors had possessed the naval and military resources at their disposal to consider such a feat.

But Cromwell's audacious Western Design did not go as planned. The fleet, setting its sights on Santo Domingo on Hispaniola, failed to capture its target, delivering Cromwell a major blow. Rather than return home disgraced and empty-handed, the expeditionary forces landed on the smaller, thinly populated island of Jamaica. Jamaica, which took years to fully conquer and settle, became the first Atlantic colony the English state captured from another European power. Its conquest, the historian Carla Gardina Pestana observes, "reconfigured the geopolitics of the central Caribbean, opening it to non-Spanish colonizers and traders." For England specifically, the conquest of Jamaica "moved the Caribbean to the center of the Atlantic economy, furthering the scope for slave-based production of tropical crops." Jamaica's eventual success as a plantation colony, one whose sugar production and demand for enslaved African labor ultimately rivaled that of Barbados, transformed the English Crown's Atlantic empire into a slave empire.

It is easy to underestimate the lasting impacts of the Interregnum era on English history due to the return of the Stuart monarchy in 1660. But the experimental republican period between 1649 and 1660 proved transformative. After the Stuart restoration, Oliver Cromwell's conquest of Jamaica enabled the island to join Virginia as the second royal colony. Jamaica may have initially seemed like a poor consolation prize to contemporaries, but in a matter of decades it fundamentally reshaped the English Atlantic world. As a result of its immense slavery-derived wealth, Jamaica emerged as the jewel in the crown of the eighteenth-century British Atlantic empire. The restored Stuart monarchs' investment in the forced importation and enslavement of hundreds of thousands of Africans would make this future possible.

CHAPTER 6

ROYAL ADVENTURERS

O n May 29, 1660, Charles II arrived in London on his thirtieth
birthday to claim the hereditary birthright long denied him—
accession to the thrones of the three kingdoms of England,
Scotland, and Ireland. As Charles and his younger brothers, the dukes of
York and Gloucester, processed toward Whitehall Palace accompanied by
twenty thousand men on horse and foot shouting and brandishing their
swords, throngs of spectators gathered to witness the restored monarch's
reentry. The capital thrummed with excitement, and the fresh morning
air hung heavy with celebration. Trumpets sounded, parish church bells
pealed, and fountains flowed with wine. King Charles, tall and slim, wearing a French wig of lush, dark curls over his graying hair, was pleased
with his reception. His extended absence from his native kingdom must
have been his own fault, Charles reportedly remarked; everyone seemed
rapturous at his return. With the elated screams of Londoners still ringing in his ears, Charles swore before the House of Lords to "not only be
a true Defender of the Faith, but an asserter of the laws and liberties of
My Subjects."

After eleven years of republican experimentation, the English Commonwealth and Cromwellian Protectorate had collapsed, ushering in a
fresh slate for the institution of the monarchy and the Stuart dynasty.
Charles and his brothers had spent their formative years in hardscrabble
exile on the Continent, traveling the courts of Europe seeking allies and
appointments. Having returned triumphantly to England by invitation
of Parliament, the Stuarts sought to reinstate monarchal power, oversee
the expansion of England's overseas trade and dominions, increase royal
revenue, and build their own personal fortunes. In addition to his own

debts incurred in exile, Charles had inherited undischarged debts accumulated by his executed father, Charles I, and the interregnum regimes. To strengthen his constitutional position and enjoy the full benefits of kingship, Charles needed money. The means to achieve these ends lay in the Crown's primary instrument of power: the royal prerogative, which empowered the monarch to regulate foreign trade and exercise administrative oversight over English colonies.

From the outset of his reign, Charles II embraced the ambitious imperial project initiated by the Commonwealth government and Cromwellian state during the 1650s. Yet, like his early-Stuart predecessors, he identified as the head of an English royal empire, a royal empire that was transatlantic, commercial, and maritime, yoked together by allegiance to the sovereign. Overseas territorial acquisitions and economic exploitation promised to enrich the mother country and supplement royal revenues. Charles continued the Navigation Acts, requiring colonists to trade exclusively with English-built, bound, or staffed vessels; and he approved Parliament's list of certain enumerated goods, including sugar and tobacco, that must first land in England even if destined for a foreign port. Although Parliament assured Charles an annual income of £1.2 million, including revenues raised through customs and excise duties, the king's ordinary income fell short of expectations. Financial insecurity undermined Charles's attempts to reinstate strong monarchal authority. The king therefore looked for opportunities to exercise his royal prerogative and shore up his financial position.

Even before the reality of the Crown's deficient finances became apparent, King Charles attempted to exert control over England's imperial, commercial, and military affairs. His goal was plain: to generate revenue for his government and personal coffers and so secure the future of his reign. Fortunately for Charles's long-term purposes, the restored king had inherited a powerful, though deeply indebted, navy from Oliver Cromwell, "a naval force such as no English monarch had ever possessed." The king hoped the navy Cromwell had built to protect England's new regime during the 1650s would enable him to master the seas at the expense of foreign rivals and yield treasure. He promptly appointed his younger brother James, duke of York, Lord High Admiral of England. James intended to put English sea power to use and profit financially from his command of the navy.

When their royal cousin Prince Rupert of the Rhine arrived at the Stuart court in late September 1660, he quickened pulses with tales of untapped African gold mines. Rupert claimed that while sailing up the Gambia River in 1652 he had heard rumors of a mine consisting of "a firm rock of gold of a great bigness, which might countervail the greatest charges as may be expended in finding of it." James required little convincing. Less than a week after Rupert's arrival at court, Samuel Pepys, clerk of the acts at the Navy Office, heard "the Duke speak of a great design that he and my Lord of Pembroke have, and a great many others, of sending a venture to some parts of Africa to dig for gold ore there. They intend to admit as many as will venture their money, and so make themselves a company." Persuaded the overseas enterprise held merit, Charles loaned the adventurers five ships from his Royal Navy: *Amity, Sophia, Griffin, Henrietta,* and *Kingsdale.*

On December 18, 1660, as the expedition departed for Guinea, the king issued a charter to The Company of Royal Adventurers into Africa. Deploying his royal authority to regulate foreign commerce, he granted exclusive trading rights to the Royal Adventurers over an extensive stretch of West African coastline, from Cape Sallee in modern Morocco to the Cape of Good Hope at the southern tip of the continent, for one thousand years. The company's monopoly was supported by a joint-stock structure; only subscribers who invested at least £250 could legally participate in the English trade with West Africa. Boosted by the Stuart monarchy's support, the Royal Adventurers amassed subscriptions from members of the royal family, peers, courtiers, and well-connected merchants with colonial interests. Subscriptions by prominent royals and courtiers included King Charles (£800); James, duke of York (£3,600); the Queen Mother, Henrietta Maria (£400); the king's sister Henrietta Anne, duchess of Orléans (£400); Prince Rupert (£800); and the king's favorite, the duke of Buckingham (£800). Chronically short of funds, the king never paid more than £560 of his pledged subscription.

Loosely governed by a committee of six, the Royal Adventurers plotted to investigate the upper course of the Gambia River, unearth gold mines, and bring home fabulous riches from Africa. Charles II supported this speculative endeavor with great enthusiasm. Two-thirds of any gold deposits extracted from African mines would belong to the king, the other third to the company. The prospect of locating untapped gold deposits in West Africa had motivated English adventurers for generations. Other commodities also proved attractive. Multiple African products fetched a high price in European and other markets, including ivory, dyewoods, hides, and spices—and enslaved captives sought after for their labor and persons and traded like any other product.

Although the company's original charter did not mention slave trading, the duke of York's instructions as Lord High Admiral to ship captains and agents involved in the first expedition reveal that the Royal Adventurers' initial objectives included human trafficking. Acquiring African captives to sell into slavery in the Iberian world formed a component of the company's scattershot moneymaking strategy. Investors aspired to discover gold, erect forts for defense and commerce, and trade with locals for valuable commodities, including enslaved people, on the West African coast. James directed Captain Holmes, commander of the first venture, to call at Madeira and order "the *Kingsdale* or *Griffin* to go away with William Usticke to the Canaries, to treat about the sale of the Negroes where he is to be ready to join with you as you pass by the Canaries." In sealed letters to be opened upon arrival at the Gambia River, James instructed company factors to trade for "Negroes, hides and other goods," then to load England-bound cargo on *Sophia* and *Griffin*. Agents directed to build trading outposts or sail up the Gambia River in search of gold mines received separate orders.

The duke of York's directives indicate that the company planned to sell African captives to Portuguese and Spanish planters on the islands off the West African coast or, failing that, to potential buyers in Spain or Portugal. James told Usticke, the agent tasked with acquiring and vending enslaved people, to return "to the Canaries and in the way to touch at the Azores and Madeiras and sell what Negroes you can and take in goods for them or bills [of exchange] or money to be sent home with the *Sophia*." Not yet equipped for transatlantic slaving enterprises, the Royal Adventurers proposed offloading any remaining human cargo in Iberia's slaving hubs on the return voyage. "If you cannot sell all the Negroes in those places," the duke clarified, "you are to go with the *Griffin* to Cádiz or

Lisbon, and to be careful to send the returns you make of them home for England." He privately ordered John Stokes, the *Amity* captain, to assist Usticke "in the sale of the Negroes or other part of the cargo at any places where he shall be directed." With Crown support and the Royal Navy at his disposal, James sought to use the first venture to gather invaluable commercial intelligence.

The prospect of gold and quick riches, above all, motivated the Stuarts to invest in the West African trade within months of the Restoration. But the Crown and the earliest investors in the Royal Adventurers recognized the profit potential of trafficking in enslaved Africans. The duke of York reminded company factors to keep meticulous records, taking care to note "at Cádiz at Lisbon the Madeiras or other places, what merchants you sell your Negroes or other commodities to [so] that the same persons may be traded withal another time." Establishing a record of sales would help to build an international slave-trading network, ensure that company shareholders and the king received their due, and lay the groundwork for successive commercial transactions. When the Royal Adventurers' poorly informed search process for West African gold mines failed, a basic grasp of the logistics of slaving enabled it to pivot to a more lucrative business strategy.

In May 1662, as part of the Restoration government's scheme to expand England's commercial and imperial interests overseas and prop up the king's waning income, Charles II married Catherine of Braganza, sister of Alfonso VI, the Portuguese king. A few days after her arrival in Portsmouth, the royal couple wed during a secret Catholic marriage service held in Catherine's bedchamber, followed by a private Anglican service officiated by the bishop of London. Charles, infamous throughout his reign for his unabashed sexual appetites and numerous mistresses and illegitimate children, expressed a distinct lack of passion for his Portuguese wife. Describing his new bride in a letter to the Lord Chancellor, the earl of Clarendon, the king framed his negative assessment of Catherine's beauty in neutral terms. "There is nothing in her face that in the least degree can disgust one," he commented. A devout woman who had lived a sheltered life in Portugal, Catherine was viciously mocked at court for her olive complexion, old-fashioned clothes, and unflattering hairstyle.

Contemporaries described her in unfavorable terms as "small for a woman and a shade tall for a dwarf," possessing a narrow face, pointed chin, large mouth, and buckteeth.

Shifting the court's focus away from Catherine's physical appearance to her intellect proved challenging. The queen spoke neither English nor French when she first arrived in 1662. Catherine communicated with Charles exclusively in Spanish. Most of her attendants returned to Portugal, leaving her isolated. To her dismay, Catherine encountered her new husband's then-mistress, Barbara Villiers, Lady Castlemaine, during the royal couple's honeymoon at Hampton Court Palace. Barbara, by all accounts the most powerful woman at court and an exceptional beauty, had recently given birth to her second illegitimate child by the king, a son named Charles. Both mother and baby were in residence at Hampton Court. Dismissing his wife's tears of protest, Charles kept Barbara close at hand, appointing her to the queen's household as Lady of the Bedchamber. Barbara, Catherine soon discovered, was only the first of a slew of royal mistresses with whom she would have to contend.

Like all royal marriages, the union of Charles II and Catherine of Braganza was a calculated diplomatic match arranged to satisfy broader political, military, and financial aims. To augment his insufficient income and satisfy his lavish tastes, the restored king needed funds. And his new bride came with a huge dowry. Portugal promised Charles a fortune in exchange for assurances of English assistance against Spain and the commercial rivalry of the Dutch and liberty of worship for Catherine. Per the terms of the marriage treaty, her unprecedented dowry consisted of two million *cruzados*, around £300,000 at the time—the largest marital inducement ever offered to an English monarch. Yet Portugal could not raise the hard currency to pay up in full. The king's representatives spent years at the Portuguese court in Lisbon attempting to chase down the unpaid remainder of Queen Catherine's dowry. In 1670, Charles noted that "our good Brother the Prince of Portugal" still owed him nearly a third of the promised dowry.

Apart from coin, Catherine's dowry included commercial concessions and benefits that held the potential to crystallize Stuart imperial ambitions. Portugal ceded Bombay (modern Mumbai) on the west coast of India and the port of Tangier in North Africa to Charles and permitted

English merchants to trade with Portuguese Brazil and the East Indies. The Restoration government expected great things from these overseas acquisitions. Acquiring a toehold in India and a trading station in the Mediterranean fed into the government's vision of an expansive, self-sufficient English maritime empire. The Anglo-Portuguese marriage treaty offered "transcendent advantages for the advancement of the trade and Empire of this kingdom, the like hath not been offered in this age," proclaimed the Lord Chancellor in a speech to the House of Lords prior to the union of Charles and Catherine.

Claiming those far-flung advantages was much easier said than done. In 1668, after his government struggled to locate and seize "the island of Bumbye" from the resistant Portuguese residents, Charles transferred control of Bombay to the East India Company. Strategically located and with an excellent natural harbor, Bombay became the focal point of the East India Company's operations on the west coast of India. Tangier, a heavily fortified Moorish port city seized by the Portuguese in 1471, offered a Mediterranean base around which King Charles envisioned orienting an expanding seaborne empire. But it was not to be. Tangier failed to attract foreign merchants and their business; the garrisoned port faced repeated attacks by Moroccan forces, necessitating costly defense and state support. Strapped for cash, the Restoration government could not afford to put sufficient resources into a distant North African outpost "surrounded by an always suspicious and increasingly hostile Muslim world." In 1684, Charles evacuated and abandoned Tangier when the garrison fell to the empire of Morocco.

Imperial developments in the Atlantic world proved more promising for the Stuart monarchy. Charles retained Jamaica as a royal colony, despite promising to restore the island to Spain if he regained his throne. He welcomed the addition of Jamaica to his growing transatlantic empire. With its strategic location near Spanish America, considerable size, and abundant natural resources, Jamaica held enormous potential as a profit-generating plantation colony. To fulfill its destiny, the island needed intrepid settlers loyal to the Crown and an army of laborers. In December 1661, Charles issued a proclamation to encourage the peopling of the island. He offered prospective Jamaican colonists all the rights and privileges of English subjects and land grants of thirty acres, plus more land for additional family members, including servants and enslaved workers. James Ley, third earl of Marlborough, aspiring governor of Jamaica and a member of the king's new Council for Foreign Plantations, argued that harnessing the island's full capacities would require a sizable population of enslaved Africans. He advised Charles to persuade the Royal Adventurers to make Jamaica "the staple for the trade of Blacks as they shall think fit to be sold to the inhabitants for goods" and to purchase one hundred African captives from the company for dispersal to planters on the island.

King Charles launched England into the transatlantic slave trade as part of a much larger imperial ambition in the Atlantic world. He sought to provide the captive labor force that a growing commercial and territorial empire underpinned by theological justifications might require. Crown support for slave trading and the growth of coerced labor in the English plantation colonies aligned with the Restoration government's economic and religious goals. In December 1660, as the Royal Adventurers initiated their first West African venture in the king's ships, Charles instructed his Council for Foreign Plantations to provide Anglican ministers for the Caribbean and North American colonies and "to consider how the natives and slaves may be invited and made capable of baptism in the Christian faith." The following year, in a "Draft of an Act for the Baptizing and Better Ordering of Negroes and Infidels in the King of England's Plantations in America," the king's council encouraged missionaries to baptize enslaved people. Through Christian conversion the growing numbers of "strong and able" Africans laboring in the English colonies "will be reduced in short time to great civility," with no impediment posed to the rights and authority of enslavers, the council maintained. From the Crown's perspective, Christian conversion was not only compatible with slavery but also a tool of the state to impose and sustain social control.

Aware of conditions on the ground, Caribbean authorities hesitated to implement royal directives related to the spiritual lives of the enslaved. Colonial officials recognized the primacy of local customs and laws related to the institution of slavery. In September 1661, the assembly of Barbados passed "An Act for the better ordering and governing of Negroes," the first comprehensive slave code in the English Atlantic. The Barbadian code characterized "Negro slaves" as a "heathenish, brutish, and uncertain dangerous kind of people," too alien and unruly to be governed by laws applicable to English subjects. The legislature granted enslavers extensive power over the lives, labor, and bodies of enslaved men, women, and children.

Lawmakers used the term "Christian" to refer to anyone who was not a slave, underscoring the presumed religious identities of free and enslaved people. In 1663, after dragging his heels, Francis, Lord Willoughby, royal governor of Barbados and the Leeward Islands, advised the Barbados assembly to pass an act recommending "the christening of Negro children and instruction of all adult Negroes." The assembly, composed of representatives drawn from the island's slaveholding planter elite, rejected Willoughby's request. The planters feared that proselytizing among enslaved people offered a potential route to freedom. Christian conversion threatened to blur the social and religious distinction between bondsmen and -women and their enslavers, potentially weakening planter control over the institution of slavery.

Thousands of miles away in London, King Charles lacked the ability to impose his will from afar—especially related to the religious instruction of people deemed chattels and held in hereditary bondage. Although the king weighed in on religious affairs in his North American and Caribbean colonies, the true extent of his influence over colonial matters was limited. Besides, supplanting the commercial dominance of the Dutch, developing lucrative trade with Spanish America, and boosting his inadequate finances took precedence. Promoting the expansion of English trade with West Africa to the benefit of Crown revenues demanded his attention. However, the fledgling Royal Adventurers proved disappointing in this regard. Major Robert Holmes captured two small islands in the Gambia River held by the Dutch and Courlanders (Courland was a Baltic duchy in modern Latvia), renaming them Charles and James Island after his royal benefactors. Holmes sent several cargoes of ivory, wax, and hides back to England but located no gold mines. In late 1662, after losing six vessels to the Dutch and failing to collect the full capital subscribed, the Royal Adventurers petitioned King Charles for a new charter.

Granted on January 10, 1663, the second charter captured the shifting objectives of both the Royal Adventurers and the Stuart monarchy: from

Figure 6.1. Seal of
The Company of Royal
Adventurers of England
Trading into Africa, 1663.

speculative gold hunting to earning a steady revenue through human trafficking and the expansion of coerced African labor in the plantation colonies. In the history of English commercial relations with West Africa, the
revised monopoly patent granted to The Company of Royal Adventurers
of England Trading into Africa was the first to address slave trading in
explicit terms. Exercising his royal prerogative to govern foreign commerce, King Charles granted the company sole control over the "buying
and selling bartering and exchanging of for and with any Negroes Slaves
Goods wares and Merchandize whatsoever." He prohibited his subjects
from engaging in the African trade without the license and consent of
the Royal Adventurers. The ships and cargoes of independent traders who
defied the king would be seized at will and confiscated by the company or
the Royal Navy. Half the value of interlopers' forfeited goods—including
African captives subsequently sold into slavery—would go to the king,
the other half to subscribers. Charles included a clause specifying that
the Crown would automatically receive half of all prizes in addition to
personal dividends and prize shares based on the amount of the monarch's
personal subscription.

As the Royal Adventurers concentrated on securing a share of the
transatlantic slave trade, the king and his inner circle continued to top

the list of subscribers. James, duke of York, pledged £2,400, and Prince Rupert £800. Seeking to "complete His Majesty's adventure of £6,000 in the Royal Company," King Charles pledged an additional £5,200 on top of his original £800, as well as £400 in Queen Catherine's name. The fund from which the king's and queen's subscriptions was to be paid remained uncertain until Charles instructed the Lord Treasurer to draw from incoming customs revenue. The king subscribed such large sums of money in the Royal Adventurers that he could not keep his promises. By 1665, the Royal Adventurers felt compelled to petition Charles to direct the Lord Treasurer to pay an outstanding sum of £7,600 he owed to the company.

To make up for his cash-flow problem, the king publicly advertised his strong personal support for the Royal Adventurers and its monopoly over the transatlantic slave trade. Issuing precise instructions for the design of the company's common seal, he specified that it include "on the one side an elephant supported by two Blackamoors, and on the other the image of our Royal person." The official seal featured a shield bearing an elephant and castle and the coat of arms of the duke of York, flanked by two Africans naked from the waist up. A helmet, royal crown, and winged Admiralty anchor rest above the shield, and the company's motto, "*Regio floret patrocinio commercium, commercioque Regnum*" ("By royal patronage trade flourishes, by trade the realm"), encircles the whole. The association between the monarchy and England's first official slave-trading company could not have been clearer.

In an era when the Dutch dominated the West African trade and many in England and the colonies resented the chartered privileges granted to the Royal Adventurers, royal support was crucial. But it did not guarantee success. The Dutch fiercely opposed foreign competitors attempting to operate in their sphere of influence, and independent English traders flouted the royal monopoly on a regular basis. Despite these obstacles, the company's intimate ties to the monarchy and the state resources at its disposal proved attractive to subscribers. The new administrative structure of the Royal Adventurers elevated James, duke of York, to the position of governor; beneath him a subgovernor, deputy governor, and court of assistants oversaw day-to-day management and commercial affairs. Men in leadership positions, excepting members of "the Royal Blood and family," were required to take an oath pledging loyalty to the king. Assurances of royal assistance and protection, particularly naval defense, enhanced the outlook and business prospects of the Royal Adventurers from its inception.

With the ink dry on its second monopoly charter from the king and an overt focus on trafficking in enslaved people, the company attracted additional merchants and other businessmen with colonial interests, including owners of Caribbean sugar plantations. Discussions were held to consider the most effective means of acquiring African captives and selling them into slavery in the English plantation colonies and Spanish America. Competing for commercial traffic on the West African coast would inevitably draw the Royal Adventurers into conflict with the Dutch. Through alliances with local rulers, the Dutch had established dominion over much of the Gold Coast, and they intended to prevent the English from erecting forts and participating in the transatlantic slave trade. Consequently, the company resolved that "what cargo shall hereafter be sent to the coast of Africa shall be laden aboard sufficient ships of force." Only a convoy of manned warships provided by King Charles would enable the Royal Adventurers to carry on the Guinea trade in the face of Dutch opposition.

The Royal Adventurers rolled out an ambitious agenda to supply enslaved Africans to the English Caribbean colonies and Spanish America simultaneously. In January 1663, in response to a petition from the Barbados Council and Assembly to Charles II requesting a transatlantic slave trade free from monopoly, James, duke of York, pledged the Royal Adventurers would deliver three thousand African captives to Barbados and other Caribbean islands annually, at £17 per head. A month later, the company negotiated an additional arrangement with the Genoese merchants Domenico Grillo and Ambrosio Lomellino, holders of the asiento contract with the Spanish Crown for the delivery of enslaved Africans. It committed to disembarking three thousand African captives per year in the English Caribbean exclusively for transshipment to Spanish America. Spain's Philip IV, however, vetoed the contract before ratification. He insisted that the asiento holder not subcontract with foreign nations, though he relaxed this policy the following year.

In 1664, due to royal officials in London exempting the asiento ships and agents from the Navigation Acts, the Royal Adventurers signed a new slaving contract with Grillo and Lomellino. The contract angered English planters in the Caribbean, who claimed the monopoly company was failing to deliver an adequate supply of enslaved Africans at fair rates for their own use. By 1666, based on surviving records identifying captive numbers and place of disembarkation, the Royal Adventurers had disembarked around 8,778 Africans in Barbados, 4,445 in Jamaica, and 1,250 in St. Kitts, Suriname, and Nevis; another 5,107 individuals had perished during the Atlantic crossing. In exchange for Spanish silver, a total of 1,718 Africans were delivered to asiento agents for transshipment to Spanish ports. Although the Royal Adventurers had pledged to deliver far greater numbers of enslaved Africans to the asientistas in the Caribbean, from the perspective of English colonists, the loss of these captives detracted from the overall labor supply available for local purchase. Obliged to buy enslaved people on credit, English planters opposed asiento factors siphoning away coerced laborers sought for their own cane fields.

Building a profitable transatlantic slaving network entailed the work of many hands, some of which were based in England's Caribbean plantation colonies. The company relied on the assistance of often uncooperative colonial administrators and self-interested agents to receive and sell arriving captives, manage English-bound shipments, and rebuke independent traders who repeatedly infringed on its monopoly. On behalf of the Royal Adventurers, Charles issued instructions to colonial governors and factors ordering them to prevent interlopers from landing and selling cargoes of enslaved Africans illegally in the Caribbean islands. The company issued monetary rewards to colonial officials who looked out for its interests. For example, Sir Thomas Modyford, speaker of the Barbados assembly, served as the company's agent on the island. After his appointment as governor of Jamaica in 1664, Modyford was rewarded for his continued service. The Royal Adventurers paid him £300 per year to oversee its affairs in Jamaica, ensuring that "the laborious part of the business be upon other hands." Modyford was also presented with £250 and a plate service "as a particular testimony of kindness and respect of this Company." Not until 1669, after the Royal Adventurers had fallen into dire financial straits, did the governing board vote to cut off Modyford's allowance.

To secure trading privileges in West African regions dominated by the Dutch, the Royal Adventurers followed their rival's lead and engaged in bribes and diplomatic gift-giving. Adopting the tactics of their Portuguese predecessors and rivals, Dutch West India Company officials routinely courted the favor of African rulers by offering gifts. Generous gift-giving enabled European outsiders to build relationships with and obtain trading rights from the rulers of various African kingdoms and states. In July 1664, for example, the company sent a parcel of gifts to the ruler of the kingdom of Allada in the Bight of Benin, to build trust and secure its commercial position. The presents intended for the "great king of Ardra" (the European interpretation of Allada) included a crown with a lining of crimson velvet and an accompanying decorated letter from the duke of York, "Brother to the King of England." James explained that the crown served as a token of esteem for the African king, representing "the badge of the highest authority." Unlike crowns gifted to European monarchs, however, the crown for the king of Allada was made of gilded brass, not gold, and embellished with colored glass instead of gemstones. How the ruler of Allada might have responded to this gift remains unknown. A Dutch fleet commanded by Admiral de Ruyter intercepted the English vessel carrying the crown, and de Ruyter brought it home as a trophy of war. The crown never reached its intended recipient.

Royal symbolism infused a wealth of material objects associated with and derived from the African trade. A royal warrant issued by King Charles on December 24, 1663, ordered the master of the Royal Mint to stamp "a little elephant in such convenient place" on all coins struck from gold or silver supplied by the Royal Adventurers. Impressing the emblem of the Royal Adventurers on these coins indicated their African origin, serving as "a mark of distinction from the rest of our gold and silver monies, and an encouragement unto the said Company." Whether stamped with an elephant or not, the gold coins became commonly known as "guineas" in recognition of their provenance. Prior to the introduction of banknotes in 1694, English money consisted of coins of gold and silver and, to a lesser extent, of copper and tin. Much of this coinage went abroad for use in international trade, and its value was based on precious metal content. Fluctuating in value, the guinea stabilized at twenty-one shillings in the early eighteenth century.

The English sovereign controlled the production of coinage as an

Figure 6.2. Guinea featuring Charles II
and elephant, 1663.

extension of the royal prerogative, a practice originating in the early medieval era. Designed to evoke a reverence for the monarchy, English coins
were associated with royal representation and the power yielded by the
sitting monarch. Coinage production and circulation depended on the
amount of bullion flowing into the country, and for centuries the English
generally held "that it was the Crown's duty to provide and maintain an
adequate supply." The message King Charles broadcast by including an
elephant under his bust on guineas and other coins with African provenance was at once wide-ranging and specific. Through the enterprising
trade of a Crown-backed monopoly company, England's gold and silver
bullion supply was being replenished and melted into coin, a material
demonstration of the benefits of Stuart rule and the royal prerogative.

The irony was that King Charles was broke. So was his younger brother
James. Despite Parliament's best efforts to provide generously for the king
and his heir, Charles's ordinary revenues and the duke of York's subsidies
continued to fall short. As government expenditures soared and royal indebtedness swelled, the Stuart brothers were advised to cut household
expenses and explore new revenue streams. Overseas commercial schemes
offered the surest means of boosting royal income. For monarchs, the
seventeenth-century economist Thomas Mun recommended, "the gain of
their foreign trade must be the rule of laying up their treasure." Charles
and James pursued the monopoly trade with West Africa, among other
ventures, to help resolve their deepening financial problems. In September
1663, a court newsletter announced that the duke of York was set on "in-

creasing his income by fitting out a frigate, of which he is sole owner, for Guinea, where it is to coast for three years." The king issued a warrant to the duke of York and the Royal Adventurers, granting use of his ships *Welcome*, *Sophia*, and *Rosebush* for the Guinea venture. Charles instructed the company to return the ships in good condition within eighteen months and to outfit and repair them in the interim.

To secure new subscribers, the Royal Adventurers published a list of current shareholders displaying the names of King Charles and Queen Catherine, the duke of York, and Prince Rupert prominently under its official seal. It advertised meetings of the general court in the king's palace at Whitehall, highlighting the royal family's involvement and attendance to the public. James played a central role in the reconstituted company. More than simply an honorary governor, he did everything within his power to ensure its success. He attended company meetings on a regular basis and held them in his own royal apartments. The duke of York subscribed an additional £2,000 in May 1664 and paid the money he owed in consistent installments, cementing his leading stake in the company. In contrast, Charles stalled on his payments. Repeated petitions to the king arguing that his prompt payment would set an example for other tardy subscribers achieved little. Charles simply lacked the funds to deliver on his promises. He assisted the Royal Adventurers in other, equally critical ways, however, chiefly by loaning stocked and manned warships from his Royal Navy to protect English forts and merchant vessels on the coast of Africa.

As heir presumptive until Queen Catherine gave birth to a child and Lord High Admiral, the duke of York had a direct line to the king and influence over naval affairs. The Lord High Admiral's most important task was deciding on the deployment of warships in consultation with the Crown. Owing to the "notoriously vague" patent of office of the Lord High Admiral, Charles had final say over naval policy, and he routinely exerted his royal prerogative. Having the ear of the king was thus crucial if James hoped to realize any financial gains from a hazardous overseas trade. In his capacity as Lord High Admiral and governor of the Royal Adventurers, James grasped the importance of controlling the international sea-lanes. English trading vessels required convoy protection in African waters and along the transatlantic trading routes. Without proper maritime defense, company ships were vulnerable to the depredations of pirates and the Dutch. The Dutch claimed that they held an uncontested right to dominion over the African trade, having conquered Portuguese-controlled territories on the Gold Coast. The Dutch Republic possessed a superior naval force and was willing to use it to thwart English inroads into West Africa.

From the duke's lodgings at Whitehall, the Royal Adventurers plotted to expand their slaving operations in Africa and the Americas at the expense of the United Provinces. The Dutch, resentful of English encroachments, attacked company ships and hampered English attempts to establish a regular trading operation. In this highly competitive and hostile atmosphere, the company struggled to deliver the African captives promised to Grillo and Lomellino for Spanish America while also maintaining a supply of enslaved laborers to the English plantations. As tensions between the English and Dutch escalated, the company reminded the king of the necessity of royal protection. Trading ventures were vulnerable to attacks without a convoy of warships to accompany merchant vessels to and from the West African coast. Although an Anglo-Dutch conflict threatened to disrupt trade and supply lines between Africa and the Caribbean, the Royal Adventurers increasingly pressed for war. If the English did not check their international rival's pretensions to universal maritime and commercial dominion, the Dutch would attain mastery of the seas and foreign trade.

Fears of Dutch supremacy motivated the aggressive stance of the Royal Adventurers and the Crown toward the United Provinces in West Africa. After the capture of Dutch forts at Cape Verde and Cape Coast by Robert Holmes in 1664, the Dutch plotted retribution. At the Hague, the States General of the United Provinces pronounced English aggression against Dutch settlements and vessels on the West African coast tantamount to open war. Charles II's tepid response to the company's brazen seizure of Dutch property in West Africa "fails to reassure that these acts will not be repeated," the States General resolved. That fall, the Dutch admiral de Ruyter retaliated, attacking English forts all along the Gold Coast. The English lost every outpost except for their main fortress at Cape Coast Castle, confirming, it seemed, that the Dutch would not rest until they had eliminated their commercial rivals in West Africa.

King Charles, appalled by the quick loss of English forts in West Africa, sought revenge against the Dutch Republic. "Reflecting on the injuries done by the Dutch, their want of due reparation thereof, their hostile preparation, and their having already dispossessed our subjects of places on the coast of Africa," Charles wrote to the duke of York in his capacity as Lord High Admiral, "we have prepared a fleet, whereon you, at your own instant desire, are to embark, hinder the Dutch from passing into the channel, destroy them if they resist, and order all their ships to be seized in any port." He ordered his younger brother to grant letters of marque to English seamen against the subjects of the United Provinces, encouraging the seizure of Dutch vessels and crews "on account of the wrongs offered by the Dutch East and West India Companies to British subjects." As further evidence of Crown favor, the king permitted some of the prize ships and goods taken from the Dutch on the African coast to be turned over to the Royal Adventurers for their own use. Charles, for instance, granted the Dutch prize vessel the *Golden Lion* to the Royal Adventurers as "his Majesty's free gift" in April 1666.

De Ruyter's triumphs on the West African coast dealt a financial blow to the Royal Adventurers and King Charles and served as a source of national embarrassment. "I hear fully the news of our being beaten to dirt at Guinea by de Ruyter and his fleet," lamented Samuel Pepys on December 22, 1664, "to the utter ruin of our Royal Company, and reproach and shame to the whole nation." Rivalry over the transatlantic slave trade contributed directly to the Second Anglo-Dutch War (1665–67), which was fought to a significant extent in West African and Caribbean waters. As hostilities between the English and Dutch intensified, the Company petitioned the king for assistance "to support a trade which brings in £200,000 to £300,000 gold per annum to your Majesty's mint" and was also "absolutely necessary to the very being of your Majesty's American plantations which will be rendered utterly useless if they have not a constant supply of Negro servants." A Dutch monopoly of the transatlantic trade in African captives would compel England's plantation colonies to rely upon foreign merchants for labor supplies, to the detriment of colonial security, national wealth, and the king's imperial vision.

King Charles wholeheartedly agreed. He characterized the Dutch as "clearly the aggressors" for attacking English shipping and "acting hostilely against the English in Africa." Yet the timing of the Dutch conflict proved disastrous for Charles and the fledgling African Company. The Second Anglo-Dutch War overlapped with an outbreak of the bubonic plague in London in 1665, followed by the Great Fire of London the next year, depleting the Exchequer. The Crown hovered on the edge of bankruptcy. War curtailed English commerce in West Africa and stalled shipments of enslaved captives to the Caribbean, exacerbating the financial difficulties of the Royal Adventurers. Company vessels stationed in or arriving at the coast of Africa were conscripted into the king's naval service to defend English trading outposts against Dutch attacks. Sponsoring fresh ventures to Africa during the Anglo-Dutch conflict, the Royal Adventurers reiterated to Charles, demanded "royal protection and assistance," specifically in the form of warships to protect company vessels and cargoes.

But Charles barely had the money to cover naval expenses and the salaries of seamen. While loans from the East India Company and the corporation of London kept him afloat, the king's ability to offer material assistance to the Royal Adventurers had flagged considerably by 1666. Declining trade and rising costs also aggravated the shortage of capital in the form of liquid assets available to the Royal Adventurers. The entire transatlantic slaving operation relied on the extension of credit. English merchants consigned cargoes of goods to agents stationed in West Africa; they, in turn, consigned shipments of captives to colonial factors. Lacking coin, many planters and other colonists purchased enslaved Africans by means of credit extended for a set period. This system gave the Royal Adventurers leverage over colonial planters and, from the perspective of directors in London, generated goodwill toward the company's monopoly. However, collecting on unpaid bonds in colonies with legislatures and courts dominated by the planter elite proved difficult and, in some cases, impossible.

By contrast, selling African captives to foreign asiento agents capable of paying in Spanish American silver served the interests of both the Royal Adventurers and the monarchy. Persuaded of the financial benefits by the duke of York, King Charles permitted asiento vessels and agents to land in his Caribbean islands and trade for enslaved people and goods imported from England. Using Jamaica as an entrepôt for supplying enslaved captives and merchandise to nearby Spanish ports offered English merchants and the Stuart monarchy the opportunity to drain the Spanish empire of bullion. The king was unmoved by his Caribbean subjects' arguments that selling the healthiest African captives to the asiento agents undercut their own labor needs and contraband trade with Spanish America. Facilitating the flow of Spanish coin into the English treasury was his government's top priority.

As deliveries of enslaved captives to the Caribbean plantations slowed during the Second Anglo-Dutch War, colonial hostility to the Royal Adventurers' monopoly over the West African trade spread. Facing public scrutiny, the company published a tract intended to attract new subscribers and defend its royal monopoly. Without a chartered company under Crown protection, England risked losing its share of the transatlantic slave trade, it pointed out; "and thereby His Majesties dominions in America in apparent hazard to be rendered useless in growing their plantations, through want of that usual supply of servants which they have hitherto had from Africa." Critics disagreed, countering that when the "Guinea trade for Negroes was formerly free to all adventurers," planters were "plentifully supplied with Negroes upon reasonable terms, without which they cannot subsist." In its defense, the company articulated a case for the value of its monopoly to England, the Caribbean colonies, and the Crown. "Plantations were never so well supplied during the pretended freedom of trade for Blacks, as they have been by this Company, since they were established, nor his Majesties revenue by customs larger," it maintained.

Still, public bluster failed to address the root problem. The Royal Adventurers had run out of liquid capital and owed creditors £57,000 that it could not repay. Beginning in 1668, the company issued licenses to independent traders and consortiums in a bid to remain solvent. A group known as the Gambia Adventurers leased the right to trade in the northern parts of West Africa for seven years at an annual rent of £1,000. Even as the Royal Adventurers floundered, between 1663 and 1668 a total of 27,489 African captives embarked in company ships in ninety-eight separate recorded voyages. Of this total, 20,747 individuals survived the perilous Middle Passage to disembark—overwhelmingly in Barbados as the first port of call. Ten years into the Restoration, the necessity and profit-generating potential of the transatlantic slave trade had become evident to royal, court, and mercantile interests. Despite the company's financial failure resulting from the combined impact of the Dutch war on trade and the shortage of liquid capital from unpaid colonial debts and subscriptions, abandoning the transatlantic slave trade was inconceivable.

As he entered the second decade of his reign, Charles remained desperate for hard currency. The Second Anglo-Dutch War had essentially wiped out the Exchequer and increased the Crown's mounting debts. Charles never received the full income nominally granted to him by Parliament, leaving him with an annual deficit of £300,000 to £400,000 and inadequate funds to meet the national expenditure. Parliament's generosity toward the king had cooled in the intervening years since the Restoration; it would only vote him taxation to meet extraordinary needs. Charles looked for a way to free himself from a dependency upon inadequate parliamentary subsidies. He encouraged the public to buy bonds and loan money to the government, and he turned to France, where his cousin Louis XIV governed absolutely, for an answer.

On May 22, 1670, Charles signed the secret Treaty of Dover, agreeing to support France in a war against the Dutch and return England to the Roman Catholic faith at a suitable future date in exchange for an annual cash subsidy. Within months, the king's agreement to support Louis XIV's attack on the United Provinces was an open secret at court. That this policy would inevitably lead to a renewal of hostilities with the Dutch Republic, but with France as the primary aggressor, offered a silver lining: Once at war, the Dutch would have fewer naval vessels available to defend the Gold Coast. The time appeared ripe for a major reinvestment in the transatlantic slave trade.

PART II

EXPANSION

CHAPTER 7

THE ROYAL AFRICAN COMPANY

In October 1671, with the king's full support, the general court of the Royal Adventurers voted to reconstitute the company and raise a new stock of at least £100,000. Subscriptions ultimately exceeded this minimum, amounting to £111,100. Meetings were to be held at the African House in London unless James, duke of York, specified otherwise. In 1672, Charles issued a new patent to The Royal African Company of England, granting it sole control over all English trade in African "commodities"—including "Negro Slaves"—for one thousand years. To enforce the terms of the African Company's royal monopoly, the king authorized it to erect Admiralty courts on the African coast to "hear and determine all cases of forfeiture and seizures of any ship or ships goods and merchandises" trading without the company's permission. Subjecting interlopers to the company's own Admiralty jurisdiction overseas allowed it to use a heavy hand to compel compliance, an exceptional power that generated controversy at the time. Charles endowed the African Company with state-like privileges, including "full power to make and declare peace and war with any of the heathen nations" along Africa's Atlantic coastline.

The 1672 charter marked a new era of commercial success for the Royal African Company (RAC) and a dramatic expansion of England's share of the transatlantic slave trade, from 33 percent to 74 percent during the first decade of its existence. The African Company, as historian William Pettigrew points out, "shipped more enslaved African women, men, and children to the Americas than any other single institution during the entire period of the transatlantic slave trade." From 1672 to 1688, during the reigns of Charles II and James II, nearly 100,000 Africans from the Bight of Benin, Bight of Biafra, Gold Coast, West Central Africa, Senegambia, Sierra Leone, and other regions fell victim to its slave-trading activities across some 330 recorded transatlantic voyages. Approximately 76,000 of these individuals survived the Atlantic crossing, which averaged seventy days, to disembark in the Americas—in the majority of cases in the English Caribbean colonies.

Noting the rough numbers of individuals who lost their lives during the Middle Passage at any point in time fails to capture the raw human experience of the Atlantic crossing. The slave ship imposed its own cruel order, notes historian Marcus Rediker, "one designed to objectify, discipline, and individualize the laboring body through violence, medical inspection, numbering, chaining, 'stowing' below decks, and various social routines, from eating and 'dancing' to working." Historians estimate that 10 percent of slaving vessels experienced insurrections staged by African captives. Uprisings and high mortality rates laid bare the staggering human costs of the transatlantic slave trade. Nevertheless, neither the African Company nor the Stuarts expressed qualms about investing in and profiting from a business centered on dehumanization, coercive control, and extreme human misery and death.

Backed politically by the Stuart monarchy, the African Company invested in the building of new fortified trading bases and the strengthening of older forts along the West African coast. The bulk of this activity took place on the Gold Coast and in the Bight of Benin, where the trade consisted primarily of enslaved captives and gold. Tenuously situated, RAC forts relied on the goodwill of local rulers for their continued existence. By the 1680s, the company was shipping enslaved Africans from eight different sites on the Gold Coast, three small islands in the northern Senegambian region, and at Ouidah in the Bight of Benin. If they survived the harrowing journey across the Atlantic, traumatized captives disembarked months later in the English plantation colonies: usually in Barbados or Jamaica, but also in the Leeward Islands of Nevis, St. Kitts, Antigua, and Montserrat. Virginia, too, received a small proportion of enslaved captives. Stationed in the colonies, African Company agents awaited the arrival of slaving vessels. Charged with managing the processing and sale of enslaved people, agents collected coin, credit slips, and payments in the form of sugar and other commodities from purchasers.

Subscribing £3,000, the duke of York remained the largest African Company shareholder, and he made regular payments toward his subscription. He was again voted governor and retained that position until he fled to France in December 1688 during the Glorious Revolution. King Charles, still massively indebted and short on funds despite receiving about £125,000 per year in French subsidies between 1671 and 1677, maintained his track record of failing to pay. In October 1674, the court of assistants petitioned the king for the money he owed the African Company after its reconstitution. Although he had subscribed £7,600 to the Royal Adventurers, the king's outstanding balance stood at £6,057. He now owed the RAC 10 percent of his original subscription, or £760, and an additional £5,297 to satisfy the defunct company's creditors. The king was not the only royal in arrears: Prince Rupert had also failed to pay £510 of his £1,600 subscription.

Lacking liquid currency to spare, Charles opted to cover his debt to the African Company in kind. He instructed James, as Lord High Admiral, to direct the Royal Navy to provide provisions for the RAC's use. James ordered his officers to supply the RAC with victuals needed to outfit two ships and feed sixty-five seamen for twelve months as well as sixty men stationed at Cape Coast Castle for six months, plus supplies for eighty-five men for one month at sea. The king also furnished the company with naval stores such as sails, cables, warps, and cords. King Charles used his executive control over the Royal Navy to offer material assistance to his state-backed slaving enterprise. This aid proved invaluable.

The African Company was closely associated with Stuart royal policies and interests. As it increased its market share over the transatlantic slave trade, the Stuarts profited in multiple ways. Regular shipments of African captives to England's plantation colonies, particularly to Barbados and Jamaica as the first ports of call, increased the population of enslaved laborers on sugar plantations across the colonial Caribbean. John Scott, an early visitor to Barbados, reported that the cultivation of sugarcane was "managed principally by Negro slaves," who undertook the most laborious and dangerous tasks. With the king's consent, Jamaica served as an entrepôt for Spanish agents seeking to purchase enslaved Africans for Spanish America. Meanwhile, beginning in 1674, Chesapeake tobacco

planters could rely on the semiregular arrival of RAC slaving vessels bearing captives directly from West Africa, primarily the ports of Gambia and
New Calabar in the Bight of Biafra. An uptick in the transatlantic slave
trade to the Chesapeake, both licit and illicit, ultimately encouraged the
large-scale adoption of slavery in the region.

Import duties on colonial sugar and tobacco, the production of which
was fueled by coerced labor, were important sources of revenue for
Charles II and his successor, James II. By 1687, sugar and tobacco customs revenue comprised one-third of total Crown revenue; subsequent
monarchal regimes would also benefit financially from colonial staples
produced by enslaved Africans. The income derived from the expansion
of the transatlantic slave trade, overseas commerce, and colonial agricultural production offered a boon to the chronically underfunded monarchy.
Once no longer in desperate financial straits, the Stuart kings could avoid
summoning Parliament and silence the voices of critics concerned with
the direction of monarchal policy and potential abuses of the royal prerogative.

Throughout the 1670s and 1680s, James, first as duke of York and then
as king, exerted his sway on behalf of the RAC at court and within the
Royal Navy in official and unofficial capacities. In 1673, James resigned
from the Admiralty and the Privy Council after Parliament passed the
Test Act to root out closeted Catholics holding public office, civil or military. Yet James retained his Admiralty office in Scotland, Ireland, and the
American and Caribbean plantations, regions of the English empire to
which the Test Act did not apply. He also influenced Admiralty affairs
behind the scenes, even after King Charles appointed an Admiralty commission to replace him. Samuel Pepys, who through his naval colleagues
purchased enslaved Africans, privately noted James's attendance at multiple Admiralty meetings, though Pepys did not record the duke's presence
in the official minute book.

Even as the duke of York's open Catholicism and marriage to the Catholic Mary of Modena transformed him into a divisive public figure, the
African Company highlighted his name in published lists of shareholders
designed to attract new subscribers. His lucrative entanglement with the
monopolistic transatlantic slaving company was widely known. Between
1676 and 1688, as competition from independent traders intensified and

the price of enslaved captives fell, the African Company borrowed money to pay a 10 percent dividend to shareholders on eleven occasions. James received RAC dividends totaling £3,551 and later sold his shares for £5,730. His personal profit from investing in the forced trafficking of tens of thousands of Africans amounted to at least £6,281.

This substantial sum does not include the cash gifts James received from the RAC. Recognizing the fruits borne of the duke of York's outsized royal influence, the governing board rewarded him in coin for services rendered. On June 26, 1677, the General Court ordered the court of assistants to present James with 500 guineas as an acknowledgment of thanks for his many favors on the company's behalf. Members gifted the purse of guineas to the duke of York three days later. Within weeks James also received a 10 percent dividend. In January 1678, a month after James was paid his second dividend of the year, the General Court resolved to gift him an additional present of 500 guineas for "extraordinary service." Eschewing specifics, the governing board expressed its appreciation for "his great condescension to take notice and continued care of this Company's affairs." So long as the Stuarts remained on the throne, ongoing Crown support promised to safeguard the African Company's monopoly privileges.

For the Royal African Company to secure a majority market share of the transatlantic slave trade, and for the Stuart monarchy to profit from its business, enforcement of the monopoly charter against illegal slaving was vital. Charles used his royal prerogative to uphold the RAC's monopoly to the full extent of his abilities. In November 1674, the king issued a proclamation to deter illicit slaving. Despite the enormous expense of building and maintaining forts, the costs of which the RAC alone had borne "to the great benefit of this Our Kingdom," his subjects had sent ships to West Africa to engage in illegal slaving for their own personal advantage. Private trade to Africa or the Caribbean, the king reiterated, was strictly prohibited. Interlopers, if caught, faced arrest and seizure of their ships and cargo, including enslaved Africans, "for Our Use, according to our Royal Charter granted to the said Company, upon pain of Our High Displeasure, and as they will answer the contrary at their perils." Still, such threats made little impact on independent traders seeking to earn a profit from transatlantic slaving.

King Charles deployed England's first major slave-trading company as an arm of the state. He commanded colonial officials and the Royal Navy to enforce the RAC's monopoly. He authorized the deployment of warships to cruise the West African coast, defending English forts and factories and convoying transatlantic deliveries of captives. To discourage independent merchants, Charles backed the African Company's right to seize interlopers and their cargoes and prosecute them in juryless vice-admiralty courts. In 1676, the deputy governor formally thanked both King Charles and the duke of York for their "continual patronage of the company's interest." In truth, the Stuarts' interests were aligned with those of the African Company; acting in the company's interest served their own. The extraordinary powers held by the RAC to defend its monopoly represented an extension of the royal prerogative. The Stuarts' efforts, however, failed to prevent independent traders from conducting business in West African or Caribbean waters in defiance of their sovereign. Advocates of free trade pushed to gain a share of the transatlantic slave trade irrespective of royal commands.

In 1676, Charles II loaned the RAC his royal warship *Hunter*, under the command of one Captain Dickinson, to cruise the West African coast in search of independent merchants trading illicitly. While on patrol, Dickinson seized two ships captained by interlopers, *Anne* and *John & Mathew*; the prize proceeds, worth £2,800, were split among the king, the RAC, and Captain Dickinson. Charles received a payment of £1,400 for his half-share of the prize money. To intercept independent merchants whose ships slipped past patrols in West African waters, sailing across the Atlantic laden with illicit cargo and enslaved captives, Charles supplied a man-of-war, *Constant Warwick*. Under the king's directive, *Constant Warwick* cruised the Caribbean, attempting to spot and seize illegal vessels before they disembarked African captives for sale in English plantation colonies hungry for coerced laborers. But one royal warship stood little chance against a sea of interlopers determined to infringe upon the company's monopoly.

In England and the colonial Caribbean, calls to constrain the abuse of the royal prerogative power to create monopolies grew in the late 1670s. The Stuarts had granted numerous monopolies to trading companies, ostensibly to regulate commerce but primarily for their own financial benefit. The RAC exemplified this abuse owing to its intimate connection to its royal benefactors: King Charles and the heir apparent, the duke of York. As one subscriber crowed privately, "we fare never the better at this time by having the Duke of York for our Governor." Critics argued that the RAC's monopoly over the West African trade—and the transatlantic slave trade as the most important component of that commerce—confirmed the absolutist pretensions of the Stuarts. Despite intense demand for enslaved Africans in England's plantation colonies, the king had closed the market to his subjects and directed slaving revenue streams into royal coffers.

Charles II strategically used his royal prerogative power to appoint judges receptive to defining African bondspeople as a legitimate form of property. Because planters relied on credit extended by the RAC to purchase enslaved Africans, profits from slaving only accrued to shareholders and the king if enslaved people were legally defined as chattel. Sir Richard Rainsford, the chief justice of the Court of King's Bench, made this legal innovation possible. In *Butts v. Penny* (1677), Rainsford ruled that "Negroes, being usually bought and sold among merchants, as merchandise, and also being infidels," could be treated as simple property under the Navigation Acts. This meant enslaved individuals could be bought, sold, and inherited as goods and litigated over for unpaid debts. The sovereign power of the ruling monarch facilitated the expansion of transatlantic slaving as well as the legalization of slavery in England's Atlantic empire. Yet the RAC's Stuart-sponsored monopoly was extremely unpopular and costly to enforce.

In response to mounting criticism, the RAC attempted to convey the value of its royal monopoly to the public and Parliament. In 1678, it oversaw the minting of forty thousand guinea coins stamped with an elephant. The guineas illustrated the extent to which the company had enriched the nation, not just shareholders. In a pamphlet published in 1680, the RAC defended the public "utility and advantages" of its monopoly. In addition to exchanging superfluous English merchandise for gold, ivory, wax, and other valuable commodities, the RAC's involvement in "the Negro Trade" had yearly "furnish[ed] with vast numbers of servants all His Majesties American Plantations, and that upon large credit and time given to the planters for payment; who at this present owe to the company more than £100,000." Crucially, the RAC supplied a steady stream of coerced laborers to colonial planters without depleting England of its native population. The importation of agricultural products, such as sugar, tobacco, molasses, and indigo, produced by enslaved labor completed the circle. "So that the riches of that part of the world, (being the result and product of industry and labor) is in good measure owing to the *Royal African* Company."

Caribbean colonists found these arguments unpersuasive and self-serving. They opposed the RAC's monopoly and the king's interference in local affairs, welcoming illicit slaving vessels and engaging in contraband trade themselves. Colonial resistance to imperial directives prompted Charles to resort to threats and punitive measures. In January 1681, Sir Henry Morgan, famed pirate turned deputy governor of Jamaica, received a copy of the king's proclamation against interlopers. He was ordered strictly "to aid and assist any factors or substitutes of the Royal African Company or others deputed by them in the seizing and taking all such ships and vessels Negroes and other commodities in whose hands soever they may be found." If Morgan faced local opposition, Charles empowered him to raise "such forces as may be necessary for the suppression of any tumultuary or riotous resistance that may be made in contempt of our authority." Far more than the RAC's trade was on the line. At stake was the legitimacy of the king's royal prerogative. "Fail not at your peril," Charles warned Morgan.

As countless independent merchants openly defied the RAC's monopoly over the West African trade, monitoring company property and profits became a priority. At their forts on the African coast, English agents corralled men, women, and children into underground prisons or holding pens to await the arrival of slave ships. Paid to facilitate the transport and sale of captives, African Company factors looked at individuals of all ages and saw only human commodities. Agents bound the wrists and ankles of captives with iron shackles and frequently requested new supplies of iron restraints from England. Subject to these dehumanizing conditions and made to perform menial tasks demanded by agents, captives broke free of their holding cells and fled the forts. To track commodified human beings, the RAC turned to a method employed by enslavers in Iberia, on the West African coast, and in the Americas since the late

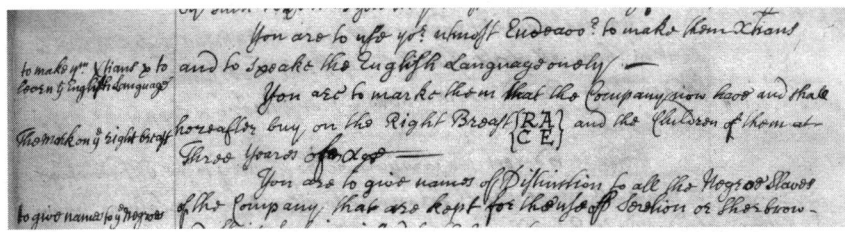

Figure 7.1. The RACE mark used to brand "castle slaves."

fifteenth century: "marking" bondspeople—including young children—with a hot branding iron, also known as a "fire mark."

Branding dehumanized and further commodified Africans, signifying their status as company property rather than human beings. Letters sent from London indicate that the RAC routinely directed agents to brand so-called "castle slaves": the enslaved Africans employed in its coastal factories. Agents based at the smaller satellite forts, where iron brands and shackles were in short supply, may have engaged in the practice to a lesser extent than their counterparts based at the company's headquarters at Cape Coast Castle. In instructions issued on August 29, 1699, and sent to factors at Cape Coast Castle, the governing board addressed the matter of branding directly. "It has been customary to mark the Company's Negroes with their mark; we believe it can be no inconvenience to renew that method," advised the directors. One of the usual marks branded into the flesh of African individuals purchased by the company, both adults and children, took the form of an acronym: RACE, for the Royal African Company of England. "You are to mark them that the Company now has and shall hereafter buy on the right breast RACE and the children of them at three years of age," directors instructed John Freeman, an agent stationed at Sherbro.

The RAC used other marks to distinguish women, men, and children it classified as human property. In at least one instance, in 1694, African captives forced to embark on *Hannibal*, captained by Thomas Phillips, were branded on the shoulder or chest with an H, to represent the ship that bore them across the Atlantic. However, the RAC typically reserved branding for the hundreds of individuals consigned to labor on the company's behalf in its coastal forts and factories, referred to as "castle slaves."

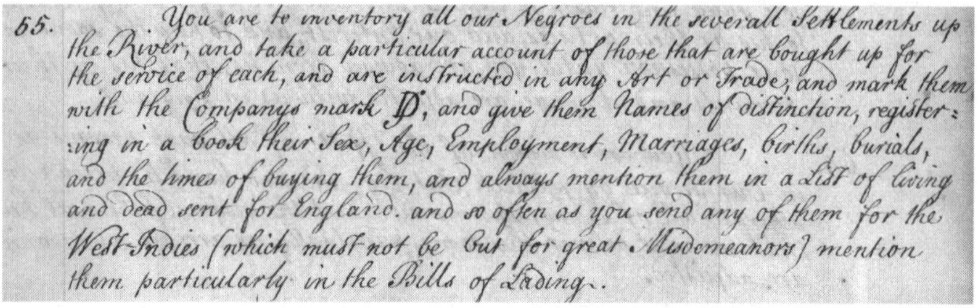

> 55. You are to inventory all our Negroes in the severall Settlements up the River, and take a particular account of those that are bought up for the service of each, and are instructed in any Art or Trade; and mark them with the Company's mark Ð, and give them Names of distinction, register-ing in a book their Sex, Age, Employment, Marriages, births, burials, and the times of buying them, and always mention them in a List of living and dead sent for England. and so often as you send any of them for the West-Indies (which must not be but for great Misdemeanors) mention them particularly in the Bills of Lading.

Figure 7.2. The DY mark used to brand "castle slaves."

In surviving copies of nineteen different letters dispatched to West Africa between 1720 and 1741, the African Company instructed its chief agents to inventory "all our Negroes" and brand those retained for use in West Africa "with the Company's mark." In four of these letters, sent in 1720, the mark is specified: DY (with the Y superimposed over the D). Decades after James II was deposed and the Stuart dynasty collapsed, DY retained its significance as a brand prescribed by RAC officials to assert ownership of Africans.

In 1735, John Atkins, a naval surgeon who visited the Gold Coast and Cape Coast Castle in the early 1720s, published an account of his travels. Atkins corroborated the continued usage of irons bearing the initials of the RAC's first governor to brand enslaved people well into the eighteenth century. He observed that the African Company "mark them still D.Y. Duke of York, to perpetuate the ignominy of his headship to that trade." Regardless of the mark employed, searing the breasts or shoulders of Africans with burning irons was a method used to facilitate a wider system of capitalistic violence, one predicated on mass commodification and dehumanization. By obscuring the humanity of bondspeople and transforming them into mere products and tools wielded by enslavers, branding signified the most overt attempt to claim ownership over Black bodies previously understood as human.

CHAPTER 8
ROYAL COMMODITIES

In December 1682, royal officials paid £50 to the elderly Scottish courtier Randall MacDonnell, the marquis of Antrim, "for a black his said Majesty bought of him." Antrim's ties to the Stuarts stretched back half a century. In addition to pledging military support for the Royalist cause during the civil war era, Antrim's wife, Catherine, was the former widow of King Charles I's murdered chief minister, George Villiers, duke of Buckingham. The gender, age, and origin of the Black individual Antrim sold to Charles II is unknown. So too is the precise fate the king had in mind for this enslaved person. Yet the chances that Charles intended to keep this particular African bondsperson at court, perhaps to serve as an attendant to one of his many mistresses, are quite high. Exhibiting an enslaved Black page garbed in bright livery with a collar around their neck had become the height of court fashion. The king and members of his inner circle led the vanguard.

Comparatively few people in late seventeenth-century England witnessed the brutality of the transatlantic slave trade or Atlantic colonial slave system firsthand. Slavery links nevertheless infused the later Stuart cultural and material world. The English smoked tobacco produced by enslaved African labor; they sweetened food and drink—tea, coffee, and chocolate—with Caribbean sugar that enslaved people planted, harvested, cultivated, and processed; they invested in transatlantic slaving and related industries; and they purchased bondspeople to serve in a variety of capacities in their homes and businesses. Londoners encountered African-descended people in the capital's streets and households on a routine basis. Most, but not all, were enslaved; and those who had fled bondage sought to blend in and carve out lives as free subjects. After the Restoration, advertisements for enslaved runaways of African descent, mostly young men who had fled their enslavers, appeared with increasing frequency in London newspapers.

The presence of enslaved Black attendants dressed in opulent livery—particularly children and young adults—was all the rage at Whitehall, in aristocratic and wealthy merchant households, and in portraiture. Exhibited as exotic objects of display, whether in person or in artwork, enslaved attendants of African ancestry signified the wealth, prestige, and imperial connections of their enslavers. To decorate their country and city houses, prominent individuals commissioned portraits featuring anonymous Black attendants and marble busts of "Blackamoors" carved in the Italian or Spanish style, with a collar encircling their necks. While artists may have based their designs on real individuals, the inclusion of unnamed enslaved pages in Stuart material culture served to enhance the status and whiteness of English subjects. At court, in private households, or in artwork presented to public view, bondspeople of African descent were rarely treated as individuals in their own right.

In addition to Prince Rupert, who inspired the later Stuarts' quest for African gold, several of Charles II's mistresses incorporated enslaved individuals into their portraits as a strategic form of self-representation. A portrait of the actress Nell Gwyn dating from the 1670s, privately held by her descendants until it was sold in 2011, depicts the king's most infamous lover suggestively preparing sausages while a young Black attendant peers over her shoulder. Dressed in red livery and wearing a silver collar, the enslaved page holds a tray and awaits his enslaver's command. Gwyn, clothed ironically in virginal white, peers at the viewer with a coy smile; her breasts are partially exposed as she stuffs the sausage casings. The portrait playfully associates sexual appetites and indulgences with the fulfillment of the royal will, even though it does not directly depict King Charles. To do so was unnecessary. Known for his dark hair and swarthy complexion and his sponsorship of African slaving, Charles was nicknamed "Black boy." Gwyn, a commoner and royal mistress, is of higher status than her anonymous enslaved attendant. Yet both figures represent commodified bodies available for royal consumption.

The king's aristocratic mistresses also turned to portraiture to advertise

Figure 8.1. *Prince Rupert of the Rhine*, seventeenth century.

Figure 8.2. *Nell Gwyn Preparing Sausages*, 1670–79.

their sexual power as recipients of the king's desire who possessed intimate access to royal wealth and patronage. Not long after first visiting England in 1670 as a maid of honor to the king's sister Henrietta, duchess of Orleans, who died soon after returning to France, Louise de Kéroualle was invited to court. She held a dual position as maid of honor to Queen Catherine and mistress to King Charles. Never one to hide his infidelities,

Figure 8.3. *Louise de Kéroualle, Duchess of Portsmouth, with an unknown female attendant.* Pierre Mignard, 1682.

Charles gave her a suite of rooms at Whitehall and the title duchess of Portsmouth in 1673. In Pierre Mignard's portrait of the duchess, a young Black female attendant offers her mistress red coral and a conch full of pearls—treasures associated with the Caribbean. The duchess, whose arm is draped maternally across the girl's shoulders, has adorned her attendant in sumptuous clothing and a pearl choker reminiscent of a slave collar. The child's dark skin illuminates the duchess of Portsmouth's alabaster complexion and plump, rosy cheeks, a nod to the king's affectionate nickname for his mistress, "Fubbs."

The diarist John Evelyn witnessed the magnificence of the duchess of Portsmouth's suite of rooms with his own eyes. In 1675 he was "casually showed the Duchess of Portsmouth's splendid apartment at Whitehall, luxuriously furnished, and with ten times the richness and glory beyond the queen's," everything of "incredible value." Eight years later, in October 1683, Evelyn visited her dressing room in the company of the king and expressed his astonishment and thinly veiled disgust at the volume of its riches, "beyond anything I had ever beheld." "Japan cabinets, screens, pendulum clocks, huge vases of wrought plate, tables, stands, chimney fur-

Figure 8.4. *Hortense Mancini,
Duchess of Mazarin, as Diana.*
Benedetto Gennari, 1684.

niture, sconces, branches, brasiers, etc, they were all of massive silver and
without number, besides of his majesty's best paintings," he exclaimed.
Incorporating an enslaved attendant in her portrait offered evidence of
the exalted status of the duchess of Portsmouth. A second portrait of the
duchess, attributed to Sir Godfrey Kneller, principal royal painter to the
Stuart monarchs, also includes a young Black female attendant—perhaps
the same child depicted by Mignard. It is reasonable to suppose that the
enslaved child served the duchess in her apartment at Whitehall, a striking physical manifestation of royal favor.

Hortense Mancini, duchess of Mazarin, another of the king's famed
mistresses, arrived at the English court in 1676 accompanied by a Black
page named Mustapha. Niece of Cardinal Mazarin, Louis XIV's former
chief minister, the duchess had fled an unhappy marriage in France and
spent a period ensconced in a house in Chelsea as Charles II's lover, with
Mustapha and other liveried pages by her side. Mustapha is one of the
few enslaved attendants at the Stuart court whose name was recorded. In
Benedetto Gennari's portrait of the duchess of Mazarin, commissioned
in 1684, she is represented as Diana, goddess of the hunt. Bare-breasted

and holding a spear, she is surrounded by four dark-skinned enslaved boys and two white hounds. All are wearing collars. The portrait, shocking both then and now in its explicit and casual embrace of bondage and gendered racial domination, offers insight into courtly attitudes toward the enslavement of African peoples in later Stuart England. All three portraits of Charles II's mistresses deploy the bodies and presence of subservient Black children to convey monarchal favor and white female sexuality.

By the final years of Charles II's reign, Stuart imperial designs relied heavily on the expansion of African slave trading and enslavement. But the decision to treat bondspeople as mere property, in both a legal and a cultural sense, exacerbated their mistreatment at the hands of enslavers. It encouraged colonists to conceptualize enslaved individuals as *things* with an inherent economic value, to downplay their obvious humanity in pursuit of ever greater profits. The emergence of colonial slave statutes classifying enslaved individuals as chattel, or movable, personal property, and real estate distinct from rights-bearing English subjects captured this horrifying shift. Enslaved people, however, did not act like things. They did not submit to their enslavers' commands without question. The contradiction rooted in English slave law—that the enslaved were at once things and capable of human criminal intent—confirmed the complexities built into the Atlantic slave system.

In contrast to Spanish and French kings, whose colonial slaving regimes were governed by royal decree, English monarchs rarely intervened to restrain the abuse of bondspeople in their colonies. By custom and law, individual enslavers in the English plantations exercised nearly unchecked power over their human chattel. Only in the most extreme circumstances, such as a lax penalty for the intentional murder of an enslaved person, did the Crown refuse to confirm colonial slave legislation. "A fine is imposed on all such as willfully and wantonly kill a Negro," wrote the Lords of Trade to the governor of Jamaica in 1683. "The king will not confirm this clause, which seems to encourage the willful shedding of blood. Some better provision must be found than a fine to deter men from such acts of cruelty." Unbridled homicidal violence against the enslaved made a mockery of English assertions that hereditary bondage under benevolent Christian masters improved the lives and moral characters of Africans.

Whether Africans and Indigenous peoples could become members of the Anglo-Christian community remained a matter of contention. English justifications for the dispossession and enslavement of Africans and Native peoples fit within a theological framework that demarcated between Christians and infidels and heathens. This ideology, which fueled earlier Christian crusades and overseas colonization efforts, derived from arguments that nonbelievers were enemies of Christ and therefore suitable targets for just war and perpetual slavery. In the English Atlantic empire, the uncertain legal status of enslaved individuals who converted to Christianity prompted questions about the future of the colonial slave system. Charles II resolved to encourage baptism among non-Christians, noting that conversion would not alter the legal status of enslaved individuals. The Virginia legislature codified the rule that baptism was incapable of conferring freedom in 1667, and other colonies followed suit. Parliament neither passed an imperial slave code nor clarified the legal status of enslaved individuals in England, leaving the matter subject to interpretation by the courts.

Religion and the future of the succession in the Crown's three kingdoms also remained in doubt. After Queen Catherine's third miscarriage, in June 1669, Charles II realized his marriage was unlikely to prove fruitful; his wife had failed to fulfill her purpose. The absence of a legitimate heir to the throne intensified the duke of York's dynastic significance. After impregnating Anne Hyde, the daughter of the Lord Chancellor, James had reluctantly agreed to marry her in September 1660. The match produced two surviving female children, Mary and Anne—both of whom would embrace Protestantism. With fears of popery rampant in England, James imperiled his dynastic position by following his wife's example and converting to Catholicism in 1669. His rejection of Protestantism, obvious from his refusal to receive Communion according to Anglican rites at the Easter service in 1671, "gave exceeding grief and scandal to the whole nation, that the heir of it, and the son of a martyr for the Protestant religion, should apostatize," lamented one contemporary. "What the consequence of this will be, God only knows, and wise men dread."

If James, duke of York, became king of the three kingdoms, a practicing Catholic would serve as supreme governor of the Church of England. Such an outrage would undermine the established Church to the detriment of the king's many Protestant subjects. As Parliament pressed for James's removal from the succession during the Exclusion Crisis, Charles ordered his younger brother and heir into exile in Flanders and then Scotland between 1679 and 1682. The king, cushioned financially by French subsidies and increased customs revenue, avoided calling Parliament. He bided his time until the House of Commons held a Tory majority committed to the principle of monarchal hereditary right. Just a few short years later, Charles was dead.

In February 1685, when King James II ascended the throne following the death of Charles II, he remained intent on strengthening the power of the Crown and profiting from the transatlantic slave trade. James retained his position as governor of the Royal African Company and issued a proclamation defending its royal monopoly two months after his accession. As king, James used his patronage of the RAC to protect its financial interests. In response to African Company petitions, he ordered the governors of Barbados, the Leeward Islands, and Virginia to prosecute and severely punish interlopers with fines, imprisonment, and the confiscation of their vessels and goods. He instructed the Royal Navy to patrol African and Caribbean waters for pirates and illegal traders. James profited personally from the African Company's monopoly control over the transatlantic trade in African captives and at the state level from the expansion of coerced labor in the plantation colonies. In 1686 and 1687, annual customs revenue from Chesapeake tobacco and Caribbean sugar alone averaged £150,000.

King James's contact with Africans and people of African descent was confined to the limited number of enslaved attendants he either sold or gifted to his friends at court. Although he professed a deep commitment to Catholicism, James's conscience was not troubled by his investment in human trafficking or African bondage. The only concern he expressed for enslaved people related to the state of their souls in his capacity as head of the Church of England. King James, like his elder brother, Charles, recommended the baptism of enslaved Africans. He also explicitly clarified that conversion did not equate to freedom. At a Privy Council meeting James said "that the Negroes in the plantations should all be baptized," noted Samuel Pepys, "exceedingly declaiming against that impiety of their masters prohibiting it, out of a mistaken opinion that they would be *ipso facto* free." His stance ran counter to the opinions and practices of his slaveholding colonial subjects. Despite widespread opposition to calls to convert enslaved people to Christianity in England's plantation colonies, "his Majesty persists in his resolution to have them christened, which piety the Bishop blessed him for," remarked John Evelyn.

But religion ultimately proved King James's undoing. He offended his Protestant subjects by invoking his dispensing powers to disregard the Test Act and appoint Catholics and dissenters to public office alongside Anglicans. The birth of a son, James Edward, in June 1688 was the final straw. If the prince survived to adulthood and ascended the throne, the king's son would perpetuate Catholic rule in the three kingdoms. That prospect was intolerable to many. In the weeks after the birth of James Edward, leading Whig and Tory politicians issued an invitation to William of Orange, a Dutch stadtholder and the husband of James's Protestant daughter Mary, to invade England. They assured the Dutch prince that the English people would rally to his side in opposition to their unacceptable Catholic sovereign.

The collapse of James II's government came swiftly on the heels of William's landing at Torbay at the head of a major expeditionary force on November 5, 1688. As William's army of around twenty-one thousand men advanced steadily toward the capital, officers and soldiers in the English king's field army defected or retreated. Queen Mary of Modena fled to France with the Prince of Wales in early December. Under duress, James II escaped London for the second and last time shortly before Christmas and followed his wife and son to France. To fund his flight abroad, James sold his substantial stock in the Royal African Company and the East India Company. The recipient of the king's £3,000 of RAC shares was James Graham, keeper of the privy purse and a close associate of the king. Graham accompanied James during his flight to France and loaned him money on the security of the king's shares in the two trading companies. By March 1689, James II's divestment from the African Company he had long championed was complete. After three years on the throne, the Stuart king returned to a life of exile on the Continent; only this time it was permanent.

CHAPTER 9

SLAVERY AND THE GLORIOUS REVOLUTION

I n early January 1689, the Royal African Company's court of assistants held a pressing meeting at their African House headquarters
on Leadenhall Street in London. Two weeks earlier, King James II,
the African Company's longtime governor and royal patron, had fled into
exile in France, severing the monopoly company's close ties to the Stuart
monarchy. The African Company's future was not the only thing in limbo
in the wake of the king's flight. Characterized as an "abdication" by the
Whigs, who favored strengthening Parliament at the expense of the monarchy, and a "desertion" by the Tories, who stood for royal prerogative and
hereditary right, King James's sudden departure left behind a monarchal
power vacuum and a divided nation. Parliament grappled with the political implications of the king's absence, however involuntary. While their
interpretations of James II's departure from England differed, Whigs and
Tories agreed that the country needed a sovereign. Both parties sought "a
lawful path out of an unlawful situation."

Backed by Whig supporters and a sizable military force, William of
Orange offered himself as a solution to the nation's troubles. Usurping
James II's dynastic right as a hereditary monarch, William called for a
parliamentary convention to determine England's constitutional future.
Now that James had supposedly abjured his realm, William was intent on
wielding executive power—even if he had to share it with his wife, Mary,
the eldest daughter of England's absent king. Assembling in late January
and February, the Convention Parliament debated whether to recognize
William and Mary as the new joint sovereigns. While the Whigs and Tories deliberated over who should fill the vacant throne or if there should
instead be a regency, the RAC cast its lot with the prince of Orange.

The African Company filled its own leadership void by inviting the Dutch prince who had chased their former governor and king out of the country to take his place. To sweeten the offer, the court of assistants presented William with £1,000 of stock, "which his Highness was pleased to accept of and promised that he would do the Company all the kindness lay in him." Edward Colston, the deputy governor of the Royal African Company—whose controversial statue in Bristol would be toppled and chucked into the harbor by protesters centuries later—initiated the £1,000 transfer. By midmonth, word spread throughout the capital that William of Orange had agreed to assume the RAC governorship. Although unprecedented, the company's gift of stock to William was probably a secondary factor when he agreed to serve as governor. William desired the English throne, and at the time his political fate rested in the hands of the specially assembled Convention Parliament. While the RAC's invitation to William to take James II's place may not have enhanced his political stature in England, it nonetheless served his cause.

William of Orange held regal pretensions but was not yet certain of the Crown. Serving as honorary governor of a major joint-stock company intimately associated with the Stuarts demonstrated the growing weight of his influence. It also signaled his commitment to dynastic continuity. He aimed to displace James on the English throne; the RAC governorship represented a first step on that path. Weeks before the parliamentary declaration proclaiming William and Mary joint sovereigns on February 6, 1689, William became the public face of the monopoly slave-trading company the Stuarts had long championed. Like his Stuart predecessors, William understood the monetary value and imperial magnitude of the transatlantic slave trade. The Dutch prince had invaded England in anticipation of war with France, but his political position remained tenuous. Needing sufficient funds to finance the coming war effort, he would use any means possible to generate revenue and strike the French on land and at sea. As the head of the Dutch Republic, moreover, William's government was already reliant upon and tied to African trafficking and enslavement.

A contemporary tract recounting the prince of Orange's unopposed landing near Exeter in November 1688 claimed that he marched at the head of an impressive army of horse and foot, his banners proclaiming

"The Protestant Religion and the Liberties of England." Led by two hundred armored men on horseback, his army included thousands of foot soldiers, among whom were supposedly "200 Blacks, brought from the plantations of the Netherlands in America, having on embroidered caps lined with white fur, and plumes of white feathers, to attend the horse." This description of William's grand procession from Exeter to London is almost certainly apocryphal. Other eyewitness accounts make no mention of the presence of numerous enslaved attendants. But the story illustrates English awareness of the significance of coerced African labor in the Dutch plantation colonies, in addition to the dominant role of Dutch merchants in the transatlantic slave trade. Amsterdam, Europe's central trading hub, processed a significant portion of sugar from the Caribbean plantations; the sugar industry dominated Amsterdam's economy by the late seventeenth century. Tales of William's arrival with a mass of enslaved African attendants, specially brought from "the plantations of the Netherlands in America," reinforced the Dutch prince's imperial prowess.

Ultimately, the Glorious Revolution and William III's replacement of James II on the English throne led to the Royal African Company losing its market share of the transatlantic slave trade and its royal monopoly. After years of intimacy with Charles II and James II, the RAC could not shake its close association with the old Stuart dynasty and its gross abuses of royal power. The company's monopoly subsequently came under increasing attack. Yet, as honorary governor, William did what he could to serve the company's interests. He also used the RAC to aid his military campaigns against France while he supported and benefited from England's transatlantic slave trade and African bondage in the colonies. The association between the monarchy, England's overseas empire, and the bodies and labor of people of African descent endured well after the accession of William and Mary and into the eighteenth century. Coinage, portraiture, and the presence of enslaved Black attendants at Hampton Court and Kensington Palace made these links explicit. The mint continued to stamp elephant and elephant and castle provenance marks on gold and silver coins, impressed under the monarchs' conjoined busts and, after Mary's death in 1694, William's bust.

Preserving the Stuart royal tradition of Black court attendants, a hand-

Figure 9.1. *Equestrian portrait of William III.* John Smith, after Sir Godfrey Kneller, 1689.

ful of enslaved pages worked in William and Mary's palaces. Whether in person or in art, enslaved attendants played supporting yet highly visible roles in court culture, their presence a regular reminder of the material rewards of the transatlantic slave trade and colonial slavery. In English portraits commemorating the Glorious Revolution, William III is depicted in armor on horseback. He is assisted by an unnamed liveried Black page who holds his helmet while the prince's army marches in the background. Dutch portraits of the prince of Orange, produced years before he invaded England, similarly depict William with an anonymous enslaved attendant. Visualized as marginal and subservient, Black pages were typically situated behind or off to the side of their master or mistress in seventeenth-century European portraiture. Wearing collars and other unmistakable signs of enslavement, they signaled the stature, power, or beauty of the portrait's principal white subject. While the downfall of James II led to the decline of the RAC and loss of its monopoly charter, reliance upon the bodies and labor of Africans to bolster royal prestige and wealth remained pervasive.

The constitutional settlement following the Glorious Revolution fundamentally redefined the political role and powers of the monarchy. William and Mary's acceptance of the Declaration of Rights before Parliament offered them the Crown—later embodied in law as part of the

Bill of Rights (1689)—permanently curtailed royal authority. Parliament placed limitations on the extent of the prerogative powers enjoyed by the monarchy, which had generated intense, recurring controversy under the Stuarts. Constitutionally, Parliament would henceforth reign supreme. Monarchs could no longer claim an authority by divine right to ignore or suspend laws; neither could they levy taxes without parliamentary consent nor prevent Parliament from meeting regularly.

William III's intense focus on the threat of France led him to accept a diminution of royal authority in exchange for grants of taxation and annual revenue from Parliament to defeat Louis XIV. William and Mary were voted customs revenue, worth an estimated £577,507 annually, for only four years instead of life. Parliament renewed this grant in 1694 for another five years. Funding for sustained warfare and the related growth of the navy and army required parliamentary approval. Taxes increased and government indebtedness rose as a result of short-term, high-interest borrowing; but strategic limitations on Crown revenues hamstrung William's ability to abuse royal power. Through control over the fiscal infrastructure of the state, Parliament brought the Crown to heel.

The English Bill of Rights of 1689 did not address the constitutionality of monopoly privileges granted by royal prerogative. But the Royal African Company's inability to enforce its charter after James II's flight was glaringly apparent. Hostility toward Crown-chartered monopoly companies, kept in check by the Stuart monarchs, found expression in court cases, petitions, pamphlets, and parliamentary debates. Within months of the accession of William and Mary, John Holt, chief justice of the Court of King's Bench, ruled in *Nightingale v. Bridges* that "no man is to be dispossessed of his property but by *legale judicium parium suorum*"— that is, the legal judgment of his peers in a jury trial. Charles II had unlawfully permitted the RAC to erect a court of Admiralty to proceed against and confiscate the persons, vessels, and human and other property of English subjects who infringed on its royal monopoly. After quietly halting its seizure of interloping vessels and instructing agents not to detain private traders, the RAC informed King William that it had become "necessary to get the charter confirmed by Act of Parliament." Supporters and critics of the African Company's monopoly over the transatlantic slave trade wasted little time articulating their opposing stances publicly.

In January and March 1690, the RAC petitioned the House of Commons to pass a bill confirming the letters patent granted to it by Charles II. Merchants and planters interested in Jamaica and Barbados, as well as independent ship captains whose vessels had been confiscated and condemned as prizes by the African Company, submitted counterpetitions. A transatlantic slave trade open to all Englishmen, critics insisted, would keep "the American plantations much better supplied with negroes, to the great augmentation of the king's revenue, and wealth and trade of the nation in general; and other nations, who trade there, would be beaten out of the trade." After weighing the arguments and evidence presented by both sides in the debate, the Commons resolved in December that forts supported by a regulated company were necessary to carry on the African trade. But with the country now embroiled in William III's war with France, other matters of national importance took precedence. Parliament delayed acting on the statute sought by the RAC.

Deliberations over the legitimacy and utility of the RAC's monopoly unleashed a flurry of parliamentary petitions and printed pamphlets, the overwhelming majority of which favored free trade. Critics pointed to the African Company's charter as an example of the Stuarts' blatant misuse of the royal prerogative. Arriving from across Britain and its Atlantic colonies, petitions and pamphlets supporting the deregulation of the transatlantic slave trade numbered in the hundreds. A representative example is a scathing tract written by William Wilkinson, a private slave trader. He attacked the African Company for its oppressive treatment of interlopers, which, he said, severely limited the supply of enslaved Africans to the plantation colonies. In 1685, a Royal Navy vessel patrolling for interlopers had captured William and his crew, including his brother Henry, near the Gambia River. Their ship and cargo were confiscated, and the Wilkinson brothers and their fellow crewmen were imprisoned in a dungeon at Cape Coast Castle. While awaiting trial before a vice-admiralty court, Henry Wilkinson had committed suicide.

William Wilkinson was determined to hold the RAC accountable for his brother's death and its collusion with the Stuart monarchy to oppress independent traders. Protective only of its own financial interests, he asserted, the African Company bound the hands of planters, ensuring that they "shall never be furnished with the Negroes sufficient to follow their business with satisfaction." The company showed no mercy to fellow English subjects attempting to earn a living from slaving. The African Company's control over the transatlantic slave trade brought ruin and dishonor to the nation and impaired Crown revenue and imperial growth, Wilkinson concluded. He appealed to William and Mary and to Parliament to act in the interests of justice and grant English merchants unrestricted access to the slave trade.

Other critics echoed Wilkinson's view, arguing that the African Company's monopoly over the slave trade represented a gross abuse of royal prerogative power. The Stuart monarchs had denied their subjects the "right and liberty to trade to Africa" solely for their own financial benefit. Economic growth in England's Atlantic empire had stalled as a result. The company, "having had the monopoly of Negroes, and consequently selling them at excessive rates, hath cramped and crippled the plantations in a grievous manner." The complaints of private traders went hand in hand with a growing consensus among Caribbean and Chesapeake planters that a free trade in enslaved Africans would resolve their pressing labor needs.

Unlike his Stuart predecessor, William III played virtually no role in the day-to-day affairs of the Royal African Company. Yet he supported the RAC's monopoly and benefited financially from his position as honorary governor and shareholder. Three months after William received a 10 percent dividend of £100 in April 1691, the company voted to quadruple the value of each proprietor's stock without payment. The general court issued an order on July 30, "That every £100 adventure shall be made £400, and that the members have credit given them accordingly." William's £1,000 of RAC stock thus became worth £4,000. The following month, William and Mary jointly received a £500 transfer of RAC shares from James Graham, the man to whom James II had transferred £3,000 of RAC shares to fund his exile in France. Graham had sold three-quarters of the African Company shares he had acquired from King James when the barons of the Exchequer ordered him to give up the remaining portion to the joint monarchs.

Graham's transfer of shares to William and Mary followed a legal determination by the attorney general that the stock, being held "in right of the Crown," now belonged to the joint sovereigns. Hence by August 1691 William III held RAC shares in his own right worth £4,000 and an additional £2,000 together with his wife, Mary II. In October 1692, the king received a 3 percent dividend of £129; the joint monarchs received a £64.10 dividend. After Queen Mary's sudden death in late December 1694 at age thirty-two from smallpox, William held £6,000 of RAC shares outright. But Mary's demise and the absence of her hereditary legitimacy threatened the king's grip on power. James II and his Jacobite supporters cast William III as a usurper, who had taken a throne that was not his by blood. French support for the Jacobite cause, and the unpopularity of the Dutch king's expensive wars and his aloof, foreign manner in England, exacerbated the uncertainty of William's reign as sole monarch.

Royal African Company stock dividends received by William, and William and Mary jointly prior to her death, amounted to small, essentially insignificant sums. However, the customs revenue the Crown derived from tobacco and sugar—colonial exports produced overwhelmingly by the forced labor of enslaved Africans—was substantial, totaling nearly £1 million in the 1690s alone, an average of £100,000 per year. By the end of the seventeenth century, wealthy colonists in the Chesapeake had followed the lead of their counterparts in the Caribbean sugar islands by investing heavily in enslaved labor, and "these men and women produced vast quantities of tobacco for their masters." In the Chesapeake colonies, the enslaved population rose from a recorded number of 4,611 individuals in 1680 to 19,617 by 1700, ultimately dwarfing the number of white servants in the region. Due to the ubiquity of African slavery in the Caribbean colonies by the late seventeenth century, in 1700 there were six times as many Africans in bondage in the English Caribbean as there were in all of mainland North America.

From private traders to French privateers and merchants, the RAC faced multiple threats to its slaving operations after the Glorious Revolution. Between 1688 and 1697, the clash between France and England and its allies, coupled with French incursions on the West African coast, undermined the African Company's market share of the transatlantic slave trade. After receiving a commission from William and Mary "empowering them to commit hostilities, and annoy the enemy in all places within their jurisdiction," the company sent orders to John Booker, their chief agent at James Island in the Gambia River, to take hostile action against the French. Booker had arrived at James Island shortly before the accession of William and Mary and renamed the island and fort in honor of England's new sovereigns. Agents rarely used the new name in practice, however, preferring "James Fort" for their former patron. In January and February 1693, Booker led two successful expeditions that captured France's Senegal and Gorée trading forts. The English partially demolished Gorée after taking French cannons, provisions, and goods, including twenty-four hundred ivory tusks. Although a subsequent French expedition recaptured both forts in June, the RAC's short-lived victory against the French stimulated a new round of parliamentary petitions and counterpetitions related to the transatlantic slave trade.

To encourage parliamentary endorsement of its royal monopoly, the African Company presented several witnesses who provided evidence on its behalf to the House of Commons. In 1694, a naval commissioner, a former agent, and the company's chief accountant testified that protecting English trading interests on the West African coast, from both local natives and other Europeans, required coastal forts. Forts were also a substantial ongoing expense. The company's opponents countered with their own witnesses, including a customs official who claimed that greater numbers of English ships set out for West Africa to the benefit of the Crown's revenue when the trade was open. Captain Robert Porton, an independent trader, maintained that African merchants preferred conducting business with interlopers rather than the African Company because they sold at lower prices. "The plantations would be much plentifuller served with negroes, by an open trade," he reasoned.

The Commons weighed these differing opinions but delayed acting, prompting another petition by the Royal African Company in the fall of 1694 to secure its monopoly. A group of planters and merchants with ties to Barbados submitted a counterpetition, dismissing the African Company's claim to possess the sole trade with West Africa by right of royal charter. "The pretended charter is only an illegal patent, which would exclude all other his Majesty's subjects from trading to Africa," they wrote.

By placing the immensely profitable transatlantic slave trade in the hands of a single corporate body tied to the monarchy, the Stuarts had abused their royal prerogative. The RAC embodied the previous monarchal regime and deserved to be held to account.

Several major developments overlapped in 1695 to shift the political debate over the future of the African trade: an escalating currency crisis in England, imperiled shipping lanes arising from William III's war with France, and the Scottish Parliament's grant of a perpetual monopoly over trade with Africa and Asia to the Company of Scotland Trading to Africa and the Indies (known as the Darien Company). Only a year after the Bank of England's founding, confidence in the government and the nation's monetary system plummeted due to the steady debasement of English currency and shortage of good coin. The basic unit of exchange, the silver crown, had lost its face value, compromising public trust in coin and credit. The price of stock shares in the Bank of England, a novel financial institution originally proposed to help finance the war effort, declined. King William struggled to support his continental army financially while French privateers wreaked havoc on English overseas trade.

The Scottish Parliament's launch of the Darien Company raised concerns that English and foreign merchants would use it as cover to engage in piracy overseas under Scottish colors. The terms of the Darien Company's charter allowing it to trade for a period without paying customs also raised the ire of England's mercantile and seafaring community. Critics pointed out that English overseas trade was, in contrast, "clogged with customs," so "they will undersell us." Consequently, the House of Lords resolved to present an address to King William, outlining "the great prejudice, inconveniences, and mischiefs" that would arise from the Scottish company. The king responded by prohibiting English merchants and planters in the Caribbean from selling to Scots, which doomed their designs in the region. William III also claimed ignorance when Scottish expeditions to plant a colony on the isthmus of Panama angered the Spanish Crown.

In 1696, while the future legality of the RAC's Crown-chartered monopoly remained in limbo, William III established a new Board of Trade, answerable to the Privy Council. Tasked to play an advisory role and propose methods to make the colonies more profitable for the Crown, the Board of Trade conducted an inquiry into the state of the transatlantic slave trade and its impact on colonial economic productivity. Merchants and planters connected to the Chesapeake colonies weighed in on the debate for the first time. The plantations in Virginia and Maryland, they insisted, would generate twice the quantity of tobacco presently produced if planters were supplied with sufficient enslaved Africans. More coerced laborers would lead to greater agricultural output, lower prices, and enhanced revenue for the king, because "one Negro will make as much tobacco in a year as must pay £30 or £40 custom in England." According to this logic, each African bondsperson who crossed the Atlantic and survived the brutal conditions to disembark in England's plantation colonies constituted a future sum of money for the royal coffers. The material gains accrued from the transatlantic slave trade and coerced African labor in the Chesapeake and Caribbean plantations benefited colonists, merchants, and the Crown alike, they maintained.

Chesapeake planters and merchants allied themselves with fellow opponents of the RAC's monopoly in England and the Caribbean colonies in hopes of expanding their own access to enslaved Africans. While the African Company had directed some of its slaving vessels to disembark in the Chesapeake in the preceding decades, the region was greatly underserved in comparison to the Caribbean. In contrast to its main commercial hubs in Barbados and Jamaica, there were no permanent salaried company factors stationed in the Chesapeake to process newly arrived African bondspeople and sell them to buyers. Instead, through prearranged contracts, the RAC consigned human cargoes in advance either directly to Chesapeake purchasers or to prominent merchants who acted as middlemen. From the perspective of colonists in Virginia and Maryland, ad hoc RAC deliveries of enslaved Africans failed to address the region's pressing labor needs. Beginning in the 1680s, the indentured servant trade to the plantation colonies declined rapidly due to decreased birth rates and rising real wages in England. The acute shortage of agricultural workers in the Chesapeake threatened to impact plantation yields and, by extension, the monarchy's bottom line. Planters increasingly pivoted to coerced African labor to produce most of the region's tobacco.

The transformation of the Chesapeake's labor force took place over a generation and increased the region's reliance on the transatlantic slave trade. In January 1686, *Speedwell*, a 120-ton slaving vessel captained by Marmaduke Goodhand, set out from London for James Island on the Gambia River in Senegambia. After spending three months purchasing a total of 217 enslaved Africans on behalf of the RAC, *Speedwell* departed for the Chesapeake plantation colonies in early June. It arrived eight weeks later in Maryland, bearing 192 terrified and exhausted bound individuals who had survived the horrific Atlantic crossing. Per the RAC's instructions to Goodhand, the enslaved Africans who disembarked in the Potomac River were to be delivered into the hands of three merchant planters for distribution to buyers: Christopher Robinson, Richard Gardiner, and Edward Porteus.

Members of the politically influential Chesapeake gentry, all three men owned large tobacco plantations and engaged in transatlantic commerce. Presumably, they sold the 192 enslaved Africans delivered by *Speedwell* in groups of lots to local planters in the Chesapeake, retaining a handful of bondspeople for their own estates. Robinson, a future member of the Virginia Council and House of Burgesses, and briefly secretary of state prior to his death in 1692, owned Hewick plantation in Middlesex County, Virginia. Gardiner owned multiple estates in St. Mary's and Charles County, Maryland, and in Virginia near the Rappahannock River. A merchant and tobacco planter, Porteus owned multiple plantations in Virginia; the largest was a 692-acre estate along the York River called New Bottle in Gloucester County. It is Porteus's life and lineage that is of greatest interest to the present study.

A wealthy merchant planter, Edward Porteus maintained strong connections to colonial political leaders. In 1693, the governor of Virginia included him in a list as a "gentleman of estate and standing" recommended for appointment to the Council of State. According to his will, dated February 23, 1694, when Porteus died in 1700 his wife, Elizabeth, inherited one-third of his estate as well as furniture, a horse and saddle, and "the time his English servant maid Betty has to serve, and his Negro girl Cumbo." Unlike the servant Betty, who labored under a contract, Cumbo possessed no rights. Edward Porteus regarded her as a possession, bound to serve his widow for life and to pass her enslaved condition on to any future children she may bear.

Edward Porteus's son, Robert, inherited the remaining two-thirds of his estate, including land, stock, servants still under contract, and enslaved individuals of African origin and descent. The elder Porteus specified that "Negroes and servants [were] to be kept on his plantations, also the stock, and the produce sent yearly to England." Appointed to the Virginia Council in 1713, Robert Porteus was a high-ranking member of Virginia's propertied elite until he moved with his second wife and children to England around 1720, settling first in York and then in Ripon. After leaving Virginia, Porteus continued to profit from New Bottle plantation and its enslaved workforce as an absentee owner.

Generations later, Frances Smith, a direct descendant of Robert Porteus, married Claude Bowes-Lyon. The Bowes-Lyons' granddaughter was Elizabeth Bowes-Lyon, wife of King George VI and mother of Queen Elizabeth II. Hence, through his maternal line, Britain's present monarch, King Charles III, is a direct descendant of Virginia planters who exercised ownership over African men, women, and children and profited from their coerced labor. The Church of England also has a link to colonial Virginia and African enslavement through one of Robert's sons, the Reverend Beilby Porteus, bishop of London from 1787 to 1809. In 1758, Beilby and his brother inherited their father's New Bottle plantation in Virginia and subsequently benefited financially from the sale of the estate and its enslaved workers.

As the parliamentary deliberations over the Africa trade dragged on without resolution, the ongoing public debate clarified the extent to which those involved—merchants, planters, agents, legislators, and government officials—understood the risks inherent in long-distance trade in human beings. Africans did not migrate voluntarily to the Americas and submit to permanent hereditary bondage under English and other European colonists of their own accord. They ran away, sickened and feigned illness, refused to work, rebelled, engaged in self-harm, and died. Calculated to commodify people and deny their humanity, the Atlantic slave system was predicated on violence and coercive control.

Commanding obedience from captives, whom enslavers conceptualized as goods rather than persons, demanded extreme ruthlessness. "This mind-set was a fundamental prerequisite of slave trading," argues the historian Nicholas Radburn. Concerns about Africans fighting back against their enslavers—on West African beaches, at sea, and in the Caribbean and North American colonies—remained top of mind. By the end of the seventeenth century, enslaved uprisings and alleged conspiracies had occurred in Bermuda, Barbados, Jamaica, Antigua, and Virginia. Repeated scares convinced English observers that enslaved people would look for any opportunity to "murder all their masters." Yet this fear failed to dampen the rising demand for greater access to the transatlantic trade in enslaved Africans and to their forced labor.

William III's position as king enabled him to steer English foreign policy in a direction that suited his geopolitical aims. Containing France was his foremost objective. Waging an expensive land and sea war against France to secure the revolutionary settlement and balance of power in Europe dominated his reign from 1689 to 1697. Raids and attacks by the French navy and privateers threatened the English and Dutch seaborne trade upon which the economies and plantation colonies of both countries relied. The Nine Years' War placed the English government under enormous financial stress, adding £32 million to the national debt. Even with the doubling of taxes, government revenue fell as the state bureaucracy and English navy and army swelled in size and trade fell.

In September 1697, William III and Louis XIV signed the Treaty of Ryswick, ending the Nine Years' War inconclusively after months of negotiations. Louis XIV officially recognized William as king of England, Scotland, and Ireland but refused to expel James II from France involuntarily, despite William's insistence. The French king's unwillingness to send his cousin and fellow monarch, James Stuart, far away from the British Isles or to stop referring to the fallen monarch as king fostered an atmosphere of mutual distrust between William and Louis. Although peace appeared temporary, at best, the reprieve in the wartime depredations on commerce fueled a resurgence of overseas trade. Confronted with a changing commercial and financial landscape, English long-distance merchants clamored to try their hand at high-risk, high-reward endeavors such as slave trading.

Alert to the growing numbers of independent traders preparing cargoes for Africa, the RAC appealed to Parliament for permission to sell its forts to a friendly foreign power. After Parliament denied this request outright and hostilities with France concluded, the Court of Assistants appealed directly to King William to intercede on the Company's behalf. A petition to the king, dated December 1697, detailed how Charles II had used his sovereign authority to grant subscribers to its joint-stock dominion over the African trade, "to the very great advantage of all your Majesty's plantations in America, till the breaking out of the late war with France." The disruptions of the late war and activities of interlopers had cost the RAC £400,000 in losses, the petition detailed, making further trade and the preservation of essential coastal forts impossible, "unless encouraged and supported by your Majesty." With William holding the role of governor and the future of the African trade under consideration by Parliament, royal defense of the African Company's monopoly remained vital. At the very least, the company hoped to persuade the king to support its bid for financial support from the independent traders for maintaining its existing forts on the West African coast.

William III received a detailed report from the African Company outlining its proposed strategy for the African trade and the preservation of England's coastal forts. The plan included reserving trade in the northern parts of Guinea exclusively for the company while opening the trade from Cape Mount to the Cape of Good Hope to all English subjects on payment of a duty—including "£5 per head on all Negroes imported into any of His Majesty's plantations or elsewhere." The duty would support existing English forts and castles, an indispensable expense because the African natives, the company alleged, "are a people so treacherous and barbarous that no treaties of peace will oblige them, and they watch all opportunities to kill and steal." A separate document listed the forts maintained by the RAC, outlining the numbers of white men, company "gromettoes" (enslaved workers), guns, and vessels assigned to each. Spread across eight coastal forts, the African Company employed 553 white men, owned 292 bondspeople, and boasted 368 guns and 126 vessels attending the forts. To the king, this documentation served as evidence of the value of retaining an English defensive presence on the West African coast.

In 1698, Parliament resolved the matter of the African trade over which it had deliberated for eight years with no resolution. In the six weeks following the initial introduction of the Africa trade bill in February, Parliament received petitions from planters and merchants connected to Virginia and Maryland, Barbados, Jamaica, the Leeward Islands, and Montserrat. Proponents for an open trade with Africa sought above all that "negroes may be brought to the plantations cheap," as the Barbados petitioners put it. Only petitioners associated with the smaller Caribbean islands, which received fewer slaving vessels and no extension of credit from interlopers, supported the continuation of the RAC's monopoly. In June 1698, the company's representations to the king and Parliament, and the opinion of the Board of Trade, led to the passage of "An Act to settle the trade to Africa." It authorized English subjects to engage in the African trade on payment of a 10 percent duty to the RAC on all goods imported or exported, excepting gold and captives, to support the expense of operating its coastal forts and factories. The law went into effect on June 24 for a period of thirteen years.

At the time, the act looked like a coup for the African Company, proof of its continued influence with the government. Parliament, though supportive of open trade, had not yet abandoned support for the Crown-sponsored company responsible for establishing English bases on the West African coast and expanding the transatlantic slave trade to the plantation colonies. Whether they used the RAC's West African forts or not, the independent traders would play a role in their maintenance. A court newsletter characterized the 1698 act as a compromise approach to the African trade, "which will now be carried on with more ease to the plantations, in respect to the furnishing them with negroes, as well as advantage to the company."

In the long run, however, the 1698 act transformed former interlopers into legal traders. It signaled the beginning of the end for the Crown-sponsored African Company. Independent traders, based in the capital and outports like Liverpool and Bristol, rushed to profit from their newly legal status, driving up the purchase price of enslaved individuals in West Africa and in England's plantation colonies. In the first four years, out of 81,879 African women, men, and children forced to embark for the Americas in English ships, 67,068, or 82 percent, sailed in vessels operated by independent traders, and one in four would not survive the harrowing passage to disembark.

The RAC bemoaned the impact of the legalization of the independent traders on its business activities and rapidly declining profits. In the interim, it attempted to use its relationship with King William, who continued to serve as governor, to its best advantage. In March 1700, in response to African Company petitions, William III sent letters on its behalf to Barbados, Jamaica, and other colonies to help recover unpaid debts and encourage the company's trade in enslaved Africans. The king's interest in the African Company's success stemmed from his awareness of the value of the agricultural commodities produced by enslaved Africans in England's plantation colonies and the ongoing need for coerced laborers. As the Board of Trade reported to the king, "from your Majesty's plantations in America great quantities of sugar, tobacco, and other goods are annually imported, exceeding much in value the goods sent thither." The planting and harvesting of valuable plantation commodities "is best carried on by the labor of Negroes," the Board emphasized. "We humbly conceive it convenient that all encouragement should be given, that the said colonies be supplied plentifully with Negroes and at the cheapest rates." The future of England's Atlantic empire depended on African trafficking and enslavement.

William III relied on the forced labor of African peoples in many facets of his life as king: to help cover expenses associated with the operation of his government, to fund overseas warfare, and to serve in his royal palaces. Two years before his death, the king commissioned a marble bust of an unnamed enslaved Black attendant from the Anglo-Flemish sculptor John Nost the Elder. The Black man's identity remains unknown, though commentators later described the bust as a portrait of "a negro, a supposed favorite servant of William III." Nost also created a full-length statue of the king made of lead, featuring him dressed as a Roman emperor, by commission of the City of London. Although few monuments were erected to commemorate William III during his lifetime, one unrealized plan proposed for St. James's Square envisioned a brass statue of the king "trampling down popery, breaking the chains of bondage, slavery, etc." King William came to embody the Glorious Revolution and the protection of English people's rights and liberties. However, the chains broken by William did not apply to those that bound Africans forcibly trafficked to the Americas—nor even to his own enslaved attendant.

The bust commissioned by William III depicts an ebony-colored Af-

Figure 9.2. Bust of an enslaved man.
John Nost, c. 1700.

rican man dressed in a delicate cream-colored shirt adorned with a scal-
loped collar and richly bejeweled band. His head is covered in a feathered
turban, and a collar encircles his neck. Originally displayed in the great
hall at Kensington Palace, the bust was later relocated to the center of the
king's dressing room at Hampton Court, where it remained exhibited to
palace visitors for centuries. The enslaved status of the bust's anonymous
Black subject was undeniable to all who saw it. As an observer remarked
nearly two hundred years after the bust's production, "encircling the throat
is a carved white marble collar, with a padlock, in every respect like a dog's
metal collar." As recently as 2023, the bust was exhibited to the public in
the queen's gallery in Kensington Palace, included among other so-called
"home comforts" and "beautiful treasures" collected by William and Mary.
Like their Stuart predecessors, eighteenth-century British monarchs
would continue to acquire and display material objects associated with
African slavery for years to come.

CHAPTER 10

THE PROMISE OF VAST RICHES

I n November 1700, international warfare appeared imminent in Europe when Carlos II, the enfeebled Spanish king, died shortly after naming the grandson of Louis XIV, the French prince Philip Anjou, as his sole heir. Stretching from the Iberian Peninsula to the Low Countries, across the Atlantic to the Americas, and even to the distant Philippines and beyond, the immense and wealthy Spanish empire was a highly coveted prize. Louis XIV moved troops into Spain in the name of Philip V and refused to exclude his grandson from the French succession. To curtail French ambitions, William III negotiated the Grand Alliance with Austria, Holland, and the German electors of Brandenburg-Prussia, Hanover, and the Palatinate. The coalition agreed to prepare for war to force a partition of the Spanish empire. Louis XIV remained defiant and raised the political stakes. He recognized James II's son, James Francis Edward (the Pretender), as James III of England after the death of the deposed king in September 1701. Dynastic reasons motivated Louis: By recognizing the Pretender as the rightful king of England, he upheld hereditary monarchy and challenged Parliament's ability to dictate the succession.

Three months earlier Parliament had reinforced the Glorious Revolution's constitutional provisions by passing the Act of Settlement. The act decreed that if William III or Princess Anne of Denmark, James II's remaining Protestant daughter, died without heirs, the Crown would pass to the nearest living Protestant heir, the Electress Sophia of Hanover and "the heirs of her body, being Protestants." In May 1702, the Grand Alliance declared war on France and its allies, launching what became known as the War of the Spanish Succession. In England, a new sovereign would steer the nation through its next major international conflict. William III had died two months earlier following a fatal riding accident. On March 8, Queen Anne ascended to the throne at age thirty-seven. Despite seventeen pregnancies, Queen Anne would also die childless, ending the Stuart dynasty.

In poor health and practically an invalid at her succession, Queen Anne was immediately thrown into an exorbitant war that cost £50 million. The War of the Spanish Succession drained her government's coffers dry and ratcheted up the national debt eightfold over ten years. Known as Queen Anne's War in the American colonies, the international conflict pitted the English, French, and Spanish and their Indigenous allies against one another for control of eastern North America and the Caribbean. It led to a spike in commissioned privateering that gave rise to the Golden Age of Atlantic piracy after hostilities ceased. The war years also saw the invention of "Great Britain," with the passage of the 1707 Act of Union linking Scotland politically to England and Wales. High taxes motivated thousands of Britons to seek their fortunes in the North American and Caribbean colonies and to pursue long-distance trading opportunities. As the settler population of the British plantation colonies expanded, demand for coerced labor grew apace. Independent traders, now legal, dominated the lucrative transatlantic slave trade during Anne's reign, embarking with a total of 127,967 African individuals carried to the Americas against their will, versus the Royal African Company's 31,355.

Held by right of the Crown, William III's RAC slaving shares passed automatically to Anne at his death, giving the queen a large stake in the struggling monopoly company. The RAC promptly invited Queen Anne's husband, Prince George of Denmark, generalissimo of all the queen's forces by land and sea and Lord High Admiral until his death in 1708, to serve as governor. As the titular head of the Admiralty, Prince George held the ability to offer critical assistance to the company by recommending the deployment of Royal Navy vessels to patrol the shipping lanes off the West African coast. RAC directors sought to benefit from the material advantages long derived from royal patronage, routinely petitioning George and Anne for naval assistance and the protection of English slaving vessels.

During the first two months of Queen Anne's reign, the RAC twice petitioned the queen for warships to patrol the West African coast. It petitioned Prince George a further five times for naval protection in 1702 alone, seeking naval vessels to cruise along southern Guinea to "support Her Majesty's subjects in their trade and to preserve them from all insults of Her Majesty's enemies." In March 1703, the company petitioned both Anne and George for a naval convoy to accompany six RAC slaving vessels bound for West Africa to "export to the plantations more than 2,000 negroes." Without Crown naval support and protection, the directors asserted, England's West African coastal forts could fall to the French or other enemies, starving the queen's plantation colonies of much-needed enslaved African laborers. "All which misfortunes would be the more grievous to the Company at this time when they have the great honor of His Royal Highness being their governor." To lose England's share of the transatlantic slave trade under Queen Anne and Prince George's watch would besmirch the monarchy's reputation.

As in previous Stuart reigns, though to a lesser extent than was possible under Charles II and James II, the Royal African Company appealed to and relied upon the monarchy for diplomatic and material support. Queen Anne aided the company's attempts to reclaim vessels and African bondspeople seized as prizes by foreign powers during the War of the Spanish Succession. In response to repeated petitions requesting royal assistance against French privateers, she sent letters to colonial governors on the RAC's behalf and approved the deployment of warships from her Royal Navy to cruise African and Caribbean waters. The queen, like the company whose slaving interests she defended, treated African women, men, and children confiscated by the enemy as stolen property, not as people.

In his capacity as Lord High Admiral, Prince George also responded favorably to RAC petitions. The directors requested privateering commissions and Royal Navy warships to patrol the West African coast and accompany their slaving vessels across the Atlantic to the Caribbean and North American colonies. He granted letters of marque to company ship captains, permitting them to attack French ships and subjects in Atlantic waters. Ordering convoys to secure the shipping lanes between West Africa and British America and the Caribbean, George issued instructions to the captains of the warships *Oxford*, *Hastings*, *Poole*, and *Chester*, for instance, to protect the company's coastal forts and "annoy the enemy." Subject to pulmonary disorders and unable to undertake active military service due to his reduced health, the prince—like his ailing wife—exercised his royal influence over the African trade and imperial affairs from afar.

Crown support could not make up for the African Company's poor financial state and the opposition it faced from a growing community of politically active independent traders based in London. In the winter of 1708, the company appealed for an end to open trade to Queen Anne, who referred the petition to the Board of Trade for consideration. Launching an inquiry into the state of the African trade, the commissioners held hearings, examined witnesses, and gathered evidence related to the supply of enslaved Africans to the colonies since the 1698 act went into effect. Upon request, colonial governors in the Caribbean, Chesapeake, and New England submitted returns on the numbers of African bondspeople who had disembarked in their respective colonies and which traders had carried them there and at what rates. The returns indicated that the activities of the independent traders had dramatically increased the supply of enslaved Africans in the colonies, though with a corresponding upsurge in prices. Monopoly had delivered insufficient numbers of coerced laborers at low prices; in contrast, free trade had increased the flow of enslaved Africans to the Americas at higher prices. Yet most colonial governors favored ready access to coerced African laborers over a return to the African Company's monopoly.

The Board of Trade's inquiry reignited a pamphlet war, with tracts written by or on behalf of independent slave traders predominant. Arguments in favor of free trade emphasized the explosion of slave trading that had taken place since the summer of 1698. One author noted that in the first four years after Parliament opened the transatlantic slave trade, independent traders had carried seventy-five thousand African individuals to the Caribbean and Chesapeake plantations. The RAC, by comparison, transported a total of sixty-four thousand bondspeople in the twenty-seven years between 1680 and 1707. "And as Negroes are of the utmost necessity for cultivating the product of the plantations, which could be worth nothing to the nation without such hands," those responsible for "carrying the greatest numbers of Negroes thither, seem to deserve the most encouragement," the author concluded. The independent traders had expanded the delivery of enslaved Africans to the plantation colonies fivefold since Parliament deregulated the slave trade, another proponent of free trade claimed. Planters in Virginia and Maryland, formerly "forced to work alone on their own land bare-foot and bare-legged," benefited most of all, using the coerced labor of Africans provided by the independent traders to produce vast quantities of tobacco.

Independent traders and their supporters presented the dramatic uptick in the volume of slave trading as a wholly positive good for the colonies, Britain, and the Crown—irrespective of its devastating impact on the lives of African peoples. To quiet the minds of those who might question the morality of buying and selling Africans, one author claimed that all the bondspeople purchased by Englishmen had been either condemned to death or slavery by the laws of their respective countries or were prisoners of war. "And these are the persons we buy in Guinea and sell to our plantations in America; where they change their country only, and not their condition, unless it be for the better." Another anonymously authored tract focused specifically on the deliveries of enslaved Africans to Barbados, Jamaica, and Antigua during the decade following the act of 1698. Out of a total of eighty thousand enslaved people who disembarked in the three Caribbean islands, over seventy thousand, or roughly 80 percent, were delivered by the independent traders. When the African Company's monopoly remained in force, an annual average of five thousand Africans arrived in England's plantation colonies; with trade open, the annual average had doubled to nearly nine thousand. Time and again, the people carried out of Africa against their will to satiate labor demands in the British colonies were reduced to mere numbers in account books.

In published rebuttals to the independent traders, RAC representatives articulated a case for the necessity of a steady cultural arbiter between English traders and African rulers and natives. Only a joint-stock company, "national in its constitution" and committed to maintaining costly West African forts and settlements for the public good, could prevent the African trade from falling into disorder. Driven by envy and greed, independent traders cared only for their own private interests. They demanded the liberty to trade in West Africa even if their presence prompted African merchants to "impose treble the price on Negroes, that the Company before bought them at." While the company emphasized the need for coastal forts as a justification for maintaining its Crown-sponsored monopoly, colonial interests focused on the rising cost of enslaved Africans. Planters in Barbados noted that the price of a bondsperson had increased from £13 to £16 when the RAC monopolized the trade to £25 to £40 since Parliament deregulated the slave trade; consequently, they expressed their support for a monopoly joint-stock company. Appealing to Queen Anne, eighty-five Barbadian colonists petitioned the Crown to explain that the independent traders had pushed up prices and supplied insufficient numbers of Africans to the island.

On October 28, 1708, during the initial stages of the Board of Trade's inquiry into the African trade, Prince George of Denmark died at age fifty-six, leaving behind a bereft Queen Anne. The African Company, having lost its royal governor and patron, asked the queen to take his place. Anne agreed to assume the governorship of the RAC, playing an honorary role. She approved the dispatch of warships to the West African coast on the company's behalf but otherwise allowed the inquiry to proceed without royal interference. The Board of Trade's deliberations took place over a period of four years, from 1708 until 1712, when the expiration of the 1698 act handed a decisive and lasting victory to the independent traders. The drawn-out inquiry clarified the extent to which the expansion of slave trading benefited Britain and its Atlantic empire, argued the commissioners, especially the North American colonies and Jamaica, an island "more concerned in the negro trade than all the other British plantations." No longer forced to pay a duty to maintain the African Company's forts, independent traders in London, Bristol, Liverpool, and other outports invested in the transatlantic slave trade. This outcome satisfied the intention of the Board of Trade, which had concluded "that there can be no doubt but that a trade so profitable in itself and necessary for the plantations ought to be preserved and improved."

The RAC took the opposite approach, pronouncing the expiration of the 1698 act an automatic restoration of its royal monopoly. In letters to agents stationed on the West African coast, it ordered them to treat all independent traders as interlopers acting in defiance of the company's charter. As agents at Cape Coast Castle were reminded, "the privilege of the sole trade thereof [was] granted to the Company by the Crown of

England, which title is equivalent and altogether as good as any plant-ers have to their particular plantations in America." If bloodshed re-sulted from a conflict with interlopers in defense of the company's coastal possessions or trade, "the damage must be borne by the trespassers and wrongdoers." Although the RAC continued to advise its agents that inter-lopers had no right to trade in West Africa, its monopoly had dissolved in favor of unregulated free trade. After 1712, its forts fell into disrepair and its market share of the transatlantic slave trade plunged. Only the prospect of trafficking enslaved Africans to Spanish America offered a temporary lifeline to the former monopolistic African Company.

In April 1713, the War of the Spanish Succession concluded with the Treaty of Utrecht and Philip V, Louis XIV's grandson, confirmed on the Spanish throne. After two years of drawn-out peace negotiations, Britain had achieved many of its commercial and imperial objectives. The thrones of France and Spain were to remain separate and the Netherlands in-dependent. France, formally recognizing England's Protestant succession, renounced support for the Jacobite cause and ceded territories in North America and the Caribbean to Britain. Yet the war was costly. It had taxed British resources and added an unprecedented £9.5 million to the national debt. During the lengthy peace negotiations, Queen Anne and her repre-sentatives had pushed for the right to supply enslaved Africans to Spanish America—a contract currently held by the French Guinea Company—as a means of resolving Britain's public debt. "France's main design is the en-grossing of all the wealth of the West-Indies," proponents argued, "which, if not prevented, will not only repair all her former losses, but enable her to arrive at universal empire in Europe." With a French Bourbon secured on the Spanish throne, preventing France from maintaining its trading partnership with Spanish America was "the only means to balance the ex-orbitant power of France, and to secure our new trade to the West-Indies."

During the negotiation process, Queen Anne prioritized restoring the balance of international trade and attaining British access to the markets and mineral wealth of Spanish America. In a speech to the House of Lords outlining the proposed treaty terms on June 6, 1712, Queen Anne disclosed that Britain's contribution to the war effort, as well as her own diplomatic role, entitled the nation to "some distinction in the terms of peace." "I have insisted, and obtained," she announced, "that the asiento or contract for furnishing the Spanish West-Indies with negroes, shall be made with us for the term of thirty years, in the same manner as it had been enjoyed by the French for these ten years past." Britain had officially won the *asiento de negros*, a sought-after contract granting the holder the exclusive right to supply enslaved Africans to Spain's colonies in the Americas. Lacking an imperial or trading presence in West Africa, Spain relied upon foreign contractors to satiate its colonists' incessant demand for coerced African labor. Italian, Portuguese, and French companies had previously held the asiento contract with Spain before it passed into Queen Anne's eager hands.

The asiento contract represented a potentially valuable commercial agreement between the Spanish monarch and foreign merchant syndicates or Crowns. It required the contract holder, or the *asientista*, to deliver annually to Spanish America 4,800 *piezas de Indias*—that is, 4,800 healthy adult males. The asientista would pay duty on the first 4,000 African captives delivered to Spanish America, regardless of whether the supplier met this quota; 10 percent of the overall slaving profits accrued to the king of Spain. Queen Anne and her advisers expected the asiento to yield substantial financial rewards, not only from legal trade but also from contraband traffic. Permission for British ships to enter Spanish American waters offered a gateway to its closed, fiercely guarded colonial markets. King Philip V permitted Britain, as the asientista, to send one ship annually to the fairs in Porto Bello, Cartagena, and Veracruz with five hundred tons of merchandise for sale duty-free. To Queen Anne personally, he granted permission to send two additional 600-ton annual ships, duty-free. Although Philip V extended limited legal access to his Spanish American markets, he provided Britons with ample opportunities for illicit trade.

Queen Anne transferred the asiento contract to the South Sea Company (SSC), a joint-stock company proposed in the spring of 1711 by her chief minister, Sir Robert Harley, later earl of Oxford and Lord Treasurer. Formed by an act of Parliament, the SSC was created to address Britain's immense national debt. The British government encouraged owners of government debt to swap those illiquid holdings for liquid shares in the South Sea Company that could be traded on the emerging London stock exchange. Awarding the SSC an economic monopoly on the transatlantic slave trade to Spanish America bolstered the perceived value of the stock and encouraged public subscription. By statute, the SSC was guaranteed a yearly payment from the Exchequer of £568,279, or 6 percent of the debt capitalized by the company, plus £8,000 in management charges, paid for by excise taxes on wine, vinegar, and tobacco.

The queen opened the South Sea subscription books for private holders of government bonds on June 27, 1711, and then announced the refinancing scheme to the British public in September. In the interim, on August 20, 1711, diplomatic negotiations on the asiento were concluded. She appointed the SSC's directors from among her favorites, most of whom were Tories with ambitions of extracting Spanish bullion and establishing a territorial empire in South America. The success of the South Sea Company scheme relied on the Crown, government creditors, and the investing public buying into the notion that the right to supply enslaved Africans to Spanish America would, as Harley proclaimed, "yearly bring vast riches from Peru and Mexico into Great Britain." Britons held immense faith in the profit potential of the transatlantic slave trade and its presumed necessity for colonial agricultural systems. As Daniel Defoe stated in 1713, "no African trade, no Negroes; no Negroes, no sugars, gingers, indigoes, etc.; no sugars, etc., no islands; no islands, no continent; no continent, no trade; that is to say, farewell all your American trade, your West-Indian trade." The same assumption applied to Spain's empire in the Americas. To maintain an advantage in the competitive world of plantation production and global trade, access to a steady stream of coerced laborers was key. According to this worldview, both traffickers and purchasers of enslaved Africans benefited in kind.

Queen Anne was already convinced. Her government presumed, correctly, that the SSC would attract additional investors in government-backed debt by offering the prospect of a dividend connected to the company's slave-trading profits. Pleased at having secured the asiento concession for Britain, Anne promised to extend the SSC her royal favor and protection. The monarchy was publicly associated with the company's establishment and commercial prospects from its inception. Anne herself was one of the largest shareholders. During the first subscription period in 1711, the queen converted £553,358 worth of her own securities into

SSC stock; and the offices of the Army, Navy, Ordnance, Victualling, and Transport converted an additional £231,126. As a result of these early investments, the monarch and the British state held extensive financial interests in transatlantic slaving—beyond the annual revenues accrued from customs duties on slave-produced colonial staples in Britain's Atlantic empire.

Although the specific amount of government bonds converted by private individuals was not public knowledge, in 1712 the SSC published a list of shareholders qualified to vote for governor, sub-governor, and deputy governor. An asterisk placed next to a shareholder's name indicated the minimum amount subscribed and the number of votes assigned. Consisting of a total of twenty-three asterisks, the queen's substantial security conversions were made on her behalf by six prominent men, including James Bridges, duke of Chandos and paymaster of the forces abroad—and a future director of the Royal African Company. Holding securities in a public-private enterprise that functioned as a bank enabled Anne and the various departments of her government to receive their money back in the form of interest payments. Like the RAC and its close association with the Stuarts, the SSC advertised its intimacy with the monarchy and foundation as a slave-trading entity. The queen's investment signaled her faith in converting government debt into shares in a corporation with monopoly privileges over the transatlantic slave trade to Spanish America.

Early on, the Tory SSC directors envisioned establishing a territorial presence in South America from which they could discover mines, process incoming slave ships, funnel precious metals back to Britain, and dominate the Spanish American trade. The directors' initial plan entailed planting a colony in Valdivia, in southern Chile, and erecting additional strategic outposts throughout South America to more readily supply Spanish colonists with merchandise and enslaved Africans. To set their ambitious imperial designs in motion, the directors of the SSC petitioned Queen Anne's secretary of state, Henry St. John, Viscount Bolingbroke, for twenty warships, forty transport ships, and four hundred troops.

On March 13, 1712, Bolingbroke reported that Queen Anne had responded favorably to the South Sea Company's request, before dramatically scaling back her verbal commitment the following year. She offered to supply ships and men sufficient for "carrying on and securing the [asiento] trade"—but not establishing a British colony in South America. To that end, the queen instructed Bolingbroke to order the Lords Commissioners of the Admiralty to loan the SSC two vessels from her Royal Navy. Anne earmarked *Angelsea* and *Warwick* to carry merchandise to the annual fairs in South America, as the asiento contract permitted. Her indebted ministry prioritized launching the asiento as soon as possible per the terms of the Treaty of Utrecht. Sending a British expeditionary force to South America to plant a colonial settlement far exceeded the resources available to the Crown.

Facilitating the delivery of the annual quota of enslaved captives from West Africa to Spanish America proved challenging for the fledgling company. The SSC directors lacked experience trading with South America or the Caribbean and possessed minimal knowledge of commercial conditions on the West African coast. Chosen for their financial savvy and political connections, the directors placed much of the business of acquiring enslaved Africans into the experienced hands of subcontractors. Turning first to the Tory-supported RAC was a logical choice. Early proponents of the South Sea Company scheme, such as Daniel Defoe, argued that it would benefit and help revamp the "sinking, and near expiring Royal African Company." Forced to compete with independent traders to supply African bondsmen and -women to the British plantation colonies, the former monopoly company would now have "an opportunity of vending great numbers of Negroes to the Spaniards." Supplying enslaved Africans to the closed markets of Spanish America offered the struggling former monopoly company a potential lifeline, one its directors were keen to grasp.

In July 1713, the SSC negotiated directly with the RAC, attempting to secure the most favorable terms. The directors requested the African Company's proposal for delivery of 4,800 "healthful and sound" Africans at the ports of Buenos Aires, Cartagena, Porto Bello, Veracruz, or Jamaica by the spring of 1714. On August 20, the two companies reached a tentative agreement for "supplying a considerable number of Negroes for the service of the asiento," though neither party was entirely satisfied with the terms of the arrangement. The RAC instructed its factors on the African coast to procure suitable captives and hold them in reserve for Span-

ish America, "some sorts of Blacks not being proper for those markets."
Both companies were aware of the asiento stipulations regarding enslaved
workers: The Spanish Crown required two-thirds of the delivered Africans to be men or adolescent boys between the ages of ten and forty,
with no more than 10 percent of the total to fall between the ages of ten
and sixteen. To meet these precise specifications, the directors mapped
out a plan to acquire batches of enslaved Africans across the company's
coastal factories. Ouidah and Cape Coast Castle would provide the majority of the bondspeople required for the asiento. The northern Gambia
base would supply the remaining enslaved Africans, acquired from the
surrounding region and the factories in Sierra Leone and Sherbro.

As the SSC directors moved forward with their plan to use the RAC to
supply the first shipments of enslaved Africans to Spanish America, the
tardy start of the asiento became a matter of increased concern. Sir James
Bateman, the sub-governor, asked for more time, writing to Bolingbroke
that "it has been altogether impossible for the South Sea Company to
enter upon the said contract of asiento for the 4,800 Negroes." Even with
the local connections and assistance of the RAC, the SSC could not meet
the minimum quota of four thousand enslaved Africans upon which they
would have to pay a duty to the Spanish Crown before May 1714. Moreover, before the asiento could get under way, the directors urgently sought
to address the allocation of profits. To their dismay, the SSC discovered
that the king of Spain retained 25 percent of overall profits and Queen
Anne an additional 22.5 percent. Such an arrangement guaranteed that
nearly half of the asiento slaving proceeds would accrue to the Spanish
and British Crowns, not to SSC investors.

As Anne saw it, she had secured a highly desirable slave-trading contract with Spain "sufficiently profitable" to the South Sea Company and
beneficial to the nation. The queen threatened "to recall what she designed
as a favor to your company" if the SSC hedged any further. Two months
later, Anne granted two additional warships to the SSC, *Suffolk* and *Bed-
ford*, staffed and supplied with eight months of provisions at the Royal
Navy's expense. The queen did not expect the SSC to cover the costs associated with her ships, Bolingbroke informed the Admiralty, "because
the expense would go a great way towards eating out the profits and that
which Her Majesty designs as a favor and encouragement to her subjects

would in this manner prove of little to no advantage to them." Anne was anxious for the asiento she had secured on her country's behalf to prove successful both financially and politically.

Yet, from the SSC's perspective, another unwelcome financial surprise lay in the fine print of the asiento. Anne had allocated an additional 7.5 percent of the overall slaving profits to Manuel Manassas Gilligan, a Catholic merchant, sometime smuggler, and naturalized Dane with knowledge of Spanish America. The queen had sent Gilligan as an envoy to Madrid to negotiate the asiento on her behalf. More grating still, Gilligan's share did not require him to invest any money in the endeavor. So, while the SSC would handle the administration of the asiento, it would receive a mere 45 percent of the profits. The directors considered this arrangement financially unfeasible. The reduced profit margin failed to warrant the substantial expenses and logistics involved in managing the slave trade to Spanish America. In December 1713, the SSC requested that the queen and Gilligan either relinquish their personal shares in the asiento or supply a due proportion of capital up front alongside the company's. Neither Anne nor Gilligan complied.

As fall gave way to winter, the South Sea Company's directors, dissatisfied with the financial arrangements of the asiento, continued to stall. On Christmas Eve 1713, Queen Anne fell seriously ill, and she remained unwell throughout the entire month of January 1714. With the future of Britain's Protestant succession hanging in the balance, the British public waited with bated breath to see if the queen would survive. Anne rejected appeals to invite George, the electress of Hanover's son, to England to take his seat in the House of Lords and wait for her to die. "Nothing can be more dangerous to the tranquility of my kingdoms," she wrote to her relations in Hanover. In mid-February 1714, Anne's health improved in time for her to open Parliament, but everyone realized her days were numbered. The South Sea Company directors again pushed for concessions from the queen—namely, that the 30 percent share of the asiento profits reserved for Anne and Gilligan be relinquished to the SSC. But Queen Anne, explained Bolingbroke, remained unmoved by their claim that retaining only 45 percent of the profits would doom the company and its shareholders financially.

On June 8, 1714, the Electress Sophia died and her son, George, became heir presumptive to the British throne. Anne remained supportive
of George while refusing to permit him to take up residence in London.
Following an appeal by the House of Commons, the queen finally agreed
to surrender her share of the asiento to the SSC. Anne retained an interest
in 10 percent of the profit from the two licensed ships and 5 percent of the
three-fourths profit of the annual ship. The South Sea Company directors
thanked the queen while begging her to convince Gilligan to release his
7.5 percent cut of the asiento. Worried the postponement would alienate
the Spanish and result in loss of revenue, the queen commanded the SSC
to "now proceed vigorously in carrying on the asiento." Convinced Anne
would relent, the directors delayed moving forward without confirmation
that Gilligan would pay up front or relinquish his asiento share.

Two weeks before her death, Anne received another memorial and address from the SSC requesting her assistance with Gilligan. But she
refused to revoke the share of the asiento that she had secured for Gilligan as a reward for his loyal service. Anne no doubt went to her grave
frustrated with what she saw as the SSC's mismanagement of the asiento.
"I wish you good success in carrying on your trade and hope you will
make a better use, than you have hitherto done, of what I have bestowed
upon you," she admonished the SSC directors only days before her death.
When Queen Anne died on August 1, 1714, following an illness characterized by vomiting, fatigue, and convulsions, only two of her promised
ships had sailed for South America on the SSC's behalf. The company
had, however, already dispatched ships to West Africa to procure enslaved
captives from the RAC.

With Gilligan's royal patron out of the way, the SSC directors sprang
into action, appealing to the Lords Justices to intervene on the company's
behalf. The Lords Justices ruled that Gilligan would have to pay £8,000,
the amount covering his proportion of the initial investment, or forfeit
his stake in the asiento. Faced with this unfortunate prospect, Gilligan
relinquished his share in the asiento three months after Anne's death.
By November 1714, the SSC had acquired the right to 75 percent of the
asiento profits and was ready to proceed. To the directors' delight, the new
Hanoverian king, George I, agreed to uphold the late queen's promises

related to the asiento, including naval support for the South Sea Company. The king held great optimism regarding Britain's control over the legal slave trade to Spanish America. And he was not alone. Soon after arriving in Britain, his eldest son and heir, George, Prince of Wales, requested SSC shares and agreed to serve as governor. Although the Stuart regime had given way to the age of the Hanoverians, Crown support for transatlantic slave trading and African enslavement remained as robust as ever.

CHAPTER 11

THE CROWN AND THE ASIENTO

Just after midday on August 1, 1714, five hours after Queen Anne died in her bed at Kensington Palace, cannons fired in the capital and heralds proclaimed her successor, George Ludwig, elector of Hanover, king of Great Britain. Six weeks passed before George I, aged fifty-four and in no hurry, arrived on September 18 to claim the British throne. Britain's new sovereign possessed only a rudimentary understanding of spoken English, yet his accession proceeded smoothly. Nearly a decade earlier, Parliament had accounted for the potentially hazardous time gap that might follow the queen's demise and arrival of the new monarch. Passed in 1706, the Regency and Naturalization Acts had established the Protestant succession in law and accorded Sophia of Hanover and her Protestant children the status of English subjects.

Prior to Queen Anne's death, Jacobite supporters alleged that Prince James Edward Stuart, the Pretender, would renounce Catholicism in exchange for regaining his royal birthright, thereby superseding George Ludwig's claim to the British throne. But Jacobite hopes did not come to pass. While relief rather than enthusiasm characterized the general public's response to George I and the Hanoverian succession, many English statesmen rejoiced at the return to experienced, manly kingship. The accession of a Protestant soldier-king, "as able to handle the scepter, and wield the sword, as he is to wear the Crown," portended well for Britain's future as an imperial power. Indeed, George I proved as committed to the expansion and defense of Britain's slave empire and invested in slaving profits as his Stuart predecessors had been.

After years of painstaking negotiations over the terms of the asiento with Queen Anne, the South Sea Company also recognized the perils and opportunities afforded by the accession of a new monarch. Immediately after George landed in England, the SCC congratulated the new king on his safe arrival. King George, who inherited both his father's and Queen Anne's SSC shares, was predisposed to look favorably on the company. William III's government had owed his late father, Ernst Augustus, £9,375 in unpaid subsidies for the Hanoverian army. This sum had formed part of the calculus of public debt subsumed by the SSC. Although George sought repayment in cash for the arrears of subsidies owed to the Hanoverian army, the British government offered him South Sea Company stock instead. In December 1711, he followed the lead of the government's other creditors and converted the unpaid debt into shares. The following year the SSC included George's name with three asterisks next to it in a published list of government creditors and shareholders qualified to vote for governor, sub-governor, deputy governor, and director.

King George arrived at St. James's Palace accompanied by his longtime mistress, Melusine von der Schulenburg (known as the duchess of Kendal after 1719) and the couple's three illegitimate daughters, whom she passed off as her "nieces." George had previously divorced and confined his wife, Sophia Dorothea of Celle, after her conviction for adultery. He would never again marry and have an official queen consort. Also joining the king was Sophia Charlotte von Kielmansegg, his illegitimate half-sister, rumored by the English court to be his incestuous mistress, though their relationship was platonic.

Two Turkish men, Mohammed and Mustapha, both of whom George had taken into his service during his military campaigns against the Turks in 1686, accompanied the king as members of his inner household. Their elevated role as grooms of the king's chamber, and their personal apartments located near George's in St. James's Palace, provoked envy among the English members of the monarch's court. Mohammed, as keeper of the king's closet, enjoyed the highest right of access to Britain's sovereign. He also paid George's bills as the effective keeper of the king's privy purse. Traditionally held by nobles, these influential positions signaled the esteem in which King George held the two Turkish men. Mohammed and Mustapha left a permanent mark on royal architecture; their mid-1720s portraits by William Kent may still be viewed on the grand staircase fresco leading to the king's state apartments at Kensington Palace.

A reclusive monarch, George I eschewed formal court etiquette and preferred to live quietly, cloistered in his palaces with his inner circle. The king's aloof lifestyle prevented his new subjects from warming to him. Far more welcome and acceptable to the public were George's sociable thirty-one-year-old son and heir, Prince George Augustus, and his wife, Princess Caroline of Ansbach. Caroline arrived in London in mid-October with two of their three daughters, Amalie and Caroline, in tow; Anne, a toddler too ill to travel, temporarily stayed behind. When the royal family decamped to England, King George ordered the couple's seven-year-old son, Frederick, to remain in Hanover under the supervision of his great-uncle Prince Ernest Augustus as evidence of the dynasty's continued commitment to the Electorate. Royal grandchildren were deemed property of the Crown, and none was more important than the eldest son. George and Caroline had no say in the matter. The move to England would ultimately destroy their relationship with Frederick.

Created Prince of Wales on September 22, Prince George spoke fluent English with a heavy German accent, as did his livelier and more well-liked wife, Princess Caroline. He attended cabinet and Privy Council meetings, acting as an interpreter for his father. To Prince George's disappointment, the king prevented his heir from holding a governmental role or assuming military command. (During the War of the Spanish Succession, Prince George had fought in the campaign in the Low Countries against France, serving with distinction during the Battle of Oudenarde.) Relations between the two Georges were strained from the first, and Prince George's inability to participate in military matters only heightened his resentment against his father. Adorned in robes of state and crimson velvet, with Mary Stuart's crown on his head, the Prince of Wales added a sense of dynastic grandeur to his father's coronation ceremony in Westminster Abbey on October 20. King George, after wearing the crown fashioned for Queen Anne, instructed the goldsmith Samuel Smithin to transfer the royal jewels to a new, lighter frame constructed of gold and silver and decorated with crosses and fleur-de-lis.

Three weeks after George I's accession, Parliament granted the new

Figure 11.1. George I's imperial
state crown, 1714.

king £700,000 a year in civil list revenue to support the operation of
his government and royal household. This included servicing the royal
family's sweet tooth through the monthly purchase of twenty pounds of
refined sugar, thirty pounds of double refined sugar, and eight pounds
of powdered sugar for the king's table. To George's chagrin, Parliament
reserved £100,000 of his allotted civil list revenue exclusively for the
household of the Prince of Wales. Prince George had access to funds
unavailable to previous princes of Wales, enabling him to establish his
own princely household and court and aggravating tensions between father and son. Because the civil list sum granted to the king was based
neither on royal expenditure nor guaranteed revenue streams, it proved
as problematic and insufficient for George as it had for his predecessor,
Queen Anne.

The inadequacy of the sources from which Crown revenue was drawn
remained a glaring issue throughout the reign of George I. So too did
the national debt, which stood at £48 million in 1714 and continued to
mount. The total interest burden of around £3 million consumed half the
government's revenues, and saddling the public with higher taxes during
peacetime was not an option. Britain's financial dilemma considerably enhanced the allure of trade with Spanish America and the illusion of quick
profits. Whether by force or license, tapping into the region's riches had

gripped the imagination of Englishmen and -women since the reign of Elizabeth I.

Prevented from taking an active role in government, Prince George, like other princes of Wales historically, struggled to fill his time with meaningful employment and lead a lifestyle worthy of his station. In a bid for financial independence, he expressed interest in acquiring shares of South Sea Company stock three months after arriving in England. Delighted to accommodate the Prince of Wales, the SSC directors extended to him both stock shares and the position of governor. On Christmas Day, 1714, the company published a list of subscribers and placed Prince George's name with three asterisks next to it prominently at the top, signaling a minimum £5,000 investment. "I have not anything more at heart than the promoting and encouraging the trade of the nation," the Prince of Wales wrote in his acceptance of the SSC governorship on January 3, 1715. He promised "to promote upon all occasions the interest of the Company," with the added caveat that "not being versed in matters of commerce I shall always leave the whole management thereof to the court of directors." Prince George's response was music to the directors' ears. After he swore the formal oath as governor in early February, the SSC rushed to advertise its connection to the new royal family in the London gazettes.

Prince George spent the spring of 1715 acquainting himself with the affairs of the South Sea Company since its establishment. He left matters of governance entirely in the hands of the directors. During this period the SSC focused its energies on getting the slave trade to Spanish America up and running and sending ships with merchandise to the annual fairs in South America. The SSC directors appealed to George I to honor his royal predecessor's authorization for the use of two additional Royal Navy ships, and the king readily complied. Prince George gifted venison to the SSC and ingratiated himself with its directors. In February 1716, when the directors presented Prince George with his annual £500 allowance as governor, he returned the money, assuring them "that he should be always ready to do the Company all the service he could." SSC directors praised the Prince of Wales for his patronage and generosity and requested that he sit for a formal portrait by Sir Godfrey Kneller. Completed the following year, the prince's portrait hung in a position of prominence in the

South Sea House, trumpeting royal investment in the company and its slave trade with Spanish America.

Delivering 4,800 enslaved Africans annually to Spanish America to fulfill the asiento was an enormous undertaking for the recently formed SSC. Some South Sea Company slaving vessels embarked from West Africa and sailed straight to the Spanish American mainland, primarily destined for Buenos Aires. The company also established a central base of operations in Jamaica, where it bought and sold enslaved people and "refreshed" exhausted African captives en route to Spanish America. For enslaved people, the dehumanizing "refreshment" process entailed an intimate inspection of their nude and shackled bodies by agents, in addition to being washed and rubbed with oil and then crowded into a pen to await transshipment to Spanish America. South Sea Company agents were dispatched to ports on the Spanish American mainland, including Buenos Aires, Havana, Santiago de Cuba, Cartagena, Portobello, Panama, and Veracruz, to establish factories where they received incoming human cargoes. Agents based in British Caribbean hubs provided slaving captains with certificates permitting them to trade in Spanish waters as temporary SSC representatives.

Using Jamaica as a strategic Caribbean base from which to manage the inter-imperial leg of the asiento had its drawbacks. By 1714, as the SSC's assumption of the asiento was underway, enslaved people made up 90 percent of the island's overall population. Concerned that the demographic imbalance imperiled the colony's safety, Jamaican officials attempted to attract more permanent white settlers, including foreigners, to counterbalance the island's enslaved African majority. At the same time, planters complained that South Sea Company slaving agents would siphon the healthiest Africans away from Jamaica for sale to Spanish colonists, limiting local availability and driving up prices. The asiento also threatened to cut into the profits of British merchants in Jamaica by curtailing the island's long-flourishing illicit trade with Spanish America. "The private trade from Jamaica to the coast of New Spain," observed one resident, "has been very considerable, and brought more money into her Majesty's dominions in a year than the contract can, admitting the 4,800 Negroes, or more, should be taken off yearly by the Spaniards, so tis to be feared, that this contract will soon put an end to the said trade." These concerns were legitimate. To protect their own profits, the SSC directors asked James Stanhope, George I's secretary of state, to instruct the Royal Navy to seize illegal slaving vessels bound for Spanish coasts.

Beginning in the late seventeenth century, the Jamaica House of Assembly had imposed a duty of ten shillings per head on all enslaved Africans imported into the colony and twenty shillings per head on every bondsperson exported from Jamaica. It opted to renew these duties even after the Spanish Crown awarded the asiento to Britain and the SSC made Jamaica its base of operations in the Caribbean. Designed both to obstruct the asiento and augment the colony's revenue, the act did not distinguish between enslaved individuals purchased on the island and then exported and African captives landed there en route to Spanish shores. The South Sea Company directors objected to the duty imposed by the assembly. They argued that it penalized the SSC for landing in Jamaica to obtain water, food, and medical care for Africans in need of so-called "refreshment" after the Atlantic crossing. If required to pay a hefty export duty, slaving vessels would forgo stopping in Jamaica altogether and proceed straight to Spanish ports, resulting in sickly cargoes and higher mortality rates. Although the SSC demanded the act's repeal, Jamaica's London agents countered that the levy would impact slave traders equally, not just South Sea Company shareholders.

The Jamaica assembly renewed the duty annually, imposing a per head fee on slaving vessels that docked at the island's ports. Appealing to their royal patron for relief, the SSC directors submitted a memorial to George I. They claimed that requiring payment for every enslaved African who docked in a Jamaican port or came ashore only briefly before transshipment to Spanish America was discriminatory against British subjects. King George, receptive to the company's concerns, asked the Board of Trade to weigh in on the legality of the Jamaican act. It resolved that while Jamaican officials could lawfully levy a duty on the king's subjects who purchased enslaved Africans in Jamaica and then exported them off the island, demanding a duty for "Negroes brought thither only for refreshment" in transit to Spanish shores was unreasonable. In January 1718, George ordered the act's repeal. But this did not prevent the Jamaica assembly from passing new legislation detrimental to the interests of the

SSC. Jamaican authorities exploited the distance between Kingston and London; it took time for Crown officials to receive, assess, and repeal colonial acts. In the interim, the colony profited from the delay.

Competition between British slaving interests, at home and in the Atlantic colonies, remained fierce in the early eighteenth century. Open access to the transatlantic slave trade accelerated a surge in independent slave trading. By aligning itself with the Tory government and securing the South Sea Company contract to supply enslaved captives for the asiento, the African Company initially survived the deregulation of the British slave trade. By the summer of 1714, however, the RAC's economic and political position had worsened. The SSC owed the African Company £7,695. As the debt went unpaid and the RAC's share of the transatlantic slave trade diminished, its stock sank to a new low. Additionally, Queen Anne's death cut the RAC's personal ties to the monarchy and led to the fall of the Tories from power. When George I inherited his royal predecessor's RAC stock at his accession, it had declined in value by 90 percent. Due to the company's ongoing financial distress and its inability to compete with the independent traders, RAC stock would never recover its former overly inflated value.

The Royal African Company nonetheless saw the arrival of a new monarch and dynasty as a potential opportunity to salvage its trade and future business prospects. Securing King George's support would improve the company's political position, which had weakened since the attack on its royal monopoly in the 1690s. Within weeks of Queen Anne's death, the general court of the RAC elected George I governor. Although George's role was entirely honorary, the company wasted no time preparing a petition to present to the new king. A month after King George arrived in England, he received a detailed account of the history of the African trade from the company. The RAC recounted how, following the grant of letters patent from Charles I in 1672, it had built multiple factories in West Africa at great expense and developed a flourishing transatlantic trade to the benefit of the nation and the Crown.

In explicit terms, the RAC explained to the new monarch how the wealth accruing to Britain from the transatlantic slave trade depended on the mass commodification and exploitation of African peoples. "That the happy fruit of the Company's adventure and expenses in gaining these possessions in Africa was the cheapness of Negroes, for they bought Negroes cheap in Africa," RAC directors informed the king, "and sold them cheap in the British plantations in America which cheapness of Negroes was the very foundation that caused such an improvement and growth of the sugar plantations by the Negro's labor." After detailing the extent to which its rights were undergirded by the principle of the royal prerogative, the African Company beseeched King George to recommend its cause favorably to Parliament.

By courting the patronage of George I, the RAC tried to renew its former intimacy with the British monarchy. When the directors petitioned the king for naval assistance on the West African coast during his first year on the throne, they reminded him of the historically close relationship between the Crown and the African Company. "Your Majesty's royal predecessors have been graciously pleased from time to time," they wrote, "to assist the Company with two or more men of war for the support of their factories." They requested that the king send at least two warships amply supplied with marines, provisions, stores, and ammunition to defend the company's settlements and agents on the coast. Preservation of Britain's trade with Africa, "so important to this your Majesty's kingdom and the plantations," necessitated his royal protection.

On July 5, 1715, RAC leadership attended King George in person at St. James's Palace. On the company's behalf, Sub-governor William Paston, earl of Yarmouth, and Deputy Governor James Blake presented him with exotic animals and precious metals emblematic of the riches of West Africa: a tiger, a catlike civet, guinea hens, green birds (probably parakeets), and gold nuggets. George graciously received their gifts and "admitted all the gentlemen present to kiss his hand." The animals soon joined the evolving royal menagerie housed for centuries at the Tower of London.

The RAC requested King George's support in its ongoing contest against multiple commercial rivals in West Africa: interlopers, pirates, other European nations, and the South Sea Company. In multiple petitions it claimed that the seventeenth-century royal charter originally granted by Charles II gave the Royal African Company prestige in comparison to more recently formed corporations. Choosing to support the

RAC offered evidence of the Hanoverian dynasty's commitment to regal precedent. After all, it was "upon the encouragement of your Majesty's royal predecessors," the directors argued, that the Stuart-backed company "first entered into the undertaking of gaining a trade in Africa." Increasingly under threat, the African trade remained of great importance to Britain and "especially to the sugar islands, which could not be managed without Negroes from Africa, besides the considerable trades carried on from Jamaica in Negroes to the Spanish coast, and from Africa to this kingdom in gold and elephant's teeth."

Presented as a means of boosting George's personal finances in return for royal sponsorship and all that entailed, the company offered to loan the king a third of a million pounds at 5 percent interest. While this proposed scheme came to nothing, the company contemplated shifting focus from transatlantic slaving to trade with the African interior. Competing with numerous separate traders for a dwindling share of the transatlantic slave trade had led to huge financial losses. If the African Company hoped to survive the era of deregulation, a new approach seemed warranted.

To supply Spanish America with enslaved Africans, the South Sea Company relied upon its own slaving vessels—several of which bore the names of members of the royal family—and slave ships subcontracted from the RAC and independent traders. But like previous asientistas seeking to profit from supplying Spanish colonists with enslaved laborers, the SSC failed to meet its contractual obligations. Between 1714 and 1718, South Sea Company agents or their representatives embarked 13,102 enslaved persons—purchased from the Bight of Benin, Gold Coast, West Central Africa, Madagascar, and Senegambia—for Spanish America. A recorded 10,521 individuals survived the nightmarish Middle Passage to disembark either in Spanish ports, primarily Buenos Aires, or in the British Caribbean for so-called "refreshment" en route to their final destination. That means that nearly a quarter of their fellow captives perished during the Atlantic crossing. Obligated to deliver a quota of 19,200 enslaved Africans to Spanish shores during that time frame, and to pay a duty of £34,000 to the Spanish Crown on a minimum of 16,000 bondspeople, the SSC fell short.

Meanwhile, the contraband slave trade to Spanish America flourished.

Mark for Negroes hereafter

Figure 11.2. South Sea Company
brand for African captives
destined for Spanish America.

As they had prior to Britain's official receipt of the asiento, Jamaican traders smuggled thousands of enslaved Africans to Spanish customers, and at lower prices than the SSC. Monopolies on slaving imposed by the Spanish and British Crowns were resisted by their respective colonial subjects, who continued to engage in illicit trade. Already an uphill battle, earning a profit from the monopoly asiento contract proved challenging in an age of ubiquitous illegal commerce between British and Spanish merchants. This competitive context led the SSC to instruct its agents to brand the bodies of Africans to signify their legal commodification under the terms of the asiento contract. When African captives destined for Spanish ports arrived in Jamaica or Barbados as the first port of call, they met South Sea Company agents waiting with hot irons.

South Sea Company directors instructed agents to brand African women, men, and children destined for Spanish shores with the "Company's mark." The brand consisted of the SSC seal topped with George I's state crown. On March 8, 1715, the company issued an official instrument, distributed to agents in Jamaica and Barbados as well as to royal officials throughout Spanish America, certifying "the mark henceforward to be put upon the bodies of the Negroes to be sold and disposed in the Spanish West Indies, for and on account of this Company and of the said

Asiento, is and shall be according to the mark in the margin of this instrument." The instrument included a visual representation of the mark so that Spanish officials could recognize it seared onto the bodies of African captives acquired legally. That the brand devised by the SSC featured a crown was a strategic choice. Supported by Queen Anne and her Hanoverian successor, George I, and his eldest son, the Prince of Wales, the company touted its intimacy with the British monarchy as a badge of honor.

Beginning in the 1720s, agents in Jamaica also began branding Africans with the letter *A* (for *asiento*) as they passed through the island on their way to Spanish America. The introduction of the second mark suggests that SSC agents may not have always strictly observed the practice of branding, despite orders from London. In 1718, the SSC directors reminded Dudley Woodbridge, the agent in Barbados, "to take care Negroes be marked with the Company's mark." Branding African individuals with the arms of the South Sea Company, or an *A*, denoted their status as human property fated for Spanish markets. The brand enabled Spanish officials to count the numbers of enslaved captives disembarking from licensed British vessels, a method that theoretically deterred interlopers from claiming a share of the asiento. A practice widely adopted by European traders and colonial enslavers, human branding served as "a form of receipt marking legal passage and provenance."

Commonly referred to as the Royal Asiento Company, the SSC broadcast its close connection to the British monarchy whenever possible. The directors invited the SSC's governor, the Prince of Wales, to attend the ceremonial launch of its newest ship, *Royal Prince*, which the prince himself had christened. Although relations between King George and his heir remained tense, the SSC used Prince George as a liaison to Britain's more remote and recurringly absent sovereign. In September 1716, for example, South Sea Company directors attended the Prince of Wales at Hampton Court Palace to present a formal address to the king, who had not yet returned from his annual summer in Hanover. Speaking on his father's behalf, the prince declared that "the Company need not doubt of His Majesty's protection and that himself on all occasions would do them what service lay in his power." But the more popular Prince George would not stand in for his father in Britain for long.

Behind the scenes, the king and his heir avoided each other's company and rarely spoke. In public, they disagreed over matters of policy, and the prince avoided cabinet meetings and encouraged his supporters to vote against the ministry. Rallying around the Prince of Wales, the leaders of the opposition in Parliament widened the growing wedge between father and son. In November 1717, the simmering resentments between King George and his heir erupted into a bitter feud following the christening of the Prince of Wales's second son, George William. Brooking no input from the child's incensed parents, the king selected his grandson's name and chose his godparents. After the tense christening, George expelled his eldest son and daughter-in-law from St. James's Palace, insisting that their children remain behind.

The prince and princess of Wales relocated to Leicester House and drew members of the opposition, both Tories and discontented Whigs, into their orbit. The royal family's quarrel heightened after George William died at the age of four months, while the Waleses were forcibly separated from their children. Prince George blamed the king, and the chasm between them widened. Leicester House became the unofficial meeting place for the opposition party, and George I refused to see anyone who frequented the rival court of his eldest son and heir. The rift in the royal family caused problems for courtiers, palace staff, and statesmen and weakened the prince's position. From his house in Leicester Square, the Prince of Wales could not compete with the power of the king and the grandeur of his court at the palaces of St. James, Kensington, or Hampton Court.

In January 1718, prior to the company's annual election, the Prince of Wales wrote to the South Sea Company directors stating that he would step aside as governor in favor of the king. His father had recently purchased £10,000 of South Sea Company shares, he explained. Informed of the king's investment, the prince decided to decline the honorary SSC governorship that he had held since 1715 in favor of his father. His decision, he clarified, stemmed from "no other consideration but my duty to the King and the honor and advantage I think it would be to your Company to be under the personal and more immediate protection of His Majesty." The patronage of the Prince of Wales, as fruitful as it had been for the company, paled in comparison to having the reigning monarch serve as governor. Not only had the king personally invested in SSC shares, but word of his acceptance of the governorship was bound to attract the attention of the investing public.

The SSC rushed to seize the opportunity. Presenting an address to King George, the court of directors sought to "acknowledge with the greatest sense of gratitude the many marks of your royal favor, which the Company have received ever since your Majesty's happy accession to the Crown, and in particular the Honor done them in becoming a proprietor in their stock." "They therefore do in the most humble and dutiful manner," the directors continued, "beseech your Majesty will be graciously pleased to grant them the further honor of using your royal name for their Governor in the ensuing election." After meeting with George I and receiving his consent to serve as governor on February 1, the SSC published its address to the king in the *Post Man* and *Daily Courant*. King George received the court of directors at St. James's again a week later. In response to their effusive thanks, he promised the company his "favor and protection." In honor of Britain's sovereign, the SSC christened its newest ship *Royal George* and paid for listings in London newspapers advertising its imminent departure for the annual fairs at Cartagena and Portobello. It replaced the portrait of the Prince of Wales hanging in South Sea House with a portrait of King George.

Yet even the king's patronage could not prevent hostilities with Spain from disrupting overseas trade and dealing a major financial blow to the SSC. Britain may have held the asiento, but strategic issues from the War of the Spanish Succession remained unresolved. In 1718, in response to Philip V's attempts to regain Italian possessions lost in 1713, Britain formed a pact with Austria, France, and Holland, known as the Quadruple Alliance, to check Spanish ambitions. The War of the Quadruple Alliance lasted for two years, during which period the Spanish Crown suspended the asiento and seized SSC factories and goods in Spanish America. The embargo on trade and confiscation of South Sea Company property was financially ruinous for the company. Although the directors protested that the asiento granted the British six months to remove their goods and agents from Spanish soil following a declaration of war between the two Crowns, the Spanish seized South Sea assets, including merchandise and enslaved captives awaiting sale. Following the outbreak of war, British merchants also suffered loses to Spanish privateers in Caribbean waters.

After the Quadruple Alliance dealt Spain a series of decisive military defeats, a chastened Philip surrendered in January 1720. Spain's humiliating trouncing at the hands of its major European rivals forced the Spanish Crown to uphold its historic pledges made under the Treaty of Utrecht, including commercial concessions granting foreign powers access to Spanish America. Upon receiving word of Spain's capitulation, the SSC directors reminded George I of the seizure of their property and his previous assurances of royal protection. During the first months of the war, George had assured the SSC of "his firm resolution to use his utmost endeavors to procure you a just satisfaction for any damages you have received and hereafter receive from the Spaniards." Now, as he discussed terms of accommodation with Philip, the king renewed his promise to pay "particular regard" to the company's interests. Like his son, the Prince of Wales, the king had returned his annual £500 allowance as governor of the SSC and responded supportively to entreaties to assist the company's bid for full satisfaction from Spain for its losses. George overlooked the SSC's inability to meet its annual asiento quota and wartime financial setbacks. The king, along with many other influential Britons, had invested in the company; the Crown was committed to its survival.

In fact, nearly all of Britain had become entangled with the affairs of the South Sea Company. In 1719, the company proposed assuming the entire British national debt, a sum of approximately £30 million, converting it into new South Sea Company shares. This scheme would convert high-interest debts into low-interest, readily tradeable company shares, benefiting all parties. Its success, of course, depended on the stock value rising. John Aislabie, chancellor of the Exchequer, supported the proposal; the hefty bribe he received certainly helped. In April 1720, he persuaded his fellow MPs to vote for the measure.

By this point, in a transparent attempt to influence George I and encourage the public to invest, South Sea Company directors had gifted the king's half-sister, Sophia Charlotte, and his mistress, the duchess of Kendal, £15,000 of company shares apiece; the duchess's so-called nieces received £5,000 each. The king, supporting the venture, pledged £100,000 in SSC stock, paying £20,000 for his first installment. Supported by funds from the civil list, the king's investment delighted the company and contributed to the speculative mania for South Sea stock. The directors commended George for "permitting your royal name to be placed at the head of the subscriptions for enlarging their capital stock."

In mid-June, as the king and his court prepared to depart for Hanover, George ordered Aislabie to sell all his South Sea Company shares. The next installment on his subscription was due, and the king lacked the funds to cover it. Aislabie returned with £106,400 in cash from the sale, the bulk of which the SSC secretary had gifted to the king. George resolved immediately to reinvest his earnings in the slaving company. Rumors concerning the resumption and enlargement of the slave trade to Spanish America and access to South American silver mines, fed by South Sea executives, attracted thousands of new subscribers hoping to make a quick profit. The king summoned the chancellor, explaining that he wished "to have the whole sum laid out again in the purchase of South Sea stock and subscriptions." Aislabie dissuaded the king from sinking the entire amount into the company, "for that the stock was carried up to an exorbitant height by the madness of the people." Given the public frenzy for South Sea Company stock, the chancellor reasoned it "must fall"—and likely soon. Aislabie advised him to invest in steady, low-risk land taxes instead. George dismissed Aislabie as a "timorous man." He invested £70,450 in the SSC, holding back £35,950 for land tallies. The king then departed for Hanover.

Lured by the prospect of increased shareholder value resulting from profits derived from the slave trade to Spanish America, the British public snapped up SSC shares, driving up the stock price. After peaking at £1,000 per share in August, the market price of South Sea Company stock began to decline rapidly thereafter as shareholders rushed to sell, precisely as Aislabie had feared. On August 19, Aislabie wrote to Hanover asking for further instructions regarding the SSC shares held by the king, the duchess of Kendal, and her so-called nieces. As he waited for a reply, the chancellor held tight and took no action; he knew that acting without permission might anger the king. Worse still, liquidating the king's shares could lead to public panic, fueling a mass sell-off. But Aislabie's hesitation on George's behalf proved unwise.

South Sea Company stock fell sharply, from £1,000 on August 17 to £190 on September 28. The precipitous decline increased selling and the stock price plummeted even lower. Shareholders who purchased stock entirely on credit went bankrupt. Virtually overnight, thousands of Britons, including members of the aristocracy, faced financial ruin. The rapid collapse of SSC stock provoked a public outcry. When word of the company's financial downfall reached the king in Hanover, George was outraged. The Lords Justices urged him to return to London at once to address "the universal calamity to which your government may be exposed." That Aislabie had not sold his South Sea Company stock at a favorable rate before the crash magnified the king's ire and frustration.

On September 27, the duchess of Kendal wrote from Hanover to upbraid Aislabie for his failure to respond to changing market conditions to the benefit of herself and the king. Given the volatility of SSC stock, awaiting orders from Germany was not only unnecessary but also detrimental. "The whole has been left to your own judgment, to sell and buy as you would think it the most profitable and convenient," she explained; "for it cannot be pretended that at such a distance as we are a good and positive resolution could be taken in the right time, since those matters are every moment subject to great alterations." She chastised him for simply watching, paralyzed by inaction as panic gripped the market and SSC shares plummeted in value. "I hope you will be so kind as to take a little care of our interest, if it is not so great a disturbance in your other affairs," the duchess quipped. Having received their stock as gifts, the duchess of Kendal and her "nieces" later profited from their South Sea Company holdings but to a far lesser extent than if Aislabie had sold their shares before the 1720 crash.

The king remained in Hanover through mid-October, even as his ministers repeatedly expressed their misgivings about the mood of the capital and pressed George to return home. Londoners had taken to the streets after the collapse of the South Sea bubble; the government feared revolutionary upheaval. When the public learned that King George had reappeared in London on October 21, the public furor quieted down and SSC shares rose slightly. Sweeping recriminations and a parliamentary investigation soon followed. The investing public demanded retribution. Parliament conducted an audit of the company's records and attempted to compensate victims by seizing substantial portions of the directors' estates.

Barred from sitting on the boards of other companies or holding government office, South Sea Company executives bore the brunt of the blame. Chancellor Aislabie was expelled from the House of Commons and committed to the Tower of London for defrauding the public.

Many Britons lost substantial fortunes when the South Sea Company bubble burst, but the king was not among them. George "lost a fairy fortune, like many of his subjects," historian John Carswell observes; "but Aislabie's prudence left him a substantial gainer on his original outlay of £20,000." Once SSC shares stabilized and the king's land tallies were sold, he gained a total of £45,304 on his initial investment. In the wake of the 1720 Bubble, it took nearly two years for the financial system to stabilize. Yet the South Sea Company remained "an efficient and committed slaver," rebounding from the financial setback. George I continued to offer his support to the SSC and to serve as its governor. Royal honor demanded that the Hanoverian king protect the reputation of British credit, at home and abroad.

Factors other than honor were also at play. A recent analysis of the historical financial data related to the SSC concludes that the "Asiento and Asiento-related slave trading increased the British central government surplus by 16%," suggesting that earnings generated from the transatlantic slave trade to Spanish America bolstered Britian's fiscal capacity. Funds derived from slaving, in turn, "could be utilized to enhance a military capacity necessary for securing an empire." Further reinforcing the British monarchy's centuries-old links to slavery, the Hanoverian kings embraced any opportunity to use the bodies and labor of enslaved Africans to achieve their own ends.

CHAPTER 12

THE KING'S SLAVES

War with Spain and the South Sea Company bubble disrupted the limited legal commerce between Britain and Spanish America, enabling piracy and contraband trade to flourish. Sir Robert Walpole, the new Lord of the Treasury and chancellor of the Exchequer, worked to restore public confidence in the government and British credit and overseas commerce. By 1721, the SSC had appointed new directors, resumed the asiento trade with Spanish America, and convinced King George I to maintain his patronage of the company and continue as its governor. Although Spanish royal officials restored some of the company's merchandise and money seized during the war, the compensation process was complicated and disputed by both sides.

South Sea Company agents reopened factories across Spanish America, and the Spanish Crown attempted to crack down on illicit smuggling. In March, the South Sea Company resumed its contract with the Royal African Company to supply three thousand enslaved Africans destined for Spanish markets. Required to be "good, sound, healthy and merchantable Negroes," twenty-four hundred were to be derived from the Gold Coast and Ouidah in the Bight of Benin, and the remaining six hundred from Angola. To fulfill the remainder of the asiento contract, the company worked with private traders and instructed enslavers to supply human cargoes that were two-thirds male and primarily between the ages of sixteen and thirty.

As a result of competition from other European slave traders and piracy on the coast of West Africa, the RAC failed to meet its specified quota of three thousand captives for the asiento. But according to the African Company, South Sea Company agents in Jamaica sold the enslaved

Africans it landed on the island to local customers, claiming they did not meet Spanish specifications. South Sea Company agents in Jamaica received a commission whenever they sold an individual African into slavery in the SSC's name, even if the purchaser was not the intended recipient in Spanish America. The SSC directors concluded that the shortage of Africans for the asiento stemmed from their own agents colluding with smugglers and complicit Spanish officials. To meet its annual quota of forty-eight hundred enslaved Africans, the SSC determined that it needed to purchase around seven thousand Africans to account for losses arising from illness, suicide, piracy, and shipwrecks. The plan entailed purchasing enslaved people primarily from Ouidah, Angola, and the Gold Coast and disembarking the survivors in Jamaica for "refreshment" followed by dispersal to Spanish American ports. South Sea Company officials viewed the nearly one-in-three loss rate of enslaved Africans as the necessary cost of doing business with Spanish America.

Both George I and the Prince of Wales remained shareholders and public supporters of the SSC during the resumption of the asiento in the early 1720s. In December 1723, the king and his heir were listed at the top of the SSC's published list of subscribers. Their individual investments had dropped to £5,000 and £1,000, respectively. The renewal of the legal traffic of enslaved people to Spanish America made no difference to the flourishing inter-imperial contraband trade. Neither George I nor Philip V had curbed rampant smuggling or piracy. British and Spanish merchants and sailors conducted regular clandestine voyages between Anglo-Caribbean territories and Spanish America. Jamaica, a sloop voyage away from numerous Spanish ports, lay at the heart of an inter-imperial illicit trading ring in goods and human commodities, and Spanish coin was the primary medium of exchange.

Cognizant that Britain benefited from the flow of Spanish American bullion to its Caribbean islands, King George and his advisers supported the interests of the SSC while simultaneously turning a blind eye to illegal smuggling. The Spanish Crown, meanwhile, launched a concerted campaign against the Anglo-Spanish contraband trade, authorizing coast guards and privateers to seize British vessels carrying illegal goods. South Sea Company agents were restricted to their assigned ports, forbidden from journeying inland to sell enslaved Africans or merchandise. The heavy-handed tactics used by the Spanish coast guards subjected the vessels of authorized traders to inspection and, in some cases, unlawful confiscation, angering the British mercantile community.

Wars, piracy, and vessel seizures repeatedly disrupted the asiento to Spanish America. During the second trading period, grievances mounted between the South Sea Company and Spanish officials, focused mostly on illicit commerce, fraud, bribery, and suspicion of British agents. SSC directors petitioned local Spanish officials and Philip V to reinstate their full asiento privileges guaranteeing peaceable official trade, including the right to deploy licensed slaving vessels and an annual ship to Spanish American ports. In addition to appeals to Spanish authorities, they repeatedly asked George I to intercede on the SSC's behalf. Directors complained of the "insults and indignities" to which the Spanish had subjected company employees "in breach of the asiento," particularly the repeated detainment of their ships.

By the late 1720s, aggressive Spanish seizures of British vessels and property became a point of escalating contention, leading to renewed hostilities between the British and Spanish Crowns and a suspension of the asiento from 1727 to 1729. During this minor war, Spanish officials confiscated the effects of the SSC and placed British merchants under house arrest prior to compulsory expulsion from Spanish ports. The war interrupted official trade lines and resulted in financial losses for the South Sea Company. Even as peace talks with Spain progressed, Spanish officials and coast guards persisted in seizing British ships, goods, factories, and subjects.

By the time the Treaty of Seville ended the second Anglo-Spanish war in November 1729, a new Hanoverian monarch sat on the British throne. On June 11, 1727, en route to his native Hanover, George I died after suffering a fatal stroke during the crossing. It took four days for the news to reach England. His eldest son, George Augustus, became King George II at the age of forty-three, the first Prince of Wales to succeed his father since Charles I in 1625. Few in Britain mourned the passing of the elderly Hanoverian king, who had kept his subjects at a distance. Nonetheless, the reign of George I had brought political stability to the realm and the British succession and enhanced fiscal military capacity.

George II's accession occurred smoothly, and he inherited his father's commitments to imperial expansion and slaving. Jacobite hopes for a national revolt, fanned by the birth of Charles Edward (the Young Pretender) in 1720, were disappointed. The king's ministers assured foreign courts that he would continue his father's policies. George expressed his intention of playing a heavy hand in foreign policy, particularly regarding Europe, and intervening in military affairs related to the army, but not the navy. Continuing in the role of prime minister, Robert Walpole secured an annual civil list of £800,000 for the new king, who had accumulated sizable debts as Prince of Wales. Mirroring his own experience as heir apparent, George II clashed repeatedly with his eldest son, Prince Frederick, who arrived in England from Hanover in 1728 with virtually no memory of his parents. The king refused to allow Frederick the same annual allowance he had enjoyed as Prince of Wales, prompting his heir to develop political links with the opposition Whigs.

In addition to consuming copious amounts of sugar regularly, George II became entangled with African enslavement to a greater extent as king than he had as Prince of Wales. In his capacity as head of the Royal Navy, the king stamped his approval on Rear Admiral Charles Stewart's suggestion that the Crown purchase "seasoned Negroes, boys and men," to labor in Jamaica's naval dockyards. Stewart, charged with constructing a naval base in northeastern Jamaica on Navy Island, reported that constant labor shortages had delayed the project. Unable to withstand the disease environment, British sailors sent to assist in the base's construction died in large numbers. Adopting a racial view shared by many Britons at the time, Stewart assumed that enslaved men of African descent were innately better suited to handle the rigors of the tropics. But paying exorbitant prices to hire skilled enslaved laborers was neither cost-effective nor efficient, he argued. Instead, the British navy could purchase and employ its own skilled enslaved labor force. Stewart recommended the Crown specially train these enslaved men and boys as "apprentices to the master caulker, carpenters or builder, or whoever are the naval officers, in order to be brought up to their several trades as caulkers, ships carpenters, or otherwise."

Buying enslaved Africans to serve the Royal Navy in Jamaica would save the Crown money, Stewart maintained, because "his Majesty has paid dear for the Negroes he had been obliged to hire." Besides, he added, "the King has been the only person in this country not served by Negroes." As the Navy Board in London considered his proposal, Stewart moved forward and purchased sixty enslaved individuals on the Crown's behalf. These men and boys, and later women and girls, became known as the "King's Negroes." In March 1732, in a report to the Admiralty, the Navy Board confirmed that it had officially approved Stewart's purchase of enslaved men and boys on the Crown's behalf, even though the king had never purchased or owned enslaved people before. To have a specialized enslaved workforce employed in the king's name at the Royal Navy's Caribbean dockyards obligated Stewart to ensure that they received appropriate training.

Pleased that his superiors had approved his proposal, Stewart assured the Navy Board that after the initial outlay required to purchase the enslaved workers, the so-called "King's Negroes" would pay for themselves. He would encourage their self-sufficiency by allowing them to fish and plant kitchen gardens. To prevent the enslaved workers in the king's service from fleeing, Stewart wrote that he took particular care to feed, clothe, and provide rum allowances to them at a higher standard than the "customs of the country." As he explained to the Admiralty, "they are Cormantees and are esteemed the best sort in the country but are most sensible of good or bad usage; therefore, I shall think it prudent to give them no cause to leave the King's servitude." The British used the term "Coromantee" to designate Akan speakers from the Gold Coast, whom they associated with military prowess and a propensity to rebel against enslavers.

By the spring of 1732, Stewart had also taken it upon himself to add to the numbers of the "King's Negroes" by buying enslaved women. He rationalized his decision, explaining that "it is important to provide wives for the men, and women can be put to work." Despite Stewart's insistence that the Crown's enslaved workforce received far better treatment than enslaved people generally in Jamaica, the "King's Negroes" remained a flight risk. "The negro who ran away some time ago has been caught," Stewart noted in April 1732. He ordered the recaptured runaway "be chained and kept to work on the island," a visible example to others tempted to abandon the king's service in favor of a chance at freedom.

The Crown was directly involved in the exploitation of coerced African labor through its reliance on enslaved workers at multiple naval dockyards in the Caribbean. The Royal Navy also purchased enslaved men and women known as the "king's negroes" or the "king's slaves" to man the Antigua naval yard at English Harbor. Technically owned by the Crown, the majority of the "king's negroes" were trained as caulkers; others were trained as smiths, sawyers, and carpenters. They had distinct opportunities available to them due to the location and nature of their work. In addition to careening and repairing British naval vessels by turning the ships on their sides for hull maintenance, they surveyed stores, unloaded naval ships, and served on the night watch. The dockyard provided unique opportunities for the enslaved to receive and share news, monitor the movements of the navy, engage in theft, and plot individual escapes or collective uprisings. Yet the demographic realities and disease environment of the British Caribbean made the presence of the so-called "king's slaves" in the yard worth the risk to the British state.

As king, George II retained his previous ties to the South Sea Company, attempting to ensure that the company and the British state continued to profit from the asiento to Spanish America. Soon after congratulating the new monarch on his accession, the SSC approached George to serve again as governor, this time as Britain's sovereign. "Your Majesty having always shown a just regard to the prosperity of trade and commerce, the known fountains of the wealth, power, and grandeur of this nation," the directors hoped he would "take them under your royal countenance and protection." King George, accepting the SSC governorship for the second time, reassured the company that it "might depend on his protection."

Within months the SSC had presented George II with a laundry list of grievances against Spain. The Spanish Crown, determined to reinstate its historic monopoly over territory and trade in the Americas, had allowed its coast guards to seize foreign vessels indiscriminately during peacetime—including those trading under the auspices of the South Sea Company. Matters deteriorated for the SSC during the two years of warfare that followed, and the directors repeatedly turned to the monarchy for support. When the negotiations with Spain began in 1729 to end the hostilities, the directors prayed the king would seek justice and financial restitution on the company's behalf. "You may depend upon the continuance of my utmost endeavors for the service and satisfaction of the South Sea Company," George assured the SSC.

Between 1730 and 1734, the Spanish seized twelve South Sea Company ships for contraband activity, negatively impacting the company's trade and the price of its stock. Smugglers, moreover, had glutted Spanish American markets with enslaved Africans, making it impossible for the SSC to provide the 4,800 African bondspeople per year stipulated in the asiento contract. Independent traders, most of whom were based in Jamaica, resented the SSC's attempts to dominate trade with Spanish America. They justified their extra-legal activity by arguing that the company's monopoly negatively impacted British subjects and the nation as a whole. By 1736, although George II still served as the SSC's governor, the king's name was no longer displayed at the top of the list of prominent subscribers. With contraband trade and piracy rife on top of strained diplomatic relations, war between the two empires appeared inevitable to the SSC, as did the loss of its assets in Spanish America.

The outbreak of Anglo-Spanish warfare in the fall of 1739 was a long time coming. Lasting three years before being subsumed by the War of the Austrian Succession, the War of Jenkins's Ear grew out of tensions over illicit trade in Spanish America. The lead-up to the war began in 1731 with an incident involving Captain Robert Jenkins, an English merchant accused by the Spanish of trading illegally in the Caribbean. A Spanish raiding party stopped Jenkins and boarded his vessel off Havana, Cuba. While inspecting his ship for contraband, the Spanish coastal guards detained Jenkins and delivered summary justice, slicing off his ear and stealing his cargo. An outraged Jenkins returned to England and presented his grievance against the Spanish to King George II. Seeking to keep the peace, the Crown chose neither to intervene on Jenkins's behalf nor to chastise him for smuggling. The king's ministers adopted the attitude that "a Prince cannot be responsible for any of his subjects carrying on a commerce forbidden under treaty." The event received little attention in Britain at the time.

As Spanish seizures of British ships and sailors increased in the late 1730s, so too did the public's ire. In the fall of 1738, after Jenkins had reportedly brandished his severed ear while testifying in the House of

Commons, the British public demanded revenge against Spain. While Jenkins's story of disfigurement at the hands of Spanish agents was probably exaggerated, "Behold!" Britons could now claim, "there was the ear itself to tell the story." In response to widespread public outcry, Parliament authorized British warships to seize Spanish vessels, thus instigating a war with Spain contrary to the pacific policy of Robert Walpole, the prime minister. Britain entered the war confident it would lead to Spain's capitulation, followed by a dramatic expansion of inter-imperial trade. The British press widely defended and shared this assumption.

Far more than clashes over shipping and illicit trade provoked conflict between Britain and Spain. In the 1730s, the British settled in regions that pressed up against Spanish-controlled territories, specifically in disputed lands to the south and southwest of the Carolinas. Founded in 1732 and named in honor of George II, Georgia was the first British colony to ban slavery and large landholdings, preferring instead small farms worked by free families. The trustees encouraged white settlement as a means of maximizing the number of able-bodied men capable of bearing arms and defending the frontier. British colonization in this region posed a threat to the Spanish empire's northern borderlands. By right of first discovery and occupation, Spain claimed possession of the southern Atlantic coast and had established missions and small garrisons on the present-day Georgia coast as an extension of the province of Florida. After the founding of Charleston in 1670, an English settlement named after Charles II and formally recognized by Spain that same year in the Treaty of Madrid, English colonists had pushed southward, encroaching upon territory claimed by Native nations and Spain.

During the first decades of settlement, South Carolina attracted numerous migrants from the English Caribbean. The region's agricultural potential appealed to prominent Barbadian sugar planters, who arrived with coerced African labor forces and established a system of plantation slavery. As profitable yet labor-intensive crops such as rice and indigo predominated, South Carolina's enslaved population expanded dramatically. Enslaved Africans constituted the dominant demographic by the early eighteenth century. The perceived social and moral danger posed by an enslaved majority to industrious Christian colonists, coupled with Spanish and Native peoples threatening the security of the borderlands, prompted the Georgia trustees to reject the South Carolina model. Still, some colonists insisted that only slavery would assure economic prosperity. British territorial expansion into the Carolinas and Georgia pushed the Spanish into a defensive posture, creating a contest for empire that encompassed the Atlantic world.

For the SSC, which saw its South American factories destroyed during the Wars of Jenkins's Ear and the Austrian Succession, Anglo-Spanish conflicts in the 1730s hammered the final nail into its coffin. The company had for years considered the asiento unprofitable due to Spanish impositions and the brisk illegal trade conducted between smugglers and complacent customers and officials at Spanish South American and Caribbean ports. As financial losses accumulated, the directors petitioned King George for a release from the asiento contract. They also warned British factors stationed throughout Spanish America of the likelihood of impending hostilities but could not prevent the detainment of South Sea Company employees and the confiscation of goods. While Spanish officials later released SSC agents, they refused to return seized merchandise, including African captives in transit.

Anticipating this result, the SSC appealed to the king and moved to abandon the official slave trade to Spanish America altogether in the weeks before the conflict began. The asiento, set to expire in 1743, had lost its utility as an investment incentive and prospective money-generating scheme. After decades of commercial disputes between Britain and Spain, the company's exclusive right to supply enslaved Africans to Spanish America had proved more trouble than it was worth. Open warfare interrupted inter-imperial smuggling and illegal slave trading as well, though illicit Anglo-Spanish commercial networks remained profitable for those willing to venture the risk.

In December 1739, Admiral Sir Edward Vernon led a squadron of nine ships in a successful assault on the key Spanish port of Portobello, the main shipping point for silver from South America to Spain. News of this early victory buoyed British hopes. Vernon became a national hero at home, lauded as a true Protestant and loyal Briton willing to stand up to Catholic tyranny. Over the following year, George II's government assembled the largest amphibious assault force ever sent to the Americas by a European power. In March 1741, Admiral Vernon, at the helm of a massive fleet of 186 ships and approximately twenty-nine thousand men, led a failed siege of Cartagena, a heavily fortified Spanish fortress on the coast of modern Colombia. The outnumbered Spanish defenders repelled the invading British forces, many of whom succumbed to yellow fever, and Vernon retreated after six weeks of fighting. When he regrouped and attempted to salvage his reputation by attacking Santiago de Cuba and Panama, those campaigns also resulted in defeat or were abandoned. Vernon had led twenty thousand men to their deaths and was stripped of his command of British naval forces in the Caribbean.

Warfare between Britain and Spain and their allies continued for another six years as European powers divided over the succession of Maria Theresa, the eldest daughter of Charles VI, the hereditary Habsburg monarch and Holy Roman Emperor. Charles VI had died without sons or male grandchildren in 1740, sparking an international dispute over his throne. While Britain and France clashed in North America and India, Vernon's successor, Admiral Sir Charles Knowles, had no better luck taking the Spanish Caribbean strongholds of Santiago de Cuba or Havana. When hostilities finally ceased in 1748, the asiento had officially expired and, with it, Britain's legal, though strictly limited, access to Spanish American markets.

Long a source of contention between Britain and Spain, the asiento slave trade had undermined the Spanish Crown's ability to control the movement of people, specie, and products within its own empire. The peace treaty of Aix-la-Chapelle included a four-year extension on Britain's hold of the asiento as compensation for wartime interruptions. This agreement did not hold. Two years later Spain pressed for a new commercial treaty with Britain and the termination of the asiento. In exchange for a payment of £100,000 to the SSC and the extension of improved privileges to British merchants within Spain itself, Britain ceded its rights to the asiento and the annual ship. British dreams of extracting the famed wealth of Spanish America through a monopoly on the legal trade in enslaved Africans had evaporated.

Profiting from the sale and coerced labor of people of African descent, however, remained an imperial and economic imperative. Sugar, a laborious, time-sensitive crop, had emerged as the most valuable British import, funneling more tax revenue into the Exchequer annually than any other commodity. As sugar production in the British Caribbean expanded rapidly and consumption rates of sugar soared at home, the Caribbean islands claimed a greater share of Britain's global trade. Nearly all of the sugar imported into Britain was retained for domestic consumption, with Ireland taking the greatest share of sugar re-exports. The laxly enforced Molasses Act of 1733 levied prohibitive duties on foreign sugar and molasses imported into British America, where the mainland colonies were nominally bound by the Navigation Acts; it also prohibited Ireland from importing French sugar and sugar by-products. Because of the protection afforded to Britain's sugar market, British sugar consumers paid more relative to customers in continental Europe, fueling a steady contraband trade in foreign sugar and molasses in the British Isles and the mainland colonies. The high price of British sugar did not lessen the public's sweet tooth, even if domestic consumers essentially subsidized Caribbean planters. Sugar, once an exotic luxury good, was a common staple in eighteenth-century British households.

The rising consumer demand for sugar and other plantation crops cultivated by an enslaved workforce stimulated the escalation of British transatlantic and intra-American human trafficking and colonial slavery. Throughout the Atlantic world, Britons were deeply entangled in an imperial system undergirded by the forced exploitation of the labor and bodies of enslaved men, women, and children. Outside of the Caribbean sugarcane belt, planters in Virginia and Maryland relied on coerced labor to grow primarily tobacco for export. In the Carolina-Georgia low country, enslaved people cultivated rice and indigo, a natural blue dye extracted for use in textile industries, and only the importation of new coerced laborers could maintain the enslaved population. While colonists employed fewer numbers of enslaved Africans and Native people in the New England and the Middle Atlantic colonies of New York, Pennsylvania, and New Jersey, the institution of slavery nonetheless played a central role in the development of their economies. These colonies supplied foodstuffs, livestock, timber, and manufactured goods to the Caribbean and southern plantation colonies in return for sugar, molasses, tobacco, and other staples, and New Englanders engaged in the transatlantic and Indian slave trades.

Prominent carriers of African bondspeople to the Americas as early as the 1670s, British merchants surpassed the Portuguese to dominate the transatlantic trade in enslaved people during the reign of George II. In the decades after parliamentary deregulation of the transatlantic slave trade, western ports such as Liverpool and Bristol flourished, drawing countless Britons into the lucrative business of transatlantic slaving. Speculative, competitive, and hazardous, the transatlantic slave trade attracted participants and investors of all social classes. Although human captives resisted enslavement and commodification, staging recurring uprisings on transatlantic slaving vessels, slave trading offered an avenue of profit generation that many Britons embraced. Merchants, shipbuilders, insurance companies, banks, brokers, manufacturers, refiners, common sailors, shopkeepers, the British government, the Crown, and consumers, among others, benefited from human trafficking and coerced labor.

Except for a handful of Quakers and Anglican evangelicals, few Britons criticized the Atlantic slave system during the first half of the eighteenth century. Censure, when expressed, was directed at colonial planters and slave traders rather than at the British policymakers who encouraged the expansion of slave trading and human bondage, or the domestic consumers who enjoyed the fruits of enslaved labor. "In the British Isles, there was a predisposition among some to judge slaveholding critically," notes historian Christopher Leslie Brown, "but that impulse was tempered by an almost complete acceptance of the value of slavery to the colonies and the empire." For early critics, Christian conversion and benevolent mastery offered the solution to the moral problem posed by the permanent, hereditary exploitation of enslaved people, not freedom or English subjecthood.

By the era of the Hanoverian succession, the Church of England had strengthened its position in British North America. Although three thousand miles away in England, the later Stuart monarchs, William III and Anne, became tightly linked with colonial churches and the conversion of people of Indigenous and African descent through the work of the Society for the Propagation of the Gospel in Foreign Parts (or SPG). Founded by royal charter in 1701 as the official missionary arm of the Church of England, the SPG sent Anglican clergymen to sites throughout Britain's Atlantic empire to promote religious conformity and convert Native peo-

ple and enslaved Africans to Protestantism. Queen Anne was praised as
a "Royal Christian heroine" for supporting the SPG's "bloodless crusade."
In response to a request from the SPG, in 1714 the queen issued royal
letters endorsing general collections in the capital and port cities to raise
money for the SPG's evangelizing work in the colonies. Prior to Anne's
death, the society appointed a select committee to "propose proper methods for the conversion of the Negroes in Her Majesty's Plantations and
Colonies in America."

The Hanoverian monarchs built upon the strong association between
the society's spiritual mission in the colonies and the Crown. Shortly after
his ascension to the British throne, George I commended the SPG for
"engaging in so pious and useful an undertaking which shall always meet
with my favor and encouragement." Following Queen Anne's lead, he issued royal letters in 1718 calling for general collections throughout England to support the SPG's proselytizing and conversion efforts in North
America and the Caribbean. Royal bounty helped to fund the salaries
of colonial clergymen and support church building and the shipment of
Bibles and religious tracts.

When SPG missionaries turned their attention to proselytizing among
the enslaved in colonial North America and the Caribbean, they, like the
Quakers before them, met indifference and fierce opposition from colonists. Stationed in St. James Goose Creek, South Carolina, the reverend
Francis Le Jau wrote frequently to the SPG about his efforts to catechize
and baptize bondsmen and -women. He reported witnessing scenes of
routine brutality, which compelled him to "condemn the barbarous usage
of many masters to their slaves, esteeming them no other than beasts."
By April 1710, the society had resolved that its design "does chiefly and
principally relate to the conversion of heathens and infidels." The SPG
promoted an idealized, paternalistic model of mastery, whereby Britons
could justify the hereditary subjugation of Africans by encouraging their
voluntary conversion to Christianity.

In time, individual clergymen based in the North American and Caribbean colonies became owners of plantations and enslaved people, often through gifts and bequests. So too did the society on an institutional
level. Church of England clergy attempting to put abstract missionary
ideals into practice while operating slave estates faced many obstacles.

In 1710, Christopher Codrington, a Barbadian planter, bequeathed two plantations and three hundred enslaved individuals to the SPG. In his will, Codrington expressed his intention that the society manage the plantations in Barbados and retain his enslaved workforce and their descendants in perpetuity, while simultaneously establishing a school. Unlike most Caribbean planters, Codrington favored the conversion of enslaved people; but he was also firmly committed to the maintenance of the colonial racial order. The SPG petitioned Queen Anne for assistance securing the Codrington plantations and embraced the bequest as an opportunity to lead by example, to profit from the coerced physical labor of Africans while evangelizing among those in bondage.

From London, the SPG envisioned the Codrington estates as a colonial laboratory for demonstrating the compatibility of slavery and Christianity in the Crown's Atlantic empire. What better way to showcase the fruits of the Church of England's missionary work among enslaved Africans than through model, benevolent mastery? SPG leadership instructed the managers of its estates "to use the slaves belonging to the two plantations late of General Codrington with greater humanity and tenderness than is commonly practiced by planters." Despite these instructions, the treatment of enslaved people on the Codrington plantations was far from humane, however. Harsh conditions led to high mortality rates. Like other enslavers, the SPG became dependent upon the regular purchase of African captives arriving in slave ships to operate its plantations. When Codrington College finally opened in 1745, it did not accept pupils of African descent, whether free or enslaved. Anglican efforts to bring "heathens and infidels" into the fold in the king's name justified and overlapped with the exploitation of their bodies and labor.

The Church of England's long-term investment in African enslavement is also evident in the financial rewards reaped from a fund known as Queen Anne's Bounty. Established in 1704 to support clergy at smaller benefices, Queen Anne's Bounty invested in the South Sea Company and accepted benefactions from wealthy individuals whose income derived from the transatlantic slave trade and colonial slavery. As a recent Church of England investigation uncovered, from 1723 to 1777, Queen Anne's Bounty funds not used to purchase land from which poor clergy received supplemental income were almost exclusively invested in South

Sea Company annuities. Although the South Sea Company abandoned the trafficking of enslaved Africans to Spanish America in 1739, Queen Anne's Bounty had by that point already accumulated investments in South Sea Company annuities with a value of around £204,000, roughly "equivalent to about £443 million in today's terms."

Britain's eighteenth-century Atlantic empire was a slave empire and the Caribbean colonies its linchpin. But it was not the only European slave empire. In the face of mounting competition from French sugar producers, many feared Britain's sugar islands teetered on the brink of ruin. British commentators urged Parliament and the Crown to recognize both the extent to which the sugar colonies undergirded the Atlantic economy and the pressing need to shore up their weaknesses. Despite "their vast importance to the trade, navigation, wealth, and power of this nation," argued a contemporary pamphleteer, the British sugar colonies were being outpaced by the larger, better situated, more productive French sugar islands, especially Saint-Domingue. "No one is ignorant that the navigation of France owes all its increase and splendor to the commerce of its sugar islands, and that it cannot be kept and enlarged otherwise than by this commerce," the author emphasized. Unspoken was the double role played by enslaved people—as coerced laborers and inheritable chattel—in driving the enormously profitable commerce of the French Caribbean colonies. Britain's sugar islands were equally reliant on enslaved Africans.

During the reign of George II, the Crown was fully aware of the immense commercial and geopolitical importance of the Caribbean colonies and the profits the sugar islands afforded to the British state. The value of slave-produced British sugar imports from the Caribbean steadily climbed throughout the eighteenth century, outstripping imports of any other commodity in Britain's world trade. Taxes on sugar comprised a large share of the British Crown's annual income from customs revenue, exceeding land tax, miscellaneous taxes, and stamps. As a result, the requests and concerns of Caribbean planters and merchants who constituted the powerful West India lobby garnered the attention of Parliament and the king.

Wealthy, well connected, and vocal, the West India lobby hired London agents to represent their interests and oppose the passing of parliamentary legislation prejudicial to the islands. Caribbean plantation profits translated into social advancement, material wealth, and political influence in Britain. And enslaved labor underwrote it all, sight unseen. The sugar colonies, kept afloat by the regular arrival of slave ships bearing bound laborers to replace the individuals who succumbed under the crushing labor conditions, devoured hundreds of thousands of Africans forced to feed the Atlantic plantation complex. But their utter dependence on the colonial slave system also made British planters in the Caribbean the most vulnerable of the king's subjects in the Americas.

Susceptible to internal and external threats, ranging from armed revolts staged by enslaved people to foreign invasion as well as devastating hurricanes and earthquakes, the sugar islands driving the imperial Atlantic economy relied on British supplies and sea and manpower for defense. To the British Crown, the incomparable value of the sugar colonies made them worth preserving at almost any cost. And the cost was immense. Not only did the institution of slavery create a permanent state of war between enslavers and the enslaved, but the vast profits derived from slavery also drove competing European powers into expensive, drawn-out conflicts with Britain over territory and natural and human resources. Insulated from the horrors of plantation slavery in England, George II kept his royal hands clean while benefiting financially from human trafficking and coerced labor in his Atlantic empire. As his ministers considered how best to preserve Britain's slave empire and respond to the growing threat of France in the Atlantic world, the king fixed his attention chiefly on European affairs. He also sought to exercise control over his own family.

Relations between George II and Frederick, Prince of Wales, remained frosty. Although the birth of a son, George William Frederick (the future George III), on June 4, 1738, improved Frederick's standing at court and secured his dynastic legacy, the king continued to regard his eldest son and heir with disdain. Even Prince Frederick's sudden death from a cold in March 1751 at age forty-four failed to elicit affection or sympathy from his distant father. "This has been a fatal year for my family," King George remarked around Christmas. "I have lost my eldest son, but I was glad of it." He ordered the government to keep his eldest son's funeral expenses to a minimum. When Frederick was laid to rest in the Hanoverian vault, no one from the royal family attended the service. Frederick, the Prince of Wales, never had his chance to make his mark on the Hanoverian dynasty. But he left behind a son and heir who would.

With his father dead and buried, only Prince George's aged and distant grandfather stood in the way of the shy twelve-year-old boy and the British throne. The prospect filled the young George with alarm. A month after Frederick's death the king elevated Prince George to Prince of Wales and earl of Chester. George II chose to retain the income from the duchy of Cornwall for himself rather than passing it on to his grandson. Soon thereafter the Prince of Wales was taken in hand by a series of harsh, dull tutors entrusted with his princely education. As the teenaged George studied the English constitution and a range of traditional academic subjects, exhibiting some curiosity but limited academic aptitude, his grandfather's government steered Britain into another international military contest. This would be no minor war.

French expansion in North America and the Caribbean threatened British trade, livelihoods, liberty, and state revenue streams. Consequently, Britons of all classes supported an aggressive policy against the French. "Tis by our trade that the revenue arises, and to that likewise is owing the extraordinary value of our lands," noted one representative author; "from both which are obtained the necessary supplies, that must enable the Crown to protect the subject, and the subject thereby encouraged to defend the Crown." Securing the future security and development of Britain's Atlantic empire demanded curbing French imperial ambitions, and that required bloodshed. In May 1756, Britain formally declared war against France; a month later, France responded in kind with its own declaration of war. The Iberian powers opted to remain neutral, but not for long. Erupting initially in North America, the conflict between Britain and France would ultimately spread to four continents, become global in scale, and last seven years. It would increase the size and population of the British Empire, nearly double Britain's national debt, further entrench African slavery in the Atlantic colonies, and shape the course of the future George III's reign.

PART III

RUPTURE

CHAPTER 13

BRITAIN'S SLAVE EMPIRE

Officially declared in 1756, the Seven Years' War pitted Britain and France and their allies against each other for imperial domination in North America and across the globe. Britain sought to halt French encroachments on the weakly defended frontiers of its American colonies, thereby both securing and expanding the borders of British territory. In the decades after the Treaty of Utrecht in 1713, France had recognized the Iroquois Confederacy and the Six Nations belonging to it—(from east to west) Mohawks, Oneidas, Tuscaroras, Onondagas, Cayugas, and Senecas—as subjects of the British Crown. Beginning in the 1720s, Shawnee, Delaware, and Iroquois tribes migrated west and southward into the Ohio Valley in pursuit of abundant land, game, and hides. As Native peoples moved into the region, British traders and speculators ventured in their wake, claiming they held a legal title to lands settled by the subjects of their king.

While the Iroquois and other Native nations worked toward their own objectives in the Ohio country, including territorial preservation and sovereignty, the British attempted to gain an imperial foothold. The French too clambered into the region, erecting outposts, enlisting Native trading partners, and claiming jurisdiction. As the British and French each declared ownership over the Ohio country, hostilities escalated. Native peoples were caught in the middle, embroiled in a European power struggle over disputed lands in eastern North America.

By the early 1750s, George II's government considered France the greatest threat to British national security and worldwide imperial interests. British ministers feared that France aimed to establish a universal monarchy in Europe, supported by wealth gained from overseas territorial expansion and commerce. Viewing Britain's maritime predominance and Atlantic empire as vital to the nation, the British public supported a foreign policy dedicated to maintaining British naval power and colonial acquisitions at France's expense. Checking the ambitious designs of the French ensured the protection of British interests. Officials in Britain held that establishing British North America on a lasting foundation depended on westward expansion and sharply delineated boundaries between French and British territories. To be hemmed in, confined to a relatively narrow strip along the eastern seaboard, forever entangled in border disputes over land and resources, would doom British America.

The growing French presence in the Caribbean also threatened to halt Britain's advance. In addition to impinging upon so-called "neutral" islands—St. Lucia, Dominica, St. Vincent, and Tobago—that the two European powers had agreed to leave uncolonized, the French had taken the lead in the race to produce valuable export crops, particularly sugar, in Saint-Domingue, Martinique, and Guadeloupe. While Britain and its colonies consumed the sugar its Caribbean islands produced, the French sugar business dominated the valuable European re-export market. The success of France's Caribbean sugar industry enabled it to maintain a favorable balance of trade and claim an increasing share of the world sugar market, disadvantaging British sugar producers. Just as it did in the British Caribbean, coerced African labor drove French sugar production, which depended in turn on the regular arrival of slaving vessels bearing fresh captives.

British traffickers continued to dominate the transatlantic slave trade, far surpassing the Portuguese in overall numbers of enslaved Africans carried to the Americas. During the first half of the eighteenth century alone, British vessels embarked from West African ports with a total of roughly 975,000 captives, of whom approximately 167,000 individuals perished during the Atlantic crossing. The majority of survivors disembarked in the Caribbean slave colonies, chiefly Jamaica or Barbados, as the first port of call, with ports in mainland North America absorbing the second largest proportion of captives. In 1750, after more than two decades of subsidizing the RAC with annual taxpayer-funded grants, Parliament dissolved the Stuart-era corporation. It erected a new holding company, the Company of Merchants Trading to Africa, to administer

Britain's West African forts for the public benefit. Vying to defend their respective commercial and territorial interests in North America and the Caribbean, the British and French Crowns envisioned expansive imperial futures predicated on the exploitation of Africans and the dispossession of Indigenous peoples.

The Seven Years' War, also known as the French and Indian War in North America, began poorly for Britain even before the official declaration of hostilities. With the assistance of Native allies, the French repelled a British expeditionary force sent to dislodge them from Novia Scotia in 1755. The French also seized Minorca, a strategic Mediterranean base, and the British government collapsed under the weight of the public outcry. For months, George II found himself without a viable ministry. Once the war was officially underway, the French made progress capturing Hanover, George II's beloved ancestral home, and took British forts on Lake Ontario in Canada and Lake George in New York.

A leading member of the patriot Whig opposition, William Pitt the Elder, appointed secretary of state for the Southern Department in 1757, altered Britain's declining fortunes. He viewed the war as an opportunity to expand Britain's maritime empire and permanently undercut French overseas commerce. Pitt argued that Britain should spare no expense waging war against its chief imperial rival. Headed by Prime Minister Thomas Pelham-Holles, duke of Newcastle, the Newcastle-Pitt ministry overseeing the war effort consisted of a coalition between the Whig establishment and parliamentary opposition forces led by Pitt. Carried to power by a flood of popular discontent directed at the government, Pitt pushed for the rapid expansion of Britain's army and navy. He supported the grant of subsidies to European forces battling France on the Continent, recognizing that strategic gains elsewhere depended on keeping French forces occupied.

Retrospectively lauded by the British public as the patriotic champion of British liberty, Pitt helped to turn the tide of the war in Britain's favor. "He warded off the evil hour that seemed approaching; he infused vigor into our arms; he taught the nation to speak again as England used to speak to foreign powers; and so far from dreading invasions from France, he affected to turn us into invaders," declared the English writer and

politician Horace Walpole. In July 1758, the British captured the French
fortress at Louisbourg and gained control of the upper Ohio Valley by
conquering Fort Duquesne, renamed Fort Pitt, in November.

But it was 1759 that proved transformative as Britain achieved signal
victories in multiple theaters of war. British forces seized Fort Niagara
and the French stronghold of Quebec, leading to the fall of Canada the
following year; captured the French Caribbean colony of Guadeloupe,
"perhaps of as great consequence to the Crown of England, as any other
in subjection to it in America; of infinite prejudice to the trade and commerce of the French, our natural and inveterate foe"; and took Gorée Island, a French slaving outpost off the coast of Senegal. At sea, British
squadrons intercepted and smashed French Mediterranean and Atlantic
fleets intent on invading England. Britain prevented an invasion on home
soil and secured mastery of the seas. Meanwhile, on the Continent, a defeat by Anglo-German forces compelled France to abandon its designs on
Hanover. Through the East India Company, Britain also won important
successes against the French in India. Ecstatic, the British people celebrated their nation's year of unrivaled military triumphs, and "church bells
were threadbare with ringing for victory."

As Britain gained the upper hand over France, enslaved individuals
monitored the disruptions occasioned by war. Colonial officials also drew
Africans and people of African descent into imperial conflicts. Deploying unprecedented numbers of regular soldiers to North America and the
Caribbean during the Seven Years' War, the British government relied
upon colonial assemblies to raise additional troops locally. In mainland
North America, enslaved and free men of African ancestry joined multiracial provincial companies, serving alongside British colonists. By the
eighteenth century, colonial militias and provincial companies commonly
contained men of African origin and descent, but regional variations
shaped the nature and extent of their service. In the mainland southern
colonies, local officials preferred to consign African-descended free and
enslaved men to servile or noncombatant positions under officers. But
authorities placed arms in the hands of Black men during periods of crisis.
In New England and the Mid-Atlantic—northern regions where people
of European ancestry held majorities (Connecticut excepted)—colonial

laws required all free men between the ages of sixteen and sixty to report for militia duty. With their enslaver's permission, bondsmen were also recruited to bear arms or to fight in their owner's stead.

In the British Caribbean, where the introduction of monoculture sugarcane production led to the engrossment of arable land by elite planters, the declining white population left colonial authorities little choice but to arm people of African descent. Local statutes compelled free Blacks and people of African and Indigenous ancestry to contribute to local militias. In Jamaica, British colonists spent decades attempting to subdue the Maroons, free descendants of formerly enslaved Africans who had fled their plantations and established sovereign communities in the island's mountainous interior. After a peace treaty signed in 1739, the Jamaican government recognized the Maroons' autonomy and land rights; in exchange, the Maroons pledged to return runaways and provide martial assistance during slave revolts and foreign invasions.

Except for Barbados, with a greater proportion of British colonists relative to other islands, the Caribbean islands lacked sufficient able-bodied white men to furnish the British army with volunteers during the Seven Years' War. Instead, Jamaica and the Leeward Islands contributed thousands of enslaved and free men of African ancestry to serve as armed combatants and military laborers or pioneers. Even in the face of widespread slaveholder opposition, the British military and colonial officials armed enslaved men to fight for the empire. Imperial warfare also opened fissures in colonial slave zones through which brutalized, hostile workers attempted to strike back against their oppressors.

In Jamaica, Britain's most valuable Atlantic possession and largest colonial slave society, enslaved people remained alert to the convulsions of the Seven Years' War. They waited for an opportune moment to exploit the defensive gap left on the island by the absence of British troops, stretched thin across the Caribbean theater. Beginning on Easter Monday, April 7, 1760, thousands of enslaved people under the leadership of an Akan warrior named Tacky staged a series of coordinated uprisings across Jamaica known as Tacky's Revolt. British troops, with the assistance of the Maroons, shot and killed Tacky on April 12, displaying his severed head on a pike in Spanish Town. Yet it took more than a year for the colonial militia to quash the insurrection. The largest uprising by enslaved people in the eighteenth-century British Atlantic, Tacky's Revolt resulted in the deaths of more than a thousand enslaved people, sixty British colonists, and sixty free people of African descent.

On October 25, 1760, six months after Tacky and his fellow rebels declared war on the Crown's most important sugar colony, Britons confronted a rupture of a different sort. The aged George II collapsed in the royal water closet during his early morning toilet, probably from a stroke, and hit his head and expired. Out riding in Kew when he received the news, his twenty-two-year-old successor, George III, readily took his grandfather's seat on the British throne. His time had come.

Young, eager, and inexperienced, George had a different vision in mind for his reign. He consciously presented himself as a Patriot King, devoted to Britain and committed to ruling above party. At his first cabinet meeting, George expressed grief for the king, love for his native country, and "determination to prosecute the just and necessary war in which the country was then engaged, in the manner most likely to bring on an honorable and lasting peace in concert with his allies." Still, the war's ongoing price tag was staggering. Although Pitt's costly war measures offered Britain a path to military victory, the Newcastle-Pitt administration had mired the country in debt. And the global conflict was far from over. To George, concluding the war and resolving the public debt would enable him to tackle his own priorities: reforming the nation's politics and morals.

The young king had his own personal will, but George did not develop it in isolation. In 1755, four years after the unexpected death of his father, Prince Frederick, George had formed a close relationship with his tutor, John Stuart, 3rd Earl of Bute. A charismatic Scottish noble and former intimate of Frederick's, Bute was appointed George's Groom of the Stole, the effective head of the prince's royal household, in 1756. Provoking George II's indignation and the envy of other politicians and courtiers, Bute exercised enormous influence over the Prince of Wales. The first tutor to serve as a true mentor to the impressionable prince, Bute had painted George an idealized vision of Britain as it should be once he became king. A reformed Britain that, while still rigidly hierarchical and rooted in hereditary privilege, would serve as an exemplar of virtue, parsimony, and duty. An indifferent student by his own account, Prince George understood that he lacked the scholarly knowledge and experience to improve British politics and society on his own. Without a trusted mentor to guide him, he risked being overwhelmed by older, opinionated ministers. Bute, therefore, would serve as George's bulwark against the machinations of politicians and their allies both inside and outside the government.

As George inherited an Atlantic slaving empire, the coerced trafficking and enslavement of Africans fit uneasily within his idealistic worldview. His early writings as a teenaged Prince of Wales offer insight into his evolving perspective on the transatlantic slave trade and human bondage. One recent biography of George III cites the king's manuscript essays from the mid-1750s as proof that the monarch was "a convinced abolitionist" before ascending to the throne. But this argument fails to capture the complexity of developing eighteenth-century assessments of the Atlantic slave system. Once shared primarily among Quakers and evangelical Protestants, intellectual consensus regarding the "abstract injustice" of the institution of slavery had become commonplace. The moral problem of slavery had begun to weigh on minds. But the stark realities of global imperial and commercial competition overrode considerations of morality. In the eyes of many British commentators, George III included, African slavery remained a necessary evil.

While studying history and politics as a young man, George considered the arguments put forward by Europeans to defend the transatlantic trafficking and enslavement of Africans. "But what shall we say to the European traffic of Black slaves," he mused, "the very reasons urged for it will be perhaps sufficient to make us hold this practice in execration." By using the term *execration*, or abhorrence, George conveyed his intense dislike of the rationales typically used to justify slaving, none of which he found persuasive. First, George noted, his contemporaries argued that cultivating the Americas required the labor of enslaved Africans. Or, more to the point, that the price of popular commodities like sugar and tobacco would skyrocket without coerced African labor. Second, that Africans—mischaracterized by some Europeans as "Black, wooly headed with monstrous features"—were physiologically suited for hard labor in tropical climes. Finally, that Africans' alleged lack of civility and common sense warranted European intervention and supervision. "Such are the

arguments for an inhuman custom wantonly practiced by the most enlightened polite nations in the world," George concluded; indeed, "there
is no occasion to answer them for they stand self-condemned." He was
deeply skeptical of generalized European justifications for the mass enslavement of Africans. But cynicism does not equate to abolitionism.

George contemplated African bondage while reading book fifteen of
Baron Charles de Montesquieu's *Spirit of the Laws*, a classic Enlighten-
ment political treatise first published in 1748. Book fifteen focuses on
slavery, and the young Prince of Wales took extensive notes as he read.
Most of his scribbles paraphrased Montesquieu's words. Prince George
also added his own commentary as he saw fit. According to Montesquieu,
it was against the law of nature for masters to perpetually enslave captive
laborers, because slaves should have the opportunity to someday become
free subjects. Montesquieu nonetheless defended Europeans' enslavement of Africans and colonial systems of permanent, hereditary bondage.
"Weak minds exaggerate too much the wrong done to the Africans," he
asserted. European nations regularly negotiated treaties with one another,
so if they had not yet agreed to end the transatlantic slave trade in the
interests of "humanity and compassion," Montesquieu reasoned, then the
trade must be just. A collective of sovereign nations linked by a shared
commitment to Christianity, European powers would only participate in
a traffic that aligned with the tenets of their common faith.

As a Prince of Wales preparing to assume the reins of government,
George admitted that he found Montesquieu's line of reasoning unpersuasive. He maintained that the enslavement of Africans arose largely
from environmental and political circumstances outside of their control.
"The true origin of the right of slavery," the prince wrote, "must be found
in the nature of things." In all despotic countries outside the temperate
zone, such as Asia and Africa, "freemen have no better resource than that
of becoming slaves to tyrants." Europeans, in contrast, had long "breathed
liberty, conquered like free men, and imparted more or less that invaluable
blessing to those they vanquished." While the young George III condemned African slavery as an immoral practice, he nonetheless saw the
world through a hierarchical lens.

George's tutors had taught him to place Christian Europeans—and
Protestant Britons particularly—above all other nations. That some of the

Figure 13.1. *HRH George, Prince of Wales.* Bernard Baron, 1755.

world's peoples lived under the yoke of despotism and fell victim to bond-age was part of the natural order, however regrettable. This rationaliza-tion did not make slave trading or hereditary slavery right; but it enabled the future monarch to accept both practices as imperatives of empire. George's subjects would expect him to defend Britain's imperial interests. Portraits of him as Prince of Wales show the subjugation and exploitation of African-descended people as an explicit part of George's royal inher-itance. Indeed, his concerns about the illegitimacy of African slavery did not affect his consumption habits. At Kew and Saville House, the Prince of Wales and family consumed sixty-nine pounds of treble refined sugar, twenty-three pounds of double refined sugar, fourteen pounds of powdered sugar, and four pounds of Lisbon sugar in November 1758 alone.

Over his own subjects, George aspired to rule as a consummate "Pa-triot King." He longed to earn the respect and admiration of his subjects as the monarchal "residence of true piety and virtue." Succeeding to the

British throne encouraged his "hopes of restoring my much-loved country to her ancient state of liberty." To achieve these ends, George released a royal proclamation encouraging godliness and set out to free his beloved country from excessive debt, according to the instructions and aspirations of his two primary role models: his deceased father Prince Frederick and his mentor Bute. Unlike the previous Hanoverian monarchs, George III intended to prioritize his British subjects and reside permanently in London; Hanover would play second fiddle to Britain.

George announced his intention of working with Whigs as well as Tories and placing the country's financial needs above his own. George's grandfather, George II, had denied him the chance "of convincing the world that I am neither unworthy of my high situation, nor of the blood that fills my veins" by joining the army at the outset of the Seven Years' War. Having studied the history of Crown revenues instead of bearing arms, George sought to demonstrate his worthiness by asking Parliament for a fixed annual civil list of £800,000. While George II had received a similar ordinary income on paper, he retained any surpluses of yearly revenues (such as fluctuating excise and customs duties) voted by Parliament. George III's income was set in stone. In the decades ahead, as the king's family expanded, inflation surged, and his finances proved inadequate, George would bitterly regret his early insistence on an inflexible income.

From the early years of his reign, George III exhibited a dogged commitment to following whatever path he had set for himself. This personality trait would complicate his early relationships with politicians during the first years of his reign and haunt him later in life. But it proved fortuitous in his choice of a wife. The new king, described as tall, fair, blue-eyed, and graceful in the bloom of youth, set his sights on a German Protestant bride, the seventeen-year-old Princess Charlotte of Mecklenburg-Strelitz. Biddable, healthy, and possessed of many childbearing years ahead of her, Charlotte met his criteria for a suitable royal spouse. She was likewise a product of the same Eurocentric worldview that strategically reinforced the subservient status of Africans. The couple were married on September 8, 1761, and George's coronation in Westminster Abbey took place two weeks later. Buoyed by the royal wedding and news of the capture of the French Caribbean colony of Dominica, optimism reigned in Britain. Except for his preferment of Lord Bute and agenda of political inclusivity

Figure 13.2. *Queen Charlotte, when Princess Sophie Charlotte of Mecklenburg-Strelitz, with a Servant.* Johann Georg Ziesenis, c. 1761.

toward the Tories, which alienated the Whigs, the young king enjoyed a high level of public goodwill.

Mere weeks after George III's coronation, the Seven Years' War ramped up. Six months of labored peace negotiations between Britain and France disintegrated. Claiming that "the unexpected violence offered on the part of the English" instigated the war between the Crowns in the first place, the French king Louis XV also blamed Britain for the failure of peace. He activated a prearranged clandestine defensive alliance with King Charles III of Spain. For aiding France, Spain would receive Louisiana west of the Mississippi and New Orleans. Pitt, the lone member of George III's cabinet pushing to capture the annual Spanish treasure fleet as the bold opening salvo of a declared war against Spain, resigned in October 1761. His exit from the cabinet mid-war alarmed the nation and dampened the new king's popularity. How could Britain bring the war to a triumphant conclusion when "it was Mr. Pitt alone that gave motion to the whole machine"? Spain, forgoing its previous posture of neutrality, belied by the depredations of Spanish privateers on British vessels, formally entered the war on the side of France in November. The remaining members of the king's cabinet moved forward with a plan to squeeze France by capturing Martinique, one of its principal Caribbean sugar islands.

The capitulation of the French in Canada enabled Britain to reallocate its military resources to the Caribbean, where the Crown intended to attack French and Spanish possessions. King George and his ministers and military officers were convinced of the utility of arming enslaved and free men of African descent for military campaigns in Caribbean waters. A well-known death trap for new arrivals from Britain, the Caribbean theater posed fatal risks to the health of soldiers and sailors. Jamaica was especially deadly; tropical diseases struck down thousands of men stationed on the island every year. Jamaica's reputation as the graveyard of the British Navy and Army discouraged recruitment. As George Keppel, third Earl of Albemarle, put it: "the soldiers and sailors cannot possibly work in this country." High mortality rates also meant that the amount spent on Jamaica's military establishment far exceeded that of other British colonies.

Knowing this, the Crown preferred to send seasoned African bondsmen into battle in the Caribbean to preserve the lives of British soldiers and seamen. In January 1762, a British expeditionary force assailed Martinique with the assistance of nearly three thousand enslaved men recruited from the Caribbean colonies. The island fell the following month, as did St. Lucia, Grenada, and St. Vincent soon after. George III then turned his attention to an esteemed prize that had long eluded his royal predecessors: Havana, Cuba. The greatest military stronghold in the western hemisphere, Havana was the fortified heart of Spain's empire in the Americas.

Enlisting men of African origin and descent, both enslaved and free, to aid the military campaign formed a central pillar of the Crown's offensive strategy. On February 15, 1762, George III issued confidential instructions to Albemarle, commander in chief of the British expedition against Havana, to collect a regiment of five hundred free Blacks and two thousand enslaved Africans in Jamaica. Judging the free and enslaved men of African ancestry "of great use in the operations you are directed to undertake," the king informed Albemarle that he had ordered William Henry Lyttelton, the governor of Jamaica, to assemble them for the Crown's "immediate service." In correspondence with Albemarle, however, Lyttelton explained that Jamaican slaveholders, wary of losing their valuable human property without compensation, refused to release enslaved individuals for the expedition until the government agreed to terms of payment. He also claimed that assembling a corps of free Blacks in Jamaica posed innumerable challenges. In the absence of the coercion to which enslaved men were subject, free Jamaicans of African descent resisted joining the expedition against Havana on King George's behalf. The prospect of re-enslavement by an enemy army was far too high.

In April, to address the concerns of planters, Jamaica's colonial legislature passed an "Act for providing two thousand Negroes for the immediate service of His Majesty." The wartime legislation guaranteed masters a per diem rate for each enslaved person contributed to Britain's combined land and sea attack on Havana. Masters would receive additional payment, not to exceed £70 per individual, "for all and every Negro or Negroes who may be killed, lost, or rendered useless in the expedition or shall not return to his owner within twelve months." After learning that the governor of Jamaica had failed to raise a separate corps of free Blacks to fight on his behalf, King George expressed his displeasure. "His Majesty is much concerned that your Lordship has been disappointed of so useful a corps as the free Negroes from Jamaica must have proved," his secretary informed Albemarle. Yet because the Crown had agreed to compensate the owners of enslaved men in Jamaica joining the invading force, "we hope your lordship will receive more slaves from thence than you seem to expect." To achieve victory, George III intended to wield individuals of African ancestry as instruments of war, whether as armed combatants, pioneers, or laborers. While enormous risk attended the deployment of coerced laborers to expand Britain's brutal Atlantic slave empire, the king and his military commanders embraced the gamble. The British military's reliance on enslaved and free Black soldiers under his predecessor, George II, had demonstrated their immense value to the empire.

On June 7, a massive British joint naval and army fleet, consisting of roughly ten thousand sailors, twelve thousand soldiers, two thousand enslaved Africans, and six hundred free militiamen of African descent, laid siege to Havana. Grossly outnumbered, the Spanish spent months attempting to repel the invaders. They even offered assurances of freedom to enslaved Africans who took up arms against the British forces. By August 11, after yellow fever wiped out about five thousand British soldiers and land battles another five hundred, Spain's seemingly impregnable Caribbean bastion had fallen. But Havana cost many British lives. Thousands of additional British troops succumbed to yellow fever after the Spanish surrendered, and new recruits arriving from North America faced the same fate.

Spanish colonists, familiar with Britain's devotion to sugar cultivation in its Caribbean islands and predominance in the slaving industry, attempted to make the best of shifting imperial circumstances. As Britain opened Havana for business, hundreds of merchant vessels arrived to engage in trade, including slave ships bearing African bondspeople. During the British occupation of Havana, Cuba's enslaved population increased by approximately 80 percent, a boon to the island's fledgling sugar industry. While the British held the Spanish stronghold for only ten months, they left behind an enduring legacy of intensifying sugar production and African bondage. "It was a harbinger of a new Cuba," notes historian Ada Ferrer, "and a lasting one."

At St. James's Palace in London on August 12, George III and Charlotte celebrated an equally consequential national triumph. The eighteen-year-old queen had given birth to the royal couple's first child: George Augustus Frederick—created Prince of Wales, duke of Cornwall, and earl of Chester the same month. The birth of an heir coincided with the surrender of Havana thousands of miles away. Outside the windows of St. James's Palace, the Royal Navy paraded through the capital with treasures seized from a Spanish galleon, worth over half a million in sterling. "All was joy, merriment, and gladness in London," remarked a royal servant. George and Charlotte, the latter of whom was continuously pregnant for the next two decades, would welcome a total of fifteen children in the coming years; three would die in infancy or at an early age. During the fall of 1762, British forces achieved further military victories, recapturing

St. John's, Newfoundland, from France and taking Manila in the Spanish Philippines. The British, having roundly defeated the French and Spanish, seemed favored by divine providence. Yet the worsening state of the country's finances motivated the king and his ministers to push for an immediate end to the lengthy, expensive war.

Peace preliminaries were soon back on the table, culminating in the Treaty of Paris on February 10, 1763. To Britain France surrendered Canada, territory east of the Mississippi except New Orleans, its African possessions in Senegal and the Gambia, and huge provinces in southern and eastern India. France received fishing rights off Newfoundland and the Gulf of St. Lawrence—the richest cod grounds in the world—and the return of Martinique, Guadeloupe, and Gorée, its West African slaving station. Of the so-called "neutral islands," the treaty awarded Dominica, St. Vincent, and Tobago to Britain and St. Lucia to France. Britain restored Havana to the Spanish, acquiring Florida and all of Spain's possessions east of the Mississippi in exchange. "I think it a noble peace," George concluded, "and Florida a good compensation for Cuba."

Underwhelmed by the enormity of Britain's gains, some politicians, including William Pitt, pronounced the treaty concessions a miscalculation. Instead of retaining valuable Caribbean territories, Britain had accepted Florida, dismissed as a largely uninhabited, "useless territory" with minimal trade. Much of Canada fared no better in these critical assessments. Additionally, by restoring Martinique and Guadeloupe to the French, "the peace does not diminish in the least the power of France in the West Indies." With access to the sugar produced by enslaved people's labor, argued Pitt in the House of Commons, "we have given her [France] the means of recovering her prodigious losses and of becoming once more formidable to us at sea." Sugar producers in the Caribbean colonies, whose interests were protected by Britain's closed market, further feared that additional competition from newly acquired French or Spanish islands would drive down sugar prices. Territory in mainland North America mattered greatly, but Caribbean sugar islands financed maritime empires.

British politicians were not the only ones disgruntled by the terms of the peace. So were Native peoples. European negotiators had ignored the detrimental impact of Britain's newly acquired supremacy in North America and the wider Atlantic on Indigenous peoples. At the conclusion of the war, the French and British did not seek the input of the Native nations occupying the Great Lakes and Saint Lawrence and Ohio River Valley lands that the two powers had spent years contesting. While Native peoples had learned to coexist with the French, who adopted Indigenous customs and chiefly attempted to trade rather than settle in disrupted regions, the British aimed to plant large-scale settlements on Indigenous lands. Forgoing the diplomatic tactics adopted by their French rivals, British colonial officials routinely treated Indigenous peoples disrespect-fully, dismissing their customs and cultural values. To save costs, British commanders refused to participate in the gift-giving rituals used by Na-tive peoples to form alliances with outside groups. Rumors spread that the British intended to seize Native lands and interfere with the fur trade.

In May 1763, Pontiac, an Ottawa-Ojibwe leader, and his Native allies launched a series of targeted attacks on British garrisons, beginning near Fort Detroit. Waged to expel the British from the Great Lakes region, Pontiac's War resulted in the deaths of around two thousand civilians, four hundred British soldiers, and an unknown number of Native peo-ples. Escalating Anglo-Native frontier violence and instability occasioned George III to issue a royal proclamation on October 7, 1763. Referring to "the extensive and valuable acquisitions in America, secured to Our Crown by the late definitive treaty of peace," the proclamation delineated the boundaries of British North America and extended Crown protection to Indian country. To stem encroachments on Native lands by individual colonists and the bloodshed that invariably followed, the king ordered the establishment of a reserve of hunting grounds west of the Appala-chians for "the several Nations or Tribes of Indians, with whom We are connected." Only the Crown and its representatives could negotiate land transfers in Indian country; the Crown also claimed first right to purchase any lands sold by Native nations. Pontiac and his allies had fought to protect their lands and autonomy. But the proclamation articulated the British Crown's claim to exercise sovereignty over North America and Native nations.

The royal proclamation of 1763 organized Britain's newly acquired territories into four jurisdictions: Quebec, East and West Florida, and Grenada, the latter of which encompassed the Lesser Antillean islands of Dominica, Grenada, the Grenadines, St. Vincent, and Tobago (often referred to as "the Ceded Islands"). Despite the continued presence of Kalinago and Afro-Indigenous communities in the Lesser Antilles, the proclamation did not acknowledge their existence. It failed to establish a boundary between current and prospective European colonists and unconquered Indigenous peoples—numbering roughly three thousand—in the Eastern Caribbean islands ceded to the British Crown.

This omission was strategic. In the aftermath of the Seven Years' War, Britain had enormous debts to pay and a global empire to maintain. Long after European colonizers assumed they had eradicated Amerindians from the region, Indigenous peoples occupied lands Britons coveted. When King George and his ministers considered the future of the Ceded Islands, they envisioned profitable agricultural production fueled by enslaved African labor. "That plantation-centered vision of the islands' future had no room for 'Indians,'" contends historian Melanie Newton. Attracting British colonists to unsettled territories required incentives, fertile land ripe for agricultural production by enslaved Africans chief among them.

On March 26, 1764, George III issued a proclamation to encourage "the speedy settlement" of Dominica, Grenada, the Grenadines, St. Vincent, and Tobago. The king detailed his plan for the imminent survey and sale of "such lands in the said islands, as are in our power to dispose of, into allotments for plantations of different size and extent, according as the nature of land shall be more or less adapted to the growth of sugar, coffee, cocoa, cotton, or other articles of beneficial culture." The Crown intended to set aside land in the Ceded Islands for military and other public purposes, as well as allotments to lease to French colonists who elected to remain under British rule. None, however, was reserved for existing Indigenous communities—"as if no such people existed," the eighteenth-century planter and historian Bryan Edwards later reflected.

On the islands of Dominica and St. Vincent respectively, British surveyors reported that fifty to sixty Kalinago families and up to two thousand Black Caribs (Garifuna) occupied territory ripe for plantation development. Preserving hunting grounds for Native communities—dismissed by British observers as "all equally savage and barbarous"—on small islands with limited arable land undercut British imperial designs. The presence of the Garifuna, a hybrid Afro-Indigenous group, proved especially disconcerting to British colonizers. They not only complicated Eurocentric racial classifications associating African ancestry and dark skin with enslavement. Their sovereign existence outside European control also offered a potential lifeline to enslaved freedom seekers—just as George III's government considered extending land grants to planters "in proportion to their number of Negroes."

British officials charged with surveying and distributing uncultivated tracts of land on St. Vincent saw no place for the Garifuna in a plantation colony. Land commissioners and colonial authorities argued that the incorporation of people of African descent into Indigenous communities nullified claims to ancestral territory. Appointed to manage the sale of Crown lands in the Ceded Islands, Sir William Young created an ethnographic portrait of the Vincentian Carib population that served British imperial interests. While surveyors estimated that up to two thousand Indigenous people inhabited the lush windward portion of the island, Young speculated few were truly "native Caribs." Instead, he alleged, the overwhelming majority consisted of "Black Caribs," racial impostors "who owe their origin to a ship freighted with negroes from Africa to Barbados and wrecked on these coasts." "Their forefathers amidst the general distress escaped to shore and found in a desert island a release from their bondage," Young contended. Masquerading as Caribs, the descendants of Africans fleeing slavery had merged with and dispossessed the island's Native inhabitants. Consequently, although the Black Caribs had adopted Indigenous cultural practices and spoke the Carib language, they occupied prime territory to which they lacked a legitimate ancestral claim.

Government officials and British commentators accepted Young's assessment of the Garifuna's origins and Indigenous illegitimacy at face value. Only "a miserable remnant" of the former expropriated Carib population inhabited St. Vincent, wrote Bryan Edwards in his general history of the British Caribbean. Over several generations, a fierce "race of people" alien to the region, though "long distinguished, however improperly, by the name of the *Black* Caribs," had eliminated the Amerindian community and fraudulently assumed its place. The presence of the African usurpers prevented the full implementation of the Crown's sugar cultivation scheme on an island "perfectly adapted for the growth of sugar." In 1764, William Young had predicted that St. Vincent "will very soon be classed among the best, most valuable of our sugar colonies." For his vision to bear fruit, the Garifuna simply needed to relocate to St. Lucia, Martinique, or a less fertile area of St. Vincent. But the Garifuna defied Young's expectations. When colonial surveyors attempted to build a road on the windward side of the island, armed warriors blocked access to their territory and "denied any subjection to the Crown of Great Britain." Thwarted by the Garifuna's refusal to submit to British rule, the island assembly informed King George that "his leniency to so worthless a set of savages will hurt his faithful, loyal and obedient subjects."

Like Anglo-Native conflicts in the Great Lakes region of North America, disputes over land in the Ceded Islands stemmed from British expansionist ambitions that denied Indigenous claims to territorial sovereignty and linked African ancestry with hereditary bondage. Whether of Native, African, or multiple ancestries, non-Europeans in territories claimed by the British Crown were expected to submit to George III. As a colonial official declared, "the Indians and Negroes not versed in the political, logical, and metaphysical jargon of the Europeans, could not be made to understand how a sovereign, whose authority they did not acknowledge, could give away their lands." In the Lesser Antilles, Indigenous dispossession and African enslavement were fundamental requisites for British colonial development and imperial prosperity. If so-called "Caribbean or wild Negroes" refused to acknowledge the authority of the British Crown and impeded the allotment and sale of land suitable for sugar cultivation on islands "belonging to Us," King George supported their subjugation and forcible removal. The honor of the Crown and expansion of Britain's Atlantic slave empire was at stake.

The Garifuna, accounting themselves a sovereign and free people, were equally determined to resist any attempts by European colonizers to seize their territory. Asking "what king was this of Great Britain?" they denied George III's royal authority and right to survey, claim, or occupy their lands. In April 1772, deteriorating conditions on St. Vincent provoked a controversial war between the island's Afro-Indigenous inhabitants and its British occupiers. Faced with what British officials labeled a recalcitrant body of "rebellious savages" who refused to submit willingly to

Crown rule, King George and his ministers approved the deployment of troops to St. Vincent to reduce the Garifuna "to a due submission to his Majesty's authority and government."

As the conflict dragged on for months, debates about the morality and necessity of the military expedition against the Black Caribs ensued in Parliament and the popular press. Britons questioned the legitimacy of the Crown's campaign against the Garifuna, an "innocent" people intent on preserving their liberty and property. Nevertheless, George III's government concentrated on "the reduction of the Savages." In February 1773, after ten months of conflict, the Garifuna capitulated. They signed a treaty with the British agreeing to surrender a portion of their lands for plantation development and to swear allegiance to King George. The Crown's cause had proved victorious on St. Vincent. But assertions of royal and parliamentary sovereignty over the North American colonies would soon inspire the greatest challenge of George III's reign.

CHAPTER 14

ATLANTIC REVOLUTIONS

anaging George III's post-1763 overseas dominions and multitude of subjects—including thousands of French and Spanish Catholics and Indigenous and African peoples, and millions of individuals in India—posed logistical and financial difficulties for the imperial state. Peopling, defending, and establishing Crown authority in conquered and ceded territories required effective administration. It also demanded substantial increases in government revenue. As George III and his ministers assessed Britain's balance sheets after 1763, the profits of the Crown's Atlantic slave empire appeared largely untapped and potentially vast. The British government needed money to pay for the war and the continued deterrent presence of troops in North America. The national debt, expanding from around £75 million in 1754 to £133 million in 1763, had nearly doubled and it continued to climb; annual interest payments cost British taxpayers more than £4 million. Although Britons at home could take pride in the extent of their nation's overseas empire, they groaned under the weight of heavy taxes. In stark contrast, Anglo-American and Caribbean colonists paid relatively little in taxes while enjoying a higher standard of living than the king's metropolitan subjects.

In the halls of Parliament and Whitehall, politicians agreed that generating revenue in the North American and Caribbean colonies, whose safety the war had secured, offered a solution to the nation's fiscal problems. The royal customs officers charged with upholding laws already on the books had failed to keep pace with rampant smuggling in the colonies. Laxly enforced, existing taxes on colonial trade produced inadequate returns for Britain's treasury. The time had come for British colonists to help shoulder the burden of taxation associated with the costs of administering the empire. Given the coin spent and lives lost in defense of British America and the sugar islands, George III supported extracting revenue from his Atlantic territories. "I have no wish but what is for the advantage of my country," the king claimed. To defray the costs of imperial administration, including the maintenance of troops overseas, Parliament passed legislation to raise funds in the colonies, including the Sugar Act of 1764, the Stamp Act of 1765, and the Townshend Acts of 1767. Colonists, to their outrage, were not consulted.

The British Parliament's attempt to exert its will on the colonies provoked public condemnations and accusations of metaphorical enslavement from American commentators. James Otis, in his popular pamphlet *The Rights of the British Colonies Asserted and Proved*, denounced the new revenue taxes as an infringement of colonists' constitutional and natural rights. Taxing the colonies without the endorsement of their local representative assemblies reduced free British subjects "to a state of slavery," he contended. In contrast to Britons in the mother country governed by just laws, observed Rhode Island's governor Stephen Hopkins, those "whose property may be taken from them by taxes, or otherwise, without their consent, and against their will, are in the miserable condition of slaves." John Adams and Thomas Jefferson, both lawyers and future founding fathers, argued that colonial Americans jealously guarded their constitutional liberties and refused to be treated, in Adams's words, "more like slaves than Britons." Oppressive taxation imposed on the colonies, Jefferson concluded in an appeal addressed to George III and later published, offered plain evidence of "a deliberate, systematic plan for reducing us to slavery."

Popular fury directed against the Stamp Act, requiring colonial publishers to print on paper stamped in Britain, resulted in violent protests, a boycott of British goods that damaged trade, and appeals to the British government. American colonists, aware that Parliament had authored the policies against which they objected, fixed their rising anger on the Lords and Commons rather than the king. But their discontent was also "directed at the entire regime of George III, and especially at Parliament, of which the king was an essential part, rather than the person of the king." Even as Parliament considered repealing the Stamp Act, King George never wavered in his unshakeable commitment to the British constitution and "the right of the Mother Country to tax its colonies." In February 1766, the House of Commons resolved to "firmly and steadily support His Majesty in all such measures as shall be necessary for enforcing the obedience due to the law from all His Majesty's subjects in every part of his dominions and for restoring order and tranquility to the colonies." Although Parliament repealed the Stamp Act the following month, it did so alongside a Declaratory Act, proclaiming that, as "his Majesty's dominions in America," the colonies "have been, are, and of right ought to be, subordinate unto, and dependent on the imperial crown and Parliament of Great Britain."

The dispute with the king's subjects in North America was far from over. At its core lay divergent conceptions of empire, sovereignty, and the role of the monarch and Parliament in Britain's largely self-governing overseas dominions. George III's American subjects envisioned a British Empire characterized by colonial legislative autonomy and negotiation with the king and Parliament. The British government, in contrast, sought to exercise parliamentary sovereignty throughout the empire. To the colonists, if the king failed to protect his subjects from Parliament's repeated and tyrannical violation of their rights, he had breached their contractual constitutional relationship. Some politicians in Britain sympathized with the American colonists; but many supported the Crown's stance that the Americans must accept their subordinate place in the empire and submit to the mother country. It seemed extraordinary, remarked one official to George III, that "the whole continent is our own, and that we find no opposition there except from our own subjects." The matter came to a head in December 1773, when colonists in Massachusetts dumped hundreds of chests of tea into the Boston harbor in protest of a tea tax passed by Parliament. The Boston Tea Party motivated Parliament, confident in its absolute sovereignty over the colonies, to pass punitive legislation that ultimately led to revolution.

On the eve of the American Revolution, American colonists raged against Parliament's unchecked power to levy taxes without the consent of colonial assemblies. They railed against the king's inability to use his royal prerogative to intervene in the imperial dispute in their favor. For the previous century, following the Glorious Revolution, the monarch had occupied a subordinate position to Parliament. Parliament held legal supremacy, and political stability rested on the balance between the sovereign, Lords, and Commons. Britons, the king's colonial subjects, and even the French praised this constitutional arrangement as evidence of the superiority of the English model of government. "The English are the only people upon earth who have been able to prescribe limits to the power of kings by resisting them," observed the French philosopher Voltaire, "and who, by a series of struggles, have at last established that wise government, where the prince is all-powerful to do good, and at the same is restrained from committing evil." The English royal prerogative, noted another French observer approvingly, had long approximated "a ship completely equipped, but from which the Parliament can at pleasure draw off the water, and leave it a-ground; as also set it again afloat by granting subsidies."

Yet, despite Parliament's avowed dominance, the monarch remained the symbolic linchpin of the eighteenth-century British Empire. Reverence for the British sovereign created a shared sense of unity and belonging, binding the disparate regions and peoples of the empire together. This was especially true in North America, where "the monarch apart from Parliament became the primary and common imperial link, the empire's living embodiment." Devotion to the Hanoverian monarchs, at best lukewarm at home, was fierce among British North Americans, who championed the king and royal family in public celebrations, political rituals, and print culture. Lacking affinity for or representation in Parliament while praising the king's justice and prerogative, the American colonists increasingly identified the monarch's subordinate status as a liability. George III's powerlessness to rein in the alleged abuses of the multitude—as embodied and enacted by the Commons—had soured his relationship with his American subjects, resulting in what they saw as political enslavement.

The British, including George III, dismissed American complaints equating parliamentary taxation with slavery as hyperbolic and hypocritical. Although Britons across the social spectrum profited from the transatlantic slave trade and colonial slavery, and some held individuals of African descent in bondage at home and abroad, the British public generally imagined slaveholding as something distasteful that happened exclusively in the plantation colonies. The sheer number of people of African and, to a far lesser extent, Indigenous descent enslaved in British America and the Caribbean offered evidence of the inferiority of colonial institutions and social norms.

Slavery's ubiquity in North America illustrated the baseness of colonists and made a mockery of their claims to act as defenders of British liberty. "If there be an object truly ridiculous in nature, it is an American patriot," wrote Thomas Day in 1776, "signing resolutions of independency with one hand, and with the other brandishing a whip over his affrighted slaves." Failing to admit the full consequences of their avowed principles betrayed the Americans' self-serving inconsistency. "If there be certain natural and universal rights," Day continued, "I wonder how the unfortunate Africans have incurred their forfeiture." King George asserted that the Americans only pretended to be paragons of liberty and had rejected imperial authority for selfish motives. The colonists had "boldly thrown off the mask and avowed that nothing less than a total independence of the British legislature will satisfy them."

American colonists' antipathy initially found expression in the repudiation of parliamentary authority. Yet their tone shifted decisively as the king's hard-line stance toward them became known. Long-held admiration for the monarchy shattered. The rebelling colonists now placed blame squarely on the shoulders of George III, charging him with negligence and complicity in Parliament's crimes against them. Working hand in hand with Parliament, the king had conspired with British politicians to deny his American colonists their birthright. This shifting stance toward monarchal authority is most evident in the Declaration of Independence, which ended with a litany of grievances directed specifically at the king. One complaint, however, was removed from the final ratified version of the Declaration: the accusation leveled by Thomas Jefferson, who owned more than six hundred enslaved people during his lifetime (his own children among them), that George III had perpetuated the institution of slavery by preventing colonial assemblies from halting the transatlantic slave trade.

Across the Chesapeake, many slaveholders shared concerns that the demographic dominance of enslaved people of African ancestry deterred the migration of European-descended settlers to the region. Additionally, they feared that newly arrived African captives, lacking familial and cultural roots in the American South and inured to warfare, would incite revolts, endangering the stability of colonial slave society. The Virginia legislature had previously debated and attempted to tax the transatlantic and intra-American slave trades on multiple occasions, laying duties on enslaved imports from outside the colony. In response to complaints from colonists, the House of Burgesses repealed some of these duty impositions at the local level; others the Crown disallowed due to mercantile petitions from Bristol, Liverpool, and elsewhere.

In 1772, the Burgesses, confident the colony's majority enslaved population was self-sustaining, petitioned George III for a prohibition on the importation of enslaved Africans. The numerical dominance of the enslaved, legislators explained, "greatly retards the settlement of the colonies with more useful inhabitants, and may, in time, have the most destructive influence"—namely, "endangering the very existence of your Majesty's American dominions." When the Crown, governed by the Board of Trade's advice, rejected Virginia's renewed attempt at regulation, Benjamin Franklin was not surprised. "The interest of a few merchants here [in Britain] has more weight with government than that of thousands at a distance," he mused.

The Crown's refusal to allow the Virginia legislature and other colonial assemblies to curtail the importation of enslaved Africans left behind residual resentment that overflowed in fury during the revolutionary era. Jefferson captured this long-standing grievance against George III in a pamphlet published in 1774 and in the preambles of his drafts of the Declaration of Independence and the Virginia constitution. He simultaneously blamed George III for perpetuating African slavery in his American colonies and prompting enslaved people to rebel in his name. Jefferson charged the king with violating the "most sacred rights of life and liberty in the persons of a distant people who never offended him, captivating and carrying them into slavery in another hemisphere, or to incur miserable death in their transportation thither." Worse still, "he is now exciting those very people to rise in arms among us, and to purchase that liberty of which he deprived them, by murdering the people upon whom he also has obtruded them." A proclamation issued by Virginia governor Lord Dunmore in November 1775 "for the more speedily reducing this colony to a proper sense of their duty, to His Majesty's Crown and dignity," appalled

Figure 14.1. Detail, *The Death of Major Peirson, 6 January 1781.* John Singleton Copley, 1783.

southern slaveholders. Declaring martial law, Dunmore offered freedom to any indentured servant or enslaved person who joined the British army. As up to two thousand enslaved people fled to Dunmore's encampment, horrified slaveholders in Virginia and across the Chesapeake feared the worst: the combined catastrophic loss of life and property as their bondsmen and -women fell in with the enemy and took up arms. The alliance of British soldiers and enslaved people threatened to destroy the estates and authority of slaveholders and turn the tide of war against the rebellious colonists. George Washington branded Dunmore "an arch-traitor to the rights of humanity." He issued a modest counteroffer in January 1776, encouraging the Continental Army to recruit free Blacks, though not enslaved men. Although Americans hesitated to arm enslaved people, both sides recognized the critical role individuals of African ancestry would play during the conflict.

Jefferson considered the king's deployment of enslaved and free Africans against the French and Spanish—Britain's traditional enemies—a far cry from unleashing the power of the enslaved against his own subjects. By supporting Dunmore's ruthless tactics, George III had perpetrated the ultimate betrayal, "paying off former crimes committed against the liberties of one people, with crimes which he urges them to commit against the lives of another." The king had used the trafficking, enslavement, and unlawful emancipation of Africans to his own benefit. Recognizing the divisiveness of the issue, congressional delegates excised Jefferson's passage condemning slavery as an evil imposed on the colonies by the Crown from the Declaration.

As American colonists leveled allegations of imperial tyranny and metaphorical enslavement against George III, British writers, satirists, and even the king himself rebuked their claims. If taxing Americans constituted a form of slavery—and "slavery is a miserable state, we have often been told"—Samuel Johnson quipped, then "how is it we hear the loudest yelps for liberty among the drivers of Negroes?" "They consider themselves as emancipated from obedience, and as being no longer the subjects of the British Crown." Unwilling to obey the laws of the empire and pay their just share of taxes, while simultaneously profiting from coerced labor, Americans had proved themselves the antithesis of honorable Britons.

American hypocrisy offended George III. He expressed his disgust that one might "suppose the Americans poor mild persons who after unheard of and repeated grievances had no choice but slavery or the sword; whilst the truth is, that the two [sic] great lenity of this country increased their pride and encouraged them to rebel." Glossing over their nation's preeminent role in the transatlantic slave trade, British commentators denigrated Americans as venal enslavers. Slavery neither existed in Britain nor was it permitted by the British constitution, asserted Ambrose Serle, a clerk in the American department for the British secretaries of state. "Negroes here, wherever they have been slaves before, experience something like natural rights, and are emancipated in a moment by setting foot upon our liberating shores," Serle declared.

That Serle and other Britons felt confident in such a claim arose from the ruling of Lord Chief Justice Mansfield in the landmark 1772 *Somerset v. Stuart* case. James Somerset was an enslaved man brought from colonial Virginia to London by his master, Charles Stewart, in 1769. In October 1771, Somerset fled from Stewart's household, seeking freedom in the capital. Stewart hired agents to pursue Somerset. They recaptured him the next month and smuggled him in chains onto a ship soon bound for Jamaica. After abolitionists spread word of Somerset's predicament, the lawyer Granville Sharp arranged for his release under writ of habeas corpus—the protection against unlawful detention—until he could plead Somerset's case in the Court of King's Bench.

Unfolding over the course of eight hearings between December 1771 and June 1772, *Somerset v. Stuart* attracted considerable public attention. London's West India lobby, concerned about the possible outcome, provided Stewart, Somerset's master, with financial support for his defense. English judicial precedent seemed to favor Stewart. A 1729 opinion of two Crown law officers, Sir Philip Yorke and Charles Talbot, stated that enslaved individuals retained their status as chattel property in England and could be legally compelled by their enslavers to return to the plantation colonies. In 1732, to encourage the slaving industry and trade with the plantation colonies, Parliament had legally classified "negroes" as a form of property—like houses, lands, and other "hereditaments and real estates" liable to be "seized, extended, sold, or disposed of, for the satisfaction of debts." "Lands, houses, negroes, &c." owned by British subjects in the plantation colonies were also subject to seizure in cases of debts owed to the king or his successors. Despite this, Mansfield determined that Stewart could not force Somerset to return to Jamaica against his will. If an enslaved person absconded while resident in the mother country and had not committed a criminal offense, English common law disallowed their forcible recapture and deportation.

Mansfield's narrow judgment in *Somerset* did not outlaw slavery in England. Nonetheless, his ruling made it virtually impossible for enslavers to retain their grip on bondspeople who fled enslavement in the metropole. In his determination, Mansfield pronounced slavery "so odious that nothing can be suffered to support it but positive law." And no such law existed in England. Still, aware of the economic value of coerced African labor in the plantation colonies, Mansfield subsequently tried to limit the implications of his ruling. He noted that his determination related only to James Somerset, an individual enslaved man, and went "no further than that the master cannot by force compel him to go out of the kingdom." But his ruling produced a sea change in the treatment of enslaved freedom seekers. It essentially rendered slavery unconstitutional in England, thereby shifting the blame for the institution onto American and Caribbean shoulders. "Lord Mansfield," claimed the chief justice's nineteenth-century biographer, "first established the grand doctrine that the air of England is too pure to be breathed by a slave."

The press disseminated the *Somerset* decision to nearly every corner of the British Atlantic world. It emboldened British and American abolitionists and inspired enslaved individuals in the colonies to flee in anticipation of ultimately reaching English soil. The language in Mansfield's ruling, as one British commentator remarked, "is remarkably strong against the slavery of negroes, and every other new slavery attempted to be introduced into England." This interpretation caught on like wildfire, and Granville Sharp and other abolitionists encouraged its spread. The *Somerset* verdict influenced a wave of similar legal cases brought by enslaved individuals against their masters and mistresses, including in Scotland. The 1778 case *Knight v. Wedderburn* established that, by default, Scottish law also disallowed forcible recapture of bondspeople and hence slavery itself. Joseph Knight, enslaved in Jamaica since childhood, had escaped from his master, John Wedderburn, after relocating with him to Scotland. The Court of Sessions, Scotland's highest court, considered the question of whether Wedderburn had the right to compel Knight's return. After much debate, the justices ruled in Knight's favor, extending legal protections to enslaved freedom seekers across Britain.

Colonial critics pointed out that the slavery question was hardly cut-and-dried. More than a century of Crown and parliamentary support for the transatlantic slave trade undermined the British state's claims of innocence. Encouraged by royal authorization and acts of Parliament, British subjects had invested in the hazardous business of human trafficking and African bondage, both domestically and in the plantation colonies. Now, it seemed, any enslaved person with the means to sue for their freedom could do so in Britain—and win. This jurisdictional quagmire enraged colonial American and Caribbean commentators.

Benjamin Franklin scoffed at the notion that Britons were blameless. Britain continued to dominate and profit from the transatlantic slave trade "while it piques itself on its virtue, love of liberty, and the equity of its courts in setting free a single negro." In his retort, the Jamaican planter Edward Long detailed the extensive historical links between the monarchy and the transatlantic slave trade, originating with Elizabeth I and escalating with the Stuarts' launch of the Royal African Company. In

1712, he noted, Parliament had become entangled as well when it stated that the trafficking of "Negroes" to the plantation colonies at reasonable rates was "highly beneficial to this kingdom" and "ought to be open to all the king's subjects." Parliament determined that the Crown, with public funds, should maintain Britain's African coastal forts for the nation's benefit. The historical record plainly evidenced the culpability of the British monarchy, government, and people for the perpetuation of slave trading and colonial slavery.

The *Somerset* decision provoked an outcry among enslavers and incited Black activism and unrest that overlapped with the unfolding conflict between the American colonies and the British government. But nothing alarmed colonial slaveholders more than the emancipatory policies of the British military during the Revolutionary War. Indeed, for the hundreds of thousands of individuals held in bondage in Britain's Atlantic empire, slavery was anything but academic or metaphorical. Enslaved people working in sugarcane fields, or on tobacco, rice, indigo, and cotton plantations, faced grueling labor conditions, inadequate food, shelter, and clothing, and high morbidity and mortality rates. They had no control over their bodies, children, or relationships and could be separated from loved ones at a moment's notice. Tasked with field, domestic, and reproductive labor, and subject to sexual abuse, enslaved women bore the brunt of slavery's most dehumanizing aspects. Given the brutal conditions of bondage, enslaved people embraced the opportunity to turn the conflict between the British Crown and its American subjects to their advantage—just as American and British military leaders and officials sought to use them in return.

Because opportunities for enslaved people to serve in the Continental Army were strictly limited, those seeking freedom primarily fled to, supported, and fought alongside the British. They did so even before the British army announced its official emancipatory recruitment policy. Rebel fears that enslaved individuals were motivated by a thirst for vengeance worked to Britain's advantage on the ground. British military officials viewed ad hoc wartime emancipation as a means to a specific end: the preservation of Britain's Atlantic slave empire. Moving forward without Crown approval, Virginia's royal governor, Lord Dunmore, formed the

Royal Ethiopian Regiment, which boasted hundreds of escapees wearing uniforms inscribed with the phrase "Liberty to slaves" by the fall of 1775. Neither George III nor Lord North, the prime minister, ordered other military commanders in the field to emulate Dunmore. But thousands of enslaved and free people of African descent nonetheless flocked to the British banner, leading to the formation of informal companies of Black pioneers. To his superiors, Captain William Dalrymple of the Twentieth Regiment of Foot praised enslaved and free African Americans born in the Chesapeake as a potential asset to Crown forces.

While George III and his ministers failed to embrace Dunmore's emancipatory strategy as their own military policy, they took the presence of enslaved people into consideration while plotting the course of the war. The king's cabinet pushed for an expedition against the middle and southern slaveholding colonies, which, "from the great number of their Negro slaves, and the small proportion of white inhabitants," made them vulnerable targets. Demographic imbalances and racial anxieties arising from slavery could serve the Crown's cause. In several of the middle and southern colonies, ministers surmised from Whitehall, the laboring people "from whence the soldiery can only be procured is chiefly composed of Negroes, whom the new states justly esteem so many intestine enemies, and therefore will not trust them in arms." Rebels in the slaveholding colonies shuddered at the prospect of arming their majority enslaved populations. Who then was left to defend these territories from British forces?

Familiar with the local terrain, eager to engage in battle for freedom, and, in some case, veterans of African wars, the enslaved offered benefits to the military commanders on both sides who embraced their service. But their valuable contribution to the war effort called into question the racial assumptions of supposed Black inferiority that Europeans and Euro-Americans had used to justify African enslavement for centuries. It also posed risks to a plantation system reliant upon the permanent, hereditary bondage of Africans. Britons as well as Americans understood these risks. In 1778, during a debate in the House of Commons over the North ministry's conduct of the war, Edmund Burke condemned the British military's policy of arming enslaved Africans. He warned of "the horrible consequences that might ensue from constituting 100,000 fierce barbarian slaves, to be both the judges and executioners of their masters." If

Figure 14.2. Detail, *Soldiers in Uniform.* Jean Baptiste Antoine de Verger, 1781.

enslaved men aided the British to crush the Americans, Burke predicted, then a race war would inevitably follow and "another massacre ensue." Lord North, defending Dunmore's emancipatory strategy, retaliated that he had never intended former bondsmen and -women to murder their former enslavers, "but only to take up arms in defense of their sovereign." The British government pressed forward cautiously with the tactical employment of enslaved individuals in the Crown's name during the Revolutionary War. That the rebel commanders, driven by necessity, gradually relaxed their initial policy of blanket opposition to arming bondspeople alleviated at least some concerns in London. In 1779, George Washington, desperate for manpower, accepted a proposal to raise a regiment of enslaved men from Rhode Island. In exchange for releasing bondsmen for military service, their masters received compensation from the public purse. But Washington opposed a more ambitious proposal to arm several thousand enslaved Black men in South Carolina and Georgia, judging the plan too risky. As the conflict dragged on and the supply of white manpower decreased, however, the rebels begrudgingly followed the British example. Revolutionary commanders recruited emancipated individuals of African descent from New England down to the Chesapeake. Historians estimate that, across multiple states, roughly five thousand enslaved and free Blacks enlisted and fought for liberation on the side of the American rebels. African American veterans who survived the war later applied for pensions from the United States government.

In comparison, tens of thousands of individuals of African descent joined George III's cause, constituting up to a quarter of the British force. In 1778, after Dominica fell to the French, the recruitment of free and enslaved Blacks to defend the Caribbean colonies began in earnest. Colonial and British authorities put enslaved men and women to work building fortifications and serving as sailors, pioneers, soldiers, nurses, and foragers. The governor of Jamaica created a regiment of free men of African ancestry with the full support of militia commanders, though the Jamaica assembly harshly criticized his decision. Brigadier General Edward Mathew, stationed at St. Lucia, procured thousands of enslaved soldiers from Charleston and multiple islands, forming what became the British Caribbean's first permanent Black army regiment.

The engine of Britain's Atlantic slave empire, the sugar islands contributed a key source of revenue to the British Crown. To a near universal extent, Britain's Caribbean colonies were dominated demographically by enslaved people of African origin and ancestry. They also relied on Britain for military support, manufactured goods, and incoming slaving vessels bearing replacements for their overworked and brutalized pool of coerced laborers. Exposed to external threats from foreign enemies and outnumbered internally by hostile enslaved populations, the Caribbean colonies remained loyal to Britain throughout the Revolutionary War. They had little choice.

The value of the Caribbean sugar islands to Britain assured a heightened level of defense from the Crown. During George III's lifetime, a stream of Caribbean planters had returned to the mother country, flaunting their newfound slavery-derived wealth, social prominence, and political connections. The king may have disapproved of the absentees' gauche behavior, but his government needed their sugar revenues. "Sugar, sugar, eh? All that sugar! How are the duties, eh, Pitt, how are the duties?" George is said to have remarked to William Pitt the Younger as a Jamaican planter passed by in his opulent carriage during the king's visit to Weymouth. After France and then Spain moved beyond providing clandestine aid to the Americans in 1778, allying formally with Britain's rebellious colonial subjects, George received intelligence that his Caribbean colonies faced extreme risk. "The object now is to make a serious attack upon the English West India Islands, to conquer them," he noted. Equally aware of the lucrative nature of slave-produced sugar, other European powers knew Britain's sugar islands commanded a high value as prizes.

From London, George and his ministers strategized about how best to protect the Caribbean colonies from French and Spanish designs. "Our islands must be defended even at the risk of an invasion of this island," the king wrote to the First Lord of the Admiralty in September 1779; "if we lose our sugar islands it will be impossible to raise money to continue the war." The king voiced particular concern about Jamaica and Barbados, the two most valuable slave colonies belonging to the British Empire. "Troops must be sent sufficient to secure Jamaica and Barbados, the capital islands belonging to this island," he urged; "we must run any risks rather than not secure them if in addition to this it can be found practicable to undertake any attack on St. Domingue it would be highly desirable." As the king reminded his military commanders, "it is by bold and manly efforts nations have been preserved, not pursuing alone the line of home defense." Keeping Britain's Atlantic slave empire intact was worth the heavy price.

Three years into the Revolutionary War, the king demonstrated his commitment to the cause by sending his third son, Prince William (the future William IV), to sea as an entry-level midshipman in the Royal Navy. Convinced the loss of the American colonies would sink Britain's global reputation and persuade Canada and the sugar islands to follow suit, George III devoted everything he had to winning the war—including his own son. George believed that a naval career—a "noble profession"— would prove the making of William, then age fourteen. He insisted the prince submit obediently to the duties of a humble midshipman, receiving "no marks of distinction." William, like other members of the Royal Navy, was expected to serve the king valiantly and bring honor and glory to the British Crown. Of course, the conduct of the king's son mattered infinitely more than that of other sailors. "Though when at home a prince," the king advised William, "you are only a boy learning the naval profession; but the prince so far accompanies you that what other boys might do, you must not." George trusted his third son would remember his royal duty.

Prince William's naval enlistment during the conflict with America inspired popular ballads praising him as Britain's "bulwark in war." "He's royal, he's noble, he's chosen by me; Britain's isle to protect and reign prince of the sea," affirmed the author of "The Royal Sailor."

In June 1779, William joined the warship *George* and spent the first years of his service in European waters attached to the Channel Fleet. In 1781, he proceeded to the coast of North America under Admiral Robert Digby's command, remaining primarily in New York, before transferring to *Warwick* under Lord Howe and cruising the Caribbean. He arrived in Port Royal, Jamaica, in February 1783 to great fanfare. Despite his father's wishes that William should receive no special favors, the planter elite treated Prince William in a manner befitting an esteemed royal guest. His naval service would have a lasting impact on the future monarch and shape his views of Britain's Atlantic slave empire and the institution of slavery.

As the only member of the royal family to visit British North America and the Caribbean, Prince William gained unique insight into the limits of Crown authority in its overseas dominions. He also witnessed firsthand the extent to which British subjects in the Caribbean colonies had established plantation societies built on enslaved labor. In September 1781, upon arriving in British-occupied New York City, William saw loyalists calling out "God bless King George!" At the same time, he noticed the empty pedestal that had once displayed his father's statue before rebels melted it down to make bullets. When word spread of the teenaged prince's presence in New York, American military commanders spotted an opportunity. In March 1782, George Washington praised a scheme proposed by Colonel Matthias Ogden to capture Prince William and Admiral Digby and convey them to the Continental Congress. After Washington's sources informed him that the British had surrounded the prince with extra sentries, he abandoned the abduction plot.

Prince William's time spent being wined and dined in Jamaica at the close of the Revolutionary War, shortly after the arrival of slaveholding loyalists fleeing revolutionary America, proved eye-opening. He glimpsed

a British colonial slave society firsthand and luxuriated in Caribbean hospitality. In the spring of 1783, he also briefly visited two other colonial
slave societies: Cape Français in French Saint-Domingue and Havana in
Spanish Cuba. These formative experiences molded William into a fierce
proponent of African trafficking and hereditary bondage. Jamaican planters expressed their gratitude to the prince, informing him that "your presence in Jamaica at this crisis, is highly acceptable to his Majesty's faithful
subjects. Threatened as we have been by the machinations of powerful and
ambitious enemies, we behold in your person, the future champion for
the liberties of mankind." The Jamaican planters certainly did not have
the liberties of enslaved people in mind when they lauded the prince.
Neither did William when he responded: "I am truly sensible of the polite
attention that has been shown to me from the hour of my arrival. I view
the island of Jamaica with infinite satisfaction; and the advantages I find
it yields to the mother country, must, from duty as well as inclination,
forever claim my best wishes." In time, slaveholders in Jamaica would
discover they had gained a valuable ally in the young prince. The prince
provided royal approval and respectability to the pro-slavery cause as public opinion in Britain turned against it with intense force.

Throughout the entirety of the Revolutionary War, George III refused
to imagine a future in which the American colonies gained their independence from Britain. To the very last, he held that conceding to the
Americans "would annihilate the rank in which the British Empire stands
among the European states." Losing a costly war against his own subjects
would wreck his personal reputation as Britain's sovereign and dim the
glory and dignity of the institution that he embodied. George bullied his
ministers into continuing the war and insisted the Americans would soon
yield. But the defeat of British troops at Yorktown ultimately forced his
hand. On February 4, 1783, after negotiating peace terms with America,
France, and Spain, he declared a formal end to hostilities with America.
His former subjects had rejected his rule and severed his Atlantic slave
empire in two. The king, dumbfounded by the immensity of the loss and
its expense, never fully recovered from the blow.

For the close to twenty thousand enslaved people of African descent,
including women and children, who had escaped to British camps across

North America in pursuit of freedom, the end of the war brought great uncertainty. Contemporary estimates suggest that about half of these individuals—referred to as "Black loyalists"—chose to depart revolutionary America alongside British loyalists and soldiers. The Black loyalists joined a total of approximately sixty thousand loyalist individuals who departed North America for other regions of the British Empire. As Crown forces evacuated from the British-controlled seaports of New York City, Charleston, Savannah, and Saint Augustine, they facilitated the dispersal of the loyalists throughout the Anglo-Atlantic world. About five thousand Black loyalists, mostly male, emigrated to Britain, landing primarily in London. The rest headed north to seek opportunities in frigid Nova Scotia, or south to subtropical Jamaica and the Bahamas in the company of white loyalist slaveholders and their bondsmen and -women, or even farther afield across the Atlantic to establish the colony of Freetown, in Sierra Leone.

Everywhere they went, Black loyalists confronted a myriad of obstacles related to their status as marginalized refugees of war and free subjects of the Crown descended from enslaved ancestors. Local conditions and attitudes in their new host societies shaped their diversity of experiences after the war. Yet all faced challenges and hardships in a British imperial world sustained by enslavement and lines of distinction based on race. The individuals who ended up in the British capital, within striking distance of George III himself, found a community of free people of African descent numbering ten thousand on the low end of estimates. Concentrated in the East End, London's growing free Black community offered a lifeline to newly arrived, disoriented Black loyalists. Disembarking in the capital of the British Empire with nothing but the clothes on their backs and promises of liberation, Black loyalists confronted a British public and government unprepared to welcome or assist them, a handful of abolitionists excepted.

CHAPTER 15

ABOLITION AND THE
SONS OF AFRICA

One day in the fall of 1786, George, Prince of Wales, received an unexpected delivery at Carlton House, his residence in London. It came from Quobna Ottobah Cugoano, a free Black man, one of approximately forty-two hundred individuals of African descent then living in London. The parcel contained several published works focused on the cruelty of the transatlantic slave trade and the appalling treatment of enslaved people in Britain's Caribbean colonies. The accompanying letter, signed "John Stuart," Cugoano's alias, implored the heir to the throne to peruse the enclosed "little tracts" and "consider the case of the poor Africans who are most barbarously captured and unlawfully carried away from their own Country and cruelly enslaved by many under the British Government." African captives, Cugoano emphasized, "are treated in a more unjust and inhuman manner than ever known among any of the Barbarous Nations in the World." At the time, Cugoano worked as a domestic servant for the fashionable portrait painters and miniaturists Maria and Richard Cosway, who lived two blocks from the prince's Carlton House residence. Employment in the household of Richard Cosway, principal painter to the Prince of Wales from 1785, granted Cugoano regular, direct access to aristocrats, artists, and politicians. Cugoano used his position in proximity to influential Britons and members of the royal family to full advantage to further the cause of abolition.

A fortuitous stroke of luck found Cugoano, a former enslaved man, living down the street from the Prince of Wales during the early years of the grassroots movement to abolish the British slave trade. The Cosways, "set afloat by royalty on the full tide of good fortune," as one observer put it, occupied the central apartment of Schomberg House at No. 88

Pall Mall. Previously owned and renovated by the Irish artist John Astley, No. 88 featured a bright attic studio with a large three-light window overlooking St. James's Park and grand, ornately decorated drawing rooms in which the very best of London high society regularly assembled. Thomas Gainsborough, the leading portrait artist in England in the late eighteenth century and a favorite painter of George III, lived in the western wing of Schomberg House, next door to James Christie's famous auction rooms. The concentration of artists and galleries in the neighborhood had transformed Pall Mall into a flourishing upscale center for art and entertainment. Maria Cosway, a woman of musical and artistic abilities famed for her blue eyes and abundance of golden curls, hosted popular weekly salons and Sunday concerts "sanctioned by his Royal Highness the Prince of Wales, and some of the highest fashionables of the day." Schomberg House's formal back gardens stretched south nearly to the border of the Carlton House Gardens, heightening the strategic social value of No. 88 for the Cosways—and Cugoano.

Raised from humble circumstances to opulence, Richard Cosway reveled in his newly acquired standing as a royal artist, and the presence of Ottobah Cugoano in his household only enhanced Cosway's status. His extravagant lifestyle and "ridiculously foppish" clothing earned him the title of the "Macaroni Miniature Painter." Cosway spent a fortune outfitting No. 88 to attract and impress London's upper echelon as they visited for portrait sittings and entertainment. He filled his public rooms with elaborate decorations and sumptuous furniture, including a carved and gilded sitter's chair, befitting his position as the official court painter to the Prince of Wales, an heir apparent widely considered the most conceited and profligate man in Britain. To trumpet his elevated social standing, Cosway attired Cugoano, his Black personal servant, in flamboyant bespoke livery. According to Cosway's earliest biographer, Cugoano performed his duties at Schomberg House in one of two vivid costumes: crimson silk trimmed with lace and gold buttons or plush Genoese crimson velvet—the latter outfit absurdly reminiscent, critics sneered, of the footmen at the Vatican.

Ottobah Cugoano likely entered Richard Cosway's service through informal London social networks or a newspaper advertisement. In Georgian Britain, royals and prominent Englishmen often employed Black manservants, particularly in the public roles of butler and valet, due to their association with the riches of Britain's Atlantic slave empire. Nobles and aspiring members of the professional classes followed the lead of George I, George II, and the sons of George III, all of whom retained Black servants. A highly visible symbol of their employer's wealth and prestige, servants of African descent engaged by great men typically engaged in light domestic duties. They served at table, answered the door, delivered calling cards and messages, and ran errands dressed in highly distinguishable livery.

John Montagu, the 4th earl of Sandwich and First Lord of the Admiralty from 1771 to 1782, employed a Black valet for many years named James, to whom he left a small bequest in his will as a reward for loyal service. Retaining Black attendants ran in his family. In a portrait of the Montagues by William Hogarth dating from the 1730s, an unnamed young Black attendant dressed in green and red livery holds out a silver tray to the gathered party. Admiral George Brydges Rodney, a well-known British naval hero, sent his unnamed "faithful African" on numerous odd jobs around London, like delivering messages to the Prince of Wales. The anonymous Black servant reportedly attended Lord Rodney on his deathbed. Surviving Georgian records and portraits indicate that domestic servants of African origin and ancestry were, as the scholar Gretchen Gerzina remarks, "silent witnesses to and participants in eighteenth-century English life."

Fortunately, however, not all Black Georgian servants remained silent. An African born in 1729 on a slave ship departing Guinea bound for the Spanish Caribbean, the musician and epistolary writer Ignatius Sancho was brought to England as a child and later educated and employed by the powerful Montagu family after he escaped slavery. Through his subsequent promotion to the position of valet for George Brudenell, the duke of Montagu, who served as captain of Windsor Castle and governor of the Prince of Wales and duke of York, Sancho gained access to the royal family and an elite circle of contacts. In 1768, he even had his portrait painted by the king's preferred artist, Thomas Gainsborough. After Sancho left the Montagu household in 1773, he opened a successful grocery shop in Westminster, which enabled him to become the first person of African descent to vote in a British general election, and he achieved minor celebrity status as the first Black composer to publish his music in Britain. Following Sancho's death in December 1780, his friends collected and published two volumes of his correspondence in 1782, with the intention of "shewing that an untutored African may possess abilities equal to an European." At the same time, Sancho's biographer, Joseph Jekyll, characterized him as an "extraordinary Negro," undercutting the broader impact of his life and example as a successful, multitalented Black Briton.

Sancho's *Letters* were well received by the British public, and he posthumously became the most celebrated Afro-Briton of his day. His published correspondence mostly sidestepped contentious topics, including African trafficking and enslavement, "a subject that sours my blood." Sancho's professed support for the monarchy enhanced his popular appeal. "His majesty, God bless him!" Sancho wrote. "It is too much the fashion to treat the royal family with disrespect—zeal for politics has almost annihilated good manners." Expressed in a letter to the son of a London bookseller in 1778, Sancho's limited remarks about the slave trade capture his hesitancy to accuse the British people or king of wrongdoing. "I am sorry to observe," he lamented, "that the practice of your country (which as a resident I love—and for its freedom—and for the many blessings I enjoy in it—shall ever have my warmest wishes—prayers—and blessings); I say it is with reluctance, that I must observe your country's conduct has been uniformly wicked in the East—West Indies—and even on the coast of Guinea." Regrettably, he concluded, "the grand object of English navigators—indeed of all Christian navigators—is money—money—money—for which I do not pretend to blame them." Sancho held Christian Europeans in general accountable for encouraging "petty kings" in West Africa to engage in warfare to sell their rivals' captured subjects into slavery. He carefully avoided laying the sin of slavery solely at the feet of Britons or their monarch.

To a lesser extent than Ignatius Sancho, Ottobah Cugoano also left behind a paper trail. What little we know about his background before he entered the employment of the Cosways comes from his own words, recorded in an abolitionist tract he published with assistance from London's free Black community in 1787. Born around 1757 in the Fante village of Agimaque on the coast of present-day Ghana, Cugoano described how his innocent and carefree childhood ended abruptly at the age of thirteen when slave traders raided his village. He and roughly twenty other Fante adolescents were kidnapped, marched in chains to a coastal fort, and forced aboard a slave ship. Over the following weeks, his enslavers conveyed Cugoano and his terrified companions in "a state of horror and slavery" across the Atlantic, ultimately disembarking in Grenada. Cugoano remained enslaved on the British island for nearly two years toiling in a "slave-gang" until his master, Alexander Campbell, a Grenadian sugar planter, brought Cugoano with him on a trip to England in late 1772.

Cugoano and Campbell arrived in London only months after Chief Justice Lord Mansfield's widely publicized decision in the *Somerset* case declaring it illegal for enslavers to recapture enslaved runaways in England and compel them to return to the plantation colonies. Runaway advertisements in newspapers confirm that hundreds of bondsmen and -women fled their enslavers in eighteenth-century Britain prior to Mansfield's narrow ruling in Somerset's favor. However, Mansfield's comments that "no master ever was allowed here to take a slave by force to be sold abroad" generated shock waves that reverberated across the country and throughout the British Atlantic. Many people at the time, including colonists who had returned home with enslaved attendants and members of London's Black community, misinterpreted the ruling as a tacit emancipation for all enslaved persons resident or touching upon English soil.

Cugoano claimed his freedom soon after arriving in London, though it is unclear if he simply took flight into the crowded streets of London or if his master turned him out in the wake of the *Somerset* decision. The first possibility is more plausible. Years later, in 1790, Cugoano's former master, Campbell, testified as a pro-slavery witness before a committee of the House of Commons. Based on his public defense of slavery, it's unlikely that he would have released Cugoano from bondage willingly. Regardless of how he became free, Cugoano, a vulnerable Fante youth lacking kin or connections, must have feared for his personal safety. On August 20, 1773, on the advice of "some good people," Cugoano was baptized as "John Stuart" (also spelled "Stewart" or "Steward") at St. James's Church, Piccadilly. He strategically adopted an Anglo-Christian identity, he explained, so that he "might not be carried away and sold again." While

Figure 15.1. *Richard Cosway, Maria Cosway and Ottobah Cugoano.*
Thomas Rowlandson, 1784.

Christian baptism would not have prevented his re-enslavement, Cugoano avoided using his real name in public from that point forward. "I have only put my African name to the title of the book," he acknowledged fourteen years later.

Over the next decade, Cugoano strengthened his ties with London's free Black community, learned to read and write in English, and became a devout Anglican. By 1784, he had entered the service of Maria and Richard Cosway. Cugoano was featured in an etching by Richard Cosway, which the prince regent later purchased, serving grapes to the couple in an idealized depiction of the Schomberg House gardens. While Cugoano spent his days and evenings working as a domestic servant, he devoted his spare time to the cause of abolition. He joined the former enslaved man and mariner Gustavus Vassa, better known as Olaudah Equiano, in a London-based group of more than two dozen Black political activists known as the Sons of Africa. Unknown at the time, Equiano would within a decade become the most renowned person of African descent in the British Atlantic world. The Sons of Africa was the first all-Black abolitionist organization and corresponding society composed of former enslaved men, sailors, soldiers, and loyalists who had supported Britain and George III during the American Revolutionary War. Throughout the mid- to late 1780s and 1790s, the Sons of Africa held meetings, networked with white activists, published abolitionist tracts, wrote letters to newspapers, and lobbied members of the royal family and Parliament to end Britain's transatlantic slave trade.

In the aftermath of the British Crown's loss of the North American colonies in 1783 came an influx of hundreds of Black loyalists into London. Desperate to defeat the American rebels and restore royal authority, British colonial administrators such as Lord Dunmore had promised liberty to bondsmen and -women who deserted their enslavers and served the loyalist cause in some capacity. Tens of thousands escaped from rebel plantations and took the British up on their offer. Some later carried written documentation, signed on George III's behalf, confirming their freedom in exchange for loyal service. Spreading insurrection and recruiting Black soldiers to fight for the king was a pragmatic wartime strategy characterized by on-the-spot decision-making and minimal royal oversight. "The British liberated to win a war, not promote emancipation," emphasizes historian Christopher Leslie Brown. After hostilities ceased, the British—with George III's support—felt obligated to honor their commitments and refused to return Black loyalist freedom seekers to their former American enslavers.

Vexing George Washington, George III approved of the evacuation of Black loyalists to Nova Scotia, the Caribbean islands, England, and beyond in the aftermath of the Revolutionary War. But Britain's king put little thought into the Black loyalists' future. Although they expected to be treated as free British subjects, Black loyalists arriving in London faced unemployment, public hostility, and crippling poverty. No social structures existed to help Black loyalists find work or receive charity. Granville Sharp, the abolitionist lawyer responsible for bringing about the *Somerset* ruling, reported his distress at seeing "the present set of unfortunate Negroes that are starving in our streets." The majority had arrived as seamen and "Royalists from America," after faithfully serving King George III, "and are thereby entitled to ample protection, and a generous requital," Sharp observed.

In January 1786, a voluntary committee formed to provide relief for London's Black poor and relocate those who were willing to migrate to the new West African settlement of Sierra Leone. Later that same year, Cugoano began tapping into his connections to prominent men and members of the royal family to further the cause of abolition. He recognized that Britain could not offer true security to free people of African descent while slave trading and hereditary racial bondage remained legal in the colonies. On July 28, Cugoano and another member of the Sons of Africa named William Greene contacted the celebrated abolitionist Granville Sharp to ask for legal assistance. They informed him that Samuel Jeffries, owner of a large sugar estate in Jamaica, had recaptured a former enslaved man, Henry Demaine, and carried him against his will aboard a ship set to embark for the Caribbean plantations. Cognizant that time was of the essence, Sharp acted without delay. He arranged for Demaine's release and reported Jeffries to the authorities less than three days later—and not a moment too soon. Rescued only minutes after the captain had ordered the ship's anchor raised and its sails unfurled, Demaine "confessed that he had intended to have jumped into the sea as soon as it was dark; choosing rather to die than be carried into slavery." The swift actions of Cugoano, Greene, and Sharp saved Henry Demaine from a cruel fate.

After all that he'd heard about Sharp from Equiano and the London newspapers, Cugoano must have been relieved that the lawyer remained committed to abolishing the transatlantic slave trade and preserving the fundamental rights of free Blacks on British soil. Praised repeatedly as an "indefatigable friend of mankind" by the Sons of Africa, Sharp was the obvious first choice to oppose the illegal seizure and attempted deportation of a former enslaved man. He had assisted the abolitionist cause on multiple occasions and served as a trusted point of contact between white abolitionists and London's Black community. Three years earlier, on March 19, 1783, Olaudah Equiano (Gustavus Vassa) had brought the now infamous case of the slave ship *Zong* to Sharp's attention. "Gustavus Vassa, a negro, called on me," Sharp recorded in his journal, "with an account of 130 negroes being thrown alive into the sea from on Board an

English slave ship." After investigating the incident, Sharp learned that in late 1781 the crew of *Zong*, a Liverpool-registered slave ship bound from Cape Coast, near Elmina, to São Tomé and then on to Jamaica, had committed mass murder, callously casting African captives "alive into the sea with their hands fettered." Sharp determined to assist Equiano, whom he later described as an "honest, sober man," to bring the perpetrators of the *Zong* massacre to justice.

According to eyewitnesses, this horrific incident occurred after *Zong* had entered the Caribbean Sea and a crew member spotted leaking water casks with Jamaica still roughly eight days' sailing time away. On an overcrowded slave ship, routinely subject to the ravages of disease, malnutrition, and violence, a water shortage could lead to devastating consequences. *Zong* had sufficient water for everyone on board for another week and a half, on full rations. But a navigational error resulted in the ship accidentally sailing past Hispaniola. This ill-timed discovery compounded the perils of the ship's position. Rather than rationing everyone's water while the ship sailed back to Jamaica, the crew threw 132 African men, women, and children overboard to drown. Filing an insurance claim for the loss of their human "cargo," the crew reasoned, was preferable to arriving with sickly, dehydrated captives who would fetch a poor price at the slave market. "If there be any necessity at all in the case," Sharp concluded, "it is the necessity (incumbent upon the whole nation) to put an immediate stop to the slave trade."

After Cugoano had helped to rescue Henry Demaine, he set his sights on a far more ambitious venture: striking at the root of African oppression by shutting down Britain's transatlantic slave trade. Accomplishing this herculean task, he knew, would require the Sons of Africa to influence and work with white abolitionists, members of Parliament, sympathetic nobles, and, most important, members of the royal family. Well placed at Schomberg House, a stone's throw from royalty, he sent letters to newspapers, wrote an account of his experiences as a victim of the British slave trade, and reached out twice to the Prince of Wales and once to George III to entreat them to back the abolitionist campaign. In personally appealing to the British monarch and wider royal family, Cugoano followed in the footsteps of generations of enslaved people in North America and the Caribbean who had petitioned the monarchy for relief from colonial oppression and equated the king with benevolence and liberty. He also followed the lead of abolitionists on both sides of the Atlantic who recognized the immeasurable value of royal endorsement, notwithstanding George III's lengthy track record of robust support for and defense of the slave trade and colonial slavery.

The first organized abolitionist efforts in Britain concentrated on moving Parliament to pass legislation against the transatlantic slave trade and encouraging George III and members of the royal family to publicly support the slaves' cause. As early as 1776, David Hartley, an MP for Hull sympathetic to the abolitionist cause, introduced a resolution in the House of Commons condemning the slave trade as "contrary to the laws of God, and the rights of men." He displayed shackles on the House's table to illustrate his point, but the motion was easily defeated. Years passed before abolitionists again challenged the trade politically. In 1783, London Quakers formed the first official anti-slavery committee in Britain and submitted a petition to the House of Commons calling for an end to the transatlantic slave trade.

The Quaker abolitionist Anthony Benezet, a founder of the American anti-slavery movement, sent a package to Queen Charlotte on August 25, 1783, nine months before his death. Along with a letter, he enclosed "some tracts which I believe faithfully describe the suffering conditions of many hundred-thousands of our fellow creatures of the African race." He urged Charlotte to attend to the tracts in hopes that she would support the abolitionist cause in favor of "so large a part of mankind." After Parliament rejected the first abolitionist petition, London Quakers printed some eleven thousand copies of Benezet's 1784 book, *The Case of Our Fellow Creatures, the Oppressed Africans*. Copies were sent to King George, Queen Charlotte, the Prince of Wales, and members of the clergy and both Houses of Parliament. The court painter Benjamin West, an American expatriate and former Pennsylvania Quaker, used his close association with the queen to present her with several more of Benezet's books on the slave trade later that year. Approaching the British royal family for their endorsement formed a critical component of transatlantic abolitionist strategy from the beginning.

Prior to contacting the Prince of Wales for assistance in 1786, Cugoano waited upon and observed the heir to the throne for many months as George sat for portraits and attended weekly concerts and social events at the Cosways' residence. The rhetorical strategy Cugoano adopted in his letters to the Prince of Wales suggests an intimate level of awareness of George's grandiose sense of self-importance as next in line to occupy the British throne. Sending a collection of anti-slavery tracts to Carlton House, Cugoano pressed the Prince of Wales to consider the African slave trade and bondage in light of his future historic legacy. "Should your Highness endeavor to release the oppressed and put a stop to that iniquitous traffic of buying and selling Men," he underscored, "all generous minds would admire you; the wise and virtuous would praise you . . . and your Name would resound with applause from Shore to Shore and in all the records of Fame be held in the highest Esteem throughout the Annals of time." Despite the superficial nature of their acquaintance, Cugoano seems to have understood that the Prince of Wales could only be maneuvered—if at all—by appeals to his vanity.

The following year, Cugoano sent the Prince of Wales a leatherbound copy of his newly published book, *Thoughts and Sentiments on the Evil and Wicked Traffic of the Slavery and Commerce of the Human Species*, the first anti-slavery text written by a former enslaved African in Britain. Noting that it contained the opinions of "an African against all manner of Slavery and oppression," Cugoano encouraged George to read and carefully consider what he, a Black man who had experienced the Middle Passage and enslavement in the British Atlantic empire firsthand, had written. He reminded the prince that Africans kidnapped and sold into slavery lacked official ambassadors "to demand restitution for the injuries which the Europeans have pursued against us"; therefore, "we can nowhere lay our case more fitly than at the feet of your Highness and if it meets with your approbation we have no doubt of your proving our Advocate."

By championing the righteous cause of oppressed Africans, "this meritorious act would rejoice the Hearts of all the true Sons of Liberty throughout your Royal Father's Dominions and it may be hoped in Days yet remote but in Gods good time that your Highness might thereby sway a greater and happier Empire than any British monarch did before." Although there is no record of George's response to Cugoano's passionate entreaties, he was not moved to join the abolitionists. But the Prince of

Wales did retain the original copy of Cugoano's *Thoughts and Sentiments* in his library at Carlton House. It is now held by the Royal Collection, a material reminder that the earliest abolitionists, including former enslaved individuals, tried—and failed—to secure the support of the current and future king of Britain for the slaves' cause.

Cugoano also sent a copy of his anti-slavery book to George III and the British statesman Edmund Burke, hoping that they "and all good Christians" would approve of his arguments against the trafficking, abuse, and enslavement of Africans. To persuade the king, he adopted a different tactic than the strategy he employed to appeal to the Prince of Wales. Cugoano must have assumed that persuading the British sovereign and head of the Church of England to back the cause of abolition necessitated an appeal to his sense of Christian duty and moral righteousness. "The cause of justice and humanity," Cugoano clarified, "are the only motives which induced me to those thoughts and sentiments on the evil of slavery with a view to the natural liberties of Men which your Majesty as a Sovereign will be pleased to support." George III, though maligned by the rebellious American colonists as a tyrant, had acquired a reputation in Britain, and particularly among members of the free Black community, as a just and enlightened monarch.

Yet even as Cugoano aimed to persuade George III to aid the abolitionists, his *Thoughts and Sentiments* lambasted British monarchs and other "kings of Europe" for establishing, defending, and continuing to reap profits from the transatlantic slave trade. For three centuries, European monarchs had permitted their subjects to buy and sell African captives as slaves and to compel them to labor without pay. Dismissing concerns about the sinfulness of the slave trade, Europeans justified its continuation by claiming that Africans would benefit from exposure to Christianity under benevolent white masters. But the slave system was the opposite of benevolent, Cugoano pointed out.

In the British Caribbean, most enslavers opposed the practice of religion among their bondspeople and treated them with extreme brutality. The widespread failure to instruct enslaved men, women, and children in Christianity gave the lie to the religious justification allegedly sanctioning African slavery. "Wherefore, if kings or nations, or any men that dealeth unjustly with their fellow-creatures, to ensnare them, to enslave them, and to oppress them, or suffer others to do so, when they have it in their power to prevent it, and yet they do not, can it ever be thought that God will be well pleased with them?" Cugoano questioned. Royal commitment to the Church and God's will surely did not entail fostering Britain's trafficking and oppression of African-descended people in perpetuity for naked financial gain.

The most radical anti-slavery text of its era, Cugoano's tract explicitly accused Britain's monarch of risking eternal damnation in exchange for national and personal profit. It articulated a bold attack on both the institution of the monarchy and on George III personally. White abolitionists avoided faulting the king or his royal predecessors for complicity in the slave trade, focusing instead on appeals to royal justice and mercy. But Cugoano pointed out what critics and supporters of the transatlantic slave trade understood equally: that Charles II had officially entered England into the "barbarous traffic" in Africans in the seventeenth century by granting a monopoly charter to the *Royal* African Company. The Stuart monarchs and their descendants had knowingly invested in an immoral slave-trading company that Cugoano described with distaste as "unworthy" of its historic association with the royal family. The king and his relations occupied the most exalted position in British society. Yet as the descendants and beneficiaries of England's first major investors in the transatlantic slave trade, George III and members of the royal family set a poor example for British subjects to emulate.

Cugoano knew the horrors of the Atlantic crossing and the suffering endured by Africans forced to labor in the British plantation colonies all too well. After experiencing bondage firsthand, he had faced precarity on the streets of London and years of domestic work in the homes of wealthy white elites. He had no intention of holding back his disgust for the British people and the sovereign who had profited from his enslavement and ignored the ongoing anguish and death of countless Africans. Britons involved in the transatlantic slave trade, Cugoano wrote, "traffic in the human species; and dreadful and shocking as it is to think, it has even been established by royal authority, and it is still supported and carried on by a Christian government." He cast blame for "such an exceeding evil and wicked traffic" not on slave traders or Caribbean planters alone but on "all of the inhabitants of Great Britain." Above all, the blame for the continued atrocities of slaving fell heaviest upon the shoulders of Britain's sovereign. "Kings and great men," Cugoano emphasized, may be "considered as more particularly guilty." Unless George III took decisive action, "preserving thousands of fellow sufferers from inevitable destruction," God would exact divine retribution on Britain's monarch and his complicit subjects. By demanding an end to British slave trading and the dismantling of the entire Atlantic slave system, Cugoano adopted a divisive stance eschewed by white abolitionists for another four decades. White abolitionists hesitated to push for full emancipation for both pragmatic and racially motivated reasons, maintaining that the enslaved were not yet ready for freedom. By contrast, Cugoano demanded an immediate end to Britain's trafficking and enslavement of Africans as well as their inclusion in the political community as free subjects. He launched the most direct assault on slavery of any writer in Britain at the time— whether Black or white. "But why should total abolition, and an universal emancipation of slaves, and the enfranchisement of all the Black people employed in the culture of the colonies, taking place as it ought to do, and without any hesitation, or delay for a moment, even though it might have some seeming appearance of loss either to government or to individuals, be feared at all?" he exclaimed. In the mid-1780s, few in Britain would have agreed with him.

While Cugoano's lone call for full and immediate emancipation fell on deaf ears, support for abolishing the British slave trade gained political and social traction in the late 1780s. Authors and activists of African descent played an increasingly critical role in shaping public opinion. At the time of its initial publication, Cugoano's *Thoughts and Sentiments* garnered minimal attention. However, the abridged second edition of his book, published in 1791, received the support of 168 subscribers, including aristocrats, politicians, and eminent artists, such as Sir Joshua Reynolds, Joseph Nollekens, James Northcote, and his employer, Richard Cosway, among others. Cugoano's connections and repeated appeals to London's elites had paid off.

Prior to his death, the date and cause of which remain unknown, he wrote to his friend and ally Granville Sharp to share his plans. Cugoano intended to open a school for young Afro-Britons in England and to recruit voluntary settlers for a second attempt to settle Black loyalists in Sierra Leone. Tragically, Cugoano disappeared from the historical record after 1791, before accomplishing either goal. The efforts of abolitionists and the Sons of Africa continued unabated. The movement Cugoano helped to ignite flamed anew and spread across Britain, soon reaching even the far corners of its Atlantic slave empire.

CHAPTER 16

A ROYAL DEFENSE

O n May 22, 1787, a London-based committee featuring evangelicals and Quakers connected to the 1783 abolition petition to Parliament, as well as the Anglican abolitionists Granville Sharp and Thomas Clarkson, founded the Society for Effecting the Abolition of the Slave Trade. "A society has lately been formed here for the purpose of opposing the slave trade," Sharp informed his brother, John. "Though the members are chiefly Quakers, I thought it my duty when invited to join them in so just a measure," he noted; "and I wish for the honor of the Church of England that some of our dignified clergy would subscribe to it." The London Abolition Society thus set out to mobilize public opinion against the transatlantic slave trade.

To initiate this task, Clarkson volunteered to travel around the country, distributing abolitionist books and pamphlets, forming provincial subcommittees, and gathering evidence about the cruelties of the trade. His first tour included the major slave ports of Bristol and Liverpool and the northern industrial towns of Manchester and Lancaster. Through Clarkson's efforts, the society built an extensive network of local and regional correspondents stretching across Britain. Clarkson helped to sow the seeds that gave rise to numerous provincial abolition committees responsible for organizing the largest mass petition campaign in British history.

As members of the London Abolition Society plotted their campaign, the Royal Academy of the Arts launched its annual summer exhibition at Somerset House, off London's Strand. Founded with the support of George III in 1768, the Royal Academy was independently run by its artist members but benefited from royal patronage. It functioned as a multipurpose school of learning, a major site of public art exhibitions, and

Figure 16.1. *The Exhibition of the Royal Academy.* Pietro Antonio Martini, 1787.

Figure 16.2. *George IV, when Prince of Wales, with a Black page.* Joshua Reynolds, 1786–87.

the foremost arbiter of artistic taste in Georgian Britain. The royal family attended previews of the academy's show every year at Pall Mall and Somerset House, enhancing the institution's national prominence. The 1787 show featured a full-length portrait of the Prince of Wales by Sir Joshua Reynolds, elected the first president of the Royal Academy, as the showcase of the exhibition. Although George III had knighted Reynolds in 1769 as a special mark of distinction to the academy, the king held no particular regard for the artist and rarely sat for him. By courting the heir to the throne instead, Reynolds had, perhaps unwittingly, irked the king and strained the academy's relations with the monarchy.

Reynolds's portrait of the Prince of Wales, awarded pride of place at the exhibition, served to advertise publicly the academy's visible association with the royal family. In the painting, the heir to the throne stands in his robes of the Order of the Garter while a young Black manservant reaches across George's waist to adjust his belt. The Prince of Wales dominates the portrait physically, towering over the unnamed Black attendant garbed in royal red and gold livery. Small in stature, the Black manservant faces away from the viewer, his facial features obscured in shadow. His attention is focused solely on the person of the Prince of Wales. Pale-skinned and rosy-cheeked, the heir apparent stands regally before a classical marble column; the ostrich feathers and clouds in the background accentuate both his whiteness and the extensive reach of the empire he will inherit. George takes no notice of either the Black page or the viewer. He stares off into the distance, secure in his privileged hereditary status as Britain's future monarch.

But the public response to Reynolds's portrait of the Prince of Wales undermined rather than enhanced royal dignity. George III delivered the first blow. When the king and queen, accompanied by several of the royal princesses, previewed the Royal Academy show, George III snubbed Reynolds's portrait of his eldest son. In the weeks that followed this initial embarrassment, the London press savaged it. The portrait, critics universally agreed, depicted the Prince of Wales as stiff and overly formal, slightly distorted, and effeminate. The inclusion of the Black manservant touching George's waist heightened the negative criticism. The Prince of Wales was mortified. Rather than temporarily smoothing over tensions between George III and his heir over the shocking state of the latter's finances, Reynolds's portrait, and the overwhelmingly critical response it elicited, increased the acrimony within the royal family.

Over the course of the previous year, the Prince of Wales had accumulated over £100,000 in unpaid debts while renovating his Carlton House residence. His father flatly rejected George's appeal for royal financial assistance. If the prince hoped to resolve his "present embarrassed and distressed situation," only one option remained: "appealing to the justice and generosity of the nation in Parliament." To George III's utter mortification, Britons were forced to bail out their future king. Initial press criticism of Reynolds's portrait of the Prince of Wales therefore drew overt connections between the unflattering depiction of George and the empty state of his royal purse. "At first sight, some singularities stand out—and catch immediately," remarked the *World*. "Amongst these is one of a *black robing the Prince of Wales*—on a supposition, we suppose, that from his humbled state he has no *white servant* left. His highness seems to take it very patiently, and the black is pushing him about as he pleases." Not long after the Royal Academy show opened, Parliament granted the Prince of Wales an unprecedented sum of £101,000 to cover his substantial debts.

His eldest son's inability to live modestly and set a suitable example of proper royal decorum infuriated George III. Dismissing the king's outrage, the prince preferred to describe his ballooning financial difficulties as "very misfortunate" but necessary. He justified his mounting expenses as essential to making Carlton House "more adapted to the residence of a Prince of Wales." George's notion of what made a residence suitable for an heir apparent differed dramatically from his father's. Indeed, his inability to pay his debts did not stop the Prince of Wales from accumulating numerous manservants, for example, including more than two dozen gentlemen of the bedchamber. Given this context, it is unsurprising that the *Morning Herald* and several other papers read the insertion of the Black attendant in the portrait as an allegorical satire about the Prince of Wales's humbled financial state and public shame. "The Prince is in his robes of State,—and a BLACK appears in the art of stripping them off." To be intimately disrobed by a Black servant signaled how far the heir to Britain's throne and overseas empire had fallen.

In April of the following year, Sir Joshua Reynolds wrote directly to the Prince of Wales. He reminded him that "the only picture that he has finished of His Royal Highness since the account last year, is a whole-length with a black servant which is still at his house, the price of that is two hundred Guineas." Predictably, the prince expressed no interest in purchasing his controversial portrait. He refused to discuss it further or view it again. The portrait remained in Reynolds's studio, ignored and unwanted, until the artist's death in February 1792. Nine months later, the Prince of Wales finally agreed to purchase the hated portrait of himself with the Black servant, as well as the only other copy, from Reynold's executors, for a total of £393.15s. He knew that purchasing both copies would prevent the reviled portrait from falling into the wrong hands, displayed to the viewing public in a London gallery for centuries to come. The original portrait is now housed in a private collection at Arundel Castle. As the Prince of Wales intended, it remains difficult to view in person or to reproduce publicly.

By February 1788, the efforts of the London Abolition Society to spread the word about the evils of the transatlantic trade in enslaved Africans had finally begun to bear fruit. Thomas Clarkson recounted how "there was among people a general feeling in behalf of the wrongs of Africa," resulting in public meetings and thirty-five petitions to Parliament from different regions of the country. In response to the "ferment in the public mind," George III ordered the Privy Council Committee for Trade and Plantations to investigate Britain's commercial relations with Africa and the slave trade. Word of the king's instructions spread to London's Black community. The Sons of Africa moved quickly, hoping to capitalize on the potential for government action against the slave trade. Olaudah Equiano offered to testify before the Board of Trade about the appalling conditions of British slaving vessels. But the board chose not to interview any former enslaved people.

Like other abolitionists before him, Equiano appealed directly to the British monarchy. On March 21, 1788, he petitioned Queen Charlotte to intercede with George III on behalf of his enslaved African brethren. "Your Majesty's well-known benevolence and humanity emboldens me to approach your royal presence, trusting that the obscurity of my situation will not prevent your Majesty from attending to the sufferings for which I plead," he wrote. "Yet I do not solicit your royal pity for my own distress; my sufferings, although numerous, are in a measure forgotten. I supplicate your Majesty's compassion for millions of my African countrymen, who groan under the lash of tyranny in the West-Indies." He signed his petition, "The oppressed Ethiopian."

The Queen, while receiving his appeal "most graciously," neither responded to nor acted upon Equiano's request. Her indifference did not deter him. Devoted to championing the cause of abolition, he wrote numerous letters to newspapers, to influential white abolitionists such as Granville Sharp, and to key members of government, including Prime Minister William Pitt and Sir William Dolben, MP for Oxford University and a vocal advocate for improving conditions on slaving vessels. "Many people felt the strength of his voice," observes historian Miles Ogborn, thanks to Equiano's near constant abolitionist efforts in person as well as print. To maximize his impact on the public, Equiano set to work writing his own autobiography as an African man subject to human trafficking and enslavement at the hands of the British. He described how, like his friend Ottobah Cugoano, he had endured "horrors of every kind" during the Middle Passage and bondage in the Atlantic plantation colonies, before ultimately securing his freedom and relocating to England.

On May 26, 1788, Sir William Dolben proposed a bill to regulate, for a limited trial period, the shipping and carrying of enslaved Africans in British vessels. Putting the general question of abolition aside for the moment, Dolben announced that the time had come for the House to remedy "a most crying evil": the cramped, inhumane conditions on slave ships. "When put on shipboard the poor unhappy wretches were chained to each other hand and foot and stowed so close," he explained, like "herrings in a barrel." Stuffing shackled captives together into tight, poorly ventilated spaces, with less than a foot and a half allotted per person, inevitably produced high rates of disease and death. If it acted promptly, Parliament could save thousands of lives. Dolben's measure outlined restrictions on the total number of enslaved individuals allowed on a British vessel in proportion to its tonnage. It also required ship captains to let fresh air into the underdecks, to distribute wholesome provisions to the captives, and to pay bonuses to the crew if less than 3 percent of enslaved Africans died on a transatlantic voyage.

Opposition to Dolben's proposed bill emerged immediately from Bristol and Britain's slaving capital, Liverpool. Liverpool merchants submitted multiple petitions protesting the imposition of any new restrictions on a "Branch of Traffic which has been carried on for more than Two Centuries." Encouraged by both the monarchy and Parliament, they maintained, investment in the African slave trade had accelerated Liverpool's

254 THE CROWN'S SILENCE

position as a leading British port for international trade, second only to London. The African Committee of Liverpool, dominated by powerful slave traders, strongly opposed Dolben's measure and made its hostility known to members of government. "In effect, My Lord, it involves the total ruin of the bulk of the African Commerce," wrote John Tarleton, a Liverpool chamber member and leader of the opposition movement, to Charles Jenkins, Lord Hawkesbury, president of the Board of Trade. "The attack through Sir William Dolben is so sudden and unlooked for, that I have only time to say at present it is determined here to give it every opposition in our power," concurred Samuel Green, secretary of the Liverpool African Committee. "The question is too great for so hasty a decision."

Dolben's timing was astute. His apprehensions about the human costs of the British government's neglect and inaction, despite the known cruelties of the slave trade, echoed the concerns of Britons across the country. What he proposed appeared sensible, measured, and timely. Despite multiple letters of protest from the agent for Jamaica and Liverpool merchants, who argued that the new legislation would imperil the £1 million Liverpool residents had invested in the slave trade and threaten to raise "great Commotions" in the British Caribbean colonies, both Houses passed the bill two months later. George III gave his royal assent to Dolben's bill to regulate slaving vessels on July 11, 1788. The king complained, however, to the British home secretary that the Commons had rushed the bill through too quickly, necessitating substantial corrections in the House of Lords. As Britain's sovereign and the pro-slavery interest saw it, the abolitionist reformers were trying to move too fast, too soon.

By the time Parliament reconvened in September 1788 after a two-month recess, George III had fallen ill. He would vacillate between states of lucidity and extreme mental instability for the next six months, throwing the political establishment into an uproar. On November 5, 1788, the first day the king's physicians described him as "deranged"—talking incessantly, unable to sleep, racing around the palace in his nightshirt, and shrieking until his voice grew hoarse—a note about George III's poor health appeared in the *Morning Herald*. Having caught wind of the king's status, the London press had begun spreading news of George's ill health to the public.

The "very indecent and improper" press coverage of the king's illness scandalized Queen Charlotte and the Prince of Wales. Prince George issued a warning to the media threatening to prosecute "with the utmost severity" any newspaper editor who dared to discuss his father's health without the royal family's permission. The tumultuous circumstances surrounding the so-called "madness" of George III have complicated the archival trail of royal involvement during the first year of the parliamentary slave-trade debate. Discussions of the king's mental state and future prospects, and the threat his inconsistent health posed to the nation and political order, dominate the surviving materials from fall 1788 and spring 1789 preserved in the Royal Archives at Windsor Castle.

Although Britain's king may have retained a quiet conviction from his youth of slavery's inherent sinfulness, George III was at core a deeply pragmatic ruler, committed above all to protecting his empire. Publicly, George kept his cards close to his chest. But his advisers and family members understood that his priorities lay with preserving and expanding British territorial acquisitions, wealth, and prestige, not with humanitarian campaigns. For the king, Britain and its interests came first; prudence would always triumph over sentiment. George III self-identified as an enlightened monarch and "a patron for Europe's civilizing mission." British worldwide expansion, and the simultaneous spread of British customs, manners, and legal traditions overseas, gave the king immense pride.

At the same time, the prospect of losing ground on the global map of imperial domination and, as he put it, "consequently falling into a very low class among the European states," kept George III up at night. While he avoided speaking his mind in public, the debate over the future of Britain's transatlantic slave trade mattered to the king because it threatened to jeopardize his long-term imperial ambitions. Losing the thirteen American colonies had already cleaved his Atlantic empire into two, increasing the strategic value of the Caribbean colonies. George III's strategy during the abolition debate is strikingly similar to the royal family's approach to the issue of slavery and racism more broadly in the centuries since his reign: protect the monarchy and its reputation; protect Britain and the British Empire; and, on record, say as little of substance as possible while positioning that silence as laudably apolitical.

While the mature George III avoided discussing the slave trade in public in the late 1780s and 1790s, and struggled with repeated bouts of mental illness, his third son, William, duke of Clarence, made his opinion widely known. The duke of Clarence fervently supported the continuation of the British slave trade and colonial slavery. On multiple occasions he proclaimed publicly that the transatlantic slave trade was necessary to sustain Britain's imperial strength and prosperity. More important, the duke defended the Atlantic slave system as humane. There is no evidence that the duke of Clarence, unlike his father, found African bondage morally repugnant, either as a young man or as an adult. He defended slavery because, in his words, he had seen it with his own eyes while serving in the Royal Navy and believed in the benevolence of the institution. As the only member of the royal family to set foot in North America and to witness plantation slavery firsthand in the British Caribbean, the duke claimed that his personal experiences gave him special insight.

Not long after he went to sea in 1779, Prince William informed George III that the Royal Navy had exposed him to many new sights and experiences, including corporal punishment. "I have seen the manners practiced in the world, and things begin to appear to me in a very different light from what I had seen them before. I have seen martial discipline kept up and the severity arising from it executed," he noted. Daily exposure to the strictness of military discipline, with harsh punishments inflicted for even minor infractions, desensitized Prince William to violence. He assumed enslaved people in the Caribbean were "comparatively in a state of humble happiness," well treated by British masters and far removed from the "gross barbarism of the Africans on the slave coast." In 1785, he was promoted to the rank of lieutenant and sent on a tour of the British Isles. Confident in his own views, he informed his father that the inhabitants of the Scottish Highlands "are in a more miserable state than the Negroes in the West Indies." Once, while complaining to George III about his lack of freedom in comparison to other young men, he accused his father of trying to "keep me under like a slave."

On April 10, 1786, Prince William received his commission to serve as captain of the twenty-eight-gun frigate *Pegasus*, under the command of Horatio Nelson. He sailed for the Americas, stopping first in Nova Scotia, and spent fifteen months stationed in the Caribbean. His last appointment on active service in the Royal Navy ended with the return of his frigate to England in April 1789. William's health had suffered during his years spent in the sugar islands. He succumbed to a series of debilitating fevers and contracted a painful case of gonorrhea. Both the prince and his doctor blamed the hot climate and petitioned George III for his return, but his father dismissed their concerns. But William's poor health did not prevent him from indulging in everything on offer in Caribbean slave society: elaborate dinners, drinks, cards and gambling, balls, and lechery. "I am sorry to say that I have been living a terrible debauched life, of which I am heartily ashamed and tired," he admitted to his older brother, the Prince of Wales, in October 1788. "I must in the West Indies turn over a new leaf, or else I shall be irrevocably ruined."

During William's visits to Jamaica in the late 1780s, colonial officials and the planter elite lavished the prince with praise and hospitality as a goodwill gesture of the island's loyalty to the Crown, just as they had done in 1783. Jamaican authorities trusted George III would take note of the warm reception given to his third son on the island and hold colonial Jamaica and the interests of its inhabitants in particular regard. As the mood of the British public soured against Caribbean slaveholders, Crown support for Britain's largest Atlantic slave colony remained vital. "The attention shown His Royal Highness, the Duke of Clarence, during his stay here has been highly pleasing to the King," Governor Clarke confirmed to the council and assembly; "and it will naturally incline His Majesty to be particularly attentive to the interests of his faithful and loyal subjects of this island." Jamaican slaveholders had found a dedicated and vocal advocate in Prince William, the duke of Clarence, whose political support lent royal legitimacy to their cause.

Soon after returning home from the Caribbean in the spring of 1789, Prince William made it his mission to defend the transatlantic slave trade. He sought to protect the livelihood of the Caribbean planters who had welcomed him into their homes and generated substantial annual revenue for Britain. Stephen Fuller, Jamaica's London agent, reported to the Jamaica House of Assembly that he was "dedicating the whole of my time to this important question," and he eagerly welcomed royal support. Confident George III and his family would side with the slave interest, Fuller arranged for copies of Jamaica's new Consolidated Slave Bill and reports of the assembly to be submitted to the king and royal family for their inspection. When, in 1790, Prince William was created duke of Clarence and entered the House of Lords, he declared his willingness to serve as a witness on behalf of the West Indian slaveholders. Knowing this, Fuller waited personally on their Royal Highnesses George, Prince of Wales; Frederick, duke of York (the king's second son); William, duke of Clarence (the king's third son); Ernest Augustus, duke of Cumberland (the king's fifth son); and William Frederick, duke of Gloucester (the king's nephew) to persuade the royals to vote as a block against abolition. All but the duke of Gloucester, who ultimately joined the abolitionists, pledged their support.

While the royal family gathered its forces to defend the slave trade behind the scenes, the Sons of Africa actively campaigned alongside the London Abolition Society to increase public awareness of the injustice and brutality of slavery. The most prominent Black activist in Britain at the time was Olaudah Equiano. In 1789, he published his autobiography, *The Interesting Narrative of the Life of Olaudah Equiano, or Gustavus Vassa, The African*, which sold out immediately. An instant popular success, the book flew through multiple editions and Equiano grew rich off the royalties. The *Interesting Narrative* recounted Equiano's remarkable life story as a young African boy kidnapped from modern-day Nigeria and sold into slavery at age eleven. He claimed he had labored on plantations in Barbados and Virginia, spent several years at sea enslaved under an officer of the Royal Navy, and eventually scraped together enough money to purchase his freedom. After working as a merchant and sailor, Equiano settled in England and joined the abolitionist cause. He traveled throughout Britain promoting his gripping account of slavery and campaigning against the transatlantic slave trade until his death, in March 1797.

While Equiano's distinctive, first-person perspective made an enormous impact on the public, no one in Britain had as much influence as George III or the members of the royal family. To win the monarchy's support was vital. Consequently, both sides of the slavery debate beseeched the king and his inner circle for their patronage. Months after the duke of York, the king's second son, married Princess Frederica Charlotte of Prussia at Buckingham Palace in November 1791, proponents of the West Indian sugar-abstinence campaign petitioned the newest royal to subscribe to the boycott. Supporters hoped to persuade the duchess of York, an authority on taste and fashion, to abstain from the use of Caribbean sugar in her own household, "not doubting," one commentator observed, "that the example of her royal highness would be followed by every person of rank in the kingdom"—including her husband. "Let sugar never be brought into your presence!" urged one commentator. "Let it be proscribed [in] your household, till its connection with fraud, robbery, and murder, be entirely broken! Engage on the same side your Royal Consort! He will not be able to resist solicitations directed to so worthy an object, and coming from you."

Better still, the example set by the duchess of York might influence King George and Queen Charlotte. "Her majesty, so famed for her private and domestic virtues, and her piety;—the King, whom his subjects gladly hail as the father of his people; but following the example of their amiable daughter-in-law, in discouraging a villainous trade, by rejecting the produce of it, will display their humility, as well as their humanity, and their other good qualities." Roughly three hundred thousand households across Britain participated in the West Indian sugar boycott of 1791–92, and much of the support for the campaign stemmed from women. Members of the royal family, while perhaps reducing their overall consumption levels, continued to partake of sugar produced by coerced labor. During the era of the boycott, the king and queen enjoyed numerous sweet fruit tarts (cherry was a particular favorite) while dining at Kensington Palace; and kitchen staff regularly purchased twelve pounds of "Lisbon sugar" and up to six pounds of "treble [refined] sugar" for the royal household.

Critics of the slave trade argued that it was the king's duty to exhibit moral leadership and call for the end of British participation in a cruel and evil traffic. If the king and members of the royal family rejected opportunities to champion the cause of oppressed Africans, what did their indifference say about Britain's national character and the dignity of its imperial project? "The protection of the oppressed, and the punishment or restraint of oppressors, is a task worthy of a great nation and an illustrious prince," claimed the author of one abolitionist tract. "Ending the slave trade furnishes ample matter for doing honor to the British people, Senate, and Crown, wiping off the infamy already contracted." Voluntarily acknowledging and rectifying historic wrongs would demonstrate the superiority

Figure 16.3. *Anti-Saccharrites, or John Bull and His Family Leaving Off the Use of Sugar.* James Gillray, 1792.

of Britain's constitutional monarchy. Yet the royal family routinely dashed abolitionists' hopes. As the chief beneficiaries of a centuries-old system of entrenched hereditary privilege, the royals distrusted any popular initiative that smacked of radicalism. They coordinated the opposition from behind the scenes and held their tongues publicly, refraining from openly assisting a movement that might prove detrimental to the monarchy's interests.

The British press took notice, and satirists did not spare the royal family. Even if the royals appeared to endorse a worthy cause—such as the boycott of West Indian sugar—the monarchy's support was mocked as apathetic at best. Produced in 1792, James Gillray's caricature of the royal family depicts Queen Charlotte's feeble attempts to persuade her six daughters to embrace unsweetened tea during the sugar-abstinence campaign. Displaying a mouth of rotten and missing teeth, Queen Charlotte urges the melancholy princesses to refrain from sugar. "You can't think how nice it is without sugar," she urges," and consider how much work you'll save the poor Blackamoors by leaving off the use of it!" "And above all," the queen continues, "remember how much expense it will save your poor Papa!" For King George, a notorious spendthrift, mock participation in the sugar boycott offered the ideal excuse to rein in royal household expenditure. Whatever seeming sympathy the monarchy displayed for the suffering of enslaved Africans, satirists hinted, the royals were wholly motivated by self-interest.

By the early 1790s, the abolitionist cause had gained significant traction across Britain. Hundreds of thousands of men and women across the social spectrum were calling for an end to the slave trade and rejecting the consumption of West Indian sugar and rum. But the momentum was short-lived. The anti-slavery movement became increasingly tainted by association with the blood spilled in revolutionary France and the unprecedented slave rebellion in Saint-Domingue. The storming of the Bastille in Paris and the attack on the French Crown and nobility struck terror into the hearts of Britain's aristocracy and royal family. For the pro-slavery faction, the violent upheavals of the French Revolution and related insurgency in France's most valuable Caribbean slave colony served as a cautionary tale about the dangers of fanaticism. Unchecked, idealism could plunge an entire country into carnage and instability, imperiling the welfare of its people, economy, and empire.

As Europe descended into crisis in the wake of revolutionary unrest in France and Saint-Domingue, proponents of slavery expressed a growing sense of frustration with the strength of abolitionist support among the British public. Popular enthusiasm for abolition of the transatlantic slave trade, they argued, stemmed from "a mistaken idea of humanity or to court popularity." Despite the British public's zeal for the abolition campaign, the first bill presented in the House of Commons in 1791 to end the British slave trade was defeated. In 1792, a second abolition bill proposing a gradual end to the trade passed the Commons but was subsequently defeated in the House of Lords. The duke of Clarence and his allies formed a voting bloc against the measure. The slaving interest consoled itself with the belief that the sole aim of the gradual abolition bill passed in the Commons was "to satisfy the popular frenzy against slavery" rather than effect actual change.

Writing to his brother John, a slave trader based in Kingston, Jamaica, Robert Taylor, a member of the West India interest, expressed his belief that the British government sought merely to placate the public rather than undermine the Atlantic slave system. "I'm very well satisfied that the present ministers, notwithstanding appearances, are no friends to the abolition," he explained, "and that they will favor the West Indian interest as much as they can, consistent with the attention that must be paid to public opinion." But in an era of profound revolutionary turmoil, public opinion could be mercurial. After Louis XIV and Marie Antoinette lost their heads to the guillotine's blade in 1793, and the Reign of Terror eviscerated the old regime in France, a wave of reactionary conservatism swept across Britain, engulfing the abolition movement. The campaign to end the transatlantic slave trade ground to a halt; abolitionists would not regain their previous momentum until the dawn of the new century.

George III held that the preservation of his kingdom's future security and the established order in Europe demanded a swift response to the French threat. Radicalism was contagious. Revolutionaries had hacked away at ancient European royal and aristocratic lineages and caused France to lose the most profitable slave colony in the world. "Every tie of religion, morality and society not only authorizes but demands" resistance to radical agitation in France and beyond, the king declared. As the abolitionists lost ground, William, the duke of Clarence, the strongest pro-slavery supporter of George III's sons, remained publicly active on behalf of the slaving interest.

On March 21, 1793, he presented two petitions in the House of Lords, one on behalf of the West India lobby and the other from the merchants of Liverpool, requesting a delay in the consideration of the slave trade. "William made a *most incomparable* speech on the slave trade," the Prince of Wales later wrote to his younger brother the duke of York. He gleefully described how William had convinced the Lords that the "principles of the abolition of the slave trade were synonymous and congenial to the general tenants of the [French] National Convention." His argument that promoters of abolition and French revolutionaries were one and the same thrilled slavery supporters. Expressing gratitude to the duke of Clarence specifically, the Jamaica assembly noted how much the colony appreciated "his indefatigable exertions, and very able and spirited arguments in our support, in the debate in the house of lords on this bill, which, in a very great measure, contributed to its rejection."

Jamaica's slaveholding interests delivered several addresses of thanks to their royal patron and presented the duke of Clarence with expensive gifts. These included a star set in diamonds and a silver plate service commissioned by the Jamaica House of Assembly from Rundell and Bridge, the Royal Goldsmiths, the latter of which remains among the Royal Collections. He dined by invitation at the club of the Jamaican absentee planters in London and attended meetings of the West India lobby. Authors of pro-slavery tracts dedicated their books to the duke of Clarence, "in testimony of the justice and ability which His Royal Highness has already manifested upon that important question." Both the royal family and abolitionist leaders were aware of his connection to the pro-slavery faction and leadership in the House during the slavery debate. In the spring of 1792, his sister Augusta Sophia sent him a present of a fine writing desk, "on which I think you may place your papers on the Slave Trade." Thomas Clarkson later recalled with not a little bitterness how abolition faced "considerable opposition" in the Lords, spearheaded by the duke of Clarence and, to a lesser extent, his royal brothers.

The pro-slavery lobby praised the duke as the royal face of their cause, and he was widely regarded as a formidable enemy of abolition. Indeed, several Liverpool captains christened their slaving vessels *Duke of Clarence* in his honor. Yet some suspected the stance of the king's third son on the slave trade originated with a more illustrious source. Writing to the Jamaica assembly in March 1795, the Jamaica agent Stephen Fuller commented that the West India interest owed more to George III than they realized. "His Majesty is a true friend to the colonies. I am of opinion we owe more to him than is generally known in regard to the defeat of the absurd attempt of abolishing the Slave Trade, which I think we will hear no more of." Fuller's instinct was correct. George III ensured that his ministers did not sponsor abolition as a cabinet measure, a point confirmed by a speech the duke of Clarence delivered in the House of Lords. "The Bill was not a Cabinet measure," he observed, "nor was it an object of ministers to support it as a measure of administration." While George III refrained from battling over the slave trade in public, he prevented Crown officials from supporting the cause of abolition.

The king's sustained opposition to abolition was evident in his displeasure with Prime Minister William Pitt the Younger, who had emerged as a great critic of the transatlantic slave trade. Pitt was easily led by others, George III told Henry Dundas, secretary of state for war and the colonies. Dundas had introduced resolutions for a gradual abolition of the slave trade as a means of thwarting calls for immediate abolition. Rather than acting in concert with the Crown on important matters such as the question of the slave trade, the king maintained, Pitt blindly succumbed to the influence of radicals. "I am certain he has all along sided with us in opinion, for his arguments have not been of his own," George III wrote to Dundas, "but as on the Slave Trade a display of those hatched by others." Britain's sovereign suspected the abolitionists had made the prime minister their mouthpiece in the Commons, even though Pitt shared his sovereign's concerns about the potential negative consequences of abolishing the transatlantic slave trade for the British Empire. George III remained opposed to ministerial sponsorship of abolition throughout Pitt's tenure as prime minister.

An unpublished "Memorandum Supporting West India Possessions," composed by George III in 1796, suggests that when he considered the benefits and drawbacks of abolishing the slave trade, only the prospect of insurrection gave him pause. The potential for the contagion of Black freedom to spread from revolutionary Saint-Domingue to Britain's nearby slave colonies, particularly Jamaica, concerned the king. Though he opposed the complete abolition of Britain's transatlantic slave trade, by the mid-1790s he was expressing an openness to restrict the total number of Africans each colony could import per year to maintain internal enslaved populations. Slowing the arrival of new captives from West Africa, he figured, would lessen the possibility of a catastrophic revolt. "In order to prevent the danger from the Negro population, continually augmented by fresh importations from Africa," George III outlined, "it seems to me indispensable, to limit the importation to such numbers only, as on an average of two or three years, may appear sufficient to keep up the population to its present amount, and afterwards, as the internal population may augment, to reduce the Importation gradually, from time to time." Once planters managed to keep up the enslaved population through natural increase, reliance on the transatlantic slave trade would decrease gradually every few years.

In public, the king remained above the political fray as his constitutional position required. He took a close interest in the abolition debate but desisted from sharing his royal opinion with the British people. The duke of Clarence, however, earnestly engaged in the parliamentary slavery dispute, to which London newspapers devoted extensive coverage. When the duke voiced strong opposition to the abolition of the transatlantic slave trade in the House of Lords, the British press publicized his remarks. So did the West India lobby. His personal experience in the Royal Navy, the king's son detailed, informed his wholehearted support for the pro-slavery interest. "I mention this, my Lords," he reiterated, "as an eye-witness and a resident for some years amongst those West India planters, I may bear witness to their good conduct, to their humanity, and to the care and attention of their slaves." Writing to his friend Lord Horatio Nelson, Clarence reflected that his efforts in support of the West India interest dominated his time during the renewed slave trade debate in 1799. "I was earnestly engaged in Parliament upon the slave trade for several weeks." The extent to which George III approved of his son's passionate defense of slavery and public friendship with the West Indian lobby is somewhat murky. Yet the cautious approach adopted by members of the king's cabinet is highly suggestive of the king's stance toward the abolition question.

The extant records of George III's ministers capture royal directives that the king either failed to put to paper or later fell through the cracks of his voluminous archive. Concerned he would provoke the king's displeasure, Lord Liverpool, president of the Board of Trade and Foreign Plantations, pled "indisposition" to avoid attending a cabinet meeting called by Pitt on July 11, 1799. Pitt wanted to discuss new limitations on Britain's slave trade that he intended to propose in the next session of Parliament. "As Lord Liverpool understood from His Royal Highness," he wrote to the duke of Clarence, "it was the king's determination that any business of this sort, should never be made a cabinet measure." Therefore, he feigned illness, assuming "he should act contrary to His Majesty's intentions if he was present at this cabinet." Lord Liverpool also informed Pitt that "he did not think he was justified in pledging himself on a question in which the property of His Majesty's subjects was so greatly concerned." Potentially compromising his relationship with the king was not worth the political risk, and Lord Liverpool hoped the duke of Clarence would "make His Majesty acquainted with this transaction."

Still, some of George III's ministers counseled him to consider adopting a policy of gradual abolition once it became clear that other major powers would do the same. Ending the British slave trade, they contended, would accomplish very little unless all of Europe and the Americans participated. Additionally, the Caribbean planters preferred an incremental approach permitting them to retain a measure of control over local circumstances and shape their own destiny. Rather than support an act of Parliament, the king could issue a royal proclamation "to prohibit the importation of slaves into any or all of the colonies until the colonial legislatures shall have respectively provided some means to encourage the marriage and increase of such slaves as are now in the colonies." According to this proposal, if George III required colonial legislatures to "encourage" bondsmen and -women to marry and reproduce, the king could effectively maintain the enslaved population in his plantation colonies without recourse to slaving vessels. A royal proclamation could produce the desired outcome—the end of Britain's transatlantic slave trade—without undercutting the institution of slavery or imperiling the economic future of the sugar colonies. The king, however, preferred to let matters play out in Parliament in the interim.

In 1805, George III's newly appointed secretary of state, John Jeffreys Pratt, earl of Camden, revisited the possibility of a royal proclamation. He advised the king to prohibit the importation of enslaved Africans into conquered colonies, specifically Trinidad. Exceptions to the rule should occur only when "necessary to keep up the present Stock." National security concerns motivated this directive, he assured the king, and "do not in any degree involve any decision upon the opinions which are entertained on the general question of the slave trade." The king consented to issuing the proclamation, "provided it be clearly understood not to encourage a system that if ever adopted in the ancient colonial possessions of the kingdom in that part of the globe that he must clearly [view] as in the teeth of public faith." By this George meant that a blanket ban on the trafficking of Africans would undermine public confidence in his commitment to upholding the rights of British subjects in the Caribbean colonies.

For centuries, first Tudor and then Stuart and Hanoverian monarchs had invested in and defended the transatlantic slave trade and encouraged their subjects to employ enslaved labor in Britain's Atlantic empire. In George's view, abolishing the slave trade to Britain's "ancient" Caribbean possessions "would disgrace the honor and justice of the British legislature which has ever fostered the British Islands and has no more right from ideas of false philanthropy to affect the property of British settlers than it would have to prevent the cultivation of land in Great Britain." Couched in patriotic terms, the royal proclamation of 1805 was followed a year later by the 1806 Foreign Slave Trade Act, which prevented Britain from supplying enslaved workers to foreign powers. The legislation passed with widespread support. By prohibiting British subjects from trafficking Africans to the conquered colonies and foreign countries, the act eliminated one-third of Britain's slaving commerce in one fell swoop.

Opposition to a general abolition bill remained even after the political context shifted in the abolitionists' favor. France was no longer a major sugar-producing threat to Britain; its former sugar powerhouse, Saint-Domingue, had become Haiti, the first free Black republic in the Americas. Abolishing the transatlantic slave trade, abolitionists argued, would protect the Caribbean colonies from the arrival of potentially militant Africans capable of fomenting rebellion. The pro-slavery establishment, however, saw the situation differently. If word of abolition reached the sugar colonies, bondsmen and -women would follow their African-descended brethren in Haiti and rise against and cut down their enslavers—in which case blood would stain the king's own hands.

On the eve of the passage of the Abolition Act in January 1807, Edmund Lyon, Jamaica's London agent, pointed out to then–prime minister William Grenville that the Stuart monarchs had initiated the transatlantic slave trade by "Royal Charter and Proclamations." Since the seventeenth century, both the monarchy and Parliament had repeatedly confirmed that enslaved Africans were a legitimate form of property capable of being bought, sold, inherited, bequeathed, and collected for debts. Ending the transatlantic slave trade signified "an attempt to promote the purposes of humanity to the Sons of Africa at the expense of an immense sacrifice of the lives of British Subjects and of British property." For Britons to assume that enslaved people would not equate abolition of slaving with emancipation was a fool's errand, he warned. "The doctrine which condemns the trade, by which Negroes are imported into the West Indies in a state of slavery, cannot be true to its own principle, except it advances one step further, and seeks to annihilate all slavery." Lyon's counsel captures a central pillar of the pro-slavery argument: that abolishing the slave trade constituted a betrayal of the Crown's historic commitments to its colonial subjects for the supposed benefit of Africans, who would immediately demand full freedom. To support abolition was to invite bloodshed and threaten not only the property but also the very lives of the king's subjects in the Caribbean plantation colonies.

On February 23, 1807, after nearly a quarter century of activism on the part of campaigners, Black and white, Parliament passed the Act for the Abolition of the Slave Trade. This hard-fought victory took place with virtually no support from the royals, most of whom remained opposed to abolition. Both the duke of Clarence and Prince Augustus Frederick, the duke of Sussex, George III's sixth son, spoke in opposition to the bill in the House of Lords. Thanks to their efforts, the abolitionist William Wilberforce feared the cause might, once again, face defeat. But though the king's sons voted as a bloc to prevent the landmark bill from passing, they were outnumbered. Only their cousin the duke of Gloucester "opposed the example of his royal relations on this subject in behalf of an helpless and oppressed people," Thomas Clarkson later wrote. Characterizing the transatlantic slave trade as a "cruel and criminal traffic" and a "foul stain on the national character," the duke of Gloucester voted for its dissolution. He would continue to dedicate himself to the cause of abolition while his more influential royal cousins dragged their heels.

British slave ships were prohibited from carrying on the trade as of January 1, 1808; but this made little impact on the lives of the seven hundred thousand individuals who remained enslaved in the Caribbean. In concert with the Sons of Africa and supportive members of the British public and government, London's Society for Effecting the Abolition of the Slave Trade had achieved an important milestone. Yet much work remained. It is doubtful that Ottobah Cugoano, had he lived to see the occasion, would have been satisfied with the mere abolition of the British transatlantic slave trade. He had dedicated his life to advocating for the end of African trafficking and enslavement, making one of the first cases in Britain for Black freedom and reparative justice. Like Lyon, the Jamaica agent, he assumed the longer enslaved men and women waited for full emancipation and proper Christian treatment, the greater their righteous wrath—and rightly so.

As Cugoano wrote in the concluding paragraph of his *Thoughts and*

Sentiments, "the voice of our complaint implies a vengeance, because of the great iniquity that you have done, and because of the cruel injustice done to us Africans." "And if it is not harkened unto," he warned, "it may yet arise with a louder voice, as the rolling thunder, and it may increase in the force of its volubility, not only to shake the leaves of the most stout in heart, but to rend the mountains before them." Cugoano sounded a cautionary note. By dismissing the repeated pleas of oppressed Africans, Britons had knowingly invited violent retribution. In the years ahead, his words would prove prophetic.

PART IV

SILENCES

CHAPTER 17

THE AFRICAN INSTITUTION

On March 28, 1807, three days after George III approved the passage of the Abolition Act, William Wilberforce hastened to Chandos Street in Marylebone to call on the king's nephew, Prince William Frederick, second duke of Gloucester and Edinburgh. Fresh off a hard-fought landmark legislative victory, Wilberforce had already devised the next steps for the British abolitionist movement. He proposed the establishment of an African Institution for "promoting civilization and improvement in Africa," and he sought Gloucester's support. A member of the House of Lords with a public voting record, the duke had acquired a reputation as the sole royal advocate for the abolitionist cause.

His abolitionist sympathies stood in stark contrast to the pro-slavery position articulated by his cousin Prince William, duke of Clarence. A mouthpiece for the West India lobby since the late 1780s, Clarence continued to declare that abolishing the transatlantic slave trade would weaken Britain's maritime strength. The two royal cousins were, in the words of historian Suzanne Schwartz, "situated at opposite ends of the political scale on abolition"; and, as members of the most illustrious family in Britain, their opposing public stances proved highly influential. While abolitionists surmised that more prominent senior royals, including the king, sympathized with Clarence on the slavery question, gaining Gloucester's support offered a boon to their cause. Attaching a royal name to future anti-slavery endeavors and leveraging the duke's high-ranking connections to influence government policy promised to amplify the post-1807 abolitionist movement.

Wilberforce and his fellow abolitionist campaigners viewed Parliament's passage of the Abolition Act as a glorious, unprecedented achievement. But they understood that the "great work" of abolition remained unfinished. For the Abolition Act to prove effective, the British state needed to enforce it. British abolitionists also assumed that the entire continent of Africa awaited "improvement" along the lines envisioned by Christian humanitarian capitalist reformers. Abolishing the British slave trade did not mean the end of profitable commerce with Africans. Rather, it marked a shift to trade in legitimate goods—not human commodities— and so-called free labor. In practice, the execution of this agenda entailed spreading European political economy and Christian civilization in Africa through the imposition of British norms and economic ambitions. To Wilberforce's delight, the duke of Gloucester concurred with his vision. He supported the foundation of an African Institution dedicated to enforcing abolition and improving Africa. Offering his "most cordial support, and his interest with any friends of the cause who might be most accessible to him (the Archbishop of Canterbury, &c.)," Gloucester brought his royal influence to bear on the issue of slavery.

In mid-April, the duke of Gloucester presided over a private, nascent gathering of the African Institution. Attendees shared "a sense of the enormous wrongs which the natives of Africa have suffered in their intercourse with Europe," and they consequently sought to "adopt such measures as are best calculated to promote their civilization and happiness." Formed on the heels of the Abolition Act, the African Institution offered a vehicle for elite abolitionist campaigners to channel their reforming energies into an ambitious new scheme. Yet, from the outset, members allowed paternalistic racial assumptions regarding Africans to guide their project for imperial reform and the suppression of slave trading. They arrogantly lumped together African peoples of whatever nation into an indistinguishable brutish mass; they also assumed that all Africans supposedly required enlightened European Christian guidance to attain a higher state of civilization.

Chaired by the duke of Gloucester, the African Institution's first official meeting took place on July 15, 1807, at Freeman's Hall on Queen Street. Meeting attendees, among whom were members of the nobility, Anglican clergy, politicians, and government ministers, invited the duke to accept the office of president and patron. The institution announced its grand plan "to introduce the blessings of civilized society among a people sunk in ignorance and barbarism and occupying no less than a fourth part of the habitable globe." The enormity of this proposed goal, subscribers admitted, might strike critics as rash and impossible to accomplish. But experience had shown that "the combined efforts of a few private men, or even the energies of a single mind, have sufficed to effect great revolutions in the opinions, the manners, the laws, and civil condition of a whole people, nay even of a great portion of mankind." The African Institution rejected European assessments of African inferiority as "degrading to the character of the negro race." Written principally by slave-trading apologists, negative characterizations of Africans were easily dismissible as self-serving "hostile testimony," it underscored. But members also held that if Africans resisted the institution's civilizing mission, their opposition offered proof of the necessity and worthiness of British intervention. In the early nineteenth century, Eurocentric racial assumptions infused anti-slavery and pro-slavery discourse alike.

As a well-connected member of the royal family, the duke of Gloucester played a critical role in the African Institution's efforts to shape the British government's policies toward West Africa and the Caribbean during this period. He served as the spokesperson of the institution, chaired regular meetings, corresponded with subscribers and critics, submitted petitions to Parliament, and used his international network of contacts to promote the suppression of the transatlantic slave trade. In Thomas Clarkson's influential 1808 history of the abolition movement, he paid a "tribute of respect" to the duke for voting against the royal family. Sending Gloucester an autographed copy of the book upon its publication, Clarkson noted that "I have no doubt that the perusal of it will occasion you frequently to rejoice, that you have lent your aid, in so distinguished a manner, towards the promotion of the same cause." As both men knew, it was a cause that required champions with access to the halls of power.

On March 26, 1808, the one-year anniversary of the royal assent to the Abolition Act, Gloucester chaired a celebratory meeting of abolitionist campaigners at the Freemasons' Tavern in London's West End. Attendees toasted the king and royal family, the British armed forces, the MPs who played an instrumental role in shepherding the milestone legislation through the Lords and Commons, and the newly formed African Institution. Gloucester addressed the assembled crowd, delivering a "brief, but energetic" speech on the historic nature of Britain's Abolition Act. "It was an act that reflected the highest credit on everyone concerned in it," the duke exclaimed; "whether considered with a view to its policy, its justice, or its humanity." The African Institution underscored to attendees the necessity of tracking the act's enforcement and putting pressure on other countries to follow Britain's lead.

Curbing the illicit trafficking of Africans by British subjects and influencing foreign powers to abolish their own slave trades topped the list of immediate aims. If other countries filled the void left by Britain's exit from the transatlantic slave trade, the trafficking of enslaved Africans would continue unabated. Britain would thus be disadvantaged economically without achieving its "great object." "In short, it is evident that whilst any one nation is allowed to continue the trade without interruption, she will afford an opening to all the rest," explained the Liverpool abolitionist William Roscoe to the duke of Gloucester. Until Britain prevailed on other nations to give up the trade, both the abolitionist cause and the British imperial economy remained vulnerable.

Passed during the Napoleonic Wars (1803–13), Britain's Abolition Act had outlawed British subjects from participating in the transatlantic slave trade and declared illicit slaving vessels and their cargoes contraband eligible for capture. To enforce the law while reducing the expenses borne by the British state, the Crown incentivized anti-slave-trade activities. It demanded the involuntary conscription of Africans released from slave ships into indentured servitude, apprenticeships, or military service. It promoted military operations against human trafficking on the West African coast and the forced enlistment of men and boys into the British armed services. African men, women, and children seized by the Royal Navy were "condemned as prize of war, or as forfeited, to the sole use of his Majesty, his heirs, and successors." In exchange for handing over captured Africans, known as "Prize Negroes" and later as "Liberated Africans," to colonial authorities, British military officers received financial rewards: £40 per man, £30 per woman, and £10 per child under the age of fourteen.

Deliverance from slave ships carried a steep price. To compensate the British government for its liberating activities, colonial officials charged with processing "such natives of Africa as shall be so condemned" held the right "to enter and enlist the same, or any of them, into his Majesty's land or sea service, as soldiers, seamen, or marines, or to bind the same or any of them, whether of full age or not, as apprentices, for any term not exceeding fourteen years." Africans liberated from slavery lost their autonomy and the power to shape their own destinies. Once captured and turned over to the colonial government or Admiralty, so-called "Prize Negroes" ceased to exist as individuals separate from the will of the British state. While not technically enslaved, their freedom of choice and action was rendered null for the remainder of their natural lives: "Indentures of apprenticeship and enlistments to be as effectual as if the party, being of full age, on good consideration, had bound himself apprentice, or had voluntarily enlisted," the act specified. Britons, not Africans, would determine what form liberation took and the nature and extent of the compensation individuals captured from slaving vessels owed to the Crown.

Freetown, Sierra Leone played a key role in calculations of both the African Institution and the British government for combating illegal slave trading off the West African coast. Founded originally as an experimental self-governing agricultural colony for free people of African descent, Sierra Leone was the brainchild of the natural scientist Henry Smeathman and Quaker and Anglican abolitionists. Smeathman envisioned a free settlement in West Africa manned by former enslaved people and Black loyalists, whose combined efforts would demonstrate the potential financial returns of free labor and act as a beacon of civility for surrounding West African communities. Freetown received about four hundred destitute Black Londoners in 1787 and another twelve hundred Black loyalists from Nova Scotia in 1792. Granville Sharp and other abolitionists envisaged the colony in utopian terms: a place for free Blacks to live independently and prosper beyond the shadow of slavery. But the Sierra Leone experiment upset their expectations. Slave trading and enslavement loomed large on the West African coast; slavery-adjacent trade was unavoidable. Poor planning and management, corrupt suppliers, hard red soil that made farming difficult, French incursions, and misunderstandings with local rulers caused the colony to falter.

During the 1790s, as warfare with revolutionary France dampened British enthusiasm for the Sierra Leone scheme, Black settlers became increasingly frustrated with the unrealistic expectations foisted upon them from London. They staged a rebellion against the Sierra Leone Company that was crushed in the fall of 1800 following the arrival of 551 Maroons exiled from Jamaica by way of Nova Scotia. By this point, the small Sierra Leone colony faced economic ruin. In 1804, Zachary Macaulay, the former governor of the Sierra Leone Company, testified before Parliament about the financial disasters that had befallen the colony since its inception. Macaulay blamed the settlement's failure on recalcitrant Black settlers and the persistence of slave trading in the region, both of which, he claimed, had dashed British attempts to civilize West Africa.

On January 1, 1808, the same day the Abolition Act took effect, Sierra Leone became a Crown colony and Britain's first West African colony. In April, two months prior to the start of his appointment as the new royal governor of Sierra Leone, Thomas Perronet Thompson received orders from the king's cabinet "to condemn within the colony all such Negroes as shall be brought in captured as prize or shall be forfeited to His Majesty." A devout evangelical Christian, Thompson had assumed he would assist Africans liberated from slave ships to become "a free and hardy peasantry." Instead, his orders from London demanded that he force apprenticeships on liberated Africans that resembled, in his mind, "actual slavery."

The British Crown used Sierra Leone as a base for patrolling the West African coast and intercepting illegal slaving vessels. Africans liberated from slave ships by the Royal Navy were compelled to work as indentured servants or to accept apprenticeships of indeterminate length in order to strengthen the British armed forces and plug labor shortages. From the moment he arrived in Freetown, Thompson vehemently opposed the colony's mock apprenticeship system. He wrote outraged reports to Lord Castlereagh, the foreign secretary, and his abolitionist colleagues in London, complaining that coerced African labor flourished unchecked in Freetown under the guise of liberation.

Thompson's condemnation of the situation in Sierra Leone disturbed and embarrassed his supporters in England, particularly Wilberforce,

Gloucester, and other prominent members of the African Institution. His accusations imperiled their personal reputations and the future of the Sierra Leone colony. Apprenticeship, they insisted, did not equate to enslavement. The African Institution deemed it a vital intermediate step on the path to full freedom. Thompson stood on his principles and refused to back down. His governorship was consequently short-lived. After being recalled, a bitter and resentful Thompson returned to England in 1810. Although he requested meetings with government ministers and pressed for a public inquiry, Thompson was effectively silenced by the British government and abolitionist interests—at least for the moment.

Five years after Thompson had questioned the apprenticeship system in Sierra Leone, the Crown colony and the African Institution faced another attack from within. Robert Thorpe, Sierra Leone's former chief justice, published a scathing pamphlet in which he accused the African Institution of complicity in the illicit trafficking and enslavement of Africans. Thorpe alleged that the African Institution's self-funded annual reports, trumpeting educational and agricultural achievements in West Africa, were "disgraceful," published to "delude a liberal nation" and advance the directors' reputations. Not even £50 annually had "been beneficially applied for Africa out of their funds since the Institution was established," he asserted.

Under pressure from the institution's well-connected directors, the Crown had recalled Thomas Perronet Thompson because he refused to lie about the deplorable conditions on the ground. Africans liberated from slaving vessels "never received any instruction; nor was an effort ever made, to restore them to their connections and country." Instead, officials in Sierra Leone consigned them to forced labor or military conscription. "Thus, the Abolition Act is to give us slaves without purchase, by seizing them from our allies," Thorpe concluded. His public accusations marred the African Institution's reputation, offered fodder to the proslavery West India lobby, and ensured he would never again work for the Colonial Office.

Between 1808 and 1863, the British landed approximately ninety-nine thousand "liberated" Africans intercepted from slaving vessels at Freetown alone. Except for a small percentage of individuals caught up in the intra-African trade, most of the Africans who disembarked in Sierra Leone as so-called condemned prizes were destined for bondage in the Americas. Each year, the shores of Freetown swelled with new arrivals, mostly Yoruba and Igbo people from modern Nigeria, who had fallen under British sovereignty after their liberation from a slaving vessel. They had escaped enslavement by returning to an area of West Africa under British control. Whether enslaved or free, their lives were no longer their own. The British government and abolitionists reasoned that Africans rescued from slave ships would gratefully submit to Crown rule. In exchange for their release from permanent, hereditary bondage, liberated Africans were required to engage in compulsory military service, agricultural production, or other forms of industry for the colony. As opposed to slavery, this "free labor" would foster British imperial progress in Africa, civilize the continent's inhabitants, and repay the debt owed to the state.

The first British court with an anti-slavery mandate, the vice-admiralty court in Freetown determined the fates of African individuals liberated from slave ships. But the court's primary purpose involved tracking the flow of money: inventorying, auctioning, and redistributing the cash value of any illicit property, including enslaved people, captured at sea. Financial and military rewards encouraged the capture of slave ships by naval vessels, and Freetown's vice-admiralty court, though thin on official oversight and scruples, was meant to ensure the equitable distribution of payments. The subsequent fates of the African women, men, and children released from the holds of slaving vessels and nominally freed received far less consideration. Assigned a cash value by the court, liberated people remained fungible commodities translated into money in the eyes of the law. They automatically became the legal property of the Crown within the imperial order, and their bodies and labor retained a cash value. Their status as Crown property qualified liberated Africans for enlistment in the British armed forces, apprenticeship, or general labor on land or sea.

The vice-admiralty court in Freetown recorded a total of 10,022 Africans captured from slaving vessels between 1808 and 1817, and 60 percent were men and boys. About a third of these men, and some boys, were forcibly impressed into the Royal African Corps on permanent military service for the Crown. A dedicated unit established in 1800 to garrison British territories in West Africa, the Royal African Corps had a poor reputation. Prior to 1808, British convicts were used as a means of protecting regular recruits from the hazards of tropical service. Other liberated males were enlisted into the British West India regiments, formed in 1795 to defend the Caribbean colonies and preserve the lives of British soldiers. "The whole of our Africa corps, and a great part of the West India regiments that serve in the West Indies, are supplied from the liberated Africans at Sierra Leone," an imperial official later testified in the House of Lords.

To aid compliance, men who enlisted in the Royal African Corps were assigned wives from among the pool of liberated women and girls, who had the least amount of control over their fates. Those who remained in the struggling Sierra Leone colony laboring as so-called "apprentices"—a problematic term designed to conceal exploitative realities on the ground—supported day-to-day operations. The end of Britain's legal slave trade did not preclude the Crown from benefiting materially from Africans captured from slaving vessels.

British abolitionists accepted the fact that illegal slave trading would persist in the Atlantic world after the Abolition Act went into effect. The government of the United States had also banned the importation of enslaved Africans, effective January 1, 1808. But American citizens routinely flouted the law, which authorities in Washington, D.C., rarely enforced. Brazil and Cuba, the two largest Iberian slave societies in the Americas, attracted the business of numerous slaving vessels in the early nineteenth century. The British press informed the public that "Spanish Cuba, and the Portuguese Brazils, have been extending their cultivation by means of a vast influx of slaves from Africa," with up to eighty thousand enslaved Africans carried to those destinations in a single year. Both colonies fiercely opposed abolition and threatened independence from their respective mother countries rather than submit to the end of the transatlantic slave trade. Between 1808 and 1820, around 841,000 enslaved Africans disembarked from slaving vessels in the Americas, and 77 percent of these ships flew Portuguese flags. American, French, Spanish, Dutch, and British flags flew on nearly all of the remaining slaving vessels.

Given this broader international context, the African Institution espoused three primary objectives early on. First, it wanted to ensure the enforcement of the British Abolition Act by lobbying for the interception of suspicious ships at sea, with stiff penalties imposed on offenders. Next, it sought to eradicate the traffic in enslaved Africans through international treaty agreements banning the transatlantic slave trade in all regions. The British Royal Navy lacked the resources to single-handedly suppress a profitable trade carried on by numerous actors across vast distances. Allowing foreign powers to funnel enslaved workers into rival plantation colonies also threatened Britain's imperial and maritime dominance. Finally, the institution aimed to implement ameliorative policies in Britain's Caribbean colonies, ensuring enslaved people received more humane treatment at the hands of slaveholders. Achieving this latter end, the African Institution maintained, would require British officials to conduct comprehensive surveys of the enslaved population. Only by amassing accurate demographic data would the British state be able to monitor illicit slave trading and assess evolving conditions on plantations. Curtailing the effects of the transatlantic slave trade on Africa was the primary goal "against which, chiefly we raise our voices," Wilberforce claimed, "as constituting a sum of guilt and misery, hitherto unequalled in the annals of the world."

Whether focused on the plight of Africans on the continent or enslaved people of African origin and descent in the Caribbean colonies, British campaigners made sweeping generalizations about their mental capacities, moral habits, and fitness for freedom. Reformers held that participating in and being commodified by the transatlantic slave trade and colonial plantation regimes had kept Africans and people of African ancestry in a state of arrested darkness, unable to share in the light of Christian civilization. A self-identified champion of oppressed Africans, Wilberforce described enslaved people as "depraved and debased." "Would you raise them from this depressed condition, remember the disease is of a moral nature."

Eradicating human trafficking from the West African coast, contended the African Institution, "might produce little effect in civilizing Africa, unless something could be done to counteract those pernicious habits which the slave trade had nourished." Subscribers therefore appointed themselves "the guardians of the best interests of Africa, pledged to promote the social and moral improvement of her uncivilized tribes." Convinced of the urgency of their reforming campaign, abolitionists refused to consider the possibility that African peoples, whether free or enslaved, possessed sophisticated political lives and cultures as well as their own understanding of moral agency.

British commentators, including those with ties to the colonial Caribbean, assumed that enslavement had negatively impacted the behaviors and morals of Africans and their bound descendants. Arresting the transatlantic slave trade held the potential to transform plantation society insofar as it resulted in greater care and instruction of enslaved people. "The change of life from the savage wilds of Africa to the insulated fields of the West Indies consists chiefly in severe compulsion to labor and rigorous personal restrictions," wrote Stephen Gaisford, a former resident of the British Caribbean. Under these debased conditions, he argued, individual and collective racial improvement among the enslaved was impossible.

Beilby Porteus, the bishop of London (and an ancestor of Britain's current sovereign), urged Caribbean slaveholders to reconcile themselves to the end of the slave trade by promoting natural increase among the enslaved. Doing so required "the careful and assiduous instruction of your slaves, both children and adults, in the principles of the Christian religion, and a strict attention to the regulation of their moral conduct." According to Porteus, without the fear of God guiding their behavior, the enslaved population would inevitably decline, overwhelmed by the "ardent and impetuous passions of an African constitution." The British, whatever their ideological position, were convinced that the condition and character of enslaved people needed improvement as they advanced toward eventual freedom.

For evidence of moral reform in a post-slavery society, British abolitionists looked with some trepidation to Haiti. The lone free Black nation in the Caribbean Sea surrounded by European-dominated colonial slave regimes, Haiti offered a "crucial test case for ideas about race, slavery, and the future of the Caribbean." The extreme violence unleashed during the Haitian freedom struggle against France and in the aftermath of Haitian independence in 1804 had alarmed British observers. Yet the ascendance of Henry Christophe, a former enslaved man born in St. Kitts, who had seized power in northern Haiti and sought to forge diplomatic ties with

Britain, inspired cautious optimism among abolitionist campaigners. In 1807, disputes over the form of government the young nation would take split Haiti into two competing provinces: the southern Republic of Haiti, headed by President Alexandre Pétion, and the Kingdom of Haiti in the north, led by Henry Christophe, who adhered to monarchal rule and was pronounced King Henry I in 1811.

Initially, Henry's presumption of royal status scandalized the British press. The notion of a Black hereditary monarchy—originating in the bloodline of a former enslaved man—flew in the face of monarchal inimitability and ancient pedigree. Worse still, Henry did not stop at the royal office. Prior to his self-styled coronation, during which he offered a toast to "My brother, the King of Great Britain," Henry released an edict creating a hereditary Haitian nobility. British newspaper reports described how the new Haitian king had ennobled dozens of his favorite generals and colonels in one fell swoop, "some made princes, some dukes, some counts, some barons, and some chevaliers," to the astonishment of "the gaping multitude, little used to such sights." In an era when American citizens were rejecting hereditary dynasties and striving to disentangle their young republic from the grip of Britain's political and cultural influence, Henry's actions seemed to make a mockery of monarchal rule.

While Henry's overnight regal status in a former French slave colony made him an international cause célèbre, in the eyes of British abolitionists he was a rising star. His embrace of constitutional monarchy and hereditary aristocracy appealed to their sensibilities. Henry also declared that his kingdom would not seek to interfere with its slaveholding neighbors, assuaging concerns about the potential spread of revolutionary fervor to Britain's Caribbean colonies. Encapsulated by the release of his Code Henry, the Haitian king strove to implement labor and educational reforms and to extend Christian civility to his subjects. To achieve these ends, he initiated correspondence with both Wilberforce and Clarkson. Clarkson claimed that Henry praised the "English nation" for its "generosity toward Africa" and asked for the African Institution's assistance to civilize and improve Haiti. The two men would correspond and discuss their ambitions for Haiti for years to come.

As he explained to Clarkson, King Henry aspired to institute a world-class educational system in his kingdom. Through improved education, "the first duty of sovereigns," his subjects would overcome the weight of racial prejudice and "soon astonish the world by their knowledge." Henry's admiration of Britain and belief in his providential duty to forge a new path forward for Haiti aligned with Clarkson's and other abolitionists' sense of their own historical importance. At a dinner held by the African Institution at the Freemasons' Tavern, Wilberforce delivered a toast in King Henry's honor. From English artisans, Henry ordered a large state saddle of Genoese crimson and yellow velvet studded with gold, along with a saddle cloth embroidered with his coat of arms and matching velvet harnesses for eight horses. He purchased a scepter, robes, and crown embedded with "diamonds which his sable majesty furnished" as well as coats of arms for high-ranking members of the Haitian nobility. "The King of Haiti seems resolved to be behind hand no monarch, Oriental or European, in the external magnificence of exalted rank," proclaimed the *Morning Post* in a mocking manner.

Prince Saunders, a freeborn Black emigrant from Boston inspired by the Haitian revolution, became an adviser to King Henry on the recommendation of British abolitionists. Saunders visited London in 1815 and forged relationships with influential Britons, visiting the homes of William Wilberforce, Thomas Clarkson, and Sir Joseph Banks, president of the Royal Society. In 1816, while still in London, Prince Saunders published the *Haytien Papers*. Consisting of extracts of Haitian state papers and policies, royal proclamations, and legal codes, Saunders's lengthy work praised Henry's monarchal regime. Exemplars of Black liberty and independence, the inhabitants of the kingdom of Haiti broadcast that "it is our will to found, in this new world, an hereditary monarchy," rooted in the bloodline of Henry Christophe.

Although British commentary on the reign of King Henry entailed a degree of skepticism or even satire regarding the appropriateness of his exalted position, the British press became more amenable to the prospect of a Black king capable of liberating his country from French tyranny. Through monarchal rule and the emulation of British norms, Henry had reestablished order in Haiti's political and social life. But the kingdom of Haiti's promise was short-lived. The subsequent violent end of Henry's reign and his suicide in October 1820, which led to Haitian reunification, reconfirmed British prejudices about Black liberation and dashed the hopes of the African Institution. Praising King Henry's passion for genuine reform, Wilberforce concluded that his birth in bondage and "the degrading effects of slavery" had played a hand in the dissolution of his fleeting, ill-fated kingdom.

As events unfolded in Haiti over which the British had no influence, abolitionist campaigners continued to turn to Crown-controlled Sierra Leone as a potential model for a free Black society. Freetown, though mired in controversy over apprenticeship, appealed to people of African descent seeking to carve out an existence away from the racial inequities of slave society. In 1810, Paul Cuffe, a Quaker ship captain of mixed African and Indigenous ancestry from Massachusetts, embarked on two transatlantic voyages to Freetown. He aimed to establish trading relations with Britain's first West African colony and develop a potential emigration scheme for free African Americans. The son of a Wampanoag woman and a formerly enslaved man of Ashanti origin, Cuffe was a maritime entrepreneur, devout Quaker, and anti-slavery advocate with connections to abolitionist organizations on both sides of the Atlantic. As Cuffe's reputation and influence grew, British abolitionists saw him as a potential partner in the economic development of Sierra Leone and surrounding West African coastal communities. To decrease the region's reliance on human trafficking, Cuffe proposed improving agricultural production and international shipping capabilities. In July 1811, he sailed from Freetown to London at the invitation of the African Institution.

While in London, Cuffe consulted with the directors of the African Institution and met with the organization's royal president and patron, the duke of Gloucester. Receptive to his proposals, Wilberforce applied on the African Institution's behalf to Earl Bathurst, secretary of state for war and the colonies, to permit Cuffe to trade with Freetown and to extend a land grant to him for future settlement. Both Cuffe and the African Institution envisioned African American emigrants playing a leading role in Sierra Leone. They would establish profitable commercial enterprises, promote the spread of Christianity, and prove instrumental in halting African slave trading and enslavement. "I have cause to rejoice in having found many who are inclined to listen and attend to the precepts of our holy religion," Cuffe wrote following his positive reception in London. He prayed that "our brethren who live in distant lands and are held in bondage, and groan under the galling chain of slavery; that they may be liberated and enjoy the liberty which God has granted unto all his faithful saints." But increasing tensions between Britain and the United States over maritime policies and British naval impressment shattered the ambitions of Cuffe and the African Institution. In the midst of impending war, plans for African American emigration to Sierra Leone were scuttled.

By the 1810s, George III's mental faculties had declined to the point that the Prince of Wales was sworn in as regent on February 6, 1811. Unfinished business related to Britain's campaign for the universal abolition of the transatlantic slave trade and the amelioration of slavery in the Caribbean colonies now fell on his shoulders. While the prince regent had previously sided with the duke of Clarence in opposition to Britain's Abolition Act, his position shifted after its enactment and his elevation to regent. Lobbying by the African Institution had influenced government attitudes and policies post-1807, and the prince regent confirmed the king's existing Tory ministers in office. That June, in acknowledgment that the "illicit trade in slaves had so greatly increased, that if not effectually checked, it seemed as if it would shortly exceed that slave trade which had been abolished," Parliament passed the Slave Trade Felony Act. The act made slave trading by British subjects a felony punishable by imprisonment, hard labor, or fourteen years transportation. But curbing illicit trafficking among Britons also meant eradicating the legal slave trades carried out by other nations whose flags flew from slaving vessels as they crossed the Atlantic.

Unlike Britain, other major slave-trading nations exhibited little interest in discontinuing the transport of enslaved people from Africa to the Americas. Under pressure, Portugal had agreed to geographic limitations on slaving, while resisting British demands for immediate and total abolition. Spain, too, opposed outlawing its slave trade. In the United States, a clandestine transatlantic trade in enslaved Africans overlapped with an expanding domestic slave trade. American citizens, the African Institution argued, dominated the contraband trade of African captives on the high seas "in defiance of the laws of their own country." The hesitance of other nations to ban slave trading or to devote resources to the enforcement of existing laws prompted British abolitionists to support heavy-handed suppression tactics to urge foreign governments to adopt universal abolition. The British Royal Navy regularly seized and searched American vessels crossing the Atlantic, regardless of their cargoes, and impressed U.S. citizens into the British navy. Britain's interference with American maritime rights and neutral trade, among other factors, contributed to the War of 1812.

By declaring war against Britain, America defended its revolution and rejected the notion that the Crown held the right to reclaim U.S. citizens as natural-born subjects of the British Empire against their will. Americans insisted that the British used the pretext of the Napoleonic Wars and slave-trade suppression to seize U.S. vessels and citizens, reducing them "to a quasi-colonial status." The War of 1812 officially ended in a draw in December 1814, with both countries agreeing to "use their best endeavors" to promote the complete abolition of the transatlantic traffic in enslaved Africans. Britain pledged to return "possessions" taken from Americans during the conflict, including thousands of enslaved people who fled behind British lines. As they had during the American Revolutionary War, British forces welcomed self-liberated individuals and enlisted former enslaved African Americans in the armed forces. Britain never delivered on its promise to return freedom seekers to their American masters. Instead, the Crown eventually paid more than $1.2 million to American slaveholders in compensation for the 3,601 enslaved individuals who had escaped bondage under British banners.

CHAPTER 18

A VERY PRECARIOUS TENURE

After Napoleon's abdication in April 1814 paved the way for the restoration of the Bourbon monarchy in France, British abolitionists feared peace would lead to the revival of France's dormant transatlantic slave trade. During the Napoleonic Wars, Britain had seized a slew of French and Dutch territories, including St. Lucia, Tobago, Demerara, Essequibo, Berbice, Martinique, and Guadeloupe, among others. Should Britain return former possessions to France and enable that country to resume a "nefarious traffic" in enslaved Africans, "little comparatively will have been achieved for Africa by all the generous efforts of this country."

At a public meeting chaired by the duke of Gloucester, the African Institution launched a campaign to petition the government in favor of universal abolition of the transatlantic slave trade. Abolitionists called upon the British public "to impress upon the minds of His Majesty's ministers the unspeakable importance of establishing a general convention among the European powers for that purpose." Once France officially banned slave trading, they reasoned, Portugal and Spain would follow. Reviving the public pressure campaign used to optimum effect to secure the 1807 Abolition Act, Gloucester and Wilberforce submitted petitions signed by hundreds of thousands of Britons to the Lords and Commons. Leading campaigners assured the government that the French Crown would succumb to pressure exerted by the monarchs of allied nations, and Britain especially as the leading maritime power.

Yet the intentions of France's newly restored King Louis XVIII differed radically from the wishes of abolitionists and their supporters in Britain. During the peace talks in Paris, Lord Castlereagh, Britain's head negotiator, discovered that Louis refused to acquiesce to British demands related to the transatlantic slave trade. Suspicious of Britain's motives for attempting to secure immediate abolition, French representatives argued that their nation's honor and future economic security hung in the balance. While Louis concurred that "all the Powers of Christendom" should work together to abolish a "traffic repugnant to the principles of natural justice and of the enlightened age in which we live," the interests of the French people had tied his government's hands. When Castlereagh returned to London after negotiating the Paris peace treaty, which contained an article permitting France to restore its transatlantic slave trade for another five years, the foreign secretary faced sharp criticism from abolitionists.

Wilberforce could barely contain his horror. As he exclaimed in the Commons, Castlereagh had allowed France, "just risen from the weight of iron despotism," to pivot toward Africa and sacrifice the lives of countless innocent people for economic gain, unleashing evils that "could not be remedied by exertions of benevolence during the space of two or three centuries." Wilberforce moved to present an address to the prince regent, who had assumed the reins of government in 1811 as a result of George III's incapacity, urging him "to procure a final and universal extinction of the slave trade."

Abolitionists once again used the press and grassroots networks to rally the British people, generating a groundswell of denunciations against the treaty's slave-trade article. The national response left no doubt as to the public mood. Across a total of 1,370 separate parliamentary petitions, more than a million Britons registered their discontent with the terms of the treaty and appealed for immediate universal abolition. The pleas of the public moved the ministry and the British monarchy to action, Thomas Clarkson reported. Writing to Louis XVIII "with his own hand," the prince regent requested that the French king agree to the immediate abolition of the slave trade as a personal favor to him. During the ongoing diplomatic discussions with France over the slave-trade issue, Clarkson also used his connection to the duke of Gloucester to influence the British chain of command. He wrote a letter to Gloucester in which he explained the dangers of allowing France to resume its slave-trading activities.

Mindful of political calculations, Clarkson understood that Louis's reputation among his subjects was at stake. He thus recommended a pragmatic solution: namely, that the British government offer France a territorial concession—an island such as Tobago, for example—in exchange for acquiescing to immediate abolition. A diplomatic exchange would prevent the French Crown from appearing weak. Gloucester shared Clarkson's letter with the chancellor of the Exchequer, who laid it before Prime Minister Liverpool. "Thus, I cannot doubt that government will make an offer to France of some equivalent or other," Clarkson noted; "and, if it should, I cannot but think that I shall have been instrumental in obtaining it." If Clarkson styled himself the wheel of change, Gloucester was its grease. While lacking the prestige of the king's sons, the duke, remarked a French noble to Clarkson's wife, "has claims to the eyes of good men of every country even if he were not a prince." The support of a man of royal blood added legitimacy to the abolitionists' cause and opened doors on an international level.

In the lengthy struggle to end the transatlantic slave trade, abolitionists coveted the support of Czar Alexander I of Russia. In addition to meeting with Alexander himself during the czar's visit to London and promoting the anti-slavery cause, the duke of Gloucester provided a letter of introduction for Clarkson to wait on Alexander during his attendance at the Congress of Vienna. To the royal duke and British abolitionists, Alexander professed his support for the anti-slavery cause. Still, the czar proved a lukewarm ally, hesitant to act without international consensus.

Convening from the fall of 1814 through the summer of 1815, the Congress of Vienna consisted of a series of diplomatic meetings designed to establish a stable postwar order in Europe. Castlereagh, subject to pressure from his own country, pushed other European powers to adopt universal abolition of the transatlantic slave trade as a shared humanitarian goal. His influence resulted in the adoption of a nonbinding international declaration against the transatlantic slave trade in February 1815. Though vague and ineffectual, the Vienna Declaration elevated a humanitarian concern into a principle of international law for the first time and laid the foundation for subsequent anti–slave trade treaties. When Napoleon, after escaping from exile on Elba that same month, returned to Paris and abolished the French slave trade to curry British favor, he inadvertently aided the anti-slavery cause. In the aftermath of Napoleon's final defeat at Waterloo in June, Louis XVIII's twice-restored regime confirmed the immediate ban of the French slave trade. But enforcement was another matter.

As Britain exerted diplomatic and naval pressure on foreign slave-trading powers to support immediate abolition, the African Institution returned to Paul Cuffe's plans for settling free African Americans in Sierra Leone. Abolitionist leaders assumed that much work remained to convert liberated Africans in Freetown into productive subjects of the Crown. Writing to Earl Bathurst, the institution's leader William Allen requested that the government permit Cuffe to sail to the Sierra Leone colony to conduct trade and settle "a few Black persons of good moral character and of some little property who are acquainted with the treatment of cotton, coffee, tobacco, and other tropical produce." The wealthy Quaker seaman had impressed Allen and his African Institution colleagues with his assessment of Sierra Leone's fertility and potential for cash-crop cultivation. Cuffe, Allen assured Bathurst, "is highly respected wherever he is known and that from the experience which the institution has had of his disposition and abilities they are fully persuaded that he will materially assist in promoting the prosperity of the colony." The institution agreed to aid African Americans willing to relocate to Freetown with Cuffe's assistance and urged the Crown to provide them with free plots of land and farming equipment upon arrival. "Clarkson and I are both of the mind that the present opportunity for promoting the civilization of Africa, through the means of Paul Cuffe, should not be lost," Allen emphasized.

The following year, Cuffe transported thirty-eight African American emigrants to Freetown, provisioning them at his own expense and with some financial assistance from the African Institution. The British government granted the new arrivals small plots of land in town and agricultural plots for farming. Sir Charles MacCarthy, the royal governor of Sierra Leone, anticipated increased yields of tropical produce for export following the arrival of Cuffe's African American settlers. But like the free Blacks who preceded them to Freetown, many of the settlers arriving with Cuffe demonstrated a reluctance to farm as a means of gaining economic self-sufficiency. Cuffe assured MacCarthy that numerous African Americans had placed their names on the waiting list for Freetown. He returned to the United States to gather additional recruits for the colony but died in 1817 before making another voyage to West Africa. The African Institution had lost yet another collaborator in its struggle to advance Sierra Leone economically and bring Christianity and civilization to the continent.

While British abolitionists attempted to influence government policy toward both Sierra Leone and foreign slave trading, they simultaneously pushed for increased imperial surveillance in Britain's Caribbean colonies. So long as Spain and Portugal resisted complete abolition, British subjects could illicitly purchase enslaved Africans from foreign agents. In Trinidad, a British Crown colony acquired from the Spanish in 1802, an order in council obligated colonists to register the enslaved people they owned. This entailed recording names, ages, birth and death dates, and labor assignments. Abolitionists argued that a centrally imposed register would prevent British subjects from engaging in the contraband trade in enslaved Africans, especially under the guise of foreign flags. In July 1815, Wilberforce introduced a bill in the House of Commons to establish a permanent imperial registry of all enslaved individuals in the British Empire. The registry bill met fierce opposition from Caribbean planters and the West Indian lobby in London, who argued that Parliament could not impose its will on self-legislating colonies like Barbados and Jamaica. Defending their rights as freeborn British subjects, the Barbadian and Jamaican assemblies rejected the registry bill as unconstitutional. They also warned British politicians and the public that once word of Wilberforce's proposed bill reached the ears of enslaved people, they would misinterpret it as an imperial emancipation bill.

Supporters and opponents of the proposed registry bill disagreed over the British imperial government's right to interfere in colonial governance. Parliamentary oversight in the form of a registry act, urged the African Institution, "is most urgently wanted, in order to secure the effect, to obtain the benefits, and demonstrate the sincerity, of our own reformation." Without a census of the existing enslaved population in the British Caribbean, it would be impossible to ensure that colonists had not smuggled in new bondsmen and -women illegally from Africa. Caribbean planters dismissed the proposed central registry as "a rash and unconstitutional privation of their property and privileges." Should Parliament approve the measure, "not emancipation, but destruction, and inevitable ruin will be the consequence of the general insurrection it will produce," they warned. On January 19, 1816, at a meeting convened by public advertisement at the London Tavern, the West Indian lobby attacked the imperial slave registry as a "baseless system of most grievous oppression, striking eventually all the properties, liberties, characters, and lives of His Majesty's faithful subjects in the West India colonies." After months of contentious public debate, the Tory ministry rejected the bill as an infringement of the rights of Caribbean colonists.

When news of an insurrection in Barbados, Britain's oldest, most stable Caribbean slave colony, reached London later that spring, pro-slavery supporters pointed to Wilberforce's registration bill as the root cause. On Easter Sunday, April 14, 1816, half a century after Tacky's Revolt rocked colonial Jamaica, enslaved people in Barbados staged the first and only armed rebellion in the island's history. That the revolt occurred in Barbados, a small, deforested island with the largest proportion of British colonists and a majority Creole enslaved population, shocked Caribbean slaveholders. According to contemporary assessments, fragmentary accounts of Wilberforce's failed imperial registry bill had reached a small number of literate enslaved women and men with access to newspapers. They concluded that the local assembly had thwarted the resolve of the British Parliament, blocking an important step on the path to full emancipation. Abolitionist supporters scoffed at the suggestion that a central registration calculated to confirm their "servile condition" in any way resembled a declaration of emancipation, "and yet we are gravely told that the Negroes mistook the one for the other."

Whether enslaved people in Barbados misunderstood the true purpose of the registry bill is beside the point. They intended to grasp freedom for themselves irrespective of the intentions of abolitionists in Britain. Over a period of several months, enslaved men holding positions of relative privilege on plantations as rangers and drivers tasked with monitoring the performance of field gangs painstakingly planned and coordinated an armed uprising. The insurrection, known as Bussa's Rebellion, began on Bayley's Plantation in the southeastern parish of St. Philip, led by an African-born Igbo enslaved man called Bussa. Little is known about Bussa's background, other than his status as a chief ranger, a position that afforded him greater independence and freedom of movement. Armed primarily with machetes and farming implements, the rebels set seventy cane fields and great houses ablaze, destroying a quarter of the year's total sugar crop. The revolt spread rapidly, drawing in hundreds and perhaps thousands of enslaved men and women across southern, central, and even northern parishes. On the mostly flat island of Barbados, plumes of black smoke could be seen for miles. The insurgents used arson not only to sow chaos and strike at the source of their enslavers' profits but also to convey signals to co-conspirators.

The poorly armed insurgents stood no chance against the armed forces sent to subdue them, however. Within three days, local militias and Black soldiers from the 1st West Indian Regiment had put down the insurrection with their superior firepower. One white civilian and one Black soldier were killed in the process of suppressing the uprising. Among the enslaved, fifty individuals died in battle, including Bussa; seventy were summarily executed in the field, and three hundred more were taken to Bridgetown for questioning and trial. Colonial officials executed about half of the prisoners, displaying their decapitated remains in public as a warning to others. The remainder were forcibly transported off the island, primarily to Belize. Under examination and no doubt torture, enslaved rebels testified that some among their number had either seen or heard rumors about newspaper reports that Wilberforce intended to free them all. Fragmentary political news from London filtered back to the enslaved community, overlapping with assumptions about the benevolence of both Parliament and the British monarchy toward African bondswomen and -men in the Crown's Caribbean colonies.

Authorities in Barbados immediately blamed abolitionists, and Wilberforce specifically, for inciting the rebellion. After extracting confessions from prisoners, Colonel Edward Codd concluded that the "chief cause" of the insurrection stemmed from the spread of misinformation among the island's enslaved population. A false notion, he wrote, had "pervaded the minds of those misguided people since the proposed introduction of the registry bill, that their emancipation was desired by the British Parliament." He alleged that neither ill treatment at the hands of their masters nor discontent with their enslaved status had motivated the rebels to action. Instead, the enslaved insurrectionists claimed that "the island belonged to them and not to white men, whom they proposed to destroy, reserving the females, whose lot in case of success is very easy to conceive." As colonial officials described it, the enslaved insurgents aspired to liberate themselves, overthrow the colonial plantation regime, and attain mastery of the island and all its female inhabitants, Black as well as white. Newspapers in Britain reported that "the insurrection appeared to be very extensive, and the blacks most ferocious," reiterating the dangers faced by Barbadian colonists. The investigation later conducted by the Barbados assembly concluded that the political activities of Wilberforce and his fellow abolitionist campaigners in Britain had convinced enslaved people that emancipation was imminent.

While the motives ascribed to the enslaved rebels by colonial officials must be viewed with a degree of skepticism, the leaders of the uprising carried white cotton flags covered with slogans and illustrations that offer insight into their intentions. The original flags have unfortunately not survived, but an illustration of an "extraordinary emblematic flag" borne by the rebels was preserved. The enslaved rebels called their movement an "endeavor" and displayed variations of the slogan "Happiness remains forever with endeavorance." The leaders of the uprising adopted imagery associated with Britain and its monarchy, including multiple crowns, Britannia and a lion, a warship flying the flag of St. George, and a redcoated soldier holding a pike with the banner "Royal G.R. [Georgius Rex] endavourance for ever." A Black couple clothed in fashionable Regency attire stands beneath one of the crowns, offering their loyalty to the British sovereign. Military symbols—muskets, banners, and a drum—and references to Britannia and God favoring "endavourance" indicate the presumed support of Britain's temporal and spiritual authorities for their cause.

According to colonial officials and witnesses, the enslaved insurgents counted on receiving military aid from the Black West Indian regiment and then scattered in astonishment when they discovered their miscalculation. As the rebels burned cane fields, great houses, and provision grounds in an attempt to raze the plantation slave system, their African-descended brethren in arms joined British militiamen and soldiers to cut them down. "The insurgents did not think our men would fight against Black men, but thank God they were deceived," wrote a Barbadian eye-

Figure 18.1. Sketch of a flag taken from the insurgent slaves at Barbados, 1816.

witness. Rather than interpreting the insurrection as an attempt by enslaved people to secure the freedom denied them as subjects of the Crown, British commentators saw only Black violence and disorder, incited by abolitionist agitators in London. The 1816 Barbados rebellion, historian Dexter Gabriel points out, should have "served as warning to colonists that enslaved people had their own vernacular readings of the political landscape, perceiving themselves as agents, even colonial subjects, in securing liberty." Political developments in Britain may have influenced the timing of the uprising, but the desire to claim liberation on their own terms and participate in colonial society as free subjects of the Crown compelled enslaved Barbadians to action.

In the wake of the Barbados insurrection, Wilberforce abandoned his proposal for a central registry of enslaved people administered by the British government. But he deflected any responsibility for the uprising. Caribbean planters, he and his fellow abolitionist campaigners contended, had brought the revolt upon themselves. Through their heated conversations, "even in the presence of their slaves," and furious published outbursts in colonial newspapers and pamphlets, their opposition to the registry bill in Parliament had reached the enslaved population. Planters had responded to the proposed registration measure with incendiary hyperbole, claiming abolitionists intended to emancipate their enslaved property and incite them to revolt against their masters.

Caribbean enslavers alone shouldered the blame for emboldening bondswomen and -men through their gross misrepresentation of the objectives of the registry bill. After decades of listening to their enslavers accuse abolitionists in Britain of aiming to free them at once, "the slaves themselves begin to believe it, and to take measures for securing the privilege," Wilberforce concluded. "In short, the artillery they had loaded so high against us, bursts among themselves, and they impute to us the loading and pointing of it." To avoid bloodshed in the Caribbean colonies, it was not for politicians thousands of miles away in London to alter their behavior but rather planters on the spot.

The Commons approved an address to the prince regent asking him to condemn the violence in Barbados, and Wilberforce approved. The Barbadian legislature also petitioned the prince regent, protesting the imposition of any future imperial registration bill on the colony. "We beg leave to deprecate in the strongest terms, all legislative interference between masters and slaves, as leading to consequences directly opposite to the professed object of these deluded philanthropists," they wrote. Misguided abolitionists excited unrealistic expectations among the enslaved, "encouraging an insubordination necessarily productive (if not of still more horrid evils) of that very severity which they seem most anxious to restrain." The registry matter was not entirely put to bed, however.

On behalf of the Crown, Bathurst instructed the Caribbean colonial assemblies to keep their own registers of enslaved people and to send copies to the ministry in London. Barbados, Jamaica, and other colonies soon made a show of enacting their own local registration bills, none of which carried real weight. The African Institution reassured subscribers that parliamentary intervention remained a possibility if local registration measures failed to produce results. Yet it was the actions of enslaved people, not cautious politicians in London, who had shifted the needle. The armed revolt in Barbados heightened anxieties across the British Caribbean. Planters, sensing that their bondsmen and -women "seem to cherish feelings of deep revenge," dreaded nightfall. The Barbados legislature appealed to the prince regent for military support. In the words of one terrified Barbadian colonist, "We hold the West Indies by a very precarious tenure."

On January 29, 1820, George III died, at the age of eighty-one, and the reigning prince regent ascended to the throne as King George IV. Queen Charlotte had preceded her husband in death in 1818. During their many decades on the throne, neither sovereign had aided the campaign to abolish the transatlantic slave trade, despite repeated appeals for support from former enslaved individuals and abolitionists. Nor had they publicly commemorated the passage of Britain's landmark Abolition Act. But those details did not prevent commentators at the time from associating both deceased monarchs with the great cause, especially now that Britain had emerged as the self-proclaimed standard-bearer for abolition.

Charlotte and the princesses "expressed great satisfaction" at the elimination of that "nefarious and abominable traffic which had so long been a disgrace to a free country," claimed the queen's biographer. "What an example to his family and his subjects, was the unblemished moral character of George III," eulogized an obituary author; the king's memory "will be dear to his subjects, and his death be considered a national evil." Over the course of his sixty-year reign, asserted another royal biographer, Britain's beloved sovereign had extended "the right hand of fellowship to the Asiatic and the African, the stranger and the slave." By assenting to the abolition bill after a twenty-year struggle, wrote a nineteenth-century historian, George III had enabled Britain "to set an example to the world, which neither the philanthropists of the French republic, nor those of the United States of America, has been sufficiently magnanimous to exhibit."

George IV, while responsive to public pressure calling for his intervention with foreign powers to halt their slaving activities, appears to have held indifferent personal views on abolition. In answer to an 1814 address from the House of Lords requesting that the prince regent entreat the monarchs of major slave-trading nations to support the suppression of the trade, George committed to "such measures as might appear best calculated for accomplishing the objects of it." Yet, despite the "strong condemnation of the crime by all the great powers of Europe, and by the United States of America" at the Congress of Vienna—an achievement that Parliament partly attributed to the diplomatic exertions of the prince regent—the measures adopted to suppress the trade remained woefully inadequate. Year after year, slaving vessels continued to forcibly transport hundreds of thousands of Africans across the Atlantic and into slavery in the Americas, "keeping a large portion of the globe in darkness and barbarism." House of Commons addresses pressing for his royal assistance in the complete abolition of the traffic in African captives elicited no assurances from George, both as regent in 1818 and as king in 1822.

At the start of George IV's reign, British abolitionists began to admit that their incremental approach to universal slave-trade abolition and amelioration in the Caribbean colonies had produced few substantive results. Abolishing Britain's transatlantic slave trade and exerting pressure on rival European powers to follow suit had not ended the traffic in enslaved Africans. It had not compelled planters in the sugar islands to improve enslaved people's daily lives or prepare them for the eventual possibility of freedom. By the early 1820s, the French, Portuguese, and Spanish kings had succumbed to British pressure and pledged to prohibit their subjects from engaging in the slave trade on the African coast. But enforcement was uniformly lax. Britain pushed for "right to search" agreements enabling the Royal Navy to board and inspect foreign vessels on the high seas suspected of transporting illegal cargoes of enslaved people. While the Iberian powers agreed, France refused the right of search to the British navy. Meanwhile, Brazil, newly independent after three centuries of Portuguese control, insisted on maintaining its slave trade. British abolitionists had tried to cut at the root of the supply, but the trafficking and enslavement of African women, men, and children had not withered.

In 1821, James Cropper, a wealthy Liverpool East Indian sugar merchant, reached out to Wilberforce and the directors of the African Institution to pose a serious question: Would the transatlantic slave trade ever truly end so long as colonial slavery flourished? In recent years, Wilberforce and his abolitionist colleagues had quietly contemplated the same thorny issue. Uttering it aloud would confirm the inflammatory charges leveled against them by Caribbean slaveholders for nearly four decades. Cropper spoke the words others hesitated to voice publicly. Abolishing the slave trade, he observed, "is but one step though a very important one;

but Africa is not relieved from her oppression, nor the sons of Africa from their cruel bondage, all this remains yet to be done, and if the African Institution desires the object, it must embrace the obvious means." Tackling the institution of slavery itself. Cropper suggested the formation of a new society devoted to the gradual and final extinction of slavery. He proposed that it concentrate on disseminating facts about the Atlantic slave system to the public, to "prove to the country that the time is approaching for the deliverance of these poor oppressed beings from their cruel bondage." The society needed to convey a simple message: Ameliorating the condition of enslaved people meant nothing without emancipation.

Wilberforce shared Cropper's dissatisfaction with the anti-slavery movement's limited gains. He agreed that the time had finally come to declare war on the colonial enslavers' way of life. However, the head of the abolitionist party in Parliament was now infirm and going blind; his days of fiery activism were behind him. As Wilberforce looked for a successor, he fixed on Thomas Fowell Buxton, the young, evangelical MP for Weymouth and a director of the African Institution. In Wilberforce's appeal to Buxton, dated May 24, 1821, he explained that "every consideration of religion, justice, and humanity" had motivated his fight on behalf "of the negro slaves in our trans-Atlantic colonies." Now he sought to form a partnership with a younger, like-minded campaigner so that "if I should be unable to commence the war," Wilberforce detailed, "and still more if, when commenced, I should (as certainly would, I fear, be the case) be unable to finish it, I do entreat that you would continue to prosecute it."

Buxton waited more than a year before deciding to accept the role. Although daunted by the prospect of filling Wilberforce's eminent shoes, he had already aired his concerns about the ineffectiveness of the African Institution to fellow directors. "I told them it was certain we once had the confidence of the country; and it was now certain the public knew little and cared little on the subject," he remarked to his wife, Hannah. As Buxton saw it, the organization had "sunk into a state of comparative inactivity." Its gentlemanly efforts to glad-hand British ministers and foreign dignitaries into supporting the cause had proved largely ineffectual. The transatlantic slave trade flourished to a shocking extent, innumerable people of African descent remained enslaved in the Americas, and the moral outrage of the British public toward slavery had dimmed. Reigniting the campaign demanded boldness.

The official title of the new anti-slavery organization founded in London in 1823 suggests what that boldness looked like in practice. The Society for the Mitigation and Gradual Abolition of Slavery Throughout the British Dominions (better known as the Anti-Slavery Society) declared its hazy intentions in convoluted language. Key leaders from the previous abolition campaign—Zachary Macaulay, Thomas Clarkson, and William Allen—remained in place, with Wilberforce playing a mostly symbolic role. Clarkson agreed to embark on another tour of England and Wales to promote the establishment of men's auxiliary anti-slavery societies. Meanwhile, Buxton advocated on the cause's behalf in Parliament.

In May 1823, Buxton announced his intention of leading a cautious campaign against the institution of slavery. He introduced a motion in the House of Commons that slavery "ought to be gradually abolished throughout the British dominions," with implementation managed from London. "The object at which we aim at is the *extinction of slavery*," he clarified, "not, however, the rapid termination of that state; not the sudden emancipation of the negro," but slow and cautious steps as "shall gently conduct us to the annihilation of slavery." Buxton, the new Anti-Slavery Society's parliamentary mouthpiece, condemned slavery as a national sin while insisting that it be allowed to die a slow, almost tranquil death.

In response, George Canning, the Tory foreign secretary and leader of the Commons, introduced three counter resolutions skillfully crafted to stop the British anti-slavery movement in its tracks. The West India lobby remained powerful, and many MPs held direct and indirect links to slavery. Canning preferred to let the Caribbean legislatures set the pace for any potential changes to the plantation system and the status of their human property. He proposed that Parliament adopt measures to ameliorate the condition of the colonial enslaved population; that lawmakers remain attuned to the progressive improvement of enslaved people; and that equal consideration be granted to the safety and property rights of Caribbean colonists in the process.

In sum, Canning's resolutions included provisions for improving the slave system while also placing the onus on the enslaved to prove—somehow—that they ultimately deserved freedom. By stressing that their release from bondage should not inconvenience the slaveholders who held them as legal property, he also extended the timeline for emancipation. Grasping that Canning's vague proposals would place the reins of amelioration into the self-interested hands of planters, Buxton attempted to counter. But he was pushed aside. Wilberforce seconded Canning's resolutions, hoping to build a foundation for the future "conversion of the slaves into a free peasantry." Canning's watered-down resolutions won the day.

As on previous occasions, snippets of metropolitan news and Canning's resolutions crossed the Atlantic and cut a path across Caribbean sugarcane fields and into the quarters of enslaved women and men. In British Demerara, a plantation colony in South America annexed from the Dutch in 1814, rumors spread among the enslaved population that Parliament and the Crown had granted them freedom but local authorities refused to comply with the order. Tensions were already high in the colony. Governor John Murray, dismissing directives from London to ameliorate labor conditions and curtail harsh punishments, such as the flogging of women, tightened restrictions on the enslaved population. He restricted and monitored their attendance at the chapels of the London Missionary Society, introducing a pass system for worship.

On August 18, 1823, about ten thousand enslaved men and women in Demerara rose in armed rebellion. The revolt was sudden and quelled by the militia and 1st West India Regiment within forty-eight hours. Murray claimed he had encountered a band of armed rebels on the road who demanded immediate emancipation. "They were tired of being slaves; their good king had sent orders that they should be free, and they would not work anymore." As on numerous prior occasions, his report suggested, parliamentary debates about the future of the colonial slave system had inspired insurrection.

At least one hundred enslaved insurgents were killed during the Demerara uprising and forty plantations damaged or destroyed. Except for the ringleaders, Governor Murray offered to pardon rebels who put down their weapons and submitted to interrogation. Under questioning, the reprieved rebels implicated a British pastor from the London Missionary Society named the Reverend John Smith. Smith had arrived in the colony

in 1817 and thereafter devoted his attention to ministering to a congregation of enslaved worshippers at Bethel Chapel. Smith, the rebels alleged,
had encouraged the insurrection through his biblical teachings; he had
strategically used chapel meetings to spread discontent among the enslaved population. Colonial officials locked Smith up, tried him by court-
martial, and sentenced him to death as a co-conspirator. Not wanting to
make a martyr of Smith, Murray wrote to George IV and requested a
royal pardon for the condemned reverend. But Smith languished and died
in prison before the king could respond.

News of the white missionary's death while in the hands of colonial
slaveholders divided the press and horrified the metropolitan public. Incensed Britons and dissenting congregations bombarded Parliament with
petitions. For anti-slavery proponents, Smith's unfair trial and tragic demise vindicated the charges they had repeatedly leveled against Caribbean
slaveholders. Precisely as colonial officials in Demerara had feared, in the
months and years after the revolt John Smith became known in evangelical and anti-slavery circles as the "Demerara martyr." Sent to one of the
king's distant dominions to save the souls of enslaved people, Smith had
paid the ultimate price for his selfless Christian labors. His death inspired
a greater public backlash than the executions of all the enslaved rebels
combined. Both the Demerara insurrection itself and the brutal response
of colonial authorities offered confirmation that the plantation system demanded improvement. To many Britons, trusting Caribbean planters to
reform the colonial slave regime without imperial intervention appeared
nothing short of folly.

CHAPTER 19

THEY WOULD BE FREE

O n Christmas Eve, 1823, three months after British forces had crushed the Demerara insurrection, Jamaican magistrates marched eight enslaved men to the public gallows in St. Mary's parish and hanged them for "rebellious conspiracy." "No distinction could be made amongst them," claimed Jamaica's governor, William Montagu, duke of Manchester, "as all were equally guilty, and four of them positively refused to turn king's evidence." What they were guilty of, according to authorities, was engaging in seditious talk on Frontier estate and daring to "imagine the death of the white people of the said parish." It began on the evening of December 16, when the planter Andrew Roberts scolded William, an enslaved domestic, for dawdling. William retorted by predicting in an ominous manner that his master would have a "bad Christmas." Alarmed, Roberts grilled William for additional details. He knew that bondspeople often timed revolts for holiday periods when planters dropped their guard, and the enslaved community enjoyed a rare period of relative autonomy.

Under interrogation, William claimed that his father, James Sterling, an enslaved laborer at nearby Frontier estate, had told him that "the negroes were going to rise, and walk all about and murder everybody." Roberts rushed to inform the local authorities, who rounded up the alleged ringleaders the next morning. Hearsay evidence provided by a smattering of enslaved witnesses confirmed the accused had boasted that on Christmas Day "they would be free." Magistrates in St. Mary's wasted no time. By December 19, the local court had tried and convicted Sterling and seven other enslaved men implicated in the alleged insurrection plot. The conspirators were sentenced to death by hanging before the holidays as a deterrent to the island's enslaved population.

In late 1823 and 1824, Governor Manchester reported to Earl Bathurst that he had received intelligence of unrest among the enslaved in four different parishes: St. Mary's, St. George's, St. James's, and Hanover. Although he claimed the localized disturbances occurred independently of one another, Manchester and his colonial informants assumed the conspirators shared the same goal: to obtain their freedom by force and massacre their enslavers. The governor maintained that he deeply regretted executing the ringleaders but hoped "this example of severity had the effect of intimidating others who were prepared for mischief." Trials of enslaved individuals accused of rebellious conspiracy unfolded over a period of eight months.

In all, Jamaican magistrates tried fifty-six enslaved men for supposedly plotting insurrections and executed twenty-two of them. The remaining accused received sentences of transportation, imprisonment, corporal punishment, or pardons from the governor. Such precautionary measures promised to "restore the colony to its former tranquility," Manchester assured the imperial government. Circumstances on the island and throughout Britain's Atlantic empire compelled Jamaican authorities to crack down on subversive talk among the enslaved. Officials could not allow bondspeople to believe "that they were entitled to their freedom and that the cause they had embraced was just and in vindication of their own rights." The maintenance of slavery depended on both the denial of rights to the enslaved and their acceptance of that marginalized, subservient status.

In December 1824, a secret committee appointed by the Jamaica assembly to investigate the previous year's rebellious plots published its report. It claimed that cruel treatment had not incited would-be insurgents to conspire against their enslavers. Instead, frequent parliamentary discussions related to Britain's colonial enslaved population had fostered their collective design, kindling a flame "which will be extinguished only in blood." The committee declared that the convicted ringleaders made their motives plain at their executions, proclaiming that they felt "contented and happy till they imbibed the notion that the king and Wilberforce had made them free." Anti-slavery advocates in Britain scoffed at this assertion, noting that Jamaican reports and newspaper coverage of the trials omitted references to "any confession of the kind." Whether the plots were inspired by events in Britain or entirely fabricated, observed the Anti-Slavery Society, planters in Jamaica had benefited from them politically. They simply attributed the unrest to parliamentary and Crown support for the amelioration of slavery. Alleged conspiracies served colonial enslavers' interests by bringing the efforts of abolitionists and the government into disrepute as "productive of blood and devastation," Zachary Macaulay wrote.

In May 1823, under public and parliamentary pressure, the British Crown adopted an official policy of slavery amelioration, or improvement. The government aimed to reform the slave system by persuading colonial assemblies to amend their slave codes. Improved conditions would supposedly instill among the enslaved a sense of moral and civic responsibility that would pave the way to their eventual freedom. Reforms included scaled-back use and monitoring of corporal punishments; the prohibition of the flogging of enslaved women and freedom for all female infants born after 1823; time off for religious instruction and the abolition of the Sunday market for sabbath observance; promotion of monogamous Christian marriages and the encouragement of reproduction among the enslaved; and admission of the evidence of enslaved individuals in colonial courts, among other interventions.

These piecemeal ameliorative measures were a far cry from full freedom. "It was not emancipation but amelioration, not revolution but evolution," remarks the Caribbean historian Eric Williams. "Slavery would be killed with kindness." To enact its reforming agenda, the government issued orders in council to the Crown colonies of Trinidad and British Guiana. The older legislative colonies, which controlled 80 percent of the empire's enslaved population, received circular dispatches from London recommending implementation of the amelioration measures. For the reforming scheme to work, securing the cooperation of colonists across the British Caribbean was imperative, but this posed innumerable challenges. Anti-slavery campaigners appealed to legislators in Jamaica, Barbados, and other self-governing colonies to submit to the Crown's will. "The Negro slavery of the British colonies," William Wilberforce pointed out, constituted "a system of the grossest injustice, of the most heathenish irreligion and immorality, of the most unprecedented degradation, and unrelenting cruelty."

But such arguments fell on deaf ears. Caribbean officials pronounced the ameliorative directives a blatant attack on their constitutional rights. They blamed agitation of the issue in Parliament for disturbances among the enslaved population and demanded redress for the property losses that would follow emancipation. In petitions to George IV, Caribbean planters and their agents in London complained that the actions of Parliament and the Crown's ministers had imperiled their lives and the sanctity of their property, "so repeatedly and so solemnly recognized by your Majesty, your royal predecessors, and the Parliament of Great Britain." Only fair financial compensation, they argued, could possibly make up for the Crown's betrayal of its slaveholding subjects. By 1824, William, duke of Clarence, a decades-long ally of the Caribbean planters and merchants, wrote that he was "broken hearted on the subject of the West Indies."

While Governor Manchester initially hoped the Jamaica assembly would compromise and revise portions of the island's slave code to satisfy imperial directives, he met a solid wall of resistance. As he admitted privately to Earl Bathurst, Jamaican planters exhibited "a great reluctance to part with power over the slave," and to a greater extent "than might have been expected in the present age." They viewed with suspicion any measure designed "to raise the slave above his present level, and any approach toward civilization as a release from that subjection which habit teaches them to think essential to the existence of slavery."

The imperial circulars dispatched from London overlapped with news of the Demerara revolt, fraying nerves in Jamaica. Rumors of enslaved conspiracies confirmed planters' worst fears and allowed them to vent their rage against those whom they held in subjugation. In 1826, a House of Commons investigation determined that the so-called evidence brought against the executed conspirators in Jamaica collapsed under the barest scrutiny. British lawmakers sought to distance themselves from the "violation of justice displayed in those trials," which had resulted in unjust death sentences "wholly unwarranted by proof." Time and again, the brutality of colonial slaveholders demonstrated the pressing need for imperial intervention in the British Caribbean.

In the wake of the Demerara revolt and the alleged conspiracies in Jamaica, the Anti-Slavery Society articulated a case for gradual emancipation that appeared too extreme to some and too timid and ineffectual to others. Modifying the Atlantic slave system to satisfy misguided humanitarian aims risked the economic foundation of the Caribbean colonies, pro-slavery supporters contended. Nothing could be more foolish when it was impossible "to wish for colonies more productive of benefit to the mother country." Britons had the right to intervene in the colonial slave system, Thomas Clarkson retorted, because the oppressed persons in question are "fellow subjects" of the Crown. The elected assemblies of the slave colonies not only refused to take action to improve conditions for enslaved people but also insulted the dignity of Britain's most revered institutions: the monarchy and Parliament. Rather than submitting to the recommended imperial reforms, the colonial legislatures had avowed "to resist to the utmost the benevolent intentions of the King and the Parliament towards their slaves."

While government ministers proposed ameliorative reforms to the colonial slave system in the king's name, and abolitionists beseeched him to expunge "our deep-sunk national stain," throughout the process George IV urged caution. He directed his representatives to deliver a speech on his behalf at the opening of Parliament in February 1824 recommending MPs exercise "calmness and discretion" and that they allow prudence to temper zeal. "To excite exaggerated expectations in those who are the objects of your benevolence, would be as fatal to their welfare as to that of their employers," the king warned.

Regarding slavery, many middle-class Britons, and women especially, were done with caution by the mid-1820s. While the king counseled restraint, dozens of ladies' anti-slavery associations whose members insisted on parliamentary action sprang up across the country. British women campaigners pledged to boycott slave-produced sugar and agitate on behalf of "Negro emancipation." They pushed for a new and enlightened era when "the unhappy Children of Africa shall no longer be treated as beasts, no longer be bought and sold, and branded like cattle; and when the torturing and degrading cart-whip shall no longer fall on the persons of helpless Negro Slaves," or infants torn from their mothers' breasts.

Female anti-slavery activists characterized enslavers' exploitation of bondswomen in colonial slave societies as an affront to British norms and Christianity. If the treatment of women and children served as the touchstone of a culture's civilization, by any measure Britain and its empire had failed. Women campaigners focused their efforts on raising the consciousness of fellow Britons, "determined to awaken (at least in the bosom of English *women*) a deep and lasting compassion, not only for the *bodily sufferings* of female slaves, but for their *moral degradation*." They appealed to British lawmakers to remove "the bitter cup of slavery" from the lips of Africans subject to bondage in the king's dominions.

No campaigner in Britain demanded action on the slavery question as urgently as the Quaker activist Elizabeth Heyrick. In her blockbuster pamphlet *Immediate, Not Gradual Emancipation*, Heyrick lambasted members of the all-male Anti-Slavery Society for their overly cautious approach. She pointed out the immediacy of the issue for the British public and highlighted concrete steps consumers could take to effect change. "The perpetuation of slavery in our West India colonies, is not an abstract question, to be settled between the government and the planters," she wrote. "It is a question in which we are *all* implicated; we are all guilty." She urged the British public to boycott Caribbean products, especially sugar, and to pressure Parliament and the Crown to act immediately. As intended, Heyrick's fiery language inflamed popular passions and signaled a critical shift in approach among anti-slavery advocates. She stressed that actions taken by British consumers, and particularly female purchasers of domestic products, could manipulate the market and deliver instantaneous results: the annihilation of the colonial slave system.

Heyrick's rhetoric and demands flew in the face of the gradualist campaign adopted by the Anti-Slavery Society. She rejected their moderate, painfully unhurried approach. By advocating for emancipation at a distant date, Britain's leading abolitionists had enabled Caribbean colonial legislatures to dismiss imperial recommendations. Thomas Clarkson, at least, sensed the shift in public opinion. While his society colleagues remained in the capital, Thomas Clarkson had set out on horseback to promote the cause of gradual emancipation. During his travels he confronted Britons hungry for swift action on the slavery question. "Everywhere people are asking me about *immediate abolition*," he jotted in his diary.

Heyrick had tapped into and amplified the nation's growing impatience. Claiming, as the Anti-Slavery Society insisted, that enslaved people must first demonstrate their moral worthiness for freedom struck her as hypocritical and detrimental to the cause. "We have no right, on any pretext of expediency or pretended humanity, to say 'because you have been made a slave, and thereby degraded and debased, therefore, I will continue to hold you in bondage until you have acquired a capacity to make a right use of your liberty,'" she argued. "Give the slave his liberty, in the sacred name of justice, give it to him at once." Heyrick called on the public to agitate en masse, commenting that "a noble duke [e.g. Clarence] besought Parliament *not to meddle with the alarming question*," when reformers first campaigned for the abolition of the slave trade. When had the Crown or the landed elite ever spearheaded the dismantling of an entrenched system of inequality?

In June 1825, the Anti-Slavery Society launched a new magazine, the *Anti-Slavery Monthly Reporter*, to share slavery-related news from across the British Empire and the globe with the public. Evolving over the years in title and focus, the magazine would play a central role in Britain's anti-slavery campaign and remain in circulation until 1840. Edited by founder Zachary Macaulay, the *Reporter* assembled detailed information on colonial conditions and developments for the parliamentary campaign and local anti-slavery committees. For provincial readers, it reprinted the proceedings of the Anti-Slavery Society meetings held in London, over which the duke of Gloucester continued to preside. Through accounts of colonial resistance to amelioration and cruelty toward enslaved people, it galvanized members of auxiliary societies to keep up the pressure on their elected representatives and the British Crown. The *Reporter* garnered a paid circulation of over twenty thousand, not including the numerous groups and individuals across the country who borrowed copies. Soon after the first issue's release, the *Reporter* became the standard reference reached for by MPs. Whenever lawmakers sought factual evidence during slavery debates, Wilberforce would say: "Let us look it up in Macaulay."

The *Anti-Slavery Reporter* aided the society's call for a new round of parliamentary petitions, which Macaulay reprinted in full for magazine readers. In July 1826, the *Reporter* stated that the House of Commons had received 674 anti-slavery petitions during its previous session and the Lords a similar number. Containing tens of thousands of signatures, the petitions expressed the sentiments of entire counties and towns, Macaulay contended, and captured the personal views of individual Britons across the social spectrum. If the government doubted the nation's commitment to the anti-slavery cause, the nature and extent of the petitions spoke volumes. "The merits of the great question at issue have been fully canvassed," the *Reporter* proclaimed. The unambiguous result: "an almost universal conviction, on the part of the public, that the slavery which prevails in our colonies is opposed to the spirit of our holy religion, to the genius of the British constitution, to the principles of humanity and justice, and to every sound view even of our commercial interests." Using the *Reporter* to spread the word, the society promoted the purchase of free-labor sugar from India, encouraged boycotts of slave-produced sugar, and pushed for the end of preferential duties for Caribbean produce.

With raw data at their disposal and public sympathy in their favor, anti-slavery campaigners looked for cracks in their opponents' lines of defense. The belligerent response of assemblies in the legislative colonies to the government's amelioration recommendations was widely known and discussed. George IV's advisers acknowledged that "the resolutions so strongly urged upon them in your Majesty's name" had strained relations between the Crown and its Caribbean possessions. "Great care and circumspection will be requisite," they reasoned, "to ward off the dangers which might arise both to this country and to the most valuable foreign possessions of your Majesty's Crown." Defenders of colonial slavery dismissed the British public as rash and impatient, too impassioned to assess the situation with the calm sobriety it warranted. It cost overwrought Britons nothing "to involve these most valuable possessions of the Crown's in indiscriminate ruin," observed a Jamaican planter. The king understood this better than anyone, and he proceeded accordingly.

But other Britons remained unconvinced by monetary arguments. Despite centuries of slavery-derived profits accruing to the British monarchy, state, and economy, some questioned the true value of the Caribbean colonies to the nation. Britain had long provided a protected market for West Indian produce, with the cost borne directly by metropolitan consumers through higher market prices. "For whose pecuniary benefit then is this system maintained?" wondered John Taylor, a Liverpool cotton merchant. "Not for that of the *British* people, nor of the 700,000 Blacks, nor of any great portion of even the 70,000 whites resident in the colonies." Ultimately, the Atlantic slave system benefited only "a small number of individuals, styling themselves West Indian proprietors and merchants." As to whether enslaved people of African origin and descent aspired to strike off their chains and participate in civil society as free subjects of the Crown, the question "is at once answered, by their well-known wish to emancipate themselves."

Caribbean planters and supporters countered that enslaved Africans knew neither their own minds nor their best interests. Overzealous activists in the mother country had led them astray with false promises of liberation. More important, in contrast to their enslavers, bondsmen and -women lacked the constitutional rights of freeborn Britons; they were merely a valuable "species of property" owned by the king's subjects. The wishes of the enslaved population therefore failed to enter the equation.

Pro-slavery authors repeatedly offered readers partial, self-serving history lessons, outlining how nearly two centuries had passed since Stuart kings first encouraged their subjects to settle the Caribbean islands by royal charter and granted them land and the right to self-government. "The charters by which the Crown confirmed their privileges to the colonies, are held to be as sacred as any institution in England which may have become identified with the law of land," argued Alexander McDonnell, a propagandist for the West India lobby. Parliament had subsequently authorized the acquisition of private property in enslaved Africans, just as successive sovereigns had offered due protection to Caribbean colonists' persons and property. "It is not freedom that revolts the minds of West Indians," insisted one Caribbean planter, "but the loss of property and the total ruin of their temporal interests." As far as the king's slaveholding subjects were concerned, when humanitarian impulses in government clashed with constitutionally protected property rights, the latter must always prevail.

Abolitionists fought back by linking themes of unchecked planter tyranny to monarchal abuses of power. If Parliament had successfully restrained the previously concentrated power of the British sovereign in 1689, why not that of the slaveholder? The conduct of Caribbean colonists suggested that they had appointed themselves absolute monarchs over their enslaved laborers.

"It is plainly derogatory to the constitutional power and glory of the Crown," wrote the abolitionist James Stephen, "that the mass of the colonial population, like the vassals of feudal barons, should have intermediate sovereigns, to whom, much more than to the king or his laws, their allegiance must be paid." In Caribbean slave society, "the master, to them is everything, and the monarch an empty name. They find that they are subjects by the sword only, not the scepter." What should offend every loyal Briton is this, Stephen concluded: "The authority of the sovereign is so degraded as to be actually made subordinate and ministerial to that of the master." While mechanisms of coercion underwrote contractual labor relations in Britain, the law exercised a restraining hand over masters that was absent in colonial slave societies.

Anti-slavery proponents pointed out that even schoolboys understood the extent to which slaveholding planters had twisted and undermined the British constitution and authority of the sovereign. Although approached with "deference and humility" by George IV's representatives, colonial slaveholders had pronounced themselves uncommonly exempt from the authority of king and Parliament. They rejected imperial calls for reform such that "neither King, Lords, nor Commons, nor all of them together had power to make *them* (the colonists) submit to the projected innovations of their slave system." Preferring to exercise an arbitrary power antithetical to British liberty, the planters repeatedly insulted the Crown to which they owed allegiance. Their desire to govern "unchecked as a despotic sovereign" over their bondswomen and -men had degraded their status as civilized British subjects.

In private letters to abolitionists, members of the nobility claiming to share concerns about despotic Caribbean enslavers expressed support for gradual emancipation. As the earl of Bristol wrote to Thomas Clarkson, he was moved by "your feelings toward the Blacks." He also worried that the result of heightened public frenzy for the slaves' cause might be "to retard emancipation to a very distant period; or to produce a state of insubordination and violence as horrible as slavery itself." The slaveholders' refusal to yield left everyone uneasy. But few at the time expected resident or absentee Caribbean planters to acquiesce to British imperial demands without dispute. Too much wealth was at stake.

Admittedly, some abolitionists conceded, in previous eras both the British monarchy and Parliament had encouraged the expansion of African trafficking and enslavement in the plantation colonies. England's most revered institutions had thus "sanctioned and instigated the planters, by bounties, protecting duties, &c. to embark their capital in slave speculations." But no more. "Our eyes are now opened to its atrocity. We will neither encourage nor connive at it any longer." Still, how blameless was the current British sovereign and government? A potentially explosive issue related to Britain's slave empire was hiding in plain sight: continued Crown ownership of enslaved people in its overseas dominions. In the 1820s, as fierce debates over gradual emancipation unfolded in Parliament and saturated the popular press, British officials addressed for the first time the question of what should be done with so-called "Crown slaves"—individuals purchased by or forfeited to the Crown.

CHAPTER 20

FREE SUBJECTS OF THE CROWN

B y the early nineteenth century, the British sovereign technically owned thousands of enslaved people. The largest number of individuals fell into the Crown's possession through purchase for government use and enrollment in the British armed forces. Crown representatives throughout the Atlantic empire procured enslaved men and women for employment on public works involving hard or specialized labor, such as building roads and forts or maintaining naval dockyards and vessels. Over a century of warfare in the hazardous Caribbean theater had demonstrated the immense value of seasoned men of African origin and ancestry to the British army and navy. From 1795 through the end of Britain's legal transatlantic slave trade, the Crown bought 13,400 enslaved men to serve in the West India Regiment at a total cost of £925,000—making the king the single largest purchaser of enslaved people in the British Empire.

After 1808, Crown officials forcibly conscripted African men and boys liberated from illegal slaving vessels into the West India Regiments and Royal African Corps for life. The British monarch's title to "prize Negroes" justified their compulsory enlistment. A revised mutiny act passed the same year as the Abolition Act declared the Crown's previously enslaved soldiers free so long as they served actively in the British armed forces. The act protected freed Black soldiers from the prospect of re-enslavement within the king's dominions. But there was, of course, a catch: Black soldiers had to serve for life and were excluded from pension schemes.

Apart from bondsmen and -women purchased for governmental or military purposes, people of African birth or descent became the property of the Crown primarily through forfeiture, conquest, and escheat (the reversion of property to the monarchy when a decedent dies intestate, with no heirs). Commonly a result of treason, the practice of forfeiture transferred ownership of land and property from a private subject to their sovereign. Enslaved individuals also came into the Crown's possession in this manner. In 1796, after sixteen months of conflict, British forces quelled a devastating and costly uprising in Grenada, known as Fédon's rebellion. Initiated by free people of African and French ancestry and enslaved men and women, the revolt occurred after Britain regained control of the island following a period of French occupation. Declaring French-speaking free whites and free and enslaved rebels of African descent guilty of high treason, the Grenada assembly confiscated insurgents' estates and property, including bondspeople. Colonial authorities transported four hundred rebels to the British penal colony of Honduras. In the aftermath of the insurrection, hundreds of enslaved men, women, and children owned by proprietors charged with treason came into the possession of the Crown and produced profits for the king's treasury.

The Crown also acquired enslaved individuals employed in the public works departments of foreign governments through conquest, as in the case of multiple territories taken during the Napoleonic Wars. In 1804, the British conquered the Dutch colony of Berbice, and four plantations and 791 enslaved people became the legal property of George III. Another common means by which the Crown assumed ownership of human property involved colonial subjects dying without a will or a legitimate spouse or heirs. When enslavers in the king's dominions died intestate, their property—including human property—automatically escheated to the British sovereign. Upon application to the king and payment of a transfer fee, natural relations could receive grants of escheated property vested in the Crown. By this means, ownership of enslaved individuals transferred back into the hands of private subjects. Uncontested human property escheated to the British sovereign was sold in the king's name and for his benefit at public auction. Finally, judicial sentences handed down to enslaved people convicted of committing crimes against the colonial state could result in forfeiture of their persons to the Crown.

Regardless of how enslaved individuals came into the monarchy's possession, abolitionists operating within the British government identified their presence in the slave colonies as an opportunity to put ameliorative theories into practice. If so-called "Crown slaves" thrived under improved conditions and more humane treatment, their advancement held the potential to set an example for colonial enslavers generally to emulate. In 1813, Zachary Macaulay, then secretary for the Berbice Commission, recommended that Crown agents pay special attention to the moral and religious instruction of enslaved people owned by the king. He also urged the Crown's representatives in the slave colonies to avoid leasing or attempting to sell "this species of property." It reflected poorly on the monarchy if enslaved individuals technically owned by the British sovereign were hired out and overworked or sold and then subsequently mistreated or sent to an early grave. Treasury officials agreed with the thrust of Macaulay's conclusions. But at the time, neither Macaulay nor members of the king's ministry proposed manumission as a potential option for "Crown slaves." They continued to view enslaved men and women in the king's possession as property, not subjects worthy of freedom.

In the 1820s, as the anti-slavery movement gathered steam, the matter of enslaved people owned by and escheated to the Crown assumed a new sense of urgency after Britain adopted slavery amelioration as official imperial policy. Sir Charles Maxwell, the newly appointed governor of Dominica and St. Kitts, first raised the issue in 1819 but received no response. In 1823 he tried again. Writing to the Colonial Office for guidance, he inquired if "his Majesty might be pleased to grant these people their freedom, as in the case of slaves illegally imported." Maxwell suggested that George IV release bondspeople who came into his possession "instead of their being retained or sold as slaves for the benefit of the Crown or relinquished to persons by whom they would be kept in a state of bondage." As a rule, treating escheated human property like Africans liberated from slaving vessels appeared preferable to subjecting them to public sale in the king's name. By this point, a handful of escheated enslaved people had also petitioned for their own freedom, yet no general principle existed.

Working as a legal adviser to the Colonial Office, James Stephen Jr., son of the famous abolitionist by the same name, considered the matter of enslaved people escheated to the Crown. He drew up an influential report in 1823 that generated several years of controversy within the government and ultimately shaped British imperial policy. Stephen observed that the case of enslaved individuals escheating to the Crown had become commonplace, owing to the significant number of free persons of multiple ancestries of illegitimate birth. This meant that "if any such person dies intestate, and without children born in marriage, the slaves of which he or she may have been seized will of course escheat." He urged the king's officials to adopt a general rule on the subject, namely that the Crown would henceforth free any escheated enslaved persons, excepting those whose age, infirmity, or troublesome behavior prevented their manumission. That many free people of mixed African and European ancestry in the colonial Caribbean owed their existence to coercive, illicit sexual unions between white men and enslaved women was an unacknowledged subtext of his report.

Earl Bathurst approved of Stephen's recommendations and endorsed their implementation as a general Crown policy. But treasury officials disagreed. They argued that the nearest relatives to the deceased had a stronger claim to escheated human property than the enslaved individuals had to their own persons. Placing a moratorium on selling bondspeople for the king's benefit was acceptable only if the claims of natural relations took precedence before any manumissions. Otherwise, this new rule "would inflict a great and undeserved hardship upon many persons having equitable claims to the property." Enslaved people, in other words, remained bare commodities subject to the more pressing property rights of British subjects. Even as the imperial government advised colonial legislatures to improve conditions for enslaved people in George IV's name, it continued to conceptualize women, men, and children of African descent as intrinsically chattel.

The Anti-Slavery Society and its supporters seized on the unresolved issue of enslaved people escheating to the Crown in the king's overseas dominions. Abolitionist campaigners attacked the practice as "a monstrous system of oppression," one that dishonored the monarchy and the British nation by "the Crown aiding, and profiting by, the wrong." Due to their owner's intestacy, enslaved individuals were thrown, like other forfeited property, "into the hands of his majesty" and treated no better than beasts. "His majesty, instead of protecting them as subjects, and giving them freedom, is made to sell them into interminable bondage, even separating, in some cases, the nearest and dearest connections, and all for his own profit, or that of his officers." It was odd, mused the *Westminster Review*, that in the push for the gradual abolition of slavery in Britain's Atlantic empire "many lesser means of emancipation are allowed to pass by unnoticed." It pointed specifically to "slaves escheated to the Crown," noting that the king had acquired ownership of 948 individuals in Jamaica alone between 1807 and 1821. "The more natural course, with a truly paternal government, would have been to give these slaves their liberty, instead of producing so large a mass of misery for the sake of an almost imperceptible increase of the revenue." Why had Britain's sovereign not led the way?

Behind the scenes, the matter of "Crown slaves" was quietly under review by the Colonial Office. Starting in 1822, the British imperial government dispatched London-based barristers to the Caribbean colonies, and throughout the king's dominions, to report on laws, courts, and the administration of justice. Essentially "royal fact finders," the commissioners of inquiry acquired colonial legal information for the Crown and made recommendations for imperial reform. As they toured the sugar islands, the commissioners investigated the process of enslaved people falling to the British sovereign by escheat, among many other legal matters. Due to the absence of a uniform policy, escheat procedures varied across the Caribbean colonies, the commissioners learned. But nowhere were escheated bondspeople considered "virtually freed" by virtue of coming into the king's possession. Their fates followed one of two standard paths: They either became the property of the deceased owner's kin by application to the king or fell into the hands of a receiver charged with disposing of escheated human property "for the advantage of the Crown." In the colonial Caribbean, even the king and his representatives benefited financially from the enslavement, ruthless separation, and sale of African-descended individuals and families.

The findings of the commissioners appeared to confirm anti-slavery campaigners' arguments about the inhumanity of Britain's slave empire. To draw public attention to an unjust colonial slave system in which all were implicated, including the king, abolitionists highlighted a particularly shocking escheat case. On August 7, 1823, following the deaths of two planters intestate, nineteen bondspeople attached to separate Barbados estates became escheats of the Crown. Among them were a total of four family units of father and son (Quow and Caesar), mother and son (Orange and October), parents and children (Abel and Lubbah and Thomas, Kitty, and Becky), sisters and a brother (Deborah, Sukey, Betsey, Polly, and Thomas) and their children (James, the infant son of Sukey; Betsey's children, Caroline, Grace, and Medorah; and Richard, Polly's son). Less than two weeks after these enslaved individuals came into the possession of the Crown, Lionel Parke, the king's receiver general in Barbados, held a public auction. He permitted a total of thirteen different planters to purchase and split the family units. The net proceeds of the sale of enslaved individuals escheated to the Crown—the "price of blood," as the Anti-Slavery Society put it—were paid into the king's treasury.

The Crown-sanctioned separation of parents and children at a public auction demonstrated the complicity of the British monarchy and state in the most callous aspects of slavery. Quow and Caesar and Orange and October were each purchased by different slaveholders. Abel and Lubbah were separated from their three children, Thomas, Kitty, and Becky, each of whom went to a separate enslaver. Five different planters purchased the sisters and brother family unit. While eighteen-month-old James, who was too young to be separated from his mother, remained with Sukey, Betsey lost her daughter Medorah, age nine, during the auction. Polly and her son, Richard, age eleven, fled prior to the auction rather than face the prospect of separation. They remained at large and the Crown did not benefit from their sale. "What is it but a slave trade, more disgraceful than even that of Africa," protested the Anti-Slavery Society, "by which the King of Great Britain has been made to enrich himself by the sale into perpetual slavery of seventeen of his liege subjects, whose dearest ties have been burst asunder by the process?" The cruelty committed in the king's name knew no bounds.

In 1830, after years of wavering, the British government reconsidered its policy regarding enslaved people escheated to the Crown. Two years earlier it had issued free certificates confirming the freedom of all involuntarily apprenticed Africans liberated from slaving vessels. This decision established a precedent for the treatment of so-called "Crown slaves," however obtained, as did reports from colonies such as Antigua testifying to the good behavior of liberated Africans post emancipation. Returning to the opinion of James Stephen, the Colonial Office validated the soundness of his recommendation that the Crown as a rule should not sell, grant, or retain bondspeople that fell into its possession. British imperial officials opted to make one exception for a large estate in Grenada with "a numerous gang of slaves," which the Crown had operated under the supervision of a colonial agent since its forfeiture in 1796.

Following decades of Crown ownership of the Grenada property, the Colonial Office elected to return the estate and its three hundred enslaved laborers to the natural heirs of the original owner. Manumitting "a multitude of slaves" simultaneously posed too grave a risk to colonial slave society, imperial officials determined. Securing the continued bondage of these individuals under new ownership, "subject to resumption by the Crown should ill usage of the slaves be proved," was the wisest course in this "anomalous case." "Slaves worked for the profit of the Crown are not likely to be so hard worked as when they are worked for the profit of an individual," the Colonial Office reasoned. Nevertheless, in all other future instances, releasing enslaved people escheated to the Crown from "bitter servitude" was preferable. The institution of the monarchy would thus avoid being implicated as an enslaver. Racial assumptions also played a role in this imperial policy shift. British officials identified the relatives applying for grants of escheated bondspeople typically as "low colored people," who, they alleged, "make notoriously the most oppressive masters of slaves." Better for Britain's king to appear blameless than for free people of African and multiple ancestries to benefit financially.

In March 1831, the circular announcing Britain's new policy of liberation for enslaved people escheated to the Crown went out to the governors of all slave colonies, Mauritius excepted. "The King's Government have felt it their duty humbly to represent to His Majesty, that this is a species of property which many considerations concur to recommend that the Crown should forthwith relinquish," the dispatch explained. Colonial officials were ordered to "place them upon the footing of other free persons of African birth or descent, and left to seek their own subsistence," like the liberated Africans emancipated by the Crown in 1828. Zachary Macaulay, who had already attacked the British sovereign's ownership of human property as a "disgrace to the Crown and to the country," found fault with the plan to manumit only enslaved individuals escheated to the Crown. The king still retained some twenty-five hundred persons "in a state of slavery" in his overseas possessions, Macaulay noted. "Crown slaves" resided in Mauritius, Grenada, Berbice, Demerara, Trinidad, Antigua, and Tobago. "These slaves of the king ought all forthwith to be declared free, and to have adequate portions of the Crown lands assigned them." Who better to receive freedom and land than men and women formerly owned in the king's name, "that they might be thus converted to a free and happy peasantry."

Later that year, the Colonial Office ordered the manumission of all enslaved individuals belonging to the Crown, regardless of how they had come into the king's possession. While abolitionists praised the decision "as satisfactory as it was honorable to his majesty's government," and "productive of economical, peaceful, and happy results," others later dismissed it as a half-measure destined to fail. Emancipating only the king's bondspeople was bound to send the wrong message to the vast general enslaved population, especially in Britain's largest and most valuable sugar colony. "The slaves in Jamaica once more believed that the King of England had given them their freedom," one of Wilberforce's biographers commented. "Was not the manumission of Crown slaves proof of it?"

On June 26, 1830, following the death of the deeply unpopular George IV, whose only legitimate heir, Princess Charlotte, had died in 1817, his younger brother ascended to the throne as William IV. Sixty-four, deeply conservative, and a known champion of slaveholders, William remained as opposed to emancipation as he had been to the abolition of the transatlantic slave trade. "The king is no Abolitionist," as one member of government put it. Half a century after visiting the Caribbean colonies while serving in the Royal Navy, Britain's sovereign still maintained that "the slaves were the happiest people in the world."

Despite the king's personal sympathy for Caribbean planters, his accession triggered a general election that offered abolitionists an opportunity to sweep candidates into office who supported the public's calls for emancipation. Popular pressure to change the electoral system and expand the franchise to middle-class men weakened and split the Tories, led by the duke of Wellington. When Parliament met in November 1830, Wellington's inability to form a government ushered into power a coalition of Whigs and liberal Tories led by the reform-minded Earl Grey. Grey, though a member of the landed elite and "averse to the agitation of any great questions that are not actually forced upon him," proved amenable under pressure to revisiting the issue of emancipation.

Within months, the new government offered a concession to the vocal abolitionist faction in the Commons, approving the liberation of bondspeople belonging to the Crown. Nevertheless, when Thomas Fowell Buxton addressed the declining enslaved population in the Caribbean in April 1831 and introduced a motion in support of general emancipation, Grey was indifferent. Speaking on the government's behalf, Viscount Howick, Earl Grey's son and the undersecretary of state for the colonies, implored the House to consider the matter with extreme caution. Immediate emancipation posed dire risks to both the enslaved and to Caribbean planters.

Howick clarified that the government had no viable proposal in hand for freeing enslaved people. Consequently, "until some safe and practical plan of emancipation is laid down before the House, I shall protest against the adoption of resolutions, which could have no other possible effect but that of irritating the master, and of exciting in the breast of the slave expectations which must be disappointed." The debate on the motion was postponed and Parliament dissolved. The Anti-Slavery Society, realizing it had lost ground to the West India lobby, formed a committee dedicated to rousing the public to promote the cause of immediate emancipation. While British lawmakers dragged their heels, "the signs of the times are all for reform," remarked the MP and diarist Charles Greville, "and against slavery."

The disturbing true story of Mary Prince, the first former enslaved woman to publish an autobiography in Britain, offered abolitionists the boost the movement needed to inspire political action. Over forty years had passed since the initial publication of the compelling first-person narratives written by the Sons of Africa activists Ottobah Cugoano and Olaudah Equiano. At a time when many middle-class women in Britain had joined female anti-slavery societies and signed petitions in favor of immediate emancipation, Prince offered exceptional insight into the experience of Caribbean enslavement from the perspective of an African-descended woman.

Published in 1831, *The History of Mary Prince, a West Indian Slave*, differed from the late eighteenth-century autobiographies released by her formerly enslaved male counterparts in a critical way, however. Prince's dictated account reached the eyes of the public only after heavy mediation by British anti-slavery campaigners, who used her first-person tale of enslavement to elicit sympathy. While abolitionist influence and parliamentary witness testimonies undoubtedly shaped the narratives published by Cugoano and Equiano, illiteracy prevented Prince from exercising any authorial control over her life story. Her gender and racial status also precluded Prince from playing a key role in the British anti-slavery movement beyond the publication of her autobiography.

Born enslaved in Bermuda around 1788, Mary Prince was separated from her family at a young age and repeatedly sold to new, increasingly brutal owners. She engaged in various forms of arduous coerced labor in Bermuda, Turks Island, and Antigua. Prince recounted numerous examples of harsh treatment she and other enslaved individuals, both male and female, faced at the hands of their enslavers: whippings, floggings, sexual abuse, and outright murder. In the mid-1820s, Prince secretly joined the Moravian church in Antigua and soon after met and married Daniel James, a free Black carpenter and widower who had purchased his own freedom. When her enslaver, John Wood, discovered that the Moravians had permitted Prince to marry in their chapel without his permission, he "flew into a great rage." Margaret Wood, incensed by Prince's illicit marriage to a greater extent than her husband, "stirred up Mr. Wood to flog me dreadfully with the horsewhip," Prince recounted. She described the acute suffering she endured as a married woman severely flogged by her master for behaving like a good Christian.

To maintain control over Mary Prince's life and labor, her enslavers refused to sell her or permit her to save money and obtain her own freedom. Voicing the desire to secure her eventual release from bondage so angered Mrs. Wood that she chastised Prince as "a black devil." The Woods repeatedly beat her, straining her relationship with her husband, James, who was helpless to assist his enslaved wife. Prince's legal status as the property of another negated his marital rights as her husband. In 1828, Prince accompanied the Woods to London, serving as their cleaner and laundress while they enrolled their daughters in school. She continued to suffer physical abuse at the hands of her enslavers. Later that year, after learning that English law prohibited the re-enslavement of freedom seekers, Prince fled and found her way to the offices of the Anti-Slavery Society. While working in the household of the society's secretary, Thomas Pringle, she dictated her autobiography to the abolitionist Susanna Strickland. Pringle edited Strickland's manuscript account of Mary Prince's life. He posed queries to Prince as he revised the autobiography and then published it at his own expense.

Mary Prince had shared her heart-wrenching narrative of enslavement, she said, to move the British people to reject deceptive claims about the supposed happiness of enslaved people. "I feel great sorrow when I hear some people in this country say, that the slaves do not need better usage, and do not want to be free," Prince grieved. "I say, not so. How can slaves be happy when they have the halter round their neck and the whip upon their back?" Could any human being feel content, she argued, when they "are disgraced and thought not more of than beasts? And are separated from their mothers, and husbands, and children, and sisters, just as cattle are sold and separated?" Prince's narrative, as Pringle intended, provided a damning account of the lived experience of slavery from a Black woman's perspective. It strategically emphasized the helplessness of enslaved people, especially abused women and children, and their reliance upon British saviors.

Mary Prince's autobiography concluded with a powerful appeal to the British public. "This is slavery. I tell it to let English people know the truth," Prince declared. "I hope they will never leave off to pray God, and call loud to the great King of England, till all the poor blacks be given free, and slavery done forevermore." For if Britain's sovereign only knew "how cruelly we are used," he would abolish the slave system at once. "I have heard say he is good; and if he is, he will stop it if he can." A just and benevolent monarch, she hinted, would protect the most vulnerable of his subjects, not facilitate their brutal mistreatment and exploitation.

William IV was not known for his benevolence, however. Far from it. Throughout his life he had professed little sympathy for the plight of enslaved people in the Crown's dominions. Abolitionists, government ministers, Caribbean planters and their metropolitan advocates, and the public writ large knew this. As duke of Clarence, he had vocalized his opinions on slavery loudly and with great frequency—in the House of Lords, at meetings and dinners hosted by the West India lobby, and in print. Pro-slavery authors continued to dedicate pamphlets to Clarence, as a royal who "can fully appreciate the accuracy of any statement respecting the colonial system."

On the eve of William IV's accession, pro-slavery advocates reminded the British public of the king's long history as their ally. "The West India body owe a great debt of gratitude to His Royal Highness the Duke of Clarence," noted one Caribbean planter, "who has *uniformly patronized* them from the earliest period of their persecutions." The patronage of a royal prince—now heir apparent—who had visited the Caribbean was "*doubly valuable to the planters*, both from his *most exalted rank* in the British empire, and from his personal knowledge of the situation and treatment of the negro population in the West India colonies." William IV was nothing short of an impediment to the abolitionist cause. Whether he would grant the royal assent to an emancipation act remained in doubt. Even with widespread popular support in Britain for immediate emancipation, it is possible that the anti-slavery agenda may have remained in suspension for years to come.

But the actions of enslaved people themselves changed the course of history. As intelligence of the new campaign for immediate emancipation reached Jamaica, enslaved men and women shared information with one another while outraged planters contemplated their options. Some Jamaican slaveholders proposed sending mass petitions to the king for support; others considered seceding from the British Empire altogether. Identifying with Britain's former American colonists, Jamaican planters characterized themselves as aggrieved subjects of the Crown, repeatedly insulted and subject to unmerited metropolitan intervention. Demands for civil equality from free people of African and multiple ancestries, who outnumbered British colonists in Jamaica two to one, exacerbated the concerns of slaveholders.

In a bid to build a political alliance, the Jamaica assembly passed an act removing the legal disabilities attached to free men of non-European ancestry in February 1830; but the unresolved slavery issue weighed heavily on the island. To tamp down potential unrest among the enslaved and cool the inflamed tempers of planters, William IV issued a royal proclamation in June 1831. The king proclaimed "that the slave population in our said colonies and possessions will forfeit all claim on our protection, if they shall fail to render entire submission to the laws, as well as dutiful submission to their masters." He intended to disabuse bondspeople of a dangerous notion they had been "erroneously led to believe, that orders have been sent out by us for their emancipation." The king had given no royal command for their freedom.

Colonial officials across the British Caribbean printed and widely distributed William IV's proclamation. Enslaved people, suspicious of the intentions of slaveholding authorities, doubted the proclamation's legitimacy. Recent political developments in Britain seemed to suggest that the king supported their liberation from bondage and would soon set them free. On December 27, 1831, during Jamaica's holiday celebrations, enslaved insurgents around Montego Bay staged a large-scale insurrection. Many of those involved in the rebellion adhered to the Baptist faith and had spent time among missionaries who preached patience on the path to emancipation. One of the chief instigators of the rebellion was Samuel Sharpe, a literate enslaved man and regular speaker at the Baptist mission. He had read the Bible and concluded that "the white man had no more right to make a slave of me than I have to make a slave of the white man." As rumors spread that the British imperial government intended to emancipate bondspeople in the king's dominions, Sharpe organized resistance planning meetings under the guise of religious gatherings. He admitted the planters would "put some of us to death" for refusing to work; "but they cannot hang and shoot us all, and if we are faithful one to another, we must obtain our freedom." Liberty was worth self-sacrifice.

Carefully plotted over many months, Jamaica's Baptist War, also known as the Christmas Rebellion, began on the morning of December 27. Sharpe had advocated nonviolence and passive resistance, but the insurrection took on a life of its own. Aiming for maximum impact and property destruction, the rebels torched over a hundred estates. A British eyewitness later described seeing fires "raging in all directions." Terror gripped the island, and the governor declared martial law. "Military noise and bustle usurped the place of the cheerful festivities of Christmas." Colonists fled for safety to the sound of drumbeats as the militia marched to meet the insurgents. "All was confusion and dismay," a resident reported. Colonial forces managed to suppress the rebellion by the first week of January 1832, killing at least 207 enslaved people. The property damage was extensive—over £1 million in losses. Targeting plantation houses and buildings and sugarcane fields instead of planters, the insurgents had exercised restraint against their enslavers.

The same could not be said of the Jamaican government's response in the aftermath of the revolt. In all, 519 enslaved men and women lost their lives during and after the rebellion in comparison to a total of fourteen British colonists. While the death toll disproportionately impacted the Black population, colonial authorities came down hard on the enslaved population in the king's name. They conducted hasty sham trials, paraded convicted rebels through the streets in oxcarts, and staged the brutal public executions of 312 individuals. Officials left bodies on public display for weeks until unceremoniously dumping them in unmarked mass graves.

One of the last to face execution, Samuel Sharpe refused to apologize for the rebellion he had initiated, though he regretted its result. "All I wished was to be free," he reportedly told spectators after ascending the gallows; "all I wished was to enjoy that liberty which I find in the bible is the birthright of every man." Although colonial authorities silenced his dissenting voice, Samuel Sharpe died a martyr to the cause of emancipation. Centuries later, after Jamaica's political independence in 1962, Samuel Sharpe became a national hero. In 1975, the Jamaican government gave Sharpe the posthumous title the Right Excellent Samuel Sharpe. His portrait was featured on $50 and $500 Jamaican banknotes. In 1976, Charles Square in Montego Bay was officially renamed Sam Sharpe Square. On August 1, 2007 (Emancipation Day), a marble monument was erected in Sam Sharpe Square in his honor.

Scrambling to cast blame for the uprising on anyone but themselves, Jamaican officials and planters directed their wrath at local missionaries for allegedly fomenting the Christmas Rebellion. Magistrates imprisoned six Baptist missionaries accused of complicity in the insurrection; bands of irate colonists rounded up and tarred and feathered other missionaries and damaged or destroyed twenty chapels. Some of the remaining missionaries fled Jamaica in fear for their lives, using the rebellion to plead the case for emancipation in Britain. Colonial officials proposed introducing more restrictive measures to police the island's enslaved population and prevent another uprising. But the political tides had turned against Caribbean slaveholders in Britain. Confronted with the prospect of endless insurrections, the government acknowledged that it could ill afford to delay plans for general emancipation. Britain's Atlantic slave empire extracted too heavy a price.

After news of the Baptist War reached Britain, and missionaries expelled from Jamaica shared eyewitness accounts with the public, anti-slavery momentum gathered strength throughout 1832. Parliament's passage of the Reform Bill in June expanded the size of the electorate and created new constituencies in northern industrial towns. The Anti-Slavery Society capitalized on the moment, deploying a chunk of its budget to send skilled lecturers on tours to promote immediate emancipation among the newly enfranchised. The speakers' fiery oratory drew large crowds, and the society published popular lectures. As word of the society's anti-slavery lecture circuit spread, more and more Britons traveled long distances to attend. In the fall of 1832, the society published lists of parliamentary candidates with their stances on immediate abolition, contesting seats both new and established in local and national newspapers. Meanwhile, in the Commons, Buxton and his select committee attacked the exaggerated claims and self-interested arguments peddled by the West India lobby and its supporters. All these tactics impacted the outcome of the 1832 general election, resulting in 104 pro-emancipation members in the new Commons and a loss of seats for the West India interest.

None of this swayed the king. He looked with skepticism on the government succumbing to the will of the populace on "popular questions likely to be rejected by the House of Lords." William IV had long opposed expanding suffrage to middle-class men, dismissing the Reform Bill as an example of "one of those wild projects which have sprung from revolutionary speculation." But he had lost the point and bowed to political pressure. On the question of emancipation, the king seemed unwilling to budge. The Jamaican insurrection, in his mind, had confirmed the barbarism of the enslaved population and the dangers inherent in discussing their potential liberation in Britain. In a letter to Viscount Goderich penned in the summer of 1832, the king wrote that abolishing slavery in the Caribbean islands would result "in the loss of all those colonies."

And to what end? As a young man in the naval service, he had witnessed colonial slavery firsthand. William remained convinced that emancipation would reduce bondspeople "from a state of comparative ease and comfort to one of misery and starvation." More important, their liberation "would ruin the proprietors," with catastrophic economic consequences for the British Empire. Unlike most of his subjects, the king's opinion had not evolved with the times.

On February 5, 1833, the king's opening speech to Parliament omitted the subject of emancipation entirely, surprising both sides of the debate. The previous month, Grey's cabinet had begun considering a provisional scheme for the release of Britain's colonial enslaved population from bondage. Although the potential date recommended for emancipation, January 1, 1835, was two years away, the government's plan needed to be ironed out, approved, and set in motion. But first, the Crown sought feedback from the alarmed West India lobby, which objected vehemently to the scheme and threatened a trade boycott. By ignoring the government's emancipation plan, despite announcing that "never, at any time, did subjects of greater interest and magnitude call for your attention," William IV conveyed his own opposition to Parliament. Following the king's speech, a demoralized Buxton inferred that the "government had given up all idea of emancipating the slaves." Britain's monarch preferred to ignore the plight of the enslaved.

Cautiously optimistic, planters and merchants with slavery interests speculated that emancipation was now a dead letter. The king's resolve to block the abolitionists from bringing ruin to his Caribbean colonies had not wavered. In a brazen move, the Jamaica assembly sent a petition to William IV reminding him of what was at stake and where the colonists' loyalties lay above all: with the slave system. Jamaican planters, they submitted, preferred "to be released from their allegiance" to the Crown rather than consent to the emancipation of their bondswomen and -men. Quoting William IV when he was duke of Clarence, pro-slavery commentators emphasized that enslaved people "*were in a state of humble happiness*" and consequently perfectly content to remain enslaved under civilized British masters. For slavery supporters, the words of a king who had once visited the Caribbean colonies carried more weight than the autobiographies and actions of enslaved people themselves and their advocates.

Virtually everyone in Britain and its slave colonies assumed the government had abandoned emancipation for the foreseeable future. Undaunted, the Anti-Slavery Society turned up the heat. Hoping to attract public and media attention, members arranged an emergency convention at Exeter Hall on the Strand, a grand venue with a large auditorium. Hundreds of delegates arrived from across Britain, pledging to do everything within their power to bring about the "immediate and entire abolition" of slavery. On April 19, 1833, 330 anti-slavery delegates processed solemnly from the Strand to Downing Street, stopping in front of Number 10. They hand delivered a memorial to Earl Grey and his cabinet calling for the end of slavery in the British dominions. Moved by the public display of anti-slavery sentiment, Grey vowed to reconsider the government's position. As one commentator wrote, the memorial, "presented by such a body and in such a manner, seemed to be, under providence, the means of sealing the doom for Negro colonial slavery!" At the same time, women anti-slavery advocates were circulating an emancipation petition that attracted over 187,000 signatures, the largest and weightiest single anti-slavery petition in British history. The British people, having answered the slavery question, awaited the government's response.

On May 14, the date set for the opening discussion of the emancipation bill, Buxton and three other MPs hauled the massive featherbed-sized women's petition into the House of Commons. Its sheer physical heft spoke volumes. The 187,157 female signatories formed part of the 1.3 million Britons who signed petitions favoring immediate emancipation in 1833. Edward Smith Stanley, the colonial secretary, rose and delivered a speech outlining the government's proposed emancipation plan. Enslaved people would be emancipated on August 1, 1834. But there was a catch: To preserve the plantation system, freed people would be apprenticed to their former enslavers for twelve years. Their former masters would have the right to claim three-fourths of their time during the apprenticeship period. The Crown would appoint special magistrates empowered to adjudicate disputes and flog those who refused to work. In a concession to enslavers, the government would pay £15 million to compensate for the loss of their human property. Loud objections raised by both abolitionists and the West India interest resulted in much debate and a revised plan. The government agreed to reduce the terms of post-emancipation apprenticeships to six years for field-workers and four for domestic and skilled laborers. Slaveholders were assured £20 million in compensation, paid for out of the public purse.

Both apprenticeship and compensation proved controversial at the time. The former scheme appeared calculated to extract coerced labor from previously enslaved people, preventing them from attaining full freedom and establishing independent lives. The latter confirmed that the British government and monarchy recognized enslaved people as legal property assigned a monetary value. Compensating planters, reiterated anti-slavery activists, denied the humanity and rights of enslaved people while awarding blood money to their enslavers. From the government's perspective, however, compensation was the price of securing colonial co-operation. Although Buxton stated flatly that bondspeople "do not belong to the planters in justice or right, and they never did," he and his fellow society leaders ultimately conceded. Compensation was the evil necessary to carry the bill. On August 28, 1833, three weeks after William Wilberforce's well-attended funeral, at which the king was noticeably absent, the Emancipation Act received royal assent. In the end, despite concerns that he would withhold his assent, William IV gave way. Members of the king's cabinet convinced him that the idea for emancipation—a doomed endeavor—had originated with himself. The mighty experiment of Black freedom was certain to fail, ultimately proving the king right.

Although slavery was abolished in the British Empire after August 1, 1834, true liberation remained out of reach for hundreds of thousands of African-descended people in the colonial Caribbean. Emancipation altered their legal status from chattel property to free subjects of the Crown. Yet the apprenticeship system implemented throughout most of the British Caribbean left freed people impoverished and propertyless, with no prospects for economic mobility or land ownership. Intended theoretically to prepare enslaved people as they transitioned to full freedom, apprenticeship subjected freed men and women to continual bondage in exchange for bare-bones housing and rations.

Required to labor up to forty-five hours per week for their former enslavers without compensation, freed people occupied a liminal space in colonial society, still required by law to work without pay for their former enslavers, who received compensation for the supposed manumission of their human property. In a few colonies with relatively small populations, including Antigua, Barbuda, and Bermuda, full emancipation came into immediate effect. Yet strict new laws limited freed people's political and economic participation and freedom of movement in these colonial societies, confining people of African ancestry to underpaid labor and, in many cases, destitution.

The Emancipation Act stipulated that stipendiary magistrates specially appointed from Britain would oversee the apprenticeship system; power over the bodies and lives of freed people officially shifted from individual masters to the state. Tasked with resolving disputes between apprentices and their former enslavers, stipendiary magistrates held court once a week to hear complaints. Their supervisory positions obligated them to visit plantations with over forty apprentices every fortnight. As Crown representatives, the stipendiary magistrates alone had the right to punish perceived transgressions. The apprenticeship system transferred the power over corporal punishment once exercised by private enslavers into the hands of the king's intermediaries. "Stipendiary magistrates, appointed by the Crown, uninfluenced by the local assemblies, free from local passions," Stanley, the colonial secretary, had outlined in the Commons, "will watch over and protect the negro in his incipient state of freedom." By assigning outsiders to manage relationships between apprentices and their former enslavers, the British government had intended the new system to exhibit an impartiality absent under slavery. On paper, the administration of justice by the stipendiary magistrates would be fair and free of bias.

New arrivals from Britain came to rapid conclusions about the African-descended freed population based on their own ingrained cultural and racial assumptions. John Anderson, a stipendiary magistrate sent to St. Vincent, for instance, exhibited little sympathy for freed people. In his diary he noted that he was "greatly disappointed with the appearance of the Negro population." He had read about their alleged "symmetry, muscular power, or the like" but instead found that even the young women "so much disclose of the African, as in their coarser features to detract from the milder graces which civilization may partially have begun." None of their supposed "physical deformity" stemmed from ill usage, Anderson wrote. "Whatever may have been the wrongs of the slave in remote periods of the accursed traffic in human flesh," he mused, "the apprenticed laborer cannot complain of any want which is not readily supplied." To Anderson, the apprenticeship system had radically transformed the daily experiences of freed people overnight. But changing what he considered their inherent nature would take far longer.

Few apprentices left behind written records of their personal experiences. Yet their collective actions demonstrate their growing discontent with the terms of freedom prescribed by the British imperial government. After years of waiting for emancipation, apprentices found the oppressive system imposed in the king's name unjust and incongruous. What was freedom if it entailed prolonged servitude and threats of abuse without adequate wages? Many apprentices regarded themselves as fully free, possessing the same rights and liberties as other British subjects. Being subject to compulsory labor despite their release from hereditary bondage was a bitter pill to swallow.

James Williams, an apprenticed teenager in Jamaica, dictated his struggles after emancipation to Joseph Sturge, a Birmingham-based Quaker activist who purchased the young man's freedom and brought him to England. As Williams described it, the apprenticeship system was worse than slavery. Embittered by the loss of their chattel property, Jamaica's former slaveholding class treated their apprentices appallingly. Williams recounted regular occurrences of overwork, physical abuse, insufficient provisions, no time off for holidays, and floggings and imprisonment for minor or fabricated infractions. Denied control over their former human property by the British Parliament, Jamaican planters exacted revenge on the bodies of newly freed people. "I have heard my master say, 'Those English devils say, we to be free, but if we is to [be] free, he will pretty well weaken we, before the six and the four years be done,'" reported Williams. "'We shall be no use to ourselves afterwards.'" Under the guise of a more palatable name, apprenticeship had replaced the institution of slavery with an equally brutal form of coercion.

Across the British Caribbean, freed people resisted apprenticeship from the outset and specifically referenced the king's will as their justification. On St. Kitts they pledged to strike, "being convinced from the King's Proclamation that they are to have unrestricted freedom." In the colony of Essequibo in British Guiana, freed men mobilized and rejected the terms of apprenticeship. Pointing to their new status as free men, they said the "King's order" guaranteed they would work fewer hours now that they were no longer enslaved. In Jamaica, apprentices in St. Mary's parish went on strike until they received proof that William IV, and not the colonial assembly, had devised the compulsory apprenticeship system.

When Governor Sligo first announced that Jamaica's enslaved population would be freed on August 1 yet subject to apprenticeship, he had admonished them to "be obedient and good subjects to our good king, so that he may never have cause to be sorry for all the good he has done for you." But coerced apprenticeships were a poor substitute for freedom. The Crown's bait and switch confused freed people. As striking apprentices put it to local authorities: "1st. Is it the king's law? 2nd. Would you swear that the king make it? 3rd. Did not the Jamaica House make it?" Presented with a coercive new labor system that colonial officials characterized as a gift from William IV to his formerly enslaved subjects raised their suspicions. The association between the British monarch and justice remained as resilient as it had during slavery.

Reenergized by reports of mistreatment, violent reprimands, and unrest in the Caribbean colonies, anti-slavery leaders launched a publicity campaign against the apprenticeship system. Despite the £20 million in compensation the British government had awarded to enslavers, slavery persisted in the king's dominions, observed the *British Emancipator*. "The demon has but changed its name." In October 1836, the abolitionists Joseph Sturge and Thomas Harvey, accompanied by several associates, embarked for the Caribbean to assess apprenticeship for themselves. Over a period of five months, Sturge and Harvey visited multiple Caribbean colonies, spending the bulk of their time in Jamaica and Barbados.

Upon returning to Britain, they published a detailed description of their tour, recounting what they saw and heard on estates throughout the region. Their account was harrowing. The men had witnessed apprentices receiving severe punishments meted out by magistrates and their subordinates: floggings, whippings, solitary confinement, and hard labor in the workhouses for men; imprisonment and hard labor in the workhouses, exhausting stints on the treadmill, and illegal floggings for women; and penal gang work in the fields for both sexes. Punishments were incurred for infractions ranging from alleged negligence and insolence to theft of food and desertion. Apprenticeship under the Crown's magistrates constituted "another system of violence and unrighteous oppression" and was neither humane nor impartial.

William IV's death at age seventy-one on June 20, 1837, offered anti-slavery campaigners a fresh opportunity to appeal to the British Crown for support. The elderly, pro-slavery king had been replaced by his much younger, fresh-faced niece, Victoria Alexandrina. When the eighteen-year-old Queen Victoria ended the reign of her unpopular Hanoverian uncles at her accession, she embodied the nation's aspirations for change. Her gender, traditionally viewed as a liability by statesmen, boded well for a campaign involving thousands of British women. The anti-slavery movement had sought a receptive monarch, and Victoria appeared ideal. Anti-slavery sentiment had grown in strength throughout Victoria's childhood, and it remained fashionable in women's circles across the country. British women campaigners aimed to arouse the queen's personal sympathies by pointing to the physical abuse of female apprentices. Male anti-slavery activists and establishment figures assumed they could mold the young queen and convince her to support the cause of mercy and justice.

Drawing Queen Victoria's attention to the plight of apprenticed Africans formed a central component of anti-slavery strategy. On August 1, 1837, the three-year anniversary of Emancipation Day, the queen received a petition from the women of Scotland "on behalf of 700,000 of your Majesty's subjects, held as Negro apprentices in the British colonies." They requested she begin her reign with "an act of justice and benevolence, which would be a bright example to other nations," by "setting the oppressed free." During Victoria's levee at St. James's Palace on February 14, 1838, Thomas Fowell Buxton presented a petition to the queen signed by nearly half a million women from across the British Isles calling for full freedom for apprentices. Lord Henry Brougham, founder of the *Edinburgh Review* and a keen anti-slavery advocate, carried piles of petitions demanding an immediate end to apprenticeship into the House of Lords daily. "To the merciful sovereign of a free people," he said in an address to Victoria, "I call aloud for mercy; to the hundreds of thousands in whose behalf half a million of her Christian sisters have cried aloud that their cry might not have risen in vain." Rarely had British petitioners or MPs looked to William IV or George IV for mercy for enslaved or freed people of African descent.

Reviving anti-slavery pressure during the first year of Victoria's reign had a twofold purpose: sweeping candidates into the House of Commons who supported an early end to apprenticeship; and garnering the queen's support for the cause. On March 14, 1838, anti-slavery delegates from across England held a special meeting in Exeter Hall to consider "the most efficient means of securing the immediate extinction of the apprenticeship." In a packed auditorium of five thousand persons, Lord Brougham made a case for the significance of Queen Victoria's monarchal influence and historical legacy. All the world would know that the final extinction of slavery in the British dominions occurred on Victoria's watch. "I think our young and lovely Queen herself might be almost thankful that it has been delayed until now, that it may take place under her sanction, if not accelerated by her expressed wish," Brougham said, "and that thousands of slaves in her Majesty's dominions may associate her name with the glorious deed of justice, and shout with glad and joyful exultation 'Victoria forever.'"

The audience erupted into applause following Lord Brougham's speech. In contrast to her pro-slavery uncle and predecessor on the throne, Queen Victoria served the anti-slavery movement's purposes. Like Britannia, the female personification of the nation, Victoria embodied Britain's idealized identity as a liberal imperial power, spreading British values, culture, and racial supremacy across the globe. Breaking the chains of bondage within her own dominions was only the first step in the Victorian expansion of British humanitarian influence in the wider world.

Set to expire on August 1, 1838, the four-year apprenticeship term for domestics and skilled laborers was fast approaching. Lobbied heavily by anti-slavery activists, Parliament debated whether to honor the terms of the 1833 legislation guaranteeing planters that apprenticed field-workers would labor uncompensated for a total of six years. The British government simultaneously reassessed imperial labor needs post-emancipation, experimenting with various immigration schemes, including convicts from the British Isles and indentured workers from India and China. In this context, forms of bond labor perceived as legitimate could re-

Figure 20.1. *Extinction of Colonial Slavery Throughout the British Dominions*, 1834.

place the illegitimate exploitation of people of African ancestry that had persisted in the wake of emancipation. Britain owed a moral debt to people of African descent that it had not yet paid. Government support for the shift away from African bondage to other forms of exploitative labor offered assurances that the socioeconomic and racial order would be maintained after slavery. Hoping to avoid parliamentary intervention in local affairs once and for all, colonial legislatures resolved to dissolve apprenticeship altogether on August 1, 1834.

Across the British Caribbean, freed men and women greeted their emancipation with hope and outpourings of affection for Queen Victoria. Brougham had predicted that Victoria would be remembered as a merciful emancipator. He was right. Former enslaved people and their descendants would equate liberation from bondage with her reign for generations to come. The colonial government pushed this interpretation of events from the beginning. "The first day of August next is the happy day when you will become free," the governor of Jamaica, Sir Lionel Smith, announced in his proclamation abolishing slavery. "Recollect what is expected of you by the people of England who have paid such a large price for your liberty."

Above all, Smith declared, they expect you to behave "as the Queen's good subjects."

On the evening of July 31, a crowd of roughly ten thousand surrounded a procession winding its way through the streets of Kingston. Marching at the front, Jamaican officials waved a banner proclaiming "OUR GRACIOUS QUEEN VICTORIA!!" The use of royal imagery at this moment was deliberate. A symbol of national unity, Queen Victoria engendered feelings of loyalty and belonging among newly freed people in Britain's former slave colonies. "Victoria became the touchstone in how they understood a new relationship to British monarchs, and to the empire that they represented." After centuries of hereditary bondage, liberated individuals had at long last attained the status of free subjects of the Crown—though they remained under the authority of local planter-dominated colonial assemblies. Provided no tools with which to fashion new lives after slavery, emancipated people were forced to shape their own destinies while their former enslavers received financial compensation from the British government.

Generations and even a new millennium would pass as free people of African ancestry waited for the British sovereign to acknowledge and atone for the cumulative, enduring impact of slavery on their lives and communities.

Today, their descendants are ready for this long silence to break.

EPILOGUE
SORROW AND REGRET

A dense mass of people crowded around Exeter Hall's heavy wooden doors on the morning of June 1, 1840. Behind them pressed some six thousand men and women in a lengthy queue snaking down the Strand and along the Thames. Although the event began at eleven o'clock, many had arrived with their admission tickets in hand up to five hours earlier. With the doors besieged and the throng of thousands growing restless, stewards admitted attendees into the building hours early. By ten o'clock, no empty seats remained in the immense auditorium; hundreds of disappointed ticket holders were turned away. The packed great room at Exeter Hall buzzed with anticipation. The first meeting of the Society for the Extinction of the Slave Trade, and for the Civilization of Africa (known as the African Civilization Society) was about to begin, and the upper echelons of the organization included a who's who of peers, government ministers, and prelates. And the morning's main attraction was a royal prince.

Members of the public had rushed to acquire tickets to the official launch of the African Civilization Society and lined up hours in advance for a reason. They craved a sight of Queen Victoria's new husband, Prince Albert of Saxe-Coburg and Gotha, who was set to deliver his first public speech since marrying Britain's sovereign. Albert had arrived in England and wed Victoria in the Chapel Royal of St. James's Palace amid national pageantry and effusive celebrations on February 10. Three months later the queen's new husband had agreed to serve as president of the African Civilization Society, a new abolitionist organization launched by Thomas Fowell Buxton to combat the foreign slave trade by promoting civilization, commerce, and Christianity in Africa.

Once "it was advertised that Prince Albert had consented to take the Chair" at the society's first public meeting, a frenzy took hold and "every effort was made by the public to obtain the necessary passports of admission," a delighted attendee told Thomas Clarkson. In the lead-up to the meeting, the society appointed Clarkson one of its many vice presidents. His invitation included a note about the participation of the queen's new husband. "We have done ourselves the honor of making you a Vice President," the society informed the eighty-year-old abolitionist campaigner, "which I am sure you will not object to, especially when you hear that Prince Albert has consented to be the President." Clarkson was thrilled.

The British people clamored to see Queen Victoria's consort in the flesh and to witness his entrance into public life. For a newly arrived foreign prince, avoiding domestic issues and embracing abolition as a means of "civilizing" Africa played well before the British public. As word of Albert's involvement in the African Civilization Society spread, so too did Britons' eagerness for the cause. The London correspondent for the *New York Herald*, the most widely read newspaper in the United States, remarked in disgust, "I find all the English nearly abolitionists, and at present there is a perfect *negro mania* in London." Fervent popular support for the anti-slavery movement, the author claimed, offered an excuse for the British Crown and government to meddle in the affairs of other nations. "It is good to be dyed black if you come up to London, for negro love is filling all ranks, from Prince Albert and the Queen down to her poorest subjects." By gracing the African Civilization Society's meeting with his presence, Victoria's husband broadcast the reigning monarch's unspoken sensibilities to the wider world.

The meeting coincided with the final week of the Royal Academy's exhibition featuring work by J. M. W. Turner, including his masterpiece *Slavers Throwing Overboard the Dead and Dying, Typhoon Coming On (Slave Ship)*. Capturing the unspeakable horrors of the transatlantic slave trade, the painting reimagines the 1781 *Zong* incident. It suspends time, forcing viewers to witness and admit culpability for the aftermath of the ship captain's decision to force 133 sickly enslaved people overboard to capitalize on the terms of his insurance policy. Turner accompanied the *Slave Ship* with lines from "Fallacies of Hope," an unpublished poem he composed

Figure Ep.1. *Slave Ship.* J. M. W. Turner, 1840.

in 1812, decrying the callousness of the transatlantic trafficking of millions of human beings.

Widely recognized as one of the most explicit anti-slavery paintings of the nineteenth century, Turner's *Slave Ship* was panned by critics at the time. The *Morning Chronicle*, in a representative assessment, pronounced it "puerile and ridiculous." But Turner's haunting painting captures not only Britain's nineteenth-century pivot away from slavery-derived profits and toward anti-slavery but also its attempt to expunge prior investment in the traffic and enslavement of Africans from the national record. In 1805, the thirty-year-old artist had invested in a speculative Jamaican venture tied to the Dry Sugar Work estate, located near Spanish Town, the profits of which depended entirely on the labor of enslaved Africans.

Turner invested in what was known as a tontine, a business scheme enabling speculators to buy shares in a pooled fund in exchange for an annuity that increases each time a participant dies. The investment documents clarified that the venture's financial success hinged on "a large gang of negroes; the money is therefore to be laid out in the purchase of the negroes." Enslaved people increased in value over time, Turner and other prospective investors were assured, enabling stakeholders "to double the amount of their first prize, after allowing any casual loss by death." That Turner regretted his ethical shortcomings as a young man is manifest in the themes of his artistic work decades later. Yet he remained silent on the matter of his own complicity in Britain's Atlantic slave system, allowing the *Slave Ship* to speak for itself.

Knowing Prince Albert would open the meeting of the African Civilization Society and draw a vast crowd of eager Britons, Thomas Fowell Buxton took special care crafting his speech for the occasion. He saw the prince's presence as an opportunity to build consensus among diverse branches of the embattled international anti-slavery movement and attract new subscribers. The African Civilization Society was Buxton's creation. Its launch would mark the first time the abolitionist cause had received the royal seal of approval from the consort of a reigning monarch. Prince Albert's willingness to serve as the organization's president and elevate the proceedings with his regal presence offered confirmation that Victoria's sympathies lay with the abolitionists.

The anti-slavery movement could finally count the British monarch and members of the royal family as firm allies. Both Prince Albert and William IV's widow, Queen Adelaide, donated money to the society. Although the dowager queen did not attend the meeting in person, she asked Buxton to convey her approval of "any plan which, by diffusing the blessings of Christianity, the comforts of civilized life, and the means of education, may gradually extinguish the dreadful export of slaves from Africa, and all the horrors consequent upon that detestable traffic." To the delight of the British public, the Crown and senior members of the royal family had, at last, embraced the cause of enslaved people and imperial liberalism.

A few minutes before eleven o'clock, Prince Albert appeared on the stage to open the business of the day. As stewards ushered the prince to his chair, he received a standing ovation from the audience. Shouts rang out, women waved their handkerchiefs, and Albert bowed repeatedly to the assembled crowd. An organist struck up a rendition of "God Save the

Queen," but his efforts were drowned out by riotous yelling and clapping. Albert waited until a veil of silence had descended over the auditorium. He then delivered his first public speech as the queen's consort and a senior member of the British royal family. Noting that he had accepted the invitation to preside over the meeting because of "a conviction of its paramount importance to the great interests of humanity and justice," Albert kept his remarks brief and to the point.

"I deeply regret that the benevolent and persevering exertions of England to abolish that atrocious traffic in human beings (at once the desolation of Africa and the blackest stain upon civilized Europe) have not as yet led to any satisfactory conclusion," he said. "But I sincerely trust that this great country will not relax in its efforts until it has finally, and forever, put an end to a state of things so repugnant to the spirit of Christianity, and the best feelings of our nature." Cheers erupted, and the prince paused until they had subsided. "Let us therefore trust that providence will prosper our exertions in so holy a cause," Albert continued, "and that under the auspices of our queen and her government we may at no distant period be rewarded by the accomplishment of the great and humane object, for the promotion of which we have this day met."

Thunderous applause followed Prince Albert's speech. According to one observer, although his remarks were "imperfectly heard" because of the commotion of the audience, no one cared. The substance of his speech mattered less than the fact that the prince had agreed to attend the society's opening meeting. "Everyone seemed to link with his presence and feelings, those of her amiable Majesty the Queen, and received him, as though (independent of his own professions) he was conveying the feelings and sympathies of her much-loved Majesty to her loyal and humane subjects." Other speakers who took the stage after Albert expressed similar sentiments.

Prince Albert's commitment to abolition would send a message to the entire world, they held. Detailing the need to convince "the natives of Africa" to prefer "peaceful industry" to the "vile traffic in blood," former (and future) conservative prime minister Robert Peel pointed to Albert. "We can feel assured that it will make an impression upon the mind of a barbarous people when they shall hear, as they will hear, and can understand," he claimed, that the queen of Britain's husband is "a zealous advocate for the total extinction of the traffic in slaves." "It will be known that Prince Albert, the consort of Britain's Queen, has taken the chair at this meeting," proclaimed the Reverend George Clayton; "it will tell in Germany, it will tell in France, it will tell among the nations of the Continent of Europe, it will tell across the Atlantic and among our Western brethren." Today, he concluded, "we have seen here the prince borrowing luster from the British throne, reflecting back that luster upon our high and holy cause." Royal patronage reinforced a growing public conviction that British imperial rule would act as a catalyst for progress and civilized Christian advancement across the globe.

The day after the African Civilization Society's first meeting, Thomas Fowell Buxton wrote a euphoric letter to his wife, Hannah. The meeting, he exclaimed, "went off to perfection." In the long history of the abolitionist movement, "such a meeting surely never took place or anything like it, only think of our having got Prince Albert." For organizers, one of the goals of inviting Albert to preside was to "show the absence of all party spirit." Crown endorsement meant far more than political neutrality. It carried substantial weight with the public. The British press covered the launch of the African Civilization Society in breathless terms, remarking on the presence of Queen Victoria's consort—"the right hand of the throne." The *Morning Chronicle* praised Albert for his decision to choose "this auspicious opportunity of lending the weight of his high station, his influence, and, we are happy to add, likewise of his virtues and his intellect, to, perhaps, the holiest, greatest cause that could occupy the mind and direct the energies of man." Prince Albert had delivered his speech "with perfect distinction, dignified emphasis, and with the slightest possible foreign accent," noted the *Morning Post*.

Thomas Clarkson's poor health had prevented him from attending the much-anticipated meeting of the African Civilization Society. Several weeks later, however, he rallied and delivered the opening remarks at the first meeting of the British and Foreign Anti-Slavery Society, also held at Exeter Hall, on June 24. Another royal presided over the Anti-Slavery meeting: the queen's uncle, the duke of Sussex. "It is a great pleasure to me to think that another illustrious person of the royal family has distinguished himself on the same way on a similar occasion," Clarkson told the audience, in reference to Albert's recent appearance on the same stage.

Although Parliament wielded supreme political authority, the anti-slavery events of June 1840 demonstrated the profound cultural power of the British royal family. No one knew it at the time, but that summer Prince Albert had issued the first of what would become many future statements of regret for Britain's historic role in the transatlantic slave trade and enslavement of millions of Africans: statements without teeth or legal implications; statements carefully crafted to highlight Britain's abolition efforts and erase centuries of racial exploitation and violence by omission.

In the twenty-first century, beginning with the commemoration of the bicentenary of the 1807 Abolition Act, representatives of the British government and members of the royal family issued multiple pro forma statements of regret for slavery. Whether consciously or not, they followed Prince Albert's lead. In an article published in the *New Nation*, a small-circulation Black newspaper, in November 2006, then–prime minister Tony Blair expressed "deep sorrow" for the "active role" Britain played in the expansion of the transatlantic slave trade. He praised the abolitionists who campaigned for its cessation and underscored Britain's laudable position as "the first country to abolish the trade." Blair avoided making a formal apology, however. As the prime minister's legal advisers had cautioned, "saying sorry could also mean admitting liability to an individual or group claiming compensation." In March 2007, during a joint press conference with the Ghanaian president, John Agyekum Kufuor, a journalist asked Blair why he had not apologized. "I have said we are sorry, and I say it again," Blair remarked.

Tony Blair's off-the-cuff comment carried no official weight. At a state event held in Ghana commemorating the bicentenary of the abolition of Britain's transatlantic slave trade the British prime minister returned to his prepared remarks. "It is right that this anniversary is being marked today here in Ghana's Elmina Castle, the scene of such inhuman abuse, and in cities across the UK—in Liverpool, Hull, Bristol and London which played their part in this deplorable trade," Blair said. "It is an opportunity for the United Kingdom to express our deep sorrow and regret for our nation's role in the slave trade and for the unbearable suffering, individually and collectively, it caused." Asked again why the British government refused to apologize officially, a cabinet representative responded that "there are some who want a further statement, but we believe that we must now look to the future."

But the past has an uncomfortable way of encroaching upon the present and irrevocably shaping the future. The vast loans the British government took out to fund compensation in the 1830s—worth billions in today's money—were not paid off by British taxpayers until 2015. That is the same year Britain's prime minister, David Cameron, whose ancestors were among the wealthy enslavers who benefited from compensation, traveled to Jamaica on a state visit. Delivering a prepared speech to Jamaica's parliament, Cameron commented on "the long, dark shadow" cast by slavery, without mentioning Britain's historic perpetuation of that institution for the sake of profit. "Slavery was and is abhorrent in all its forms," he remarked. "It has no place whatsoever in any civilized society, and Britain is proud to have eventually led the way in its abolition." Dismissing the prospect of slavery reparations, Cameron expressed his desire to "move on from this painful legacy and continue to build for the future."

Cameron's explicit focus on the future during his 2015 visit to Jamaica was calculated. Forward-looking statements accept no responsibility for past injustices and their lingering consequences for descendants. Caribbean states, too, looked forward that year—joining together to form the CARICOM Reparations Commission to lobby former colonial powers such as Britain, France, and Portugal to apologize for slavery and initiate reparatory justice. "The region wants to put this terrible history behind it," said Sir Hilary Beckles, chairman of the CARICOM commission, in June 2015, "but brushing crimes under the carpet will not serve to enhance the region's self-respect and international perceptions of our dignity as young nations." Silence, he implied, cannot undo or repair the wrongs of the past. Moving forward demands a reckoning with slavery and its legacies. We need to grapple with history to understand how we got here and where we are going.

During the final years of Queen Elizabeth's reign, the British monarchy faced repeated demands for redress over its historic involvement in the transatlantic slave trade and expansion of African enslavement. In 2018, Prince Charles waded into the public conversation. During a state visit to Ghana, he addressed "the appalling atrocity of the slave trade," which, he said, had "left an indelible stain on the history of our world." Like Prince Albert and Prime Ministers Blair and Cameron before him, Charles highlighted Britain's contributions to the international abolition struggle in the nineteenth century. "While Britain can be proud that it later led the way in the abolition of this shameful trade, we have a shared responsibility to ensure that the abject horror of slavery is never forgotten," he told an audience in Ghana.

Three years later, Prince Charles addressed the crowd during the ceremony marking Barbados's historic transition to a republic. The state of the world had shifted dramatically since he last touched on the issue of Britain's involvement in the transatlantic slave trade in Ghana. The Covid-19 pandemic, the Black Lives Matter movement, the departure of Harry and Meghan as senior royals, and mounting calls for the monarchy to own up to its own historic role had snowballed. Charles chose his words with care. Referring once again to "the appalling atrocity of slavery, which forever stains our history," he focused on the path forward for Barbadians. "Your long journey has brought you to this moment," Charles declared.

During a misguided royal tour in the Caribbean in March 2022, Prince William echoed his father's sentiments. "I want to express my profound sorrow," William said. "Slavery was abhorrent, and it should never have happened." Speaking at a Commonwealth summit in Rwanda that summer, Charles revisited the issue of slavery and its afterlives. "I cannot describe the depths of my personal sorrow at the suffering of so many," he noted, "as I continue to deepen my own understanding of slavery's enduring impact." The remarks of the then–heir apparent suggested a tacit understanding on the part of the British monarchy that the past endures in the present.

On May 30, 2023, the law firm Leigh Day hosted a public event at the House of Commons to address the question of whether there is a legal basis for a claim for reparations for the transatlantic slave trade. Speaking remotely from Jamaica, Dr. Verene Shepherd, a renowned slavery scholar and vice chair of the CARICOM Reparations Commission, argued that the moral imperative and legal case for reparations will depend greatly on the evidence mustered by historians and other experts. The documentary record is critical. "Enslavers boasted about their crimes in archival documents, assuming victims would never access these records, or not caring if

they did," Shepherd commented. Fraught, heartbreaking, and intention-
ally designed to legitimize and minimize colonial violence, the archive of
slavery also lays bare historical complicity.

This book has mined an extensive archival trail of historical links to slavery that lead straight to the British monarchy. From Elizabeth I onward,
British sovereigns sponsored and protected slaving through their control
of the military. They used royal proclamations and orders in council to
incentivize colonists to purchase enslaved Africans. They supported the
passage of colonial slave laws defining enslaved people as property that
could be bought, sold, bequeathed, inherited, collected for debts, and escheated to the Crown when enslavers died intestate. They wove transatlantic slaving into state finances and benefited financially from revenues
drawn from colonial goods produced by enslaved people. They impressed
enslaved men and recruited liberated Africans against their will to defend
Britain's Atlantic slave empire in exchange for freedom from slaving vessels. They used inter-imperial wars to increase the number of plantation
territories and enslaved laborers under British control and even outright
owned thousands of enslaved people in the Crown's name well into the
nineteenth century.

What steps the British monarchy takes next, if any, remain to be seen.
Due to constitutional limitations, monarchs must speak on the advice of
ministers and operate within the boundaries of government policy. In recent years, both Tory and Labour prime ministers have rejected calls to
apologize for slavery or to discuss the possibility of reparations, preferring,
as they say, to look forward and focus on pressing current-day issues. Yet
time and again history reminds us that it is impossible to live in a present
decoupled from the past. "The past does not exist independently from
the present," Michel-Rolph Trouillot rightly insists. "Only in the present
can we be true or false to the past we choose to acknowledge."

As the oldest person in British history to succeed to the throne, and
following his 2024 cancer diagnosis, Charles III must realize that his reign
is tightly time-bound. Endless vistas no longer stretch out before him. He
may, perhaps, possess a unique sense of urgency. "None of us can change
the past," remarked King Charles in his opening speech at the biennial
Commonwealth Heads of Government Meeting in Apia, Samoa, on Oc-

tober 25, 2024. "But we can commit with all our hearts to learning its lessons and to finding creative ways to right inequalities that endure." Will he follow his mother's example and pass the burden of silence on to future generations to carry? Or will Charles, speaking in concert with the British government, acknowledge and seek to redress historical injustices as a means of promoting a more equitable present?

The world waits.

ACKNOWLEDGMENTS

This book would not exist without the critical support of multiple institutions and individuals along the way. Although my debts are many, I will try to be concise. I am grateful to the Omohundro Institute and the Georgian Papers Programme—especially Karin Wulf and Oliver Walton—for supporting my research in the Royal Archives at Windsor Castle at an early stage of the project. A visiting fellowship from the Eccles Centre for American Studies at the British Library soon after enabled me to spend a vital month in the manuscript reading room. When Covid-19 hit, I—like many scholars concerned about the pandemic derailing their research—despaired for the future of this book. Fortunately, the Library Company of Philadelphia extended a remote semester-long fellowship to me and access to its rich early-modern collections. Librarians tendered research aid to fellows from afar, and I particularly benefited from Erika Piola's kind assistance. Virginia Commonwealth University provided essential financial support in the form of a VCU Arts, Humanities, and Social Sciences grant from the Office of the Vice President for Research and Innovation as well as research and travel funds from the College of Humanities and Sciences, the History Department, and the Humanities Research Center. Special thanks to VCU staff members Andrea Wight, Kathleen Murphy, Alexis Finc, and Brian McNeill for their vital administrative assistance.

I wrote the first chapter of this book during a winter residency at MacDowell in New Hampshire. At MacDowell I met playwrights, poets, documentarians, musicians, novelists, and graphic artists, among others, and have never felt so inspired. Thank you to the administrative and kitchen staff at MacDowell and to the other artists who were in residence for your warm welcome. I drafted the bulk of the book manuscript as a National Endowment for the Humanities Sabbatical Fellow at the American Philosophical Society in Philadelphia. My deep gratitude to the APS and its dedicated staff, especially Adrianna Link and Michelle Craig McDonald, for their generous support. My fellow APS fellows offered continuous intellectual curiosity and comradery: Zara Anishanslin, Christopher Roy, Michael Ortiz, Alexandra Lamiña, Nayanika Ghosh, and Andrea Miles. The friendship of Anthea Butler and Oliver Franklin, both of whom encouraged me to leave my cubicle and experience the city, enriched my year in Philadelphia.

Numerous colleagues and friends read chapter drafts and offered their insights, questions, and suggestions: Greg Smithers, Catherine Ingrassia, Shermaine Jones, Oliver Speck, Carolyn Eastman, Mary Caton Lingold, Michael Dickinson, Sarah Meacham, Adin Lears, Ryan Smith, and other members of the premodern writing group. Four historians generously agreed to read the entire manuscript: William Pettigrew, Ana Lucia Araujo, Nicholas Radburn, and Rebecca Goetz. I am enormously grateful to Will, Ana, Nick, and Becky for taking the time to read the book and share their expertise and feedback. Others wrote letters of support on my behalf, helping me to secure the funding necessary to research and write this book, or offered encouragement and words of wisdom over the years: Richard Godbeer, Susan Amussen, Trevor Burnard, Manuel Barcia, Ana Lucia Araujo, Simon Newman, Ann McGrath, Sathnam Sanghera, Miranda Kaufmann, Dana Rabin, Liz Covart, Marcus Rediker, Natalie Zacek, Laura Clancy, Sureka Davies, Jessica Parr, Anna Law, Neil Kennedy, Deb Harkness, and Kathleen Wilson. Although Trevor is sadly no longer with us, he served as a mentor and intellectual touchstone throughout my career. I miss him and can only hope to follow his example. While finishing the book, I benefited from the opportunity to collaborate with *Guardian* journalists and researchers on the "Cost of the Crown" series. My thanks to David Conn, Maya Wolfe-Robinson, and Desirée Baptiste.

Working with my fabulous editor, Rakia Clark, at Mariner has been a dream. We clicked during our first meeting and have shared the same vision for the book ever since. Rakia pushed me in all the right directions, and I imagine every one of her authors feels as lucky as I do to have her in their corner. My gratitude to Rakia, Ivy Givens, Brian Moore, Bob Castillo, Kelly Cronin, Liz Psaltis, and everyone at Mariner for their tireless work on the book. Alia Hanna Habib, my incomparable agent, championed this book from day one and helped make it possible for me to get it into the hands of readers. Many thanks to Alia, Sophie Pugh-Sellers, Joy Fowlkes, Gabe Sherman, and the entire team at the Gernert Company.

Finally, as always, I am grateful for the support of my family and friends—both near and far: Richard, Carolyn and Kevin, Kristin and Shannon, Tracy and Mike, Emilie and Craig, Rivka and Mary Caton, Ana Lucia and Becky, Michael, Jessica, Vivian, Brian and Monic, Lori, Bridget and Aaron, Brooke and Lauren, Emma and Nathan, Brenda and Paul, David and Evie, Val and Charlie, Katelyn and Hongbae, Bryan and Kelsey, Jane and Mike, and, most of all, Greg, Gwyneth, and Simone. My husband, Greg, provided the steady encouragement, feedback, caregiving, and household labor that made this book possible. Our daughters, Gwyneth and Simone, lived with this book for years and kept me going through pandemic lockdown, international travel, lengthy out-of-state sabbaticals, and tight deadlines. To the three of them, I offer my deepest gratitude and inexpressible love.

NOTES

ABBREVIATIONS

ADM	Admiralty Series, The National Archives, UK
AHR	*American Historical Review*
BHO	British History Online, https://www.british-history.ac.uk
BJL	Brynmor Jones Library, University of Hull
BL	British Library, Manuscripts Department
BOD	Bodleian Library, Oxford University
CCPHH	*Calendar of the Cecil Papers in Hatfield House: Volume 14, Addenda*, BHO, https://www.british-history.ac.uk/cal-cecil-papers/vol14
CO	Colonial Office Series, The National Archives, UK
Cornell	Cornell University Press
CP	Clarendon Press
CSPC	Calendar of State Papers, Colonial
CSPS1	*Calendar of State Papers, Spain (Simancas), Volume 1, 1558–1567*, ed. Martin A. S. Hume (1892; repr. Kraus, 1971)
CSPS2	*Calendar of State Papers, Spain (Simancas), Volume 2, 1568–1579*, ed. Martin A. S. Hume (1892; repr. Kraus, 1971)
CUP	Cambridge University Press
DUP	Duke University Press
EUP	Edinburgh University Press
GRO	Gloucester Record Office, Gloucester
HL	Henry E. Huntington Library, San Marino, California
HSP	Historical Society of Pennsylvania, Philadelphia
HUP	Harvard University Press
ICS	Institute of Commonwealth Studies, Senate House, University of London
IUP	Indiana University Press
JHUP	Johns Hopkins University Press
LOC	Library of Congress
LSE	London School of Economics
LSUP	Louisiana State University Press
LUP	Liverpool University Press
MUP	Manchester University Press
NAS	Northamptonshire Archives Service

NYUP   New York University Press
OUP   Oxford University Press
PA   Parliamentary Archives, London
PC   Privy Council Series, The National Archives, UK
PM   Palgrave Macmillan
PP   *Parliamentary Papers*
PSUP   Pennsylvania State University Press
PUP   Princeton University Press
RA   Royal Archives, Windsor Castle
RAC   Royal African Company
RL   Rubenstein Library, Duke University
SP   State Papers Series, The National Archives, UK
SSC   South Sea Company
Stock   L. F. Stock, ed., *Proceedings and Debates of the British Parliament Respecting North Amer-ica*, 5 vols. (Washington, D.C.: Carnegie Corporation, 1924–41)
TBP   The Boydell Press
TNA   The National Archives, UK
T 70   Royal African Company Series, The National Archives, UK
UBCP   University of British Columbia Press
UC Press University of California Press
UCP   University of Chicago Press
UDP   University of Delaware Press
UGAP   University of Georgia Press
UIP   University of Illinois Press
ULP   University of London Press
UMP   University of Missouri Press
UNCP   University of North Carolina Press
UNMP   University of New Mexico Press
UOP   University of Oklahoma Press
UPenn   University of Pennsylvania Press
UPF   University Press of Florida
UVAP   University of Virginia Press
UWIP   University of the West Indies Press
VMHB   *Virginia Magazine of History and Biography*
Voyages Slave Voyages (www.slavevoyages.org)
WCL   William Clements Library, University of Michigan, Ann Arbor
WMQ   *The William and Mary Quarterly*, 3rd series
YUP   Yale University Press

AUTHOR'S NOTE

xvii   *"the word* slave*":* Vanessa M. Holden, "'I was Born a Slave': Language, Sources, and Considering Descendant Communities," *Journal of the Early Republic* 43, no. 1 (2023): 75–83, here 76. See also Tiya Miles, *All That She Carried: The Journey of Ashley's Sack, A Black Fam-*

ily Keepsake (Random House, 2021), 287–89; P. Gabrielle Foreman, et al., "Writing about 'Slavery'? This Might Help," https://docs.google.com/document/d/1A4TEddDgYslX-hlKez LodMIM71My3KTN0zxRv0IQTOQs/edit [accessed July 17, 2023].

PROLOGUE: I SEE AND KEEP SILENT

1   *arrived at Westminster:* Guzman de Silva to the King, June 27 and July 22, 1564, *CSPS1*, 364–66. Silva's relationship with the queen is detailed in Carole Levin, *The Reign and Life of Queen Elizabeth I: Politics, Culture, and Society* (PM, 2022), 119–22.

1   *approximately £3,000:* K. R. Andrews, *The Spanish Caribbean: Trade and Plunder, 1530–1630* (YUP, 1978), 127.

2   *"I will try":* Silva to the King, July 31, 1564, *CSPS1*, 366–70.

2   *Elizabeth offered to loan him:* Harry Kelsey, *Sir John Hawkins: Queen's Elizabeth's Slave Trader* (YUP, 2003), 18–19.

3   *"over 50,000 ducats":* Silva to the King, October 1, 1565, *CSPS1*, 483–86. In 1554, the Privy Council estimated a single Spanish ducat as being worth 6s, 8d. *Acts of the Privy Council of England: Volume 4, 1552–1554*, ed. John Roche Dasent (London, 1892), 410.

3   *60 percent return:* Kelsey, *Sir John Hawkins*, 31–32.

3   *enormous losses:* Schedule of losses for which John Hawkins claimed compensation, 1569, SP 12/53, ff. 6v–7v.

3   *"hideously persistent":* Rowan Williams, "Sermon to Commemorate the Abolition of the Slave Trade," March 27, 2007, http://rowanwilliams.archbishopofcanterbury.org/articles.php/1432 /slavery-is-gods-grief-sermon-at-westminster-abbey.html.

4   *"face our history":* Ibid.

4   *he then invited worshippers:* "Abolitionists Remembered in Westminster Abbey Service, *Anglican Communion News Service*, March 28, 2007, https://www.anglicannews.org/news/2007/03 /abolitionists-remembered-in-westminster-abbey-ceremony.aspx.

4   *"You should be ashamed!":* David Smith, "You, the Queen, Should be Ashamed!" *Guardian*, March 27, 2007, https://www.theguardian.com/uk/2007/mar/27/race.world1.

4   *Operation Truth 2007:* "Operation Truth 2007: Challenging Abolition Myths 2007," *Ligali Organization*, December 18, 2006, https://www.pacma.org.uk/ligali/article.php?id=589.

5   *"You should say sorry!":* Daniel Blake, "Protestor Disrupts Westminster Abbey Slave Abolition Service," *Christian Today*, March 28, 2007, https://www.christiantoday.com/article/protester .disrupts.westminster.abbey.slave.abolition.service/10139.htm.

5   Video et taceo: Susan Bridgton, *New Worlds, Lost Worlds: The Rule of the Tudors, 1485–1603* (Penguin, 2007), 287.

5   *"They impose a silence":* Michel-Rolph Trouillot, *Silencing the Past: Power and the Production of History* (Beacon, 1995), 118.

5   maangamizi *or* maafa: See esp. Marimba Ani, *Let the Circle Be Unbroken: The Implications of African Spirituality in the Diaspora* (Red Sea Press, 1994); Maulana Karenga, "The Ethics of Reparations: Engaging the Holocaust of Enslavement," June 22, 2001, https://ncobra.org/resources /pdf/Karenga%20-THE%20ETHICS%20OF%20REPARATIONS.pdf; Katarina Schwartz, *Reparations for Slavery in International Law: Transatlantic Enslavement, the Maangamizi, and the Making of International Law* (OUP, 2022).

5   *"The queen has to say sorry":* Smith, "You, the Queen, Should be Ashamed!"

5   *"madman":* Stephanie Merritt, "'Madman' Who Asked the Queen to Say Sorry," *Observer*, December 15, 2007, https://www.theguardian.com/world/2007/dec/16/race.uk.

5   *"the British monarchy, government and church":* Toyin Agbetu, "My Protest Was Born of Anger, Not Madness," *Guardian*, April 3, 2007, https://www.theguardian.com/theguardian/2007/apr/03/features11.g2.

6   *requested for centuries:* See esp. Sir Hilary Beckles, *Britain's Black Debt: Reparations for Caribbean Slavery and Native Genocide* (UWIP, 2013); Ana Lucia Araujo, *Reparations for Slavery and the Slave Trade: A Transnational and Comparative History* (Bloomsbury, 2017).

6   *Jamaica's Rastafarian community:* Frank Jan van Dijk, *Jahmaica: Rastafari and Jamaican Society, 1930-1990* (1993; repr. ISOR, 2023), 80, 156-57, 189.

6   *Rastafarians renewed their request:* "Rastas Want Meeting with Britain's Queen," CNN, February 17, 2002, https://www.latinamericanstudies.org/jamaica/rastas.htm.

6   *"We regret and condemn":* "Mixed Reactions to Queen Elizabeth's Visit," *Jamaica Gleaner*, February 25, 2002, https://jamaica-gleaner.com/article/esponsored/20220225/mixed-reactions-queen-elizabeths-visit.

6   *November 30, 2021:* Danica Coto, "Barbados Bids Farewell to British Monarchy, Becomes Republic," AP News, November 30, 2021, https://apnews.com/article/queen-elizabeth-ii-barbados-rihanna-b1633f7f26427c0cb62ebe8f32b77fa1.

7   *Barbados has lit:* Kate Chappell and Brian Ellsworth, "Commonwealth Nations Face Hurdles to Follow Barbados's Republican Path," *Reuters*, November 30, 2021, https://www.reuters.com/world/americas/commonwealth-nations-face-hurdles-follow-barbados-republican-path-2021-11-30/.

7   *Queen Elizabeth II's death:* Amy Gunia, "Queen Elizabeth's Passing Could Push Some Countries to Alter Their Ties to the British Monarchy," *Time*, September 9, 2022, https://time.com/6212004/queen-elizabeth-republicanism-anti-monarchy/.

7   *ten-point reparation plan:* "Ten Point Action Plan," CARICOM Reparations Commission, https://caricomreparations.org [accessed June 3, 2022].

7   *Black Lives Matter protests:* Jason Silverstein, "The Global Impact of George Floyd: How Black Lives Matter Protests Shaped Movements Around the World," June 4, 2021, CBS News, https://www.cbsnews.com/news/george-floyd-black-lives-matter-impact/.

7   *slavery apologies:* Hanna Ziady, "Bank of England Joins British Companies in Apologizing for Slavery," CNN, June 19, 2020, https://www.cnn.com/2020/06/19/business/bank-of-england-slavery-apology/index.html.

7   *calls in Commonwealth realms:* Anna Fleck, "Which Nations Want to Cut Ties with the British Monarchy?", *Statista*, September 28, 2023, https://www.statista.com/chart/30904/commonwealth-countries-who-would-vote-to-become-a-republic/.

CHAPTER 1: THE FIRST ROYAL SLAVE TRADER

11   *the Portuguese Crown's complaints:* Complaints of the Portuguese Ambassador, April 8, 1561, SP 70/25, f. 25.

11   *"although unprecedented":* Queen Elizabeth to the King of Portugal and the Queen Regent, and Safe Conduct for the Portuguese, April 24, 1561, SP 70/25 ff. 91–93.

11   *The queen commanded:* The Queen to the Lord Admiral, April 30, 1561, SP 70/26 ff. 3–4; the
     Queen to the Lord Admiral, June 28, 1561, SP 12/17, f. 94.

12   *the Portuguese had erected:* See esp. A. J. R. Russell-Wood, "Settlement, Colonization, and Inte-
     gration in the Portuguese-Influenced World, 1415–1570," *Portuguese Studies Review* 15, no. 1–2
     (2007): 34; Toby Green, *A Fistful of Shells: West Africa from the Rise of the Slave Trade to the Age
     of Revolution* (UCP, 2019), 127–29, 134–37.

12   *modest Royal Navy:* At her accession, Elizabeth inherited thirty-four royal ships and galleys,
     only twenty-two of which the Admiralty deemed seaworthy in March 1559. List of the queen's
     ships, February 20, 1559, SP 12/2, f. 107; the Admiralty's recommendation regarding the
     queen's ships, March 20, 1559, BOD, Rawlinson MSS C840, ff. 46-48.

12   *Captain John Lok:* "Certain articles delivered to John Lok . . . September 8, 1561," in *The Prin-
     cipal Navigations . . .* , ed. Richard Hakluyt (London, 1589; 1598–1600), 52–53; James A. Wil-
     liamson, *Sir John Hawkins: The Time and the Man* (CP, 1927), 55.

12   *"going to buy and sell":* Bishop Quadra to the Duchess of Parma, September 27, 1561,
     CSPS1, 140.

12   *In his dispatches:* Quadra to the King of Spain, September 13 and November 17, 1561, *CSPS1*,
     139, 144.

13   *Lok's Guinea expedition:* "A letter of M. Iohn Lok to the worshipfull company of Marchants
     aduenturers for Guinie, written 1561 . . ." in Hakluyt, ed., *Principal Navigations*, 53–54.

13   *signed a new contract:* Indenture and Charter-party between the Queen and Thomas Lodge,
     1562, SP 12/26, ff. 87–97.

13   *"not only the merchant ships":* Throckmorton to the Queen, March 6, 1562, SP 70/35, f. 78.

13   *to defend Portugal's exclusive claim:* The King of Portugal's claim to the Guinea Trade, May 20,
     1562, SP 70/37, ff. 121–23.

13   *Captain Rutter's expedition:* "The relation of one William Rutter . . . touching a voyage set out to
     Guinea in the yeere 1562," Hakluyt, ed., *Principal Navigations*, 54–56.

14   *Hawkins hunted for Africans:* Kelsey, *Sir John Hawkins*, 14–15, 21.

14   *"would be detestable":* The quote attributed to Elizabeth I first appeared in John Hill, *The Naval
     History of Britain from the Earliest Periods* (London, 1756), 292. Anthony Benezet repeated
     Hill's claim in *A Caution and Warning to Great Britain* (Philadelphia, 1766), 28, and again in the
     expanded 2nd edition, *A Caution to Great Britain and Her Colonies* (1766; repr. London, 1784),
     36. Thomas Clarkson popularized Elizabeth's supposed quote in *The History of the Rise, Progress,
     and Accomplishment of the Abolition of the African Slave-Trade by the British Parliament*, 2 vols.
     (London, 1808), I: 40–41. More recent works repeating the quote include Daniel Mannix and
     Malcolm Cowley, *Black Cargoes: A History of the Atlantic Slave Trade* (Viking, 1962), 22; Nick
     Hazelwood, *The Queen's Slave Trader: John Hawkyns, Elizabeth I, and the Trafficking in Human
     Souls* (Harper, 2004), 91.

15   *a second-rate power:* Alison Games, *The Web of Empire: English Cosmopolitans in an Age of Explo-
     ration, 1560–1660* (OUP, 2008), 6–7.

15   *Mary Tudor forcibly wrenched:* Eamon Duffy, *Fires of Faith: Catholic England Under Mary Tudor*
     (YUP, 2010), 25–27, 81–83; Anna Whitelock, *Mary Tudor: England's First Queen* (Penguin,
     2016), 317–18.

15   *Her treasury was virtually empty:* Wallace T. MacCaffrey, *Elizabeth I: War and Politics, 1588–
     1603* (PUP, 1992), 59–62.

15   *"For whosoever commands the sea":* Sir Walter Raleigh, *Judicious and Select Essayes and Obser-*
      vations by that Renowned and Learned Knight, Sir Walter Raleigh Upon the First Invention of
      Shipping . . . (London, 1650), 20.

16   *Spain claimed sovereignty:* Timothy Walker, "European Ambitions and Early Contacts: Diverse
      Styles of Colonization, 1492–1700," in *Converging Worlds: Communities and Cultures in Colonial*
      America, ed. Louise A. Breen (Routledge, 2012), 28–30.

16   *Portugal asserted its dominance:* John Blake, *Europeans in West Africa, 1540–1560*, Volume 1
      (1942; repr. Hakluyt Society, 2010), 18–21; Malyn Newitt, *The Portuguese in West Africa,*
      1415–1670: A Documentary History (CUP, 2010), 8; Green, *A Fistful of Shells,*127.

16   *Treaty of Tordesillas:* Tamar Herzog, *Frontiers of Possession: Spain and Portugal in Europe and the*
      Americas (HUP, 2015), 5–6.

16   *Roman legal notion of possession:* Detailed in Lauren Benton and Benjamin Straumann, "Acquir-
      ing Empire by Law: From Roman Doctrine to Early Modern European Practice," *Law and*
      History Review 28, no. 1 (2010): 1–38.

17   *dispossession and enslavement of Native peoples:* On Native slavery in Spanish America, see Erin
      Woodruff Stone, *Captives of Conquest: Slavery in the Early Modern Spanish Caribbean* (UPenn,
      2021), 29–75; Héctor Díaz-Polanco, *Indigenous Peoples in Latin America: The Quest for Self-*
      Determination, trans. Lucia Rayas (1997; repr. Routledge, 2018), 23–37.

17   *launched slaving raids:* Erin Stone, "War and Rescate: The Sixteenth-Century Circum-
      Caribbean Indigenous Slave Trade," in *The Spanish Caribbean and the Atlantic World in the Long*
      Sixteenth Century, ed. Ida Altman and David Wheat (UNP, 2019), 48–49.

17   *flouted the new royal laws:* David M. Lantigua, *Infidels and Empires in a New World Order: Early*
      Modern Spanish Contributions to International Legal Thought (CUP, 2020), 149–50.

17   *Indigenous slavery:* See esp. Ruth Kerns Barber, *Indian Labor in the Spanish Colonies* (UNMP,
      1932); Andrés Reséndez, *The Other Slavery: The Uncovered Story of Indian Enslavement in Amer-*
      ica (Houghton Mifflin Harcourt, 2016); Alan Gallay, *The Indian Slave Trade: The Rise of the*
      English Empire in the American South, 1670–1717 (YUP, 2008).

17   *Bartolomé de Las Casas:* Bartolomé de Las Casas, *Brevísima Relación de la Destrucción de las*
      Indias (Seville, 1552). See also Daniel Castro, *Another Face of Empire: Bartolomé de Las Casas,*
      Indigenous Rights and Ecclesiastical Imperialism (DUP, 2007).

18   *altered the demographic makeup:* Stone, "War and Rescate," 60–61.

18   *Edward IV sought permission:* D. B. Quinn, "Edward IV and Exploration," *Mariner's Mirror* xxi
      (1935): 275–84.

18   *"willingly permits his subjects":* Quoted in Blake, *Europeans in West Africa*, 295.

18   *"regions or provinces":* Letters Patent from King Henry VII to Johan Cabot and Sons, March 5,
      1495/96, CO 5/283, f. 11.

18   *Henry rewarded Cabot:* Reward to John Cabot, September 26, 1497, TNA, E 101/414/6, f. 90;
      Grant of a £20 pension to John Cabot, December 13, 1497, TNA, C 82/171.

19   *"what they have discovered":* Dispatch of Pedro de Ayala to Ferdinand and Isabella, July 25, 1498,
      in *The Precursors of Jacques Cartier, 1497–1534: A Collection of Early Documents Relating to the*
      Early History of the Dominion of Canada, ed. H. P. Biggar (Government Printing, 1911), 28–29.

19   *"an enormous land":* Quoted in Felipe Fernández-Armesto, *Amerigo: The Man Who Gave His*
      Name to America (Random House, 2008), 144.

19   *granted new letters patent:* R. A. Skelton and James A. Williamson, *The Cabot Voyages and Bristol*
      Discovery Under Henry VII (Routledge, 2016), 235–36.

19   *Anglo-Iberian commercial networks:* See Gustav Ungerer, *The Mediterranean Apprenticeship of British Slavery* (Verbum, 2008), 15–28; Heather Dalton, "'Into speyne to selle for slavys': English, Spanish, and Genoese Merchant Networks and Their Involvement with the 'Cost of Gwynea' Trade before 1550," in *Brokers of Change: Atlantic Commerce and Cultures in Pre-Colonial Western Africa*, ed. Toby Green (OUP, 2012), 91–123; James A. Williamson, *Maritime Enterprise: 1485–1588* (CP, 1913), 215–19.

20   *made three expeditions:* Williamson, *Hawkins of Plymouth*, 29.

20   *"one of the savage kings":* "A Briefe relation of two sundry voyages made by the worshipful M. William Haukins of Plimmoth . . . in the yeere 1530 and 1532," Hakluyt, *Principal Navigations*, vol. 2 (London, 1599), 700–701.

20   *"I doubt not":* William Hawkyns to Cromwell, 1536, SP 1/113, f. 154.

20   *English merchants were pursuing:* Robert Brenner, *Merchants and Revolution: Commercial Change, Political Conflict, and London's Overseas Traders, 1550–1653* (CUP, 1993), 4–14.

20   *trading English merchandise:* Andrews, *Trade, Plunder, and Settlement*, 102; James McDermott, *Martin Frobisher: Elizabethan Privateer* (YUP, 2001), 31–32.

20   *a voyage sponsored:* "A Voyage made out of England unto Guinea . . . in the yeere of our Lord 1553," Richard Hakluyt, ed., *Principal Navigations*, 16 vols. (London, 1589; 1598–1600), II: 11–13. See also Andrews, *Trade, Plunder, and Settlement*, 106–107.

21   *Frobisher remained:* McDermott, *Martin Frobisher*, 40–42.

21   *"Moors and Negroes":* "The Second Voyage to Guinea . . . in the Yere 1554," Hakluyt, ed., *Principal Navigations*, II: 331.

21   *African coastal brokers:* Ana Lucia Araujo, *Humans in Shackles: An Atlantic History of Slavery* (UCP, 2024), 71.

22   *West African gold producers:* Green, *A Fistful of Shells*, 132–33.

22   *compelled private merchants:* Andrews, *Trade, Plunder, and Settlement*, 109–110.

22   *"the unlawful traffic":* In reference to alleged unlawful traffic of English merchants in Guinea, 1555, SP 69/7 f. 149.

22   *"Portugal makes a claim":* Meeting at Hampton Court, July 18, 1555, PC 2/7, f. 283.

22   *The Privy Council directed:* Meeting at Grenewiche, December 30, 1555, PC 2/7, f. 345.

22   *"common usage of the world":* Quoted in Williamson, *Maritime Enterprise*, 289.

23   *repeated Privy Council attempts:* See Meeting at St. James's, July 7, 1556, PC 2/7, f. 451; Privy Council meeting at Eltham July 29, 1556, PC 2/7, f. 465; Privy Council meeting at Eltham, August 7, 1556, PC 2/7, f. 473; Privy Council meeting at Eltham, July 1556, BL, Cotton Nero B/I, f. 54.

23   *uncertain ground:* John Edwards, *Mary I: England's Catholic Queen* (YUP, 2011), 265, 341; David Loades, *Elizabeth I* (Hambledon, 2003), 131–34.

23   *Her Tudor predecessors:* Arthur Bryant, *The Elizabethan Deliverance* (Williams Collins, 1980), 24.

24   *sought fresh intelligence:* Loades, *Elizabeth I*, 202; McDermott, *Martin Frobisher*, 48–49.

24   *"none of the people":* Declaration of Martin Frobisher, 1562, SP 70/37, f. 151. See also Martin Frobisher's declaration for the traffic in Guinea, May 27, 1562, BL, Cotton Nero B/I, f. 65.

25   *"the more Christian people":* The King of Portugal's Claim to the Guinea Trade, May 20, 1562, and Reply to the Spanish Ambassador, May 27, 1562, SP 70/37, ff. 121–23, 153–59.

25   *"ambition of profit":* Replication of the Ambassador of Portugal, June 7, 1562, SP 70/38, f. 48.

25   *Elizabeth deemed it:* Cecil to Challoner, June 8, 1562, and Answer to the Portuguese Ambassador's Replication, June 15, 1562, SP 70/38, ff. 75, 110–16.

25 *"He joins the name":* Second Replication of the Portuguese Ambassador, June 19, 1562, SP 70/38, f. 146.

25 *Hawkins grew up:* On Hawkins's early life, see Williamson, *Sir John Hawkins,* 63–77; Kelsey, *Sir John Hawkins,* 4–12; Hazelwood, *The Queen's Slave Trader,* 4–8.

26 *"Negroes were very good merchandise":* "The first voyage of the right worshipfull and valiant knight sir John Hawkins . . . ," Hakluyt, *Principal Navigations,* vol. 3 (London, 1600), 500.

26 *Investors included:* John Stow, *The History and Survey of the Cities of London and Westminster,* 2 vols. (London, 1753), II: 78; James Williamson, *Sir John Hawkins: The Time and the Man* (CP, 1927), 83–85.

27 *Three small ships: Voyages,* https://www.slavevoyages.org/voyage/database (accessed June 2, 2023).

27 *circumnavigate the globe:* Harry Kelsey, *Sir Francis Drake: The Queen's Pirate* (YUP, 1998), 211–23.

27 *"got into his possession":* "The first voyage of the right worshipfull and valiant knight sir John Hawkins . . . ," Hakluyt, ed., *Principal Navigations,* III: 500.

27 *According to Portuguese witnesses:* Williamson, *Sir John Hawkins,* 83–85.

27 *vend their human cargo:* "The first voyage of the right worshipfull and valiant knight sir John Hawkins . . . ," Hakluyt, *Principal Navigations,* III: 500.

28 *"her own subjects":* Elizabeth to Philip II, remonstrating against the seizure of English merchants and ships, March 17, 1563/64, BL, Cotton Vespasian C/VII, f. 289.

CHAPTER 2: UNDER THE QUEEN'S COMMAND

29 *Jesus of Lübeck:* James A. Williamson, *Sir John Hawkins: The Time and the Man* (CP, 1927), 94. In March 1563, Elizabeth loaned the *Jesus* to the earls of Pembroke and Leicester for a voyage to the coasts of Africa and America. It is unclear whether this voyage took place. See Warrant for delivery of the ship *Jesus,* March 8, 1563, SP 12/28, f. 3.

29 *naval assessors valued:* Navy Vessels, March 1545, SP 1/194, f. 126.

29 *£500 bond:* Certificate by William Wynter, October 23, 1565, SP 12/37, f. 172.

29 *queen's royal standard:* While commanding *Jesus,* Hawkins flew the St. George flag—a red cross on a white background, regarded as England's battle flag—and the royal standard. When he encountered the Spanish fleet, he strategically pulled down the St. George flag and flew only the royal standard. See Roy C. Strong, *The Cult of Elizabeth: Elizabethan Portraiture and Pageantry* (UC Press, 1977), 181–82; Williamson, *Sir John Hawkins,* 184.

29 *slave trade to Spanish America:* See esp. Marc Eagle and David Wheat, "The Early Iberian Slave Trade to the Spanish Caribbean, 1500–1580," in *From the Galleons to the Highlands: Slave Trade Routes in the Spanish Americas,* ed. Alex Borucki, David Eltis, and David Wheat (UNMP, 2020), 47–72.

30 *Silva explained:* Guzman de Silva to the King, July 31, 1564, *CSPS1,* 370.

30 *Philip commanded Silva:* The King to Guzman de Silva, August 6, 1564, *CSPS1,* 370.

31 *"command the said ships":* Request of the Ambassador of Portugal, November 19, 1564, and the Queen's Answer, November 24, 1564, SP 70/75, ff. 49, 98.

31 *Her subjects:* Elizabeth to the King of Portugal, November 26, 1564, BL, Cotton Nero B/I, f. 85.

31 *Hawkins's fleet of four ships: Voyages,* https://www.slavevoyages.org/voyage/database#results (accessed July 2, 2023).

31 *narrative of the second voyage:* "The voyage made by M. John Hawkins . . . in An. Dom. 1564,"

Hakluyt, *Principal Navigations*, vol. 3 (London, 1600), 501–21. The following paragraphs draw from Spark's account.

31 *"In this island"*: Ibid., 504. On the Mane, see Andreas Massing, "The Mane, the Decline of Mali, and Mandinka Expansion Towards the South Windward Coast," *Cahiers d'études africaines* (1985): 21–55; Walter Rodney, "A Reconsideration of the Mane Invasions of Sierra Leone," *Journal of African History*, viii (1967): 219–46.

32 *"dispatched his business"*: Ibid., 505.

32 *"no man should traffic"*: Ibid., 507.

32 *"armada of the queen's majesty"*: Ibid., 511–12.

33 *"courageous worth"*: Quoted in Harry Kelsey, *Sir John Hawkins: Queen's Elizabeth's Slave Trader* (YUP, 2003), 33, 226.

33 *"some of the merchants here"*: Guzman de Silva to Philip II, November 5, 1565, *CSPS1*, 503–504.

35 *"trade of capturing"*: Guzman de Silva to Philip II, February 4 and March 23, 1566, *CSPS1*, 522–23, 534–35.

35 *a different plan:* Preparations are detailed in Lewes to Cecil, October 14, 1566, and Lewes to the Council, October 31, 1566, SP 12/40, ff. 182, 211.

35 *Posted a £500 bond:* Bond of John Hawkyns of Plymouth, October 31, 1566, SP 12/40, f. 213.

36 *"knew not how"*: Quoted in Harry Kelsey, *Sir Francis Drake: The Queen's Pirate* (YUP, 1998), 25.

36 *"load Negroes in Guinea"*: Hawkins to the Queen, September 16, 1567, SP 12/44, f. 16.

36 *third slaving expedition:* Described in Sir John Hawkins, *A True Declaration of the Troublesome Voyadge of M. Iohn Haukins to the Parties of Guynea and the West Indies, in the yeares of our Lord 1567. and 1568* (London, 1569).

37 *warring African forces:* Dean Snow, *The Extraordinary Journey of David Ingram: An Elizabethan Sailor in Native North America* (OUP, 2023), 40–43.

37 *"we thought it"*: Hawkins, *A True Declaration of the Troublesome Voyadge*.

37 *"made me great promises"*: Guzman de Silva to Philip II, January 3, 1568, and March 27, 1568, *CSPS2*, 1, 12.

37 *"thank her for forbidding"*: The King to Guzman de Silva, April 6, 1586, *CSPS2*, 14.

37 *"reasonable trade"*: Hawkins, *A True Declaration of the Troublesome Voyadge*.

38 *the ensuing battle:* Ibid.

38 *Hawkins staggered back:* His arrival home is described in William Hawkins to Cecil, January 20, 1569, SP 12/49, f. 77.

38 *"treason of the Spaniards"*: John Hawkins to William Cecil, January 25, 1569, SP 12/49, f. 83.

38 *account of the voyage:* A journal by John Hawkyns of the . . . voyage made with the *Jesus* and the *Mynion*, 1567, 1568, [March] 1569; and Hawkins to Cecil, March 1, 1569, SP 12/49, f. 85, 116.

38 *schedule of losses:* List of lost goods and equipment, 1569, SP 12/53, ff. 6v-7v. The most accurate transcription is in Gary Paul Baker and Craig Lambert, "William Fowler, Sir William Garrard, Sir John Hawkins and the Sixteenth-Century Atlantic Slave Trade," *English Historical Review* 139, no. 598–599 (2024): 687–88.

39 *"best kind of stature"*: Ibid.

39 *supported his formal complaint: Spanish Documents Concerning English Voyages to the Caribbean, 1527–1568* (The Hakluyt Society, 1928), 9–10.

39 *"a great spoil"*: Spoils of John Hawkins, December 1568, SP 70/104A, ff. 89–90.

39 *Elizabeth demurred:* Elizabeth to Sebastian, King of Portugal, January 2, 1569, SP 12/49, f. 1.

39 *"pricked to the heart"*: Portuguese Ambassador's Reply, December 1568, SP 70/104A, f. 91.

40   *revenge against Spain:* Neil Hanson, *The Confident Hope of a Miracle: The True Story of the Spanish Armada* (Knopf, 2007), 54.

40   *Regnans in Excelsis:* See esp. Aislin Muller, *The Excommunication of Elizabeth I: Faith, Politics, and Resistance in Post-Reformation England, 1570–1603* (Brill, 2020), 114–40.

40   *the 1570s saw:* Andrews, *Trade, Plunder, and Settlement*, 111–12.

40   *death of King Sebastião:* Andrew C. Hess, *The Forgotten Frontier: A History of the Sixteenth-Century Ibero-African Frontier* (1978; repr. UCP, 2010), 100–101; Laura Fernández-González, *Philip II of Spain and the Architecture of Empire* (PSUP, 2021), 97–99.

41   *Dom António:* Gordon K. McBride, "Elizabethan Foreign Policy in Microcosm: The Portuguese Pretender, 1580–89," *Albion* 5, no. 3 (1973): 193–210.

41   *struck a deal:* The conditions of the grant required for trading on the Guinea Coast, with names of the Merchants that desire it, and An answer to the petition of the Merchants of Taunton, for their trade to Guinea, 1587, BL, Lansdowne Vol/55, ff. 74, 76.

41   *issued a royal charter:* Privy Council Meeting, February 26, 1588/89, PC 2/15, f. 413.

41   *terms of a separate contract:* Mario Alberto Nunes Costa, "D. António e o Trato Inglês da Guiné (1587–1593)," *Boletim Cultural da Guiné Portuguesa* 8, no. 32 (1953): 683–797, here 717–18.

41   *Spanish Armada:* See esp. James McDermott, *England and the Spanish Armada: The Necessary Quarrel* (YUP, 2005); Colin Martin and Geoffrey Parker, *Armada: The Spanish Enterprise and England's Deliverance in 1588* (YUP, 2023).

41   *Portuguese had minimal influence:* Christopher R. DeCorse, "Early Trade Posts and Forts of West Africa," in *First Forts: Essays on the Archaeology of Proto-colonial Fortifications*, ed. Eric Klingelhofer (Brill, 2010), 212.

42   *lacked sufficient motivation:* McBride, "Elizabethan Foreign Policy in Microcosm," 193–210.

42   *the queen granted:* Ungerer, *The Mediterranean Apprenticeship of British Slavery*, 84–89.

42   *"we think it advisable":* Declaration by the Queen, January 1598, SP 12/266, f. 48. On the limitations and achievements of this era, see Lior Blum, "Empire Later: England and West Africa, 1553–1631, and the Foundations of English Dominance in the Region in the Late Seventeenth Century," (Ph.D. Dissertation, University of Southampton, 2019), 115–18.

42   *community of African descent:* Imtiaz Habib, *Black Lives in the English Archives, 1500–1677: Imprints of the Invisible* (Routledge, 2016), 72–74; Laura Hunt Yungblut, *Strangers Settled Here Among Us: Policies, Perceptions and Presence of Aliens in Elizabethan England* (Routledge, 1996), 31–34; Michael Guasco, *Slaves and Englishmen: Human Bondage in the English Atlantic World* (UPenn, 2014), 104, 108.

43   *ordering the expulsion:* On Elizabeth's expulsion orders, see esp. Kim F. Hall, "Reading What Isn't There: 'Black' Studies in Early Modern England," *Stanford Humanities Review* 3 (1993): 23–33; Emily Bartels, "Too Many Blackamoors: Deportation, Discrimination, and Elizabeth I," *Studies in English Literature, 1500–1900* 46, no. 2 (2006): 305–322; and Emily Weissbourd, "'Those in Their Possession': Race, Slavery, and Queen Elizabeth's 'Edicts of Expulsion,'" *Huntington Library Quarterly* 78, no.1 (2015): 1–19.

43   *"black-mores":* Walter Raleigh, *The History of the World* (London, 1614), L2r.

43   *ordered the deportation:* Bartels, "Too Many Blackamoors": 308–309.

44   *"diverse blackamoors":* Meeting at the Court of Greenwich, July 11, 1596, PC 2/21, f. 304.

44   *an open warrant:* An open warrant to the Lord Mayor of London, 1596, PC 2/21, f. 306.

44   *a "very good exchange":* Ibid.

44   *permitted Casper van Senden:* Casper van Senden, merchant of Lubeck, to the Queen, c. No-

vember 1600, "Cecil Papers: 1600," in *CCPHH*. See also Miranda Kaufmann, "Caspar van Senden, Sir Thomas Sherley and the 'Blackamoor' Project," *Historical Research* 81, no. 212 (2008): 366–371.

44   *"masters of the blackamoors":* Ibid.

45   *"negars and blackamoors":* An open letter about Negroes brought into England, 1601, PC 2/21, f. 304.

45   *never signed off:* Kaufmann, "Caspar van Senden, Sir Thomas Sherley and the 'Blackamoor' Project," 369.

45   *range of occupations:* See esp. Miranda Kaufmann, *Black Tudors: The Untold Story* (Oneworld, 2017).

CHAPTER 3: THE WORLD OF 1619

46   *English narratives:* Catherine Loomis, *The Death of Elizabeth I: Remembering and Reconstructing the Virgin Queen* (PM, 2010), 20–26.

46   *rode north:* Alexander Lord Elphinstone to the Master of Gray, March 28, 1603, SP 14/1, f. 15.

46   *Carey later claimed:* Sir Robert Carey, *The True Narration of the Entertainment of His Royal Majesty* (London, 1604), 63.

46   *the accession:* Proclamation by the Lord Mayor of London and Privy Council, declaring the hereditary right of King James to the Crowns of England, France, and Ireland, March 24, 1603, SP 14/1/1.

46   *proceeded slowly:* Richard A. McCabe, "Panegyric and Its Discontents: The First Stuart Succession," in *Stuart Succession Literature: Moments and Transformations*, ed. Paulina Kewes and Andrew McRae (OUP, 2019), 19–36.

47   *"true pattern of divinity":* King James, *The Trew Law of Free Monarchies* (1598; repr. London, 1603).

47   *"righteous and just king":* *The Kings Maiesty's Speech, as it was Delivered by Him in the Upper House of the Parliament . . . on Munday the 19. day of March 1603 . . .* (London, 1603).

47   *"King of Great Britain":* By the King. A Proclamation concerning the king Majesty's Stile, of King of Great Britain, &c. October 20, *1604,* in *Stuart Royal Proclamations, Vol. 1: Royal Proclamations of King James I, 1603–1625,* ed. James F. Larkin and Paul L. Hughes (OUP, 1973), 95.

48   *ordered ship captains:* The King to all captains of ships, abroad on martial affairs, May 1603, SP 14/1, f. 253; *Proclamation by the King,* June 23, 1603, in *Stuart Royal Proclamations,* I: 30.

48   *Intent on peace:* Pauline Croft, "Rex Pacificus, Robert Cecil and the 1604 Peace with Spain," in *The Accession of James I: Historical and Cultural Consequences,* ed. Glenn Burgess, Jason Lawrence, and Rowland Wymer (PM, 2006), 140–54.

48   *privateering:* K. R. Andrews, "Caribbean Rivalry and the Anglo-Spanish Peace of 1604," *History* 59, no. 195 (1974): 1–17.

48   *fragile peace arrangement:* By the King. Proclamation on the Treaty with Spain, July 8, 1605, in *Stuart Royal Proclamations,* I: 42.

48   *fair game:* On English notions of colonization and dispossession, see esp. Robert A. Williams, *The American Indian in Western Legal Thought: The Discourses of Conquest* (OUP, 1992), 193–225; Allen Greer, *Property and Dispossession: Natives, Empires and Land in Early Modern North America* (CUP, 2018), 191–240.

49   *Richard Hakluyt:* Richard Hakluyt, *A Discourse of Western Planting, Written in the Year 1584,* 2

vols., ed. Charles Deane (Cambridge, 1877). See also Peter C. Mancall, *Hakluyt's Promise: An Elizabethan's Obsession for an English America* (YUP, 2007).

49   *century of inflation:* David Loades, *Elizabeth I* (Bloomsbury, 2003), 292.

49   *James inherited:* Tim Harris, *Rebellion: Britain's First Stuart Kings, 1567–1642* (OUP, 2014), 117.

49   *Charters included practical benefits:* Alvin Rabushka, *Taxation in Colonial America* (PUP, 2008), 31–32.

50   *"overseas charters projected:"* Philip Stern, *Empire, Incorporated: The Corporations that Built British Colonialism* (Belknap, 2023), 18.

50   *Virginia charter authorized:* James Horn, *A Land as God Made It: Jamestown and the Birth of America* (Basic Books, 2005), 35–37.

50   *the Virginia Company alone:* Benjamin Woolley, *Savage Kingdom: Virginia and the Founding of English America* (HarperCollins, 2008), 18.

50   *hopes of finding gold:* Horn, *A Land as God Made It*, 40–41.

51   *"The Powhatan":* Karen Ordhal Kupperman, *Pocahontas and the English Boys: Caught Between Cultures in Early Virginia* (NYUP, 2019), 3.

51   *various Algonquian dialects:* Helen C. Rountree, *The Powhatan Indians of Virginia: Their Traditional Culture* (UOP, 1989), 7–8.

51   *recognized by the state of Virginia:* See Sandra F. Waugaman and Danielle Moretti-Langholtz, *We're Still Here: Contemporary Virginia Indians Tell Their Stories* (Palari Publishing, 2000).

51   *"cruel diseases":* "Observations by George Percy," in *Narratives of Early Virginia, 1606–1625*, ed. Lyon G. Tyler (Scribner, 1907), 21.

51   *"God (being angry with us)":* John Smith, *A True Relation of Such Occurrences and Accidents of Noate as Hath Hapned in Virginia Since the First Planting of That Colony* (London, 1608).

51   *granted in May 1609:* Grant to the Earls of Salisbury, Suffolk, Southampton, and Pembroke, and others, of incorporation as the Virginia Company, May 27, 1609, SP 14/141, f. 38.

51   *the winter of 1609–10:* Virginia Bernhard, *A Tale of Two Colonies: What Really Happened in Virginia and Bermuda?* (UMP, 2011), 126.

52   *"houses to dwell in":* For the Plantation in Virginia; Or Nova Britannia (London, 1609).

52   *"the greater part":* "The Proceedings of the English Colonies in Virginia," in *Narratives of Early Virginia*, 180.

52   *conflict with the Powhatans:* David A. Price, *Love and Hate in Jamestown: John Smith, Pocahontas, and the Start of a New Nation* (Knopf, 2003), 117; Thomas S. Kidd, *American Colonial History: Clashing Cultures and Faiths* (YUP, 2016), 69.

52   *island of Bermuda:* Michael J. Jarvis, *In the Eye of All Trade: Bermuda, Bermudians, and the Maritime Atlantic World, 1680–1783* (UNCP, 2010), 11–19.

53   *teenage daughter, Metoaka:* Rebecca Anne Goetz, *The Baptism of Early Virginia: How Christianity Created Race* (JHUP, 2012), 49–55.

53   *praised John Rolfe:* David. R. Ransome, "Pocahontas and the Mission to the Indians," *VMHB* 99 (1991): 81–94.

53   *"daughter of a King":* Chamberlain to Carleton, August 1, 1613, SP 14/74, f. 101.

53   *"witness his marriage":* Ralph Hamor, *A True Discourse of the Present Estate of Virginia and the Successe of the Affaires There Till the 18 of June 1614* (London, 1615), 11, 34.

53   *"the unbridled desire":* John Rolfe to Sir Thomas Dale, in *Narratives of Early Virginia*, 240.

54   *"rejecting her barbarous condition":* John Smith, *The Generall Historie of Virginia, New-England, and the Summer Isles* (London, 1624), 122, 123.

54   *masque by Ben Jonson:* Pocahontas attended "The Vision of Delight." See *The Works of Ben Jonson,* 9 vols. (London, 1756), VI: 19–28.

54   *"The Virginian woman":* Chamberlain to Carleton, January 18, 1617, SP 14/90, ff. 55–56.

54   *Pocahontas's visit to London:* Karen Robertson, "Pocahontas at the Masque," *Signs* 21 (1996): 551–83; Cynthia J. Van Zandt, *Brothers Among Nations: The Pursuit of Intercultural Alliances in Early America, 1580–1640* (OUP, 2008), 65–66, 83–84.

54   *promoted tobacco:* See, for example, Anthony Chute, *Tabacco* (London, 1595), 1–2.

54   *the Roanoke settlement:* Karen Ordahl Kupperman, *Roanoke: The Abandoned Colony* (Rowman and Littlefield, 2007), 52.

55   *"so precious estimation":* Thomas Hariot, *A Briefe and True Report of the New Found Land of Virginia* (London, 1588), C3.

55   *critics of tobacco feared:* Sandra Bell, "The Subject of Smoke: Tobacco and Early Modern England," in *The Mysterious and the Foreign in Early Modern England,* ed. Helen Ostovich, Mary Silcox, and Graham Roebuck (UDP, 2008), 153–69.

55   *"Indian tobacco":* Philaretes, *Work for Chimny-Sweepers* (London, 1602).

55   *"the great indignities":* Anon., *A New and Short Defense of Tabaco with the Effects of the Same, and the Right Use Thereof* (London, 1602).

55   *plumes of tobacco smoke:* The English were enthralled by tobacco. See, for example, Roger Marbecke, *A Defense of Tabacco with a Friendly Answer to the Late Printed Booke Called Work for Chimny-Sweepers* (London, 1602); Sir John Beaumont, *The Metamorphosis of Tabacco* (London, 1602).

55   *English merchants imported:* John Goodman, *Tobacco in History: The Cultures of Dependence* (Routledge, 2005), 56.

56   *"And now good Countrymen":* King James I, *A Counterblaste to Tobacco* (London, 1604).

56   *shops of London tobacconists:* Bryant Lillywhite, *London Signs: A Reference Book of London Signs from Earliest Times to About the mid-Nineteenth Century* (Allen and Unwin, 1972), 44, 296; George Berry, *Seventeenth Century England: Traders and Their Tokens* (Seaby, 1988), 68.

56   *Portuguese introduced tobacco:* Daviken Studnicki-Gizbert, *A Nation Upon the Ocean Sea: Portugal's Atlantic Diaspora and the Crisis of the Spanish Empire, 1492–1640* (OUP, 2007), 117–18.

56   *"Indian weed":* Richard Brathwait, *The Smoaking Age* (London, 1617).

57   *"if all be diseased":* Barnaby Rich, *The Honestie of This Age* (London, 1614), 26; ibid., *The Irish Hubbub* (London, 1618), 46.

57   *"devilish and drunken merriments":* Stephen Jerome, *Moses His Sight of Canaan with Simeon His Dying-Song* (London, 1614), 53, 313.

57   *Farm of the Great Customs:* Robert Ashton, *The City and the Court, 1603–1643* (CUP, 1979), 20–21; Linda Levy Peck, *Court Patronage and Corruption in Early Stuart England* (Routledge, 2003), 153.

58   *into the king's hands:* Project for increase of the King's revenue by his resuming into his own hands the grant of sole importation of tobacco, December 1613, SP 14/75, f. 73.

58   *"the duty on it":* Quoted in Bell, "The Subject of Smoke," 153.

58   *saddled with debts:* Sir Thomas Edmondes to Carleton, March 13, 1618, SP 14/96, ff. 103–104.

58   *never one for frugality:* John Cramsie, *Kingship and Crown Finance Under James VI and I, 1603–1625* (TBP, 2002), 84–85.

58   *financial advisers recommended:* Notes concerning the King's revenue, 1619, SP 14/111, f. 240.

58   *growth of tobacco:* John C. Coombs, "The Phases of Conversion: A New Chronology for the Rise of Slavery in Early Virginia," *WMQ* 68, no. 3 (2011): 332–30.

58 *opportunistic assaults:* Gregory E. O'Malley, *Final Passages: The Intercolonial Slave Trade of British America, 1619–1807* (UNCP, 2014), 85–89; Mark Hanna, *Pirate Nests and the Rise of the British Empire, 1570–1640* (UNCP, 2015), 75–76.

59 *"20. and odd Negroes":* See Engel Sluiter, "New Light on the '20. and Odd Negroes' Arriving in Virginia, August 1619," *WMQ* 52, no. 2 (1997): 395–98; John Thornton, "The African Experience of the '20. and Odd Negroes' Arriving in Virginia in 1619," *WMQ* 55 (1998): 421–434.

59 *Virginia census:* Martha W. McCartney, "An Early Virginia Census Reprised," *Quarterly Bulletin of the Archaeological Society of Virginia* 54 (1999): 178–96.

59 *Anne of Denmark:* Clare McManus, *Women on the Renaissance Stage: Anna of Denmark and Female Masquing in the Stuart Court, 1590–1619* (MUP, 2002), 73–75. Claims that James VI ordered four Africans to dance naked in the snow after his wedding to Anne of Denmark in Oslo in November 1589 are unsubstantiated. The story likely originated with one of Queen Anne's twentieth-century biographers. See Ethel Carleton Williams, *Anne of Denmark: Wife of James VI of Scotland, James I of England* (Longman, 1970), 21.

59 *Anne herself wore blackface:* Jemma Field, *Anna of Denmark: The Material and Visual Culture of the Stuart Courts, 1589–1619* (MUP, 2020), 169–71; McManus, *Women on the Renaissance Stage,* 75–77.

60 *"black faces and hands":* Dudley Carleton to John Chamberlain, *1603–1624: Jacobean Letters,* ed. Maurice Lee Jr. (RUP, 1972), 68.

60 *Anne spent a fortune:* The Masque of Blackness cost between £3,000 and £4,000 to stage. See Adrian Tinniswood, *Behind the Throne: A Domestic History of the British Royal Household* (Basic Books, 2018), 57.

60 *Danish royal bloodline:* Field, *Anna of Denmark,* 168–71.

60 *full-length hunting portrait:* See Sara Ayers, "A Mirror for the Prince? Anne of Denmark in Hunting Costume with Her Dogs (1617) by Paul van Somer," *Journal of Historians of Netherlandish Art* 12, no. 2 (2020): 1–30.

60 *Her personal income:* Field, *Anna of Denmark,* 47; Frederick C. Dietz, *English Public Finance, 1558–1641,* volume 2 (1932; repr. F. Cass, 1964), 357.

60 *lease of the import duties:* [The Lord Treasurer] to the Officers of Customs of the Port of London, 1608, SP 14/40, f. 12b.

60 *Brazilian sugar producers:* Herbert S. Klein and Francisco Vidal Luna, *Slavery in Brazil* (CUP, 2010), 25–28.

61 *jeweler, George Heriot:* Dictionary of National Biography, vol. 1, ed. Leslie Stephen (London, 1885), 436.

61 *payment for a debt:* Plan devised [by Sir Edw. Coke] for payment of the Queen's debts, March 1616, SP 14/86, f. 175.

CHAPTER 4: TOBACCO AND GOLD

62 *by royal proclamation:* See Stuart Royal Proclamations, Vol. 1: Royal Proclamations of King James I 1603–1625, ed. James F. Larkin and Paul L. Hughes (OUP, 1973), no. 192, 195, 202, 203, 257, 265; Stuart Royal Proclamations, Vol. 2: Royal Proclamations of King Charles I 1625–1646, ed. James F. Larkin (OUP, 1983), no. 6, 63, 66, 73, 144, 173, 179, 184, 257, 282, 284, 291.

62 *The College of Physicians:* Certificate by the College of Physicians, December 1619, SP 14/111, f. 171; Cramsie, *Kingship and Crown Finance,* 29.

62   *"before the customs":* A Proclamation concerning the viewing and distinguishing of Tobacco in England and Ireland, November 10, 1619, SP 14/187, f. 171.

62   *limited acreage and unpredictable winds:* Virginia Bernhard, *Slaves and Slaveholders in Bermuda, 1616–1782* (UMP, 1999), 33-35.

62   *£200,000 worth of tobacco:* Jarvis, *In the Eye of All Trade,* 26–29.

63   *"one Indian and a Negro":* Nathaniel Butler, *Historye of the Bermudaes or Summer Islands,* ed. Henry Lefroy (Hakluyt Society, 1882), 84.

63   *"a most necessary commodity":* Ibid., 144.

63   *African-descended residents:* Michael J. Jarvis, *Isle of Devils, Isle of Saints* (JHUP, 2022), 64–66.

63   *farmers overplanted tobacco:* David R. Montgomery, *Dirt: The Erosion of Civilizations* (2007; repr. UC Press, 2012), 119.

63   *encroached upon Powhatan lands:* Lorena S. Walsh, *Motives of Honor, Pleasure, and Profit: Plantation Management in the Colonial Chesapeake, 1607–1763* (UNCP, 2010), 59–63.

63   *Recurrent epidemics:* Carville V. Earle, "Environment, Disease, and Mortality in Early Virginia," in *The Chesapeake in the Seventeenth Century: Essays on Anglo-American Society,* ed. Thad W. Tate and David L. Ammerman (Norton, 1979), 96–125.

63   *untenable conditions:* Anthony S. Parent, *Foul Means: The Formation of a Slave Society in Virginia, 1660–1740* (UNCP, 2003), 16–17; Letter to the Commissioners of the Navy, January 31, 1620/21, PC 2/30, ff. 400–401.

64   *"Native infidels":* Sir Thomas Wilson to the Earl of Salisbury, July 14, 1622, SP 14/132, ff. 60–61.

64   *"lawful and rightful kingdom":* Edward Waterhouse, *A Declaration of the State of the Colony and Affaires in Virginia* (London, 1622), 3, 24.

64   *altered English perceptions:* Rebecca Anne Goetz, *The Baptism of Early Virginia* (JHUP, 2012), 5, 57–59.

64   *offensive position:* Privy Council meeting at Whitehall, July 29, 1622, PC 2/31, ff. 449–450; Susan Juster, *Sacred Violence in Early America* (UPenn, 2016), 49–51.

64   *"Indian crew":* Christopher Brooke, *A Poem on the Massacre in Virginia* (London, 1622).

64   *"perfidious and inhumane people":* John Smith, *Generall Historie of Virginia, New-England, and the Summer Isles* (London, 1624), 14, 147.

65   *"against that naked people":* Privy Council meeting at Whitehall, July 29, 1622, PC 2/31, ff. 449–50.

65   *issued a proclamation:* A Proclamation Prohibiting Interloping and Disorderly Trading to New England in America, November 6, 1622, SP 14/187, f. 234.

65   *According to a census:* List of Names of the Living in Virginia, February 16, 1624, CO 1/3, No. 2; Patricia Cline Cohen, *A Calculating People: The Spread of Numeracy in Early America* (Routledge, 1999), 61–62.

66   *revoked the Company's charter:* S. G. Kingsbury, ed., *The Records of the Virginia Company of London,* 4 vols. (Government Printing Office, 1906), IV: 475.

66   *Walter Raleigh returned:* Alan Galley, *Walter Ralegh: Architect of Empire* (Basic Books, 2019), 466–70; Lior Blum, "From Scarlet to Gold: Towards Understanding the Circumstances of the Foundation of the Guinea Company in 1618," *Journal of Early American History* 13 (2023): 114.

66   *the Guinea Company:* See esp. L. H. Roper, *Advancing Empire: English Interests and Overseas Expansion, 1613–1688* (CUP, 2017), 62–85; Julie Mo Svalastog, *Mastering the Worst of Trades: England's Early African Companies and Their Traders, 1618–1672* (Brill, 2021), 45–85; Blum, "From Scarlet to Gold,": 97–117.

66 *the patent listed:* Grant of Divers Privileges to the Company of Adventurers of London, Trading into Africa, November 16, 1618, SP 14/141, f. 127. See also C. T. Carr, *Select Charters of Trading Companies, AD 1530–1707*, vol. 28 (Selden Society, 1913), 99–106.

67 *trading station:* Svalastog, *Mastering the Worst of Trades*, 62–64.

67 *"the men slain":* Account of the losses sustained by the Company of Merchant Adventurers in voyages of discovery to Ginney, Binney, and the River Gambia, in 1618, 1619, and 1620, SP 14/124, f. 233.

67 The Golden Trade: Richard Jobson, *The Golden Trade, Or a Discovery of the River Gambra and the Golden Trade of the Aethiopians* (London, 1623), 83.

67 *"a great town":* Ibid., 88–91.

68 *the Guinea Company's failure:* Blum, "From Scarlet to Gold": 99–100; Svalastog, *Mastering the Worst of Trades*, 59–69.

68 *private commercial pursuits:* Blum, "From Scarlet to Gold": 112–13.

68 *"his gracious favor":* Meeting at Whitehall, April 30, 1623, PC 2/31, ff. 681–82.

69 *"English traders":* Nethersole to Carleton, May 24, 1624, SP 14/165, f. 64.

69 *opposed to monopoly companies:* Robert Brenner, *Merchants and Revolution: Commercial Change, Political Conflict, and London's Overseas Traders, 1550–1653* (Verso, 2003), 215.

69 *"grievance in creation":* May 24, 1624, in *Proceedings in Parliament 1624: The House of Commons*, ed. Philip Baker, BHO, http://www.british-history.ac.uk/no-series/proceedings-1624-parl /may-24 (accessed September 14, 2023).

69 *Monopolies Act:* "The Monopolies Act, 1624," in *The Stuart Constitution, 1603–1688: Documents and Commentary*, ed. J. P. Kenyon (1986; rep. CUP, 1993), 62–63.

69 *substantial Crown debt:* Kevin Sharpe, *The Personal Rule of Charles I* (YUP, 1992), 124.

69 *toward coerced labor:* L. H. Roper, *Advancing Empire*, 33–36.

CHAPTER 5: OPPORTUNISTIC ENSLAVERS

70 *death of James I:* Pauline Croft, *King James* (PM, 2003), 128–29.

70 *national mood worsened:* Thomas Cogswell, *The Blessed Revolution: English Politics and the Coming of War, 1621–1624* (CUP, 1989), 311–14; Austin Woolrych, *Britain in Revolution, 1625–1660* (OUP, 2002), 18, 53–57.

70 *pushed the royal prerogative:* David Cressy, *Charles I and the People of England* (OUP, 2015), 52–54.

71 *Charles maintained prohibitions:* King Charles I, *A Proclamation Touching Tobacco*, April 9, 1625; *A Proclamation Touching Tobacco*, February 17, 1626/27.

71 *"built upon smoke":* Quoted in Pauline Gregg, *King Charles I* (UC Press, 1981), 203.

71 *£10,000 a year:* See Alexander G. Taylor, "Tobacco Retail Licenses and State Formation in Early Modern England and Wales," *Economic History Review* 72, no. 2 (2019): 448–49.

71 *"The chief spring":* Treatise by Edward Bennett, 1622, SP 14/135, ff. 118–121.

71 *Barbados attracted thousands:* Simon P. Newman, *A New World of Labor: The Development of Plantation Slavery in the British Atlantic* (UPenn, 2013), 62–63.

72 *loaned the company:* Commissioners of the Navy to the Duke of Buckingham, September 28, 1626, SP 16/36, f. 122.

72 *"an elephant's head":* Note of Articles desired from Guinea, July 31, 1625, SP 16/4, f. 227.

72 *private traders complained:* Lord President Manchester to the King, July 7, 1627, SP 16/70, f. 70.

72 *"shall be restrained":* Thomas Meautys to Sec. Conway, July 23, 1627, SP 16/71, f. 134.

73 *"the coasts of Guinea":* Lords of Admiralty to Sir John Pennington and other captains of HM ships, November 11, 1637, SP 16/353, f. 64.

73 *new monopoly charter:* Certificate by Sir Richard Young and Copy of the Order in the Court of Wards, May 26, 1631, SP 16/540/1, ff. 149, 151.

73 *£10,000 in gold:* The humble answer of the Guinny Comp unto the Remonstrance of Mr. Samuel Vassall and Comp, May 25, 1650, CO 1/11, f. 29.

73 *by royal proclamation:* Order for the issue of a proclamation relating to the patent granted . . . [for] the sole trade in Guinea and Binney, Africa, November 23, 1631, PC 2/41/416; King Charles I, *A Proclamation Concerning the Trade of Ginney, and Binney, in the Parts of Africa,* November 22, 1631.

73 *sought-after commodities:* List of Guinea import goods, February 3, 1632, PC 2/41/662.

73 *diversified its portfolio:* Sir Henry Melvin to Lords of Admiralty, November 21, 1636, SP 16/336, f. 50.

74 *recalling classical attire:* David Bindman, "The Black Presence in British Art: Sixteenth and Seventeenth Centuries," in *The Image of the Black in Western Art: From the "Age of Discovery" to the Age of Abolition,* ed. David Bindman and Henry Louis Gates, Jr. (HUP, 2010), 235–70, here 249.

74 *The Shepherds' Paradise:* Andrea Stevens, *Inventions of the Skin: The Painted Body in Early English Drama* (EUP, 2013), 105–108; Sophie Tomlinson, *Women on Stage in Stuart Drama* (CUP, 2005), 70–71.

75 *"for her beauty":* *The Shepheards' Paradise* (London, 1659), 167.

75 *Providence Island:* Karen Ordahl Kupperman, *The Other Puritan Colony: Providence Island, 1630–1641* (CUP, 1993), 152–53.

75 *The company supported:* Instructions from the Company of Providence Island to Capt. Camock, July 1, 1633, and to Capt. Collins, July 30, 1634, CO 124/1, ff. 56–58, 72–73.

75 *launched a rebellion:* Kupperman, *The Other Puritan Colony,* 165–72.

75 *attempted to thin:* The Company of Providence Island to the Governor and Council, March 29, 1637, CO 124/1, ff. 104–109.

76 *the Dutch captured:* Johannes Postma, *The Dutch in the Atlantic Slave Trade 1600–1815* (CUP, 1990), 21–22.

76 *Guinea Company of Scotland:* See Robin Law, "The First Scottish Guinea Company, 1634–9," *The Scottish Historical Review* 76, no. 202 (1997): 185–202.

76 *restrictive local customs:* See Jerome S. Handler, "Custom and Law: The Status of Enslaved Africans in Seventeenth-Century Barbados," *Slavery & Abolition* 37, no. 2 (2026): 233–55.

76 *"Negroes and Indians":* William Duke, *Memoirs of the First Settlement of the Islands of Barbados and Other Carribbee Islands* . . . (London, 1743), 20.

77 *critical pivot point:* Larry Gragg, "'To Procure Negroes': The English Slave Trade to Barbados, 1627–60," *Slavery and Abolition* 16, no. 1 (1995): 65–84; L. H. Roper, "Reorienting the 'Origins Debate': Anglo-American Trafficking in Enslaved People, c. 1615–1660," *Atlantic Studies* 20, no. 4 (2022): 540–57.

77 *5,680 enslaved Africans:* George Downing to John Winthrop, Jr., August 26, 1645, in *Documents Illustrative of the History of the Slave Trade to America,* ed. Elizabeth Donnan, 4 vols. (Carnegie Institution of Washington, 1935), I: 125.

77 *"they have bought":* John Scott, "Description of Barbados," BL, Sloane 3662, ff. 54-62.

77 *slave law:* Thomas D. Morris, *Southern Slavery and the Law, 1619–1860* (UNC, 1996), 38.

77 *regular traffic:* Richard J. Blakemore, "West Africa in the British Atlantic: Trade, Violence, and Empire in the 1640s," *Itinerario* 39, no. 2 (2015): 299–327.

77 *Nicholas Crispe:* Roper, *Advancing Empire*, 80–81.

77 *renewed the patent: Select Charters of Trading Companies, A.D. 1530–1707*, vol. 28 (Selden Society, 1913), xlv.

77 *English traders:* Vera Keller, *The Interlopers: Early Stuart Projects and the Undisciplining of Knowledge* (JHUP, 2023), 189.

78 *prioritized trade:* Jonathan Scott, *When the Waves Ruled Britannia: Geography and Political Identities, 1500–1800* (CUP, 2011), 75; Jonathan Barth, *The Currency of Empire: Money and Power in Seventeenth-Century English America* (Cornell, 2021), 72–73.

78 *"lusty Negers":* The Guinea Company to James Pope, September 17, 1651, in *Documents Illustrative of the History of the Slave Trade*, I: 126–28, 130–31.

79 *factor specially appointed:* The Guinea Company to Francis Soane, December 9, 1651, in ibid., I: 132–33.

79 *"pairs of shackles":* The Guinea Company to Bartholomew Haward, December 9, 1651, in ibid., I: 129–30.

79 *Rupert's fleet:* Narrative made by command of the Council of State, by Wm. Coxon, June 1652, SP 18/24/1, f. 88.

79 *"assaulted":* Report by Dr. Walter Walker et al. of the damage done to the *Friendship,* John Blake commander, hired by the Guinea Company for a voyage to Gambia, October 8, 1563, SP 18/41, ff. 60–62.

79 *petitioned:* The petition of the Guinea Company, July 21, 1653, SP 25/70, f. 81.

79 *by 1657:* Roper, *Advancing Empire*, 164.

79 *East India Company:* Margaret Makepeace, "English Traders on the Guinea Coast, 1657–1668: An Analysis of the East India Company Archive," *History in Africa* 16 (1989): 237–84.

80 *dramatically expanded navy:* Bernard Capp, *Cromwell's Navy: The Fleet and the English Revolution, 1648–1660* (OUP, 1989), 4–6.

80 *"cost little more":* Quoted in Barry Coward, *The Cromwellian Protectorate* (MUP, 2002), 222.

80 *"reconfigured the geopolitics":* Carla Gardina Pestana, *The English Conquest of Jamaica: Oliver Cromwell's Bid for Empire* (HUP, 2017), 2.

CHAPTER 6: ROYAL ADVENTURERS

82 *throngs of spectators:* John Evelyn, *The Diary of John Evelyn*, 2 vols., ed. William Bray (London, 1862), I: 332–33.

82 *"Defender of the Faith": The Earl of Manchester's Speech to His Majesty in the Name of the Peers, at His Arrival at White-Hall, the 29th of May, 1660* (Edinburgh, 1660).

82 *invitation of Parliament: Wednesday May 9, 1660, Resolved . . . That the Kings Majestie be Desired to Make his Speedy Return to his Parliament, and to the Exercise of the Kingly Office* (London, 1660).

83 *Charles needed money:* Tim Harris, *Restoration: Charles II and His Kingdoms, 1660–1685* (Allen Lane, 2005), 60.

83 *'the royal prerogative:* Nuala Zahedieh, *The Capital and the Colonies: London and the Atlantic Economy, 1660–1700* (CUP, 2010), 45; Abigail Swingen, *Competing Visions of Empire: Labor, Slavery, and the Origins of the British Atlantic Empire* (YUP, 2015), 57.

83 *English royal empire:* See Zach Bates, "The Idea of Royal Empire and the Imperial Crown of England," *Journal of the History of Ideas* 80, no. 1 (2019): 25–46.

83 *the Navigation Acts:* Charles II, Proclamation on the Navigation Acts, August 25, 1663, CO 1/17, f. 72.

83 *customs and excise duties:* The Great Statute, 1660, in *English Historical Documents: Volume VI, c. 1660–1714,* ed. Andrew Browning (1966; repr. Routledge, 1996), 273–81.

83 *Financial insecurity:* John Brewer, *The Sinews of Power: War, Money, and the English State, 1688–1783* (Knopf, 1989), 92; N. H. Keeble, *The Restoration: England in the 1660s* (Blackwell, 2002), 104.

83 *"a naval force":* Capp, *Cromwell's Navy,* 6.

84 *command of the navy:* R. Harding, *The Evolution of the Sailing Navy, 1509–1815* (St. Martin's Press, 1995), 95.

84 *"rock of gold":* *Memoirs of Prince Rupert, and the Cavaliers,* 3 vols., ed. Eliot Warburton (London, 1849), III: 361.

84 *"a great design":* Samuel Pepys, *The Diary of Samuel Pepys, Esquire,* ed. Lord Braybrooke (London, 1902), 77.

84 *loaned the adventurers:* Voyage to Gambia in five of the king's ships, December 7, 1660, Royal Adventurers Ships' Books, Entry book of invoices, 1660–1663, T 70/1221, f. 1.

84 *issued a charter:* Patent granted to the Royal Adventurers Trading into Africa, December 18, 1660, Chancery and Supreme Court of Judicature, Patent Rolls, TNA, C 66/2936, f. 6. See also C. T. Carr, ed., *Select Charters of Trading Companies, A.D. 1530–1707,* vol. 28 (Selden Society, 1913), 172–77.

84 *the Stuart monarchy's support:* G. F. Zook, *The Company of Royal Adventurers Trading into Africa* (The New Era Printing Company, 1919), 8, 12.

84 *royals and courtiers:* Subscriptions, September 26, 1662, Company of Royal Adventurers, Journal and Warrant Books-Home, 1662–1663, T 70/309.

85 *untapped gold deposits:* K. G. Davies, *The Royal African Company* (Octagon Books, 1975), 41.

85 *"the Kingsdale or Griffin":* Instruction for Capt Holmes, Commander in Chief for the voyage to Guinea and Private instructions for the factors in this voyage for Guinea, December 1660, Orders of the Duke of York, Lord High Admiral, 1660 to 1665, ADM 2/1725, ff. 37–46.

85 *received separate orders:* Instructions for them that are to go up to the myne in Guinea, and Instructions for the Captaine of the fort to be erected in Guinea, Admiralty Out-Letters: Duke of York, 1660–1662, ADM 2/1732, ff. 71, 72.

85 *duke of York's directives:* Instruction for Capt Holmes, Commander in Chief for the voyage to Guinea, Private instructions for the factors in this voyage for Guinea, and Private instructions for Capt John Stokes in the voyage for Guinea, December 1660, Orders of the Duke of York, Lord High Admiral, 1660 to 1665, ADM 2/1725, ff. 37–46.

86 *"what merchants you sell":* Private instructions for the factors in this voyage for Guinea, December 1660, ADM 2/1725, f. 39.

86 *the royal couple wed:* Lorraine Madway, "Rites of Deliverance and Disenchantment: The Marriage Celebrations for Charles II and Catherine of Braganza, 1661–62," *The Seventeenth Century* 27, no. 1 (2012): 79–103.

86 *"nothing in her face":* Charles II to Clarendon, May 21, 1662, BL, Lansdowne MS 1236, f. 124.

87 *"small for a woman":* Quoted in *Lorenzo Magalotti at the Court of Charles II,* trans. and ed. W. E. Knowles Middleton (Wilfried Laurier University Press, 1980), 29.

87   *husband's then-mistress:* Campbell Davidson, *Catherine of Braganza, Infanta of Portugal and Queen Consort of England* (John Murray, 1909), 117, 139; Linda Porter, *Mistresses: Sex and Scandal at the Court of Charles II* (Picador, 2020), 53.

87   *the marriage treaty:* "Treaty between Great Britain and Portugal, signed at Whitehall, 24 June 1661," in *The Consolidated Treaty Series*, 243 vols., ed. Clive Perry (Oceania Publications, 1969), VI: 327–36.

87   *"our good Brother":* Instructions to Edward Blackwell Esq. Alderman of London, appointed Treasurer for the receipt of the residue of the portion of our dear consort the Queen, 1670, SP 89/11, ff. 52–53.

88   *"transcendent advantages":* Lord Chancellor's Speech, May 8, 1661, *Journal of the House of Lords: Volume 11, 1660–1666* (London, 1767–1830), 244.

88   *Charles transferred control:* Clyde Grose, "The Anglo-Portuguese Marriage of 1662," *The Hispanic American Historical Review* 10, no. 3 (1930): 313–52; William Dalrymple, *The Anarchy: The East India Company, Corporate Violence, and the Pillage of an Empire* (Bloomsbury, 2019), 22.

88   *"hostile Muslim world":* Quoted in A. R. Disney, *A History of Portugal and the Portugal Empire: Volume Two* (CUP, 2009), 22. On the acquisition and fall of English Tangier, see esp. Tristan Stein, "Tangier in the Restoration Empire," *The Historical Journal* 54, no. 4 (2011): 985–1011; Gabriel Glickman, "Empire, 'Popery,' and the Fall of English Tangier, 1662–1684," *Journal of Modern History* 87 (2015): 247–80.

88   *Charles issued a proclamation:* Brooke N. Newman, *A Dark Inheritance: Blood, Race, and Sex in Colonial Jamaica* (YUP, 2018), 50–51.

89   *"the trade of Blacks":* Proposals concerning Jamaica by James Earl of Marlborough, November 1660, Privy Council: America and West Indies, CO 1/14, f. 56.

89   *Council for Foreign Plantations:* Warrant for a Commission, appointing the Lord Chancellor and numerous other persons named a Council for the management of the Foreign Plantations, October 25, 1660, SP 29/19, f. 74.

89   *"natives and slaves":* "Instructions for the Council appointed for Foreign Plantations," December 1660, in *CSPC*, vol. 1, ed. W Noel Sainsbury (Her Majesty's Stationery Office, 1860), 493.

89   *"strong and able":* Quoted in Anthony S. Parent, *Foul Means: The Formation of a Slave Society in Virginia, 1660–1740* (UNCP, 2003), 238.

89   *"Negro slaves":* An Act for the better ordering and governing of Negroes, 1661, Barbados Laws, 1645–1682, CO 30/2, f. 16.

90   *the term "Christian":* Newman, *A Dark Inheritance*, 50; Katharine Gerbner, *Christian Slavery: Conversion and Race in the Protestant Atlantic World* (UPenn, 2018), 45–46.

90   *"christening of negro children":* "Minutes of the Councill of Barbados," November 23, 1663, in *CSPC*, vol. 2, ed. W. Noel Sainsbury (Longmans, 1860), 6, 7.

90   *Royal Adventurers proved disappointing:* Zook, *The Company of Royal Adventurers*, 10–13.

91   *"buying and selling":* Patent granted to the Royal Adventurers Trading into Africa, January 10, 1663, C 66/3029, f. 11. See also Charles II, Royal charter granted to the Royal Adventurers Trading into Africa, 1663, BL, Sloane MS 205.

92   *list of subscribers:* Subscriptions, June 25, and August 25, 1663, T 70/309.

92   *"His Majesty's adventure":* Sir Ellis Leighton to Sec. Bennet, June 1663, SP 29/75, f. 237.

92   *instructed the Lord Treasurer:* Warrant to the Lord Treasurer to pay from the Customs to Thomas Holder, treasurer of the RAC, £5,200 as the king's subscription, and £400 as the queen's, in the said company, June 27, 1663, SP 44/15, f. 75.

92   *compelled to petition:* Petition to the King from the Royal Adventurers, 1665, SP 29/142A, f. 1. For the king's unpaid debt, see T 70/76, f. 25.

92   *"on the one side":* BL, Sloane MS 205.

92   *coat of arms:* Holly Brewer, "Slavery, Sovereignty, and 'Inheritable Blood': Reconsidering John Locke and the Origins of American Slavery," *AHR* 122, no. 4 (2017): 1050–51.

92   *ties to the monarchy:* William Pettigrew, *Freedom's Debt: The Royal African Company and the Politics of the Atlantic Slave Trade, 1672–1752* (UNCP, 2013), 122–23.

93   *alliances with local rulers:* Johannes Menne Postma, *The Dutch in the Atlantic Slave Trade, 1600–1815* (CUP, 1990), 17–21; Rebecca Shumway, *The Fante and the Transatlantic Slave Trade* (URP, 2011), 35.

93   *"aboard sufficient ships":* Meetings March 8 and 15, 1663, T 70/75, ff. 6–7.

93   *response to a petition:* Minutes of the Council and Assembly, December 18, 1662, CO 31/1, f. 77; Answer of the Company of Royal Adventurers of England . . . January 10, 1662/63, in George F. Zook, "The Royal Adventurers and the Plantations," *The Journal of Negro History* 4, no. 2 (1919): 209.

93   *negotiated an additional arrangement:* Alejandro García-Montón, *Genoese Entrepreneurship and the Asiento Slave Trade, 1650–1700* (Routledge, 2022), 121, 180–82.

94   *a new slaving contract:* Meeting June 20, 27, 1664, T 70/75, ff. 16–17.

94   *Royal Adventurers had disembarked:* See *Voyages,* https://www.slavevoyages.org/voyage/database#results (accessed March 3, 2022).

94   *total of 1,718 Africans:* García-Montón, *Genoese Entrepreneurship and the Asiento Slave Trade,* 187.

94   *issued monetary rewards:* Swingen, *Competing Visions of Empire,* 94; Zook, *The Company of Royal Adventurers,* 74.

94   *"the laborious part":* Meetings, August 5, 1664, and January 11, 1669, T 70/75, ff. 19–20, 92.

95   *Generous gift-giving:* See esp. Ana Lucia Araujo, *The Gift: How Objects of Prestige Shaped the Atlantic Slave Trade and Colonialism* (CUP, 2024).

95   *parcel of gifts:* Christina Brauner, "Connecting Things: Trading Companies and Diplomatic Gift-Giving on the Gold and Slave Coasts in the Seventeenth and Eighteenth Centuries," *Journal of Early Modern History* 20, no. 4 (2016): 408–28.

95   *"great king of Ardra":* Ibid., 410.

95   *"a little elephant":* Warrant to Sir Ralph Freeman and Hen. Slingsby, masters and workers of the Mint, to coin all the money brought into the Mint by the Royal African Company with a little elephant, December 24, 1663, SP 29/86, f. 82.

95   *English money consisted:* Sir John Craig, *The Mint: A History of the London Mint from A.D. 287 to 1948* (CUP, 1953), xiii, 7, 166; C. E. Challis, *A New History of the Royal Mint* (CUP, 1992), 338, 390–91; Emma Howard, *Coins of England & the United Kingdom (2021): Pre-Decimal Issues* (Spink Books, 2020), 344.

96   *English coins:* On the association between the monarchy and English coinage, see Rory Naismith, *Money and Power in Anglo-Saxon England: The Southern English Kingdoms, 757–865* (CUP, 2012).

96   *"the Crown's duty":* T. F. Reddaway, "The King's Mint and Exchange in London, 1343–1543," *The English Historical Review* 82, no. 322 (1967): 1–23, here 1.

96   *coins with African provenance:* The elephant or elephant and castle provenance mark was featured on gold guineas, half-guineas, double-guineas, and five-guinea pieces as well as silver

half-crowns and shillings during Charles II's reign. See Howard, *Coins of England & the United Kingdom*, 348–61.

96 *government expenditures soared:* John Callow, *The Making of King James: The Formative Years of a Fallen King* (Sutton Publishing, 2000), 118–23.

96 *"their foreign trade":* Thomas Mun, *England's Treasure by Forraign Trade* (London, 1664), 94.

97 *"increasing his income":* Newsletter, September 2, 1663, SP 29/80, f.14.

97 *issued a warrant:* Entry of warrant to Lord Admiral the Duke of York to order the delivery of the Welcome and two other ships, with all their remaining stores, to the RAC, September 5, 1663, SP 44/15, f. 190; The King to the Board of Greencloth, August 25, 1663, SP 29/79, f. 116.

97 *list of current shareholders: A List of the Royal Adventurers of England Trading into Africa* (London, 1663).

97 *It advertised meetings: Sir, His Royal Highnesse hath Appointed a Generall Court of the Company of Royal Adventurers of England, Trading into Africa, to be Holden at Whitehall, on the Eighteenth of this Instant January* (London, 1664).

97 *The duke of York subscribed:* Subscription for Royal Adventurers, May 10, 1664, Minute Books, Royal Adventurers, 1664-1672, T 70/75, f. 12.

97 *petitions to the king:* Meeting June 28, 1665, T 70/75, f. 40; Petition to the King from the Royal Adventurers, 1665, SP 29/142A, f. 1.

97 *deployment of warships:* J. D. Davies, *Kings of the Sea: Charles II, James II and the Royal Navy* (Seaforth Publishing 2017), 100, 104.

97 *"notoriously vague":* J. D. Davies, *Pepys's Navy: Ships, Men & Warfare, 1649–1689* (Seaforth Publishing, 2008), 26.

98 *The Dutch claimed:* Affidavit by William Crawford, October 20, 1662, SP 84/166, f. 175.

98 *The Royal Adventurers plotted:* Meeting, June 20, 1664, T 70/75, f. 16; Zook, *The Company of Royal Adventurers*, 93.

98 *reminded the king:* Petition of the Royal Adventurers to the King, for a convoy of ships of war, June 15, 1664, SP 29/99, f. 129.

98 *their international rival's pretensions:* Steven Pincus, *Protestantism and Patriotism: Ideologies and the Making of English Foreign Policy, 1650–1668* (CUP, 1996), 247–68.

98 *Fears of Dutch supremacy:* Gijs Rommelse, "Prizes and Profits: Dutch Maritime Trade during the Second Anglo-Dutch War," *International Journal of Maritime History* XIX, no. 2 (2007): 139–59.

98 *"fails to reassure":* Extract from the Register of the Resolutions of the States General, August 9, 1664, Hague, SP 84/171/114, f. 241.

99 *The Dutch would not rest:* Pincus, *Protestantism and Patriotism*, 261.

99 *"Reflecting on the injuries":* The King to the Duke of York, October 1664, SP 29/449, f. 63.

99 *"the wrongs offered":* Warrant for a commission to James Duke of York, Lord Admiral, to grant letters of marque and reprisal against the subjects of the States General, November 30, 1664, SP 29/105, f. 175.

99 *the prize ships:* Declaration, December 16, 1664, SP 29/106, f. 150; Warrant to Captain Holmes, January 7, 1665, SP 44/16, f. 321.

99 *"his Majesty's free gift":* The King to the Duke of York, April 6, 1666, SP 44/17, f. 180.

99 *"beaten to dirt":* Pepys, *The Diary of Samuel Pepys*, 326.

99 *"support a trade":* Petition of the Royal African Company to the King, January 2, 1665, SP 29/110, f. 3.

100 *"clearly the aggressors"*: The King's declaration, February 22, 1665, SP 29/113, f. 68.

100 *the Great Fire:* See "A true relation of that sad and deplorable fire that happened and broke out in London the 2nd of September 1666," *London Gazette*, September 10, 1666.

100 *"royal protection"*: Petition of the Royal Adventurers to the King, 1666, SP 29/186, f. 1.

100 *kept him afloat:* Brian Weiser, *Charles II and the Politics of Access* (TBP, 2003), 149–50.

100 *extension of credit:* Davies, *The Royal African Company*, 42; Lee B. Wilson, *Bonds of Empire: The English Origins of Slave Law in South Carolina and British Plantation America, 1660–1783* (CUP, 2021), 90–91.

100 *Spanish American silver:* Stanley J. and Barbara H. Stein, *Silver, Trade, and War: Spain and America in the Making of Early Modern Europe* (JHUP, 2000), 106–107.

101 *by the duke of York:* García-Montón, *Genoese Entrepreneurship and the Asiento Slave Trade*, 180–81.

101 *Jamaica as an entrepôt:* Nuala Zahedieh, "The Merchants of Port Royal, Jamaica, and the Spanish Contraband Trade, 1655–1692," *WMQ* 43 (1986): 589–91; April Lee Hatfield, *Boundaries of Belonging: English Jamaica and the Spanish Caribbean, 1655–1715* (UPenn, 2023), 30–31.

101 *"His Majesties dominions":* The Several Declarations of the Company of Royal Adventurers of England Trading into Africa Inviting all His Majesties Native Subjects in General to Subscribe, and become Sharers in their Joynt-Stock (London, 1667), 1, 6.

101 *"so well supplied":* An Answer of the Company of Royal Adventurers of England Trading into Africa (London, 1667), 5, 7, 9.

101 *African captives embarked: Voyages*, https://www.slavevoyages.org/voyage/database#results (accessed September 2, 2022).

102 *an annual deficit: Calendar of Treasury Books, 1669–1672*, vol. 3, Part I, ed. William Shaw (H. M. Stationery Office, 1908), lviii.

102 *Treaty of Dover:* Bruce G. Carruthers, *City of Capital: Politics and Markets in the English Financial Revolution* (PUP, 1996), 32–34; Ronald Hutton, "The Making of the Secret Treaty of Dover," *Historical Journal* 29, no. 2 (1986): 297–318; Davies, *The Royal African Company*, 61–62.

CHAPTER 7: THE ROYAL AFRICAN COMPANY

105 *reconstitute the company:* Meetings October 27, 1671, and October 3, 1672, T 70/100, ff. 5–8, 33–34.

105 *African "commodities":* Patent to the Royal African Company, January 18, 1672, TNA, C 66/3136, f. 10.

105 *The 1672 charter:* Copy of the Charter of the Royal African Company, 1672, T 70/1505.

105 *"shipped more enslaved":* Pettigrew, *Freedom's Debt*, 11.

105 *nearly 100,000 Africans: Voyages*, https://www.slavevoyages.org/voyage/database#statistics (accessed February 11, 2023).

106 *"designed to objectify":* Marcus Rediker, *The Slave Ship: A Human History* (Viking, 2007), 265.

106 *10 percent of slaving vessels:* See David Richardson, "Shipboard Revolts, African Authority and the Atlantic Slave Trade," *WMQ* 58 (2001): 69–92.

106 *centered on dehumanization:* For enslaved experiences during the Middle Passage, see esp. Stephanie Smallwood, *Saltwater Slavery: A Middle Passage from Africa to American Diaspora* (HUP, 2007); Rediker, *The Slave Ship*; Sowande M. Mustakeem, *Slavery at Sea: Terror, Sex, and Sickness in the Middle Passage* (UIP, 2016); Michael L. Dickinson, *Almost Dead: Slavery and Social Rebirth in the Black Urban Atlantic, 1680–1807* (UGP, 2022).

106 *RAC forts:* Davies, *The Royal African Company*, 44–45.

107 *made regular payments:* See Cash Book of the RAC, January 18, 1671/2, to December 25, 1676, T 70/216.

107 *failing to pay:* Meetings October 27, 1671, and January 14, 1672, T 70/100, ff. 5–8, 34.

107 *petitioned the king:* Meeting October 22, 1674, RAC, Minute Book: Court of Assistants, March 20, 1673, to September 28, 1676, T 70/76, ff. 24–25.

107 *ordered his officers:* James to Principal Officers, April 29, May 16, 1671, Duke of York letters, 1668–1685, ADM 2/1746, ff. 85–87.

107 *"by Negro slaves":* John Scott, The Description of Barbados, c. 1667, BL, Sloane 3662, f. 59.

107 *entrepôt for Spanish agents:* "Considerations about the Spaniards buying Negros of the English at Jamaica, etc.," February 2, 1674/75, BL, Egerton MS 2395, f. 501.

107 *Chesapeake tobacco planters:* T 70/61, ff. 3–4; *Voyages,* https://www.slavevoyages.org/voyage /database#results (accessed August 2, 2024); Lorena Walsh, "The Chesapeake Slave Trade: Regional Patterns, African Origins, and Some Implications," *WMQ* 58, no. 1 (2001): 139–70.

108 *comprised one-third:* Gross and net produce of the customs, 1679–1735, TNA, CUST 37/1.

108 *The income derived:* L. H. Roper, *Advancing Empire,* 233.

108 *influenced Admiralty affairs:* N. A. M. Rodger, *The Command of the Ocean: A Naval History of Britain, 1649–1815* (Norton, 2004), 107–108; Davies, *Kings of the Sea,* 259–61.

108 *purchased enslaved Africans:* Claire Tomalin, *Samuel Pepys: The Unequalled Self* (Knopf, 2002), 123, 177.

108 *in published lists: A List of the Names of All of the Adventurers of the Royal African Company* (London, 1676); Zahedieh, *The Capital and the Colonies,* 118.

109 *RAC dividends:* The dividends paid to James, as both duke of York and king, are in T 70/185, ff. 17, 27, 34, 43, 55, 59, 70, 78; T 70/82, ff. 5, 42.

109 *the cash gifts:* Meeting June 26, 1677, RAC Minute Book: General Court, January 10, 1671, to February 5, 1678, T 70/100, f. 39; Meeting June 28, 1677, RAC Minute Book: Court of Assistants, October 3, 1676, to July 30, 1678, T 70/77, ff. 36, 37.

109 *"extraordinary service":* Meeting January 15, 1678, T70/100, f. 40.

109 *"this Our Kingdom":* King Charles II, *By the King. A Proclamation for the Protection of the Royal African Company,* November 30, 1674.

110 *"continual patronage":* Meeting January 16, 1676, T 70/100, f. 38.

110 *the royal prerogative:* Ann M. Carlos and Jamie Brown Kruse, "The Decline of the Royal African Company: Fringe Firms and the Role of the Charter," *Economic History Review* XLIX, no. 2 (1996): 291–313; Pettigrew, *Freedom's Debt,* 23–26.

110 *loaned the RAC:* Davies, *The Royal African Company,* 106–107.

110 *payment of £1,400:* Meetings June 4 and 18, 1678, T 70/77, ff. 82, 83.

111 *"never the better":* Quoted in *Seventh Report of the Royal Commission on Historical Manuscripts* (London, 1879), 472.

111 *absolutist pretensions:* Pettigrew, *Freedom's Debt,* 24.

111 *to appoint judges:* See Holly Brewer, "Creating a Common Law of Slavery for England and its New World Empire," *Law and History Review* 39, no. 4 (2021): 765–834.

111 Butts v. Penny: Ibid., 795–96.

111 *"bought and sold":* Quoted in Janet Dine, *Companies, International Trade and Human Rights* (CUP, 2005), 140.

111 *oversaw the minting:* Meeting January 11, 1678, T 70/100, ff. 39–40.

111 *"utility and advantages":* Certain Considerations Relating to the Royal African Company of England (London, 1680), 5.

112 *received a copy:* Powell to Sir Henry Morgan, Deputy-Governor and Commander in Chief of Jamaica, January 19, 1681, and RAC, Charles II's Proclamation against interlopers in their trade, 1681, BL, Sloane MS 2724, ff. 1, 8–11.

112 *dehumanizing conditions:* Smallwood, *Saltwater Slavery,* 34.

112 *employed by enslavers:* See esp. Manuel Lucena Salmoral, "El carimbo de los indios esclavos," *Estudios de historia social y económica de América,* no. 14 (1997): 125–133; Erin Woodruff Stone, *Captives of Conquest: Slavery in the Early Modern Spanish Caribbean* (UPenn, 2021), 1–2, 37–38.

113 *"castle slaves":* See Simon P. Newman, *A New World of Labor: The Development of Plantation Slavery in the British Atlantic* (UPenn, 2013), 139–65; Rebecca Shumway, "Castle Slaves of the Eighteenth-Century Gold Coast (Ghana)," *Slavery & Abolition* 35, no. 1 (2014): 84–98.

113 *"customary to mark":* RAC to Nicholas Buckeridge, Howsley Freeman, and Samuel Wallis, Cabo Corsoe, August 29, 1699, T 70/51, f. 41.

113 *"You are to mark":* RAC to John Freeman, August 4, 1702, T 70/51, f. 137.

113 *embark on Hannibal:* Thomas Phillips, "A Journal of a Voyage Made in the Hannibal of London, Ann. 1693, 1694, From England, to Cape Monseradoe, in Africa," in *A Collection of Voyages and Travels,* ed. A. Churchill (London, 1732), 218.

114 *"all our Negroes":* See Copy of the Instructions of the Royal African Company of England to their Cheif [sic] Agents in Africa. No. 1, from 1720 to 1737, and No. 2, from 1737 to 1750, T 70/66–67.

114 *"mark them still":* John Atkins, *The Navy Surgeon; Or A Practical System of Surgery* (London, 1735), 364.

114 *commodification and dehumanization:* See esp. Katrina H. B. Keefer and Matthew S. Hopper, "Following the Trail of the Slave Trade: Branding, Skin, and Commodification," in *Stigma: Marking Skin in the Early Modern World,* ed. Katherine Dauge-Roth and Craig Koslofsky (PSUP, 2023), 89–116.

CHAPTER 8: ROYAL COMMODITIES

115 *"for a black":* Moneys Received and Paid for Secret Services of Charles II and James II, ed. John Yonge Akerman (London, 1851), 58.

115 *ties to the Stuarts:* John O'Hart, *Irish Pedigrees: Or, The Origin and Stem of the Irish Nation,* 2 vols. (Dublin, 1892), I: 532.

115 *an enslaved Black page:* Susan Amussen, *Caribbean Exchanges: Slavery and the Transformation of English Society, 1640–1700* (UNCP, 2009), 322–24; Catherine Molineux, *Faces of Perfect Ebony: Encountering Atlantic Slavery in Imperial Britain* (HUP 2012), 31–35.

115 *The English smoked tobacco:* Catherine Molineux, "Pleasures of the Smoke: 'Black Virginians' in Georgian London's Tobacco Shops," *WMQ* 64, no. 2 (2007): 327–76.

115 *sweetened food and drink:* Woodruff D. Smith, *Consumption and the Making of Respectability, 1600–1800* (Routledge, 2002), 122.

115 *African-descended people:* Imtiaz Habib, *Black Lives in the English Archives, 1500–1677: Imprints of the Invisible* (Routledge, 2017), 172–82.

116 *advertisements for enslaved runaways:* See esp. Simon Newman, *Freedom Seekers: Escaping from Slavery in Restoration London* (ULP, 2022).

116   *Exhibited as exotic objects:* Simon Gikandi, *Slavery and the Culture of Taste* (PUP, 2011), 171–74.

116   *country and city houses:* Rupert Goulding and Louis P. Nelson, "Cartography, Collecting and the Construction of Empire at Dryham Park," in *Slavery and the British Country House*, ed. Madge Dresser and Andrew Hann (English Heritage, 2013), 355.

116   *the actress Nell Gwyn:* Dayla Alberge, "Graphic Portrait of Charles II's Mistress Comes to Light," *Guardian*, June 28, 2011, https://www.theguardian.com/artanddesign/2011/jun/28/nell-gwyn-charles-mistress-painting.

116   *commodified bodies:* See esp. "'Thy Longing Country's Darling and Desire': Aesthetics, Sex, and Politics in the England of Charles II," in *Politics, Transgression, and Representation at the Court of Charles II*, ed. Julia Marciari Alexander and Catherine MacLeod (YUP, 2007), 1-32.

118   *treasures associated with the Caribbean:* Amussen, *Caribbean Exchanges*, 194; Molly A. Warsh, *American Baroque: Pearls and the Nature of Empire, 1492–1700* (UNCP, 2018), 222.

118   *"Fubbs":* J. P. Kenyon, *The Stuarts: A Study in English Kingship* (Fontana, 1970), 141.

118   *diarist John Evelyn:* Quotes are from Evelyn, *The Diary of John Evelyn*, II: 108, 188.

119   *second portrait of the duchess:* Patricia A. Matthew, "Look Before You Leap," *Lapham's Quarterly*, November 4, 2019, https://www.laphamsquarterly.org/roundtable/look-you-leap.

119   *duchess of Mazarin:* Lewis Melville, *The Windsor Beauties: Ladies of the Court of Charles II* (Victorian Heritage Press, 2005), 131–33; Susan Shifrin, "'Subdued by a Famous Roman Dame': Picturing Foreignness, Notoriety, and Prerogative in the Portraits of Hortense Mancini, Duchess Mazarin," in *Politics, Transgression, and Representation at the Court of Charles II*, 141–76.

120   *colonial slave statutes:* For a general overview, see Alan Watson, *Slave Law in the Americas* (UGAP, 1989).

120   *English slave law:* Wilson, *Bonds of Empire*, 31–33.

120   *custom and law:* Brooke N. Newman, *A Dark Inheritance: Blood, Race, and Sex in Colonial Jamaica* (YUP, 2018), 58–59, 237.

120   *"A fine is imposed":* Lords of Trade and Plantations to Lynch, February 17, 1683, *CSPC*, vol. 11: 386, no. 948.

121   *Virginia legislature codified:* Rebecca Anne Goetz, *The Baptism of Early Virginia* (JHUP, 2012), 105–106.

121   *an imperial slave code:* Ruth Paley, Cristina Malcolmson, and Michael Hunter, "Parliament and Slavery, 1660–c.1710," *Slavery and Abolition* 31, no. 2 (2010): 257–81.

121   *duke of York's dynastic significance:* Howard Nenner, *The Right to Be King: The Succession to the Crown of England, 1603–1714* (PM, 1995), 115–16.

121   *"gave exceeding grief":* Evelyn, *The Diary of John Evelyn*, II: 88.

121   *undermine the established Church:* Jacqueline Rose, *Godly Kingship in Restoration England: The Politics of the Royal Supremacy, 1660–1688* (CUP, 2011), 5–6.

122   *the Exclusion Crisis:* Callow, *The Making of King James II*, 183–84.

122   *issued a proclamation:* King James II, *By the King. A Proclamation to Prohibit His Majesties Subjects to Trade Within the Limits Assigned to the Royal African Company of England, Except Those of the Company*, April 1, 1685, in *British Royal Proclamations Relating to America, 1603-1783*, ed. Clarence S. Brigham (Burt Franklin, 1911), 137-39.

122   *ordered the governors:* James II, Orders to the Governors of Barbados, Leeward Islands, and Virginia, 1686, T 70/169, ff. 43–46.

122   *instructed the Royal Navy:* James II, Orders related to pirates on the coast of Africa, T 70/169, ff. 47–48.

122   *annual customs revenue:* Payments into the Exchequer from 1679–1687, TNA, CUST 37/1.

122   *"negroes in the plantations":* Quoted in Callow, *The Making of King James II*, 244.

123   *"his Majesty persists":* Evelyn, *The Diary of John Evelyn*, II: 234.

123   *offended his Protestant subjects:* Steven Pincus, *1688: The First Modern Revolution* (YUP, 2009), 226–28.

123   *issued an invitation:* For the text of the invitation, see E. N. Williams, *The Eighteenth-Century Constitution: Documents and Commentary* (CUP, 1960), 8-10.

123   *William's landing:* Jonathan I. Isreal, "The Dutch Role in the Glorious Revolution," in *The Anglo-Dutch Moment: Essays on the Glorious Revolution and Its World Impact*, ed. Jonathan Isreal (CUP, 1991), 124–26.

123   *sold his substantial stock:* James II stock transfer to James Graham, January 10, 1689, approved by the RAC in March 1689, RAC Books Concerning Stock, 1687–1691, T 70/187, f. 34.

CHAPTER 9: SLAVERY AND THE GLORIOUS REVOLUTION

124   *held a pressing meeting:* Meeting January 8, 1688/89, RAC Minute Book: Court of Assistants, July 19, 1687, to December 16, 1690, T 70/82, ff. 52.

124   *"abdication":* John Miller, "The Glorious Revolution: 'Contract' and 'Abdication' Reconsidered," *The Historical Journal* 25, no. 3 (1982): 541–55.

124   *"lawful path":* Richard S. Kay, *The Glorious Revolution and the Continuity of Law* (Catholic University of America Press, 2014), 55.

124   *lot with the prince of Orange:* The House of Lords was almost evenly split: fifty-one for a king, forty-nine for a regent. *The Correspondence of Henry Hyde, Earl of Clarendon, and of His Brother, Laurence Hyde, Earl of Rochester; with the Diary of Lord Clarendon from 1687 to 1690*, 2 vols. (London, 1828), II: 256.

125   *£1,000 of stock:* January 8, 1689, RAC Books Concerning Stock: Transfer Book, 1687–1691, T 70/187, f. 30; General Court held January 16, 1689, RAC Minute Book: General Court, 1678–1720, T 70/101, f. 22.

125   *trafficking and enslavement:* A. M. Claydon, *William III* (2002; repr. Routledge, 2014), 33–34; John Childs, *The Nine Years' War and the British Army, 1688–1697: The Operations in the Low Countries* (MUP, 1991), 21–23.

126   *"The Protestant Religion":* *The Expedition of His Highness the Prince of Orange for England* (London, 1688), 6.

126   *Other eyewitness accounts:* See *A Letter from a Gentleman in Exeter to His Friend in London* (London, 1688); *An Historical Account of the Memorable Actions of the Most Glorious Monarch William III . . .* (London, 1689); *Quadriennium Jacobi, Or, the History of the Reign of King James II from His First Coming to the Crown to His Desertion* (London, 1689).

126   *dominated Amsterdam's economy:* Ulbe Bosma, *The World of Sugar: How the Sweet Stuff Transformed Our Politics, Health, and Environment over 2,000 Years* (HUP, 2023), 50–52.

126   *The mint continued:* Howard, *Coins of England & the United Kingdom*, 374–77, 384–86, 392.

127   *prestige and wealth remained pervasive:* Allison Blakely, *The Black Presence in the Dutch World* (IUP, 1993), 105–106; Diane Wolfthal, *Household Servants and Slaves: A Visual History, 1300–1700* (YUP, 2022), 23, 65, 201.

128   *curtailed royal authority:* John Brewer, *The Sinews of Power: War, Money, and the English State, 1688–1713* (Unwin Hyman, 1989), 117.

128 *voted customs revenue:* William Ashworth, *Customs and Excise: Trade, Production, and Consumption in England, 1640–1845* (OUP, 2003), 21–22.

128 *hamstrung William's ability:* John Miller, *The Glorious Revolution* (1983; repr. Routledge, 1997), 47, 53–54.

128 Nightingale v. Bridges: *Nightingale and others against Bridges,* Hilary 1789, in *Reports of Cases Adjudged in The Court of King's Bench,* 2 vols., ed. Bartholomew Shower (London, 1794), I: 131–39, here 136. See also Pettigrew, *Freedom's Debt,* 31–32; Holly Brewer, "Creating a Common Law of Slavery for England and its New World Empire," *Law and History Review* 39, no. 4 (2021): 812–13.

128 *"the charter confirmed":* Meeting December 11, 1689, RAC Minute Books: General Court, 1678–1720, T 70/101, f. 24.

129 *petitioned the House of Commons:* Stock, II, 16–17, 18, 20–23, 35; Davies, *The Royal African Company,* 123–24.

129 *petitions and pamphlets:* For a full list, see Pettigrew, *Freedom's Debt,* Appendix 5, 240–46.

129 *a scathing tract:* William Wilkinson, *Systema Africanum; Or a Treatise, Discovering the Intrigues and Arbitrary Proceedings of the Guiney Company* (London, 1690).

130 *"the Negroes sufficient":* Ibid., 7–8.

130 *"right and liberty":* *The Case Between the African Company and the People of England* (London, 1692), 1.

130 *supported the RAC's monopoly:* See, for instance, William III, Instructions to the Governors of Barbados and New Hampshire, July 1696, Paper relating to the RAC, 1696–1700, BL, Sloane MS 2902, ff. 87–89.

130 *10 percent dividend:* Warrants for a dividend, April 21, 1691, RAC Minute Book: Court of Assistants, January 8, 1690, to May 16, 1693, T 70/83, f. 8.

130 *"every £100 adventure":* Meeting July 30, 1691, RAC Books Concerning Stock, 1691–93, T 70/188, f. 14.

130 *Graham had sold:* After James II transferred his stock to Graham in January 1689, Graham sold £2,500 worth to four individuals in a bid to recoup the money he had loaned the exiled monarch. See T 70/187, ff. 35–36.

131 *"right of the Crown":* *Attorney-General v. Royal African Company,* Decree, 3 Wm & M (1691), TNA, E 130/15/2/No. 9.

131 *held RAC shares:* Stock transfer August 20, 1691, and 13th dividend, October 13, 1692, RAC Books concerning stock, Journal, 1691–1693, T 70/188, ff. 32, 85; Warrants for a dividend, October 4, 1692, T 70/83, f. 63.

131 *cast William III:* Murray Pittock, *Jacobitism* (Bloomsbury, 1998), 26–27; Edward Gregg, *Queen Anne* (1980; repr. YUP, 2001), 101–103.

131 *the customs revenue:* Payments into the Exchequer from 1688–1695 and 1696–1703, TNA, CUST 37/1, nf.

131 *"vast quantities of tobacco":* Quoted in Allan Kulikoff, *Tobacco and Slaves: The Development of Southern Cultures in the Chesapeake, 1680–1800* (UNCP, 1986), 6.

131 *enslaved population rose:* Christopher Tomlins, *Freedom Bound: Law, Labor, and Civic Identity in Colonizing English America, 1580–1865* (CUP, 2010), 41; Robert William Fogel and Stanley L. Engerman, *Time on the Cross: The Economics of American Negro Slavery* (W. W. Norton, 1974), 21.

132 *"to commit hostilities":* John Campbell, *The Lives of the Admirals, and Other Eminent British Seamen,* 3 vols. (London, 1742–1744), III: 185.

132   *orders to John Booker:* J. M. Gray, *A History of the Gambia* (1940; repr. CUP, 2015), 107, 112–13.

132   *"much plentifuller served":* Stock, II, 88–93.

132   *"an illegal patent":* Stock, II, 101–102.

133   *compromising public trust:* Brian P. Levack, *Distrust of Institutions in Early Modern Britain and America* (OUP, 2022), 102–103; Julie Orr, *Scotland, Darien and the Atlantic World, 1698–1700* (EUP, 2018).

133   *the Darien Company:* Orr, *Scotland, Darien and the Atlantic World,* 52–62; Mark Hanna, *Pirate Nests and the Rise of the British Empire, 1570–1740* (UNCP, 2015), 230.

133   *"clogged with customs":* Stock, II, 132, 138.

134   *"one Negro will make":* Stock, II, 160.

134   *Chesapeake planters and merchants:* Davies, *Royal African Company,* 294–95; William A. Pettigrew, "Transatlantic Politics and the Africanization of Virginia's Labor Force, 1688–1712," in *Early Modern Virginia: Reconsidering the Old Dominion,* ed. Douglas Bradburn and John C. Coombs (UVAP, 2011), 282–83.

134   *indentured servant trade:* Allan Kulikoff, *Tobacco and Slaves,* 37–41.

135   Speedwell: On the 1686 voyage of *Speedwell,* see *Voyages:* https://www.slavevoyages.org/voyage/database (accessed September 4, 2022).

135   *the RAC's instructions:* RAC Letter Book: Letters Sent to Africa, 1685–1698, T 70/50, f. 6; RAC Letter Book: Letters Received from Africa, 1683–1698, T 70/11, f. 59.

135   *influential Chesapeake gentry:* William A. Crozier, ed., *Virginia Heraldica: Being a Registry of Virginia Gentry Entitled to Coat Armor with Genealogical Notes of the Families* (The Genealogical Association, 1908), 14; *Maryland Historical Magazine,* Volume XV (Maryland Historical Society, 1920), 27–28; Lyon Gardiner Tyler, *Encyclopedia of Virginia Biography* (1915; repr. Genealogical Publishing, 1998), 151–52.

135   *"gentleman of estate":* Quoted in *Magazine of the Society of the Lees of Virginia* 1, no. 3 (1923): 108.

135   *"Negro girl Cumbo":* Will of Edward Porteus, February 23, 1694, Principal Probate Registry Class: Will-Register Books 157–158 NOEL, Virginia Colonial Records Project, https://image .lva.virginia.gov/VTLS/CR/04793/index.html (accessed September 4, 2023).

136   *"Negroes and servants":* Ibid.

136   *Robert Porteus: Magazine of the Society of the Lees of Virginia,* 108; Governor Spotswood to the Earl of Dartmouth, March 9, 1713, in *The Official Letters of Alexander Spotswood, Lieutenant-Governor of the Colony of Virginia, 1710-1722,* ed. R. A. Brocks, 2 vols. (Virginia Historical Society, 1882–1885), I: 54–55.

136   *a direct descendant:* On these genealogical links, see Desirée Baptiste, "The King, the Archbishop, and Hereditary Slavery," *The Repair Campaign,* March 8, 2024, https://repaircampaign .org/reparations-today/the-king-the-archbishop-and-hereditary-slavery/; David Conn and Rachel Hall, "Direct Ancestors of King Charles Owned Slave Plantations, Documents Reveal," *Guardian,* April 27, 2023, https://tinyurl.com/ybs5bz3h.

136   *"a fundamental prerequisite":* Nicholas Radburn, *Traders in Men: Merchants and the Transformation of the Transatlantic Slave Trade* (YUP, 2023), 11.

137   *uprisings and alleged conspiracies:* Jason T. Sharples, *The World that Fear Made: Slave Revolts and Conspiracy Scares in Early America* (UPenn, 2020), 255, Table 1.

137   *"murder all their masters":* Evelyn, *The Diary of John Evelyn,* II: 319.

137   *enormous financial stress:* General estimate of the present state of the trade of England, January 14, 1697/98, BL, Sloane MS 2902, f. 118; Rabushka, *Taxation in Colonial America,* 273.

137 *Treaty of Ryswick:* Jonathan Barth, *The Currency of Empire: Money and Power in Seventeenth-Century English America* (Cornell, 2021), 249, 261, 285; Childs, *The Nine Years' War and the British Army,* 133–34; Edward T. Corp, *A Court in Exile: The Stuarts in France, 1689–1718* (CUP, 2004), 52–53.

137 *appealed to Parliament:* Stock, II: 187, 202–203.

138 *"very great advantage":* Meeting December 30, 1697, RAC Minute Book: Court of Assistants, September 7, 1697, to January 2, 1699, T 70/85, ff. 11–12; Petition to the king, delivered December 30, 1697, Copy of Petitions and Memorials presented by the RAC, No. 1, from December 30, 1697, to June 20, 1720, T 70/170, f. 5.

138 *£5 per head:* The RAC's proposals for the regaining and preservation of the trade to Africa, and Forts in Africa maintained by the RAC, William III, Papers relating to the African Company, 1696–1700, BL, Sloane MS 2902, ff. 89–91.

138 *company "gromettoes":* Borrowed from the Portuguese, the term "gromettoes" was used to describe the company's so-called castle slaves. See David Eltis, *The Rise of African Slavery in the Americas* (CUP, 2000), 148.

139 *10 percent duty:* The duty applied to all trade in the areas where the RAC maintained forts; redwood was subject to a 5 percent duty. See Joseph Washington, *An Exact Abridgement of all the Statutes of King William and Queen Mary, and of King William III* (London, 1701), 543–49.

139 *period of thirteen years:* Stock, II, 216–17, 222–23, 235.

139 *"be carried on":* Newsletter R. Yard to Lord Williamson, April 19, 1698, SP 32/10, f. 127.

139 *transformed former interlopers:* Davies, *The Royal African Company,* 139–40.

139 *first four years: Voyages,* https://www.slavevoyages.org/voyage/database#results (accessed June 4, 2023).

140 *William III sent letters:* William III's response to the RAC, March 26, 1700, SP 44/100, f. 381; Petition to the king, 1700, and King's letter to Sir William Beeston, Governor of Barbados, on behalf of the RAC, April 8, 1700, T 70/170, ff. 15–16.

140 *"your Majesty's plantations":* Board of Trade, Advice to King William, BL, Sloane MS 2902, ff. 173–74.

140 *"supposed favorite servant":* Sir Henry Cole, *A Hand-Book for the Architecture, Tapestries, Paintings, Gardens, and Grounds of Hampton Court* (London, 1849), 46.

140 *"trampling down popery":* Quoted in Nicola Smith, *The Royal Image and the English People* (Ashgate, 2001), 150.

141 *great hall at Kensington Palace:* See *London in 1710 from the Travels of Zacharias Conrad von Uffenbach,* trans. and ed. W.H. Quarrell and M. Mare (London, 1934), 157.

141 *exhibited to palace visitors:* William Willshire, *The Stranger's Guide to Hampton Court Palace and Gardens* (London, 1869), 54; Peter Fryer, *Staying Power: The History of Black People in Britain* (Pluto Press, 1984), 22–23.

141 *"encircling the throat":* *Chamber's Journal of Popular Literature, Science, and Art,* no. 370, vol. 8 (January 31, 1891): 65.

CHAPTER 10: THE PROMISE OF VAST RICHES

142 *warfare appeared imminent:* James Falkner, *The War of the Spanish Succession, 1701–1714* (Pen and Sword, 2015), 13–14, 26.

142 *"heirs of her body":* Act of Settlement, 1701, in *The Eighteenth-Century Constitution, 1688–1815: Documents and Commentary,* ed. E. Neville Williams (CUP, 1970), 58.

142 *a new sovereign:* Falkner, *The War of the Spanish Succession,* 35–36; Howard Nenner, *The Right to Be King: Succession to the Crown of England,* 1587–1714 (Macmillan, 1995), 232–33.

143 *into an exorbitant war:* Alvin Rabushka, *Taxation in Colonial America* (PUP, 2008), 291–95.

143 *spike in commissioned privateering:* David. J. Starkey, *British Privateering Enterprise in the Eighteenth Century* (University of Exeter Press, 1990), 90–93.

143 *invention of "Great Britain":* Linda Colley, *Britons: Forging the Nation* (1992; repr. YUP, 2005), 11–12.

143 *127,967 African individuals: Voyages,* https://www.slavevoyages.org/voyage/database#results (accessed May 5, 2022).

143 *William III's RAC slaving shares:* The Queen's stock, April 13 and June 15, 1713, RAC: Books concerning stock, 1708–1712, T 70/196, f. 155.

143 *Prince George of Denmark:* Edward Gregg, *Queen Anne* (YUP, 2001), 137.

143 *petitioning George and Anne:* See RAC petitions to the Queen, April 2 and May 5, 1702, RAC petitions to George, Prince of Denmark, July 2, August 11, September 25, October 17, and December 24, 1702, and Petitions to Prince George and Queen Anne, 1703, Petitions and Memorials presented by the RAC of England, No 1, From December 30, 1697, to June 20, 1720, T 70/170, ff. 29–33, 33–36.

144 *"Her Majesty's subjects":* Petition to HRH George Prince of Denmark and Lord High Admiral, July 2, 1702, T 70/170, f. 31.

144 *"export to the plantations":* Petition to Queen Anne, March 1703, T 70/170, ff. 34–36.

144 *letters to colonial governors:* See, for example, Queen Anne to Bermuda and Barbados, July 16, 1703, and Queen Anne to Bermuda, January 32, 1704, RAC Letter Books: Letters sent to Plantations, 1701–1715, T 70/58, ff. 42, 62; Queen Anne to the Governor of Virginia, February 7, 1707, T 70/170, f. 64.

144 *approved the deployment:* General Manchester to Pembroke, April 14, 1702, SP 44/109, f. 199; Nottingham to the Attorney, July 7, 1703, SP 44/104, f. 311.

144 *letters of marque:* Hedges to the Lord High Admiral's Council, August 10, 1704, SP 44/204, f. 422.

144 *George issued instructions:* Prince George, Memorial about instructions for the convoys, and Instructions to Capt. Moore of the *Oxford* and Capt. Stanhope of the *Hastings,* September 12, and October 1704, and Prince's instructions to Capt. Windsor of the *Poole* and to Capt. Balshen of the *Chester,* July, and September 7, 1705, T 70/170, ff. 45, 52–53, 57–58.

145 *his reduced health:* Gregg, *Queen Anne,* 160–61.

145 *state of the African trade:* Abigail L. Swingen, *Competing Visions of Empire: Labor, Slavery, and the Origins of the British Atlantic Empire* (YUP, 2015), 142; William A. Pettigrew, *Freedom's Debt: The Royal African Company and the Politics of the Atlantic Slave Trade, 1672–1752* (UNCP, 2013), 94–95; James A. Rawley, *London, Metropolis of the Slave Trade* (UMP, 2003), 62–65.

145 *"of the utmost necessity": The State of the Trade to Africa, between 1680 and 1707* (London, 1708), 1.

146 *"forced to work alone": The Case of the Separate Traders to Africa* (London, 1708), 1.

146 *"the persons we buy": Considerations upon the Trade to Guinea* (London, 1708), 28–29.

146 *deliveries of enslaved Africans: An Account of the Number of Negroes Delivered in to the Islands of Barbadoes, Jamaica, and Antego, from the Year 1698 to 1708* (London, 1709), 1–2.

146 *"national in its constitution": The Falsities of Private Traders to Africa Discovered, and the Mischiefs They Occasion Demonstrated* (London, 1708), 3.

146 *"impose treble the price":* *The Case of the Royal-African Company* (London, 1709), 2.

147 *Barbadian colonists petitioned:* *A Letter from the Most Considerable Proprietors of the Island of Barbadoes* . . . (London, 1709), 2; *The Barbados Petition, Relating to the African Trade* (London, 1710), 1–2.

147 *asked the queen:* Petition to Queen Anne from the Royal African Company, June 18, 1711, SP 34/31, ff. 48–49; Gregg, *Queen Anne*, 280.

147 *Board of Trade's deliberations:* Abstracts of various reports and representations to the queen and the House of Commons concerning the African trade, made between 3 Feb 1707/8 and 15 Mar 1711/12, SP 34/18, ff. 27–34, quotes ff. 28, 32.

147 *"the sole trade":* Letter to Seth Grosvenor, James Phipps, and Robert Bleau at Cape Coast Castle, December 8, 1712, TNA, RAC letters to Africa, September 7, 1703, to June 17, 1715, T 70/52, ff. 142–43.

148 *"France's main design":* *A Letter from an Exchange Broker to a Country Gentleman, Concerning Peace and South-Sea Stock* (London, 1711), 6.

148 *"the only means":* *A True Account of the Design, and Advantages of the South-Sea Trade* (London, 1711), 6.

149 *"I have insisted":* Quoted in Paul Chamberlen, *An Impartial History of the Life and Reign of our Last Most Gracious Sovereign Queen Anne, of Blessed Memory* (London, 1738), 407.

149 *The asiento contract:* Memorandum concerning Article 42 of the Asiento Treaty, nd, SP 35/68, part 2, ff. 101–102. For the full terms of the asiento contract, see Arthur S. Aiton, "The Asiento Treaty as Reflected in the Papers of Lord Shelburne," *Hispanic American Historical Review* 8, no. 2 (1928): 167–77; Victoria Gardner Sorsby, "British Trade with Spanish America under the Asiento, 1713–1740" (Ph.D. Dissertation, University College London, 1975), 16–18.

149 *the South Sea Company:* *Abstract of the Charter of the Corporation and Company of Merchants of Great Britain Trading to the South Seas and Other Parts of America* . . . (London, 1711).

150 *an economic monopoly:* See Steven Pincus, "Empire and the Treaty of Utrecht (1713)," in *New Worlds? Transformations in the Culture of International Relations Around the Peace of Utrecht*, ed. Inken Schmidt-Voges and Ana Crespo Solana (Routledge, 2017), 153–75.

150 *"bring vast riches":* *Cobbett's Parliamentary History of England*, vol. 6 (London, 1810), 1022.

150 *"no African trade":* Daniel Defoe, *Review* 1, no. 44, January 10, 1712/13, in *Defoe's Review: Reproduced from the Original Editions*, ed. Arthur Wellesley Secord (Columbia University Press, 1938), 89.

150 *her royal favor:* Her Majesty's Warrant, January 28, 1712/13, South Sea Company, TNA, T 48/21, 1–8; Her Majesty's Answer, June 24, 1713, SSC Records, BL, Add MS 25495, f. 63.

151 *extensive financial interests:* South Sea Company: Notebook of subscribers, c. 1711–1720, LSE Library Archives and Special Collections, GB 97 SR 0083.

151 *list of shareholders:* *A List of the Names of the Corporation of the Governor and Company of Merchants of Great Britain Trading to the South-Seas* . . . (London, [1712]), 3–4.

151 *a public-private enterprise:* John Carswell, *The South Sea Bubble* (Cressnet Press, 1960), 57; Carl Wennerlind, *Casualties of Credit: The English Financial Revolution, 1620–1720* (HUP, 2011), 197–98.

151 *initial plan entailed:* Wennerlind, *Casualties of Credit*, 217–18; Shinsuke Satsuma, *Britain and Colonial Maritime War in the Early Eighteenth Century: Silver, Seapower, and the Atlantic* (TBP, 2013), 180–82.

152 *"carrying on":* Bolingbroke to Bateman, March 13, 1712, SSC Records, BL, Add MS 25562, f. 3.

152 *the queen instructed:* Bolingbroke to the Lords Commissioners of the Admiralty, July 12, 1713, and Oxford to Bateman, October 5, 1713, BL, Add MS 25562, f. 4.

152 *hands of subcontractors:* Carswell, *The South Sea Bubble*, 57–58; Gregory E. O'Malley, *Final Passages: The Intercolonial Slave Trade of British America, 1619–1807*, 222–23.

152 *"and near expiring":* Daniel Defoe, *A True Account of the Design and Advantages of the South Sea Trade* (London, 1711), 20.

152 *SSC negotiated directly:* Meetings June 12 and July 29, 1713, BL, Add MS 25495, ff. 60, 71–72; RAC Court of Assistants to the SSC, September 11, 1713, BL, Add MS 25562, f. 6; Heads for a contract between the SSC and the RAC, September 18, 1713, T 70/38, nf.

153 *"sorts of Blacks":* RAC to Agent John Clark, Sherbro, August 16, 1713, T 70/52, f. 168. See also RAC to Seth Grosvenor, James Phipps, and Robert Bleau, Cape Coast Castle, October 22, 1713, T 70/52, ff. 177–80.

153 *"been altogether impossible":* Bateman to Bolingbroke, October 14, 1713, SSC Records, BL, Add MS 25559, f. 21.

153 *allocation of profits:* Pym to Mortimer, December 2, 1713, BL, Add MS 25559, ff. 23–24.

153 *"the expense would go":* Bolingbroke to Lords Commissioners of the Admiralty, July 17, 1713, SSC Records, 1712–1732, BL, Add MS 25562, f. 3.

154 *Manuel Manassas Gilligan:* Sorsby, "British Trade with Spanish America Under the Asiento," 16–17; Adrian Finucane, *The Temptations of Trade: Britain, Spain, and the Struggle for Empire* (UPenn, 2016), 23.

154 *the SSC requested:* Pym to Mortimer, December 2, 1713, Copies of memorials, applications, petitions, etc. from the Court of Directors of the SSC, 1711–1721, BL, Add MS 25559, ff. 23–24.

154 *Anne fell seriously ill:* Gregg, *Queen Anne*, 374–75, 377–78.

154 *"be more dangerous":* Queen Anne to the Electress Dowager, May 19, 1714, in *The Life of Queen Anne*, ed. Abel Boyer (London, 1714), 398.

154 *unmoved by their claim:* Bolingbroke to Bateman, February 5, 1713/14, BL, Add MS 25562, ff. 5.

155 *thanked the queen:* SSC Address to the Queen, 1714, SP, 34/24, f. 122.

155 *"now proceed vigorously":* Bolingbroke to Shepherd, May 17, 1714, BL, Add MS 25562, f. 11.

155 *delayed moving forward:* Meeting June 23, 1714, BL, Add MS 25495, ff. 172–73.

155 *memorial and address:* Memorial to the Queen, July 16 and 19, 1714, BL, Add MS 25559, ff. 32, 33.

155 *"wish you good success":* Queen Anne to the SSC, July 21, 1714, BL, Add MS 25495, f. 188.

155 *following an illness:* Elizabeth Lane Furdell, *The Royal Doctors, 1485–1714: Medical Personnel at the Tudor and Stuart Courts* (University of Rochester Press, 2001), 245.

155 *to the Lords Justices:* Appeal to the Lords Justices, August 17 and September 1, 1714, BL, Add MS 25559, ff. 34–37.

155 *new Hanoverian king:* Address to George I, September 1714, BL, Add MS 25559, f. 38.

156 *requested SSC shares:* Meeting December 31, 1714, SSC Records, BL, Add MS 25494, ff. 243–44.

CHAPTER 11: THE CROWN AND THE ASIENTO

157 *Queen Anne died:* An Elegy on the Death of Her Most Gracious Majesty Queen Anne, Who Dy'ed at Her Palace in Kensington, on the First of August 1714 (London, 1714); Edward Gregg, *Queen Anne* (YUP, 2001), 212.

157   *Jacobite hopes:* Howard Nenner, *The Right to Be King: Succession to the Crown of England, 1603–1714* (Macmillan, 1995), 254–55.

157   *"able to handle":* Daniel Defoe, *Strike While the Iron's Hot* (London, 1715), 19.

158   *congratulated the new king:* SSC Meeting September 22, 1714, SSC Records, BL, Add MS 25495, ff. 206–207.

158   *in unpaid subsidies: The Political State of Great Britain,* vol. 1 (London, 1711), 351; Ragnhild Hatton, *George I* (1979; repr. YUP, 2001), 69.

158   *included George's name: A List of the Names of the Corporation of the Governor and Company of Merchants of Great Britain Trading to the South-Seas . . .* (London, 1712), 3.

158   *King George arrived:* Hatton, *George I,* 128–29.

158   *Mohammed and Mustapha:* John M. Beattie, *The English Court in the Reign of George I* (CUP, 1967), 260–61; Lucy Worsley, *The Courtiers: Splendor and Intrigue in the Georgian Court at Kensington Palace* (Walker & Co., 2010), 78–81.

159   *grand staircase fresco:* See Catherine Molineux, *Faces of Perfect Ebony: Encountering Atlantic Slavery in Imperial Britain* (HUP, 2012), 18–20.

159   *King George ordered:* Hatton, *George I,* 128–29.

159   *Prince George's disappointment:* Jeremy Black, *The Hanoverians: The History of a Dynasty* (Bloomsbury, 2004), 83–84.

160   *civil list revenue:* J. M. Beattie, *The English Court in the Reign of George I* (1967; repr. CUP, 2008), 107–108.

160   *royal family's sweet tooth:* A Monthly Proportion of Spice for the King's Kitchen, Establishment Books, 1714, RA, EB/EB/49, f. 5b.

160   *the national debt:* Henry Roseveare, *The Financial Revolution, 1660–1760* (1991; repr. Routledge, 2013), 52.

160   *the allure of trade:* Paul W. Mapp, *The Elusive West and the Contest for Empire, 1713–1763* (UNCP, 2011), 118–21.

161   *SSC directors extended:* SSC Meeting December 31, 1714, BL, Add MS 25495, ff. 243–44.

161   *list of subscribers: A List of the Names of the Corporation of the Governor and Company of Merchants of Great Britain Trading to the South-Seas . . .* (1714), 1.

161   *"I have not anything":* SSC Meeting, January 3, 1714/15, BL, Add MS 25495, ff. 244–45.

161   *swore the formal oath:* SSC Meeting February 2, 1714/15, BL, Add MS 25495, f. 251.

161   *acquainting himself with:* SSC Meetings March 16 and April 13, 1715, SSC Records, BL, Add MS 25496, ff. 15–16, 23–24.

161   *royal predecessor's authorization:* Letter and enclosure to Secretary Stanhope, May 27, 1715, SP 42/14, f. 104.

161   *George gifted venison:* SCC Meeting November 30, 1715, BL, Add MS 25496, f. 83. The SSC directors dined on the venison in July 1716; see BL, Add MS 25496, f. 142.

161   *"he should be always":* Meetings February 16 and 22, 1715, BL, Add MS 25496, ff. 95–97, 98.

162   *base of operations:* Power to Jamaica Agents representing the South Sea Company, SSC Records, BL, Add MS 25575, ff. 15–16.

162   *transshipment to Spanish America:* O'Malley, *Final Passages,* 228–29.

162   *the demographic imbalance:* Brooke N. Newman, *A Dark Inheritance: Blood, Race, and Sex in Colonial Jamaica* (YUP, 2018), 17.

162   *"The private trade":* William Wood, *The Asiento Contract Consider'd* (London, 1714), 6.

163 *SSC directors asked:* SSC to James Stanhope, September 28, 1715, SSC Records, BL, Add MS 25555, ff. 29–32.

163 *to renew these duties:* Meetings December 7, 20, and 21, 1715, *Journal of the Assembly of Jamaica,* vol. 2 (London, 1824), 157, 159–60.

163 *obstruct the asiento:* Abigail L. Swingen, *Competing Visions of Empire: Labor, Slavery, and the Origins of the British Atlantic Empire* (YUP, 2015), 193–94.

163 *objected to the duty:* SSC Meeting March 6, 1716, SSC Records, BL, Add MS 25497, ff. 16–17.

163 *Appealing to their royal patron:* SSC Meetings October 23, November 6, and December 11, 1717, BL, Add MS 25497, ff. 73–74, 76, 87–90; Petition of the Court of Directors of the SSC, 1717, CO 137/12, pt. 2.

163 *"Negroes brought thither":* Board of Trade report to the King-in-Council, December 21, 1717, CO 138/16, ff. 32–33.

163 *ordered the act's repeal:* Duties on Negroes in Jamaica, January 16, 1718, in *Royal Instructions to British Colonial Governors, 1670–1776,* vol. 2, ed. Leonard Labaree (Appletone, 1935), 670–71.

164 *accelerated a surge:* David Richardson, "The British Empire and the Atlantic Slave Trade, 1660–1807," in *The Oxford History of the British Empire,* ed. P. J. Marshall (OUP, 1998), 442, 446.

164 *owed the African Company:* William A. Pettigrew, *Freedom's Debt: The Royal African Company and the Politics of the Atlantic Slave Trade, 1672–1752* (UNCP, 2013), 162.

164 *royal predecessor's RAC stock:* George I's stock, December 31, 1714, 1715, and 1719, RAC Books concerning stock, 1713–1719, T 70/197, f. 252; K. G. Davies, *Royal African Company* (Octagon Books, 1975), 80.

164 *elected George I governor:* Meeting August 24, 1714, Minute Books, RAC: General Court, 1678–1720, T 70/101, f. 162.

164 *A detailed account:* RAC Petition to the King, October 21, 1714, T 70/101, ff. 163–65.

165 *"That the happy fruit":* Ibid.

165 *petitioned the king:* Petitions to George I, April 5, and July 13, 1715, Copies of Petitions and Memorials presented by the RAC, No. 1, From 1697 to 1720, T 70/170, ff. 85–86.

165 *"the gentlemen present":* Meetings July 4 and 5, 1715, T 70/89, ff. 135, 136.

165 *evolving royal menagerie:* Caroline Grigson, *The History of Exotic Animals in England, 1100–1837* (OUP, 2016), 78-81.

165 *multiple petitions:* Quotes taken from Petitions to George I, September 16 and December 20, 1715, and August 23, 1716, T 70/170, ff. 86, 89–90, 91–92.

166 *contemplated shifting focus:* Pettigrew, *Freedom's Debt,* 164–65.

166 *bore the names:* These included *Prince, Prince of Wales, George Augustus, Crown, Anne Galley,* and *Princess Amelia.* See *Voyages,* https://www.slavevoyages.org/voyage/database#results (accessed May 4, 2024).

166 *like previous asientistas:* Jean O. McLachlan, *Trade and Peace with Old Spain, 1667–1750* (1940; repr. CUP, 2015), 27.

166 *representatives embarked 13,102: Voyages,* https://www.slavevoyages.org/voyage/database#statistics (accessed January 11, 2023).

166 *contraband slave trade:* Colin A. Palmer, *Human Cargoes: The British Slave Trade to Spanish America, 1700–1739* (IUP, 1981), 93; Gregory E. O'Malley, *Final Passages: The Intercolonial Slave Trade of British America, 1619–1807* (UNCP, 2014), 244–47.

167 *instruct its agents:* An Instrument Certifying that the seal impressed in the margin thereof is to

be used for the future for selling the Company's Negroes, March 8, 1715, BL, Add MS 25575, ff. 16–17.

167 *"the mark henceforward"*: An Instrument Certifying that the Mark in the Margin thereof is to be used for that purpose for the future, 1715, BL, Add MS 25575, ff. 17–18, 19–20.

168 *the brand devised*: Lúcio Menezes Ferreira and Gabino La Rose, "The Archaeology of Slave Branding in Cuba," in *Current Perspectives on the Archaeology of African Slavery in Latin America*, ed. Pedro Paulo A. Funari and Charles E. Orser, Jr. (Springer, 2015), 49.

168 A *(for* asiento*)*: O'Malley, *Final Passages*, 219–20.

168 *"Negroes be marked"*: SSC to Dudley Woodbridge, 1718, SSC Records, BL, Add MS 25563, f. 263.

168 *"form of receipt"*: Sherwin K. Bryant, *Rivers of Gold, Lives of Bondage: Governing Through Slavery in Colonial Quito* (UNCP, 2014), 80–81.

168 Royal Prince: See Meetings October 9 and November 6, 1717, BL, Add MS 25497, ff. 70–71, 76–78.

168 *His Majesty's protection*: Meeting September 7, 1716, BL, Add MS 25496, f. 156.

169 *the growing wedge*: Beattie, *The English Court in the Reign of George I*, 268–70.

169 *royal family's quarrel*: Hatton, *George I*, 199–200, 206–209.

169 *"no other consideration"*: SSC Meeting January 27, 1718, BL, Add MS 25497, ff. 105–106.

170 *"your royal favor"*: SSC Meetings January 27 and 31, 1718, BL, Add MS 25497, ff. 105–106.

170 *receiving his consent*: SSC Meetings February 6 and 7, 1718, SSC Records, BL, Add MS 25498, ff. 1–2.

170 *"favor and protection"*: SSC Meeting February 12, 1718, BL, Add MS 25498, ff. 3–4.

170 Royal George: Meetings March 19 and April 2, 1718, BL, Add MS 25498, ff. 20–21, 24–25.

170 *portrait of King George*: SSC Meeting January 17, 1719, BL, Add MS 25555, f. 106.

170 *Britain formed a pact*: Jeremy Black, *Politics and Foreign Policy in the Age of George I, 1714–1727* (2014; repr. Routledge, 2016), 118–20.

170 *the directors protested*: SSC Minutes January 21, 1718/19, Committee of Correspondence, SSC Records, BL, Add MS 25551; SSC to the King, September 24, 1718, SP 35/12, ff. 330–43; SSC to the King, October 22, 1718, SP 35/13, f. 28.

171 *forced the Spanish Crown*: Allan J. Kuethe and Kenneth J. Andrien, *The Spanish Atlantic World in the Eighteenth Century: War and the Bourbon Reforms, 1713–1796* (CUP, 2014), 62–66.

171 *reminded George I*: Memorial to the King, January 1720, SP 35/20, ff. 106–107.

171 *"his firm resolution"*: His Majesty's answer to the SSC, September 25 and November 12, 1718, BL Add MS 25498, ff. 60–61, 66–67.

171 *"particular regard"*: Meetings January 6 and February 20, 1719, BL, Add MS 25498, ff. 82, 99.

171 *the company proposed*: Hatton, *George I*, 251.

171 *a transparent attempt*: John Carswell, *The South Sea Bubble* (Cressnet Press, 1960), 257–58.

171 £100,000 in SSC stock: Receipt for stock in the SSC, June 1, 1720, and Account of the South Sea Stock purchased on behalf of George I, 1720, RA, GEO/MAIN/52841–52843.

172 *"your royal name"*: SSC Meeting June 11, 1720, SSC Records, BL, Add MS 25499, f. 25.

172 *George ordered Aislabie*: RA, GEO/MAIN/52841–52843.

172 *thousands of new subscribers*: Carswell, *The South Sea Bubble*, 260.

172 *increased shareholder value*: Gregory Price and Warren Whatley, "Did Profitable Slave Trading Enable the Expansion of Empire?: The *Asiento de Negros*, the South Sea Company and the Financial Revolution in Great Britain," *Cliometrica* 15 (2021): 678.

172 *began to decline:* Harold L. Vogel, *Financial Market Bubbles and Crashes: Features, Causes, and Effects* (PM, 2018), 49–50.

172 *Aislabie wrote to Hanover:* John Aislabie, Account of actions regarding South Sea stock, 1722–1727, RA, GEO/MAIN/5238–52840.

173 *faced financial ruin:* Carswell, *The South Sea Bubble*, 260–61.

173 *"the universal calamity":* Lords Justices to the King, September 21, 1720, SP 35/23, f. 99.

173 *"to sell and buy":* Duchess of Kendal to John Aislabie, September 27, 1720, RA, GEO/MAIN/52844–52855.

173 *stock as gifts:* Further recount of actions regarding South Sea Stock, 1720–1727, RA, GEO/MAIN/52848; Hatton, *George I*, 251–54.

173 *pressed George:* Charles Delafaye to Earl Stanhope, October 12, 1720, SP 35/23, f. 199; Craggs to Stanhope, October 14, 1720, SP 78/169, f. 85; Craggs to Stanhope, October 21, 1720, SP 78/169, f. 111.

173 *investing public demanded:* Lewis Melville, *The South Sea Bubble* (Small, Maynard, & Co, 1923), 211.

174 *Chancellor Aislabie: Mr. Aislabie's Two Speeches Considered; with His Tryal at Large in Both Houses of Parliament* (London, 1721), 8.

174 *"a fairy fortune":* Carswell, *The South Sea Bubble*, 261.

174 *"efficient and committed":* Helen J. Paul, *The South Sea Bubble: An Economic History of its Origins and Consequences* (Routledge, 2010), 65.

174 *"Asiento-related slave trading":* Price and Whatley, "Did Profitable Slave Trading Enable the Expansion of Empire?" *Cliometrica:* 710.

CHAPTER 12: THE KING'S SLAVES

175 *convinced King George:* Petition to the King, c. 1721, SP 35/65/30, part I, f. 45.

175 *"good, sound, healthy":* Agreement between the SSC and the RAC, March 15, 1721, SSC Records, BL, Add MS 25575, ff. 75–77.

175 *instructed enslavers:* Meeting January 2, 1721/22, SSC Records, BL, Add MS 25556, f. 20.

176 *received a commission:* Victoria Gardner Sorsby, *British Trade with Spanish America Under the Asiento, 1713–1740* (Ph.D. dissertation, University College London, 1975), 110–12.

176 *The plan entailed:* Directors to Rigby and Pratter, April 21, 1725, SSC Records, BL, Add MS 25564, f. 106.

176 *SSC's published list: A List of the Names of the Corporation of the Governor and Company of Merchants of Great Britain Trading to the South-Seas . . .* (London, 1723), 1.

176 *inter-imperial contraband trade:* Adrian J. Pearce, *British Trade with Spanish America, 1763–1808* (LUP, 2007), 23–24.

176 *a concerted campaign:* Richard Pares, *War and Trade in the West Indies, 1739–1763* (Frank Cass, 1963), 20–28.

177 *SSC directors petitioned:* Petition to the Spanish Crown from the SSC, June 27, 1723, SP 35/43/162, Part 2, f. 141.

177 *asked George I:* Memorial to King George from the SSC, July 19, 1722, SP 35/32/38, ff. 70–73; Memorial to King George from the SSC, August 23, 1722, SP 35/32/141, ff. 292–93.

177 *"insults and indignities":* Court of Directors to King George, October 12, 1726, SP 35/63/33, ff. 55–59.

177 *aggressive Spanish seizures:* Adrian Finucane, *The Temptations of Trade: Britain, Spain, and the Struggle for Empire* (UPenn, 2016), 68–69.

177 *George I died:* Jeremy Black, *The Hanoverians: The History of a Dynasty* (Hambledon and London, 2004), 84–85.

178 *George II's accession:* Paul Langford, *A Polite and Commercial People: England, 1727–1783* (1989; repr. OUP, 1998), 11–15.

178 *copious amounts of sugar:* A monthly proportion of spice etc. for the kitchen, Household Allowance Book for George II, 1727, Establishment Books, RA, EB/EB/31-31a, f.12.

178 *purchase "seasoned Negroes":* Admiral Charles Stewart to Navy Board, November 11, 1729, cited in *Naval Administration, 1715–1750*, ed. Daniel A. Baugh (Naval Records Society, 1977), 351. Stewart's naval career is detailed in John D. Grainger, *The British Navy in the Caribbean* (TBP, 2021), 124–37.

179 *"has paid dear":* Admiral Charles Stewart to Navy Board, December 29, 1730, cited in *Naval Administration*, 357.

179 *Navy Board confirmed:* Navy Board to Admiralty Secretary, March 11, 1731/32, ibid., 359–61.

179 *"they are Cormantees":* Admiral Charles Stewart to Navy Board, January 13, 1731/1732, ADM 106/842, ff. 1–3.

179 *the term "Coromantee":* Kwasi Konadu, *The Akan Diaspora in the Americas* (OUP, 2010), 122–24.

179 *"to provide wives":* Admiral Charles Stewart to Navy Board, March 15, 1732, ADM 106/842, ff. 14–15.

179 *"negro who ran":* Stewart to Navy Board, April 29, 1732, ibid., f. 22.

180 *Antigua naval yard:* Henry Snow, "Fugitive Harbour: Labour, Community, and Marronage at Antigua Naval Yard," *Slavery & Abolition* 42, no. 4 (2021): 803–26; Charles R. Foy, "The Royal Navy's Employment of Black Mariners and Maritime Workers, 1754–1783," *International Journal of Maritime History* 28, no. 1 (2016): 6–35.

180 *"might depend on":* George II to the SSC, July 21, 1727, SSC Records, BL, Add MS 25544, f. 56.

180 *presented George II:* Address to King George II, July 6, 1727, SSC Records, BL, Add MS 25556, f. 113; SSC Meetings July 4, 21, 1727, BL, Add MS 25544, ff. 55–56.

180 *turned to the monarchy:* Address to the King in Council, September 28, and Address to the King, December 22, 1727, BL, Add MS 25556, f. 117–18, 124–25.

180 *prayed the king:* Address presented to His Majesty, July 18, and December 5, 1729, BL, Add MS 25544, ff. 65–66.

181 *"may depend upon":* His Majesty's response, December 5, 1729, ibid., f. 68.

181 *the Spanish seized:* Finucane, *The Temptations of Trade*, 85–87.

181 *the king's name:* *A List of the Names of the Corporation of the Governor and Company of Merchants of Great Britain Trading to the South-Seas . . .* (London, 1736), 1, 13.

181 *War of Jenkins's Ear:* See esp. Philip Woodfine, *Britannia's Glories: The Walpole Ministry and the 1739 War with Spain* (TBP, 1998); Robert Gaudi, *The War of Jenkins' Ear: The Forgotten Struggle for North and South America, 1739–1742* (Pegasus Books, 2021).

181 *"a Prince cannot":* Horatio Walpole, Considerations relating to the Navigation and Commerce of Great Britain in America, with Respect to the Treaties with Spain, January 23, 1737/38, BL, Add MS 9131, ff. 251–71.

182 *"the ear itself":* Justin McCarthy, *A History of the Four Georges*, 4 vols. (Leipzig, 1890), II: 185.

182 *press widely defended:* Kathleen Wilson, "Empire, Trade and Popular Politics in Mid-Hanoverian Britain: The Case of Admiral Vernon," *Past and Present* 121 (1988): 96–99.

182 *Georgia was the first:* Alan Taylor, *American Colonies* (Penguin Books, 2001), 241–42.

182 *founding of Charleston:* Thomas D. Wilson, *Charleston and Savannah: The Rise, Fall, and Reinvention of Two Rival Cities* (UGAP, 2023), 47–52.

182 *South Carolina attracted:* Matthew Mulcahy, *Hubs of Empire: The Southeastern Lowcountry and the British Caribbean* (JHUP, 2014), 84–111.

183 *the Georgia trustees:* Betty Wood, *Slavery in Colonial Georgia, 1730–1775* (1984; repr. UGAP, 2007), 5.

183 *appealed to the king:* Petition of the SSC to the King, July 4, 1734, SP 36/32/117, f. 117; Address of the SSC to the King, May 15, 1735, SP 36/35/45, f. 45; Meeting September 21, 1739, SSC Records, BL, Add MS 25510.

183 *Vernon led a squadron:* Kathleen Wilson, *The Sense of the People: Politics, Culture, and Imperialism* (CUP, 1995), 142–46.

183 *amphibious assault force:* Elena A. Schneider, *The Occupation of Havana: War, Trade, and Slavery in the Atlantic World* (UNCP, 2018), 57–58; J. R. McNeil, *Mosquito Empires: Ecology and War in the Greater Caribbean, 1620–1914* (CUP, 2010), 154–55.

184 *succession of Maria Theresa:* Barbara Stollberg-Rilinger, *Maria Theresa: The Habsburg Empress in Her Time* (PUP, 2021), 79–82.

184 *Spanish Caribbean strongholds:* Schneider, *The Occupation of Havana,* 58–60.

184 *new commercial treaty:* Shinsuke Satsuma, *Britain and Colonial Maritime War in the Early Eighteenth Century: Silver, Seapower and the Atlantic* (TBP, 2013), 247.

184 *valuable British import:* Richard Sheridan, *Sugar and Slavery: An Economic History of the British West Indies* (1974; repr. Canoe Press, 1994), 496–97.

185 *British sugar consumers:* Troy Bickham, *Eating the Empire: Food and Society in Eighteenth-Century Britain* (Reaktion Books, 2020), 32–34.

185 *Outside of the Caribbean:* Ira Berlin, *Generations of Captivity: A History of African-American Slaves* (HUP, 2003), 68; Taylor, *American Colonies,* 35–36.

185 *New Englanders engaged:* Margaret Ellen Newell, *Brethren by Nature: New England Indians, Colonists, and the Origins of American Slavery* (Cornell, 2015), 4–6.

186 *surpassed the Portuguese:* David Eltis and David Richardson, *Atlas of the Transatlantic Slave Trade* (YUP, 2010), 23; Nicholas Radburn, *Traders in Men: Merchants and the Transformation of the Transatlantic Slave Trade* (YUP, 2023), 20, 24–26.

186 *captives resisted enslavement:* See esp. David Richardson, "Shipboard Revolts, African Authority, and the Atlantic Slave Trade," *WMQ* 58, no. 1 (2001): 69–92; Eric Robert Taylor, *If We Must Die: Shipboard Insurrection in the Era of the Atlantic Slave Trade* (LSUP, 2006).

186 *"to judge slaveholding":* Christopher Leslie Brown, *Moral Capital: Foundations of British Abolitionism* (UNCP, 2006), 36.

186 *the SPG sent:* See esp. Daniel O'Connor, *Three Centuries of Mission: The United Society for the Propagation of the Gospel, 1701–2000* (Bloomsbury, 2000); Andrew Porter, *Religion Versus Empire? British Protestant Missionaries and Overseas Expansion, 1700–1914* (MUP, 2004); Travis Glasson, *Mastering Christianity: Missionary Anglicanism and Slavery in the Atlantic World* (OUP, 2013).

187 *"Royal Christian heroine":* Elkanah Settle, *A Pindaric Poem on the Propagation of the Gospel in Foreign Parts* (London, 1711), iii.

187 *The queen issued:* SPG meetings April 6 and 23, 1714, Society for the Propagation of the Gospel Proceedings, HL, MSS MFilm 00589, Reel 001, 1701-1850, vol. I, ff. 374, 377.

187   *"propose proper methods":* SPG meeting May 21, 1714, ibid., vol. II, f. 382.

187   *"so pious and useful":* SPG meeting October 15, 1714, ibid., vol. III, f. 1.

187   *Royal bounty helped:* Jeremy Gregory, "The Hanoverians and the Colonial Churches," in *The Ha-noverian Succession: Dynastic Politics and Monarchial Culture,* ed. Andreas Gestrich and Michael Schaich (Routledge, 2016), 116–17; Jennifer C. Snow, *Mission, Race, and Empire: The Episcopal Church in Global Context* (OUP, 2024), 40–41.

187   *"the barbarous usage":* SPG meeting October 21, 1709, HL, MSS MFilm 00589, Reel 001, vol. I, ff. 415–16.

187   *"the conversion of heathens":* SPG meeting April 28, 1710, ibid., vol. I, ff. 478–79.

187   *individual clergymen:* An SPG missionary in North Carolina, for example, was left "a very good plantation upon which he lives, with all the houses and some household Furniture, two Slaves and their Increase for ever . . ." SPG meeting March 22, 1711, ibid., vol. II, f. 16.

188   *Christopher Codrington:* David Brion Davis, *The Problem of Slavery in Western Culture* (1966; repr. OUP, 1988), 219.

188   *petitioned Queen Anne:* SPG meeting February 8, 1710/11, HL, MSS MFilm 00589, Reel 001, vol. I, ff. 570–72.

188   *"to use the slaves":* SPG meeting February 16, 1710/11, ibid., vol. II, f. 4.

188   *far from humane:* Glasson, *Mastering Christianity,* 143–44; Katharine Gerbner, *Christian Slavery: Conversion and Race in the Protestant Atlantic World* (UPenn, 2018), 111–14; Janice McLean-Farrell and Michael Anderson Clarke, "Missions in Contested Places/Spaces: The SPG, Slavery, and Codrington College, Barbados," *Mission Studies* 38 (2021): 325–49.

188   *Church of England investigation:* See "Church Commissioners' Research Into Historic Links to Transatlantic Chattel Slavery," *Church Commissioners for England,* https://www.churchof england.org/sites/default/files/2023-01/church-commissioners-for-england-research-into -historic-links-to-transatlantic-chattel-slavery-report.pdf (accessed January 15, 2023).

189   *being outpaced by:* Padraic X. Scanlan, *Slave Empire: How Slavery Built Modern Britain* (Robin-son, 2020), 41–43.

189   *"the navigation of France":* John Bennet, *Two Letters and Several Calculations on the Sugar Colonies and Trade; Addressed to Two Committees Nominated by the West-India Merchants, &c.* (London, 1738), 6.

189   *British sugar imports:* Maxine Berg and Pat Hudon, *Slavery, Capitalism, and the Industrial Rev-olution* (Polity, 2023), 59.

189   *from customs revenue:* John Sinclair, *The History of the Public Revenue of the British Empire: Part III* (London, 1790), 25, 27.

189   *the West India lobby:* P. J. Marshall, *The Making and Unmaking of Empires: Britain, India, and America, c. 1750–1783* (OUP, 2005), 16–17; Andrew J. O'Shaughnessy, "The Formation of a Commercial Lobby: The West India Interest, British Colonial Policy and the American Revo-lution," *HJ* 40, no. 1 (1997): 71–95; David Beck Ryden, *West Indian Slavery and British Abolition, 1783–1807* (CUP, 2009), 40–82.

190   *state of war:* See Vincent Brown, *Tacky's Revolt: The Story of an Atlantic Slave Revolt* (HUP, 2020), 4–6; Trevor Burnard and John Garrigus, *The Plantation Machine: Atlantic Capitalism in French Saint-Domingue and British Jamaica* (UPenn, 2016), 128–31.

190   *a fatal year:* Quoted in Christopher Hibbert, *George III: A Personal History* (Basic Books, 1998), 14.

191   *the young George:* Jeremy Black, *George III: America's Last King* (YUP, 2006), 7–8.

191 *"Tis by our trade"*: William Perrin, *The Present State of the British and French Sugar Colonies, and Our Own Northern Colonies, Considered* (London, 1740), 50.

CHAPTER 13: BRITAIN'S SLAVE EMPIRE

195 *into the Ohio Valley:* Michael A. McConnell, *A Country Between: The Upper Ohio Valley and Its Peoples, 1724–1774* (UNP, 1992), 19–20.

195 *over disputed lands:* Daniel K. Richter, *The Ordeal of the Longhouse: The Peoples of the Iroquois League in the Era of European Colonization* (UNCP, 1992), 235; McConnell, *A Country Between,* 50–55.

196 *the British public:* Kathleen Wilson, "Empire of Virtue: The Imperial Project and Hanoverian Culture c.1720–1785," in Lawrence Stone, ed., *An Imperial State at War: Britain from 1689 to 1815* (Routledge, 1994), 128–64.

196 *growing French presence:* Fred Anderson, *Crucible of War: The Seven Years' War and the Fate of Empire in British North America, 1754–1766* (Vintage Books, 2000), 33–35.

196 *roughly 975,000 captives:* Voyages, https://www.slavevoyages.org/voyage/database#tables (accessed February 3, 2024).

196 *Parliament dissolved:* William Pettigrew, *Freedom's Debt: The Royal African Company and the Politics of the Atlantic Slave Trade, 1672–1752* (UNCP, 2013), 176–77, 205.

197 *Vying to defend:* P. J. Marshall, *The Making and Unmaking of Empires: Britain, India, and America, c. 1750–1783* (OUP, 2005), 81–83.

197 *British government collapsed:* Jeremy Black, *Pitt the Elder* (CUP, 1992), 165–67.

197 *William Pitt the Elder:* John Brewer, *The Sinews of Power: War, Money, and the English State, 1688–1783* (HUP, 1988), 169, 174–75.

197 *"he infused vigor":* Horace Walpole, *Memoires of the Last Ten Years of the Reign of George the Second,* 2 vols. (London, 1822), II: 272.

198 *"as great consequence":* An Account of the Expedition to the West Indies, Against Martinico, with the Reduction of Guadelupe, and Other the Leeward Islands; Subject to the French King, 1759 (London, 1762), 91.

198 *"church bells":* Quoted in Richard Middleton, *The Bells of Victory: The Pitt-Newcastle Ministry and the Conduct of the Seven Years' War, 1757–1762* (CUP, 2002), 146.

198 *multiracial provincial companies:* Maria Alessandra Bollettino, "Slavery, War, and Britain's Atlantic Empire: Black Soldiers, Sailors, and Rebels in the Seven Years' War" (Ph.D. dissertation, University of Texas, Austin, 2019), 41–46.

199 *subdue the Maroons:* Brooke N. Newman, *A Dark Inheritance: Blood, Race, and Sex in Colonial Jamaica* (YUP, 2018), 74–75, 86–90, 94; Michael Craton, *Testing the Chains: Resistance to Slavery in the British West Indies* (Cornell, 1982), 88–90.

199 *armed enslaved men:* Bollettino, "Slavery, War, and Britain's Atlantic Empire," 96–98; ibid., "'Of Equal or of more Service: Black Soldiers and the British Empire in the Mid-Eighteenth-Century Caribbean," *Slavery & Abolition* (2017): 510–33.

199 *Tacky's Revolt:* See esp. Brown, *Tacky's Revolt;* Trevor Burnard, *Jamaica in the Age of Revolution* (UPenn, 2020), 103–30; Jason T. Sharples, *The World That Fear Made: Slave Revolts and Conspiracy Scares in Early America* (UPenn, 2020), 185–90.

200 *his grandfather's seat:* George III, Memoirs from October 25, 1760, RA, GEO/MAIN/4.

200 *"determination to prosecute":* Memorandum on the death of George II and accession of George III, October 25, 1760, RA, GEO/MAIN/2, f. 1.

200 *his tutor:* John L. Bullion, "The Prince's Mentor: A New Perspective on the Friendship between George III and Lord Bute during the 1750s," *Albion* 21, no. 1 (1989): 34–55; Janice Hadlow, *A Royal Experiment: The Private Life of King George III* (Henry Holt, 2014), 107–112.

201 *"a convinced abolitionist":* Andrew Roberts, *The Last King of America: The Misunderstood Reign of George III* (Viking, 2021), 29.

201 *"abstract injustice":* Christopher Leslie Brown, *Moral Capital: Foundations of British Abolitionism* (UNCP, 2006), 114.

201 *a necessary evil:* Most historians agree that George III was no abolitionist. See, for example, Richard Pares, *King George III and the Politicians* (OUP, 1953), 42; G. M. Ditchfield, *George III: An Essay in Monarchy* (PM, 2002), 136; Black, *George III: America's Last King,* 333.

201 *"the European traffic":* George III, Private Papers, Essays III, Of Laws Relative to Government in General, 1750s, RA, GEO/ADD/32/873–874.

201 *"monstrous features":* Ibid.

202 *"exaggerate too much":* Baron Charles de Montesquieu, *The Spirit of Laws,* 2 vols., trans. (London, 1750), I: 196, 342.

202 *"The true origin":* George III, Private Papers, Essays III, Of Laws Relative to Government in General, 1750s, RA, GEO/ADD/32/874, 877.

202 *tutors had taught:* For the curriculum used in the instruction of George III and other British princes, see Peter Gordon and Denis Lawton, *Royal Education: Past, Present, and Future* (Frank Cass, 2003), 102–108; Aysha Pollnitz, *Princely Education in Early Modern Britain* (CUP, 2015).

203 *The Prince of Wales and family consumed:* Account of kitchen expenses for food provision to the Prince of Wales and family at Kew and Saville House, November 1758, RA, GEO/ADD/17/67/25. For monthly kitchen expenses through August 1760, see also RA, GEO/ADD/17/67/26-31.

203 *"Patriot King":* See Henry St. John, 1st Viscount Bolingbroke, *Letters on the Spirit of Patriotism: On the Idea of a Patriot King . . .* (London, 1752).

203 *"residence of true piety":* Prince George to Earl Bute, June 1757, in *Letters from George III to Lord Bute, 1756–1766, ed.* Romney Sedgwick (MacMillan, 1939), 6.

204 *primary role models:* Ibid.; Instructions from Frederick, Prince of Wales, to his son George, January 13, 1749/50, RA, GEO/MAIN/54227–54232.

204 *"convincing the world":* George, Prince of Wales, to King George II, July 20, 1759, RA, GEO/MAIN/15701-2.

204 *history of Crown revenues:* George III Essays, A Short Historical account of ye Revenue of ye Crown, c. 1755, RA, GEO/ADD/32/1648–1684.

204 *would bitterly regret:* Black, *George III,* 51–53.

204 *optimism reigned:* Ibid., 47–49.

205 *"the unexpected violence": An Historical Memorial of the Negotiation of France and England, From the 26th of March, 1761, to the 20th of September of the Same Year* (London, 1761), 4.

206 *"Mr. Pitt alone": An Earnest Address to the People of Great-Britain and Ireland: Occasioned by the Dismission of William Pitt, Esq. from the Office of Secretary of State* (London, 1761), 28.

206 *to squeeze France:* Jonathan R. Dull, *The French Navy and the Seven Years' War* (UNP, 2005), 202–206.

206 *well-known death trap:* Vincent Brown, *The Reaper's Garden: Death and Power in the World of Atlantic Slavery* (HUP, 2008), 18.

206 *"the soldiers and sailors":* Earl of Albemarle to Earl of Egremont, May 27, 1762, CO 117/1, ff. 69–72.

206 *Jamaica's military establishment:* Annual Expence of the British Colonies in North America and the West Indies, 1765, Stowe Collection, Grenville Correspondence, HL, STG Box 12, folder 30.

206 *British expeditionary force:* Stephen Conway, *War, State, and Society in Mid-Eighteenth Century Britain and Ireland* (OUP, 2006), 30-32.

206 *Havana, Cuba:* Ada Ferrer, *Cuba: An American History* (Scribner, 2021), 43–44.

207 *"of great use":* Secret instructions issued by King George III to Lord Albemarle, February 15, 1762, Lyttelton to Albemarle, and Extract of the Jamaican Act for providing Two Thousand Negroes for the Immediate Service of His Majesty, May 4 and 14, and Draught to the Earl of Albemarle, August 7,1762, CO 117/1, ff. 24–36, 67, 73–74.

207 *prospect of re-enslavement:* Gerald Horne, *The Counter-Revolution of 1776: Slave Resistance and the Origins of the United States of America* (NYUP, 2014), 189–90.

207 *"two thousand Negroes":* Extract of the Jamaican Act for providing Two Thousand Negroes for the Immediate Service of His Majesty, May 14, 1762, CO 117/1, f. 67.

207 *"so useful a corps":* Draught to the Earl of Albemarle, August 7, 1762, CO 117/1, ff. 75–76.

207 *their immense value:* The British army used enslaved people as pioneers, laborers, and soldiers during the War of Jenkins's Ear and the sieges of Martinique and Guadeloupe. See Bollettino, "'Of Equal or of More Service'": 510–33; Marshall Smelser, *The Campaign for the Sugar Islands, 1759: A Study of Amphibious Warfare* (UNCP, 1955), 37, 139–45; Richard Pares, *War and Trade in the West Indies, 1739–1763* (1936; repr. London: F. Cass, 1963). Enslaved individuals were also used in the North American theater. See, for example, Larry G. Bowman, "Virginia's Use of Blacks in the French and Indian War," *Western Pennsylvania Historical Magazine* 53 (1970): 57–63; Scott Padeni, "The Role of Blacks in New York's Northern Campaigns of the Seven Years' War," *Bulletin of the Fort Ticonderoga Museum* 16 (1999): 153–69.

208 *laid siege to Havana:* Elena A. Schneider, *The Occupation of Havana: War, Trade, and Slavery in the Atlantic World* (UNCP, 2018), 17; Daniel E. Walker, "Colony versus Crown: Raising Black Troops for the British Siege on Havana, 1762," *Journal of Caribbean History* 33, no. 1 (1999): 74–84.

208 *many British lives:* Eyewitness accounts, though spotty on specifics, capture the enormity of the undertaking and the high casualties from disease. See, for example, *An Authentic Journal of the Siege of the Havana* (London, 1762), 1, 9, 40–42.

208 *"a new Cuba":* Ferrer, *Cuba*, 53.

208 *"All was joy":* Quoted in *The Memoirs of the Court of George III*, ed. Michael Kassler (Routledge, 2016), 11.

208 *British forces achieved:* Anderson, *Crucible of War*, 498, 515–17.

209 *"a noble peace":* George III to Bute, November 8 and 10, 1762, in *Letters from George III to Lord Bute, 1756–1766*, ed. Romney Sedgwick (Macmillan, 1939), 160, 161.

209 *"have given her":* William Cobbett, *The Parliamentary History of England, from the Earliest Period to the Year 1803*, vol. XV (London, 1813), 1265.

209 *Native peoples:* Richard Middleton, *Pontiac's War: Its Causes, Course, and Consequences* (Routledge, 2007), 49–56.

210 *Pontiac's War:* William M. Fowler, *Empires at War: The French and Indian War and the Struggle for North America, 1754–1763* (Walker & Company, 2005), 275–80; Colin G. Calloway, *The Scratch of a Pen: 1763 and the Transformation of North America* (OUP, 2006), 92–96.

210 *"extensive and valuable":* George III, *By the King. A Proclamation,* October 7, 1763 (London, 1763).

211 *presence of Kalinago:* Tessa Murphy, *The Creole Archipelago: Race and Borders in the Colonial Caribbean* (UPenn, 2021), 17, 21.

211 *profitable agricultural production:* William Petty, Some Hints for the better settlements of the ceded Islands, WCL, Shelburne Papers, vol. 48, ff. 567–73.

211 *"plantation-centered vision":* Melanie J. Newton, "Counterpoints of Conquest: The Royal Proclamation of 1763, the Lesser Antilles, and the Ethnocartography of Genocide," *WMQ* 79, no. 2 (2022): 269.

211 *"the speedy settlement":* George III, *By the King. A Proclamation,* March 26, 1764, in *British Royal Proclamations Relating to America, 1603–1783,* ed. Clarence S. Brigham (Burt Franklin, 1911), 218–24.

211 *"no such people":* Bryan Edwards, *The History, Civil and Commercial, of the British Colonies in the West Indies,* 2 vols. (London, 1793), I: 377.

211 *British surveyors reported:* George Scott, A general account of the Island of Dominique, 1763, and West Indies, Abstract of several Informations & plans relative to the settling of Grenada, Tobago St. Vincent & Dominico, April 1763, Stowe Collection, Grenville Correspondence, HL, STG Box 12, folders 22, 12.

211 *"all equally savage":* Admiral Rodney, West Indies, Considerations for settling the Granadas and the other Islands ceded to Great Britain by the Definitive Treaty, 1764, HL, STG Box 12, folder 27.

212 *Eurocentric racial classifications:* See Brooke N. Newman, "Identity Articulated: British Settlers, Black Caribs, and the Politics of Indigeneity on St. Vincent, 1763–1797," in *Native Diasporas: Indigenous Identities and Settler Colonialism in the Americas,* ed. Gregory D. Smithers and Brooke N. Newman (UNP, 2014), 109–50.

212 *"in proportion to":* West Indies, Abstract of several Informations & plans, HL, STG Box 12, folder 12.

212 *saw no place:* State of the Island of St. Vincent in 1763, WCL, Shelburne Papers, West India Miscellaneous Papers, vol. 74, f. 122.

212 *truly "native Caribs":* Sir William Young, *Considerations which May Tend to Promote the Settlement of our New West-India Colonies . . .* (London, 1764), 9.

212 *"a miserable remnant":* Edwards, *The History, Civil and Commercial, of the British Colonies in the West Indies,* I: 378.

213 *"soon be classed":* Young, *Considerations which May Tend to Promote the Settlement of our New West-India Colonies,* 11.

213 *"denied any subjection":* Council meeting in Kingstown, Saint Vincent, May 10 and 24, 1769, CO 263/1, nf.

213 *British expansionist ambitions:* Newton, "Counterpoints of Conquest," 245.

213 *"the Indians and Negroes":* An account of the Neutral Islands, 1763, HL, STG Box 12, folder 23.

213 *"belonging to Us":* King George III, *By the King. A Proclamation,* March 26, 1764, in *British Royal Proclamations Relating to America, 1603–1783,* ed. Clarence S. Brigham (Burt Franklin, 1911), 218–24.

213 *"what king was this":* William Young, *An Account of the Black Charaibs in the Island of St. Vincent's; with the Charaib Treaty of 1773, and other Original Documents* (London, 1795), 38. See also Bernard Marshall, "The Black Caribs: Native Resistance to British Penetration into the Windward Side of St. Vincent, 1763–1773," *Caribbean Quarterly* 19, no. 4 (1973): 4–19.

214 *debates about the morality:* See Jack P. Greene, *Evaluating Empire and Confronting Colonialism in Eighteenth-Century Britain* (CUP, 2013), 1–19.

214 *an "innocent" people: Authentic Papers Relative to the Expedition Against the Charibbs, and the Sale of Lands in the Island of St. Vincent* (London, 1773), 58, 69.

214 *"the reduction of":* Lt. Col. William Dalrymple to Lord Barrington, December 26, 1772, RA, GEO/MAIN/1466.

214 *signed a treaty:* Young, *An Account of the Black Charaibs,* 90–97.

CHAPTER 14: ATLANTIC REVOLUTIONS

215 *multitude of subjects:* Hannah Weiss Muller, *Subjects and Sovereign: Bonds of Belonging in the Eighteenth-Century British Empire* (OUP, 2017), 7; Linda Colley, *Britons: Forging the Nation, 1707–1837* (1992; repr. YUP, 2005), 135–36.

215 *government needed money:* Colin G. Calloway, *The Scratch of a Pen: 1763 and the Transformation of North America* (OUP, 2006), 11–12.

215 *burden of taxation:* Alvin Rabushka, *Taxation in Colonial America, 1607–1775* (PUP, 2008), 728–29; John Phillip Reed, *Constitutional History of the American Revolution: The Authority to Tax* (UWP, 1987), 29–31.

216 *"I have no wish":* George III to the Lord Chancellor, January 8, 1766, RA, GEO/MAIN/287.

216 *Parliament passed legislation:* Edmund S. Morgan and Helen S. Morgan, *The Stamp Act Crisis: Prologue to Revolution* (1953; repr. UNCP, 1995), 21–27.

216 *accusations of metaphorical enslavement:* Justin du Rivage, *Revolution Against Empire: Taxes, Politics, and the Origins of American Independence* (YUP, 2017), 118.

216 *"a state of slavery":* James Otis, *The Rights of the British Colonies Asserted and Proved* (Boston, 1764), 53.

216 *"property may be taken":* Stephen Hopkins, "The Rights of Colonies Examined," in *Tracts of the American Revolution, 1763–1776,* ed. Merrill Jensen (2003; repr. Hackett, 1966), 43.

216 *"more like slaves":* John Adams, *The Papers of John Adams,* 4 vols., ed. Robert J. Taylor (HUP, 1977–1979), I: 124.

216 *"plan for reducing":* Quoted in Mary Ann Radzinowicz, *American Colonial Prose: John Smith to Thomas Jefferson* (CUP, 1984), 38.

216 *"the entire regime:* Brian P. Levack, *Distrust of Institutions in Early Modern Britain and America* (OUP, 2022), 50.

217 *"support His Majesty":* House of Commons Report, February 7, 1766, RA, GEO/MAIN/565.

217 *"his Majesty's dominions":* Quoted in Michael Zuckert, "Natural Rights and Imperial Constitutionalism: The American Revolution and the Development of the American Amalgam," in *Natural Rights Liberalism from Locke to Nozick,* ed. Ellen Frankel Paul, Fred D. Miller Jr., and Jeffrey Paul (CUP, 2005), 34.

217 *divergent conceptions of empire:* Edmund S. Morgan, *The Birth of the Republic, 1763–89* (1956; repr. UCP, 2013), 15–28; Jack P. Greene, "Transatlantic Colonization and the Redefinition of Empire in the Early Modern Era: The British-American Experience," in *Negotiated Empires: Centers and Peripheries in the Americas, 1500–1820,* ed. Christine Daniels and Michael V. Kennedy (Routledge, 2002), 267–82.

217 *"the whole continent":* Barrington, 2nd Viscount, Memorandum on the American colonies, 1766, RA, GEO/MAIN/415a.

218 *"the only people"*: Voltaire, *Letters Concerning the English Nation* (London, 1741), 43–44.

218 *"a ship completely equipped"*: J. L. de Lolme, *The Constitution of England, Or an Account of the English Government* (Dublin, 1776), 48.

218 *"the monarch apart"*: Brendan McConville, *The King's Three Faces: The Rise and Fall of Royal America, 1688–1776* (UNCP, 2006), 8.

218 *George III's powerlessness:* Eric Nelson, *The Royalist Revolution: Monarchy and the American Founding* (HUP, 2014), 1–6.

219 *"object truly ridiculous"*: Thomas Day, "Fragment of an original Letter, on the Slavery of the Negroes; written in the Year 1776," in *The English Review* (London, 1784), 470.

219 *"boldy thrown off"*: Memoranda by the King on Dispute with North American Colonies, c. 1774, RA, GEO/MAIN/1709–1711.

219 *Declaration of Independence:* Joseph J. Ellis, *American Sphinx* (Knopf, 1998), 35–36, 56; Peter Onuf, *The Mind of Thomas Jefferson* (UVAP, 2007), 170, 239–41.

219 *his own children:* See Annette Gordon Reed, *The Hemingses of Monticello: An American Family* (W. W. Norton, 2008).

220 *familial and cultural roots:* Katherine Paugh, *The Politics of Reproduction: Race, Medicine, and Fertility in the Age of Abolition* (OUP, 2017), 30–36.

220 *Virginia legislature:* See Elizabeth Donnan, ed., *Documents Illustrative of the History of the Slave Trade to America,* 4 vols. (Carnegie Institution of Washington, 1935), IV: 142–59.

220 *"greatly retards"*: Virginia Colony to George III of England, April 1, 1772, Petition Against Importation of Slaves from Africa, LOC, Thomas Jefferson Papers.

220 *"a few merchants"*: Benjamin Franklin to Richard Woodward, 10 April 1773, in *The Papers of Benjamin Franklin,* vol. 20, *January 1 through December 31, 1773,* ed. William B. Willcox (YUP), 1976), 155–56.

220 *Jefferson captured:* Jefferson Roger Wilkins, *Jefferson's Pillow: The Founding Fathers and the Dilemma of Black Patriotism* (Beacon Press, 2001), 5, 50; Ellis, *American Sphinx,* 56.

220 *"most sacred rights"*: Quoted in David Armitage, *The Declaration of Independence: A Global History* (HUP, 2007), 57.

220 *"the more speedily"*: By his Execellency the Right Honourable John Earl of Dunmore, his Majesty's Lieutenant and Governour-General of the Colony and Dominion of Virginia, and Vice-admiral of the same. A Proclamation, 1775, LOC.

221 *"an arch-traitor"*: *The Writings of George Washington from the Original Manuscript Sources, 1745–1799,* vol. 4, ed. John C. Fitzpatrick (US Government Printing Office, 1931), 167.

221 *arm enslaved people:* See esp. Sylvia Frey, *Water from the Rock: Black Resistance in a Revolutionary Age* (PUP, 1991); Cassandra Pybus, *Epic Journeys of Freedom: Runaway Slaves of the American Revolution and Their Global Quest for Liberty* (Beacon Press, 2006); Douglas R. Egerton, *Death or Liberty: African Americans and Revolutionary America* (OUP, 2009).

221 *"paying off former crimes"*: Quoted in Armitage, *The Declaration of Independence,* 57.

222 *congressional delegates excised:* Gary B. Nash, *The Unknown American Revolution: The Unruly Birth of Democracy and the Struggle to Create America* (Penguin, 2005), 208–209.

222 *"a miserable state"*: Samuel Johnson, *Taxation No Tyranny* (London, 1776), 64, 81, 89.

222 *"suppose the Americans"*: His Majesty King George III to Lord North, May 31, 1777, RA, GEO/MAIN/2564.

222 *denigrated Americans:* Jenna M. Gibbs, *Performing the Temple of Liberty: Slavery, Theater, and Popular Culture in London and Philadelphia, 1750–1850* (JHUP, 2014), 54–66.

222   *"Negroes here"*: Ambrose Serle, *Americans Against Liberty* (London, 1776), 25.

222   Somerset v. Stuart: See Francis Hargrave, *An Argument in the Case of James Sommersett, a Negro, Lately Determined by the Court of King's Bench* (London, 1772); *Somerset v. Stuart* (1772) in *Granville Sharp's Cases on Slavery*, ed. Andrew Lyall (Hart Publishing, 2017), 153–238.

223   *Yorke and Charles Talbot:* See Travis Glasson, "'Baptism doth not bestow Freedom': Missionary Anglicanism, Slavery, and the Yorke-Talbot Opinion, 1701–30," *WMQ* 67, no. 2 (2010): 279–318.

223   *legally classified "negroes":* "An Act for the more easy Recovery of Debts in His Majesty's Plantations and Colonies in America, 1732," in Jospeh Chitty, *A Collection of Statutes with Practical Utility* (London, 1829), 180.

223   *Mansfield determined:* Somerset v. Stewart, Easter 1772, in *Reports of Cases Adjudged in the Court of King's Bench from Easter Term 12 Geo. 3. To Michaelmas 14 Geo. 3*, ed. Capel Lofft (London, 1776), 1–19.

223   *"so odious":* Ibid., 19.

224   *"the grand doctrine":* Lord John Campbell, *The Lives of the Chief Justices*, 2 vols. (Philadelphia, 1851), II: 320.

224   *inspired enslaved individuals:* Alan Gilbert, *Black Patriots and Loyalists: Fighting for Emancipation in the War for Independence* (UCP, 2012), 8–9.

224   *"is remarkably strong":* *The British Magazine and General Review* (London, 1772), 504.

224   *encouraged its spread:* Peter Freyer, *Staying Power: The History of Black People in Britain* (Pluto Press, 1984), 203.

224   Knight v. Wedderburn: John W. Cairns, "The Definition of Slavery in Eighteenth-Century Thinking: Not the True Roman Slavery," in *The Legal Understanding of Slavery: From the Historical to the Contemporary*, ed. Jean Allain (OUP, 2012), 61–84.

224   *Crown and parliamentary support:* See George Van Cleve, "*Somerset's Case* and Its Antecedents in Imperial Perspective," *Law and History Review* 24, no. 2 (2006): 601–45.

224   *"it piques itself":* Benjamin Franklin, *The Private Correspondence of Benjamin Franklin* (London, 1818), 17.

224   *planter Edward Long:* Edward Long, *Candid Reflections Upon the Judgement Lately Awarded by the Court of King's Bench . . .* (London, 1772), 22–25.

225   *trafficking of "Negroes":* Ibid., 24, 25.

225   *enslaved women bore:* See esp. Jennifer Morgan, *Laboring Women: Reproduction and Gender in New World Slavery* (UPenn, 2011); Marisa Fuentes, *Dispossessed Lives: Enslaved Women, Violence, and the Archive* (UPenn, 2016); Sasha Turner, *Contested Bodies: Pregnancy, Childrearing, and Slavery in Jamaica* (UPenn, 2017).

225   *enslaved people embraced:* Matthew Mason, "North American Calm, West Indian Storm: The Politics of the Somerset Decision in the British Atlantic," *Slavery & Abolition* 41, no. 4 (2020): 723–47; Charles Foy, "Seeking Freedom in the Atlantic World, 1713–1783," *Early American Studies* 4 (2006): 46–77.

225   *ad hoc wartime emancipation:* Philip D. Morgan and Andrew Jackson O'Shaughnessy, "Arming Slaves in the American Revolution," in *Arming Slaves from Classical Times to the Modern Age*, ed. Christopher Leslie Brown and Philip D. Morgan (YUP, 2006), 180–208; Gilbert, *Black Patriots and Loyalists*, 15–45.

226   *"the great number":* Lord North to His Majesty, October 15, 1775, RA, GEO/MAIN/2196–98.

226   *"composed of Negroes":* A Plan for reducing the Colonies in the most expeditious Manner and at the least expense, 1779, RA, GEO/MAIN/3676 (1–6).

226 *enslaved offered benefits:* Morgan and O'Shaughnessy, "Arming Slaves in the American Revolution," 181–82; Frey, *Water from the Rock,* 76–77; Jack P. Greene, *Evaluating Empire and Confronting Colonialism in Eighteenth-Century Britain* (CUP, 2013), 221–22.

226 *"the horrible consequences":* Edmund Burke's speech, 1778, in *The Parliamentary History of England,* vol. 19, ed. William Cobbett and T. C. Hansard (London, 1806), 698–99.

227 *the rebel commanders:* Gary B. Nash, *The Forgotten Fifth: African Americans in the Age of Revolution* (HUP, 2006), 5–6; Judith L. Van Buskirk, *Standing in Their Own Light: African American Patriots in the American Revolution* (UOP, 2017), 1–23.

228 *quarter of the British force:* Alan Gilbert, *Black Patriots and Loyalists: Fighting for Emancipation in the War for Independence* (UCP, 2012), 123.

228 *to defend the Caribbean:* Andrew Jackson O'Shaughnessy, "Redcoats and Slaves in the British Caribbean," in *The Lesser Antilles in the Age of European Expansion,* ed. Robert Paquette and Stanley L. Engerman (UPF, 1996), 105–27; ibid., *An Empire Divided: The American Revolution and the British Caribbean* (UPenn, 2000), 175–81.

228 *"Sugar, sugar":* Quoted in Fryer, *Staying Power,* 18.

229 *"The object now":* George III, Book of Secret Intelligence, 1779 to 1782, RA, GEO/MAIN/4121. See also Larrie D. Ferreiro, *Brothers at Arms: American Independence and the Men of France and Spain Who Saved It* (Vintage, 2016), 114, 136, 320.

229 *"must be defended":* Draft of King George III to Lord Sandwich, September 13, 1779, RA, GEO/MAIN/3518.

229 *"by bold and manly":* His Majesty to Lord Sandwich, September 13, 1779, RA, GEO/MAIN/3520.

229 *making of William:* Philip Ziegler, *William IV* (Harper, 1973), 26–27; Jonas Hanway, *The Seaman's Christian Friend* (London, 1779), 107.

230 *"He's royal":* "The Royal Sailor" in *Naval Songs and Ballads,* ed. C. H. Firth (The Naval Records Society, 1908), 262–63.

230 *joined the warship:* John Marshall, *Royal Naval Biography,* vol. 1 (London, 1823), 3–5; Ziegler, *William IV,* 28–33.

230 *"God bless":* Prince William to King George III, September 27, 1781, RA, GEO/MAIN/44630–1.

230 *to capture Prince William:* George Washington to Matthias Ogden, March 28, 1782, LOC, George Washington Papers; Washington Irving, *Life of George Washington,* vol. 4 (Leipzig, 1857), 344–45.

231 *in Caribbean hospitality:* Prince William's visits are detailed in Lord Hood to His Majesty, February 28, 1783, RA, GEO/MAIN/16338–41; Lord Hood to His Majesty, April 16, 1783, GEO/MAIN/16348–9; and Lord Hood to His Majesty, May 18, 1783, GEO/MAIN/16351–2.

231 *"presence in Jamaica":* Address to His Royal Highness, Prince William, from the County of Middlesex, Jamaica, February 15, 1783, RA, GEO/ADD/MSS/4/20.

231 *"truly sensible":* *Gazette of Saint Jago de le Vega* (February 27, 1783).

231 *annihilate the rank:* His Majesty to Lord North, January 21, 1782, RA, GEO/MAIN/4407.

231 *bullied his ministers:* Black, *George III,* 239–41; Andrew Jackson O'Shaughnessy, *The Men Who Lost America* (YUP, 2013), 28–29, 34–43.

232 *"Black loyalists":* See Maya Jasanoff, *Liberty's Exiles: American Loyalists in the Revolutionary World* (Knopf, 2011), 9–10, 49–50, 357; Mary Louise Clifford, *From Slavery to Freetown: Black Loyalists After the American Revolution* (McFarland, 1999).

232 *community of free people:* Norma Myers, *Reconstructing the Black Past: Blacks in Britain, 1780–1830* (Frank Cass, 1996), 20–21.

CHAPTER 15: ABOLITION AND THE SONS OF AFRICA

233 *approximately forty-two hundred individuals:* Estimates range from forty-two hundred to ten thousand. See Norma Myers, *Reconstructing the Black Past: Blacks in Britain, 1780–1830* (Frank Cass, 1996), 29; Cassandra Pybus, *Black Founders: The Unknown Story of Australia's First Black Settlers* (UNSW Press, 2006), 45.

233 *"little tracts":* John Stuart to the Prince of Wales, 1786, Granville Sharp Papers, GRO, D/3549/13/1/S36. The "little tracts" he enclosed for the Prince of Wales may have included James Ramsey's *Essay on the Treatment and Conversion of African Slaves in the British Sugar Colonies* (London, 1784) and Thomas Clarkson's *An Essay on the Slavery and Commerce of the Human Species, Particularly the African* (London, 1786). See Ottobah Cugoano, *Thoughts and Sentiments on the Evil and Wicked Traffic of the Slavery and Commerce of the Human Species, Humbly Submitted to the Inhabitants of Great Britain by Ottobah Cugoano, A Native of Africa* (London, 1787), 15. See also Ryan Hanley, *Beyond Slavery and Abolition: Black British Writing, c. 1770–1830* (CUP, 2018), 179.

233 *"set afloat by":* Library of the Fine Arts (London, 1832), 185–86.

233 *Schomberg House:* John Thomas Smith, *Nollekens and His Times, And Memoirs of Contemporary Artists . . .* 2 vols. (London, 1828), II: 393–95.

234 *Thomas Gainsborough:* George Williams Fulcher, *Life of Thomas Gainsborough, R.A.* (London, 1856), 101–102, 150.

234 *transformed Pall Mall:* Rosie Dias, "'A World of Pictures': Pall Mall and the Topography of Display," in *Georgian Geographies: Essays on Space, Place and Landscape in the Eighteenth Century,* ed. Miles Ogborn and Charles W. J. Withers (MUP, 2004), 94.

234 *"by His Royal Highness":* Smith, *Nollekens and His Times,* 398.

234 *"Macaroni Miniature Painter":* Peter McNeil, *Pretty Gentlemen: Macaroni Men and the Eighteenth-Century Fashion World* (YUP, 2018), 105–106.

234 *official court painter:* Between 1781 and 1786, the Prince of Wales purchased a total of thirty-five miniatures, portraits, and drawings from Cosway worth a total of £651. See Bill from Richard Cosway to the Prince of Wales, 1781–1786, RA, GEO/MAIN/26792. By November 1789, the prince's collection of Cosway's paintings was valued at £5,000. See Henry Holland, Architect, List and Estimated Value of Furniture in Carlton House, RA, GEO/MAIN/25082.

234 *two vivid costumes:* George C. Williamson, *Richard Cosway R.A.* (London, 1905), 32.

235 *employed Black manservants:* James Walvin, *England, Slaves and Freedom, 1776–1838* (Macmillan, 1986), 37.

235 *a Black valet:* Andrew Jackson O'Shaughnessy, *The Men Who Lost America: British Leadership, the American Revolution and the Fate of the Empire* (YUP, 2020), 352.

235 *portrait of the Montagues:* William Hogarth, *The Montagu Family and an Unknown Attendant,* 1730–1735, Yale Center for British Art, https://collections.britishart.yale.edu/catalog/tms:407.

235 *"faithful African":* Lord Rodney to Captain Payne, May 3, 1791, RA, GEO/MAIN/38596–38597; N. W. Wraxall, *Posthumous Memoirs of His Own Time,* 3 vols. (London, 1836), II: 164.

235 *"silent witnesses":* Gretchen Gerzina, *Black London: Life Before Emancipation* (RUP, 1995), 67.

235 *Ignatius Sancho:* Vincent Carretta, "Introduction," in *Letters of the Late Ignatius Sancho, an*

African (Broadview Press, 2015), 14–19; David Olusoga, *Black and British: A Forgotten History* (Macmillan, 2016), 107–12.

236 *"an untutored African":* Ignatius Sancho, *Letters of the Late Ignatius Sancho, An African,* 2 vols. (London, 1782), I: ii, v.

236 *"subject that sours":* Sancho, *Letters of the Late Ignatius Sancho,* I: 69, II: 183, 4.

237 *"state of horror":* Cugoano, *Thoughts and Sentiments,* 5–6, 10–13.

237 *runaway advertisements:* Stephen Mullen, Nelson Mundell, and Simon P. Newman, "Black Runaways in Eighteenth-Century Britain," in *Britain's Black Past,* ed. Gretchen Gerzina (LUP, 2020), 81–98.

237 *"no master ever":* Somerset v. Stewart (1772) in T. B. Howell, *A Complete Collection of State Trials,* vol. 20 (London, 1816), 79–82.

237 *misinterpreted the ruling:* Vincent Carretta, *Equiano, the African: Biography of a Self-Made Man* (Penguin, 2005), 209; Norman S. Poser, *Lord Mansfield: Justice in the Age of Reason* (McGill-Queen's University Press, 2013), 295–96.

237 *it is unclear:* Vincent Caretta, "Introduction," in Quobna Ottobah Cugoano, *Thoughts and Sentiments on the Evil of Slavery,* ed. Vincent Caretta (1787; Penguin, 1999), xv.

237 *Campbell, testified:* Testimony of Alexander Campbell, Esquire, February 13, 1790, Great Britain, House of Commons, *Select Committee Appointed to Take Examination of Witnesses Respecting the African Slave Trade* (London, 1790), 135.

237 *"some good people":* Cugoano, *Thoughts and Sentiments,* N[ota] B[ene].

238 *the prince regent:* Purchased by George IV when Prince Regent from Colnaghi and Company for 5 shillings, July 12, 1813, RA, GEO/MAIN/27932.

238 *Sons of Africa:* Hanley, *Beyond Slavery and Abolition,* 180–82; Micah Alpaugh, *Friends of Freedom: The Rise of Social Movements in the Age of Atlantic Revolutions* (CUP, 2021), 206. Black abolitionist groups on both sides of the Atlantic adopted the moniker "Sons of Africa," claiming ties to Africa based on either birth or descent. See Manisha Sinha, *The Slave's Cause: A History of Abolition* (YUP, 2016), 125.

238 *most renowned person of African descent:* Caretta, *Equiano, the African,* xii.

239 *on George III's behalf:* Simon Schama, *Rough Crossings: The Slaves, the British, and the American Revolution* (Ecco, 2006), 2.

239 *"The British liberated":* Christopher Leslie Brown, *Moral Capital: Foundations of British Abolitionism* (UNCP, 2006), 311.

239 *arriving in London:* An estimated one thousand to five thousand Black loyalists reached London in the 1780s. See Wallace Brown, "Black Loyalists in London After the American Revolution," in *Moving on: Black Loyalists in the Afro-Atlantic World,* ed. John W. Pulis (Routledge, 1999), 103; Maya Jasanoff, *Liberty's Exiles: American Loyalists in a Revolutionary World* (Knopf, 2011), 357.

239 *"the present set":* Granville Sharp to the Archbishop of Canterbury, August 1, 1786, in *Memoirs of Granville Sharp, Esq.,* ed. Prince Hoare (London, 1820), 263.

240 *London's Black poor:* Stephen Braidwood, *Black Poor and White Philanthropists: London's Blacks and the Foundations of the Sierra Leone Settlement 1786–1791* (LUP, 1994), 23–24.

240 *abolitionist Granville Sharp:* Extracts from the Diary of Granville Sharp, 1783–1792, Granville Sharp Papers, GRO, D/3549 13/4/2, f. 36.

240 *"to have jumped":* Hoare, *Memoirs of Granville Sharp, Esq,* 247–48.

240 *"indefatigable friend":* Cugoano, *Thoughts and Sentiments,* 100.

240 *"Gustavus Vassa":* Extracts from the Diary of Granville Sharp, 1783–1792, GRO, D/3549 13/4/2, f. 36.

241 *"into the sea":* Granville Sharp to William Baker, May 23, 1783, ibid., GRO, D3549 13/1/B1.

241 *"honest, sober man":* Granville Sharp to Ann Jemima Sharp, February 1811, ibid., GRO, D3549 13/1/S6.

241 *According to eyewitnesses:* James Walvin, *The Zong: A Massacre, the Law, and the End of Slavery* (YUP, 2011), 104–105.

241 *"be any necessity":* Granville Sharp to William Baker, May 23, 1783, ibid., GRO, D3549 13/1/B1.

242 *equated the king:* Brendan McConville, *The King's Three Faces: The Rise and Fall of Royal America, 1688–1776* (UNCP, 2006), 175–82; James Gregory, *Mercy and British Culture, 1760–1960* (Bloomsbury, 2022), 112–13.

242 *"laws of God":* Thomas Clarkson, *The History of the Rise, Progress, and Accomplishment of the Abolition of the African Slave-trade by the British Parliament*, 2 vols. (London, 1808), I: 84.

242 *London Quakers:* David Richardson, *Principles and Agents: The British Slave Trade and Its Abolition* (YUP, 2022), 100–101.

242 *"the suffering conditions":* Anthony Benezet to Charlotte, Queen of Great Britain, August 25, 1783, reprinted in Wilson Armistead, *Anthony Benezet: From the Original Memoir* (London, 1859), 49–50.

242 *some eleven thousand copies:* Roger Anstey, *The Atlantic Slave Trade and British Abolition, 1760–1810* (Humanities Press, 1975), 229.

242 *painter Benjamin West:* Thomas Drake, *Quakers and Slavery in America* (YUP, 1950), 92.

243 *"Should your Highness":* John Stuart to the Prince of Wales, 1786, GRO, D/3549 13/1/S36.

243 *"an African against":* John Stuart to the Prince of Wales, 1787, GRO, D/3549 13/1/S36.

243 *"this meritorious act":* Ibid.

244 *the Royal Collection:* Vincent Carretta, "'Property of Author': Olaudah Equiano's Place in the History of the Book," in *Genius in Bondage: Literature of the Black Atlantic*, ed. Vincent Carretta and Philip Gould (UPK, 2016), 145, n3; see also https://www.rct.uk/collection/1125525/thoughts-and-sentiments-on-the-evil-and-wicked-traffic-of-the-slavery-and.

244 *"all good Christians":* Letter from John Stuart [1787], WWM/Bk/P/1/2105, Microfilm, *Politics in the Age of Revolution, 1715–1848*, Reel 10, Part 1: The Papers of Edmund Burke, 1729–1797, from Sheffield Archives and Northamptonshire Record Office (Adam Matthews Publications).

244 *"cause of justice":* John Stuart to King George III, 1787, GRO, D/3549 13/1/S36.

244 *"if kings or nations":* Cugoano, *Thoughts and Sentiments*, 94.

245 *the "barbarous traffic":* Ibid., 106.

245 *"traffic in the human species":* Ibid., iii, 109.

246 *agreed with him:* Ibid., 60–61.

246 *abridged second edition:* *Thoughts and Sentiments on the Evil of Slavery . . . Addressed to the Sons of Africa, By a Native* (London, 1791), Subscribers Names.

246 *his death:* See Vincent Carretta, *Unchained Voices: An Anthology of Black Authors in the English-Speaking World of the Eighteenth Century* (UPK, 1996), 145–47.

246 *share his plans:* John Stuart to Granville Sharp, nd, GRO, D/3549, 13/1/S36.

CHAPTER 16: A ROYAL DEFENSE

248 *"lately been formed":* Granville Sharp to John Sharp, July 19, 1787, GRO, D3549, 13/1/S.

248 *Clarkson volunteered:* John Oldfield, *Popular Politics and British Antislavery: The Mobilisation of*

Public Opinion Against the Slave Trade, 1787–1807 (Frank Cass, 1998), 38; Christopher Leslie Brown, *Moral Capital: Foundations of British Abolitionism* (UNCP, 2006), 385.

248 *the Royal Academy:* Royal Academy Laws and Regulations, December 1772, RA, GEO/MAIN/1468; Holger Hoock, *The Royal Academy of Arts and the Politics of British Culture, 1760–1840* (CP, 2003), 136–37.

250 *no particular regard:* Richard Wendorf, *Sir Joshua Reynolds: The Painter in Society* (HUP, 1996), 173–74; *George III and Queen Charlotte: Patronage, Collecting and Court Taste* (The Royal Collection, 2004), 158.

250 *irked the king:* Holger Hoock, *The King's Artists: The Royal Academy of Arts and the Politics of British Culture, 1760–1840* (CP, 2003), 176.

250 *dominates the portrait:* Paula E. Dumas, *Proslavery Britain: Fighting for Slavery in an Era of Abolition* (PM, 2016), 92.

250 *royal red and gold:* Philip Mansel, *Dressed to Rule: Royal and Court Costume From Louis XIV to Elizabeth II* (YUP, 2005), 77.

250 *George III snubbed:* Hoock, *The King's Artists*, 172.

250 *rejected George's appeal:* George III to George, Prince of Wales, May 9, 1786, RA, GEO/MAIN/31894–31895.

251 *"embarrassed and distressed":* House of Commons, April 30, 1787, in *The Speeches of the Right Honourable Charles James Fox, in the House of Commons*, 6 vols. (London 1815), III: 322–23.

251 *"At first sight":* *The World*, May 1, 1787 (London, 1787), 3.

251 *Parliament granted:* *The Parliamentary Register*, vol. 23 (London, 1788), 59.

251 *"very misfortunate":* George, Prince of Wales, to George III, September 2, 1785, RA, GEO/MAIN/31896–31897.

251 *two dozen gentlemen:* The Prince of Wales' Gentlemen of the Bedchamber, May 1787, RA, GEO/MAIN/16604.

251 *allegorical satire:* Hoock, *The King's Artists*, 175.

251 *"the only picture":* Sir Joshua Reynolds to the Prince of Wales, April 22, 1788, RA, GEO/MAIN/26793.

252 *agreed to purchase:* The Prince of Wales paid £262.10s and £131.5s, respectively, for the two paintings. See Oliver Miller, "George IV When Prince of Wales: His Debts to Artists and Craftsmen," *Burlington Magazine* 128, No. 1001 (1986): 586–92, here 588.

252 *"a general feeling":* Thomas Clarkson, *The History of the Rise, Progress, and Accomplishment of the Abolition of the African Slave-trade by the British Parliament*, 2 vols. (London, 1808), I: 469–70.

252 *Equiano offered to testify:* Carretta, *Equiano, the African*, 264.

252 *"well-known benevolence":* Olaudah Equiano, *The Interesting Narrative of the Life of Olaudah Equiano; Or, Gustavus Vassa, the African*, 2 vols. (London, 1789), II: 255–58.

252 *"most graciously":* Ibid., 255.

253 *wrote numerous letters:* Letters to Granville Sharp (December 15, 1787), William Dolben, William Pitt, and Charles James Fox (July 15, 1788), Lord Hawkesbury (March 13, 1788), and William Dickson (April 15, 1789) are reproduced in ibid., II: 326–27, 333–34, 341–44.

253 *"Many people felt":* Miles Ogborn, *The Freedom of Speech: Talk and Slavery in the Anglo-Caribbean World* (UCP, 20190), 211.

253 *"horrors of every kind":* Equiano, *The Interesting Narrative*, I: 73.

253 *"most crying evil": Journals of the House of Commons*, vol. 43 (London, 1803), 508; *The Parliamentary Register*, vol. 23 (London, 1788), 606.

253 *outlined restrictions:* James W. LoGerfo, "Sir William Dolben and 'The Cause of Humanity': The Passage of The Slave Trade Regulation Act of 1788," *Eighteenth-Century Studies* 6, no. 4 (1973): 431–51.

253 *"Branch of Traffic": Journals of the House of Commons,* vol. 43, 515.

254 *Liverpool's position:* Kenneth Morgan, "Liverpool's Dominance in the British Slave Trade, 1740–1807," in *Liverpool and Transatlantic Slavery,* ed. David Richardson, Suzanne Schwartz, and Anthony Tibbles (LUP, 2007), 14–42.

254 *"the total ruin":* John Tarleton to Lord Hawkesbury, May 25, 1788, Liverpool Papers, BL, Add MS 38416, ff. 90–91.

254 *"is so sudden":* enclosure, Samuel Green, Secretary of Liverpool African Committee, to John Tarleton, BL, Add MS 38416, f. 93.

254 *passed the bill:* Meetings on May 27, July 4, and July 8, 1788, Great Britain House of Commons, *Journals of the House of Commons* (London, 1788), 508, 644–52.

254 *his royal assent: An Act to Regulate, for a Limited Time, the Shipping and Carrying Slaves in British Vessels from the Coast of Africa,* 28 George III, c. 54 (1788), PA, HL/PO/PU/1/1788/28G3n170.

254 *the king complained:* His Majesty George III to Lord Sydney, Windsor, July 8, 1788, RA, GEO/MAIN/6450.

255 *"indecent and improper":* Prince of Wales, Windsor, November 5, 1788, RA, GEO/MAIN, np.

255 *"very low class":* George III to Lord North, March 7, 1780, RA, GEO/MAIN/3738.

255 *long-term imperial:* Jeremy Black, *George III: America's Last King* (YUP, 2006), 331.

256 *"the manners practiced":* Prince William to George III, November 24, 1779, RA, GEO/MAIN/44606–44607.

256 *"humble happiness":* Prince William to George III, August 4, 1785, RA, GEO/MAIN/44679.

256 *rank of lieutenant:* Philip Ziegler, *King William IV: The First English King in America* (Harper, 1971), 105–106.

256 *"keep me under":* Prince William to George III, March 1, 1786, RA, GEO/MAIN/44705.

257 *William's health had suffered:* Robert Wright and John Fidge, Report on the Health of Prince William, March 2, 1788, RA, GEO/MAIN/44823–44824; John Fidge to Captain Elphinstone, February 13, 1788, RA, GEO/MAIN/44818–44819; Prince William to George III, August 20, 1788, RA, GEO/MAIN/44845–44848.

257 *"sorry to say":* Prince William to George, Prince of Wales, October 26, 1788, RA, GEO/MAIN/44850.

257 *"The attention shown":* Governor Clarke's speech to the council and assembly, October 21, 1789, CO 137/88, f. 80. See also Address of the Council to Governor Clarke, and Address of the Assembly to Governor Clarke, October 21, 1789, CO 137/88, ff. 84, 89.

257 *"whole of my time":* Mr Fuller's Account as Agent for Part of the Year 1789, Stephen Fuller Papers, 1786–1796, RL, FF5643.

258 *waited personally on:* Stephen Fuller to James Pinnock, March 20, 1790, and Stephen Fuller to the Committee of Correspondence, April 7, 1790, RL, FF5643.

258 *multiple editions:* Equiano's book went through nine different official editions, and countless unauthorized editions, during his lifetime. See Carretta, *Equiano, the African,* xii.

258 *until his death:* Ibid., 366.

259 *"her royal highness": The Critical Review; Or the Annals of Literature, Extended and Improved* (London, 1792), 478; *An Address to Her Royal Highness the Duchess of York, Against the Use of Sugar* (London, 1792), 16.

259   *West Indian sugar boycott:* Oldfield, *Popular Politics and British Antislavery*, 140.

259   *sweet fruit tarts:* See dining entries for Their Majesties and purchases of sugar for the royal household in 1791–92 in Adam Crymble et al., "Three Thousand Dishes on a Georgian Table, 1788–1813—Dataset," June 23, 2023, *Zenodo*, https://doi.org/10.5281/zenodo.8070132.

259   *"restraint of oppressors":* Niel Douglas, *The African Slave Trade: Or a Short View of the Evidence, Relative to that Subject, Produced Before the House of Commons* (London, 1792), 138.

260   *mocked as apathetic:* Mimi Sheller, *Consuming the Caribbean: From Arawaks to Zombies* (Routledge, 2003), 91.

261   *the blood spilled:* On the French and Haitian revolutions, see especially Peter McPhee, *Liberty or Death: The French Revolution* (YUP, 2016); Jeremy Popkin, *A New World Begins: The History of the French Revolution* (Basic Books, 2019); Laurent Dubois, *Avengers of the New World: The Story of the Haitian Revolution* (HUP, 2004); Marlene L. Daut, *Awakening the Ashes: An Intellectual History of the Haitian Revolution* (UNCP, 2023).

261   *"a mistaken idea":* Joseph King to Lord Grenville, May 17, 1792, BL, Dropmore Papers, Add MS 59305A, f. 13.

261   *voting bloc:* Michael Taylor, *The Interest: How the British Establishment Resisted the Abolition of Slavery* (The Bodley Head, 2020), 23.

261   *"the popular frenzy":* House of Lords Minutes, May 8, 1792, RA, GEO/MAIN/6948.

261   *"very well satisfied":* Robert Taylor to John Taylor, April 7, 1792, Tailyour Family Papers, WCL, Box 6, Folder 17.

262   *reactionary conservatism:* Wil Verhoeven, *Americomania and the French Revolution Debate in Britain, 1789–1802* (CUP, 2013), 36.

262   *"tie of religion":* Quoted in Christopher Hibbert, *George III* (Basic Books, 1998), 309.

262   "most incomparable speech": The Prince of Wales to the Duke of York, April 14, 1793, RA, GEO/MAIN/44048.

262   *"indefatigable exertions": Report from the Committee of the Honourable House of Assembly, Appointed to Inquire Into the State of the Colony, as to Trade, Navigation, and Culture, &c.* (St. Jago de la Vega, Jamaica, 1800), 12.

262   *silver plate service:* Beth Carver Wees, *English, Irish, and Scottish Silver at the Sterling and Francine Clark Art Institute* (Hudson Hills Press, 1997), 162; William James Gardner, *A History of Jamaica from Its Discovery by Christopher Columbus to the Present Time* (London, 1873), 219.

263   *attended meetings:* See M915 West India Committee Minutes, Reels 2–3, ICS; David Beck Ryden, *West Indian Slavery and British Abolition, 1783–1807* (CUP, 2009), 45–46.

263   *"His Royal Highness": Letters of Alfred . . . Upon the Important Subject of the Slave Trade in General* (London, 1793), dedication.

263   *"place your papers":* Augusta Sophia to His Royal Highness, Duke of Clarence, 1792, Knightley MSS vol. III, Royal Letters and Papers, 1718–1904, BL, Add MS 46358, f. 8.

263   Duke of Clarence: *Voyages, https://www.slavevoyages.org/voyage/database* (accessed July 30, 2024).

263   *"a true friend":* Stephen Fuller to the Jamaica Assembly, March 31, 1795, in *The Correspondence of Stephen Fuller, 1788–1795: Jamaica, the West India Interest at Westminster and the Campaign to Preserve the Slave Trade,* ed. M. W. McCahill (Wiley-Blackwell, 2014), 227.

263   *"not a Cabinet measure":* May 28, 1799, House of Lords, *Woodfall's Parliamentary Reports*, vol. 3 (London, 1794), 38.

264   *"I am certain":* George III to Henry Dundas, February 6, 1796, BL, Add MS 40100, f. 169.

264 *his sovereign's concerns:* Seymour Dresher, *Pathways from Slavery: British and Colonial Mobiliza-tions in Global Perspective* (Routledge, 2018), 80–82.

264 *"prevent the danger":* George III, Memorandum Supporting West India Possessions, c. 1796, RA, GEO/MAIN/8229.

265 *the British press:* See, for example, *Morning Post*, May 21, 1799; *Substance of the Speech of His Royal Highness, the Duke of Clarence, in the House of Lords, on the Motion for the Recommitment of the Slave Trade Limitation Bill, on the Fifth Day of July, 1799* (London, 1799).

265 *"I was earnestly":* Duke of Clarence to Admiral Nelson, August 14, 1799, Nelson Papers, Vol-ume XII: August 1–September 20, 1799, BL, Add MS 34913, ff. 45–46; see also M915 West India Committee Minutes, General Meeting, May 21, 1799, Reel 2, ICS.

265 *pled "indisposition":* Copy of Lord Liverpool's Note to the Duke of Clarence, July 10, 1799, Liverpool Papers, BL, Add MS 38416, ff. 312–313.

266 *"prohibit the importation":* Joseph King to Lord Grenville, May 28, 1792, Dropmore Papers, BL, Add MS 59305A, ff. 19–22.

266 *"to keep up":* Lord Camden to George III, 1805, RA, GEO/MAIN/11666–11667.

266 *"provided it be":* George III to Lord Camden, May 1, 1805, in *The Later Correspondence of George III, Volume Four, 1802–1807*, ed. A. Aspinall (CUP, 1968), 322.

266 *"disgrace the honor":* Ibid.

267 *Foreign Slave Trade Act:* Roger Anstey, *The Atlantic Slave Trade and British Abolition, 1760–1810* (Humanities Press, 1975), 368–76; David Brion Davis, *The Problem of Slavery in the Age of Rev-olution, 1770–1823* (OUP, 1999), 443–44.

267 *"Royal Charter and Proclamations":* Edmund Lyon to Lord Grenville, January 16, 1807, BL, Add MS 59305A, ff. 116, 121.

268 *passed the Act: An Act for the Abolition of the Slave Trade*, 47 George III session 1, c. 36 (1807), PA, HL/PO/PU/1/1807/47G3s1n60.

268 *voted as a bloc:* Proceedings in the House of Lords on Slave Trade Bill, May 16, 1806, BL, Add MS 59305A, ff. 57–58. The duke of Sussex voted against the abolition bill but decades later be-came a supporter of the anti-slavery movement. See L. Gluck Rosenthal, *A Biographical Memoir of His Late Royal Highness, the Duke of Sussex* (Brighton, 1846), 52.

268 *"cruel and criminal traffic":* Clarkson, *The History of the Rise, Progress, and Accomplishment of the Abolition of the African Slave-Trade by the British Parliament*, II: 452.

268 *the seven hundred thousand individuals:* Taylor, *The Interest*, 24.

269 *"voice of our complaint":* Cugoano, *Thoughts and Sentiments*, 143.

CHAPTER 17: THE AFRICAN INSTITUTION

273 *for "promoting civilization":* William Wilberforce to Lord Grenville, March 28, 1807, Dropmore Papers, BL, Add MS 58978, f. 114.

273 *public voting record:* Joshua Wilson, *A Biographical Index of the Present House of Lords* (London, 1808), 263–65.

273 *weaken Britain's maritime strength:* The Duke of Clarence to Samuel Hawker, [1807], RA, GEO/ADD/44/10.

273 *"at opposite ends":* Suzanne Schwartz, "Royal Attitudes to the Atlantic Slave Trade and Abolition in the Late Eighteenth and Early Nineteenth Centuries," *English Historical Review* 138, no. 592 (2023): 497–527, here 498.

274 *Christian civilization:* See esp. Philip D. Curtain, *The Image of Africa: British Ideas and Action, 1780–1850* (UWP, 1964); Boyd Hilton, *The Age of Atonement: The Influence of Evangelicalism on Social and Economic Thought, 1795–1865* (CP, 1988).

274 *"most cordial support":* Wilberforce to Grenville, March 28, 1807, Dropmore Papers, BL, Add MS 58978, f. 114.

274 *"the enormous wrongs":* William Wilberforce to Lord Grenville, April 11, 1807, BL, Add MS 58978, ff. 115–16. On the African Institution, see Wayne Ackerson, *The African Institution (1807–1827) and the Antislavery Movement in Great Britain* (Edwin Mellen Press Ltd, 2005).

275 *"introduce the blessings":* Report of the Committee of the African Institution, Read to the General Meeting on 15th July, 1807 (London, 1807), iv, 9–11, 16, 21, 68–69.

275 *"tribute of respect":* Thomas Clarkson, *The History of the Rise, Progress, and Accomplishment of the Abolition of the African Slave-Trade by the British Parliament,* 2 vols. (London, 1808): II: 570–71.

275 *"I have no doubt":* Thomas Clarkson to the Duke of Gloucester, May 21, 1808, Schomburg Center for Research in Black Culture, New York, S.T. 18.

276 *"brief, but energetic":* Morning Chronicle, March 26, 1808.

276 *"whilst any one nation":* Copy of a letter from William Roscoe to HRH the Duke of Gloucester, n.d., RA, GEO/ADD/23/87, f. 29.

276 *enforce the law:* Abstract of the Acts of Parliament for Abolishing the Slave Trade, and of the Orders in Council Founded on Them (London, 1810), 24–25.

276 *"prize of war":* Formation of the Recruiting Depot on the Coast of Africa, July 28, 1812, CO 267/35.

277 *"natives of Africa":* Abstract of the Acts of Parliament for Abolishing the Slave Trade, 26; Letters Patent Establishing a Court of Vice Admiralty at Sierra Leone, May 2, 1807, ADM 5/51.

277 *Freetown, Sierra Leone:* Stephen Braidwood, *Black Poor and White Philanthropists: London's Blacks and the Foundation of the Sierra Leone Settlement, 1786–1791* (ULP, 1994), 5–12; Christopher Leslie Brown, "Empire Without America: British Plans for Africa in the Era of the American Revolution," in *Abolitionism and Imperialism in Britain, Africa, and the Atlantic,* ed. Derek R. Peterson (Ohio University Press, 2010), 84–100; Cassandra Pybus, "'A Less Favourable Specimen': The Abolitionist Response to Self-Emancipated Slaves in Sierra Leone, 1793–1808," *Parliamentary History* 26, supp. (2007): 101–12.

278 *551 Maroons:* Ruma Chopra, *Almost Home: Maroons between Slavery and Freedom in Jamaica, Nova Scotia, and Sierra Leone* (YUP, 2018), 139–59.

278 *testified before Parliament:* Richard Peter Anderson, *Abolition in Sierra Leone: Re-Building Lives and Identities in Nineteenth-Century West Africa* (CUP, 2020) 30–31.

278 *"to condemn within":* Dispatch to the Governor of Sierra Leone, April 1808, CO 267/24.

278 *"free and hardy":* Quoted in Emma Christopher, *Freedom in White and Black: A Lost Story of the Illegal Slave Trade and Its Global Legacy* (UWP, 2018), 114.

278 *wrote outraged reports:* Thompson to Castlereagh, July 27 and August 2, 1808, Sierra Leone Original Correspondence: Despatches, 1808, CO 267/24; Thompson to Nancy Barker, July 23, 1808, Papers of Thomas Perronet Thompson, BJL, DTH 4/1/455–61.

278 *particularly Wilberforce:* Wilberforce to Thompson, October 19, 1808, BJL, DTH 1/61/8.

279 *effectively silenced:* See Michael J. Turner, "The Limits of Abolition: Government, Saints, and the 'African Question,'" c. 1780–1820," *English Historical Review* 122 (1997): 319–57.

279 *former chief justice:* John McLaren, *Dewigged, Bothered, and Bewildered: British Colonial Judges on Trial, 1800–1900* (UTP, 2011), 233.

279 *"delude a liberal nation":* Robert Thorpe, *A Letter to William Wilberforce . . . Containing Remarks on the Reports of the Sierra Leone Company, and African Institution* (London, 1815), xviii, 11, 47.

279 *ninety-nine thousand "liberated" Africans:* Richard Anderson, "The Diaspora of Sierra Leone's Liberated Africans: Enlistment, Forced Migration, and 'Liberation' at Freetown, 1808 to 1863," *African Economic History* 41 (2013): 101–138, here 101.

280 *Yoruba and Igbo:* Maeve Ryan, "'A Most Promising Field for Future Usefulness': The Church Missionary Society and the Liberated Africans of Sierra Leone," in *A Global History of Anti-Slavery Politics in the Nineteenth Century*, ed. William Mulligan and Maurice Bric (PM, 2013), 37–58.

280 *this "free labor":* Second Report of the Committee of the African Institution, Read at the Annual General Meeting, on the 25 of March 1808 (London, 1808), 7–8.

280 *vice-admiralty court:* Padraic X. Scanlan, *Freedom's Debtors: British Antislavery in Sierra Leone in the Age of Revolution* (YUP, 2017), 100; Lisa Ford and Naomi Parkinson, "Legislating Liberty: Liberated Africans and the Abolition Act, 1806–1824," *Slavery & Abolition* 42 (2021): 827–46; Emma Christopher, "'Tis Enough That We Give Them Liberty'? Liberated Africans at Sierra Leone in the Early Era of Slave-Trade Suppression," in *The Suppression of the Atlantic Slave Trade: British Policies, Practices and Representations of Naval Coercion*, ed. Robert Burroughs and Richard Huzzey (MUP, 2015), 55–72.

280 *recorded a total:* Scanlan, *Freedom's Debtors*, 105, 118; Richard Anderson, "The Diaspora of Sierra Leone's Liberated Africans: Enlistment, Forced Migration, and 'Liberation' at Freetown, 1808–1863," *African Economic History* 41 (2013): 101–38.

281 *"our Africa corps":* The Sessional Papers Printed by Order of The House of Lords, Or Presented by Royal Command, in the Session 1837, vol. 23 (London, 1837), 34.

281 *assigned wives:* General statement of the disposal of the captured negroes received into the colony of Sierra Leone from 30 June 1816 to 4 September 1816, CO 267/44.

281 *a problematic term:* Suzanne Schwartz, "The Impact of Liberated African 'Disposal' Policies in Early Nineteenth-Century Sierra Leone," in *Liberated Africans and the Abolition of the Slave Trade, 1807–1896*, ed. Richard Anderson and Henry B. Lovejoy (URP, 2020), 45–65, here 58.

281 *flouted the law:* Peter Grindal, *Opposing the Slavers: The Royal Navy's Campaign Against the African Slave Trade* (I. B. Tauris, 2016), 102–103.

281 *"Spanish Cuba":* Sunday's Post, November 8, 1815, 4.

281 *threatened independence:* Ada Ferrer, "Cuban Slavery and Atlantic Antislavery," in *Slavery and Anti-Slavery in Spain's Atlantic Empire*, ed. Josep M. Fradera and Christopher Schmidt-Nowara (Berghahn Books, 2016), 134–57.

281 *around 841,000 enslaved Africans:* Leonardo Marques, *The United States and the Transatlantic Slave Trade to the Americas, 1776–1867* (YUP, 2006), 63–64.

281 *three primary objectives:* Extracts from the African Institution Reports, 1808, BOD, Papers of Sir Thomas Fowell Buxton, ff. 10–13.

282 *"chiefly we raise":* William Wilberforce, *A Letter on the Abolition of the Slave Trade* (London, 1807), 10–11.

282 *"depraved and debased":* Ibid., 246–47.

282 *"produce little effect":* Second Report of the Committee of the African Institution, 4.

282 *"the guardians of":* George Harrison, *Some Remarks on A Communication from Wm. Roscoe to the Duke of Gloucester, dated March 20, 1809 . . .* (London, 1810), 8.

283 *sophisticated political lives:* On enslaved people as political actors, see esp. Jennifer L. Morgan, *Reckoning with Slavery: Gender, Kinship, and Capitalism in the Early Black Atlantic* (DUP, 2021).

283 *"change of life":* Stephen Gaisford, *An Essay on the Good Effects Which May be Derived in the British West Indies in Consequence of the Abolition of the African Slave Trade* (London, 1811), preface, 79–80.

283 *"careful and assiduous":* Beilby Porteus, *A Letter to the Governors, Legislatures, and Proprietors of Plantations, in the British West-India Islands* (London, 1808), 5–6.

283 *"crucial test case":* David Patrick Geggus, *Haitian Revolutionary Studies* (IUP, 2002), 27.

283 *Henry Christophe:* On his life and legacy, see Marlene L. Daut, *The First and Last King of Haiti: The Rise and Fall of Henry Christophe* (Knopf, 2025).

284 *Haiti into two:* Julia Gaffield, *Haitian Connections in the Atlantic World: Recognition After Revolution* (UNCP, 2015), 153–81; Ada Ferrer, "Haiti, Free Soil, and Antislavery in the Revolutionary Atlantic," *AHR* 117, no. 1 (2012): 40–66.

284 *toast to "My brother":* Hayti (St. Domingo) Coronation of the Negro King and Queen, 2nd June 1811, *Cobbett's Political Register 20,* no. 12 (London, 1816), 383–84.

284 *"some made princes":* "The King's Ordinance for the Creating of Princes, Dukes, Counts, Barons, and Knights of the Kingdom," *L'Hemisphere, Journal Francais; Contenant Des Varietes Litteraires Et Politiques, Dedie Aux Americains Amateurs De La Langue Francaise (1809–1811),* June 30, 1811, 730.

284 *rejecting hereditary dynasties:* Tabitha McIntosh and Grégory Pierrot, "Capturing the Likeness of Henry I of Haiti (1805–1822)," *Atlantic Studies* 14, no. 2 (2017): 127–51; James Forde, *The Early Haitian State and the Question of Political Legitimacy: American and British Representations of Haiti, 1804–1824* (PM, 2020), 93–128.

284 *assuaging concerns:* Friedemann Pestel, "The 'First Crowned Monarch of the New World': Monarchical Legitimation and Symbolic Politics of Henry I of Haiti (1811–1820)," *Atlantic Studies* 19, no. 2 (2022): 255–80; St. Domingo, April 20, 1816, *Niles Weekly Register,* vol. 10 (London, 1816), 135.

284 *"English nation":* Quoted in *Henry Christophe and Thomas Clarkson: A Correspondence,* ed. Earl Leslie Griggs and Clifford H. Prator (1952; repr. UC Press, 2020), 63.

285 *"the first duty":* Henry Christophe to Thomas Clarkson, February 5, 1816, in ibid., 91–93.

285 *delivered a toast: Richmond Enquirer,* September 16, 1816.

285 *"his sable majesty": Morning Post,* December 19, 1814.

285 *Prince Saunders:* Daut, *The First and Last King of Haiti,* 428, 433–34.

285 *"it is our will":* Prince Saunders, *Haytien Papers* (London, 1816), 150.

285 *end of Henry's reign:* Leslie M. Alexander, *Fear of a Black Republic: Haiti and the Birth of Black Internationalism in the United States* (UI, 2023), 32–37; Pestel, "The 'First Crowned Monarch of the New World,'" 279.

286 *"the degrading effects":* William Wilberforce to Henry Richard Holland, December 11, 1820, BL, Add MS 51820, f. 34.

286 *"two transatlantic voyages":* Paul Cuffe, *A Brief Account of the Settlement and Present Situation of the Colony of Sierra Leone, in Africa* (New York, 1812), 4–5.

286 *a potential partner:* James Sidbury, *Becoming African in America: Race and Nation in the Early Black Atlantic* (OUP, 2007), 149–55.

286 *Cuffe consulted with: Sixth Report of the Directors of the African Institution* (London, 1812), 27.

286 *Wilberforce applied:* Wilberforce to Lord Bathurst, July 24, 1812, Sierra Leone Original Correspondence, Secretary of State, May–December 1812, CO 267/35.

286 *"I have cause":* Cuffe, *A Brief Account of the Settlement and Present Situation of the Colony of Sierra Leone,* 9–10.

287 *increasing tensions:* Sidbury, *Becoming African in America*, 156–57.

287 *sworn in as Regent:* Jeremy Black, *George III: America's Last King* (YUP, 2006), 407–408.

287 *the "illicit trade":* House of Commons, March 5, 1811, *Parliamentary Debates from the Year 1803 to the Present Time,* vol. 19 (London, 1812), 239.

287 *legal slave trades:* Jenny S. Martinez, *The Slave Trade and the Origins of International Human Rights Law* (OUP, 2012), 23.

287 *Portugal had agreed:* Lewis Hertslet, ed., *A Complete Collection of the Treaties and Conventions, and Reciprocal Regulations, at Present Subsisting Between Great Britain and Foreign Powers . . .* vol. 3 (London, 1850), 931–32; Gabriel Paquette, *Imperial Portugal in the Age of Atlantic Revolutions: The Luso-Brazilian World, c. 1770–1850* (CUP, 2013), 76.

287 *"in defiance of":* Fourth Report of the Directors of the African Institution . . . (London, 1810), 11–12.

288 *suppression tactics:* David Eltis, *Economic Growth and the Ending of the Transatlantic Slave Trade* (OUP, 1987), 106–10; Paul A. Gilje, "'Free Trade and Sailors' Rights': The Rhetoric of the War of 1812," *Journal of the Early Republic* 30 (2010): 1–23.

288 *"quasi-colonial status":* Alan Taylor, *The Civil War of 1812: American Citizens, British Subjects, Irish Rebels, and Indian Allies* (Vintage, 2010), 4.

288 *War of 1812:* Christen Mucher, "Conceptual Traffic: The Atlantic Slave Trade and the War of 1812," in *Warring for America: Cultural Contests in the Era of 1812,* ed. Nicole Eustace and Fredrika J. Teute (UNCP, 2017), 127–63; Matthew Mason, "Keeping Up Appearances: The International Politics of Slave Trade Abolition in the Nineteenth-Century Atlantic World," *WMQ* 66, no. 4 (2009): 809–32.

CHAPTER 18: A VERY PRECARIOUS TENURE

289 *"nefarious traffic":* Eighth Report of the Directors of the African Institution, Read at the General Meeting on the 23rd of March, 1814 (London, 1814), 11.

289 *"to impress upon":* Eighth Report of the Directors of the African Institution, Appendix A, 37–47.

289 *public pressure campaign:* Herbert S. Klein, *The Atlantic Slave Trade* (CUP, 2010), 191–92.

290 *Louis refused:* Fabian Klose, *In the Cause of Humanity: A History of Humanitarian Intervention in the Long Nineteenth Century* (CUP, 2022), 81–83.

290 *Paris peace treaty:* Extract from the Definitive Treaty of Peace between Great Britain and France, signed at Paris the 30th of May 1814, *The Journals of the House of Commons,* vol. 70 (London, 1815), Appendix, 999.

290 *"just risen from":* Wilberforce's speech, June 27, 1814, in Hansard, *Parliamentary Debates,* vol. 28 (London, 1814), 272, 274, 277.

290 *used the press:* Seymour Drescher, *Abolition: A History of Slavery and Antislavery* (CUP, 2009), 228–29.

290 *"his own hand":* Clarkson to unknown, 1814, Clarkson Papers: vol. III, BL, Add MS 41267A, ff. 59–61.

291 *"I cannot doubt":* Clarkson to unknown, 1814, and Prince Louis Marie François de Saint-Mauris to Mrs. Clarkson, April 18, 1815, BL, Add MS 41267A, ff. 59–61, 73.

291 *letter of introduction:* Thomas Clarkson, History of the African Institution, HL, Clarkson Papers, Box 5, ff. 15–17.

291 *the Vienna Declaration:* Betty Fladeland, "Abolitionist Pressures on the Concert of Europe, 1814–1822," *Journal of Modern History* 38, no. 4 (1966): 355–73; Jenny Martinez, *The Slave*

Trade and the Origins of International Human Rights Law (OUP, 2011), 32–33; Jeremy Black, *The Atlantic Slave Trade in World History* (Routledge, 2015), 117.

292 *"a few Black persons":* Extracts from the Minutes of a Committee of the African Institution in Sierra Leone affairs, May 18, 1815, and Allen to Bathurst, May 27 and June 15, 1815, CO 267/41.

292 *Cuffe transported:* Ackerson, *The African Institution,* 75–76; Bronwen Everill, *Abolition and Empire in Sierra Leone and Liberia* (PM, 2013), 23–24.

292 *anticipated increased yields:* MacCarthy to Bathurst, June 22, 1816, CO 267/44.

293 *imperial surveillance:* James Stephen, *Reasons for Establishing a Registry of Slaves in the British Colonies* (London, 1814), 84.

293 *The registry bill:* Melanie J. Newton, *The Children of Africa in the Colonies: Free People of Color in Barbados in the Age of Emancipation* (LSUP, 2008), 68; Christer Petley, *Slaveholders in Jamaica: Colonial Society and Culture During the Era of Abolition* (2009: repr. Routledge, 2016), 87–88.

293 *"most urgently wanted":* Reasons for Establishing a Registry of Slaves in the British Colonies: Being a Report of a Committee of the African Institution* (London, 1815), 115.

293 *"rash and unconstitutional":* George Chalmers, *Proofs and Demonstrations How Much the Projected Registry of Colonial Negroes is Unfounded and Uncalled for . . .* (London, 1816), 18.

294 *"inevitable ruin":* A Letter to the Members of the Imperial Parliament, Referring to the Evidence Contained in the Proceedings of the House of Assembly of Jamaica, and Shewing the Injurious and Unconstitutional Tendency of the Proposed Slave Registry Bill* (London, 1816), 7.

294 *a meeting convened: Morning Post,* January 30, 1816.

294 *rejected the bill:* Robin Blackburn, *The Overthrow of Colonial Slavery, 1776–1848* (1988; repr. Verso, 2011), 323.

294 *insurrection in Barbados:* Newton, *The Children of Africa in the Colonies,* 68.

294 *contemporary assessments:* Joseph Marryat, *More Thoughts Still on the State of the West India Colonies* (London, 1817), 6.

294 *"servile condition":* Remarks on the Insurrection in Barbados and the Bill for the Registration of Slaves* (London, 1816), 6.

294 *rangers and drivers:* Hilary McD. Beckles, "The Slave-Driver's War: Bussa and the 1816 Barbados Slave Rebellion," *Boletín de Estudios Latinoamericanos y del Caribe* 39 (1985): 85–110. On enslaved drivers, see Randy Browne, *The Driver's Story: Labor and Power in the World of Atlantic Slavery* (UPenn, 2024).

294 *an armed uprising:* James Leith to Earl Bathurst, April 30, 1816, and Colonel Edward Codd to James Leith, April 25, 1816, CO 28/85, ff. 8, 11–12.

295 *questioning and trial:* Barbados House of Assembly, *The Report from a Select Committee of the House Assembly Appointed to Inquire into the Origin, Causes and Progress, of the Late Insurrection* (Barbados, 1818), 27; Beckles, "The Slave-Driver's War," 87–88.

295 *the "chief cause":* Colonel Edward Codd to James Leith, April 25, 1816, CO 28/85, f. 14.

296 *As colonial officials described: Remarks on the Insurrection in Barbados, and the Bill for the Registration of Slaves . . .* (London, 1816).

296 *"the insurrection appeared":* Caledonian Mercury,* June 6, 1816; Barbados House of Assembly, *The Report,* 12.

296 *"extraordinary emblematic flag":* Sketch of a flag taken from the insurgent slaves at Barbados, 1816, TNA, MFQ 1/112.

296 *the presumed support:* David Lambert, *White Creole Culture, Politics, and Identity During the Age*

of Abolition (CUP, 2005), 109; Aline Helg, *Slave No More: Self-Liberation Before Abolitionism in the Americas*, trans. Lara Vergnaud (UNCP, 2019), 258–59.

296 *would fight against:* Colonel Edward Codd to James Leith, April 25, 1816, and Extract of a private letter, St. Ann's, Barbados, CO 28/85, ff. 11–12.

297 *"served as warning":* Dexter Gabriel, *Jubilee's Experiment: The British West Indies and American Abolitionism* (CUP, 2023), 22.

297 *"in the presence":* Wilberforce's speech, June 19, 1816, *Hansard's Parliamentary Debates*, vol. 34 (London, 1816), 1158.

298 *"the slaves themselves":* Quoted in Robert Isaac Wilberforce and Samuel Wilberforce, *The Life of William Wilberforce*, 5 vols. (London, 1839), IV: 287.

298 *reassured subscribers: Eleventh Report of the Directors of the African Institution* (London, 1817), 20.

298 *"to cherish feelings":* Wilberforce and Wilberforce, *The Life of William Wilberforce*, IV: 291.

298 *the prince regent:* Petition to His Royal Highness George Prince Regent from the Barbados Council and Assembly, January 17, 1816/17, CO 28/85, f. 85.

299 *"a very precarious":* Extract of a Letter from Barbados, June 6, 1816, ibid., f. 86.

299 *neither sovereign had aided:* J. R. Oldfield, *Transatlantic Abolitionism in the Age of Revolution: An International History of Anti-Slavery, c. 1787–1820* (CUP, 2013), 192; James Gregory, *Mercy and British Culture, 1760–1960* (Bloomsbury, 2022), 112.

299 *"great satisfaction":* W. C. Oulton, *Authentic and Impartial Memoirs of Her Late Majesty, Charlotte* (London, 1819), 375.

299 *"the right hand":* Robert Huish, *The Public and Private Life of His Late Excellent and Most Gracious Majesty, George the Third* (London, 1821), 702.

299 *"set an example":* J. R. Miller, *The History of Great Britain from the Death of George II to the Coronation of George IV* (London, 1825), 328.

299 *"appear best calculated": Journals of the House of Lords*, vol. 49 (London, 1814), 1027.

300 *"a large portion":* Ibid., 1034.

300 *Commons addresses:* Address by the House of Commons to the Prince Regent, July 7, 1818, TNA, FO 84/2; Address by the House of Commons to His Majesty, June 27, 1822, Foreign Office: Slave Trade Department, TNA, FO 84/19.

300 *"right to search":* Ian Clark, *International Legitimacy and World Society* (OUP, 2007), 52–53; Klein, *The Atlantic Slave Trade*, 193.

300 *reached out to Wilberforce:* James Cropper to William Wilberforce, May 3, 1821, in *Letters Addressed to William Wilberforce, M.P.* (Liverpool, 1822), 4–5. See also David Brion Davis, "James Cropper and the British Anti–Slavery Movement," *Journal of Negro History* 45, no. 4 (1960): 241–58.

300 *"but one step":* James Cropper to Zachary Macaulay, March 5, 1822, Clarkson Papers, vol. VIII, BL, Add MS 41267A, f. 104.

301 *"a new society":* James Cropper to Zachary Macaulay, March 12, 1822, ibid., ff. 108–109.

301 *Ameliorating the condition:* James Cropper to Thomas Clarkson, August 5, 1822, Ibid, ff. 110–11.

301 *"every consideration":* Thomas Fowell Buxton, *Memoirs of Sir Thomas Fowell Buxton, Baronet*, ed. Charles Buxton (London, 1848), 118.

301 *"I told them":* Ibid., 104–105.

302 *Anti-Slavery Society:* Kenneth Morgan, *Slavery and the British Empire: From Africa to America* (OUP, 2007), 178.

302　*a cautious campaign:* Clare Midgley, *Women Against Slavery: The British Campaigns, 1780–1870* (Routledge, 1992), 45–46.

302　"extinction of slavery": Buxton, *Memoirs of Sir Thomas Fowell Buxton,* 113.

302　*George Canning:* Scanlan, *Slave Empire,* 227–28.

303　"*conversion of the slaves*": Buxton, *Memoirs of Sir Thomas Fowell Buxton,* 115–16.

303　*British Demerara:* Emilia Da Costa, *Crowns of Glory, Tears of Blood: The Demerara Slave Rebellion of 1823* (OUP, 1994), 46, 216.

303　"*tired of being slaves*": Murray to Bathurst, Report on the Insurrection, Demerara, August 24, 1823, Demerara, 1823, CO 111/39, ff. 77–80.

303　*reprieved rebels implicated:* Private, Evidence as to the intentions of the rebel slaves, Murray, September 11, 1823, ibid., f. 90.

303　*Reverend John Smith:* Da Costa, *Crowns of Glory, Tears of Blood,* 252–53.

304　*divided the press:* See, for example, *An Authentic Copy of the Minutes of Evidence on the Trial of John Smith, a Missionary, in Demerara* (London, 1824); *The Missionary Smith . . .* (London, 1824); *The Demerara Martyr: Memoirs of the Rev. John Smith, Missionary to Demerara* (London, 1848).

CHAPTER 19: THEY WOULD BE FREE

305　"*rebellious conspiracy*": Manchester to Bathurst, December 24, 1823, Jamaica: Dispatches, 1823, CO 137/154, ff. 492–93.

305　*engaging in seditious talk:* Miles Ogborn, *The Freedom of Speech: Talk and Slavery in the Anglo-Caribbean World* (UCP, 2019), 221–22.

305　"*imagine the death*": At a special slave court, held in St. Mary's, December 19, 1823, in *Papers Relating to the Manumission, Government and Population of the Slaves in the West-Indies, 1822–1824* (London, 1825), 40.

305　"*negroes were going to rise*": Ibid., 40, 41.

306　*death by hanging:* Public hangings were still common in England. See Vic Gatrell, *The Hanging Tree: Execution and the English People, 1770–1868* (OUP, 1994).

306　"*this example of severity*": Manchester to Bathurst, January 12, 1824, CO 137/156, ff. 6–7.

306　to "*restore the colony*": Manchester to Bathurst, February 9, 1824, ibid., ff. 137–38.

306　"*entitled to their freedom*": Manchester to Bathurst, July 31, 1824, ibid., f. 304.

306　"*extinguished only in blood*": *The Edinburgh Magazine,* vol. 18, January–June 1826, 77.

306　*felt "contented and happy*": Zachary Macaulay, *The Slave Colonies of Great Britain; Or A Picture of Negro Slavery Drawn by the Colonists Themselves* (London, 1825), 49, 52.

307　*Reforms included:* Mary Reckord, "The Colonial Office and the Abolition of Slavery," *The Historical Journal* 14, no. 4 (1971): 723–34.

307　"*It was not emancipation*": Eric Williams, *Capitalism and Slavery* (1944; repr. UNCP, 2021), 158.

307　*circular dispatches:* Circular dispatches, May 28 and July 9, 1823, CO 854/1, ff. 133, 160–64.

307　"*The Negro slavery*": William Wilberforce, *An Appeal in the Religion, Justice and Humanity of the Inhabitants of the British Empire, In Behalf of the Negro Slaves in the West Indies* (London, 1823), 1, 35.

308　"*recognized by your Majesty*": Petition to the Crown by Charles Ellis, M.P., Chairman of the Standing Committee of West India Planters and Merchants, February 10, 1824, Christian Faith Society, Lambeth Palace Library, ff. 70–71.

308   *he was "broken hearted":* William, Duke of Clarence, to John Bourke, 4th Earl of Mayo, August 10, 1824, RA, GEO/ADD/4/74.

308   *"a great reluctance":* Manchester to Bathurst, and Private, Manchester to Bathurst, December 24, 1823, CO 137/154, ff. 492–93, 494–98.

308   *planters' worst fears:* Mary Turner, *Slaves and Missionaries: The Disintegration of Jamaican Slave Society, 1787–1834* (UWIP, 1998), 100–115.

308   *"violation of justice":* Jamaica slave trials, *Hansard's Parliamentary Debates,* vol. 14 (London, 1826), 1068.

309   *"to wish for colonies":* *Reflections Upon the Value of the British West Indian Colonies and of the British North American Provinces* (London, 1826), 10.

309   *"fellow subjects" of the Crown:* Thomas Clarkson, *Thoughts on the Necessity of Improving the Condition of the Slaves in the British Colonies* (London, 1823), 56.

309   *proposed ameliorative reforms:* *Report of the Committee of the Society for the Mitigation and Gradual Abolition of Slavery* (London, 1824), 10.

309   *"deep-sunk national stain":* *Thoughts on the Abolition of Slavery: Humbly Submitted in a Letter to the King* (London, 1824), 21.

309   *"calmness and discretion":* Speech of the Lords Commissioners on the opening of the Session, February 3, 1824, *The Annual Register* (London, 1824), 332–33.

309   *ladies' anti-slavery associations:* Claire Midgley, *Women Against Slavery: The British Campaigns, 1780–1870* (Routledge, 1992), 99.

309   *"Negro emancipation":* *Ladies' Association of Calne, Melksham, and their respective Neighbourhoods, in Aid of the Cause of Negro Emancipation* (Calne, 1825).

310   *"determined to awaken":* *The First Report of the Female Society, for Birmingham, West-Bromwich, Wednesbury, Walsall, and Their Respective Neighbourhoods, for the Relief of British Negro Slaves* (Birmingham, 1826), 3–4; *The Ladies' Association of Manchester and its Neighbourhood, in Aid of the Cause of Negro Emancipation* (Manchester, 1826).

310   *"not an abstract question":* Elizabeth Heyrick, *Immediate, Not Gradual Emancipation; Or, An Inquiry into the Shortest, Safest, and Most Effectual Means of Getting Rid of West Indian Slavery* (London, 1824), 4.

310   *Heyrick's fiery language inflamed:* Julie L. Holcomb, *Moral Commerce: Quakers and the Transatlantic Boycott of the Slave Labor Economy* (Cornell, 2016), 90, 106.

310   *"Everywhere people are asking":* Quoted in Bronwen Everill, *Not Made by Slaves: Ethical Capitalism in the Age of Abolition* (HUP, 2020), 50.

311   *"We have no right":* Heyrick, *Immediate, Not Gradual Emancipation,* 7–8, 12.

311   Anti-Slavery Monthly Reporter: *Anti-Slavery Monthly Reporter,* no. 1, June 30, 1825. Published from 1825 to 1830, the *Anti-Slavery Monthly Reporter* was succeeded by the *Anti-Slavery Reporter* from 1831 to 1836 and the *British Emancipator* from 1837 to 1840. See Peter C. Hogg, *The African Slave Trade and Its Suppression: A Classified and Annotated Bibliography of Books, Pamphlets and Periodical Articles* (1973; repr. Routledge, 2013), 1769.

311   *"Let us look it up":* Quoted in Ian Whyte, *Zachary Macaulay: The Steadfast Scot in the British Anti-Slavery Movement* (LUP, 2011), 191.

312   *anti-slavery petitions:* For examples, see *Anti-Slavery Reporter,* no. 6, November 30, 1825, 57–58; *Anti-Slavery Reporter,* no. 19, December 30, 1826, 287–88.

312   *"merits of the great question":* *Anti-Slavery Reporter,* no. 14, July 31, 1826, 197.

312 *free-labor sugar:* For support of free-labor sugar and equalized duties, see, for instance, *Anti-Slavery Reporter*, no. 17, October 31, 1826, 248; *Anti-Slavery Reporter*, no. 34, March 31, 1828 (London, 1828), 204.

312 *"resolutions so strongly urged":* William Huskisson to George IV, September 21, 1827, RA, GEO/MAIN/24992–24995.

312 *"these most valuable possessions":* George Wilson Bridges, *A Voice from Jamaica, in Reply to William Wilberforce* (London, 1823), 48.

312 *slavery-derived profits:* See esp. Maxine Berg and Pat Hudson, *Slavery, Capitalism and the Industrial Revolution* (Polity Press, 2023), 43–53.

312 *"For whose pecuniary benefit":* John Taylor, *Negro Emancipation and West Indian Independence: The True Interest of Great Britain* (Liverpool, 1824), 9, 7.

313 *"species of property":* Member of the Dominica Legislature, *An Appeal and Caution to the British Nation: with Proposals for the Immediate or Gradual Emancipation of the Slaves* (London, 1824), 32.

313 *"the Crown confirmed their privileges":* Alexander McDonnell, *The West India Legislatures Vindicated from the Charge of Having Resisted the Call of the Mother Country from the Amelioration of Slavery* (London, 1826), 20.

313 *"revolts the minds of West Indians":* Resident and Proprietor in the West Indies, *An Impartial Review of the Question Pending between Great Britain and Her West Indian Colonies . . .* (London, 1824), 31.

314 *"glory of the Crown":* James Stephen, *England Enslaved by Her Own Slave Colonies: An Address to the Electors and People of the United Kingdom* (London, 1826), 86.

314 *the law exercised a restraining hand:* Seymour Drescher, *The Mighty Experiment: Free Labor Versus Slavery in British Emancipation* (OUP, 2002), 13–14.

314 *"deference and humility":* Henry Nelson Coleridge, *The Young Logicians: Or, School-boy Conceptions of Rights and Wrongs* (Birmingham, 1828), 85.

314 *"neither King, Lords, nor Commons":* *The Death Warrant of Negro Slavery Throughout the British Dominions* (London, 1829), 12, 20.

314 *"your feelings toward the Blacks":* Earl of Bristol to Clarkson, March 25, 1826, BL, Add MS 41267A, ff. 140–41.

315 *"sanctioned and instigated the planters":* *Letters on the Necessity of a Prompt Extinction of British Colonial Slavery: Chiefly Addressed to the More Influential Classes* (London, 1826), 211.

CHAPTER 20: FREE SUBJECTS OF THE CROWN

316 *owned thousands of enslaved people:* See "Accounts of all Slaves now in possession of His Majesty's Government, in any of the Colonies," June 10, 1824, *PP*, vol. 24 (London, 1824), 1–49.

316 *Crown bought 13,400 enslaved men:* Roger Norman Buckley, *Slaves in Red Coats: The British West India Regiments, 1795–1818* (YUP, 1979), 55.

316 *Crown officials forcibly conscripted:* Claudius K. Fergus, *Revolutionary Emancipation: Slavery and Abolitionism in the British West Indies* (LSUP, 2013), 98–99, 185–86; Justin Iverson, *Rebels in Arms: Black Resistance and the Fight for Freedom in the Anglo-Atlantic* (UGAP, 2022), 117.

317 *known as Fédon's rebellion:* Gordon Turnbull, *A Narrative of the Revolt and Insurrection in the Island of Grenada* (London, 1796), Appendix, 100.

317 *confiscated insurgents' estates and property:* Edward L. Cox, "Fedon's Rebellion 1795–96: Causes and Consequences," *Journal of Negro History* 67, no. 1 (1982): 7–19.

317 *profits for the king's treasury:* Joseph Murryat, *An Examination of the Report of the Berbice Commissioners, and an Answer to the Letters of James Stephen, Esq.* (London, 1817), 85, 111.

317 *Dutch colony of Berbice:* "Papers Relating to the Crown Estates in the Colony of Berbice, 1816," *PP,* vol. 8, no. 509 (London, 1816), 3–4, 21; Alvin O. Thompson, *Unprofitable Servants: Crown Slaves in Berbice, Guyana, 1803–1831* (UWIP, 2002), 1–7.

317 *escheated to the British sovereign:* On this legal process, see esp. Krista Kesselring, "'Negroes of the Crown': The Management of Slaves Forfeited by Grenadian Rebels, 1796–1831," *Journal of the Canadian Historical Association* 22, no. 2 (2011): 1–29.

318 *"species of property":* Zachary Macaulay to the British Treasury, November 19, 1814, TNA, T 1/3807.

318 *reflected poorly on the monarchy:* Ibid.; Kesselring, "'Negroes of the Crown,'" 12–13.

318 *amelioration as official imperial policy:* Canning's speech, May 15, 1823, in *Select Speeches of the Right Honourable George Canning,* ed. Robert Walsh (Philadelphia, 1835), 400–10.

318 *raised the issue in 1819:* The prince regent appointed Maxwell on May 21, 1819. See *Bulletins of State Intelligence* (London, 1819), 143; Kesselring, "'Negroes of the Crown,'" 16.

318 *"his Majesty might be pleased":* Charles Maxwell to Earl Bathurst, February 5, 1823, CO 239/9. Maxwell's inquiry is also discussed in "An Account of the final Disposal of Slaves escheated to the Crown in the West Indies, 1821–31," *PP* 16, no. 121 (London, 1831), 3–5.

319 *"if any such person dies intestate":* "An Account of the final Disposal of Slaves escheated to the Crown," 3–4.

319 *"a great and undeserved hardship":* Ibid., 7–8.

319 *"a monstrous system of oppression":* *Third Report of the Committee of the Society for the Mitigation and Gradual Abolition of Slavery Throughout the British Dominions* (London, 1826), 15.

320 *"many lesser means":* *Westminster Review,* vol. 1, January–April 1824 (London, 1824), 354.

320 *under review by the Colonial Office:* Bathurst's Instructions to the Commissioners, Henry Hill, CO 318/57.

320 *"royal fact finders":* Lauren Benton and Lisa Ford, *Rage for Order: The British Empire and the Origins of International Law, 1800–1850* (HUP, 2016), 59.

320 *escheat procedures varied:* *Third Report of the Commissioners of Inquiry into the Administration of Civil and Criminal Justice in the West Indies* (London, 1827), 87.

321 *the "price of blood":* *The Further Progress of Colonial Reform* (London, 1827), 24–25.

321 *"What is it but a slave trade":* "Return of Slaves escheated to the Crown in the Island of Barbados, 1824," *PP,* vol. 24, no. 433 (London, 1824), 10.

321 *good behavior of liberated Africans: Anti-Slavery Record 2,* no. 1 (New York, 1836), 11.

322 *"a numerous gang of slaves":* "An Account of the final Disposal of Slaves escheated to the Crown in the West Indies," 9.

322 *supervision of a colonial agent:* See Alvin O. Thompson, "African 'Recaptives' under Apprenticeship in the British West Indies, 1807–1828," *Immigrants & Minorities* 9, no. 2 (1990): 123–44.

322 *"a multitude of slaves":* Horace Twiss to the Hon. J. K. Stewart, August 16, 1830, in "An Account of the final Disposal of Slaves escheated to the Crown," 9.

322 *"Slaves worked for the profit of the Crown":* Ibid., 11.

322 *"have felt it their duty":* "Copies of the several Orders sent to the Colonies for emancipating the Slaves belonging to the Crown," March 1831, *PP,* vol. 19, no. 305 (London, 1831), 3.

322 *"a disgrace to the Crown": Anti-Slavery Reader,* no. 73 (London, 1831), 153–55.

323 *the Colonial Office ordered:* Kesselring, "'Negroes of the Crown,'" 19–20.

323 *"as satisfactory as it was honorable":* Ester Copley, *A History of Slavery and its Abolition* (London, 1839), 366.

323 *"peaceful, and happy results":* G. W. Alexander, *Letters on the Slave-Trade, Slavery, and Emancipation* . . . (London, 1842), 24.

323 *"The slaves in Jamaica":* Reginald Coupland, *Wilberforce: A Narrative* (OUP, 1923), 512.

323 *"The king is no Abolitionist":* *The Holland House Diaries 1831–1840: The Diary of Henry Richard Vassall Fox, Third Lord Holland,* ed. Abraham D. Kriegel (Routledge, 1977), 209.

323 *triggered a general election:* Michael Taylor, *The Interest: How the British Establishment Resisted the Abolition of Slavery* (Bodley Head, 2020), 178–81.

324 *"averse to the agitation":* Eric J. Evans, *Parliamentary Reform in Britain, c. 1770–1918* (2000; repr. Routledge, 2013), 21–25.

324 *"safe and practical plan":* Speech of Viscount Howick, April 15, 1831, in *The Anti-Slavery Reporter,* vol. 5 (London, 1833), 86.

324 *"the signs of the times":* Charles Greville, *A Journal of the Reigns of King George IV and King William IV,* vol. 2, ed. Henry Reeve (London, 1874), 29.

324 *true story of Mary Prince:* On Prince's life, see esp. Moira Ferguson, *Subject to Others: British Women Writers and Colonial Slavery, 1670–1834* (Routledge, 1992), 281–98; Ryan Hanley, *Beyond Slavery and Abolition: Black British Writing, c. 1770–1830* (CUP, 2019), 76–96.

325 *parliamentary witness testimonies:* See Jane Webster, *Materializing the Middle Passage: A Historical Archaeology of British Slave Shipping, 1680–1807* (OUP, 2023), 440–47.

325 *"flew into a great rage":* Mary Prince, *The History of Mary Prince, A West Indian Slave* (London, 1831), 17–18.

325 *"a black devil":* Ibid., 20–22.

326 *dictated her autobiography:* Hanley, *Beyond Slavery and Abolition,* 76–77.

326 *"This is slavery":* Prince, *The History of Mary Prince,* 22–23, 44.

327 *"can fully appreciate":* Henry William Martin, *A Counter Appeal in Answer to "An Appeal" From William Wilberforce, Esq., M.P.* . . . (London, 1823), 3.

327 *"a great debt of gratitude": A Letter to the Most Honorable the Marquis of Chandos by a West India Planter* (London, 1830), 70.

328 *"will forfeit all claim": Eclectic Review,* vol. 7 (London, 1832), 247.

328 *king supported their liberation:* Mary Turner, *Slaves and Missionaries: The Disintegration of Jamaican Slave Society, 1787–1834* (UWIP, 1998), 150–51.

328 *spent time among missionaries:* Richard Hart, *Slaves Who Abolished Slavery* (UWIP, 2002), 249.

328 *"had no more right":* Henry Bleby, *Speech of Rev. Henry Bleby, Missionary from Barbadoes, on the Results of Emancipation in the British W. I. Colonies* (Boston, 1858), 11.

328 *the Christmas Rebellion:* See esp. Mary Reckord, "The Jamaican Slave Rebellion of 1831," *Past and Present* 40, no. 1 (1968): 108–125; Michael Craton, *Testing the Chains: Resistance to Slavery in the British West Indies* (Cornell, 1982), 291–321.

328 *"raging in all directions":* Theodore Foulks, *Eighteen Months in Jamaica: with Recollections of the Late Rebellion* (London, 1833), 59, 60, 62.

329 *the death toll:* Tom Zoellner, *Island on Fire: The Revolt That Ended Slavery in the British Empire* (HUP, 2020), 168, 176–77.

329 *"All I wished":* Quoted in Henry Bleby, *Death Struggles of Slavery: Being a Narrative of Facts and Incidents, Which Occurred in a British Colony, During the Two Years Immediately Preceding Negro Emancipation* (London, 1853), 113–14.

329 *died a martyr:* William Knibb, *Defense of the Baptist Missionaries from the Charge of Inciting the Late Rebellion in Jamaica* (London, 1833), 4.

329 *Sharpe became a national hero:* Jean Besson, "Missionaries, Planters, and Slaves in the Age of Abolition," in *The Caribbean: A History of the Region and Its Peoples*, ed. Stephan Palmié and Francisco A. Scarano (UCP, 2011), 324.

329 *wrath at local missionaries:* Bleby, *Death Struggles of Slavery*, 95–119; K. R. M. Short, "Jamaican Christian Missions and the Great Slave Rebellion of 1831–1832," *Journal of Ecclesiastical History* 27, no. 1 (1976): 57–72; Robin Blackburn, *The Overthrow of Colonial Slavery, 1776–1848* (1988; repr. Verso, 2011), 433–34.

330 *the Reform Bill:* J. R. Oldfield, *The Ties That Bind: Transatlantic Abolitionism in the Age of Reform, c. 1820–1865* (LUP, 2020), 45–48; B. W. Higman, "The West India 'Interest' in Parliament 1807–1833," *Historical Studies, Australia and New Zealand* 13 (1967): 1–19.

330 *published popular lectures:* See, for example, George Thompson, *Three Lectures on British and Colonial Slavery* (London, 1832).

330 *"likely to be rejected":* William IV to Earl Grey, February 4, 1831, RA, GEO/MAIN/35895–35906.

330 *"in the loss":* William IV to Goderich, June 5, 1832, Ripon Papers, BL, Add MS 40862, ff. 345–46.

331 *Crown sought feedback:* Ian Newbold, *Whiggery and Reform, 1830–1841: The Politics of Government* (PM, 1990), 115.

331 *"subjects of greater interest":* Hansard's Parliamentary Debates, vol. 15 (London, 1833), 86–90.

331 *"government had given up":* Quoted in Taylor, *The Interest*, 255.

331 *"to be released":* Greville, *A Journal*, 352.

331 *"a state of humble happiness":* Foulks, *Eighteen Months in Jamaica*, 109–110.

332 *"immediate and entire abolition":* Henry Wheatley, *London Past and Present* (London, 1891), 26.

332 *"presented by such a body":* Thomas Timpson, *The Negroes' Jubilee: A Memorial of Negro Emancipation, August 1, 1834* (London, 1834), 76.

332 *women anti-slavery advocates:* Seymour Drescher, "Women's Mobilization in the Era of Slave Emancipation: Some Anglo-French Comparisons," in *Women's Rights and Transatlantic Antislavery in the Era of Emancipation*, ed. Kathryn Kish Sklar and James Brewer Stewart (YUP, 2007), 106.

332 *featherbed-sized women's petition:* Susan Zaeske, *Signatures of Citizenship: Petitioning, Antislavery, and Women's Political Identity* (UNCP, 2003), 46; Sarah Richardson, *The Political Worlds of Women: Gender and Politics in Nineteenth Century Britain* (Routledge, 2013), 119.

332 *apprenticed to their former enslavers:* Taylor, *The Interest*, 265–67.

333 *"do not belong to the planters":* Holland House Diaries, 208.

333 *Wilberforce's well-attended funeral:* Padraic X. Scanlan, *Slave Empire: How Slavery Built Modern Britain* (Robinson, 2020), 290–291.

333 *left freed people impoverished:* James A. Thome and Joseph Horace Kimball, *Emancipation in the West Indies: A Six Months' Tour in Antigua, Barbadoes, and Jamaica in the Year 1837* (London, 1838).

334 *strict new laws:* See esp. Diana Paton, *No Bond but the Law: Punishment, Race, and Gender in Jamaican State Formation, 1780–1870* (DUP, 2004); Natasha Lightfoot, *Troubling Freedom: Antigua and the Aftermath of British Emancipation* (DUP, 2015).

334 *power over corporal punishment:* Paton, *No Bond but the Law*, 59; Dawn P. Harris, *Punishing the Black Body: Making Social and Racial Structures in Barbados and Jamaica* (UGAP, 2017), 32–34.

334 *"appointed by the Crown":* *The Debates in Parliament, Session 1833—on the Resolutions and Bill for the Abolition of Slavery in the British Colonies* (London, 1834), 79.

334 *"appearance of the Negro":* Quoted in Roderick A. McDonald, ed., *Between Slavery and Freedom: Special Magistrate John Anderson's Journal of St. Vincent during the Apprenticeship* (UPenn, 2001), 81–82.

335 *their growing discontent:* K. Woodville Marshall, "'We Be Wise to Many More Tings'": Blacks' Hopes and Expectations of Emancipation," in *Caribbean Freedom: Economy and Society from Emancipation to the Present,* ed. Hilary Beckles and Verene Shepherd (Ian Randle, 1993), 12–20.

335 *"I have heard": A Narrative of Events, Since the First of August, 1834, by James Williams, an Apprenticed Labourer in Jamaica,* ed. Diana Paton (DUP, 2001), 5.

335 *freed people resisted apprenticeship:* Swithin Wilmot, "Not 'Full Free': The Ex-Slaves and the Apprenticeship System in Jamaica, 1834–1838," *Jamaica Journal* 17 (1984): 2–10.

335 *referenced the king's will:* See Gad Heuman, "Apprenticeship and Emancipation in the Caribbean: The Seeds of Citizenship," in *Race and Nation in the Age of Emancipations,* ed. Whitney Nell Stewart and John Garrison Marks (UGAP, 2018), 107–20.

335 *"the King's Proclamation":* Nixon to Stanley, July 10, 1834, in *PP,* vol. 50, 278–82.

336 *"our good king":* Richard Robert Madden, *A Twelvemonth's Residence in the West Indies, During the Transition from Slavery to Apprenticeship* (London, 1835), 257.

336 *"Is it the king's law?":* Quoted in Heuman, "The Apprenticeship System in the Caribbean," 108.

336 *"The demon has":* British Emancipator, no. 1, December 27, 1837.

336 *embarked for the Caribbean:* Stephen Hobhouse, *Joseph Sturge: His Life and Work* (London,1919), 40–41.

336 *The men had witnessed:* Joseph Sturge and Thomas Harvey, *The West Indies in 1837* (London, 1838), 5–7, 122, 167, 218, 372.

337 *Victoria appeared ideal:* Richard Huzzey, *Freedom Burning: Anti-slavery and Empire in Victorian Britain* (Cornell, 2012), 11, 40.

337 *"your Majesty's subjects":* Petition to Her Majesty, Queen Victoria, from the [Ladies of Scotland] . . . (Glasgow, 1837).

337 *a petition to the queen:* Clare Midgley, *Women Against Slavery: The British Campaigns, 1780–1870* (Routledge, 1992), 66–67.

337 *"To the merciful sovereign":* Henry Brougham, *Immediate Emancipation: The Speech of Lord Brougham in the House of Lords on Tuesday, February 20, 1838, on Slavery and the Slave-Trade* (London, 1838), 24.

338 *meeting in Exeter Hall:* British Emancipator, March 14, 1838, 36.

338 *erupted into applause:* Ibid.

338 *a liberal imperial power:* Scanlan, *Slave Empire,* 329.

338 *reassessed imperial labor needs:* Izhak Gross, "Parliament and the Abolition of Negro Apprenticeship 1835–1838," *English Historical Review* 96, no. 380 (1981): 560–76; Kate Boehme, Peter Mitchell, and Alan Lester, "Reforming Everywhere and All at Once: Transitioning to Free Labor Across the British Empire, 1837–1838," *Comparative Studies in Society and History* 60, no. 3 (2018): 688–718.

339 *"is the happy day":* W. A. Feurtado, *The Jubilee Reign of Her Most Gracious Majesty Queen Victoria in Jamaica* (Kingston, 1890), 9–10.

340 *"OUR GRACIOUS QUEEN":* Ibid., 10.

340   *Victoria engendered feelings of loyalty:* Kennetta Hammond Perry, *London Is the Place for Me: Black Britons, Citizenship, and the Politics of Race* (OUP, 2015), 40.

340   *"Victoria became the touchstone":* Quoted in Anne Spry Rush, *Bonds of Empire: West Indians and Britishness from Victoria to Decolonization* (OUP, 2011), 51.

340   *under the authority:* See Lord Melbourne to Queen Victoria, August 13, 1838, Victorian Papers, Main Series, RA, VIC/MAIN/A/1/187.

EPILOGUE: SORROW AND REGRET

341   *first meeting of the Society:* "Extinction of the Slave Trade," *Morning Post,* June 2, 1840, "The Great Meeting for the Abolition of the Slave Trade," *Essex Standard,* June 5, 1840.

341   *to serve as president:* G. E. Anson to Buxton, May 27 and 30, 1840, Buxton Papers, vol. 19, BOD, Extracts Relating to The Abolition of Slavery.

342   *"Prince Albert had consented":* Richard N. Phillips to Clarkson, June 1, 1840, BL, Add MS 41267A, ff. 172–75.

342   *"making you a Vice President":* African Civilization Society, invitation to Clarkson, Edward North Buxton to Clarkson, May 25 and 26, 1840, BL, Add MS 41267A, ff. 162–67.

342   *"a perfect* negro mania*":* *Anti-Slavery Reporter,* September 9, 1840, 229.

342   *monarch's unspoken sensibilities:* Walter L. Arnstein, *Queen Victoria* (PM, 2003), 67.

343   *"puerile and ridiculous":* "Exhibition of the Royal Academy," *Morning Chronicle,* May 8, 1840.

343   *speculative Jamaican venture:* Sam Smiles, "Turner and the Slave Trade: Speculation and Representation, 1805–40," *British Art Journal* 8, no. 3 (2007/8): 47–54; Franny Moyle, *Turner: The Extraordinary Life and Momentous Times of J. M. W. Turner* (Penguin, 2016), 217, 225–29.

344   *"a large gang of negroes":* Quoted in Stephen J. May, *Voyage of the Slave Ship: J. M. W. Turner's Masterpiece in Historical Context* (McFarland and Company, 2014), 26.

344   *Albert would open the meeting:* Lord John Russell to Queen Victoria, May 29, 1840, RA, VIC/MAIN/A/7/41.

344   *Buxton took special care:* Notes for Buxton's speech at the Exeter Hall meeting and for his address to Prince Albert, 1840, BOD, Buxton Papers, vol. 19.

344   *"may gradually extinguish":* *Proceedings at the First Public Meeting of the Society for the Extinction of the Slave Trade, and for the Civilization of Africa, held at Exeter Hall, on Monday, 1st June, 1840* (London, 1840), 7.

345   *his first public speech:* Copy of Prince Albert's speech, The Society for the Abolition of Slavery, June 1, 1840, RA, VIC/MAIN/Z/271/1.

345   *"imperfectly heard":* Phillips to Clarkson, June 1, 1840, BL, Add MS 41267A, ff. 172–75.

345   *"the natives of Africa":* *Proceedings at the First Public Meeting of the Society for the Extinction of the Slave Trade,* 24–25, 38–39.

346   *a catalyst for progress:* On Britain's supposed global civilizing duty, see esp. Uday Singh Mehta, *Liberalism and Empire: A Study in Nineteenth-Century British Liberal Thought* (UCP, 1999); Jennifer Pitts, *A Turn to Empire: The Rise of Imperial Liberalism in Britain and France* (PUP, 2005).

346   *"went off to perfection":* Buxton to Hannah Buxton, June 2, 1840, BOD, Buxton Papers, vol. 19.

346   *"right hand of the throne":* *Morning Chronicle,* June 2, 1840.

346   *"with perfect distinction":* *Morning Post,* June 2, 1840.

346   *"It is a great pleasure":* Clarkson's speech at the meeting at Exeter Hall, June 24, 1840, BL, Add MS, f. 200.

347 *Blair expressed "deep sorrow":* "Text of Tony Blair's Statement on Slavery," November 27, 2006, *History News Network*, https://www.historynewsnetwork.org/article/text-of-tony-blairs-statement -on-slavery.

347 *"saying sorry could also mean":* "Marching to London to Hear a Single Word . . . Sorry," *Guardian*, March 24, 2007, https://www.theguardian.com/uk/2007/mar/24/britishidentity.race.

347 *"in Ghana's Elmina Castle":* "Slave Trade Shameful, Blair Says," BBC News, March 25, 2007, http://news.bbc.co.uk/2/hi/uk_news/6493507.stm.

348 *"the long, dark shadow":* "PM's Speech to the Jamaica Parliament," British Government, September 30, 2015, https://www.gov.uk/government/speeches/pms-speech-to-the-jamaican -parliament.

348 *"this painful legacy":* "David Cameron Rules Out Slavery Reparation During Jamaica Visit," BBC News, September 20, 2105, https://www.bbc.com/news/uk-34401412.

348 *"The region wants to put":* Beckles's Message of CARICOM Reparations Commission, UWI St. Augustine News, June 16, 2015, https://sta.uwi.edu/news/releases/release.asp?id=1439.

348 *"appalling atrocity of the slave trade":* "Prince Charles Says Britain's Role in Slave Trade was an Atrocity," *Guardian*, November 5, 2018, https://www.theguardian.com/uk-news/2018/nov/05 /prince-charles-says-britains-part-in-transatlantic-slave-trade-was-atrocity.

349 *"appalling atrocity of slavery":* "Prince Charles Denounces 'Appalling Atrocity of Slavery' as Barbados Becomes a Republic," *Newsweek*, November 30, 2021, https://www.newsweek.com /prince-charles-denounces-appalling-atrocity-slavery-barbados-republic-rihanna-1654318.

349 *"my profound sorrow":* "Prince William Expresses Sorrow for Slavery in Jamaica Visit," Associated Press, March 22, 2022, https://apnews.com/article/queen-elizabeth-ii-business-prince -william-slavery-barbados-bbd2d86c14f9636c6feeb1e0ad11a658.

349 *"I cannot describe":* "Prince Charles Expresses Sorrow Over Slavery in Commonwealth Speech," *Reuters*, June 24, 2022, https://www.reuters.com/world/africa/commonwealth-leaders-meet -rwanda-amid-criticism-hosts-rights-record-2022-06-24/.

349 *the law firm Leigh Day hosted:* "Reparations for the Trans-Atlantic Slave Trade: Is There a Legal Basis for a Claim?" Leigh Day, May 30, 2023, https://www.leighday.co.uk/news/news/2023 -news/reparations-for-the-trans-atlantic-slave-trade-is-there-a-legal-basis-for-a-claim/.

349 *"Enslavers boasted about their crimes":* Dr. Verene Shepherd, quoted in ibid.

350 *"The past does not exist independently":* Michel-Rolph Trouillot, *Silencing the Past: Power and the Production of History* (Beacon, 1995), 15, 151.

350 *"None of us can change the past":* His Majesty the King's Opening Speech for CHOGM 2024, October 25, 2024, https://thecommonwealth.org/news/chogm24/king-charles-opening-speech.

INDEX